D0212395

Tenth Edition

Introduction to
Mass Communication
MEDIA LITERACY AND CULTURE

Stanley J. Baran

Bryant University

McGraw
Hill
Education

INTRODUCTION TO MASS COMMUNICATION, TENTH EDITION

Published by McGraw-Hill Education, 2 Penn Plaza, New York, NY 10121. Copyright © 2019 by McGraw-Hill Education. All rights reserved. Printed in the United States of America. Previous editions © 2017, 2015, and 2014. No part of this publication may be reproduced or distributed in any form or by any means, or stored in a database or retrieval system, without the prior written consent of McGraw-Hill Education, including, but not limited to, in any network or other electronic storage or transmission, or broadcast for distance learning.

Some ancillaries, including electronic and print components, may not be available to customers outside the United States.

This book is printed on acid-free paper.

2 3 4 5 6 7 8 9 LMN 21 20 19 18

ISBN: 978-1-259-92497-2 (Looseleaf)
MHID: 1-259-92497-1

ISBN: 978-1-260-39725-3 (Bound)
MHID: 1-260-39725-4

Portfolio Manager: *Sarah Remington*
Product Developer: *Victoria DeRosa*
Marketing Manager: *Laura Young*
Content Project Manager: *Lisa Bruflodt*
Buyer: *Laura M. Fuller*
Designer: *Jessica Cuevas*
Content Licensing Specialist: *DeAnna Dausener*
Cover Image: © *Kasiaa/Shutterstock.com*
Compositor: *Lumina Datamatics*
Printer: *LSC Communications*

All credits appearing on page or at the end of the book are considered to be an extension of the copyright page.

Library of Congress Cataloging-in-Publication Data

Library of Congress Cataloging-in-Publication Data
Names: Baran, Stanley J., author.
Title: Introduction to mass communication: media literacy and culture /
    Stanley J. Baran, Bryant University.
Description: Tenth edition. | New York, NY: McGraw-Hill Education, 2019.
Identifiers: LCCN 2017045179 (print) | LCCN 2017047591 (ebook) | ISBN
    9781260154627 (Online) | ISBN 9781259924972 (looseleaf) | ISBN
    9781260154634 (softcover)
Subjects: LCSH: Mass media. | Mass media and culture. | Media literacy.
Classification: LCC P90 (ebook) | LCC P90 .B284 2019 (print) | DDC
    302.23—dc23
LC record available at https://lccn.loc.gov/2017045179

The Internet addresses listed in the text were accurate at the time of publication. The inclusion of a website does not indicate an endorsement by the authors or McGraw-Hill Education, and McGraw-Hill Education does not guarantee the accuracy of the information presented at these sites.

mheducation.com/highered

In loving memory of my mother,
Margaret Baran—
she gave me life;
and in honor of my wife,
Susan Baran—
she gave that life meaning.

From the Author

Dear Friends,

The media, like sports and politics, are what we talk about, argue over, dissect, and analyze. Those of us who teach media know that these conversations are essential to the functioning of a democratic society. We also know that what moves these conversations from simple chatting and griping to effective public discourse is media education. And regardless of what we might call the course—Introduction to Mass Communication, Introduction to Mass Media, Media and Society, or Media and Culture—media education has been part of the university for more than six decades. From the outset, the course has fulfilled these goals:

Courtesy of Stanley Baran

- Increasing students' knowledge and understanding of the mass communication process and the mass media industries
- Increasing students' awareness of how they interact with those industries and their content to create meaning
- Helping students become more skilled and knowledgeable consumers of media content and therefore more ethical and confident participants in their worlds

We now call the fulfillment of these goals *media literacy*.

A Cultural Perspective

This text's cultural orientation toward mass communication places a great deal of responsibility on media consumers. In the past, people were considered either victims of media influence or impervious to it. The cultural orientation asserts that audience members are as much a part of the mass communication process as are the media technologies and industries. As important agents in the creation and maintenance of their own culture, audience members have a moral obligation not only to participate in the process of mass communication but also to participate critically as better consumers of mass media.

Enriching Students' Literacy

The focus of this book, from the start, has been on media literacy and culture, and those emphases have shaped its content and its various learning aids and pedagogical features. Every chapter's *Cultural Forum* box poses a critical thinking dilemma based on a current social problem and asks students to work through their solution. The *Using Media to Make a Difference* feature offers chapter-specific examples of how people in and outside the media industries have employed technology to meet important cultural and social needs. And each chapter ends with a *Media Literacy Challenge* that asks students to apply what they've learned to a contemporary media issue. Literacy, in this case media literacy, is about living in, interacting with, and making the most of the world that surrounds us. That belief is the central philosophy of this text.

My Thanks to You

Thank you for teaching mass communication. There are few college courses that will mean more to our students' lives now and after they graduate than this one. Thank you, too, for considering *Introduction to Mass Communication: Media Literacy and Culture* for use in your course. I have poured the last 25 years of my career into this text and what it has to say about mass communication and the world that our interaction with the media produces. Your interest in this text confirms my passion.

—**Stanley J. Baran**

Brief Contents

Contents

PART 3 STRATEGIC COMMUNICATION INDUSTRIES   258

PART 4   MASS-MEDIATED CULTURE IN THE INFORMATION AGE   310

Preface

McGraw-Hill Connect: An Overview

McGraw-Hill Connect offers full-semester access to comprehensive, reliable content and learning resources for the Communication course. Connect's deep integration with most learning management systems (LMSs), including Blackboard and Desire2Learn (D2L), offers single sign-on and deep gradebook synchronization. Data from Assignment Results reports synchronize directly with many LMSs, allowing scores to flow automatically from Connect into school-specific gradebooks, if required.

The following tools and services are available as part of Connect for the Communication course:

Tool	Instructional Context	Description
SmartBook	• SmartBook is an engaging and interactive reading experience for mastering fundamental Communication content. • The metacognitive component confirms students' understanding of the material. • Instructors can actively connect SmartBook assignments and results to higher-order classroom work and one-on-one student conferences. • Students can track their own understanding and mastery of course concepts and identify gaps in their knowledge.	• SmartBook is an adaptive reading experience designed to change the way students read and learn. It creates a personalized reading experience by highlighting the most impactful concepts a student needs to learn at that moment in time. • SmartBook creates personalized learning plans based on student responses to content question probes and confidence scales, identifying the topics students are struggling with and providing learning resources to create personalized learning moments. • SmartBook includes a variety of learning resources tied directly to key content areas to provide students with additional instruction and context. This includes video and media clips, interactive slide content, mini lectures, and image analyses. • SmartBook Reports provide instructors with data to quantify success and identify problem areas that require addressing in and out of the classroom. • Students can access their own progress and concept mastery reports.
Connect Insight for *Instructors*	• Connect Insight for Instructors is an analytics resource that produces quick feedback related to learner performance and learner engagement. • It is designed as a dashboard for both quick check-ins and detailed performance and engagement views.	• Connect Insight for Instructors offers a series of visual data displays that provide analysis on five key insights: 1. How are my students doing? 2. How is this one student doing? 3. How is my section doing? 4. How is this assignment doing? 5. How are my assignments doing?

(Continued)

Tool	Instructional Context	Description
Connect Insight for *Students*	• Connect Insight for Students is a powerful data analytics tool that provides at-a-glance visualizations to help students understand their performance on Connect assignments.	• Connect Insight for Students offers details on each Connect assignment to students. When possible, it offers suggestions for the students on how they can improve scores. This data can help guide students to behaviors that will lead to better scores in the future.
Video Speech Assignment	• Video Speech Assignment provides instructors with a comprehensive and efficient way of managing in-class and online speech assignments, including student self-reviews, peer reviews, and instructor grading.	• The Video Speech Assignment tool allows instructors to easily and efficiently set up speech assignments for their course that can easily be shared and repurposed, as needed, throughout their use of Connect. • Customizable rubrics and settings can be saved and shared, saving time and streamlining the speech assignment process from creation to assessment. • Video Speech Assignment allows users, both students and instructors, to view videos during the assessment process. Feedback can be left within a customized rubric or as time-stamped comments within the video playback itself.
Speech Preparation Tools	• Speech Preparation Tools provide students with additional support and include Topic Helper, Outline Tool, and access to third-party Internet sites like EasyBib (for formatting citations) and Survey Monkey (to create audience-analysis questionnaires and surveys).	• Speech Preparation Tools provide students with additional resources to help with the preparation and outlining of speeches, as well as with audience-analysis surveys. • Instructors have the ability to make tools either available or unavailable to students.
Instructor Reports	• Instructor Reports provide data that may be useful for assessing programs or courses as part of the accreditation process.	• Connect generates a number of powerful reports and charts that allow instructors to quickly review the performance of a given learner or an entire section. • Instructors can run reports that span multiple sections and instructors, making it an ideal solution for individual professors, course coordinators, and department chairs.
Student Reports	• Student Reports allow students to review their performance for specific assignments or for the course.	• Students can keep track of their performance and identify areas with which they struggle.
Pre- & Post-Tests	• Instructors can generate their own pre- and post-tests from the test bank. • Pre- and post-tests demonstrate what students already know before class begins and what they have learned by the end.	• Instructors have access to two sets of pre- and post-tests (at two levels). Instructors can use these tests to create a diagnostic and post-diagnostic exam via Connect.
Tegrity	• Tegrity allows instructors to capture course material or lectures on video. • Students can watch videos recorded by their instructor and learn course material at their own pace.	• Instructors can keep track of which students have watched the videos they post. • Students can watch and review lectures by their instructor. • Students can search each lecture for specific bites of information.
Simple LMS Integration	• Connect seamlessly integrates with every learning management system.	• Students have automatic single sign-on. • Connect assignment results sync to the LMS's gradebook.

Instructor's Guide to Connect for *Introduction to Mass Communication: Media Literacy and Culture*

When you assign Connect you can be confident—and have data to demonstrate—that your students, however diverse, are acquiring the skills, principles, and critical processes that constitute effective communication. This leaves you to focus on your highest course expectations.

TAILORED TO YOU. Connect offers on-demand, single sign-on access to students—wherever they are and whenever they have time. With a single, one-time registration, students receive access to McGraw-Hill's trusted content.

EASY TO USE. Connect seamlessly supports all major learning management systems with content, assignments, performance data, and LearnSmart, the leading adaptive learning system. With these tools you can quickly make assignments, produce reports, focus discussions, intervene on problem topics, and help at-risk students—as you need to and when you need to.

Introduction to Mass Communication: Media Literacy and Culture SmartBook

A PERSONALIZED AND ADAPTIVE LEARNING EXPERIENCE WITH SMARTBOOK. SmartBook with Learning Resources is the first and only adaptive reading and study experience designed to change the way students read and master key course concepts. As a student engages with SmartBook, the program creates a personalized learning path by highlighting the most impactful concepts the student needs to learn at that moment in time and delivering learning resources—videos, animations, and other interactivities. These rich, dynamic resources help students learn the material, retain more knowledge, and get better grades.

ENHANCED FOR THE NEW EDITION! With a suite of new learning resources and question probes, as well as highlights of key chapter concepts, SmartBook's intuitive technology optimizes student study time by creating a personalized learning path for improved course performance and overall student success.

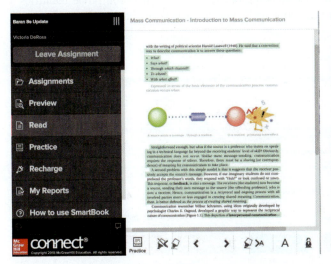
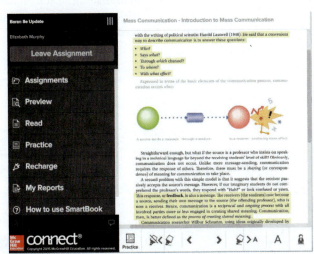

SmartBook highlights the key concepts of every chapter, offering the student a high-impact learning experience (left). Here, highlighted text and an illustration together explain the communication process. Highlights change color (right) when a student has demonstrated his or her understanding of the concept.

READER/eBOOK. Alongside SmartBook, there is also Connect eBook for simple and easy access to reading materials on smartphones and tablets. Students can study on the go without an Internet connection, highlight important sections, take notes, search for materials quickly, and read in class. Offline reading is available by downloading the eBook app on smartphones and tablets, and any notes and highlights created by students will be synced between devices when they reconnect. Unlike SmartBook, there is no pre-highlighting, practice of key concepts, or reports on usage and performance.

HUNDREDS OF INTERACTIVE LEARNING RESOURCES. Presented in a range of interactive styles, *Introduction to Mass Communication: Media Literacy and Culture* Learning Resources support students who may be struggling to master, or simply wish to review, the most important mass communication concepts. Designed to reinforce the most important chapter concepts, every Learning Resource is presented at the precise moment of need. Whether a video, audio clip, or interactive mini-lesson, each of the 200-plus Learning Resources was designed to give students a life-long foundation in strong mass communication skills.

MORE THAN 1,000 TARGETED QUESTION PROBES. Class-tested at colleges and universities nationwide, a treasury of engaging question probes—new and revised, more than 1,000 in all—give students the information on mass communication and media literacy they need to know, at every stage of the learning process, in order to thrive in the course. Designed to gauge students' comprehension of the most important *Introduction to Mass Communication: Media Literacy and Culture* chapter concepts, and presented in a variety of interactive styles to facilitate student engagement, targeted question probes give students immediate feedback on their understanding of the text. Each question probe identifies a student's familiarity with the instruction and points to areas where additional remediation is needed.

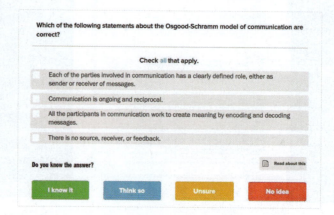

INFORMED BY THE LATEST RESEARCH. The best insights from today's leading mass communications scholars infuse every lesson and are integrated throughout the text.

FRESH EXAMPLES ANCHORED IN THE REAL WORLD. Every chapter of *Introduction to Mass Communication: Media Literacy and Culture* opens with a vignette exploring media literacy situations in our everyday lives. Dozens of additional examples appear throughout the text. Whether students are reading the text, responding to question probes, or reviewing key concepts in a learning resource, their every instructional moment is rooted in the real world. McGraw-Hill Education research shows that high-quality examples reinforce academic theory throughout the course. Relevant examples and practical scenarios—reflecting engagement with multiple forms of mass media—demonstrate how effective communication informs and enhances students' lives and media literacy skills.

BOXED FEATURES. Students must bring media literacy—the ability to critically comprehend and actively use mass media—to the mass communication process. This edition of *Introduction to Mass Communication: Media Literacy and Culture* includes a variety of boxed features to support student learning and enhance media literacy skills.

Using Media to Make a Difference boxes highlight interesting examples of how media practitioners and audiences use the mass communication process to further important social, political, or cultural causes.

Cultural Forum boxes highlight media-related cultural issues that are currently debated in the mass media to help students develop their moral reasoning and critical thinking skills.

Media Literacy Challenge boxes build on ideas from each chapter's "Developing Media Literacy Skills" section and ask students to think critically about media content they encounter in their daily lives and actually use the skills they've learned.

Video Speech Assignment

Designed for use in face-to-face, real-time classrooms as well as online courses, Video Speech Assignment allows you to evaluate your students' speeches using fully customizable rubrics. You can also create and manage peer review assignments and upload videos on behalf of students for optimal flexibility.

Students can access rubrics and leave comments when preparing self-reviews and peer reviews. They can easily upload a video of their speech from their hard drive or use Connect's built-in video recorder. Students can even attach and upload additional files or documents, such as a works-cited page or a PowerPoint presentation.

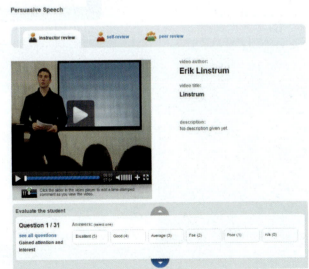

PEER REVIEW. Peer review assignments are easier than ever. Create and manage peer review assignments and customize privacy settings.

SPEECH ASSESSMENT. Connect Video Speech Assignment lets you customize the assignments, including self-reviews and peer reviews.

FEEDBACK. Connect saves your frequently used comments, simplifying your efforts to provide feedback.

Data Analytics

Connect Insight provides at-a-glance analysis on five key insights, available at a moment's notice. The first and only analytics tool of its kind, Insight will tell you, in real time, how individual students or sections are doing (or how well your assignments have been received) so that you can take action early and keep struggling students from falling behind.

Instructors can see how many learners have completed an assignment, how long they spent on the task, and how they scored.

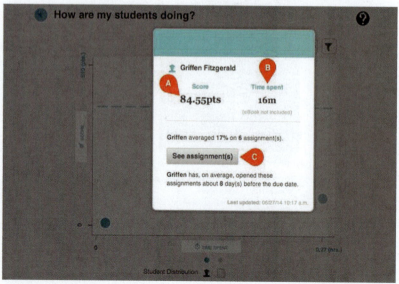

Instructors can see, at a glance, individual learner performance: Analytics showing learner investment in assignments, and success at completing them, help instructors identify, and aid, those who are at risk.

LearnSmart Instructor Reports allow instructors to quickly monitor students' activity, making it easy to identify which students are struggling and to provide immediate help to ensure those students stay enrolled in the course and improve their performance. The Instructor Reports also highlight the concepts and learning objectives that the class as a whole is having difficulty grasping. This essential information lets you know exactly which areas to target for review during your limited class time.

Some key LearnSmart reports are listed here.

Progress Overview report—View student progress for all LearnSmart modules, including how long students have spent working in the module, which modules they have used outside of any that were assigned, and individual student progress through LearnSmart.

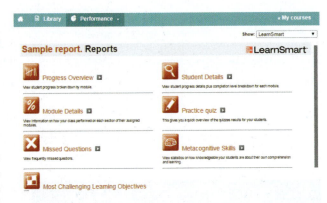

Missed Questions report—Identify specific LearnSmart probes, organized by chapter, that are problematic for students.

Most Challenging Learning Objectives report—Identify the specific topic areas that are challenging for your students; these reports are organized by chapter and include specific page references. Use this information to tailor your lecture time and assignments to cover areas that require additional remediation and practice.

Metacognitive Skills report—View statistics showing how knowledgeable your students are about their own comprehension and learning.

Classroom Preparation Tools

Whether before, during, or after class, there is a suite of Baran products designed to help instructors plan their lessons and to keep students building upon the foundations of the course.

POWERPOINT SLIDES. The PowerPoint presentations for *Introduction to Mass Communication: Media Literacy and Culture* provide chapter highlights that help instructors create focused yet individualized lesson plans.

TEST BANK. The *Introduction to Mass Communication: Media Literacy and Culture* Test Bank is a treasury of more than 1,000 examination questions based on the most important mass communication concepts explored in the text; more than 100 of the questions are new or revised for this edition.

MEDIA LITERACY WORKSHEETS. Media literacy worksheets provide students with thought-provoking questions and exercises based on the most important concepts addressed in each chapter. Students are encouraged to examine their own experiences with media and form their own opinions.

INSTRUCTOR'S MANUAL. Written by the author, this comprehensive guide to teaching from *Introduction to Mass Communication* contains lecture suggestions and resources for each chapter.

Support to Ensure Success

- **Digital Success Academy**—The Digital Success Academy on Connect offers a wealth of training and course creation guidance for instructors and students alike. Instructor support is presented in easy-to-navigate, easy-to-complete sections. It includes the popular *Connect* video shorts, step-by-step *Click through Guides,* and *First Day of Class*

materials that explain how to use both the Connect platform and its course-specific tools and features.

- **Implementation Team**—Our team of Implementation Consultants are dedicated to working online with instructors—one-on-one—to demonstrate how the Connect platform works and to help incorporate Connect into a customer's specific course design and syllabus. Contact your Learning Specialist to learn more.

- **Learning Specialists**—Learning Specialists are local resources who work closely with your McGraw-Hill learning technology consultants. They can provide face-to-face faculty support and training.

- **Digital Faculty Consultants**—Digital Faculty Consultants are experienced instructors who use Connect in their classrooms. These instructors are available to offer suggestions, advice, and training about how best to use Connect in your class. To request a Digital Faculty Consultant to speak with, please e-mail your McGraw-Hill learning technology consultant.

- **National Training Webinars**—McGraw-Hill offers an ongoing series of webinars for instructors to learn and master the Connect platform as well as its course-specific tools and features. We hope you will refer to our online schedule of national training webinars and sign up to learn more about Connect!

CONTACT OUR CUSTOMER SUPPORT TEAM

McGraw-Hill is dedicated to supporting instructors and students. To contact our customer support team, please call us at 800-331-5094 or visit us online at http://mpss.mhhe.com/contact.php

---

Changes to the Tenth Edition: Highlights

The new edition maintains its commitment to enhancing students' critical thinking and media literacy skills. New and updated material in this edition reflects the latest developments in new digital technologies and highlights the most current research in the field.

Chapter 1 Mass Communication, Culture, and Media Literacy: New examination of public and industry pushback against sexism in media; new discussion of the hostile media effect (people distrusting news regardless of its accuracy and quality)

Chapter 2 Convergence and the Reshaping of Mass Communication: New Cultural Forum box discussion of how the media underperformed in the 2016 presidential election; updated look at new means of day-and-date home delivery of Hollywood feature films; introduction of news deserts (communities starved for local journalistic resources); new examination of life in the meme culture

Chapter 3 Books: New Cultural Forum box asking if Hitler's *Mein Kampf* should be banned; updated look at the renaissance of U.S. independent bookstores; added discussion of research connecting fiction reading and empathy

Chapter 4 Newspapers: New discussion of the loss of working journalists and its impact on journalism

Chapter 5 Magazines: Updated look at some new entries in custom publishing; new Cultural Forum box on the controversy surrounding attempts to standardize and regulate sponsored content

Chapter 6 Film: Updated look at the trend of exhibitors becoming studios; enhanced discussion of how sequels and franchises are losing their luster; new overview of dynamic ticket pricing (variable pricing of tickets depending on day, time, available seats, etc.) and mention of movie palaces

Chapter 7 Radio, Recording, and Popular Music: Enhanced examination of the ethics of music piracy; new discussions of formulaic/mathematical songwriting, the use of social media to link fans with artists and their music, discussion of stream ripping (illegally downloading streaming music), and what we lose from algorithm-based streaming; new Media Literacy Challenge to find new music

Chapter 8 Television, Cable, and Mobile Video: Updated discussion of Nielsen's new ratings procedures and of satirical TV news and the 2016 presidential election; new look at skinny bundles (low-cost, limited-channel program bundles) and video streaming apps Periscope and Facebook Live

Chapter 9 Video Games: New coverage of virtual reality games; enhanced discussion of sexism and mistreatment of female players, including the Video Game Sexism Scale

Chapter 10 The Internet and Social Media: Updated examination of newer and niche social networking; new Using Media to Make a Difference box on fake news and the presidential election; new coverage of the Internet of Things and slacktivism (online activism); new Media Literacy Challenge offering a test for Internet addiction self-diagnosis

Chapter 11 Public Relations: New coverage of how to identify fake online reviews, including a new Media Literacy Challenge; updated examination of corporate social responsibility

Chapter 12 Advertising: Discussion of boutique agencies; examination of programmatic ad fraud

Chapter 13 Theories and Effects of Mass Communication: New Cultural Forum box discussing the failure of the traditional press to identify and report the economic frustration of Trump voters

Chapter 14 Media Freedom, Regulation, and Ethics: Updated coverage of the FCC and indecent programming; new discussions of how journalists should address politicians' dishonesty, the ethics of outing gay politicians who work for homophobic causes, the Corey Lewandowski CNN conflict of interest, and judging the use of anonymous sources

Chapter 15 Global Media: New Using Media to Make a Difference box examining the use of social media in developing countries for health benefit; updated coverage of social media as revolutionary and counterrevolutionary media

Acknowledgements

A project of this magnitude requires the assistance of many people. For this latest edition I benefited from several e-mails from readers—instructors and students—making suggestions and offering advice. This book is better for those exchanges. Rather than run the risk of failing to include one of these essential correspondents, I'll simply say, "Thanks. You know who you are."

Reviewers are an indispensable part of the creation of a good textbook. In preparing for the tenth edition, I was again impressed with the thoughtful comments made by my colleagues in the field. Although I didn't know them by name, I found myself in long-distance, anonymous debate with several superb thinkers, especially about some of the text's most important concepts. Their collective keen eye and questioning attitude sharpened each chapter to the benefit of both writer and reader. Now that I know who they are, I would like to thank the reviewers by name.

Shira Chess, *The University of Georgia*

Phillip Cunningham, *Quinnipiac University*

Robert F. Darden, *Baylor University*

Meredith Guthrie, *University of Pittsburgh*

Kelli Marshall, *DePaul University*

Elizabeth Behm-Morawitz, *University of Missouri–Columbia*

Pamela Hill Nettleton, *Marquette University*

Rick Stevens, *University of Colorado Boulder*

Matthew R. Turner, *Radford University*

I would also like to thank the reviewers of the first nine editions. **Ninth Edition Reviewers:** Cathy Ferrand Bullock, Utah State University; Alta Carroll, Worcester State University; Antoinette Countryman, McHenry County College; Adrienne E. Hacker Daniels, Illinois College; Lori Dann, Eastfield College; Jessica M. Farley, Delaware Technical Community College; Jeffrey Goldberg, Mass Bay Community College; Barbara J. Irwin, Canisius College; Christopher Leigh, University of Charleston; Katherine Lockwood, University of Tampa; Jodi Hallsten Lyczak, Illinois State University; Susan McGraw, Henry Ford College; Larry Moore, Auburn University at Montgomery; Travice Baldwin Obas, Georgia Highlands College–Cartersville; Luis Lopez-Preciado, Lasell College; Terri F. Reilly, Webster University; Joseph M. Sirianni, Niagara University; Sandra Luzzi Sneesby, Community College of Rhode Island; Martin D. Sommerness, Northern Arizona University; Pamela Stovall, University of New Mexico–Gallup; Joanne A. Williams, Olivet College; Joe Wisinski, University of Tampa; Robert Wuagneux, Castleton State College. **Eighth Edition Reviewers:** Lee Banville, University of Montana; Rick Bebout, West Virginia University; Bob Britten, West Virginia University; Cathy Bullock, Utah State University; James Burton, Salisbury University; Yolanda Cal, Loyola University–New Orleans; Nathan Claes, State University of New York–Buffalo; Helen Fallon, Point Park University; Ray Fanning, University of Montana; Richard Ganahl, Bloomsburg University; Paul Hillier, University of Tampa; Daekyung Kim, Idaho State University; Charles Marsh, University of Kansas–Lawrence; Susan McGraw, Henry Ford Community College; Bob Mendenhall, Southwestern Adventist University; Bruce Mims, Southeast Missouri State University; Jensen Moore, West Virginia University; Timothy Pasch, University of North Dakota; Kenneth Ross, Eastern Connecticut State University; Siobhan Smith, University of Louisville; Jeff South, Virginia Commonwealth University; Richard Taflinger, Washington State University–Pullman; Clifford Vaughn, Belmont University; Kimberly Vaupel, Henry Ford Community College; Joe Wisinski, University of Tampa. **Seventh Edition Reviewers:** Kwasi Boateng, University of Arkansas at Little Rock; Mike Igoe, Buffalo State College; Joe Marre, Buffalo State College; Sonya Miller, University of North Carolina–Asheville; Yuri Obata, Indiana University–South Bend; Danny Shipka, Louisiana State University. **Sixth Edition Reviewers:** Chris Cakebread, Boston University; Cynthia Chris, College of Staten Island; Laurie Hayes Fluker, Texas State University; Jacob Podber, Southern Illinois University–Carbondale; Biswarup Sen, University of Oregon; Lisa A. Stephens, University of Buffalo; Denise Walters, Front Range Community College. **Fifth Edition Reviewers:** Jennifer Aubrey, University of Missouri; Michael Boyle, Wichita State University; Tim Coombs, Eastern Illinois University; Denise Danford, Delaware County Community College; Tim Edwards, University of Arkansas at Little Rock; Junhao Hong, State University of New York at Buffalo; Mark Kelly, University of Maine; Alyse Lancaster, University of Miami; Carol S. Lomick, University of Nebraska at Kearney; Susan Dawson-O'Brien, Rose State College; Alicia C. Shepard, University of Texas at Austin; Tamala Sheree Martin, Oklahoma State University; Stephen D. Perry, Illinois State University; Selene Phillips, University of Louisville. **Fourth Edition Reviewers:** Kristen Barton, Florida State University; Kenton Bird, University of Idaho; Katia G. Campbell, University of Colorado; Paul A. Creasman, Azusa Pacific University; Annette Johnson, Georgia State University; James Kelleher, New York University; Polly McLean, University of Colorado; Anthony A. Olorunnisola, Pennsylvania State University; Stephen D. Perry, Illinois State University; Michael Porter, University of Missouri; Stephen J. Resch, Indiana Wesleyan University; Christopher F. White, Sam Houston State University. **Third Edition Reviewers:** Roger Desmond, University of Hartford; Jules d'Hemecourt, Louisiana State University; Deborah A. Godwin-Starks, Indiana University–Purdue University Fort Wayne; Junhao Hong, State University of New York at Buffalo; Alyse Lancaster, University of Miami; Carol S. Lomicky, University of Nebraska at Kearney; Jenny L. Nelson, Ohio University; Enid Sefcovic, Florida Atlantic University; Kevin R. Slaugher, George Mason University; Terri Toles Patkin, Eastern Connecticut State University; David Whitt, Nebraska Wesleyan University; Gary J. Wingenbach, Texas A&M University. **Second Edition Reviewers:** Rob Bellamy, Duquesne University; Beth Grobman Burruss, DeAnza College; Stephen R. Curtis, Jr., East Connecticut State University; Lyombe Eko, University of Maine; Junhao Hong, State University of New York at Buffalo; Carol Liebler, Syracuse University; Robert Main, California State University, Chico; Stephen Perry, Illinois State University; Eric Pierson, University of San Diego; Ramona Rush, University of Kentucky; Tony Silvia, University of Rhode Island; and Richard Welch, Kennesaw State University. **First Edition Reviewers:** David Allen, Illinois State University; Sandra Braman, University of Alabama; Tom Grimes, Kansas State University; Kirk Hallahan, Colorado State University; Katharine Heintz-Knowles, University of Washington; Paul Husselbee, Ohio University; Seong Lee, Appalachian State University; Rebecca Ann Lind, University of Illinois at Chicago; Maclyn McClary, Humboldt State University; Guy Meiss, Central Michigan University; Debra Merskin, University of Oregon; Scott R. Olsen, Central Connecticut State University; Ted Pease, Utah State University; Linda Perry, *Florida Today* newspaper; Elizabeth Perse, University of Delaware; Tina Pieraccini, State University of New York–College at Oswego; Michael Porter, University of Missouri; Peter Pringle, University of Tennessee at Chattanooga; Neal Robison, Washington State University; Linda Steiner, Rutgers University; and Don Tomlinson, Texas A&M University.

The tenth edition was written with the usual great support (and patience) of my McGraw-Hill Education team. The Internet may make producing a book more efficient, but it does have a big drawback—despite spending hundreds of hours "working together," I have yet to meet my teammates face to face. This, certainly, is my loss. Still, I have had few better colleagues than Lisa Bruflodt, Betty Chen, Sally Constable, Mary Ellen Curley, Victoria DeRosa, Samantha Donisi-Hamm, Esther Go, Nancy Huebner, Lisa Pinto, Sarah Remington, Jennifer Shekleton, Janet Byrne Smith, Emily Windelborn, and Laura Young. An author cannot surround himself with better people than those McGraw-Hill Education has given me.

Finally, my most important inspiration throughout the writing of this book has been my family. My wife, Susan, is educated in media literacy and a strong disciple of spreading its lessons far and wide—which she does with zest. Her knowledge and assistance in my writing is invaluable; her love in my life is sustaining; her fire—for improved media literacy and for our marriage—is empowering. My children—Jordan and Matthew—simply by their existence require that I consider and reconsider what kind of world we will leave for them. I've written this text in the hope that it helps make the future for them and their friends better than it might otherwise have been.

S.J.B.

Tenth Edition

Introduction to
Mass Communication
MEDIA LITERACY AND CULTURE

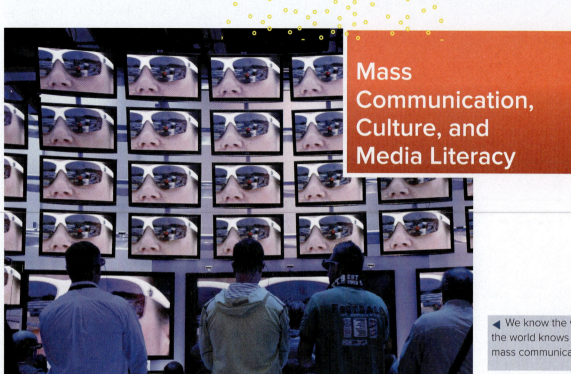

1

Mass Communication, Culture, and Media Literacy

◀ We know the world, and the world knows us, through mass communication.

©Sean Gallup/Getty Images

Learning Objectives

Mass communication, mass media, and the culture that shapes us (and that we shape) are inseparable. After studying this chapter, you should be able to

▶ Define *communication, mass communication, mass media,* and *culture*.

▶ Describe the relationships among communication, mass communication, culture, and those who live in the culture.

▶ Evaluate the impact of technology and economics on those relationships.

▶ List the components of media literacy.

▶ Identify key skills required for developing media literacy.

c 600   Wooden block printing press invented
in China

c 1000   The Chinese develop movable clay type

c 1200   Simple movable metal printing press
invented in Korea

1446   Gutenberg printing press perfected

1456 ▶ First Gutenberg Bible printed · · · · · · · · · · · · ·

1400

©North Wind Picture Archives/Alamy

1800s   Availability of printed materials spreads
knowledge that leads to the Industrial
Revolution; the Industrial Revolution leads
to the creation of the first mass audiences

1800

1830s   Publishers begin selling newspapers for a
penny and profitting from ad sales, selling
readers rather than papers

1948   Harold Laswell defines communication in
its simplest, linear form

1900

1954   Osgood-Schramm model of communication
and mass communication developed

1962 ▶ Marshall McLuhan publishes *The Gutenberg
Galaxy* and argues the advent of print is the
key to modern consciousness · · · · · · · · · · ·

1975   Carey's cultural definition of communication

©TJ Photography/PhotoEdit

2004 ▶ Dove Real Beauty campaign · · · · · · · · · · · · ·

2000

2008 ▶ Art Silverblatt identifies elements of
media literacy

2013   Term "binge viewing" enters mainstream use

2015   Bud Light's "remove 'no' from your
vocabulary" slogan is deemed culturally
insensitive; *Women's Health* magazine
bans phrases "bikini body" and "drop two
sizes" from its covers

2016 ▶ Annual global Internet traffic passed the
zetabyte threshold; Mattel introduces
fuller-figured Barbie dolls as well as
petite, tall, and a variety of skin tones,
hairstyles, and fashion styles · · · · · · · · · · ·

©Ruby Washington/The New York Times/Redux

©Mattel/Spalash News/Newscom

YOUR SMARTPHONE'S RADIO ALARM SINGS YOU AWAKE. It's Beyoncé, the last few bars of "Hold Up." The upbeat DJ shouts at you that it's 7:41 and you'd better get going. But before you do, she adds, listen to a few words from your friends at Best Buy electronics, home of fast, friendly, courteous service—"Expert Service. Unbeatable Price!"

Before you get up, though, you take a quick pass at Facebook and Instagram. But you've gotta get going now. In the living room, you find your roommate has left the television on. You stop for a moment and listen: The economy is showing stronger signs of rebounding, brightening the employment picture for new college grads; several states are considering providing free high-speed Internet to all students to improve their access to the digital world; chaos continues to sweep across the Middle East; and you deserve a break today at McDonald's. As you head toward the bathroom, your bare feet slip on some magazines littering the floor—*Wired, Rolling Stone, People.* You need to talk to your roommate about cleaning up!

After showering, you quickly pull on your Levi's, lace up your Nike cross-trainers, and throw on an Under Armour jacket. No time for breakfast; you grab a Nature Valley granola bar and your tablet and head for the bus stop. As the bus rolls up, you can't help but notice the giant ad on its side: another *Transformers* movie. Rejecting that as a film choice for the weekend, you sit down next to a teenager listening to music on his Beats headphones and playing a video game. You fire up your tablet and bury yourself in Snapchat, Twitter, and your favorite news app, scanning the lead stories and the local news and then checking out *Doonesbury* and *Garfield.*

Hopping off the bus at the campus stop, you run into your friend Chris. You walk to class together, talking about last night's *The Walking Dead* episode. It's not yet 9:00, and already you're involved in mass communication. In fact, like 60% of Americans, you're involved with media on your smartphone first thing in the morning, even before you get out of bed (Hunter, 2014).

In this chapter we define *communication, interpersonal communication, mass communication, media,* and *culture* and explore the relationships among them and how they define us and our world. We investigate how communication works, how it changes when technology is introduced into the process, and how differing views of communication and mass communication can lead to different interpretations of their power. We also discuss the opportunities mass communication and culture offer us and the responsibilities that come with those opportunities. Always crucial, these issues are of particular importance now, when we find ourselves in a period of remarkable development in new communication technologies. This discussion inevitably leads to an examination of media literacy, its importance, and its practice.

What Is Mass Communication?

"Does a fish know it's wet?" influential cultural and media critic Marshall McLuhan would often ask. The answer, he would say, is "No." The fish's existence is so dominated by water that only when water is absent is the fish aware of its condition.

So it is with people and mass media. The media so fully saturate our everyday lives that we are often unconscious of their presence, not to mention their influence. Media inform us, entertain us, delight us, annoy us. They move our emotions, challenge our intellects, insult our intelligence. Media often reduce us to mere commodities for sale to the highest bidder. Media help define us; they shape our realities.

A fundamental theme of this book is that media do none of this alone. They do it *with* us as well as *to* us through mass communication, and they do it as a central—many critics and scholars say *the* central—cultural force in our society.

Communication Defined

In its simplest form, **communication** is the transmission of a message from a source to a receiver. For more than 70 years now, this view of communication has been identified with the writing of political scientist Harold Lasswell (1948). He said that a convenient way to describe communication is to answer these questions:

- *Who?*
- Says *what?*

- Through *which* channel?
- To *whom*?
- With *what effect*?

Expressed in terms of the basic elements of the communication process, communication occurs when a source sends a message through a medium to a receiver, producing some effect (Figure 1).

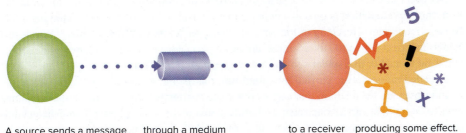

◀ **Figure 1** The Basic Communication Process.

A source sends a message   through a medium   to a receiver   producing some effect.

This idea is straightforward enough, but what if the source is a professor who insists on speaking in a technical language far beyond the receiving students' level of skill? Obviously, communication does not occur. Unlike mere message-sending, communication requires the response of others. Therefore, there must be a *sharing* (or correspondence) of meaning for communication to take place.

A second problem with this simple model is that it suggests that the receiver passively accepts the source's message. However, if our imaginary students do not comprehend the professor's words, they respond with "Huh?" or look confused or yawn. This response, or **feedback**, is also a message. The receivers (the students) now become a source, sending their own message to the source (the offending professor), who is now a receiver. Hence, communication is a *reciprocal* and *ongoing process* with all involved parties more or less engaged in creating shared meaning. Communication, then, is better defined as *the process of creating shared meaning*.

Communication researcher Wilbur Schramm, using ideas originally developed by psychologist Charles E. Osgood, developed a graphic way to represent the reciprocal nature of communication (Figure 2). This depiction of **interpersonal communication**—communication between two or a few people—shows that there is no clearly identifiable source or receiver. Rather, because communication is an ongoing and reciprocal process, all the participants, or "interpreters," are working to create meaning by **encoding** and **decoding** messages. A message is first *encoded*, that is, transformed into an understandable sign and symbol system. Speaking is encoding, as are writing, printing, and filming a television program. Once received, the message is *decoded*; that is, the signs and symbols are interpreted. Decoding occurs through listening, reading, or watching that television show.

The Osgood–Schramm model demonstrates the ongoing and reciprocal nature of the communication process. There is, therefore, no source, no receiver, and no feedback. The

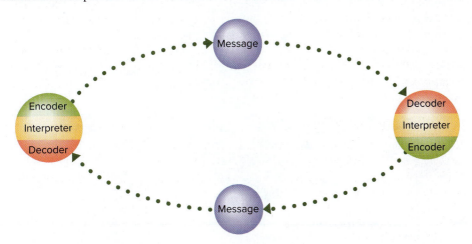

◀ **Figure 2** Osgood and Schramm's Model of Communication.
Source: Schramm, Wilbur Lang, The Process and Effects of Mass Communication. *1954*

reason is that, as communication is happening, both interpreters are simultaneously source and receiver. There is no feedback because all messages are presumed to be in reciprocation of other messages. Even when your friend starts a conversation with you, for example, it can be argued that it was your look of interest and willingness that communicated to her that she should speak. In this example, it is improper to label either you or your friend as the source—who really initiated this chat?—and, therefore, it is impossible to identify who is providing feedback to whom.

Not every model can show all aspects of a process as complex as communication. Missing from this representation is **noise**—anything that interferes with successful communication. Noise is more than screeching or loud music when you are trying to work online. Biases that lead to incorrect decoding, for example, are noise, as is a page torn out of a magazine article you want to read or that spiderweb crack in your smartphone's screen.

Encoded messages are carried by a **medium**, that is, the means of sending information. Sound waves are the medium that carries our voice to friends across the table; the telephone is the medium that carries our voice to friends across town. When the medium is a technology that carries messages to a large number of people—as the Internet carries text, sounds, and images and radio conveys the sound of music and news—we call it a **mass medium** (the plural of medium is *media*). The mass media we use regularly include radio, television, books, magazines, newspapers, movies, sound recordings, cell phones, and computer networks. Each medium is the basis of a giant industry, but other related and supporting industries also serve them and us—advertising and public relations, for example. In our culture we use the words *media* and *mass media* interchangeably to refer to the communication industries themselves. We say, "The media entertain" or "The mass media are too conservative (or too liberal)."

Mass Communication Defined

We speak, too, of mass communication. **Mass communication** is the process of creating shared meaning between the mass media and their audiences. Schramm recast his and Osgood's general model of communication to help us visualize the particular aspects of the mass communication process (Figure 3). This model and the original Osgood–Schramm model have much in common—interpreters, encoding, decoding, and messages—but it is their differences that are most significant for our understanding of how mass communication differs from other forms of communication. For example, whereas the original model includes "message," the mass communication model offers "many identical messages." In addition, the mass communication model specifies "feedback," whereas the interpersonal communication model does not. When two or a few people communicate face to face, the participants can immediately and clearly recognize the feedback residing in the reciprocal messages (our boring professor can see and hear the students' disenchantment as they listen to the lecture). Things are not nearly as simple in mass communication.

In Schramm's mass communication model, feedback is represented by a dotted line labeled "delayed **inferential feedback**." This feedback is indirect rather than direct.

▶ **Figure 3** Schramm's Model of Mass Communication.

Source: Schramm, Wilbur Lang, The Process and Effects of Mass Communication. *1954*

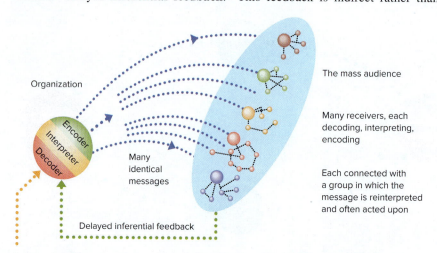

Organization

Encoder
Interpreter
Decoder

Many identical messages

The mass audience

Many receivers, each decoding, interpreting, encoding

Each connected with a group in which the message is reinterpreted and often acted upon

Delayed inferential feedback

Television executives, for example, must wait a day, at the very minimum, and sometimes a week or a month, to discover the ratings for new programs. Even then, the ratings measure only how many sets are tuned in, not whether people liked or disliked the programs. As a result, these executives can only infer what they must do to improve programming; hence the term *inferential feedback*. Mass communicators are also subject to additional feedback, usually in the form of criticism in other media, such as a television critic writing a column in a newspaper.

The differences between the individual elements of interpersonal and mass communication change the very nature of the communication process. How those alterations influence the message itself and how the likelihood of successfully sharing meaning differs are shown in Figure 4. For example, the immediacy and directness of feedback in interpersonal communication free communicators to gamble, to experiment with different approaches. Their knowledge of one another enables them to tailor their messages as narrowly as they wish. As a result, interpersonal communication is often personally relevant and possibly even adventurous and challenging. In contrast, the distance between participants in the mass communication process, imposed by the technology, creates a sort of "communication conservatism." Feedback comes too late to enable corrections or alterations in communication that fails. The sheer number of people in many mass communication audiences makes personalization and specificity difficult. As a result, mass communication tends to be more constrained, less free. This does not mean, however, that it is less potent than interpersonal communication in shaping our understanding of ourselves and our world.

Media theorist James W. Carey (1975) recognized this and offered a **cultural definition of communication** that has had a profound impact on the way communication scientists and others have viewed the relationship between communication and culture. Carey wrote, "Communication is a symbolic process whereby reality is produced, maintained, repaired and transformed" (p. 10).

Carey's (1989) definition asserts that communication and reality are linked. Communication is a process embedded in our everyday lives that informs the way we perceive, understand, and construct our view of reality and the world. Communication is the foundation of our culture. Its truest purpose is to maintain ever-evolving, "fragile" cultures; communication is that "sacred ceremony that draws persons together in fellowship and commonality" (p. 43).

What Is Culture?

Culture is the learned behavior of members of a given social group. Many writers and thinkers have offered interesting expansions of this definition. Here are four examples, all from anthropologists. These definitions highlight not only what culture *is* but also what culture *does*:

> Culture is the learned, socially acquired traditions and lifestyles of the members of a society, including their patterned, repetitive ways of thinking, feeling, and acting. (Harris, 1983, p. 5)

> Culture lends significance to human experience by selecting from and organizing it. It refers broadly to the forms through which people make sense of their lives, rather than more narrowly to the opera or art of museums. (Rosaldo, 1989, p. 26)

> Culture is the medium evolved by humans to survive. Nothing is free from cultural influences. It is the keystone in civilization's arch and is the medium through which all of life's events must flow. We are culture. (Hall, 1976, p. 14)

> Culture is an historically transmitted pattern of meanings embodied in symbolic forms by means of which [people] communicate, perpetuate, and develop their knowledge about and attitudes toward life. (Geertz, as cited in Taylor, 1991, p. 91)

Culture as Socially Constructed Shared Meaning

Virtually all definitions of culture recognize that culture is *learned*. Recall the opening vignette. Even if this scenario does not exactly match your early mornings, you probably recognize its elements. Moreover, all of us are familiar with most, if not every, cultural

	Interpersonal Communication You invite a friend to lunch.		**Mass Communication** Idiot Box Productions produces *The Walking Dead*.	
	Nature	**Consequences**	**Nature**	**Consequences**
Message	Highly flexible and alterable	You can change it in midstream. If feedback is negative, you can offer an alternative. Is feedback still negative? Take a whole new approach.	Identical, mechanically produced, simultaneously sent Inflexible, unalterable The completed *The Walking Dead* episode that is aired	Once production is completed, *The Walking Dead* cannot be changed. If a plotline or other communicative device isn't working with the audience, nothing can be done.
Interpreter A	One person—in this case, you	You know your mind. You can encode your own message to suit yourself, your values, and your likes and dislikes.	A large, hierarchically structured organization—in this case, Idiot Box Productions and the AMC television network	Who really is Interpreter A? Idiot Box Productions' executives? The writers? The director? The actors? The network and its standards and practices people? The sponsors? All must agree, leaving little room for individual vision or experimentation.
Interpreter B	One or a few people, usually in direct contact with you and, to a greater or lesser degree, known to you—in this case, your friend	You can tailor your message specifically to Interpreter B. You can make relatively accurate judgments about B because of information present in the setting. Your friend is a vegetarian; you don't suggest a steak house.	A large, heterogeneous audience known to Interpreter A only in the most rudimentary way, little more than basic demographics—in this case, several million viewers of *The Walking Dead*	Communication cannot be tailored to the wants, needs, and tastes of all audience members or even those of all members of some subgroup. Some more or less generally acceptable standard is set.
Feedback	Immediate and direct yes or no response	You know how successful your message is immediately. You can adjust your communication on the spot to maximize its effectiveness.	Delayed and inferential Even overnight ratings are too late for this episode of *The Walking Dead*. Moreover, ratings are limited to telling the number of sets tuned in.	Even if the feedback is useful, it is too late to be of value for this episode. In addition, it doesn't suggest how to improve the communication effort.
Result	Flexible, personally relevant, possibly adventurous, challenging, or experimental		Constrained by virtually every aspect of the communication situation A level of communication most likely to meet the greatest number of viewers' needs A belief that experimentation is dangerous A belief that to challenge the audience is to risk failure	

▲ **Figure 4** Elements of Interpersonal Communication and Mass Communication Compared.
(left) ©Image Source RF; (right) ©AF archive/Alamy

reference in it. *Transformers*, *Rolling Stone*, McDonald's, Under Armour, *Garfield*—all are points of reference, things that have some meaning for all of us. How did this come to be?

Creation and maintenance of a more or less common culture occurs through communication, including mass communication. When we talk to our friends, when a parent raises a child, when religious leaders instruct their followers, when teachers teach, when grandparents pass on recipes, when politicians campaign, and when media professionals produce content that we read, listen to, or watch, meaning is being shared and culture is being constructed and maintained.

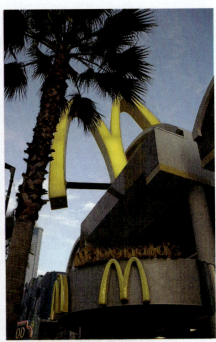

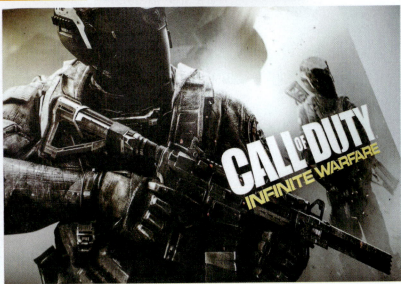

▲ These images have meaning for all of us—meaning that is socially constructed through communication in our culture. How many can you recognize? What specific meaning or meanings does each have for you? How did you develop each meaning? How closely do you think your meanings match those of your friends? Of your parents? What value is there—if any—in having shared meaning for these things in our everyday lives?

(clockwise from top left) ©Fox/Photofest; ©McGraw-Hill Education/John Flournoy, photographer; ©Rich Polk/Getty Images; ©Joe Drivas/Getty Images

Functions and Effects of Culture

Culture serves a purpose. It helps us categorize and classify our experiences; it helps define us, our world, and our place in it. In doing so, culture can have a number of sometimes conflicting effects.

LIMITING AND LIBERATING EFFECTS OF CULTURE   A culture's learned traditions and values can be seen as patterned, repetitive ways of thinking, feeling, and acting. Culture limits our options and provides useful guidelines for behavior. For example, when conversing, you do not consciously consider, "Now, how far away should I stand? Am I too close?" You simply stand where you stand. After a hearty meal with a friend's family, you do not engage in mental self-debate, "Should I burp? Yes! No! Arghhhh. . . ." Culture provides information that helps us make meaningful distinctions about right and wrong, appropriate and inappropriate, good and bad, attractive and unattractive, and so on. How does it do this?

Obviously, it does so through communication. Through a lifetime of communication, we have learned just what our culture expects of us. The two examples given here are positive results of culture's limiting effects. But culture's limiting effects can be negative, such as when we are unwilling or unable to move past patterned, repetitive ways of thinking, feeling, and acting or when we entrust our "learning" to teachers whose interests are selfish, narrow, or otherwise inconsistent with our own.

U.S. culture, for example, values thinness and beauty in women. How many women endure weeks of unhealthy diets and succumb to potentially dangerous surgical procedures in search of a body that for most is physically unattainable? How many women are judged by the men and other women around them for not conforming to our culture's standards of thinness and beauty? Why is the expression "fat shaming" in our language? Why are 40% to 60% of girls aged 6 to 12 concerned about their weight or about becoming too fat? Why do 42% of girls in first, second, and third grade want to be thinner, and why are 81% of 10-year-olds—girls *and* boys—afraid of being overweight? Why do over one-half of teenage girls and nearly one-third of teenage boys use unhealthy weight control behaviors like skipping meals, fasting, smoking cigarettes, vomiting, and taking laxatives (National Eating Disorders Association, 2016)? Why do almost 1.3 million adolescent girls in the United States have anorexia (Pai & Schryver, 2015)?

Now consider how this situation may have come about. Our parents did not bounce us on their knees when we were babies, telling us that thin was good and fat was bad. Think back, though, to the stories you were told and the television shows and movies you watched growing up. The heroines (or, more often, the beautiful love interests of the heroes) were invariably tall, beautiful, and thin. The bad guys were usually mean and fat. From Disney's depictions of Snow White, Cinderella, Belle, Jasmine, and Pocahontas to the impossible dimensions of most video game and comic book heroines, the message is embedded in the conscious (and unconscious) mind of every girl and boy: You can't be too thin or too beautiful! As it is, 69% of women and 65% of girls cite constant pressure from advertising and media to reach unrealistic standards of beauty as a major factor fueling their anxiety about their appearance (Dove, 2016). And it does not help that these messages are routinely reinforced throughout the culture, for example in the recent explosion of day spas for girls as young as 3 that "honor the feminine" while the little misses are treated "like a Kardashian" (Turkewitz, 2015, p. A1).

This message and millions of others come to us primarily through the media, and although the people who produce these media images are not necessarily selfish or mean, their motives are undeniably financial. Their contribution to our culture's repetitive ways of thinking, feeling, and acting is most certainly not primary among their concerns when preparing their communication.

Culture need not only limit. That media representations of female beauty often meet with debate and disagreement points out the fact that culture can be liberating as well. This is so because cultural values can be *contested*. In fact, today, we're just as likely to see strong, intelligent female characters who save the day like *Brave*'s Merida, *Mulan*'s Fa Mulan, and *Cloudy with a Chance of Meatballs*'s Sam Sparks as we are movie princesses who need to be saved by the hero.

Especially in a pluralistic, democratic society such as ours, the **dominant culture** (or **mainstream culture**)—the one that seems to hold sway with the majority of people—is often openly challenged. People do meet, find attractive, like, and love people who do not fit the standard image of beauty. In addition, media sometimes present images that suggest different ideals of beauty and success. Actresses Sofia Vergara, Dascha Polanco, and Mindy Kaling; singers/actresses Beyoncé and Jennifer Lopez; and comedian Amy Schumer all represent alternatives to our culture's idealized standards of beauty, and all have undeniable appeal (and power) on the big and small screens. Liberation from the limitations imposed by culture resides in our ability and willingness to learn and use *new* patterned, repetitive ways of thinking, feeling, and acting; to challenge existing patterns; and to create our own.

▲ Culture can be contested. The makers of Dove soap challenge the culture's narrow image of beauty with its "Real Women Have Curves" campaign, placing images like this on billboards and bus stops across the country, running them in national magazines, and making them the focus of its TV commercials. In 2015, the editors of *Advertising Age* magazine awarded Dove's Campaign for Real Beauty its prize as the Number 1 ad campaign of the 21st century for being "brave, bold, insightful, transparent, and authentic." Not only was it successful, they noted, in advocating that women are in control of their own definitions of beauty, but sales of Dove's products increased from $2.5 to $4 billion over the span of the campaign ("Top Ad," 2015, p. 16).
©*Ruby Washington*/The New York Times/*Redux*

DEFINING, DIFFERENTIATING, DIVIDING, AND UNITING EFFECTS OF CULTURE Have you ever made the mistake of calling a dolphin, porpoise, or even a whale a fish? Maybe you have heard others do it. This error occurs because when we think of fish, we think "lives in the water" and "swims." Fish are defined by their "aquatic culture." Because water-residing, swimming dolphins, porpoises, and whales share that culture, we sometimes forget that they are mammals, not fish.

We, too, are defined by our culture. We are citizens of the United States; we are Americans. If we travel to other countries, we will hear ourselves labeled "American," and this label will conjure up stereotypes and expectations in the minds of those who use and hear it. The stereotype, whatever it may be, will probably fit us only incompletely, or perhaps hardly at all—perhaps we are dolphins in a sea full of fish. Nevertheless, being American defines us in innumerable important ways, both to others (more obviously) and to ourselves (less obviously).

Within this large, national culture, however, there are many smaller, **bounded cultures** (or **co-cultures**). For example, we speak comfortably of Italian neighborhoods, fraternity row, the South, and the suburbs. Because of our cultural understanding of these categories, each expression communicates something about our expectations of these places. We think we can

▲ *Pretty Little Liars, Nashville,* and *The Vampire Diaries*—these three television programs are aimed at different audiences, yet in each the characters share certain traits that mark them as attractive. Must people in real life look like these performers to be considered attractive? Successful? Good? The people shown are all slender, tall, and young. Yes, they are just make-believe television characters, but the producers of the shows on which they appear chose these people—as opposed to others—for a reason. What do you think it was? How well do you measure up to the cultural standard of beauty and attractiveness represented here? Do you ever wish that you could be just a bit more like these people? Why or why not?

(top) ©ABC Family/Photofest; *(bottom left and right)* ©AF archive/Alamy

predict with a good deal of certainty the types of restaurants and shops we will find in the Italian neighborhood, even the kind of music we will hear escaping from open windows. We can predict the kinds of clothes and cars we will see on fraternity row, the likely behavior of shop clerks in the South, and the political orientation of the suburb's residents. Moreover, the people within these cultures usually identify themselves as members of those bounded cultures. An individual may say, for example, "I am Italian American" or "I'm from the South." These smaller cultures unite groups of people and enable them to see themselves as different from other groups around them. Thus culture also serves to differentiate us from others.

In the United States, we generally consider this a good thing. We pride ourselves on our pluralism, on our diversity, and on the richness of the cultural heritages represented within our borders. We enjoy moving from one bounded culture to another or from a bounded culture to the dominant national culture and back again.

Problems arise, however, when differentiation leads to division. All Americans are traumatized by horrific events such as the terrorist attacks of September 11, 2001, and the 2016 mass shooting at the Pulse nightclub in Orlando, but those tragedies are compounded for the millions of Muslim Americans whose patriotism is challenged simply because they belong to a particular bounded culture. Not only are the number of cases of violence against Muslims in America at an all-time high (Lichtblau, 2016), but the Department of Homeland Security reports that incidents of Muslim American terrorism continue to be far less common

▲ What is it about Muslim Americans that "communicates disloyalty" to some in the United States?
©Hans Millett/Newzulu/Alamy

than right-wing or antigovernment terrorism, and cooperation from the Muslim American community has been essential in its efforts to investigate domestic threats (Shane, 2016); still we continue to see examples of overt discrimination. For example, in the wake of a serious increase in hateful online and public commentary following the release of its 2015 film *American Sniper*, movie studio Warner Bros. felt compelled to issue a statement declaring that it "denounces any violent, anti-Muslim rhetoric, including that which has been attributed to viewers of *American Sniper*. Hate and bigotry have no place in the important dialogue that this picture has generated about the veteran experience"(Mandell, 2015). Muslim Americans' religion, skin color, and clothing "communicate" disloyalty to the United States to many other Americans. Just as culture is constructed and maintained through communication, it is also communication (or miscommunication) that turns differentiation into division.

Yet U.S. citizens of all colors, ethnicities, genders, nationalities, places of birth, economic strata, and intelligence levels often get along; in fact, we *can* communicate, *can* prosper, and *can* respect one another's differences. Culture can divide us, but culture also unites us. Our culture represents our collective experience. We converse easily with strangers because we share the same culture. We speak the same language, automatically understand how far apart to stand, appropriately use titles or first or last names, know how much to say, and know how much to leave unsaid. Through communication with people in our culture, we internalize cultural norms and values—those things that bind our many diverse bounded cultures into a functioning, cohesive society.

DEFINING CULTURE From this discussion comes the definition of culture on which the remainder of this book is based:

> Culture is the world made meaningful; it is socially constructed and maintained through communication. It limits as well as liberates us; it differentiates as well as unites us. It defines our realities and thereby shapes the ways we think, feel, and act.

Mass Communication and Culture

Despite the fact that culture can limit and divide, it can also liberate and unite. As such, it offers us infinite opportunities to use communication for good—if we choose to do so. James Carey (1975) wrote:

> Because we have looked at each new advance in communication technology as opportunities for politics and economics, we have devoted them, almost exclusively, to government and trade. We have rarely seen them as opportunities to expand [our] powers to learn and exchange ideas and experience. (pp. 20–21)

Who are "we" in this quote? *We* are the people involved in creating and maintaining the culture that defines us. *We* are the people involved in mass media industries and the people who compose their audiences. Together we allow mass communication not only to occur but also to contribute to the creation and maintenance of culture.

Everyone involved has an obligation to participate responsibly. For people working in the media industries, this means professionally and ethically creating and transmitting content. For audience members, it means behaving as critical and thoughtful consumers of that content. Two ways to understand our opportunities and our responsibilities in the mass communication process are to view the mass media as our cultural storytellers and to conceptualize mass communication as a cultural forum.

Mass Media as Cultural Storytellers

A culture's values and beliefs reside in the stories it tells. Who are the good guys? Who are the bad guys? How many of your childhood heroines were even slightly overweight? How many good guys dressed in black? How many heroines lived happily ever after without marrying Prince Charming? Probably not very many. Our stories help define our realities, shaping the ways we think, feel, and act. "Stories are sites of observations about self and society," explains media theorist Hanno Hardt (2007). "These fictional accounts are the constitutive material signs of a shared conversation" (p. 476). Therefore, the "storytellers" have a responsibility to tell their stories in as professional and ethical a way as possible.

At the same time, we, the audience for these stories, also have opportunities and responsibilities. We use these stories not only to be entertained but also to learn about the world around us, to understand the values, the way things work, and how the pieces fit together. We have a responsibility to question the tellers and their stories, to interpret the stories in ways consistent with larger or more important cultural values and truths, to be thoughtful, and to reflect on the stories' meanings and what they say about us and our culture. To do less is to miss an opportunity to construct our own meaning and, thereby, culture.

For example, *Women's Health* recently joined a host of other publications, promising to ban expressions like "bikini body" and "drop two sizes" from its covers (McNiel, 2016), and lingerie company Aerie vowed to no longer use photoshopped models in its ads (and saw sales surge; Mosbergen, 2016). Brewer Anheuser-Busch InBev discontinued its promotion of Bud Light as "the perfect beer for removing 'no' from your vocabulary for the night" (Schultz, 2015). And in 2016, toy maker Mattel announced that it would begin selling new versions—curvy, petite, and tall—of its formerly anatomically impossible fashion doll Barbie, all in a variety of skin tones, eye colors, and hairstyles (Abrams, 2016). In each case, the cultural conversation—on social media, among friends, and in the mass media—demanded a different, and better, way of talking about women and girls.

▲ Unchanged since 1959, the appearance of the iconic Barbie doll underwent significant alteration in 2016 after the cultural conversation demanded a different, and better, way of thinking about how real girls look.
©*Mattel/Splash News/Newscom*

Mass Communication as Cultural Forum

Imagine a giant courtroom in which we discuss and debate our culture—what it is, and what we want it to be. What do we think about welfare? Single motherhood? Labor unions? Nursing homes? What is the meaning of "successful," "good," "loyal," "moral," "honest," "beautiful," or "patriotic"? We have cultural definitions or understandings of all these things and more. Where do they come from? How do they develop, take shape, and mature?

Mass communication has become a primary forum for the debate about our culture. Logically, then, the most powerful voices in the forum have the most power to shape our definitions and understandings. Where should that power reside—with the media industries or with their audiences? If you answer "media industries," you will want members of these industries to act professionally and ethically. If you answer "audiences," you will want individual audience members to be thoughtful and critical of the media messages they consume. The forum is only as good, fair, and honest as those who participate in it.

Scope and Nature of Mass Media

No matter how we choose to view the process of mass communication, it is impossible to deny that an enormous portion of our lives is spent interacting with mass media. On a typical Sunday night, about 40 million people in the United States will tune in to a prime-time television show. Video viewing is at an all-time high and accounts for more than half of all adult Americans' leisure-time activity. Ninety-six percent of all U.S. homes have at least one set, and 95% of those homes have high-definition sets (Television Advertising Bureau, 2017). Seventy percent of TV viewers admit to **binge viewing**, watching five or more episodes of a series in one sitting, and 93% multitask while watching (Sharma, 2016), meaning the average American actually enjoys 31 hours and 28 seconds of activity in any given day (Ault, 2015). On Facebook alone, 1.8 billion people daily watch more than 100 million hours of video (Constantine, 2016). We listen to nearly four hours of music every day (Ault, 2015), and we spend more than $11 billion a year at the movies, buying just over 1.3 billion tickets (Barnes, 2017). If Facebook were its own country, its 1.8 billion monthly active users would make it the largest in the world. Facebook alone accounts for 6% of all the time the world's Internet users spend online (Smith, 2015). Sixty-three percent of American households are home to at least one person who plays video games three or more hours a week, and half of all U.S. homes have a game console, averaging two per home (Entertainment Software Association, 2016).

Just under 4 billion people across the globe are connected to the Internet, 50% of the planet's population and a 918% increase since 2000. Eighty-nine percent of North Americans use the Internet, a 196% increase since 2000 ("Internet users," 2016). Annual global Internet traffic passed the zettabyte (that's 1,000 exabytes, which is 1 billion gigabytes) threshold in 2016 and will reach 2.3 zettabytes per year by 2020. Worldwide Internet traffic has increased five-fold over the past five years and will increase three-fold over the next five years. That traffic in 2020 will be 95 times greater than it was in 2005. By 2020 nearly a million minutes of video content will cross the Internet every second, and it would take you more than 5 million years to watch all the video that will travel the Internet each month (Cisco Systems, 2016). You can see Americans' media preferences in Figure 5 and how those preferences have changed over the last few years.

Despite the pervasiveness of mass media in our lives, many of us are dissatisfied with or critical of the media industries' performance and much of the content provided. For example, only 17% of adults feel that entertainment media provide "very good" or "excellent" value (Smith, 2011). People's evaluations of the news media have also become more negative over the last decade. Their trust in each of the three major news sources—television, newspapers, and the Internet—has fallen to its lowest level since 1994, continuing a "decades-long decline in the share of Americans saying they have 'a great deal' or 'quite a lot' of confidence" in their media (Dugan, 2014). Their faith in the "media's ability to report the news fully, accurately, and fairly" has also dropped to a historic low of 32% of all Americans (Swift, 2016). Seventy percent believe that the news media have "a negative effect on the nation" (Geiger, 2016).

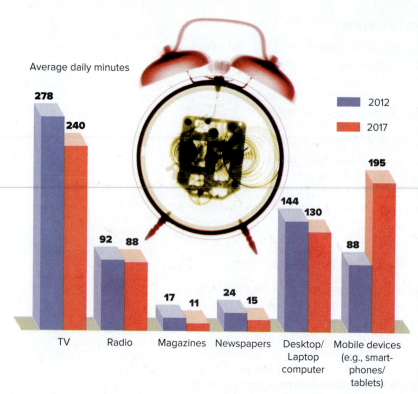

Average daily minutes

278 | 240 | 92 | 88 | 17 | 11 | 24 | 15 | 144 | 130 | 88 | 195

2012
2017

TV   Radio   Magazines   Newspapers   Desktop/ Laptop computer   Mobile devices (e.g., smart- phones/ tablets)

▲ **Figure 5** Average Number of Minutes per Day a Typical Adult Spends with Selected Media, 2012 versus 2017.

Source: eMarketer, "Growth in time spent with media is slowing," eMarketer.com, June 6, 2016. Online: http://www.emarketer.com/ Article/Growth-Time-Spent-with-Media-Slowing/1014042
©Jim Wehtje/Getty Images RF

Our ambivalence—we criticize, yet we consume—comes in part from our uncertainties about the relationships among the elements of mass communication. What is the role of technology? What is the role of money? And what is *our* role in the mass communication process?

The Role of Technology

To some thinkers, it is machines and their development that drive economic and cultural change. This idea is referred to as **technological determinism**. Certainly there can be no doubt that movable type contributed to the Protestant Reformation and the decline of the Catholic Church's power in Europe or that television changed the way members of American families interact. Those who believe in technological determinism would argue that these changes in the cultural landscape were the inevitable result of new technology.

But others see technology as more neutral and claim that the way people *use* technology is what gives it significance. This perspective accepts technology as one of many factors that shape economic and cultural change; technology's influence is ultimately determined by how much power it is given by the people and cultures that use it.

This disagreement about the power of technology is at the heart of the controversies that always seem to spring up with the introduction of new communication technologies. Are we more or less powerless in the wake of advances such as the Internet, the World Wide Web, and instant global audio and visual communication? If we are at the mercy of technology, the culture that surrounds us will not be of our making, and the best we can hope to do is make our way reasonably well in a world outside our control. But if these technologies are indeed neutral and their power resides in *how* we choose to use them, we can utilize them responsibly and thoughtfully to construct and maintain whatever kind of culture we want. As film director and technophile Steven Spielberg explained, "Technology can be our best friend, and technology can also be the biggest party pooper of our lives. It interrupts our own story, interrupts our ability to have a thought or daydream, to imagine something wonderful because we're too busy bridging the walk from the cafeteria back to the office on the cell phone" (quoted in Kennedy, 2002, p. 109). Or, as the character Dr. Ian Malcolm (played by Jeff Goldblum) said in Spielberg's 1997 *The Lost World: Jurassic Park,* "Oooh! Ahhh! That's how it always starts. Then later there's running and screaming."

Technology does have an impact on communication. At the very least it changes the basic elements of communication (see Figure 4). But what technology does not do is relieve us of our obligation to use mass communication responsibly and wisely.

The Role of Money

Money, too, alters communication. It shifts the balance of power; it tends to make audiences products rather than consumers.

The first newspapers were financially supported by their readers; the money they paid for the paper covered its production and distribution. But in the 1830s a new form of newspaper financing emerged. Publishers began selling their papers for a penny—much less than it cost to produce and distribute them. Because so many more papers were sold at this bargain price, publishers could "sell" advertising space based on their readership. What they were actually selling to advertisers was not space on the page—it was readers. How much they could charge advertisers was directly related to how much product (how many readers) they could produce for them.

This new type of publication changed the nature of mass communication. The goal of the process was no longer for audience and media to create meaning together. Rather, it was to sell those readers to a third participant—advertisers.

Some observers think this was a devastatingly bad development, not only in the history of mass communication but in the history of democracy. It robbed people of their voice, or at least made the voices of the advertisers more powerful. Others think it was a huge advance for both mass communication and democracy because it vastly expanded the media, broadening and deepening communication. Models showing these two different ways of viewing mass communication are presented in the box "Audience as Consumer or Audience as Product?" Which model makes more sense to you? Which do you think is more accurate? ABC journalist Ted Koppel told *The Washington Post,* "[Television] is an industry. It's a business. We exist to make money. We exist to put commercials on the air. The programming that is put on between those commercials is simply the bait we put in the mousetrap" (in "Soundbites," 2005, p. 2). Do you think Koppel is unnecessarily cynical, or is he correct in his analysis of television?

The goals of media professionals will be questioned repeatedly throughout this book. For now, keep in mind that ours is a capitalist economic system and that media industries are businesses. Movie producers must sell tickets, book publishers must sell books, and even public broadcasting has bills to pay.

This does not mean, however, that the media are or must be slaves to profit. Our task is to understand the constraints placed on these industries by their economics and then demand that, within those limits, they perform ethically and responsibly. We can do this only by being thoughtful, critical consumers of the media.

CULTURAL FORUM
Audience as Consumer or Audience as Product?

People base their judgments of media performance and content on the way they see themselves fitting into the economics of the media industry. Businesses operate to serve their consumers and make a profit. The consumer comes first, then, but who *is* the consumer in our mass media system? This is a much-debated issue among media practitioners and media critics. Consider the following models.

	PRODUCER	PRODUCT	CONSUMERS
Basic U.S. Business Model	A manufacturer . . .	produces a product . . .	for consumers who choose to buy or not. The manufacturer must satisfy the consumer. Power resides here.
Basic U.S. Business Model for Cereal: Rice Krispies as Product, Public as Consumer	Kellogg's . . .	produces Rice Krispies . . .	for us, the consumers. If we buy Rice Krispies, Kellogg's makes a profit. Kellogg's must satisfy the consumer. Power resides here.
Basic U.S. Business Model for Television (A): Audience as Product, Advertisers as Consumer	NBC . . .	produces audiences (using its programming) . . .	for advertisers. If they buy NBC's audiences, NBC makes a profit from ad time. NBC must satisfy its consumers, the advertisers. Power resides here.
Basic U.S. Business Model for Television (B): Programming as Product, Audience as Consumer	NBC . . .	produces (or distributes) programming . . .	for us, the audience. If we watch NBC's shows, NBC makes a profit from ad sales. NBC must satisfy its audience. Power resides here.

The first three models assume that the consumer *buys* the product; that is, the consumer is the one with the money and therefore the one who must be satisfied. The last model makes a different assumption. It sees the audience, even though it does not buy anything, as sufficiently important to NBC's profit-making ability to force NBC to consider the audience's interests above others' (even those of advertisers). Which model do you think best represents the economics of U.S. mass media?

Mass Communication, Culture, and Media Literacy

Culture and communication are inseparable, and mass communication, as we've seen, is a particularly powerful, pervasive, and complex form of communication. Our level of skill in the mass communication process is therefore of utmost importance. This skill is not necessarily a simple one to master (it is much more than booting up the computer, turning on the television, or flipping through the pages of your favorite magazine). But it is, indeed, a learnable skill, one that can be practiced. This skill is **media literacy**—the ability to effectively and efficiently comprehend and use any form of mediated communication. But let's start with the first mass medium, books, and the technology that enabled their spread, the printing press.

The Gutenberg Revolution

As it is impossible to overstate the importance of writing, so too is it impossible to overstate the significance of Johannes Gutenberg's development of movable metal type. Historian S. H. Steinberg (1959) wrote in *Five Hundred Years of Printing*:

> Neither political, constitutional, ecclesiastical, and economic, nor sociological, philosophical, and literary movements can be fully understood without taking into account the influence the printing press has exerted upon them. (p. 11)

Marshall McLuhan expressed his admiration for Gutenberg's innovation by calling his 1962 book *The Gutenberg Galaxy*. In it he argued that the advent of print is the key to our modern consciousness, because although **literacy**—the ability to effectively and efficiently comprehend and use written symbols—had existed since the development of the first alphabets more than 5,000 years ago, it was reserved for very few, the elites. Gutenberg's invention was world-changing because it opened literacy to all; that is, it allowed *mass* communication.

THE PRINTING PRESS Printing and the printing press existed long before Gutenberg perfected his process in or around 1446. The Chinese were using wooden block presses as early as 600 C.E. and had movable clay type by 1000 C.E. A simple movable metal type was even in use in Korea in the 13th century. Gutenberg's printing press was a significant leap forward, however, for two important reasons.

Gutenberg was a goldsmith and a metallurgist. He hit on the idea of using metal type crafted from lead molds in place of type made from wood or clay. This was an important advance. Not only was movable metal type durable enough to print page after page, but letters could be arranged and rearranged to make any message possible, and Gutenberg was able to produce virtually identical copies.

In addition, Gutenberg's advance over Korean metal mold printing was one of scope. The Korean press was used to produce books for a very small, royal readership. Gutenberg saw his invention as a way to produce many books for profit. He was, however, a poor businessman. He stressed quality over quantity, in part because of his reverence for the book he was printing, the Bible. He used the highest-quality paper and ink and turned out far fewer volumes than he otherwise could have.

Other printers, however, quickly saw the true economic potential of Gutenberg's invention. The first Gutenberg Bible appeared in 1456. By the end of that century, 44 years later, printing operations existed in 12 European countries, and the continent was flooded with 20 million volumes of 7,000 titles in 35,000 different editions (Drucker, 1999).

THE IMPACT OF PRINT Although Gutenberg developed his printing press with a limited use in mind, printing Bibles, the cultural effects of mass printing have been profound.

Handwritten or hand-copied materials were expensive to produce, and the cost of an education, in time and money, had made reading an expensive luxury. However, with the spread of printing, written communication was available to a much larger portion of the population, and the need for literacy among the lower and middle classes grew. The ability to read became less of a luxury and more of a necessity; eventually literacy spread, as did education. Soldiers at the front needed to be able to read the emperor's orders. Butchers needed to

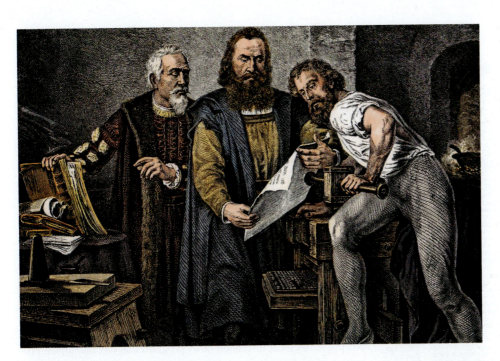

Johannes Gutenberg takes the first proof from his printing press.
©*North Wind Picture Archives*

understand the king's shopping list. So the demand for literacy expanded, and more (and more types of) people learned to read.

Tradespeople, soldiers, clergy, bakers, and musicians all now had business at the printer's shop. They talked. They learned of things, both in conversation and by reading printed material. As more people learned to read, new ideas germinated and spread, and cross-pollination of ideas occurred.

More material from various sources was published, and people were freer to read what they wanted when they wanted. Dominant authorities—the Crown and the Church—were now less able to control communication and, therefore, the people. New ideas about the world appeared; new understandings of the existing world flourished.

In addition, duplication permitted standardization and preservation. Myth and superstition began to make way for standard, verifiable bodies of knowledge. History, economics, physics, and chemistry all became part of the culture's intellectual life. Literate cultures were now on the road to modernization.

Printed materials were the first mass-produced product, speeding the development and entrenchment of capitalism. We live today in a world built on these changes. Use of the printing press helped fuel the establishment and growth of a large middle class. No longer were societies composed of rulers and subjects; printing sped the rise of democracy. No longer were power and wealth functions of birth; power and wealth could now be created by the industrious. No longer was political discourse limited to accepting the dictates of Crown and Church; printing had given ordinary people a powerful voice.

Tech writer Kevin Kelly connected printing directly to freedom and the rule of law:

When technology shifts, it bends the culture. Once, long ago, culture revolved around the spoken word. The oral skills of memorization, recitation, and rhetoric instilled in societies a reverence for the past, the ambiguous, the ornate, and the subjective. Then, about 500 years ago, orality was overthrown by technology. Gutenberg's invention of metallic moveable type elevated writing into a central position in the culture. By means of cheap and perfect copies, text became the engine of change and the foundation of stability. From printing came journalism, science and the mathematics of libraries and law. (2008, p. 48)

The Industrial Revolution

By the mid-18th century, printing and its libraries of science and mathematics had become powerful engines driving the Industrial Revolution. Print was responsible for building and disseminating bodies of knowledge, leading to scientific and technological developments and the refinement of new machines. In addition, industrialization reduced the time necessary to

▲ This page from a Gutenberg Bible shows the exquisite care the printer used in creating his works. The artwork in the margins is hand painted, but the text is mechanically printed.

©North Wind Picture Archives/ Alamy

complete work, and this created something previously unknown to most working people—leisure time.

Industrialization had another effect as well. As workers left their sunrise-to-sunset jobs in agriculture, the crafts, and trades to work in the newly industrialized factories, not only did they have more leisure time, but they also had more money to spend on their leisure. Farmers, fishermen, and tile makers had to put their profits back into their jobs. But factory workers took their money home; it was spendable. Combine leisure time and expendable cash with the spread of literacy, and the result is a large and growing audience for printed *information* and *entertainment.* By the mid-19th century, a mass audience and the means to reach it existed.

Media Literacy

Television influences our culture in innumerable ways. One of its effects, according to many people, is that it has encouraged violence in our society. For example, American television viewers overwhelmingly say there is too much violence on television. Yet, almost without exception, the local television news program that has the largest proportion of violence in its nightly newscast is the ratings leader. "If it bleeds, it leads" has become the motto for much of local television news. It leads because people watch.

So, although many of us are quick to condemn improper media performance or to identify and lament its harmful effects, we rarely question our own role in the mass communication process. We overlook it because we participate in mass communication naturally, almost without conscious effort. We possess high-level interpretive and comprehension skills that make even the most sophisticated television show, movie, or magazine story understandable and enjoyable. We are able, through a lifetime of interaction with the media, to *read media texts.*

Media literacy is a skill we take for granted, but like all skills, it can be improved. And if we consider how important the mass media are in creating and maintaining the culture that helps define us and our lives, it is a skill that *must* be improved.

Hunter College media professor Stuart Ewen (2000) emphasized this point in comparing media literacy with traditional literacy. "Historically," he wrote, "links between literacy and democracy are inseparable from the notion of an informed populace, conversant with the issues that touch upon their lives, enabled with tools that allow them to participate actively in public deliberation and social change. . . . Literacy was about crossing the lines that had historically separated men of ideas from ordinary people, about the enfranchisement of those who had been excluded from the compensations of citizenship" (p. 448). To Ewen, and others committed to media literacy, media literacy represents no less than the means to full participation in the culture.

Elements of Media Literacy

Media scholar Art Silverblatt (2008) identifies seven fundamental elements of media literacy. To these we will add an eighth. Media literacy includes these characteristics:

1. *A critical thinking skill enabling audience members to develop independent judgments about media content.* Thinking critically about the content we consume is the very essence of media literacy. Why do we watch what we watch, read what we read, listen to what we listen to? Is that story you saw on Twitter real? If we cannot answer these questions, we have taken no responsibility for ourselves or our choices. As such, we have taken no responsibility for the outcome of those choices.

2. *An understanding of the process of mass communication.* If we know the components of the mass communication process and how they relate to one another, we can form

expectations of how they can serve us. How do the various media industries operate? What are their obligations to us? What are the obligations of the audience? How do different media limit or enhance messages? Which forms of feedback are most effective, and why?

3. *An awareness of the impact of media on the individual and society.* Writing and the printing press helped change the world and the people in it. Mass media do the same. If we ignore the impact of media on our lives, we run the risk of being caught up and carried along by that change rather than controlling or leading it.

4. *Strategies for analyzing and discussing media messages.* To consume media messages thoughtfully, we need a foundation on which to base thought and reflection. If we make meaning, we must possess the tools with which to make it (for example, understanding the intent and impact of film and video conventions, such as camera angles and lighting, or the strategy behind the placement of images on a newspaper's website). Otherwise, meaning is made for us; the interpretation of media content will then rest with its creator, not with us.

5. *An understanding of media content as a text that provides insight into our culture and our lives.* How do we know a culture and its people, attitudes, values, concerns, and myths? We know them through communication. For modern cultures like ours, media messages increasingly dominate that communication, shaping our understanding of and insight into our culture.

6. *The ability to enjoy, understand, and appreciate media content.* Media literacy does not mean living the life of a grump, liking nothing in the media, or always being suspicious of harmful effects and cultural degradation. We take high school and college classes to enhance our understanding and appreciation of novels; we can do the same for media texts.

   Learning to enjoy, understand, and appreciate media content includes the ability to use **multiple points of access**—to approach media content from a variety of directions and derive from it many levels of meaning. Thus, we control meaning making for our own enjoyment or appreciation. For example, we can enjoy any one of the hit movies from the *Hunger Games* trilogy as an action-laden adventure full of explosions, danger, and romance, the perfect holiday blockbuster. But as movie buffs we might see it as a David-and-Goliath, underdog-takes-on-the-powerful-villain tale. Or we might read it as an analogy for what's happening in America's contemporary economy of growing income inequality and harshness of life for those near the bottom. Maybe it's a history lesson disguised as dystopian fiction, reminding us that our country was born of revolution against those who would rule us. Or maybe it's just a fun way to spend a Saturday night, entertained by the same industry that so delighted us with other special-effects extravaganzas, like *Fantastic Beasts and Where to Find Them*, *Doctor Strange*, and *Batman v Superman: Dawn of Justice*.

   In fact, television programs such as *Blackish*, *The Daily Show*, *The Simpsons*, *Game of Thrones*, and *Family Guy* are specifically constructed to appeal to the media literacy skills of sophisticated viewers while providing entertaining fare for less skilled consumers. *Blackish* and *The Daily Show* are produced as television comedies, designed to make people laugh. But they are also intentionally produced to provide more sophisticated, media-literate viewers with opportunities to make personally interesting or relevant meaning. Anyone can laugh while watching these programs, but some people can empathize with the daily travails of an upper-middle-class African American family working to deal with race while they pursue the American Dream (*Blackish*), or they can examine the failings and foibles of contemporary politics and journalism (*Daily Show*).

7. *Development of effective and responsible production skills.* Traditional literacy assumes that people who can read can also write. Media literacy also makes this assumption. Our definition of literacy (of either type) calls not only for effective and efficient comprehension of content but also for its effective and efficient *use*. Therefore, media-literate individuals should develop production skills that enable them to create useful media messages. If you have ever tried to make a narrative home video—one that tells a story—you know that producing content is much more difficult than consuming it. If you have ever posted to Snapchat or Instagram or uploaded a video to YouTube, you are indeed a media content producer; why not be a good media content producer?

8. *An understanding of the ethical and moral obligations of media practitioners.* To make informed judgments about the performance of the media, we also must be aware of the competing pressures on practitioners as they do their jobs. We must understand the media's official and unofficial rules of operation. In other words, we must know, respectively, their legal and ethical obligations. Return, for a moment, to the question of televised violence. It is legal for a station to air graphic violence. But is it ethical? If it is unethical, what power, if any, do we have to demand its removal from our screens? Dilemmas such as this are discussed at length in the chapter on media freedom, regulation, and ethics.

▶ *Family Guy* has all the things you would expect from a television situation comedy—an inept dad, a precocious daughter, a slacker son, a loving wife, and zany situations. Yet it also offers an intellectual, philosopher dog and an evil-genius, scheming baby. Why do you think the producers have gone to the trouble to populate this show with the usual trappings of a sitcom but then add other, bizarre elements? And what's going on in *The Hunger Games*? Is it another special-effects, explosion-laden, action-adventure holiday blockbuster? A classic David-and-Goliath movie? A historical allegory? A commentary on growing financial inequality in America?

(top) ©20th Century Fox/Courtesy Everett Collection; (bottom) ©Photos 12/Alamy

Media Literacy Skills

Consuming media content is simple. Push a button and you have images on a television or music on your car's radio. Come up with enough cash and you can see a movie or buy an e-book. Media-literate consumption, however, requires a number of specific skills:

1. *The ability and willingness to make an effort to understand content, to pay attention, and to filter out noise.* As we saw earlier, anything that interferes with successful communication is called noise, and much of the noise in the mass communication process results from our own consumption behavior. When we watch television, often we are also doing other things, such as eating, reading, or chatting on the phone. We drive while we listen to the radio. We text while we read. Obviously, the quality of our meaning making is related to the effort we give it.

2. *An understanding of and respect for the power of media messages.* We are surrounded by mass media from the moment we are born. Just about every one of us can enjoy them. Their content is either free or relatively inexpensive. Much of the content is banal and a bit silly, so it is easy to dismiss media content as beneath serious consideration or too simple to have any influence.

   We also disregard media's power through the **third-person effect**—the common attitude that others are influenced by media messages but that we are not. That is, we are media literate enough to understand the influence of mass communication on the attitudes, behaviors, and values of others but not self-aware or honest enough to see its influence on our lives.

3. *The ability to distinguish emotional from reasoned reactions when responding to content and to act accordingly.* Media content is often designed to touch us at the emotional level. We enjoy losing ourselves in a good song or in a well-crafted movie or television show; this is among our great pleasures. But because we react emotionally to these messages does not mean they don't have serious meanings and implications for our lives. Television images, for example, are intentionally shot and broadcast for their emotional impact. Reacting emotionally is appropriate and proper. But then what? What do these images tell us about the larger issue at hand? We can use our feelings as a point of departure for meaning making. We can ask, "Why does this content make me feel this way?"

4. *The development of heightened expectations of media content.* We all use media to tune out, waste a little time, and provide background noise. When we decide to watch television, we are more likely to turn on the set and flip channels until we find something passable than we are to read the listings to find a specific program to view. When we search for online video, we often settle for the "10 most shared today," or we let Netflix choose for us. When we expect little from the content before us, we tend to give meaning making little effort and attention.

5. *A knowledge of genre conventions and the ability to recognize when they are being mixed.* The term **genre** refers to the categories of expression within the different media, such as "evening news," "documentary," "horror movie," or "entertainment magazine." Each genre is characterized by certain distinctive, standardized style elements—the **conventions** of that genre. The conventions of the evening news, for example, include a short, upbeat introductory theme and one or two good-looking people sitting at a large, modern desk. When we hear and see these style elements, we expect the evening news. We can tell a documentary film from an entertainment movie by its more serious tone and a number of talking heads. We know by their appearance—the use of color, the types of images, and the amount of text on the cover—which magazines offer serious reading and which provide entertainment.

   Knowledge of these conventions is important because they cue or direct our meaning making. For example, we know to accept the details in a documentary film about the Boston Marathon bombings as more credible than those found in *Patriots Day*, the 2016 Hollywood movie about the terrorist attack.

   This skill is also important for another reason. Sometimes, in an effort to maximize audiences (and therefore profits) or for creative reasons, media content makers mix genre conventions. Is *Deepwater Horizon* fact or fiction? Is Meredith Vieira a journalist, a talk show host, or a showperson? *Extra!* and *E! News* look increasingly like CNN's reporting and the *CBS Evening News*. Reading media texts becomes more difficult as formats are co-opted.

6. *The ability to think critically about media messages, no matter how credible their sources.* It is crucial that media be credible in a democracy in which the people govern because the media are central to the governing process. This is why the news media are

sometimes referred to as the fourth branch of government, complementing the executive, judicial, and legislative branches. This does not mean, however, that we should accept uncritically everything they report. But it is often difficult to arrive at the proper balance between wanting to believe and accepting what we see and hear unquestioningly, especially when frequently we are willing to suspend disbelief and are encouraged by the media themselves to see their content as real and credible.

But media-literate people know not to discount *all* news media; they must be careful to avoid the **hostile media effect**, the idea that people see media coverage of important topics of interest as less sympathetic to their position, more sympathetic to the opposing position, and generally hostile to their point of view regardless of the quality of the coverage (Tsfati & Cohen, 2013). There are indeed very good media sources, just as there are those not deserving of our respect. Media literacy, as you'll read throughout this text, helps us make that distinction.

7. *A knowledge of the internal language of various media and the ability to understand its effects, no matter how complex.* Just as each media genre has its own distinctive style and conventions, each medium also has its own specific internal language. This language is expressed in **production values**—the choice of lighting, editing, special effects, music, camera angle, location on the page, and size and placement of headlines. To be able to read a media text, you must understand its language. We learn the grammar of this language as early as childhood—for example, we know that when the television image goes "all woosielike," the character is dreaming.

Let's consider two versions of the same movie scene. In the first, a man is driving a car. Cut to a woman lying tied up on a railroad track. What is the relationship between the man and the woman? Where is he going? With no more information than these two shots, you know automatically that he cares for her and is on his way to save her. Now, here is the second version. The man is driving the car. Fade to black. Fade back up to the woman on the tracks. Now what is the relationship between the man and the woman? Where is he going? It is less clear that these two people even have anything to do with each other. We construct completely different meanings from exactly the same two scenes because the punctuation (the quick cut/fade) differs.

Media texts tend to be more complicated than these two scenes. The better we can handle their grammar, the more we can understand and appreciate texts. The more we understand texts, the more we can be equal partners with media professionals in meaning making.

▶ *The Daily Show with Trevor Noah* offers all the conventions we'd expect from the news—background digital graphics, an anchor behind his desk, and a well-known interviewee. But it also contains conventions we'd expect from a comedy program—a satirist as host and an unruly, loud audience. Why does this television show mix the conventions of these two very different genres? Does your knowledge of those conventions add to your enjoyment of this hit program? *©Brad Barket/Comedy Central/ Getty Images*

MEDIA LITERACY CHALLENGE
Recognizing Cultural Values

Media-literate people develop *an understanding of media content as a text that provides insight into our culture and our lives,* and they have *an awareness of the impact of media on the individual and society.* So, challenge your own media literacy skills. You can do this exercise with a parent or another person older than you, or you can speculate after using the Internet to view movies and television shows from 20 years ago. Compare your childhood heroes and heroines with those of someone older. What differences are there between the generations in what you consider heroic qualities? What are some similarities and differences between the heroic qualities you and people from an earlier generation identify? Are the good qualities of your personal heroes something you can find in today's movies or TV? If so, where on TV or in film can you find the qualities you consider heroic? Which cultural values, attitudes, and beliefs, if any, do you think have influenced how heroes and heroines have changed throughout the last few decades? How have the media helped establish the values you identify as important qualities in people?

Resources for Review and Discussion

REVIEW POINTS: TYING CONTENT TO LEARNING OUTCOMES

▶ **Define** *communication, mass communication, mass media,* **and** *culture.*
- ☐ Communication is the process of creating shared meaning.
- ☐ Mass communication is the process of creating shared meaning between the mass media and their audiences.
- ☐ Mass media is the plural of mass medium, a technology that carries messages to a large number of people.
- ☐ Culture is the world made meaningful. It resides all around us; it is socially constructed and maintained through communication. It limits as well as liberates us; it differentiates as well as unites us. It defines our realities and shapes the ways we think, feel, and act.

▶ **Describe the relationships among communication, mass communication, culture, and those who live in the culture.**
- ☐ Mass media are our culture's dominant storytellers and the forum in which we debate cultural meaning.

▶ **Evaluate the impact of technology and economics on those relationships.**
- ☐ Technological determinism argues that technology is the predominant agent of social and cultural change. But it is not technology that drives culture; it is how people use technology.
- ☐ With technology, money, too, shapes mass communication. Audiences can be either the consumer or the product in our mass media system.

▶ **List the components of media literacy.**
- ☐ Media literacy, the ability to effectively and efficiently comprehend and use any form of mediated communication, consists of eight components:
  1. A critical thinking skill enabling the development of independent judgments about media content
  2. An understanding of the process of mass communication
  3. An awareness of the impact of the media on individuals and society
  4. Strategies for analyzing and discussing media messages
  5. An awareness of media content as a "text" providing insight into contemporary culture
  6. A cultivation of enhanced enjoyment, understanding, and appreciation of media content
  7. The development of effective and responsible production skills
  8. The development of an understanding of the ethical and moral obligations of media practitioners

▶ **Identify key skills required for developing media literacy.**
- ☐ Media skills include
  - ▪ The ability and willingness to make an effort to understand content, to pay attention, and to filter out noise

- An understanding of and respect for the power of media messages
- The ability to distinguish emotional from reasoned reactions when responding to content and to act accordingly
- The development of heightened expectations of media content

- A knowledge of genre conventions and the recognition of their mixing
- The ability to think critically about media messages
- A knowledge of the internal language of various media and the ability to understand its effects

KEY TERMS

communication, 4

feedback, 5

interpersonal communication, 5

encoding, 5

decoding, 5

noise, 6

medium (pl. media), 6

mass medium, 6

mass communication, 6

inferential feedback, 6

cultural definition of communication, 7

culture, 7

dominant culture (mainstream culture), 11

bounded culture (co-culture), 11

binge viewing, 15

technological determinism, 16

media literacy, 18

literacy, 18

multiple points of access, 21

third-person effect, 23

genre, 23

conventions, 23

hostile media effect, 24

production values, 24

QUESTIONS FOR REVIEW

1. What is culture? How does culture define people?
2. What is communication? What is mass communication?
3. What are encoding and decoding? How do they differ when technology enters the communication process?
4. What does it mean to say that communication is a reciprocal process?
5. What is James Carey's cultural definition of communication? How does it differ from other definitions of that process?
6. What do we mean by mass media as cultural storyteller?
7. What do we mean by mass communication as cultural forum?

8. What is media literacy? What are its components?
9. What are some specific media literacy skills?
10. What is the difference between genres and production conventions? What do these have to do with media literacy?

To maximize your study time, check out CONNECT to access the SmartBook study module for this chapter and explore other resources.

QUESTIONS FOR CRITICAL THINKING AND DISCUSSION

1. Who were your childhood heroes and heroines? Why did you choose them? What cultural lessons did you learn from them?
2. The arrival of the printing press dramatically changed history. Traditional seats of power lost influence, science flourished, and the seeds were planted for capitalism and the growth of a middle class. What effects has the Internet had on how you

live different aspects of your life? Will its ultimate impact be less than, equal to, or greater than the impact wrought by the printing press? Defend your answer.

3. How media literate do you think you are? What about those around you—your parents, for example, or your best friend? What are your weaknesses as a media-literate person?

REFERENCES

1. Abrams, R. (2016, January 28). Barbie now comes in tall, short and curvy. *The New York Times*, p. B1.
2. Ault, S. (2015, November 24). Not enough hours? *Variety*, p. 31.
3. Barnes, B. (2017, January 1). Film audiences sought fantasy escapes in 2016. *The New York Times*, p. C2.
4. Carey, J. W. (1975). A cultural approach to communication. *Communication, 2*, 1–22.
5. Carey, J. W. (1989). *Communication as culture*. Boston: Unwin Hyman.
6. Cisco Systems. (2016, June 1). White paper. *Cisco.com*. Online: http://www.cisco.com/c/en/us/solutions/collateral/service-provider/visual-networking-index-vni/complete-white-paper-c11-481360.html
7. Constantine, J. (2016, January 27). Facebook hits 100M hours of video watched a day, 1B users on groups, 80M on FB lite. *TechCrunch*. Online: https://techcrunch.com/2016/01/27/facebook-grows/
8. Dove. (2016, June 21). New Dove research finds beauty pressures up, and women and girls calling for change.

PR Newswire. Online: http://www.prnewswire.com /news-releases/new-dove-research-finds-beauty -pressures-up-and-women-and-girls-calling-for -change-583743391.html

9. Drucker, P. E. (1999, October). Beyond the information revolution. *The Atlantic,* pp. 47–57.

10. Dugan, A. (2014, June 19). Americans' confidence in news media remains low. *Gallup.com.* Online: http://www.gallup .com/poll/171740/americans-confidence-news-media -remains-low.aspx

11. eMarketer. (2016, June 6). Growth in time spent with media is slowing. *eMarketer.com.* Online: http://www.emarketer .com/Article/Growth-Time-Spent-with-Media -Slowing/1014042

12. Entertainment Software Association. (2016). Essential facts about the computer and video game industry. Online: http://essentialfacts.theesa.com/

13. Ewen, S. (2000). Memoirs of a commodity fetishist. *Mass Communication & Society, 3,* 439–452.

14. Geiger, A. (2016, September 26). From universities to churches, Republicans and Democrats differ in views of major institutions. *Pew Research Center.* Online: http://www .pewresearch.org/fact-tank/2016/09/26/from-universities -to-churches-republicans-and-democrats-differ-in-views -of-major-institutions/

15. Hall, E. T. (1976). *Beyond culture.* New York: Doubleday.

16. Hardt, H. (2007, December). Constructing photography: Fiction as cultural evidence. *Critical Studies in Media Communication,* pp. 476–480.

17. Harris, M. (1983). *Cultural anthropology.* New York: Harper & Row.

18. Hunter, D. (2014, August 29). Do you check your smartphone before getting out of bed? *Fresh Business Thinking.* Online: http://www.freshbusinessthinking.com/do-you-check-your -smartphone-before-getting-out-of-bed/

19. "Internet users in the world." (2016). Internet World Statistics, June 30. Online: http://www.internetworldstats.com/stats.htm

20. Kelly, K. (2008, November 23). Becoming screen literate. *The New York Times Magazine,* pp. 48–53.

21. Kennedy, L. (2002, June). Spielberg in the Twilight Zone. *Wired,* pp. 106–113, 146.

22. Lasswell, H. D. (1948). The structure and function of communication in society. In L. Bryson (Ed.), *The Communication of Ideas.* New York: Harper.

23. Lichtblau, E. (2016, September 18). Level of hate crimes against U.S. Muslims highest since after 9/11. *The New York Times,* p. A13.

24. *The Lost World: Jurassic Park.* (1997). Directed by Steven Spielberg for Universal Studios.

25. Mandell, A. (2015, January 30). Warner Bros denounces anti-Muslim rhetoric following "American Sniper" release. *Huffington Post.* Online: http://www.huffingtonpost .com/2015/01/30warner-bros-anti-muslim-rhetoric _n_6574742.html

26. McLuhan, M. (1962). *The Gutenberg galaxy: The making of typographic man.* London: Routledge.

27. McNiel, S. (2016, January 1). A popular women's magazine is banning "bikini body" and "drop 2 sizes" from its cover. *BuzzFeed.* Online: https://www.buzzfeed.com /stephaniemcneal/bye-bikini-body?utm_term=. cpMRpqnW7#.ksVQYA3Bo

28. Miller, J. (2016, June 13). 2016 is on track to be Hollywood's worst year for ticket sales in a century. *Vanity Fair.* Online: http://www.vanityfair.com/hollywood/2016/06/hollywood -movie-ticket-sales

29. Mosbergen, D. (2016, May 19). Since lingerie brand Aerie ditched photoshopped ads, sales have surged. *Huffington Post.* Online: http://www.huffingtonpost.com/entry/aerie-photoshop -sales-growth-2016_us_573d35d6e4b0646cbeec260c

30. National Eating Disorders Association. (2016). Get the facts on eating disorders. *NEDA.org.* Online: https://www .nationaleatingdisorders.org/get-facts-eating-disorders

31. Pai, S. & Schryver, K. (2015). *Children, teens, media, and body image.* New York: Common Sense Media.

32. Rosaldo, R. (1989). *Culture and truth: The remaking of social analysis.* Boston: Beacon Press.

33. Schramm, W. L. (1954). *The process and effects of mass communication.* Urbana: University of Illinois Press.

34. Schultz, E. J. (2015, May 4). Brewer's "whatever" problem. *Advertising Age,* p. 4.

35. Shane, S. (2015, June 25). Most U.S. attacks are homegrown and not jihadist. *The New York Times,* p. A1.

36. Sharma, A. (2016, March 23). 70 percent of US consumers binge watch TV, bingers average five episodes per sitting. *Deloitte.* Online: https://www2.deloitte.com/us/en/pages /about-deloitte/articles/press-releases/digital-democracy -survey-tenth-edition.html

37. Silverblatt, A. (2008). *Media literacy* (3rd ed.). Westport, CT: Praeger.

38. Smith, C. (2015, January 22). 105 amazing Netflix facts and statistics. *Expandedramblings.com.* Online: http:// expandedramblings.com/index.php/netflix_statistics-facts/

39. Smith, L. D. (2011, May 25). Study finds fragmentation of audience attention leads to decline in perceived value of entertainment. *PR Newswire.* Online: http://www.prnewswire .com/news-releases/study-finds-fragmentation-of-audience -attention-leads-to-decline-in-perceived-value-of- entertainment-122574018.html

40. "Soundbites." (2005, December). A better mousetrap. *Extra! Update,* p. 2.

41. Steinberg, S. H. (1959). *Five hundred years of printing.* London: Faber & Faber.

42. Swift, A. (2016, September 14). Americans' trust in mass media sinks to new low. *Gallup.* Online: http://www.gallup.com/poll /195542/americans-trust-mass-media-sinks-new-low.aspx

43. Taylor, D. (1991). Transculturating transculturation. *Performing Arts Journal, 13,* 90–104.

44. Television Advertising Bureau. (2017). TV basics. Online: https://www.tvb.org/Default.aspx?TabID=1585

45. "Top ad campaigns of the 21st century. Number 1: Dove: Campaign for Real Beauty." *Advertising Age*. Online: http://adage.com/lp/top15/#realbeauty

46. Tsfati, Y., & J. Cohen. (2013). The third-person effect, trust in media, and hostile media perceptions. *International Encyclopedia of Media Studies: Media Effects/Media Psychology, 1*, 1–19.

47. Turkewitz, J. (2015, January 3). After a spa day, looking years younger (O. K., they're only 7). *The New York Times*, p. A1.

Cultural Forum Blue Column icon, Media Literacy Red Torch Icon, Using Media Green Gear icon, Developing Media book in starburst icon: ©McGraw-Hill Education

©Pictorial Press Ltd/Alamy

Convergence and the Reshaping of Mass Communication

2

◀ Netflix's first feature film, *Beasts of No Nation*, was released worldwide day-and-date on its own streaming service and in theaters on October 16, 2015.

Learning Objectives

The mass media system we have today has existed more or less as we know it ever since the 1830s. It is a system that has weathered repeated significant change with the coming of increasingly sophisticated technologies—the penny press newspaper was soon followed by mass market books and mass circulation magazines. As the 1800s made way for the 1900s, these popular media were joined by motion pictures, radio, and sound recording. A few decades later came television, combining news and entertainment, moving images and sound, all in the home and all, ostensibly, for free. The traditional media found new functions and prospered side by side with television. Then, more recently, came the Internet, the World Wide Web, and mobile technologies like smartphones and tablets. Now, because of these new technologies, all the media industries are facing profound alterations in how they are structured and do business, the nature of their content, and how they interact with and respond to their audiences. Naturally, as these changes unfold, the very nature of mass communication and our role in that process will alter. After studying this chapter, you should be able to

▶ Summarize broad current trends in mass media, especially concentration of ownership and conglomeration, globalization, audience fragmentation, hypercommercialization, and convergence.

▶ Describe in broad terms how the mass communication process itself will evolve as the role of the audience in this new media environment is altered.

1830s Development of the mass media system as we know it today

1945 Supreme Court Justice Hugo Black claims that a free press is a condition of a free society

1900

©Interfoto/Alamy; ©CBS/photofest

1950s ▶ Television displaces radio

1950

1967 Richard Dawkins introduces the term "meme"

1974 Internet emerges

1982 60% of journalists say they had compete freedom to choose their stories, as opposed to 34% 25 years later after explosion of concentration and conglomeration

1996 ▶ DVD introduced

©Howard kingsnorth/
Getty Images RF

©fyv6561/Shutterstock RF

2004 ▶ Facebook debuts

2000

2012 ▶ Facebook buys Instagram

2014 Apple buys Beats Music; YouTube buys Twitch

2015 Actavision buys game company King Digital Entertainment; AT&T buys DirecTV; DVD sales decline; movie ticket sales hold constant, but decline as proportion of population; newspaper circulation drops 7% and newsroom staff falls by 10% from previous year; magazine industry revenue drops 4.5% from previous year; global media consumption rises 1.4% from previous year

©fyv6561/Shutterstock RF

2016 ▶ Pepe the Frog becomes a hate symbol due to meme portrayals; the press is widely criticized for quality of 2016 election coverage; Fox creates Fresco News

©Carlo Allegri/Reuters/Alamy

▲ *The Interview* had day-and-date release.

©Moviestore Collection Ltd/Alamy

©Moviestore Collection Ltd/Alamy

"WHAT'S THAT ON YOUR PHONE?"

"It's *Beasts of No Nation*, a movie about the brutality inflicted on child soldiers in Africa."

"I heard this just came out in theaters. How are you watching it on your phone?"

"Netflix released it day-and-date. It was available to stream online the same day that it first played in theaters."

"That sounds like a cool experiment. Can I watch with you?"

Day-and-date release isn't an "experiment"; filmmakers, big and small, have been using the strategy for some time. Big-budget *Snowpiercer* (2013), star-studded *Bachelorette* (2012), *Margin Call* (2011), and political documentary *Trumpland* (2016) are just some of the more successful examples. In the case of 2014's *The Interview,* the studio had little choice but to release the movie online after North Korean dictator Kim Jong-un threatened revenge against theaters because he didn't like being spoofed in an American movie. These online hits are not only good examples of day-and-date releases, but they also represent a fact of modern media life: There is a seismic shift going on in the mass media—and therefore in mass communication—that dwarfs the changes to the media landscape wrought by television's assault in the 1950s and 1960s on the preeminence of radio and the movies. Encouraged by the Internet, digitization, and mobility, producers are finding new ways to deliver new content to audiences. The media industries are in turmoil, and audience members, as they are confronted by a seemingly bewildering array of possibilities, are now coming to terms with these new media. Will you pay for movie downloads? How much? What will you pay for on-demand television programs? Would you be willing to view the commercials they contain if you could pay a bit less per show? Would you pay more or less for classic programming than for contemporary shows? Would you be willing to watch a movie or television show on a small screen? How will you listen to the radio—satellite radio or terrestrial radio or digital terrestrial radio or streamed Internet radio? If it's streamed over the Internet, is it still "radio"? You may not hold the physical newspaper in your hands, but when you access a newspaper's story on its app (abbreviation for application; software for mobile digital devices), you're reading the newspaper. Or are you? Back to day-and-date. There are technologies that provide day-and-date release for all movies from partner studios. Screening Room offers digital delivery of new releases to your home day-and-date. The set-top box costs $150, and you pay $50 for each movie. Or maybe you'd prefer Prima Cinema, the technology that allows you to watch new releases at home, for the low, low price of $35,000 (Barnes, 2016)? On which platform (the means of delivering a specific piece of media content) might you most enjoy watching your movies? Would you be willing to pay more or less for different platforms? In theater? On your tablet or phone? On a wide-screen home TV? What is the most you would be willing to pay? These are precisely the kinds of questions that audiences will be answering in the next several years. Media-literate audiences will be better equipped to do so.

Traditional Media Industries in Transition

The way we interact with the mass media is indeed changing. While this shift is good news for media consumers, it has not necessarily been beneficial for the established media industries. Just how much pain has been produced by this "perfect storm" of rapid technological change and our shifting consumption behavior?

- Although Americans spend over $11 billion a year at the movies, they continue to buy fewer tickets per person every year than they did in the 1920s (Barnes, 2017). Only 11% of Americans go to the movies once a month or more ("Changes," 2017).

- The number of music CDs sold fell 13.9% between 2014 and 2015, producing a 17% drop in the dollar value of those sales (Friedlander, 2016).

- Fifteen years ago, the four major broadcast networks commanded 61% of all television viewing. Today their share hovers around 30%. The top-rated program in 1980 was *Dallas*, viewed in more than 34% of all homes with a television; in 1990 it was *Cheers*, watched by 21% of all TV homes; today it is *Sunday Night Football*, drawing about 13%.

- The rate of decline in DVD sales increased from 10.9% in 2014 to 12% in 2015, costing the movie studios an $800 million dollar loss in their primary source of home entertainment income (Wallenstein, 2016).

- American newspaper industry revenues declined 4.4% from 2015 to 2016, and 45% over the previous 10 years (Sass, 2017).

- The U.S. magazine industry saw a 3.2% drop in advertising and circulation revenue from 2015 to 2016 (Sass, 2017).

- Listenership to American commercial AM and FM radio has fallen from 96% of Americans 12 years old and over in 2001 to 91% today, and sale of on-air advertising fell 3% between 2014 and 2015 (Vogt, 2016).

The Good News for Media Industries

Indeed, what this turmoil indicates is that the challenge facing the traditional media industries today is how to capture a mass audience now fragmented into millions of niches, that is, into increasingly smaller subaudiences. What is clear is that although we are consuming media in new and different ways, our levels of consumption are at an all-time high.

Global media consumption rose 1.4% from 2014 to 2015, driven by a 27.7% increase in mobile media usage. Across the globe, people average 177 minutes of television a day, accounting for 41% of their media engagement (Barnard, 2016). The typical American spends 10 hours and 39 minutes of screen time a day (Howard, 2016). The average American teen spends more than nine hours a day engaged simultaneously with many different screens, **media multitasking** across the TV set, the computer, video games, and handheld devices (Rideout, 2015). You can see teens' daily activity across all media in Figure 1. We watch 8 billion videos every day on Facebook (Savage, 2016) in addition to the 5 billion a day we watch on YouTube (Statistics, 2016). This does not include the 100 million hours a day of Netflix movies and TV shows streamed by its 87 million worldwide subscribers (Smith, 2016) or all of the viewing by millions of people who watch on their video game consoles or any of the growing number of other video services like HBO Now, CBS All Access, Roku, Amazon Prime, Sling TV, Hulu, and a score more. And that decline in DVD sales and rentals mentioned earlier? It's being made up by **electronic sell-through (EST)**, the buying of digital download movies that annually brings studios more than $1.6 billion in new revenue (Wallenstein, 2016). In fact, Americans are watching more videos, listening to more music, reading more often, playing more video games, consuming more news, and accessing the Internet more often than ever before; they are simply doing it in new and different ways. For media industries, these facts offer good news—readers, viewers, and listeners are out there in ever-increasing numbers, and they value the mass communication experience. These data also offer good news for literate media consumers—their consumption choices will shape the media landscape to come and, inevitably, the mass communication process itself.

Media industries face a number of challenges that promise to alter their relationship with their audiences. Concentration of media ownership and conglomeration can constrict the number and variety of voices available to audiences. Those audiences are becoming fragmented, potentially making it more difficult for media organizations to reach them. Globalization not only fragments the audience even more, but it can also make it less profitable for a media company to tailor its fare for its own homeland. Hypercommercialization might allow those companies to earn more income, but at what price to an audience awash in commercials? And fueling all this change is **convergence**—the erosion of traditional distinctions among media. As we've already seen, content typically associated with one

▶ **Figure 1** American Teens' Daily Media Usage.

Source: Rideout, V., "The Common Sense Census: Media Use by Tweens and Teens," Common Sense Media, *November 3, 2015.*

©PhotoAlto/Matthieu Spohn/Getty Images RF

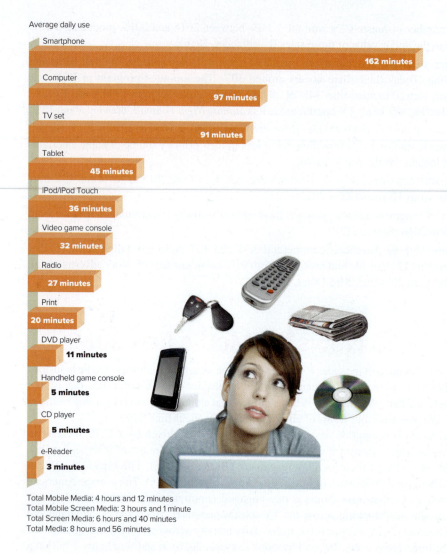

Average daily use

Smartphone	162 minutes
Computer	97 minutes
TV set	91 minutes
Tablet	45 minutes
iPod/iPod Touch	36 minutes
Video game console	32 minutes
Radio	27 minutes
Print	20 minutes
DVD player	11 minutes
Handheld game console	5 minutes
CD player	5 minutes
e-Reader	3 minutes

Total Mobile Media: 4 hours and 12 minutes
Total Mobile Screen Media: 3 hours and 1 minute
Total Screen Media: 6 hours and 40 minutes
Total Media: 8 hours and 56 minutes

medium is quite likely to be delivered by any number of other media; we, the **platform-agnostic** audience members, having no preference on which medium to consume content, seem quite content with that state of affairs.

Changes

Concentration of Ownership and Conglomeration

Ownership of media companies is increasingly concentrated in fewer and fewer hands. Through mergers, acquisitions, buyouts, and hostile takeovers, a very small number of large conglomerates is coming to own more and more of the world's media outlets. For example, in 2015 telecommunication conglomerate AT&T acquired satellite TV provider DirecTV for $49 billion, and cable company Charter Communications acquired Time Warner Cable for $57 billion. In 2016, another telecom giant, Verizon, bought Yahoo and its many Web brands (TechCrunch, Huffington Post, Flickr, and Tumblr, to name just a few) for nearly $5 billion; Internet giant Microsoft bought LinkedIn for $26 billion; and AT&T, the country's second-largest wireless carrier, was back in the acquisition market, bidding $85 billion for the multinational media and entertainment conglomerate Time Warner and its holdings such as HBO, CNN, Bleacher Reports, DC Comics, and the Warner Bros. movie studio. Media observer Ben Bagdikian reported that in 1997 the number of media corporations with "dominant power in society" was 10. Today six companies—Comcast, News Corp., Disney, Viacom, Time Warner, and CBS—own 90% of the media content consumed by Americans

(Corcoran, 2016). This **concentration of ownership** is more than an economic issue. It is a fundamental principle of our democracy that we have a right to information from a wide diversity of viewpoints so that we can make up our own minds. Democracy—rule by the people—requires an independent media. This is the crux of Supreme Court Justice Hugo Black's eloquent defense of a vibrant media in his 1945 *Associated Press v. U.S.* decision: "The First Amendment rests on the assumption that the widest possible dissemination of information from diverse and antagonistic sources is essential to the welfare of the public, that a free press is a condition of a free society." Closely related to concentration is **conglomeration**, the increase in the ownership of media outlets by larger, nonmedia companies. The threat is clear, explained Vermont senator Bernie Sanders:

> What you've got today . . . is about a half a dozen major media conglomerates that own and control the distribution of the information that the American people receive. That is a massive concentration of control. And what is never discussed about this is, What is the goal of these major media conglomerates? Is it to educate the American people? Is it to give the five sides of the issue? No. Their function as major media conglomerates, owned by very large financial interests, is to make as much money as they possibly can. . . . This is a disaster for democracy. (in Smiley, 2016)

You can read more about conglomeration in the box titled "The Quest for Profit or Serving Democracy?"

But the conflict of interest between profit and public service is only one presumed problem with conglomeration. The other is the dominance of a bottom-line mentality and its inevitable degradation of media content. *Variety*'s Peter Bart explains that the "corporate giants" that own media companies are in a "race for consolidation [that] continues to accelerate, burying movies, magazines, books, and music under still more layers of corporate number-crunchers." Wall Street, he argues, favors risk-free companies, whether they are media outlets or supermarkets (2014, p. 28). Bart was speaking of media in general. As for journalism, former CBS anchor Dan Rather added, "The larger the entities that own and control the news operations, the more distant they become" (quoted in Auletta, 2001, p. 60). New York University law professor Burt Neuborne warned:

> The press has been subsumed into a market psychology, because they are now owned by large conglomerates, of which they are simply a piece. And they (news organizations) are expected to contribute their piece of the profit to the larger pie. You don't have people controlling the press anymore with a fervent sense of responsibility to the First Amendment. Concentrating on who's sleeping with whom, on sensationalism, is concentrating on essentially irrelevant issues. (as quoted in Konner, 1999, p. 6)

Evidence for Professor Neuborne's appraisal abounds. In 1982, 60% of American journalists said they had "almost complete freedom" in selecting the stories they would cover. Now, only 34% say they can make that claim ("Hard Numbers," 2014). The number of full-time statehouse newspaper reporters fell by more than one-third between 2003 and 2014. Only 164 full-time newspaper journalists now report on the bills, debates, possible corruption, and politicians in the nation's 50 state capitals (Barber, 2014). Only 21 of 50 states currently have even one daily newspaper reporter assigned to Washington, DC, to cover Congress (Lu & Holcomb, 2016). This produces **news deserts**, communities starved for news vital to their existences (Oreskes, 2016). There is social scientific evidence that this "impoverishment of local political news in recent years is driving down citizen engagement," producing voters who are less politically active, less knowledgeable about political candidates, and less likely to vote (Hayes, 2015). And in 2015, the hottest year in recorded history, a year that saw a dramatic increase in America's level of income inequality, and a year in which there were several high-profile police shootings of young African American men and a number of deadly terrorist attacks at home and across the globe, the most-reported news story on the three largest commercial television networks—ABC, CBS, and NBC—was winter weather, not climate change, not the economy, and not the world's refugee crisis (ADT Research, 2016).

There are, however, positive observations on concentration and conglomeration. Many industry professionals argue that concentration and conglomeration are not only inevitable but necessary in a telecommunications environment that is increasingly fragmented and internationalized; companies must maximize their number of outlets to reach as much of the

▲ Winter snowstorms are pretty interesting, but are they more important than climate change, the economy, or a global refugee crisis?
©Susan Baran

divided and far-flung audience as possible. If they do not, they will become financially insecure, and that is an even greater threat to free and effective mediated communication because advertisers and other well-monied forces will have increased influence over them.

Another defense of concentration and conglomeration has to do with **economies of scale**; that is, bigger can in fact sometimes be better because the relative cost of an operation's output declines as the size of that endeavor grows. For example, the cost of collecting the news or producing a television program does not increase significantly when that news report or television program is distributed over 2 outlets, 20 outlets, or 100 outlets. The additional revenues from these other points of distribution can then be plowed back into even better news and programming. In the case of conglomeration, the parallel argument is that revenues from a conglomerate's nonmedia enterprises can be used to support quality work by its media companies.

The potential impact of this **oligopoly**—a concentration of media industries into an ever smaller number of companies—on the mass communication process is enormous. What becomes of shared meaning when the people running communication companies are more committed to the financial demands of their corporate offices than they are to their audiences, who are supposedly their partners in the communication process? What becomes of the process itself when media companies grow more removed from those with whom they communicate? And what becomes of the culture that is dependent on that process when concentration and conglomeration limit the diversity of perspective and information? Or are the critics making too much of the issue? Is this unnamed manager of newspaper chain 10/30 Communications correct when he says, "Many companies in our industry have wrongly divided their focus among many customer groups. We do not. Our customer is the advertiser. Readers are our customers' customers" (in Wemple, 2016)?

CULTURAL FORUM

The Quest for Profit or Serving Democracy?

In the aftermath of the 2016 presidential election, one in which the media not only badly judged the outcome but left many important policy issues uncovered, Joshua Benton, of the Nieman Journalism Lab, wrote, "One way to think of the job journalism does is telling a community about itself, and on those terms the American media failed spectacularly this election cycle. That Donald Trump's victory came as such a surprise—a systemic shock, really—to both journalists and so many who read or watch them is a marker of just how bad a job we did . . . The troubling morning-after realization is that the structures of today's media ecosystem encourage that separation, and do so a little bit more each day" (2016). A post-election survey offered evidence of how badly journalists failed to understand and report the true mood of many in the nation—not only did a majority, 57%, of Americans say the media had too much influence in the election, they gave that performance a grade of D+ ("Low Marks," 2016).

What were the problematic "structures of today's media ecosystem" that led to this poor grade? Two of the most commonly cited problems were directly related to the drive for profit. The first was serious cuts in the number of working journalists as media companies shed staff to bolster their bottom lines in an already tough media economy. The "brutal economics of the news business . . . decimat[ed] newsrooms around the country and [left] fewer people to grapple with what was a gargantuan story," argued *Columbia Journalism Review's* Kyle Pope (2016). The second was the degradation of the news itself, the "desperation for clicks and ratings that guarantees that civic and democratic values will always be trumped by commercial and entertainment demands," in the words of *The Nation's* John Nichols (2016)—or, as *The Guardian's* Katherine Viner (2016) put it, the profit-driven drift "away from public-service journalism and toward junk-food news." We knew all about Hillary Clinton's e-mails (which received more coverage than all other policy issues combined; Alterman, 2016) and Mr. Trump's sensitivity to his hand size and the leaked video where he describes sexually grabbing women, but there was little examination of the candidates' policies. There was not a single question on climate change in any of the three presidential debates, and a Harvard University analysis determined that only 9% of the news in the country's 10 major media outlets was devoted to issues (Hahessy, 2016). Where was reporting on economic instability and inequality? On why so many citizens now think the American Dream is exactly that, a dream? "Whatever you say about this year's election coverage," lamented *The New York Times*'s Jim Rutenberg, "it killed at the box office" (2016, p. B1).

The Internet, especially social networking sites that traded in false news and flat-out lies, was another reason often cited for the media's failure to see the true story behind Americans' great dissatisfaction with the status quo. Mr. Benton offered this evidence: "I'm from a small town in south Louisiana. The day before the election, I looked at the Facebook page of the current mayor. Among the items he posted there in the final 48 hours of the campaign: *Hillary Clinton Calling for Civil War If Trump Is Elected. Pope Francis Shocks World, Endorses Donald Trump for President. Barack Obama Admits He Was Born in Kenya. FBI Agent Who Was Suspected of Leaking Hillary's Corruption Is Dead.*" All

were lies spread far and wide online and twice as likely to be read on social media than stories from legitimate new sites (Mandese, 2016). Many critics argued that voters' reliance on unedited and unverified reports on Facebook and other Internet outlets was itself a product of traditional media's profit-motivated turn away from real to junk-food news. As mainstream news becomes more fatuous, celebrity-obsessed, and advertiser-friendly, it begins to lose its value. When only 32% of Americans have a fair or great deal of trust in the media (Swift, 2016), why shouldn't people get "news" from people they trust, someone who's like them? But, as Martin Baron, executive editor of *The Washington Post*, explained, "If you have a society where people can't agree on basic facts, how do you have a functioning democracy?" (in Rutenberg, 2016, p. B1).

Enter your voice in the cultural forum. Regardless of your favored candidate in that contentious campaign, how well do you think the media performed? Journalism professionals were nearly unanimous in their self-criticism; how much of it do you think is deserved? Does the quest for corporate profit make it more or less likely that we the people can count on the media to serve our democratic needs?

Globalization

Closely related to the concentration of media ownership is **globalization**. It is large, multinational conglomerates that are doing the lion's share of media acquisitions. The potential impact of globalization on the mass communication process speaks to the issue of diversity of expression. Will distant, anonymous, foreign corporations, each with vast holdings in a variety of nonmedia businesses, use their power to shape news and entertainment content to suit their own ends? Here in America the concern is that media companies, with an eye toward an expanding worldwide market for their fare, will tailor their content to the widest possible global audience, ignoring story and character in their television shows and movies in favor of car chases and explosions. Foreign audiences understand big-time action and adventure; nuance and subtlety don't translate as well. Abroad, the worry is that high-quality American media content will overwhelm local media industries and local cultures. As it is, almost every country in the world, including our friends in Canada, puts limits of some sort on the amount and type of U.S. media content they allow across their borders. There is, however, an alternative view to these concerns. Different people from different cultures can learn from one another through the exchange of their different media. Rather than fear the sharing of the stories we tell, we should embrace them. In addition, defenders of increased globalization point to the need to reach a fragmented and widespread audience—the same factor that fuels concentration—as encouraging this trend. They also cite the growing economic clout of emerging democracies (and the need to reach the people who live in them) and the increasing intertwining of the world's economies as additional reasons globalization is necessary for the economic survival of media businesses.

Audience Fragmentation

The nature of the other partner in the mass communication process is changing too. Individual segments of the audience are becoming more narrowly defined; the audience itself is less of a mass audience. This is **audience fragmentation**.

Before the advent of television, radio and magazines were national media. Big national radio networks brought news and entertainment to the entire country. Magazines such as *Life*, *Look*, and the *Saturday Evening Post* once offered limited text and many pictures to a national audience. But television could do these things better. It was radio with pictures; it was magazines with motion. To survive, radio and magazines were forced to find new functions. No longer able to compete on a mass scale, these media targeted smaller audiences that were alike in some important characteristic and therefore more attractive to specific advertisers. So now we have magazines such as *Psychology Today* and *Brides*, and radio station formats such as Country, Urban, and Lithuanian. This phenomenon is known as **narrowcasting**, **niche marketing**, or **targeting**.

Technology has wrought the same effect on television. Before cable television, people could choose from among the three commercial broadcast networks—ABC, CBS, NBC—one noncommercial public broadcasting station, and, in larger markets, maybe an independent station or two. Now, with cable, satellite, and Internet video streaming, people have literally millions of viewing options. The television audience has been fragmented. To attract advertisers, each channel now must find a more specific group of people to make up its viewership. Nickelodeon targets kids, for example; TV Land appeals to baby boomers; Spike aims at young men; and Bravo seeks upper-income older people.

The new digital technologies promise even more audience fragmentation, almost to the point of audiences of one. For example, cable companies have the ability to send very specific commercials not only to specific neighborhoods but even to individual homes. Television network NBC does the same in its on-demand programming. And if you've ever used an Internet search engine, you know that the ads you see are specific to you based on the history of your overall Internet use. So, too, are the search results you're offered. **Zonecasting** technology allows radio stations to deliver different commercials to specific neighborhoods, and **location-based mobile advertising**, as you no doubt know well, lets marketers directly send ads targeted at you wherever you are in that moment.

But if these audience-fragmenting **addressable technologies**—technologies permitting the transmission of very specific content to equally specific audience members—are changing the nature of the mass media's audiences, then the mass communication process itself must also change. What will happen as smaller, more specific audiences become better known to their partners in the process of making meaning? What will happen to the national culture that binds us as we become increasingly fragmented into demographically targeted **taste publics**—groups of people bound by little more than an interest in a given form of media content? Will there be a narrowing of our collective cultural experience, as media's storytelling function is disrupted because we are each listening to stories we individually preselect or that are preselected for us? "Maybe one day," wonders *Creativity* magazine editor Teressa Iezzi, "you won't be able to say anything to anyone because a common language or the ability to grapple with or laugh at something outside of your comfort zone will have fallen away" (2007, p. 11). National Public Radio's Michael Oreskes (2016) adds, "'Nichefication' may strengthen the business prospects of [media] companies, but it weakens their ability to serve the public."

There is an alternative view, however. Audience may well be fragmenting, but the interactivity encouraged and facilitated by the digital media will reconnect and reconfigure us into more numerous, more robust, more varied communities. There is indeed a lot of conversation, curiosity, and sharing taking place on social networking sites like Twitter and Facebook; yes, it can be small and juvenile, but very often it is passionate, informative, observant, clever, subversive, and maybe even community-building.

Hypercommercialism

The costs involved in acquiring numerous or large media outlets, domestic and international, and of reaching an increasingly fragmented audience must be recouped somehow. Selling more advertising on existing and new media and identifying additional ways to combine content and commercials are the two most common strategies. This leads to

hypercommercialism. The rise in the number of commercial minutes in a typical broadcast television show is evident to most viewers, as more than 17% of a prime-time broadcast network hour is devoted to commercials. Cable channels devote 21% of their program hour to commercials, in part by speeding up the video to make more commercial time available (Ember, 2016; Morran, 2015). Hypercommercialization has hit the Internet as well, as you surely know as you try to separate the brand tweets from those of the real people you follow on Twitter and work to block the endless commercials on your Facebook news feed.

▲ Jane the Virgin apparently shops exclusively at Target.
©Collection Christophel/Alamy

The sheer growth in the amount of advertising is one troublesome aspect of hypercommercialism. But for many observers, the increased mixing of commercial and noncommercial media content is even more troubling. Of course, not everyone has a problem with this practice. Angela Courtin, chief marketing officer of movie and television studio Relativity Media, explains, "We have come to an intersection of media and content where marketing is content and content is marketing" (in Downey, 2015). What do you think of these "intersections"? A typical prime-time unscripted program, for example *The Voice*, has more than 14 minutes of product placement and more than 15 minutes of actual commercial breaks, meaning that one-half of its hour is devoted to promotion. Tinder shows up regularly on *The Mindy Project*; the vice-principal on *The Fosters* loves the new school tablets so much she calls them by their full name, "the Kindle Paperwhite e-reader." The star of *Jane the Virgin* is a regular at Target, and whenever a character on any show on the FX cable channel has a beer, it's a MillerCoors product (Nussbaum, 2015). So ubiquitous has this **product placement**—the integration, for a fee, of specific branded products into media content—become, that the Writers Guild of America demands additional compensation for writing what are, in effect, commercials. The producers' response is that product placement is not a commercial; rather, it represents a new form of content, **brand entertainment**—when brands are, in fact, part of and essential to the program. Toyota, Kraft Foods, Chase credit cards, and Cigna insurance are recurring "characters" on *Top Chef*. Musical artists not only take payment to include brands in their songs; some, for example Mariah Carey, now integrate brands into their CD booklets. Music channel Vevo retroactively inserts products into already existing music videos. Celebrities like Rihanna, Kylie Jenner, and *Teen Mom* star Chelsea Houska accept payments from brands to push their wares on Instagram (Davis, 2016). *Time* and *Sports Illustrated* magazines run ads on their covers, and many e-books come not only with products integrated into their story lines but also with links to the sponsors' websites.

Sometimes hypercommercialism involves direct payments of cash in exchange for exposure rather than "mere" branding. Many television stations around the country, for example Channels 17 and 99 in Naperville, Illinois, sell entire segments of their morning news and talk shows to local businesses. Many radio stations now accept payment from record promoters to play their songs, an activity once illegal and called **payola**. It is now quite acceptable as long as the "sponsorship" is acknowledged on the air.

Again, as with globalization and concentration, where critics see damage to the integrity of the media themselves and disservice to their audiences, defenders of hypercommercialism argue that it is simply the economic reality of today's media world.

Erosion of Distinctions among Media: Convergence

Movie studios make their titles available not only on DVD and EST but for handheld video game systems as well. Cable's AMC runs a slate of **webisodes**, Web-only television shows, to accompany its hit series *The Walking Dead*. Satellite provider Dish Network offers interactive, TV remote–based play of classic video games. Magazines *Allure* and *Vanity Fair* maintain digital video channels and produce their own television shows. The iPod Nano music player contains an FM tuner. Video game consoles don't just let players download movies and television shows, surf the Internet, check their Facebook accounts, and tune in to the Weather Channel and the BBC; they also offer streaming of tens of thousands of feature films. Ken Burns unveiled his documentary series *Prohibition* on the iPad and iPhone a week before its airing on PBS, when it was simultaneously streamed over the Internet and broadcast in advance of its availability on DVD and on iTunes. You can subscribe to *National Geographic* and play its issue-matched video game online or on a smartphone. There are tens of thousands of U.S. commercial and noncommercial and foreign radio stations delivering their broadcasts over the Web.

You can read *The New York Times* or *Time* magazine and hundreds of other newspapers and magazines on a variety of screens. And what can "newspapers, magazines, and books," "radio and recordings," and "television and film" really mean (or more accurately, *really be*) now that we can access digital texts, audio, and moving images virtually anyplace, anytime via **Wi-Fi** (wireless Internet) and handheld devices? This erosion of distinctions among media is called *convergence*, and it has been fueled by three related phenomena that have overwhelmed the mass communication process all at once. First is the digitization of almost all content, making it possible to transmit and share information across all platforms. Second is the increasing data speed of both wired and wireless networks, making access to that digitized content fast, easy, and seamless. Third are the remarkably fast and ongoing advances in communication technology that make once-unimagined ideas quite possible.

The traditional lines between media are disappearing. Concentration is one reason for this convergence. If one company owns newspapers, an online service, television stations, book publishers, a magazine or two, and a film company, it has a strong incentive to get the greatest use from its content, whether news, education, or entertainment, by using as many channels of delivery as possible. The industry calls this **synergy**, and it is the driving force behind several recent mergers and acquisitions in the media and telecommunications industries. In 2012 Facebook bought photo-sharing platform Instagram for $1 billion to gain access to its app-based mobile services and to make its Facebook offerings more visual, therefore increasing the site's value to advertisers. In 2014 Apple, deciding that the future of music was streaming, not downloads, paid $3.2 billion for the headphone and music streaming company Beats Music; and YouTube, wanting to bring real-time video game play to its already massive array of channels, paid more than $1 billion for the game-streaming service Twitch. In 2015, Activision paid nearly $6 billion for King Digital Entertainment in order to move its console-bound games like *Call of Duty* and *World of Warcraft* to more mobile platforms where King, with hits like *Candy Crush*, was dominant.

▶ Convergence killed the video store, victimized by video downloads, streaming, and online rentals—products of the convergence of movies, video, and the Internet. Convergence is strangling the bookstore as well, victimized by downloads and portable e-readers, smartphones, and tablets—products of the convergence of print, the Internet, and smartphones.

(top, bottom): ©Susan Baran

A second reason for convergence is audience fragmentation. A mass communicator who finds it difficult to reach the whole audience can reach its component parts through various media. A third reason is the audience itself. We are increasingly platform agnostic, having no preference for where we access our media content. Will this expansion and blurring of traditional media channels confuse audience members, further tilting the balance of power in the mass communication process toward the media industries? Or will it give audiences more power—power to choose, power to reject, and power to combine information and entertainment in individual ways?

The New Mass Communication Process

One essential element of media literacy is *having an understanding of the process of mass communication.* Understanding the process—how it functions, how its components relate to one another, how it limits or enhances messages, which forms of feedback are most effective and why—permits us to form expectations of how the media industries and the process itself can serve us. But throughout this chapter we have seen that the process of mass communication is undergoing fundamental change. Media-literate individuals must understand why and how this evolution is occurring. We can do this by reconsidering its elements as described in Figure 4 in the chapter on mass communication, culture, and media literacy.

Interpreter A—The Content Producer

Traditionally, the content producer, the source, in the mass communication process is a large, hierarchically structured organization—for example, Pixar Studios, the *Philadelphia Inquirer,* or CBS Television. And as we saw, the typical consequence of this organizational structure is scant room for individual vision or experimentation. But in the age of the Internet, with its proliferation of **blogs** (regularly updated online journals that comment on just about everything), social networking sites such as Facebook where users post all variety of free personal content, and other websites, the distinction between content consumer and content provider disappears. Now, Interpreter A can be an independent musician self-releasing her music online, a lone blogger, a solitary online scrapbooker, or two pals who create digital videos. Traditional media outlets routinely make use of people as sources who would have once been called amateurs. For example, Forbes.com publishes the work of 1,400 contributors, and the *Dallas Morning News* maintains an unpaid network of several dozen "civilians." Fox television network stations across the country provide "citizen journalists" with an app, Fresco, that operates like a 24/7 newsroom. It assigns stories to be covered, and once the users' images and video are verified for accuracy and aired, they are paid for their work (Jessell, 2016). Internet domain company Go Daddy traditionally airs a viewer-created commercial during the Super Bowl. Tens of millions of producers, big and small, distribute their video fare on the Internet. Sites like Vuze, Joost, and Blip Networks strike financial deals with producers, again big and small, for content for their own sites and for syndication to others. And what are Snapchat's 150 million and Instagram's 500 million monthly users who upload 800 million and 80 million images a day, respectively, if not producers of a huge amount of sometimes very engaging content?

In the newly evolving model of mass communication, content providers are just as likely to be individuals who believe in something or who have something to say as they are big media companies in search of audiences and profits. Now sources themselves, they are *the people formerly known as the audience*, and it is not simply technological change that has given them voice. It is the reduction of the **cost of entry** for content production to nearly $0 that those digital technologies have wrought that has made them all creators. "Rates of authorship are increasing by historic orders of magnitude. Nearly universal authorship, like universal literacy before it, stands to reshape society by hastening the flow of information and making individuals more influential," wrote futurists Denis Pelli and Charles Bigelow. "As readers, we consume. As authors, we create. Our society is changing from consumers to creators" (2009).

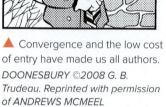

▲ Convergence and the low cost of entry have made us all authors.

DOONESBURY ©2008 G. B. Trudeau. Reprinted with permission of ANDREWS MCMEEL SYNDICATION. All rights reserved.

What are the likely consequences of this change? Will the proliferation of content sources help mitigate the effects of concentration and conglomeration in the traditional media industries? Will the cultural forum be less of a lecture and more of a conversation? Will new and different and challenging storytellers find an audience for their narratives? Does journalist William Greider (2005), speaking specifically of the news, overstate when he says, "The centralized institutions of press and broadcasting are being challenged and steadily eroded by widening circles of unlicensed 'news' agents—from talk-radio hosts to Internet bloggers and others—who compete with the official press to be believed. These interlopers speak in a different language and from many different angles of vision. Less authoritative, but more democratic" (p. 31)?

The Message

The message in the traditional mass communication model is typically mechanically produced, simultaneously sent, inflexible, and unalterable. Once AMC airs tonight's episode of *The Walking Dead*, it has aired tonight's episode of *The Walking Dead*. The consequence? Audiences either like it or don't like it. The program either succeeds or fails. But we've already seen that different commercial spots can be inserted into programs sent into specific homes. You can buy only four tracks of an artist's latest CD, add three more from an earlier release, and listen to a completely unique, personally created album. Every music-streaming service now available allows you to create your own personalized "radio station" or playlist. **RSS**, or **really simple syndication**, feeds are aggregators that allow Web users to create their own content assembled from the Internet's limitless supply of material. Some of the most popular are Bloglines, Sitrion, and Digg Reader. Users tell the aggregator what sites to collect, or their topics of interest, or even their favorite writers. As soon as any new content in their preselected categories appears online, it is automatically brought to their RSS file. The Breaking News app, for example, brings aggregated news on more than 90,000 topics to people and news organizations alike. As such, these aggregated "messages" are infinitely alterable, completely unique, and thoroughly idiosyncratic. Alternate-ending DVDs permitting viewers to "re-edit" an existing movie at home are old hat by now. But what do you think of director Steven Soderbergh's vision for a digital movie future? Some time ago he said that when theaters convert from film to digital projection, he would plan to exhibit multiple, different versions of the same film. "I think it would be very interesting to have a movie out in release," he said, "and then, just a few weeks later say, 'Here's version 2.0, recut, rescored.' The other version is still out there—people can see either or both" (in Jardin, 2005, p. 257). Well, it's more than 10 years later and digital projection is a reality. But alternate-ending movies haven't hit the big screen yet. Is it because the movie industry is content to stay with its mechanically produced, simultaneously sent, inflexible, unalterable films, or is it because we aren't ready for them yet?

What will be the impact on the mass communication process when content producers no longer have to amass as large an audience as possible with a single, simultaneously distributed piece of content? When a producer can sell very specific, very idiosyncratic, constantly changing content to very specific, very idiosyncratic, constantly changing consumers, will profitability and popularity no longer be so closely linked? What will "popular" and "profitable" messages really mean when audience members can create infinitely "alterable" messages? What will happen when the mass communication process, long dependent on **appointment consumption** (audiences consume content at a time predetermined by the producer and distributor; for example, a movie time at a theater, your favorite television show at 9:00 on Tuesdays, news at the top of the hour, your magazine in your mailbox on the third of the month), evolves more completely to **consumption on demand** (the ability to consume any content, anytime, anywhere)?

Feedback and Interpreter B—The Audience

In the traditional model of the mass communication process, feedback is inferential and delayed—what is a newspaper's circulation, what were this weekend's box office numbers for that movie, what are that program's ratings? Likewise, the audience is typically seen as large and heterogeneous, known to content producers and distributors in a relatively rudimentary way, little more than basic demographics. But digital media have changed what content creators and distributors know about their audiences (Interpreter B) because they have changed how audiences talk back to those sources (feedback). Silicon Valley marketing consultant Richard Yanowitch explains, "The Internet is the most ubiquitous experimental lab in history, built on two-way, real-time interactions with millions of consumers whose individual consumption patterns can for the first time be infinitesimally measured, monitored, and molded." Adds Google advertising executive Tim Armstrong, "Traditionally, the focus has been on the outbound message. But we think the information coming back in is as important or more important than the messages going out" (both in Streisand & Newman, 2005, p. 60).

In today's mass communication, every visit to a specific Web address (and every click of a mouse once there), every download of a piece of content, and every product bought online provide feedback to someone. But it isn't just the Internet—every selection of a channel on cable or satellite; every rental or purchase by credit card of a CD, DVD, video game, or movie ticket; and every consumer product scanned at the checkout counter or purchased from an Internet-connected vending machine is recorded and stored in order to better identify us to Interpreter A, whoever that might be. But this raises the question, Who is Interpreter A? It might be content providers who want to serve us more effectively because they know us so much more thoroughly than they once did when relying solely on demographics. Or it could be those who would make less honorable use of the feedback we so willingly provide—for example, identity thieves or a potential employer who would deny you a job because of your political or religious beliefs.

The Result

How will we use the new communication technologies? What will be our role in the new, emerging mass communication process? The world of content creators and distributors is now more democratic. Audiences, even though they may be fragmented into groups as small as one person or as large as 100 million, are better known to those who produce and distribute content, and they can talk back more directly and with more immediacy. Content, the message, is now more flexible, infinitely alterable, unbound by time and space. Clearly, for content producers there is more room for experimentation in content creation and consumption. There is less risk, and possibly even great reward, in challenging audiences. The evolving mass communication process promises not only efficiency but great joy, boundless choice, and limitless access to information for all its partners. But the technologies that help provide these gifts are in fact double-edged swords; they cut both ways, good and bad. Media-literate people, because they understand the mass communication process through which they operate, are positioned to best decide how to benefit from their potential and limit their peril.

DEVELOPING MEDIA LITERACY SKILLS

Making Our Way in the Meme Culture

At the end of his 1967 book *The Selfish Gene*, noted evolutionary biologist Richard Dawkins introduced the term *meme*. He likened them to genes, "Memes propagate themselves in the meme pool by leaping from brain to brain via a process which, in the broad sense, can be called imitation" (in Gleick, 2011). He continued his analogy, arguing that, like genes, memes compete with each other for limited resources; memes compete for attention, because without attention they cease to be. And while he was speaking of any idea that spreads from person to person in a culture, he came to accept the Internet-based meaning of **meme**, an online idea or image that is repeatedly copied, manipulated, and shared. "The meaning is not that far away from the original. It's anything that goes viral," Dawkins said. "In the original introduction to the word *meme* . . . I did actually use the metaphor of a virus. So when anybody talks about something going viral on the Internet, that is exactly what a meme is" (in Solon, 2013).

For Professor Dawkins, memes were how ideas come into being, are propagated, and (if they survive) serve their host, the culture in which they flourish. But what of Internet memes specifically? Critics of meme culture argue that the ideas most likely to be spread—go viral— are the ones most guaranteed to attract attention. So we spend (or possibly waste) time on epic fail videos and funny cat pictures with oddly spelled slogans (the I Can Has Cheezburger Meme network has hundreds of millions of page and video views each month). But maybe we aren't wasting time. Maybe we're building community by creating, viewing, and sharing ideas. "My generation turns to memes . . . so that we can connect and relate," wrote millennial college student Ashley Perling (2016, p. A24). But, ask critics, what kind of meaningful community can be built around memes like My Food Looks Funny and You're Doing It Wrong? But maybe Perling is right; as we all learned in grammar school, sharing *is* caring.

Still, unlike the traditional media that carry cultural ideas, bound as they are by economic and ethical considerations, memes "represent a new 'Wild West' in entertainment, where account holders, sometimes having millions of followers, can simply post whatever they want with little review or backlash. . . . Memes succeed in condensing [ideas] into bite-size humor, for all to find acceptable and swallow without protest" (Tulsi, 2016). After all, they're just jokes. So because they attract more life-sustaining attention than kindness and thoughtfulness, racist and misogynistic memes flourish.

Meme culture became especially relevant during the 2016 presidential election when memes were created to attack both major candidates. Social media saw endless variations of Lock Her Up and Trump's Taco Bowl memes, as well as memes consisting of fabricated quotes and figures that sought to sway voters. The platform of then-candidate Donald Trump largely consisted of securing the U.S. southern border, deporting illegal immigrants, and monitoring or completely halting the immigration of any Muslims into the United States, all promises that appealed to the alt-right, a group of white nationalists who created the benign-sounding name in an attempt to normalize their agenda. They embraced Trump as their candidate and utilized meme culture to spread their messages widely, most notably with Pepe the Frog memes. The Pepe the Frog cartoon, originally created in 2005 by artist Matt Furie and a hit meme subject on its own for years, was appropriated by white nationalists in 2016. Used in this racist manner, Pepe was declared a hate symbol by the Anti-Defamation League. Sufficiently dismayed by its vile use, Furie killed off Pepe from his comic series in 2017 (Hunt, 2017). However, the dark side of memes is that once in the culture, no one can control their use; even seemingly harmless or humorous images can spread hateful or inaccurate messages.

Memes survive because *we* spread them. They attract our attention, and we send them on to attract the attention of others. But maybe this is how it should be in our new era of mass communication. We now have the opportunity to express ourselves, however seriously or frivolously, to offer our own point of view, however well-founded or off-the-wall, all without someone else vetting us, telling us we matter. This is the Internet's great gift to mass communication. But it is its greatest challenge. What do we do with this immense freedom and the power it grants each of us? As a media-literate individual, you understand and respect the power of media messages and you know that media content is a text providing insight into our culture and our lives. So the choice is yours: how will you use the Internet and social media? Memes are easy and fun; you are free to create and share them, to have a laugh, to skewer or honor. But the Internet and social media are also sites for more meaningful personal and cultural expression. You are free to undertake that more valuable, if a bit more difficult, work. What will you do? This question and some answers run throughout this text; the lessons you draw from what you read will be your own.

◀ Pepe the Frog. The meme that put a gentler face on the hate and ignorance of white supremacy. *©Carlo Allegri/Reuters/Alamy*

MEDIA LITERACY CHALLENGE
The Fraction of Selection

An important part of being media literate is having critical thinking skills enabling you to develop independent judgments about media and media content. Challenge your own skill by predicting which media will survive and which will disappear as a result of the dramatic technological, economic, and audience-preference turmoil currently shaking the traditional media industries. Which will change and how? The answers depend on you and your media choices. In 1954, when television was doing to movies, newspapers, magazines, and radio what the Internet and smartphones are doing to today's media, communication scholar Wilbur Schramm created the *fraction of selection* to answer the question, "What determines which offerings of mass communication will be selected by a given individual?" It looks like this:

$$\frac{\text{Expectation of Reward}}{\text{Effort Required}}$$

It suggests that you weigh the level of reward you expect from a given medium or piece of content against how much effort—in the broadest sense—you make to secure that reward. Now, consider your own media consumption. For example, how do you typically watch movies: at the theater, streamed, downloaded, on disc, wait for them to come to cable? What "data" would go in your numerator? In your denominator? Create your personal formula for other media consumption as well. News on the Internet versus the newspaper? Popular music on commercial radio versus streamed from the Internet? Compare your outcomes with those of your friends. Based on your results, can you speculate on tomorrow's media winners and losers?

Resources for Review and Discussion

REVIEW POINTS: TYING CONTENT TO LEARNING OUTCOMES

▶ **Summarize broad current trends in mass media, especially concentration of ownership and conglomeration, globalization, audience fragmentation, hypercommercialization, and convergence.**

☐ Encouraged by the Internet and other digital technologies, content producers are finding new ways to deliver content to audiences.

☐ All of the traditional media have begun to see either flattening or declines in audience, yet overall consumption of media is at all-time highs.

☐ Five trends are abetting this situation—convergence, audience fragmentation, concentration of ownership and conglomeration, globalization, and hypercommercialism.

☐ Convergence is fueled by three elements—digitization of nearly all information, high-speed connectivity, and advances in technology's speed, memory, and power.

▶ **Describe in broad terms how the mass communication process itself will evolve as the role of the audience in this new media environment is altered.**

☐ Content providers can now be lone individuals aided by low cost of entry.

☐ Messages can now be quite varied, idiosyncratic, and freed of the producers' time demands.

☐ Feedback can now be instantaneous and direct, and, as a result, audiences, very small or very large, can be quite well known to content producers and distributors.

KEY TERMS

media multitasking, 33

electronic sell-through (EST), 33

convergence, 33

platform agnostic, 34

concentration of ownership, 35

conglomeration, 35

news desert, 35

economies of scale, 36

oligopoly, 36

globalization, 37

audience fragmentation, 37

narrowcasting, 38

niche marketing, 38

targeting, 38

zonecasting, 38

location-based mobile advertising, 38

addressable technologies, 38

taste publics, 38

hypercommercialism, 39

product placement, 39

brand entertainment, 39

payola, 39

webisode, 39

Wi-Fi, 40

synergy, 40

blog, 41

cost of entry, 41

RSS (really simple syndication), 42

appointment consumption, 43

consumption-on-demand, 43

meme, 44

QUESTIONS FOR REVIEW

1. What is convergence?

2. What is media multitasking?

3. Differentiate between concentration of media ownership and conglomeration.

4. What is globalization?

5. What is hypercommercialism?

6. What is audience fragmentation?

7. What are the two major concerns of globalization's critics?

8. What three elements are fueling today's rampant media convergence?

9. Differentiate among notions of content producers, audiences, messages, and feedback in the traditional view of the mass communication process and more contemporary understandings of these elements of the process.

10. What is the significance of low cost of entry?

To maximize your study time, check out CONNECT to access the SmartBook study module for this chapter and explore other resources.

QUESTIONS FOR CRITICAL THINKING AND DISCUSSION

1. Many industry insiders attribute the recent falloff in audiences for movies, recorded music, network television, DVD, radio, newspapers, and video games to changes in technology; people are simply finding new ways to access content. And while this is certainly true to a degree, others say that in this age of concentrated and hypercommercialized media, audiences are simply being turned off by content that just isn't that compelling. Would you agree with the critics? Why? Can you give examples from your own media consumption?

2. Critics of concentration of media ownership and conglomeration argue that they are a threat to democracy. What is the thrust of their concern? Do you share it? Why or why not?

3. A close reading of how the mass communication process is evolving has led some observers to argue that it is becoming less "mass" and more akin to interpersonal communication. Revisit Figure 4 in the chapter on mass communication, culture, and media literacy. From what you've read in this chapter and from your own media experience, can you make the argument that the "result" of the process has the potential to be more "flexible, personally relevant, possibly adventurous, challenging, or experimental"?

REFERENCES

1. ADT Research. (2016, January). Top 20 stories of 2015. *The Tyndall Report*. Online: http://tyndallreport.com/yearinreview2015/

2. Alterman, E. (2016, November 28). Television fail. *Nation*, pp. 6–8.

3. *Associated Press et al. v. United States*, 326 U.S. 1, 89 L. Ed. 2013, 65 S. Ct. 1416 (1945).

4. Auletta, K. (2001, December 10). Battle stations. *The New Yorker*, pp. 60–67.

5. Barber, G. (2014, July 10). Study: Statehouse press corps in decline. *National Public Radio*. Online: http://www.npr.org/sections/itsallpolitics/2014/07/10/330456166/study-statehouse-press-corps-in-decline

6. Barnard, J. (2016, June 13). Media consumption forecasts 2016. *Performics*. Online: http://www.performics.com/media-consumption-forecasts-2016/

7. Barnes, B. (2017, January 1). Film audiences sought fantasy escapes in 2016. *The New York Times*, p. C2.

8. Barnes, B. (2016, March 20). Hollywood divided over movie streaming service. *The New York Times*, p. B1.

9. Bart, P. (2014, August 19). Anti-Amazon rebels remind us bigger isn't always better. *Variety*, p. 28.

10. Benton, J. (2016, November 9). The forces that drove this election's media failures are likely to get worse. *Nieman Lab*. Online: http://www.niemanlab.org/2016/11/the-forces-that-drove-this-elections-media-failure-are-likely-to-get-worse/

11. "Changes at the multiplex." (2017, March 28). *Variety*, p. 41.

12. Corcoran, M. (2016, February 11). Democracy in peril: Twenty years of media consolidation under Telecommunications Act. *Truthout*. Online: http://www.truth-out.org/news/item/34789-democracy-in-peril-twenty-years-of-media-consolidation-under-the-telecommunications-act

13. Davis, W. (2016, November 30). FTC urged to investigate word-of-mouth companies over Instagram marketing. *MediaPost*. Online: http://www.mediapost.com/publications/article/290079/ftc-urged-to-investigate-word-of-mouth-companies-o.html

14. Downey, K. (2015, January 21). Product placement V2.0 is hot brand strategy. *TVNewscheck.com*. Online: http://www.tvnewscheck.com/article/82404/product-placement-v20-is-hot-brand-strategy

15. Ember, S. (2016, February 27). Television networks are recasting the role of commercials. *The New York Times*, p. B3.

16. Friedlander, J. P. (2016). News and notes on 2015 RIAA shipment and revenue statistics. *Recording Industry Association of America*. Online: https://www.riaa.com/wp-content/uploads/2016/03/RIAA-2015-Year-End-shipments-memo.pdf

17. Gleick, J. (2011, May). What defines a meme? *Smithsonian*. Online: http://www.smithsonianmag.com/arts-culture/what-defines-a-meme-1904778/

18. Greider, W. (2005, November 21). All the king's media. *The Nation*, pp. 30–32.

19. Hahessy, E. (2016, November 1). The US election—a policy free zone. *Pursuit*. Online: https://pursuit.unimelb.edu.au/articles/the-us-election-a-policy-free-zone

20. "Hard numbers." (2014, July/August). *Columbia Journalism Review*, p. 13.

21. Hayes, D. (2015, January 23). The decline of local news is threatening citizen engagement. *The Washington Post*. Online: http://www.washingtonpost.com/blogs/monkey-cage/wp/2015/01/23/the-decline-of-local-news-is-threatening-citizen-engagement/

22. Howard, J. (2016, July 29). Americans devote more than 10 hours a day to screen time, and growing. *CNN*. Online: http://www.cnn.com/2016/06/30/health/americans-screen-time-nielsen/

23. Hunt, E. (2017, May 7). Pepe the Frog creator kills off Internet meme co-opted by white supremacists. *The Guardian*. Online: https://www.theguardian.com/world/2017/may/08/pepe-the-frog-creator-kills-off-internet-meme-co-opted-by-white-supremacists

24. Iezzi, T. (2007, January 29). A more-targeted world isn't necessarily a more civilized one. *Advertising Age*, p. 11.

25. Jardin, X. (2005, December). Thinking outside the box office. *Wired*, pp. 256–257.

26. Jessell, H. A. (2016, March 9). Fox turns viewers into stringers with app. *TVNewsCheck*. Online: http://www.tvnewscheck.com/article/92960/fox-turns-viewers-into-stringers-with-app

27. Konner, J. (1999, March/April). Of Clinton, the Constitution & the press. *Columbia Journalism Review*, p. 6.

28. "Low marks for major players in 2016 election—including the winner." (2016, November 21). *Pew Research Center*. Online: http://www.people-press.org/2016/11/21/low-marks-for-major-players-in-2016-election-including-the-winner/?utm_source=Pew+Research+Center&utm_campaign=9e40b867cf-Weekly_Nov_23_201611_22_2016&utm_medium=email&utm_term=0_3e953b9b70-9e40b867cf-399750965

29. Lu, K., & Holcomb, J. (2016, January 7). In 21 states, local newspapers lack a dedicated D.C. reporter covering Congress. *Pew Research Center*. Online: http://www.pewresearch.org/fact-tank/2016/01/07/in-21-states-local-newspapers-lack-a-dedicated-reporter-keeping-tabs-on-congress/

30. Mandese, J. (2016, November 25). Facebookers 2.5 times more likely to read fake news, millennials least prone. *Mediapost*. Online: http://www.mediapost.com/publications/article/289778/facebook-users-25-times-more-likely-to-read-fake.html?utm_source=newsletter&utm_medium=email&utm_content=readmore&utm_campaign=98385

31. Morran, C. (2015, February 19). Cable channels speed up TV shows to cram in more ads. *Consumerist*. Online: https://consumerist.com/2015/02/19/cable-channels-speed-up-tv-shows-to-cram-in-more-ads/

32. Nichols, J. (2016, March 28/April 4). Trumped by the media. *Nation*, pp. 3–4.

33. Nussbaum, E. (2015, October 12). The price is right. *The New Yorker*, pp. 95–99.

34. Oreskes, M. (2016, November 2). Journalists can regain public's trust by reaffirming basic values. *Columbia Journalism Review*. Online: http://www.cjr.org/first_person/trust_media_coverage.php

35. Pelli, D. G., & Bigelow, C. (2009, October 20). A writing revolution. *Seed Magazine*. Online: http://seedmagazine.com/content/article/a_writing_revolution/

36. Perling, A. (2016, May 20). Addicted to meme culture. *The New York Times*, p. A24.

37. Pope, K. (2016, November 9). Here's to the return of the journalist as malcontent. *Columbia Journalism Review*. Online: http://www.cjr.org/criticism/journalist_election_trump_failure.php

38. Rideout, V. (2015, November 3). The common sense census: Media use by tweens and teens. *Common Sense Media*. Online: https://www.commonsensemedia.org/research/the-common-sense-census-media-use-by-tweens-and-teens

39. Rutenberg, J. (2016, November 7). Media's next challenge: Overcoming the threat of fake news. *The New York Times*, p. B1.

40. Sass, E. (2017, March 21). Newspaper, mag revenues fell in 2016. *MediaPost*. Online: http://www.mediapost.com/publications/article/297448/newspaper-mag-revenues-fell-in-2016.html

41. Savage, J. (2016, April 10). Top 5 Facebook video statistics for 2016. *Social Media Today*. Online: http://www.socialmediatoday.com/marketing/top-5-facebook-video-statistics-2016-infographic

42. Smiley, T. (2016, November 14). Interview with Senator Bernie Sanders. *PBS.org*. Online: http://www.pbs.org/wnet/tavissmiley/interviews/senator-bernie-sanders-2/

43. Smith, C. (2016, November 10). Netflix statistics and facts. *DMR*. Online: http://expandedramblings.com/index.php/netflix_statistics-facts/

44. Solon, O. (2013, June 20). Richard Dawkins on the Internet's hijacking of the word "meme." *Wired*. Online: http://www.wired.co.uk/article/richard-dawkins-memes

45. Statistics Brain. (2016, September 1). YouTube company statistics. Online: http://www.statisticbrain.com/youtube-statistics/

46. Streisand, B., & Newman, R. J. (2005, November 14). The new media elites. *U.S. News & World Report*, pp. 54–63.

47. Swift, A. (2016, September 14). Americans' trust in mass media sinks to new low. *Gallup*. Online: http://www.gallup.com/poll/195542/americans-trust-mass-media-sinks-new-low.aspx

48. Tulsi, A. (2016, September 26). How meme culture makes sexism easier to swallow. *Thought Catalogue*. Online: http://thoughtcatalog.com/alita-tulsi/2016/09/heres-how-meme-culture-is-making-you-blind-to-sexism/

49. Viner, K. (2016, July 12). How technology disrupted the truth. *The Guardian*. Online: https://www.theguardian.com/media/2016/jul/12/how-technology-disrupted-the-truth

50. Vogt, N. (2016, June 15). Audio fact sheet. *Pew Research Center*. Online: http://www.journalism.org/2016/06/15/audio-fact-sheet/

51. Wallenstein, A. (2016, January 6). Why 2015 home entertainment figures should worry studios. *Variety*. Online: http://variety.com/2016/digital/news/home-entertainment-spending-2015-studios-1201673329/

52. Wemple, E. (2016, October 17). Report: McNewspapers are gobbling up small-town America. *The Washington Post*. Online: https://www.washingtonpost.com/blogs/erik-wemple/wp/2016/10/17/report-mcnewspapers-are-gobbling-up-small-town-america/?utm_term=.48c5710f0959

Cultural Forum Blue Column icon, Media Literacy Red Torch Icon, Using Media Green Gear icon, Developing Media book in starburst icon:
©McGraw-Hill Education

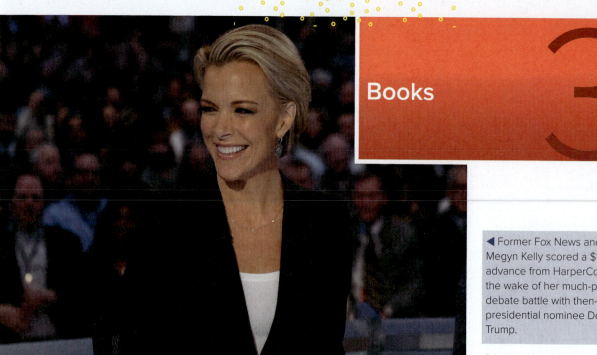

Books

3

◄ Former Fox News anchor Megyn Kelly scored a $10 million advance from HarperCollins in the wake of her much-publicized debate battle with then-presidential nominee Donald Trump.

©Andrew Harrer/Bloomberg/Getty Images

Learning Objectives

Books were the first mass medium and are, in many ways, the most personal. They inform and entertain. They are repositories of our pasts and agents of personal development and social change. Like all media, they mirror the culture. After studying this chapter, you should be able to

▶ Outline the history and development of the publishing industry and the book itself as a medium.

▶ Describe the cultural value of books and the implications of censorship for democracy.

▶ Explain how the organizational and economic nature of the contemporary book industry shapes the content of books.

▶ Act as a more media-literate consumer of books, especially in considering their uniqueness in an increasingly mass-mediated, media-converged world.

1456 First Gutenberg Bible

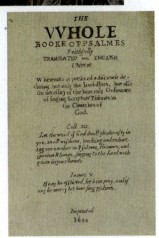

©North Wind Picture Archives

1638 First printing press in the Colonies

1600

1644 ▶ *The Whole Booke of Psalms,* first book printed in the Colonies

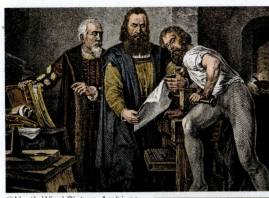

Source: Library of Congress, Prints and Photographs Division

1732 ▶ *Poor Richard's Almanack*

1700

1765 Stamp Act

1774 Thomas Paine writes *Common Sense*

©Universal History Archive/UIG/Getty Images

~1800 Continuous roll paper

1800

1807 John Wiley & Sons established

1811 Steam-powered printing press

1817 Harper Brothers established

1830 Improved pulp making

1852 ▶ Stowe's *Uncle Tom's Cabin*

1860 Dime novels appear

1861 U.S. achieves highest literacy rate in the world

1884 Linotype machine

1885 Offset lithography

©Bettmann/Corbis

1926 Book of the Month Club begins

1900

1935 Penguin Books (first paperbacks) established in London

1939 Pocket Books (paperbacks) established in the U.S.

1953 ▶ Bradbury's *Fahrenheit 451*

1960 Paperback sales surpass hardback sales for the first time

1995 Amazon.com goes online

©AF archive/Alamy

2003 Project Gutenberg and *Search Inside the Book* debut

2000

2005 Google ignites controversy with plan to scan copyrighted books

2006 Sony Reader

2007 Final *Harry Potter* book; Amazon's Kindle

2008 On-demand titles exceed number of traditional titles

2009 For first time, Amazon sells more e-books than hard-copy books in one day (Christmas Day). Espresso Book Machine

2010 ▶ iPad

2011 E–books outsell all print books on Amazon

©Oleksiy Maksymenko Photography/Alamy

▲ In the now not-so-distant future of *Fahrenheit 451*, people must memorize the content of books because to own a book is illegal.

©AF archive/Alamy

YOU JUST WALKED INTO A ROOM WHERE YOUR FRIENDS ARE ENJOYING A MOVIE THAT YOU'VE NEVER SEEN BEFORE. So there you are, watching an arresting scene from François Truffaut's 1967 adaptation of Ray Bradbury's 1953 science fiction classic *Fahrenheit 451*.

At first you can't make out what is happening. Several people are wandering about, and each person is talking to him or herself. You recognize actress Julie Christie, but the other performers and what they are saying are completely unfamiliar. You stay with the scene. The trees are bare. Snow is falling, covering everything. Puffs of steam float from people's mouths as they speak, seemingly to no one. As you watch a bit more, you begin to recognize some familiar phrases. These people are reciting passages from famous books! Before you can figure out why they are doing this, the film ends.

So you restart and watch the entire movie, discovering that these people *are* the books they have memorized. In this near-future society, all books have been banned by the authorities, forcing these people—book lovers—into hiding. They hold the books in their heads because to hold them in their hands is a crime. If discovered with books, people are jailed and the books are set afire—Fahrenheit 451 is the temperature at which book paper will burst into flames, according to Bradbury.

Moved by the film, you go to the library the next day and check out the book. Bradbury's main character, Guy Montag, a fireman who until this moment had been an official book burner himself, speaks a line that stays with you. After he watches an old woman burn to death with her forbidden volumes, he implores his ice-cold, drugged, and television-deadened wife to understand what he is only then realizing. He pleads with her to see: "There must be something in books, things we can't imagine, to make a woman stay in a burning house; there must be something there" (pp. 49–50).

In this chapter we examine the history of books, especially in terms of their role in the development of the United States. We discuss the importance that has traditionally been ascribed to books, as well as the scope and nature of the book industry. We address the various factors that shape the contemporary economics and structures of the book industry, examining at some length the impact of convergence, concentration, and hypercommercialism on the book industry and its relationship with its readers. Finally, we discuss the media literacy issues inherent in the wild success of the *Harry Potter* books.

A Short History of Books

As detailed in the chapter on mass communication, culture, and media literacy, the use of Gutenberg's printing press spread rapidly throughout Europe in the last half of the 15th century. But the technological advances and the social, cultural, and economic conditions necessary for books to become a major mass medium were three centuries away. As a result, it was a printing press and a book industry much like those of Gutenberg's time that first came to the New World in the 17th century.

Books Come to Colonial North America

The earliest colonists came to America primarily for two reasons—to escape religious persecution and to find economic opportunities unavailable to them in Europe. So, most of the books they carried with them to the New World were religiously oriented. Moreover, they brought very few books at all. Better-educated, wealthier Europeans were secure at home. Those willing to make the dangerous journey tended to be poor, uneducated, and largely illiterate.

There were other reasons early settlers did not find books central to their lives. One was the simple fight for survival. In the brutal and hostile land to which they had come, leisure for reading books was a luxury for which they had little time. People worked from sunrise to sunset just to live. If there was to be reading, it would have to be at night, and it was folly to waste precious candles on something as unnecessary to survival as reading. In addition, books and reading were regarded as symbols of wealth and status and therefore not priorities for people who considered themselves to be pioneers, servants of the Lord, or anti-English colonists. The final reason the earliest settlers were not active readers was the lack of portability of books. Books were heavy, and few were carried across the ocean. Those volumes that did make it to North America were extremely expensive and not available to most people.

The first printing press arrived on North American shores in 1638, only 18 years after the Plymouth Rock landing. It was operated by a company called Cambridge Press. Printing was limited to religious and government documents. The first book printed in the colonies appeared in 1644—*The Whole Booke of Psalms,* sometimes referred to as the *Bay Psalm Book.* Among the very few secular titles were those printed by Benjamin Franklin 90 years later. *Poor Richard's Almanack,* which first appeared in 1732, sold 10,000 copies annually. The *Almanack* contained short stories, poetry, weather predictions, and other facts and figures useful to a population more in command of its environment than those first settlers. As the colonies grew in wealth and sophistication, leisure time increased, as did affluence and education. Franklin also published the first true novel printed in North America, *Pamela,* written by English author Samuel Richardson. Still, by and large, books were religiously oriented or pertained to official government activities such as tax rolls and the pronouncements of various commissions.

The primary reason for this lack of variety was the requirement that all printing be done with the permission of the colonial governors. Because these men were invariably loyal to King George II, secular printing and criticism of the British Crown or even of local authorities were never authorized, and publication of such writing meant jail. Many printers were imprisoned—including Franklin's brother James—for publishing what they believed to be the truth.

The printers went into open revolt against official control in March 1765 after passage of the Stamp Act. Designed by England to recoup money it spent waging the French and Indian War, the Stamp Act mandated that all printing—legal documents, books, magazines, and newspapers—be done on paper stamped with the government's seal. Its additional purpose was to control and limit expression in the increasingly restless colonies. This affront to their freedom, and the steep cost of the tax—sometimes doubling the price of a publication—was simply too much for the colonists. The printers used their presses to run accounts of antitax protests, demonstrations, riots, sermons, boycotts, and other antiauthority activities, further fueling revolutionary sympathies. In November 1765—when the tax was to take effect— the authorities were so cowed by the reaction of the colonists that they were unwilling to enforce it.

Anti-British sentiment reached its climax in the mid-1770s, and books were at its core. Short books, or pamphlets, motivated and coalesced political dissent. In 1774 England's right to govern the colonies was openly challenged by James Wilson's *Considerations on the Nature and Extent of the Legislative Authority of the British Parliament,* John Adams's *Novanglus Papers,* and Thomas Jefferson's *A Summary View of the Rights of British America.* Most famous of all was Thomas Paine's 47-page *Common Sense.* It sold 120,000 copies in the first three months after its release to a total population of 400,000 adults. Between 1776 and 1783, Paine also wrote a series of pamphlets called *The American Crisis. Common Sense* and *The American Crisis* made Paine the most widely read colonial author during the American Revolution.

THE EARLY BOOK INDUSTRY After the Revolutionary War, printing became even more central to political, intellectual, and cultural life in major cities like Boston, New York, and Philadelphia. To survive financially, printers also operated as booksellers, book publishers, and sometimes as postmasters who sold stationery and even groceries. A coffeehouse or tavern often was attached to the print shop. The era was alive with political change, and print

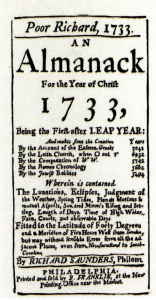

▲ First published in 1732, Benjamin Franklin's *Poor Richard's Almanack* offered readers a wealth of information for the upcoming year.

©*Universal History Archive/UIG/ Getty Images*

▲ British-born writer, patriot, and revolutionary leader Thomas Paine wrote *Common Sense* and *The American Crisis* to rally his colonial compatriots in their struggle against the British.

Source: Library of Congress, Prints and Photographs Division [LC-USZ62-46915]

shops and bookshops became clearinghouses for the collection, exchange, and dissemination of information.

The U.S. newspaper industry grew rapidly from this mix, as detailed in the chapter on newspapers. The book industry, however, was slower to develop. Books were still expensive, often costing the equivalent of a working person's weekly pay, and literacy remained a luxury. However, due in large measure to a movement begun before the Civil War, compulsory education had come to most states by 1900. This swelled the number of readers, which increased the demand for books. This increased demand, coupled with a number of important technological advances, brought the price of books within reach of most people. In 1861 the United States had the highest literacy rate of any country in the world (58%), and 40 years later at the start of the 20th century, 9 out of every 10 U.S. citizens could read. Today, nearly total literacy reigns in America.

THE FLOWERING OF THE NOVEL The 1800s saw a series of important refinements to the process of printing, most notably the **linotype** machine, a typewriter-like keyboard allowing printers to set type mechanically rather than manually, and **offset lithography**, permitting printing from photographic plates rather than from heavy, fragile metal casts. The combination of this technically improved, lower-cost printing (and therefore lower-cost publications) and widespread literacy produced the flowering of the novel in the 1800s. Major U.S. book publishers Harper Brothers and John Wiley & Sons—both in business today—were established in New York in 1817 and 1807, respectively. And books such as Nathaniel Hawthorne's *The Scarlet Letter* (1850), Herman Melville's *Moby Dick* (1851), and Mark Twain's *Huckleberry Finn* (1884) were considered by many of their readers to be equal to or better than the works of famous European authors such as Jane Austen, the Brontës, and Charles Dickens.

The growing popularity of books was noticed by brothers Irwin and Erastus Beadle. In 1860 they began publishing novels that sold for 10 cents. These **dime novels** were inexpensive, and because they concentrated on frontier and adventure stories, they attracted growing numbers of readers. Within five years of their start, Beadle & Company had produced over 4 million volumes of what were also sometimes called **pulp novels** (Tebbel, 1987). Advertising titles like *Malaeska: Indian Wife of the White Hunter* with the slogan "Dollar Books for a Dime!" the Beadles democratized books and turned them into a mass medium.

THE COMING OF PAPERBACK BOOKS Dime novels were "paperback books" because they were produced with paper covers. But publisher Allen Lane invented what we now recognize as the paperback in the midst of the Great Depression in London when he founded Penguin Books in 1935. Four years later, publisher Robert de Graff introduced the idea to the United States. His Pocket Books were small, inexpensive (25 cents) reissues of books that had already become successful as hardcovers. They were sold just about everywhere—newsstands, bookstores, train stations, shipping terminals, and drug and department stores. Within eight weeks of their introduction, de Graff had sold 325,000 books (Menand, 2015). Soon, new and existing publishers joined the paperback boom, their popularity boosted by Fawcett Publication's decision in 1950 to start releasing paperback originals. Traditionalists had some concern about the "cheapening of the book," but that was more than offset by the huge popularity of paperbacks and the willingness of publishers to take chances. For example, in the 1950s and 1960s, African American writers such as Richard Wright and Ralph Ellison were published, as were controversial works such as J. D. Salinger's *The Catcher in the Rye*. Eventually, paperback books became the norm, surpassing hardcover book sales for the first time in 1960. Today, the majority of all physical books sold in the United States are paperbacks, and bookstores generate half their revenue from these sales.

Books and Their Audiences

The book is the least "mass" of our mass media in audience reach and in the magnitude of the industry itself, and this fact shapes the nature of the relationship between medium and audience. Publishing houses, both large and small, produce narrowly or broadly aimed titles for readers, who buy and carry away individual units. This more direct relationship between publishers and readers renders books fundamentally different from other mass media. For example, because books are less dependent than other mass media on attracting the largest possible audience, books are more able and more likely to incubate new, challenging, or unpopular ideas. As the medium least dependent on advertiser support, books can be aimed at extremely small groups of readers, challenging them and their imaginations in ways that many sponsors would find unacceptable in advertising-based mass media. Because books are produced and sold as individual units—as opposed to a single television program simultaneously distributed to millions of viewers or a single edition of a mass circulation newspaper—more "voices" can enter and survive in the industry. This medium can sustain more voices in the cultural forum than can other traditional mass media. As former head of the New York Public Library, Vartan Gregorian, explained to journalist Bill Moyers (2007), when among books, "suddenly you feel humble. The whole world of humanity is in front of you. . . . Here it is, the human endeavor, human aspiration, human agony, human ecstasy, human bravura, human failures—all before you."

The Cultural Value of Books

The book industry is bound by many of the same financial and industrial pressures that constrain other media, but books, more than the others, are in a position to transcend those constraints. In *Fahrenheit 451* Montag's boss, Captain Beatty, explains why all books must be burned. "Once," he tells his troubled subordinate, "books appealed to a few people, here, there, everywhere. They could afford to be different. The world was roomy. But then the world got full of eyes and elbows and mouths" (Bradbury, 1981, p. 53). Bradbury's firemen of the future destroy books precisely because they *are* different. It is their difference from other mass media that makes books unique in our culture. Although all media serve the following cultural functions to some degree (for example, people surf the Internet's self-help sites for personal development, and popular music is sometimes an agent of social change), books traditionally have been seen as a powerful cultural force for these reasons:

- *Books are agents of social and cultural change.* Free of the need to generate mass circulation for advertisers, offbeat, controversial, even revolutionary ideas can reach the public. For example, Andrew Macdonald's *Turner Diaries* is the ideological and how-to guide of the antigovernment militia movement in the United States. Nonetheless, this radical, revolutionary book is openly published, purchased, and discussed.

- *Books are an important cultural repository.* Want to definitively win an argument? Look it up. We often turn to books for certainty and truth about the world in which we live and the ones about which we want to know. Which countries border Chile? Find the atlas. James Brown's sax player? Look in Bob Gulla's *Icons of R&B and Soul.* Books have been edited and fact-checked, unlike much of what you might find online, and they often contain information and detail that you might not know to search for.

- *Books are our windows to the past.* What was the United States like in the 19th century? Read Alexis de Tocqueville's *Democracy in America.* England in the early 1800s? Read Jane Austen's *Pride and Prejudice.* Written during the times they reflect, these books are more accurate representations than those available in the modern movie and television depictions.

- *Books are important sources of personal development.* The obvious forms are self-help and personal improvement books. But books also speak to us more individually than advertiser-supported media because of their small, focused target markets. For example,

▲ Veronica Roth's *Divergent* series and Suzanne Collins's *Hunger Games* trilogy are hugely popular sources of entertainment, escape, and personal reflection. *(left) ©CBW/Alamy; (right) ©Onsite/Alamy*

Our Bodies, Ourselves, introduced by the Boston Women's Health Book Collective in the very earliest days of the modern feminist movement, is still published today. (For more on this influential book, see the "Our Bodies, Ourselves" box.) *Dr. Spock's Baby and Child Care* has sold more than 50 million copies. J. D. Salinger's *The Catcher in the Rye* was the literary anthem for the Baby Boomers in their teen years, as is William Gibson's *Neuromancer* for many Web pioneers. It is unlikely that any of these voices would have found their initial articulation in commercially sponsored media.

- *Books are wonderful sources of entertainment, escape, and personal reflection.* Suzanne Collins, John Grisham, Stephenie Meyer, and Stephen King all specialize in writing highly entertaining and imaginative novels. The enjoyment found in the works of writers Veronica Roth (the *Divergent* series), John Irving (*The World According to Garp*, *Hotel New Hampshire*), Pat Conroy (*The Prince of Tides*, *Beach Music*), Paula Hawkins (*Girl on a Train*), and J. K. Rowling (the *Harry Potter* series) is undeniable.

- *The purchase and reading of a book is a much more individual, personal activity than consuming advertiser-supported (television, radio, newspapers, and magazines) or heavily promoted (popular music and movies) media.* As such, books tend to encourage personal reflection to a greater degree than these other media. We are part of the tribe, as media theorist Marshall McLuhan would say, when we consume other media. But we are alone when we read a book. "Books allow you to fully explore a topic and immerse yourself in a deeper way than most media today," explained Facebook founder Mark Zuckerberg on the launch of his book club, A Year of Books (in Widdicombe, 2015, p. 18).

- *Books are mirrors of culture.* Books, along with other mass media, reflect the culture that produces and consumes them.

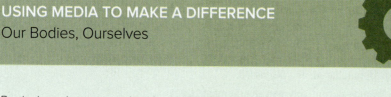

USING MEDIA TO MAKE A DIFFERENCE
Our Bodies, Ourselves

Books have been central to many of the most important social and political movements in our nation's history. *Our Bodies, Ourselves,* a book for and about women, is credited with beginning the women's health movement. The profits this book generates—some 40 years after its first appearance—continue to support what has become a worldwide undertaking. How did this influential book, with more than 4 million copies sold in 18 different languages, come into being, and how does it continue to be so influential?

The story of *Our Bodies, Ourselves* begins in 1969. That year, several women, aged 23 to 39, were attending a workshop, "Women and Their Bodies," at a women's liberation conference in Boston. They began exchanging "doctor stories." They readily came to the conclusion that most women were relatively ignorant about their bodies (and by extension, their sexuality) and that the male-dominated medical profession was not particularly receptive to their needs. So they gave themselves a "summer project." As explained by the women, who began identifying themselves as the Boston Women's Health Book Collective (Norsigian et al., 1999):

> We would research our questions, share what we learned in our group, and then present the information in the fall as a course "by and for women." We envisioned an ongoing process that would involve other women who would go on to teach such a course in other settings. In creating the course, we learned that we were capable of collecting, understanding, and evaluating medical information; that we could open up to one another and find strength and

comfort through sharing some of our most private experiences; that what we learned from one another was every bit as important as what we read in medical texts; and that our experience contradicted medical pronouncements.

Over time these facts, feelings, and controversies were intertwined in the various editions of *Our Bodies, Ourselves*.

How does *Our Bodies, Ourselves* continue to make a difference? One of the original Boston Women's Health Book Collective members, Jane Pincus, explains in her introduction to the 1998 edition:

Unlike most health books on the market, *Our Bodies, Ourselves for the New Century* is unique in many respects: It is based on, and has grown out of, hundreds of women's experiences. It questions the medicalization of women's bodies and lives, and highlights holistic knowledge along with conventional biomedical information. It places women's experiences within the social, political, and economic forces that determine all of our lives, thus going beyond individualistic, narrow, "self-care" and self-help approaches, and views health in the context of the sexist, racist, and financial pressures that affect far too many girls, women, and families adversely. It condemns medical corporate misbehavior driven by "bottom-line" management philosophy and the profit motive. Most of all, *Our Bodies, Ourselves* encourages you to value and share your own insights and experiences, and to use its information to question the assumptions underlying the care we all receive so that we can deal effectively with the medical system and organize for better care. . . . (p. 21)

You may disagree with some (or all) of the philosophy and goals of the Boston Women's Health Book Collective, but there is no argument that its book, *Our Bodies, Ourselves*, has made—and continues to make—a difference in the health of women around the world. In fact, in 2012, the Library of Congress designated *Our Bodies, Ourselves* as one of 88 "books that shaped America."

Censorship

Because of their influence as cultural repositories and agents of social change, books have often been targeted for **censorship**. A book is censored when someone in authority limits publication of or access to it. Censorship can and does occur in many situations and in all media (more on this in the chapter on media freedom, regulation, and ethics). But because of the respect our culture traditionally holds for books, book banning takes on a particularly poisonous connotation in the United States.

Reacting to censorship presents a dilemma for book publishers. Publishers have an obligation to their owners and stockholders to make a profit. Yet, if responsible people in positions of authority deem a certain book unsuitable for readers, shouldn't publishers do the right thing for the larger society and comply with demands to cease its publication? This was the argument presented by morals crusader Anthony Comstock in 1873 when he established the New York Society for the Suppression of Vice. It was the argument used in Berlin on the evening of May 10, 1933, when Nazi propaganda chief Joseph Goebbels put a torch to a bonfire that consumed 20,000 books. It was the argument made in 1953 when U.S. senator Joseph McCarthy demanded the removal of more than 100 books from U.S. diplomatic libraries because of their "procommunist" slant. (Among them was Thomas Paine's *Common Sense*.) It is the argument made today by people like those "concerned" parents of the Lamont School District in Illinois who in 2016 had the award winning young adult novel *The God of Small Things* by Arundhati Roy removed from the curriculum because it contained "inappropriate" subject matter, as well as by members of the Arkansas legislature who sought to ban Howard Zinn's *A People's History of the United States* from the state's schools because it approached "the nation's history from the perspective of marginalized and disadvantaged communities" (Young, 2017).

According to the American Library Association Office of Intellectual Freedom and the American Civil Liberties Union, among the library and school books most frequently targeted by modern censors are the *Harry Potter* series, Mark Twain's *The Adventures of Huckleberry Finn*, Harper Lee's *To Kill a Mockingbird*, John Steinbeck's *Of Mice and Men*, the *Goosebumps* series, Alice Walker's *The Color Purple*, and children's favorite *In the Night Kitchen* by Maurice Sendak. You can see the 10 most frequently banned library books of 2015 in Figure 1. With how many are you familiar? Which ones have you read?

Book publishers can confront censorship by recognizing that their obligations to their industry and to themselves demand that they resist censorship. The publishing industry and

▶ **Figure 1** Most-Challenged Library Books of 2015 (and Why They Were Challenged).

Source: Begley, S., "What the List of the Most Banned Books Says About Our Society's Fears," Time, *September 25, 2016.*

©Oleksiy Maksymenko/Alamy RF

1. *Looking for Alaska* by John Green
   Reasons: Offensive language, sexually explicit, and unsuited for age group
2. *Fifty Shades of Grey* by E. L. James
   Reasons: Sexually explicit and unsuited for age group
3. *I Am Jazz* by Jessica Herthel and Jazz Jennings
   Reasons: Inaccurate, homosexuality, sex education, religious viewpoint, and unsuited for age group
4. *Beyond Magenta: Transgender Teens Speak Out* by Susan Kuklin
   Reasons: Anti-family, offensive language, homosexuality, sex education, political viewpoint, religious viewpoint, and unsuited for age group
5. *The Curious Incident of the Dog in the Night-Time* by Mark Haddon
   Reasons: Offensive language, religious viewpoint, and unsuited for age group
6. *The Holy Bible*
   Reasons: Religious viewpoint
7. *Fun Home* by Alison Bechdel
   Reasons: Violence and "graphic images"
8. *Habibi* by Craig Thompson
   Reasons: Nudity, sexually explicit, and unsuited for age group
9. *Nasreen's Secret School: A True Story from Afghanistan* by Jeanette Winter
   Reasons: Religious viewpoint, unsuited to age group, and violence
10. *Two Boys Kissing* by David Levithan
    Reasons: Homosexuality and "condones public displays of affection"

the publisher's role in it are fundamental to the operation and maintenance of our democratic society. Rather than accepting the censor's argument that certain voices require silencing for the good of the culture, publishers in a democracy have an obligation to make the stronger argument that free speech be protected and encouraged. The short list of frequently censored titles in the previous paragraph should immediately make it evident why the power of ideas is worth fighting for. You can test your own willingness to censor in the Cultural Forum box entitled "Would You Ban a Book by Adolph Hitler? One by Milo Yiannopoulos?"

Cultural Forum
Would You Ban a Book by Adolph Hitler? One by Milo Yiannopoulos?

As 2016 began, a long-banned work showed up in German bookstores. Adolf Hitler's ultranationalist, racist, and anti-Semitic *Mein Kampf* reappeared after 70 years of censorship. Many Germans were appalled, arguing that the 1925 hate-filled tract, instrumental in the Nazi's rise to power, would further inflame the racist and xenophobic fervor that at the time of this new release seemed to be taking hold across Europe. Others were satisfied with the new version of the hateful book because, rather than a re-issue of Hitler's original version, it was a heavily annotated edition, the culmination of six years of work by scholars from the Institute for Contemporary History in Munich. Their extensively researched rebuttal of the original's 600 pages of lies and half-truths swelled the reissue to 2,000 pages. "It would be simply irresponsible to let this racist work of inhumanity wander loose in the public domain without comment," wrote the Institute's director, Andreas Wirsching (in "Germany," 2016, p. 14). Still others insisted that the book should never have been banned in the first place. Dictatorships like Hitler's ban books; democracies do not. Censorship is a sign of fear and weakness, they said. They argued that Hitler's legacy is clear to everyone: the concentration camps, the Holocaust, millions dead across the globe. What good is served by hiding the writing and thoughts of such a mad man? Enter your voice. What was the right call: maintain the ban, publish with annotation, or never ban the book at all? Can you think of any other solutions for dealing with poisonous books?

Now consider this situation, one a bit closer to home. As 2017 began, Threshold Imprints, Simon & Schuster's politically conservative imprint, signed Milo Yiannopoulos of the conservative website Breitbart News to a lucrative book deal. Mr. Yiannopoulos, who had been "permanently barred from Twitter for violating the platform's rules against hate speech and harassment," was well-known for comparing Islam to cancer, mocking transgender people, leveling anti-Semitic

insults, and suggesting that women who are harassed online should simply stay off the Internet. Many people were outraged by the book deal. A number of Simon & Schuster authors openly criticized their publisher, some promising to leave the venerable house when their current contracts expired. The *Chicago Review of Books* went as far as to promise it would not review any of the company's books for the remainder of the year. The critics' complaint was that Mr. Yiannopoulos's positions espoused "outright racism and misogyny" (Alter, 2017, p. B1). As such, many argued his book should not be published.

The question that entered the cultural forum, then, was one of censorship. Simon & Schuster's defenders argued that no matter how offensive an author's views might be, they deserve to be published. After all, censorship is censorship. Enter your voice. Do you consider the criticism faced by Simon & Schuster fair? Why or why not? How would you have handled Mr. Yiannopoulos's book as a publisher? Publish, not publish, annotate? Now revisit your solution to the question of publishing *Mein Kampf*. Do you see a distinction between the two cases? Can you make an argument that the books are different and, therefore, deserve to be treated differently? If so, what does that say about your commitment to freedom of expression? There is an old saying in publishing, "There's no such thing as a little censorship." Do you agree? Why or why not?

Aliteracy as Self-Censorship

Censors ban and burn books because books are repositories of ideas, ideas that can be read and considered with limited outside influence or official supervision. But what kind of culture develops when, by our own refusal to read books, we figuratively save the censors the trouble of striking the match? **Aliteracy**, wherein people possess the ability to read but are unwilling to do so, amounts to doing the censors' work for them. As Russian immigrant and writer Joseph Brodsky explained when accepting his Nobel Prize for Literature, "Since there are no laws that can protect us from ourselves, no criminal code is capable of preventing a true crime against literature; though we can condemn the material suppression of literature—the persecution of writers, acts of censorship, the burning of books—we are powerless when it comes to its worst violation: that of not reading the books. For that crime, a person pays with his whole life; if the offender is a nation, it pays with its history" (Brodsky, 1987).

Thirty-three percent of American high school graduates will never read a book after high school; 42% of college students won't read another one after they graduate. Eighty percent of U.S. households will not buy a single book this year (Statistic Brain, 2016). And despite evidence that small children who are read to can recognize the letters of the alphabet, can count to 20, can write their own names, and can read sooner than those who are not (National Education Association, 2015), a quarter of American kids 0 to 8 years old are read to never or less often than once a week (Zickuhr & Rainie, 2014).

Declining reading rates are important far beyond issues of academic performance. Regardless of income, reading correlates closely with quality of social life, voting, political activism, participation in culture and fine arts, volunteerism, charity work, and exercise. National Endowment for the Arts chair Dana Gioia explained a decade ago after her organization's study of Americans' reading habits: "The habit of regular reading awakens

▶ *In the Night Kitchen* and *The God of Small Things* are two popular books that frequently raise censors' ire.
(left) ©TJ Photography/PhotoEdit; (right) ©Ben Curtis/PA/Alamy

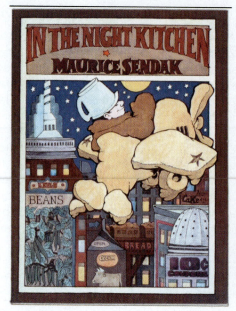

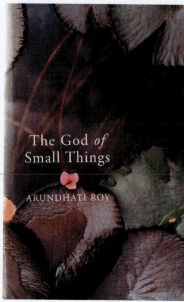

something inside a person that makes him or her take their own life more seriously and at the same time develops the sense that other people's lives are real." Added Timothy Shanahan, past president of the International Reading Association, "If you're low in reading ability . . . you're less likely to take part in activities like sports or church. Being low in literacy is self-isolating, tends to push you out of culture altogether" (all quoted in Thompson, 2007, p. C1). Another well-qualified group of experts—your parents—endorses Ms. Gioia's argument. When asked to identify the skills "most important for children to get ahead in the world today," 86% identified reading, a score second only to that of communication's 90% (Goo, 2015).

You can see Americans' book-reading rates in Figure 2. Do these data represent your frequency of reading? Do you agree with the argument that the lack of reading has consequences for our country, as well as for individuals?

▶ **Figure 2** Adult Book Reading Rates, 2011–2016.
Source: Perrin, 2016.
©Image Source/PictureQuest/ Getty Images RF

Percentage of adults who say they have engaged with books in the previous 12 months

- Read a book in any format
- Read a print book
- Read an e-book
- Listened to an audio book

	2011	2012	2014	2015	2016
Read a book in any format	79	74	76	72	73
Read a print book	71	65	69	63	65
Read an e-book	17	23	28	27	28
Listened to an audio book	11	13	14	12	14

Scope and Structure of the Book Industry

More than 300,000 traditional and nontraditional (print-on-demand, self-published, and niche) titles are published in the United States each year; Americans annually buy nearly 700 million books (Milliot, 2016b), generating $29 billion in sales (Statista, 2016). Today, more books than ever are being published. More books are being read; more people are writing books. Books that would never have been released through traditional publishers are now routinely published.

Categories of Books

The Association of American Publishers divides books into several sales categories:

- *Book club editions* are books sold and distributed (sometimes even published) by book clubs. There are currently more than 300 book club publishers in the United States. These organizations offer trade, professional, and more specialized titles—for example, books for aviation aficionados and expensive republications of classic works. The Book of the Month Club, started in 1926, is the best known; the Literary Guild and the Reader's Digest Book Club are also popular.
- *El-hi* are textbooks produced for elementary and high schools.
- *Higher education* are textbooks produced for colleges and universities.
- *Mail-order books,* such as those advertised on television by Time-Life Books, are delivered by mail and usually are specialized series (*The War Ships*) or elaborately bound special editions of classic novels.
- *Mass market paperbacks* are typically published only as paperbacks and are designed to appeal to a broad readership; many romance novels, diet books, and self-help books are in this category.
- *Professional books* are reference and educational volumes designed specifically for professionals such as doctors, engineers, lawyers, scientists, and managers.
- *Religious books* are volumes such as Bibles, Korans, and the Śruti.
- *Standardized tests* are guide and practice books designed to prepare readers for various examinations such as the SAT or the bar exam.
- *Subscription reference books* are publications such as the *World Book Encyclopaedia*, atlases, and dictionaries bought directly from the publisher rather than purchased in a retail setting.
- **Trade books** include not only fiction and most nonfiction but also cookbooks, biographies, art books, coffee-table books, and how-to books.
- *University press books* come from publishing houses associated with and often underwritten by universities. They typically publish serious nonfiction and scholarly books. Yale University Press and the University of California Press are two of the better-known university presses, and Cambridge University Press is the oldest publisher in the world.

Trends and Convergence in Book Publishing

Like all the media with which we are familiar, convergence is changing the nature of the book industry. In addition to convergence, contemporary publishing and its relationship with its readers are being reshaped by conglomeration, hypercommercialism and demand for profits, the growth of small presses, restructuring of retailing, and changes in readership.

Convergence

Convergence is altering almost all aspects of the book industry. Most obviously, the Internet is changing the way books are distributed and sold. But this digital technology, in the form of **e-publishing**, the publication of books initially or exclusively in a digital format, also offers a new way for writers' ideas to be published. In fact, many of today's "books" are no longer composed of paper pages snug between two covers. As former Random House editor Peter Osnos explained, "Unlike other printed media, books do not have advertising, so there is none to lose. They don't have subscribers, so holding on to them is not an issue either. The main challenge is to manage inventory, making books available where, when, and how readers want them. And on that score, the advances in gadgetry and the changes in popular [reading] habits over the past decade . . . have produced a major advance" (2009, p. 38). By gadgetry, Osnos means primarily e-books, print on demand (POD), and a host of electronic reading devices.

E-BOOKS In her mid-forties, Erika Mitchell, writing under the pen name E. L. James, was having some success publishing fan fiction based on the vampire novels *Twilight* as **e-books**—books downloaded in electronic form from the Internet to computers, e-readers, or mobile digital devices. This brought her to the attention of traditional publisher Random House, and working together they turned her *50 Shades of Grey* trilogy into a series of best sellers and major motion pictures. Romance writer Meredith Wild, who writes mainly after her children leave for school, has sold more than a million and a half self-published erotic novels on Amazon and other websites. This brought her a $6.5 million advance from traditional publisher Forever (Alter, 2016c). Established authors fare well, too. Stieg Larsson's smash best seller, *The Girl with the Dragon Tattoo*, and the other books in his trilogy, *The Girl Who Played with Fire* and *The Girl Who Kicked the Hornet's Nest*, have sold more digital than hard-copy editions, and big-name authors like Stephen King now routinely write works primarily for e-publication.

Popular acceptance of e-books seemed in place by Christmas Day 2009, when Amazon reported that for the first time in its history, it sold more e-books than traditional paper books in a single day. Today, e-books account for about 30% of all U.S. book sales, a number that has held steady for several years now and has seemed to peak (Milliott, 2016a). Industry experts explain the leveling off in the growth of e-books to readers' digital fatigue, an explanation bolstered by data indicating that Americans' number-one favorite activity when unplugged from their digital devices is reading books in their paper version (Birth, 2016).

Still, e-publishing's greatest impact may be on new writers. Because anyone with a computer and a story to tell can bypass the traditional book publishers, first-time authors or writers of small, niche books now have an outlet for their work. An additional advantage of e-publishing, especially for new or small-market authors, is that e-books can be published almost instantly. James Patterson has made enough money selling his books that he can wait the one to two years it typically takes for a traditional novel to be produced once it is in the publisher's hands. Rarely can new authors afford this luxury.

Another advantage is financial. Authors who distribute through e-publishers typically get royalties of 40% to 70%, compared to the 5% to 10% offered by traditional publishers. This lets aspiring writers offer their books for as little as 99 cents or $2.99, making those works more attractive to readers willing to take a low-cost chance to find something and someone new and interesting—earning writers even more sales. Traditional book publishers say their lower royalty rates are mandated by the expense of the services they provide, such as editorial assistance and marketing, not to mention the cost of production and distribution. The debate over self- versus traditional publishing is really a disagreement over the value of **disintermediation**, eliminating gatekeepers between artists and audiences. Eliminate the middlemen and more original content of greater variety from fresher voices gets to more people. Keep the middlemen and quality is assured, and while an occasional interesting work or new voice might be missed, the industry's overall product remains superior. For books, disintermediation in the form of self-publication runs the gamut from completely self-published-and-promoted works to self-publishing with an assist, with digital publishers providing a full range of services—copyediting, securing and commissioning artwork, cover design, promotion, and in some cases, distribution of traditional paper books to brick-and-mortar bookstores. And of course, there is a hybrid model, such as Amazon's Kindle Worlds, a self-publishing online platform for fan fiction where successful authors can be offered contracts and production and editing support from Amazon Publishing, the company's book division. Other major publishers such as Penguin and Harlequin now have self-publishing divisions. How successful are self-published authors? In every week of 2015, a third of the 100 best-selling Kindle books were self-published, and over the last five years, nearly 40 self-published authors have sold a million copies of their e-books on Amazon (Alter, 2016c).

Print on demand (POD) is another form of e-publishing. Companies such as Xlibris,

▲ The Espresso Book Machine—7 million titles from traditional publishers, the public domain, and self-publishers, each available in about four minutes.
©Leon Neal/AFP/Getty Images

AuthorHouse, and iUniverse are POD publishers. They store works digitally and, once ordered, a book can be instantly printed, bound, and sent. Alternatively, once ordered, that book can be printed and bound at a bookstore that has the proper technology. The advantage for publisher and reader is financial. POD books require no warehouse for storage, there are no **remainders** (unsold books returned to publishers to be sold at great discount) to eat into profits, and the production costs, in both personnel and equipment, are tiny when compared to traditional publishing. These factors not only produce less expensive books for readers but also greatly expand the variety of books that can and will be published. And although a large publisher like Oxford University Press can produce thousands of volumes a year, smaller POD operations can make a profit on as few as 100 orders. Large commercial publishers have also found a place for POD in their business, using the technology to rush hot, headline-inspired books to readers. In 2008, for the first time, American publishers released more POD titles than new and revised titles produced by traditional methods; in 2010 the ratio was more than three to one. The availability of POD books will grow even more with the continued rollout of the Espresso Book Machine, a joint effort of several major book publishers. The device, which can print and bind a 300-page book in four minutes, is available in hundreds of locations across the globe and has access to more than 7 million books available from self-publishers, a growing list of traditional publishing houses, and the public domain.

Smartphones, Tablets, and e-Readers

Many booksellers and even publishing companies themselves offer e-books specifically for smartphones, tablets, and **e-readers**, digital devices with the appearance of traditional books that display content that is digitally stored and accessed. Although earlier attempts at producing e-readers had failed, the 2006 unveiling of the Sony Reader, dubbed the iBook, proved so successful that it was soon followed by several similar devices, such as Amazon's various Kindle models, Apple's iPad, and Barnes & Noble's Nook. (In 2014 Sony discontinued its e-reader technologies.) In addition, smartphone and tablet apps like Bookari and Scribd and other e-reading alternatives such as online publisher Zinio, which makes titles available for most digital devices, and Pronoun, which offers video-enhanced books, have also appeared. Today, just under one in five American adults owns a dedicated e-reader, but because 68% have smartphones and 45% have tablets, the large majority holds in its hands the ability to read digital books (Anderson, 2015).

Nonetheless, readers have welcomed the devices and publishers have understandably responded, given the industry's belief that "any business that requires a truck these days, forget it" (Thompson, 2009). Hundreds of thousands of in- and out-of-print titles are available for **platform agnostic publishing**—digital and traditional paper books available for any and all reading devices. And those reading devices themselves will continue to evolve, with advances such as flexible screens so thin they can be rolled up and fully text-functional

▲ Amazon's Kindle, Apple's iPad, and numerous other e-readers have transformed publishing and reading.

(left) ©Kevin Dietsch/UPI/Newscom; (right) ©Oleksiy Maksymenko Photography/Alamy

e-readers that let users copy and paste text to Word documents on their computers. In anticipation of the growth of e-publishing, some traditional publishers, Dorchester Publishing for example, have abandoned bound paper books altogether.

For readers in search of almost every book ever written or for those who want to search the contents of almost every book ever written (say, for references to the Civil War even though "Civil War" does not appear in the title), there are several developments. Online bookseller Amazon has scanned every page of every in-print book into its Search Inside the Book feature. That means anyone registered (it's free, but readers must provide a credit card number) can eventually search millions of books for just about any topic or idea. The pages cannot be downloaded, and there is a limit to how much searching a given reader can do in a specified period of time. Of course, Amazon's goal is to sell more books (you just might want to order one of the books your search has uncovered), and it has developed its own POD service, CreateSpace, that instantly provides any book requested. Several nonprofit organizations are also making searchable and downloadable books available online. Project Gutenberg offers 1 million noncopyrighted classics; the Million Book Project also has 1 million government texts and older titles; the Open Content Alliance digitizes the holdings of its many member libraries; and the International Children's Digital Library and the Rosetta Project make downloadable tens of thousands of current and antique children's books from around the world.

Whereas these efforts at digitizing books have been generally well regarded, the same cannot be said for Google Print. Internet giant Google announced in late 2005 its intention to make available online 15 million books from the New York Public Library and several university libraries. The vast majority, 90%, were to be out-of-print books not bound by copyright. The problem, however, was Google's plan to hold the entire text of all works, in and out of print, on its servers, making only small, fair-use portions of copyrighted works available to Web users. Initially, many publishers agreed to participate if the complete text of their copyrighted works could be stored on *their* servers, but Google refused. Despite Google's insistence that it would protect the interests of authors and publishers as it strives to, in its own words, "organize the world's information and make it universally accessible and useful," a series of lawsuits from the Author's Guild and major publishers followed. In 2013 a federal court upheld the legality of Google Books' effort, ruling that it expanded the market for books by helping consumers discover works that they would never have otherwise known existed, and the Supreme Court's refusal to hear that case in 2016 confirmed that decision (Liptak & Alter, 2016).

Conglomeration

More than any other medium, the book industry into the 1970s and 1980s was dominated by relatively small operations. Publishing houses were traditionally staffed by fewer than 20 people, the large majority by fewer than 10. Today, however, although tens of thousands of businesses call themselves book publishers, only a very small percentage produces four or more titles a year. The industry is dominated now by the so-called Big 5 publishing houses—Penguin Random House (250 **imprints**, or individual book publishing companies), Hachette (23 imprints), HarperCollins (120 imprints), Macmillan (30 imprints), and Simon & Schuster (52 imprints)—and a few other large concerns, like Time Warner Publishing. Each of these giants was once, sometimes with another name, an independent book publisher. All are now part of large national or international corporate conglomerates (Alter, 2016b). These major publishers control more than 80% of all U.S.

book sales. Even e-publishing is dominated by the big companies, as all the major houses and booksellers maintain e-publishing units.

Opinion on the benefit of corporate ownership is divided. The positive view is that the rich parent company can infuse the imprint with necessary capital, enabling it to attract better authors or to take gambles on new writers that would, in the past, have been impossible. Another plus is that the corporate parent's other media holdings can be used to promote and repackage the books for greater profitability. Neither of these benefits is insignificant, argue many industry insiders, because book publishing is more like gambling than business. Literary agent Eric Simonoff says the industry is "unpredictable . . . the profit margins are so small, the cycles (from contract to publication) are so incredibly long" and there is an "almost total lack of market research" (quoted in Boss, 2007, p. B6). Fiction writer James Patterson, for example, suffered 12 rejections for *The Thomas Berryman Number* before Little, Brown accepted his first novel in 1976. Patterson has since rewarded his publisher with 51 *New York Times* best sellers. Since 2006, one out of every 17 hardcover books bought in America was written by Patterson (Mahler, 2010). Even J. K. Rowling's first *Harry Potter* book was rejected 12 times before finding a publisher (Flood, 2015). "It's guesswork," says Doubleday editor-in-chief Bill Thomas. "The whole thing is educated guesswork, but guesswork nonetheless. You just try to make sure your upside mistakes make up for your downside mistakes" (quoted in Boss, 2007, p. B6).

The negative view is that as publishing houses become just one in the parent company's long list of enterprises, product quality suffers as important editing and production steps are eliminated to maximize profits. Before conglomeration, publishing was often described as a **cottage industry**; that is, publishing houses were small operations, closely identified with their personnel—both their own small staffs and their authors. The cottage imagery, however, extends beyond smallness of size. There was a quaintness and charm associated with publishing houses—their attention to detail, their devotion to tradition, the care they gave to their façades (their reputations). "The act of publishing is essentially the act of making public one's own enthusiasm," reminisced Robert Gottlieb, longtime editor-in-chief at old-line houses Simon & Schuster and Knopf (in Menand, 2015, p. 80). The world of corporate conglomerates has little room for such niceties, as profit dominates all other considerations. Critics of corporate ownership see profits-over-quality at play in recent publishing practices, such as when publishers use "big data" from online e-book readership not only to determine which books get published (Alter & Russell, 2016), but also to help shape characters and story lines in books as they are being written (Miller, 2014), as well as when fans read online manuscripts and then vote on which should be published (Alter, 2014b).

Demand for Profits and Hypercommercialism

The threat from conglomeration resides in the parent company's overemphasis on the bottom line—that is, profitability at all costs. Unlike in the days when G. P. Putnam's sons and the Schuster family actually ran the houses that carried their names, critics fear that now little pride is taken in the content of books and that risk taking (tackling controversial issues, experimenting with new styles, finding and nurturing unknown authors) is becoming rarer and rarer.

Daniel Menaker, fiction editor for *The New Yorker*, explains, "Being a book editor is often, on balance, a rum game. The arts—high and low—have a way of moving forward, backward, or to the side, which leaves their servants perpetually scrambling to catch up with and make sense of their direction and their very nature. Profit, when it gets into bed with them, doesn't like the unpredictability of the arts. It tries to rationalize them and make them financially reliable. Can't be done" (2009). As a result, Jason Epstein, longtime editor at Random House and founder of Anchor Books, writes that his is an "increasingly distressed industry" mired in "severe structural problems." Among them are a retail bookselling system that favors "brand name" authors and "a bestseller-driven system of high royalty advances." He says that contemporary publishing is "overconcentrated," "undifferentiated," and "fatally rigid" (quoted in Feldman, 2001, p. 35). To Menaker, Epstein, and other critics of conglomeration, the industry seems overwhelmed by a blockbuster mentality—lust for the biggest-selling authors and titles possible, sometimes with little consideration for literary merit. Simon & Schuster recently formed a division, Keywords Press, to publish books written by Internet celebrities, signing YouTube stars Shane Dawson and Justine Ezarik, better known as iJustine. Author Michael Crichton got $40 million for a two-book deal from HarperCollins; author Tom Clancy received $45 million for two books from Penguin Putnam. Fox News anchor Megyn Kelly got a $10 million advance from HarperCollins after her debate run-in with then-presidential candidate Donald Trump. Random House offered Lena Dunham, actress, writer, and creator of television's *Girls*, $3.7 million for her first book, *Not That Kind of Girl*. As the resources and energies of publishing houses are committed to a small number of superstar writers and blockbuster books, smaller, more interesting, possibly more serious or important books do not get published. If these types of books cannot get published, they may never be written. Will we be denied their ideas in the cultural forum? We will see, but as we read earlier in this chapter, it is converged technologies like POD and e-books that may well be the vehicles that ensure those ideas have access to the forum and us to them.

Publishers attempt to offset the large investments they do make through the sale of **subsidiary rights**, that is, the sale of the book, its contents, and even its characters to filmmakers, paperback publishers, book clubs, foreign publishers, and product producers like T-shirt, poster, coffee cup, and greeting card manufacturers. For example, based on the success of his first book, *Cold Mountain*, Charles Frazier's one-page proposal for his second novel earned his publisher $3 million for the film rights alone from Paramount Pictures. The industry itself estimates that many publishers would go out of business if it were not for the sale of these rights. Writers such as John Grisham (*The Client*) and Gay Talese (*Thy Neighbor's Wife*) can command several million dollars for the film rights to their books. Although this is good for the profitability of the publishers and the superstar authors, critics fear that those books with the greatest subsidiary sales value will receive the most publisher attention.

As greater and greater sums are tied up in blockbusters, and as subsidiary rights therefore grow in importance, the marketing, promotion, and public relations surrounding a book become crucial. This leads to the additional fear that only the most promotable books will be published—bookstores are flooded with celebrity cookbooks, celebrity picture books, unauthorized biographies of celebrities, and tell-all autobiographies from the children of celebrities.

In addition, **tie-in novels**—books based on popular television shows and movies—have become more common. *Bratva* is a novel using characters from the FX Network's hit series *Sons of Anarchy*. *Homeland*, *Fringe*, and *CSI* are other TV shows that have enjoyed novelization, as is *Murder She Wrote*, which went off the air in 1996 and whose 44th book version was released in 2015 (Alter, 2015).

The importance of promotion and publicity has led to an increase in the release of **instant books**. What better way to unleash millions of dollars of free publicity for a book than to base it on an event currently trending on Twitter? Publishers see these opportunities and then initiate the projects. For example, within days of the two political parties' 2016 nominating conventions, *Trump vs. Clinton: In Their Own Words: Everything You Need to Know to Vote Your Conscience* was available for Kindle. Lost in the wake of instant books, easily promotable authors and titles, and blockbusters, critics argue, are books of merit, books of substance, and books that make a difference.

Several other recent events suggest that the demand for profits is bringing even more hypercommercialism to the book business. One trend is the "Hollywoodization" of books. Potential synergies between books, television, and movies have spurred big media companies such as Viacom, Time Warner, and News Corp. to invest heavily in publishing, buying up houses big and small. Some movie studios are striking "exclusive" deals with publishers—for example, Walden Media teams with Penguin Young Readers, Focus Films with Random House, and Paramount with Simon & Schuster. In addition, ReganBooks (owned by HarperCollins, which, in turn, is owned by News Corp.) moved its offices from New York to Los Angeles to be in a better position to develop material that has both book and film potential. Movie studios Warner Brothers, Columbia, Paramount, DreamWorks, Fox, New Line, Imagine, Tribeca, and Revolution Films have all set up operations in New York City to be closer to the source of books, magazine articles, and plays that they hope to turn into material for the big screen. Critics fear that only those books with the most synergistic potential will be signed and published. Advocates argue just the opposite—a work that might have had limited profit potential as a "mere" book, and therefore gone unpublished, just might find a home across several mutually promoting platforms. They point to *Sideways*, a small-selling book that became a best-selling book after the movie it inspired became a hit.

Another trend that has created much angst among book traditionalists is the paid product placement. Movies and television have long accepted payments from product manufacturers to feature their brands in their content, but it was not until May 2000 that the first paid-for placement appeared in a fiction novel. Bill Fitzhugh's *Cross Dressing*, published by Avon, contains what are purchased commercials for Seagram liquor. Fay Weldon followed suit in 2001, even titling her book *The Bulgari Connection*, after her sponsor, a jewelry company by the same name. *Cathy's Book*, from Perseus/Running Press, pushed Cover Girl cosmetics, but public criticism from several sources, including Consumer Alert and the *New York Times* editorial board, led the publisher to abandon product placement when the title went to paperback. As with other media that accept product placements, critics fear that content will be bent to satisfy sponsors rather than serve the quality of the work itself. Product placement in e-books has done little to allay those concerns. Embedded links in e-books can boost the potential value of a placement, making them attractive to sponsors. It is unlikely, however, that the brands used by characters will fail to deliver the sponsor's advertised benefits. For example, Hillary Carlip's 2014 *Find Me I'm Yours* is about a young woman, Mags, working at a bridal magazine and searching for love in Los Angeles. Of course, like any young person, Mags is health and weight conscious. Naturally, then, she uses the sugar substitute Sweet'N Low quite frequently throughout the novel's 356 pages, even having her nails painted to look like the product's distinctive pink packets. And although Sweet'N Low paid $1.3 million for development of the book, Mags uses a variety of other brand-name products, all of which readers can further investigate by visiting the book's 33 brand-related websites. They are unlikely to do that if those products fail Mags in some way (Alter, 2014a).

▲ First-time author Lena Dunham, creator of TV's *Girls*, landed a $3.7 million advance for her book, *Not That Kind of Girl*. ©*Charles Sykes/AP Photo*

Growth of Small Presses

The overcommercialization of the book industry is mitigated somewhat by the rise in the number of smaller publishing houses. Although these smaller operations are large in number, they account for a very small proportion of books sold. Nonetheless, as recently as seven years ago there were 20,000 U.S. book publishers. Today there are more than 80,000, the vast majority being small presses. They cannot compete in the blockbuster world. By definition *alternative*, they specialize in specific areas such as the environment, feminism, gay issues, and how-to. They can also publish writing otherwise uninteresting to bigger houses, such as poetry and literary commentary. Relying on specialization and narrowly targeted marketing, books such as Ralph Nader and Clarence Ditlow's *The Lemon Book*, a guide on buying a used car, published by Moyer Bell; Claudette McShane's *Warning! Dating May Be Hazardous to Your Health*, published by Mother Courage Press; and *Split Verse,* a book of poems about divorce published by Midmarch Arts, can not only earn healthy sales but also make a difference in their readers' lives. And what may seem surprising is that it is the Internet, specifically Amazon, that is boosting the fortunes of these smaller houses. Because it compiles data on customer preferences (books bought, browsed, recommended to others, or wished for), it can make recommendations to potential buyers, and quite often those recommendations are from small publishers that the buyer might never have considered (or never have seen at a brick-and-mortar retailer). In other words, Amazon helps level the book industry playing field.

Restructuring of Book Retailing

There are approximately 20,000 bookstores in the United States, but the number is dwindling as small, independent operations find it increasingly difficult to compete with chains such as

▲ The best-known and most successful of the online booksellers, Amazon offers potential buyers a wealth of information and services.
©Lenscap/Alamy

Barnes & Noble, Follett's, and Books-A-Million. Even giant chain store Borders (1,249 stores under its own name and Waldenbooks) was forced to file for bankruptcy in 2011 and gradually closed all its stores. The remaining chains and the independents must still contend with online retailers like Amazon; discount stores such as Target, Walmart, and Costco, which together control 30% of the American book market; the explosion of POD; and the rapid migration of books from paper to the electronic screens of laptops, tablet computers, e-readers, and smartphones.

Where the big stores have prospered it is because their size enables them to purchase inventory in bulk cheaply and then offer discounts to readers. Because their locations attract shoppers, they can also profitably stock nonbook merchandise such as audiobooks, CDs, computer games, calendars, magazines, and greeting cards for the drop-in trade. But high-volume, high-traffic operations tend to deal in high-volume books. To book traditionalists, this only encourages the industry's blockbuster mentality. When the largest bookstores in the country order only the biggest sellers, the small books get lost. When floor space is given over to Garfield coffee mugs and pop star calendars, there is even less room for small but potentially interesting books. Although big bookselling chains have their critics, they also have their defenders. At least the big titles, CDs, and cheap prices get people into bookstores, the argument goes. Once folks begin reading, even if it is less sophisticated stuff, they might eventually move on to more sophisticated material.

Independent bookstores are experiencing something of a renaissance. Today there are about 1,700 independent booksellers in the United States, operating 2,227 outlets. And although this is a big decline from the 4,000 independent bookstores of the 1990s, the number of indies has grown 23% since 2009 (Alter, 2016a). Just as important, despite sales losses experienced by the big chains, independent bookstores saw their sales increase more than 6% from 2015 to 2016 (McCarthy, 2016). They have accomplished this by using their small size and independence to their advantage, countering the chains and discount stores with expert, personalized service provided by a reading-loving staff, coffee and snack bars, cushioned chairs and sofas for slow browsing, intimate readings by favorite authors, and even neighborhood bookmobiles, book-filled vans that travel to readers. In fact, so successful have these strategies been that the big stores now are copying them. Barnes & Noble, for example, sponsors a program it calls Discover to promote notable first novels. Not only do these efforts emulate services more commonly associated with smaller independents, but they also help blunt some of the criticism suffered by the chains, specifically that they ignore new and smaller-selling books. Still, the big operations cannot or will not emulate some strategies. Specialization is one. Religious, feminist, and animal-lover bookstores exist. The availability of in-store book clubs for children or poetry fans, for example, is another small-store strategy.

Another alternative to the big chain store is buying books online. Amazon is the best known of the online book sales services. Thorough, fast, and well stocked, Amazon boasts low overhead, and that means better prices for readers. In addition, its website offers book buyers large amounts of potentially valuable information. Once online, customers can identify the books that interest them, read synopses, check reviews from multiple sources, read sample pages from a book, and see comments not only from other readers but sometimes from the authors and publishers as well. Of course, they can also order books. Although books represent only 7% of the Seattle company's $75 billion in annual revenue, it dominates book retailing, selling 40% of all new books sold every year and controlling 60% of all e-book sales (Packer, 2014). This size gives Amazon quite a bit of power in the book industry. Critics say it uses its position to extort high payments from the publishers, who have little choice but to sell their books on its site, while defenders see much benefit for readers, who get a greater variety of books at lower prices.

DEVELOPING MEDIA LITERACY SKILLS

The Lessons of Harry Potter

J. K. Rowling's series of books about youthful British sorcerer Harry Potter offers several important media literacy lessons. For example, its huge appeal to young people can be used to examine one element of media literacy, understanding content as a text providing insight into our culture and lives. Just why have these books resonated so strongly with young readers? The controversy surrounding the numerous efforts to have the series banned from schools and libraries as antireligious and anti-Christian and its status as the "most challenged" (censored) children's literature in the United States call into play the particular media literacy skill of developing the ability and willingness to effectively and meaningfully understand content.

The publishing industry classifies the *Harry Potter* books as young adult fiction. But their phenomenal reception by readers of all ages suggests these works not only have broader appeal but are in themselves something very special. The initial U.S. printing of a *Harry Potter* book is about 14 million copies—100 times that of a normal best seller. The seven *Harry Potter* books combined have sold more than 500 million copies worldwide, and two-thirds of all American children have read at least one *Harry Potter* book. The *Potter* series has been published in over 67 languages (including Greek, Latin, and "Americanized English") in more than 200 countries. *Potter* books occupy the top four spots on the all-time fastest-selling book list.

An important element of media literacy is the development of an awareness of the impact of media, and there is evidence that *Harry Potter* has helped create a new generation of readers. When the series first appeared, horror writer Stephen King wrote, "If these millions of readers are awakened to the wonders and rewards of fantasy at 11 or 12 . . . well, when they get to age 16 or so, there's this guy named King" (as quoted in Garchik, 2000, p. D10). Diane Roback, children's book editor at *Publishers Weekly,* cited "'the Harry Potter halo effect,' in which children come into stores and libraries asking for books that resemble the Rowling series" (*USA Today,* 2000, p. E4). When the final *Potter* book was released, a Scholastic Books survey of 500 *Harry Potter* readers aged 5 to 7 indicated that 51% said they did not read books for fun until they started reading the series. Three-quarters said reading the series had made them interested in reading other books (Rich, 2007). That impact seems long-lasting, as today 82% of children 12 and under report reading for fun on a weekly basis, as do nearly half of all teens ("Are Kids," 2016).

But the series has had another, arguably more important impact. There is a wealth of scholarly research on the link between reading literary fiction and developing empathy for others, for example McCreary and Marchant's "Reading and Empathy" (2016) and Bal and Veltkamp's "How Does Fiction Reading Influence Empathy? An Experimental Investigation of the Role of Emotional Transportation" (2013). The logic behind these studies is that reading literary fiction engages us with the psychological, social, and cultural complexities of life by requiring us to become someone else, transporting ourselves not only into the situations of others but into their minds. Reading *Harry Potter,* then, should have a similar impact, especially as he "is continually in contact with stigmatized groups. The 'muggles' get no respect in the wizarding world as they lack any magical ability. The 'half-bloods,' or 'mud-bloods'—wizards and witches descended from only one magical parent—don't fare much better, while the Lord Voldemort character believes that power should only be held by 'pure-blood' wizards" (Stetka, 2014). Loris Vezzali and her colleagues (2013) tested *Harry Potter*'s power to build empathy in an article entitled "The Greatest Magic of Harry Potter: Reducing Prejudice" and discovered just what media-literate people who recognize the power of well-crafted media messages would expect. Readers who read parts of the book where Harry had to deal with prejudice showed more empathy toward immigrants, homosexuals, and refugees than did those who read neutral passages. In an interview with

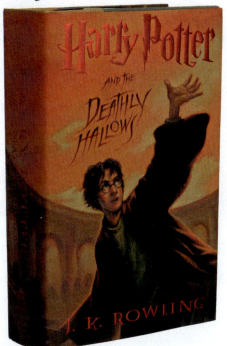

▲ Harry Potter, the wizard who launched a million readers and made them better people, too.
©*Lars Klove*/The New York Times /*Redux*

science writer Bret Stetka (2014), Professor Vezzali explained, "Unfortunately the news we read on a daily basis tells us we have so much work to do. But based on our work, fantasy books such as *Harry Potter* may be of great help to educators and parents in teaching tolerance."

MEDIA LITERACY CHALLENGE
Literacy: Limiting Access to Books in School

The *Harry Potter* books have been best sellers, but they have also been the frequent target of people who want to censor them from school libraries. You may never have read any of these works, but consider the possible reasons that parents might not want their children to read certain books without their knowledge, and then answer the following questions. To do so will call into play important components of media literacy: *the development of an understanding of the ethical and moral obligations of those who make (and dispense) media content* and *the awareness of media content as "texts" that provide insight into our culture.* Two media literacy skills are also involved: *the ability to distinguish emotional from reasoned reactions when responding to content* and *the ability to think critically about media messages.*

Your challenge is to answer these questions. Is it ever okay for groups outside the school (parents or concerned citizens, for example) to choose not to allow certain books in their schools? Why or why not? If you think it is appropriate to ask (or even insist) that movies, TV, video games, and recordings used in schools have warning labels or that parents who object to their children's exposure to that content be allowed to "opt out," would you hold books to those same controls? Should other in-school media be subject to greater control than books? Why or why not? Is it better to have children reading controversial books as long as it encourages them to read, or would it be better if those children were not reading at all? Which is the greater "evil"? You can approach this challenge as either an opportunity for personal reflection, committing your thoughts to paper, or you can set it up as a debate, for example the No Limits versus the Some Limits versus the Strong Limits.

Resources for Review and Discussion

REVIEW POINTS: TYING CONTENT TO LEARNING OUTCOMES

▶ **Outline the history and development of the publishing industry and the book itself as a medium.**
- ☐ Although the first printing press came to the colonies in 1638, books were not central to early colonial life. However, books and pamphlets were at the heart of the colonists' revolt against England in the 1770s.
- ☐ Developments in the 18th and 19th centuries, such as improvements in printing, the flowering of the American novel, and the introduction of dime novels, helped make books a mass medium.

▶ **Describe the cultural value of books and the implications of censorship for democracy.**
- ☐ Books have cultural value because they are agents of social and cultural change; important cultural repositories; windows on the past; important sources of personal development; sources of entertainment, escape, and personal reflection; mirrors of culture; and because the purchase and reading of a book is a much more individual, personal activity than consuming advertiser-supported or heavily promoted media.
- ☐ Censorship, both formal and in the form of people's own aliteracy, threatens these values, as well as democracy itself.

▶ **Explain how the organizational and economic nature of the contemporary book industry shapes the content of books.**

  ☐ Convergence is reshaping the book industry as well as the reading experience itself through advances such as e-publishing, POD, e-books, e-readers, smartphones and tablets, and several different efforts to digitize most of the world's books.

  ☐ Conglomeration affects the publishing industry as it has all media, expressing itself through trends such as demand for profit and hypercommercialization.

  ☐ Demand for profit and hypercommercialization manifest themselves in the increased importance placed on subsidiary rights, instant books, "Hollywoodization," and product placement.

  ☐ Book retailing is undergoing change; large chains dominate the business but continue to be challenged by imaginative, high-quality independent booksellers. Much book buying has also gravitated to the Internet.

▶ **Act as a more media-literate consumer of books, especially in considering their uniqueness in an increasingly mass-mediated, media-converged world.**

  ☐ The wild success of the *Harry Potter* series holds several lessons for media-literate readers, not the least of which is that people value quality media content.

KEY TERMS

linotype, 54

offset lithography, 54

dime novels, 54

pulp novels, 54

censorship, 57

aliteracy, 59

trade books, 61

e-publishing, 62

e-book, 62

disintermediation, 62

print on demand (POD), 63

remainders, 63

e-reader, 63

platform agnostic publishing, 63

imprint, 64

cottage industry, 65

subsidiary rights, 66

tie-in novels, 66

instant books, 66

QUESTIONS FOR REVIEW

1. What were the major developments in the modernization of the printing press?

2. Why were the early colonists not a book-reading population?

3. What was the Stamp Act? Why did colonial printers object to it?

4. What factors allowed the flowering of the American novel, as well as the expansion of the book industry, in the 1800s?

5. Who developed the paperback in England? In the United States?

6. Name six reasons books are an important cultural resource.

7. What are the major categories of books?

8. What is the impact of conglomeration on the book industry?

9. What are the products of increasing hypercommercialism and demands for profit in the book industry?

10. What are e-books, e-readers, and e-publishing?

To maximize your study time, check out CONNECT to access the SmartBook study module for this chapter and explore other resources.

QUESTIONS FOR CRITICAL THINKING AND DISCUSSION

1. Do you envision books ever again having the power to move the nation as they did in revolutionary or antislavery times? Why or why not?

2. Are you proud of your book-reading habits? Why or why not? For example, do you read for fun? How often do you read outside of required school material? When you do read, which genres do you prefer?

3. Under what circumstances is censorship permissible? Whom do you trust to make the right decision about what you should and should not read? If you were a librarian, under what circumstances would you pull a book off the shelves?

REFERENCES

1. Alter, A. (2017, January 12). Political storm for publishers. *The New York Times*, p. B1.

2. Alter, A. (2016a, March 28). Bookmobiles signal stores are on road to recovery. *The New York Times*, p. B3.

3. Alter, A. (2016b, March 2). New offer by Hachette for Perseus is approved. *The New York Times*, p. B4.

4. Alter, A. (2016c, January 31). A self-publisher making an imprint. *The New York Times*, pp. B1, B6.

5. Alter, A. (2015, January 4). As seen on TV: Novelizations sustain fans and gain respect. *The New York Times*, p. A1.

6. Alter, A. (2014a, November 2). E-book mingles love and product placement. *The New York Times*, p. B1.

7. Alter, A. (2014b, August 12). Publishers turn to the crowd to find the next best seller. *The New York Times*, p. B1.

8. Alter, A., & Russell, K. (2016, March 15). Moneyball for book publishers: A detailed look at how we read. *The New York Times*, p. B1.

9. Anderson, M. (2015, October 29). Technology device ownership: 2015. *Pew Research Center*. Online: http://www.pewinternet.org/2015/10/29/technology-device-ownership-2015/

10. "Are kids and teens in the U.K. and U.S. reading for fun?" (2016, November 11). *Nielsen*. Online: http://www.nielsen.com/uk/en/insights/news/2016/are-kids-and-teens-in-the-uk-and-us-reading-for-fun.html

11. Bal, P. M., & Veltkamp, V. (2013). How does fiction reading influence empathy? An experimental investigation of the role of emotional transportation. *PloS One*, 8, e55341

12. Begley, S. (2016, September 25). What the list of the most banned books says about our society's fears. *Time*. Online: http://time.com/4505713/banned-books-week-reasons-change/

13. Birth, A. (2016, February 25). Unplugging: Majority of Americans try to disconnect from tech; 45% try weekly. *The Harris Poll*. Online: http://www.theharrispoll.com/health-and-life/Unplugging-Americans-Disconnect-Tech.html

14. Boss, S. (2007, May 13). The greatest mystery: Making a best seller. *The New York Times*, pp. B1–B6.

15. Bradbury, R. (1981). *Fahrenheit 451*. New York: Ballantine. (Originally published in 1953.)

16. Brodsky, J. (1987, December 8). *Nobel lecture*. Online: http://www.nobelprize.org/nobel_prizes/literature/laureates/1987/brodsky-lecture.html

17. Feldman, G. (2001, February 12). Publishers caught in a Web. *The Nation*, pp. 35–36.

18. Flood, A. (2015, March 24). JK Rowling says she received "loads" of rejections before Harry Potter successs. *The Guardian*. Online: https://www.theguardian.com/books/2015/mar/24/jk-rowling-tells-fans-twitter-loads-rejections-before-harry-potter-success

19. Garchik, L. (2000, July 25). Death and hobbies. *San Francisco Chronicle*, p. D10.

20. "Germany: How dangerous is *Mein Kampf?* (2016, January 15). *The Week*, p. 14.

21. Goo, S. (2015, February 19). The skills Americans say kids need to succeed in life. *Pew Research Center*. Online: http://www.pewresearch.org/fact-tank/2015/02/19/skills-for-success/

22. Liptak, A, & Alter, J. (2016, April 18). Challenge to Google Books is declined by Supreme Court. *The New York Times*, p. B6.

23. Mahler, J. (2010, January 24). James Patterson Inc. *The New York Times Magazine*, pp. 32–39, 46–48.

24. McCarthy, N. (2016, August 18). Bookstores: Finally turning the page? *Statistica*. Online: https://www.statista.com/chart/5532/are-us-bookstores-finally-turning-the-page/

25. McCreary, J. J., & Marchant, G. J. (2016). Reading and empathy. *Reading Psychology*. Online: http://dx.doi.org/10.1080/02702711.2016.1245690

26. Menaker, D. (2009, September 14). Redactor agonistes. *Barnes & Noble Review*. Online: http://bnreview.barnesandnoble.com/t5/Reviews-Essays/Redactor-Agonistes/ba-p/1367

27. Menand, L. (2016, December 12). Banned books and blockbusters. *The New Yorker*, pp. 78–85.

28. Menand, L. (2015, January 5). Pulp's big moment. *The New Yorker*, pp. 62–69.

29. Miller, L. (2014, January 8). Big data's next frontier: Crowd-testing fiction. *Salon*. Online: http://www.salon.com/2014/01/09/big_datas_next_frontier_crowd_testing_fiction/

30. Milliott, J. (2016a, June 17). As e-book sales decline, digital fatigue grows. *Publishers Weekly*. Online: http://www.publishersweekly.com/pw/by-topic/digital/retailing/article/70696-as-e-book-sales-decline-digital-fatigue-grows.html

31. Milliot, J. (2016b, January 1). Print book sales up again in 2015. *Publishers Weekly*. Online: http://www.publishersweekly.com/pw/by-topic/industry-news/bookselling/article/69051-print-sales-up-again.html

32. Moyers, B. (2007, February 12). Discovering what democracy means. Online: http://www.commondreams.org/views/2007/02/12/discovering-what-democracy-means

33. National Education Association. (2015). Facts about children's literacy. Online: http://www.nea.org/grants/facts-about-childrens-literacy.html

34. Norsigian, J., Diskin, V., Doress-Worters, P., Pincus, J., Sanford, W., & Swenson, N. (1999). The Boston women's health book collective and *Our Bodies, Ourselves:* A brief history and reflection. *Journal of the American Medical Women's Association*. Online: http://www.ourbodiesourselves.org

35. Osnos, P. (2009, March/April). Rise of the reader. *Columbia Journalism Review*, pp. 38–39.

36. Packer, G. (2014, February 17 & 24). Cheap words. *The New Yorker*, pp. 66–79.

37. Perrin, A. (2016, September 1). Book reading. *Pew Research Center*. Online: http://www.pewinternet.org/2016/09/01/book-reading-2016/

38. Pincus, J. (1998). Introduction. In Boston Women's Health Book Collective (Eds.), *Our bodies, ourselves for the new century* (pp. 21–23). New York: Touchstone.

39. Rich, M. (2007, July 22). A magical spell on kids' reading habits? *Providence Journal*, p. J2.

40. Robert Gottlieb, quoted in Menand, L. (2016, December 12). Banned books and blockbusters. *The New Yorker*, 78–85.

41. Statista. (2016, September 5). Statistics and facts on the U.S. Book Industry. Online: https://www.statista.com/topics/1177/book-market/

42. Statistic Brain. (2016, September 4). Reading statistics. Online: http://www.statisticbrain.com/reading-statistics/

43. Stetka, B. (2014, September 9). Why everyone should read Harry Potter. *Scientific American*. Online: https://www.scientificamerican.com/article/why-everyone-should-read-harry-potter/

44. Tebbel, J. (1987). *Between covers: The rise and transformation of American book publishing.* New York: Oxford University Press.

45. Thompson, B. (2007, November 19). A troubling case of readers' block. *The Washington Post,* p. C1.

46. Thompson, B. (2009, June 1). At publishers' convention, is writing on the wall? *The Washington Post.* Online: http://www.washingtonpost.com/wp-dyn/content/article/2009/05/31/AR2009053102119.html

47. *USA Today.* (2000, July 9). The Potter phenomenon: It's just magic. *Honolulu Advertiser,* p. E4.

48. Vezzali, L., Stathi, S., Giovannini, D., Capozza, D., & Trifiletti, E. (2013). The greatest magic of Harry Potter: Reducing prejudice. *Journal of Applied Social Psychology,* 45, 105–121.

49. Widdicombe, L. (2015, January 19). The Zuckerberg bump. *The New Yorker,* pp. 18–19.

50. Young, S. (2017, March 13). Arkansas bill would ban Howard Zinn's writings from classrooms. *Truthout.* Online: http://www.truth-out.org/news/item/39814-arkansas-bill-would-ban-howard-zinn-s-writings-from-classrooms

51. Zickuhr, K., & Rainie, L. (2014, January 15). E-reading rises as device ownership jumps. *Pew Research Center.* Online: http://www.pewinternet.org/2014/01/16/e-reading-rises-as-device-ownership-jumps/

Cultural Forum Blue Column icon, Media Literacy Red Torch Icon, Using Media Green Gear icon, Developing Media book in starburst icon: ©McGraw-Hill Education

Newspapers 4

◀ Has reading the newspaper become old-fashioned?

©Joseph McKeown/Hulton Archive/ Getty Images

Learning Objectives

Newspapers were at the center of our nation's drive for independence and have a long history as the people's medium. The newspaper was also the first mass medium to rely on advertising for financial support, changing the relationship between audience and media from that time on. After studying this chapter, you should be able to

▶ Outline the history and development of the newspaper industry and the newspaper itself as a medium.

▶ Identify how the organizational and economic nature of the contemporary newspaper industry shapes the content of newspapers.

▶ Describe the relationship between the newspaper and its readers.

▶ Explain changes in the newspaper industry brought about by converging technologies and how those alterations may affect the medium's traditional role in our democracy.

▶ Apply key newspaper-reading media literacy skills, especially in interpreting the relative placement of stories and use of photos.

100 B.C.E. ▶ Acta Diurna in Caesar's Rome

1600

©Pixtal/agefotostock RF

Courtesy of John Frost
Historical Newspapers

1620 Corantos
~1625 Broadsides
1641 Diurnals
~1660 "Newspaper" enters the language
1665 *Oxford Gazette*
1690 ▶ *Publick Occurrences Both Foreign and Domestick*

1704 *Boston News-Letter*
1721 *New-England Courant's* James Franklin jailed for "scandalous libels"
1729 ▶ Benjamin Franklin's *Pennsylvania Gazette*
1734 The Zenger Trial
1765 Stamp Act
1791 The First Amendment to the Constitution
1798 The Alien and Sedition Acts

1700

©History Archives/Alamy

1827 The first African American newspaper, *Freedom's Journal*
1828 *Cherokee Phoenix*
1833 The penny press
1844 Introduction of the telegraph
1847 Frederick Douglass's *North Star*
1856 The New York Associated Press
1883 Pulitzer's *New York World,* yellow journalism
1889 ▶ *Wall Street Journal*

1800

©McGraw-Hill Education/Jill Braaten, photographer

1905 ▶ *Chicago Defender*
1907 United Press International
1908 *Christian Science Monitor*
1909 International News Service
1970 Newspaper Preservation Act
1982 *USA TODAY*

1900

2007 Murdoch buys *Wall Street Journal*
2009 *Christian Science Monitor* ceases daily publication; *Rocky Mountain News* shuttered; Internet overtakes paper as news source
2012 Association of Alternative Newsweeklies becomes Association of Alternative Newsmedia
2016 Number of people employed in digital publishing passes number working at newspapers; Newspaper Association of America becomes the News Media Alliance and begins accepting digital-only news sites as members; American Society of News Editors sets membership dues by monthly web traffic; Tribune Publishing becomes Tronc; Facebook offers free online training for journalists

2000

©Jack Delano/Library of Congress/
Getty Images

YOUR FRIENDS KNOW YOU HAVE A GOOD HEAD FOR MONEY, SO YOU'RE THE GO-TO PERSON FOR ALL THEIR FINANCIAL QUESTIONS. But this one was a bit out of the ordinary. Chris wanted investment advice on the best place to put a fairly sizable inheritance from a hardly known uncle. Your reply—*Newspapers!*—caused something of a stir, not only with Chris, but with just about everyone else who heard about it. Tired of defending yourself over and over again, you posted your argument on your Facebook page for the world to see:

> OK, everybody, *newspapers?* It's not as crazy as Chris makes it sound. Yes, the economics of the newspaper industry are in bad shape. But as an investment, newspapers are a good deal. They make money! You might ask why Amazon founder Jeff Bezos bought *The Washington Post* or sports mogul John Henry purchased *The Boston Globe*? Good question, but a better question is why does billionaire investor Warren Buffett own so many papers, buying 28 in the last few years alone (Zipin, 2016)? "You don't hear about community papers going out of business," Chip Hutcheson, president of the National Newspaper Association, said, "It's not the doom and gloom that major-market papers face" (in Knolle, 2016). Buffett knows newspapers are an indispensable local medium, so indispensable, his papers earn a 10% after-tax profit (better than most businesses). This not only makes him and his investors money, but now banks are also starting to look at papers again as a place to put *their* money. That means more investment, which means a better product, which means more profit. So yes, *newspapers*! Like all traditional media they are undergoing massive change, but many are still doing pretty well!

In this chapter we examine that massive change and what it means for the relationship between the newspaper and its readers. We start with a look at the medium's roots, beginning with the first papers and following them from Europe to colonial America, where many of the traditions of today's free press were set. We study the cultural changes that led to the creation of the penny press and to competition between these mass circulation dailies that gave us "yellow journalism."

We then review the modern newspaper in terms of its size and scope. We discuss different types of newspapers and the importance of newspapers as an advertising medium. The wire and feature services, important providers of newspaper content, are also highlighted.

We then detail how the relationship between medium and audience is shifting as a result of the loss of competition within the industry, hypercommercialism in the guise of commercial pressure on papers' editorial content, the positive and negative impacts of new and converging technology, newspapers' gravitation to online formats, and changes in the nature of newspaper readership. Finally, we test our media literacy skill through a discussion of how to read the newspaper—for example, interpreting the relative positioning of stories.

A Short History of Newspapers

The opening vignette makes an important point about contemporary newspapers—they are in a state of **disruptive transition**—radical change brought about by the introduction of a new technology or product—but they are working hard and often successfully to secure new identities for themselves in an increasingly crowded media environment. As a medium and as an industry, newspapers are in the midst of a significant change in their role and operation. The changing relationship between newspapers and readers is part of this upheaval. And while it's not uncommon to read or hear comments such as this one from about 10 years ago from Microsoft CEO Steve Ballmer, "There will be no media consumption left in 10 years that is not delivered over IP [Internet Protocol] network. There will be no newspapers, no magazines that are delivered in paper form. Everything gets delivered in an electronic form" (in Dumenco, 2008, p. 48), newspapers in paper form are still around. They have faced similar challenges more than once in the past and have survived.

The Earliest Newspapers

In Caesar's time, Rome had a newspaper, the **Acta Diurna** (actions of the day). It was carved on a tablet and posted on a wall after each meeting of the Senate. Its circulation was one, and there is no reliable measure of its total readership. However, it does show that people have always wanted to know what was happening and that others have helped them do so.

The newspapers we recognize today have their roots in 17th-century Europe. **Corantos**, one-page news sheets about specific events, were printed in English in Holland in 1620 and imported to England by British booksellers who were eager to satisfy public demand for information about Continental happenings that eventually led to what we now call the Thirty Years' War.

Englishmen Nathaniel Butter, Thomas Archer, and Nicholas Bourne eventually began printing their own occasional news sheets, using the same title for consecutive editions. They stopped publishing in 1641, the same year that regular, daily accounts of local news started appearing in other news sheets. These true forerunners of our daily newspaper were called **diurnals**, but by the 1660s the word *newspaper* had entered the English language (Lepore, 2009).

Political power struggles in England at this time boosted the fledgling medium, as partisans on the side of the monarchy and those supporting Parliament published papers to bolster their positions. When the monarchy prevailed, it granted monopoly publication rights to the *Oxford Gazette*, the official voice of the Crown. Founded in 1665 and later renamed the *London Gazette*, this journal used a formula of foreign news, official information, royal proclamations, and local news that became the model for the first colonial newspapers.

COLONIAL NEWSPAPERS In the colonies, bookseller/print shops became the focal point for the exchange of news and information, which led to the beginning of the colonial newspaper. It was at these establishments that **broadsides** (sometimes referred to as **broadsheets**), single-sheet announcements or accounts of events imported from England, would be posted. In 1690 Boston bookseller/printer (and coffeehouse owner) Benjamin Harris printed his own broadside, *Publick Occurrences Both Forreign and Domestick*. Intended for continuous publication, the country's first paper lasted only one day; Harris had been critical of local and European dignitaries, and he had also failed to obtain a license.

More successful was Boston postmaster John Campbell, whose 1704 *Boston News-Letter* survived until the Revolution. The paper featured foreign news, reprints of articles from England, government announcements, and shipping news. It was dull and expensive. Nonetheless, it established the newspaper in the colonies.

The *Boston News-Letter* was able to survive in part because of government subsidies. With government support came government control, but the buildup to the Revolution helped establish the medium's independence. In 1721 Boston had three papers. James Franklin's *New-England Courant* was the only one publishing without authority. The *Courant* was popular and controversial, but when it criticized the Massachusetts governor, Franklin was jailed for printing "scandalous libels." When released, he returned to his old ways, earning himself and the *Courant* a publishing ban, which he circumvented by installing his younger brother Benjamin as nominal publisher. Ben Franklin soon moved to Philadelphia, and without his leadership the *Courant* was out of business in three years. Its lasting legacy, however, was demonstrating that a newspaper with popular support could indeed challenge authority.

In Philadelphia, Benjamin Franklin established a print shop and later, in 1729, took over a failing newspaper, which he revived and renamed the *Pennsylvania Gazette*. By combining the income from his bookshop and printing businesses with that from his popular daily, Franklin could run the *Gazette* with significant independence. Even though he held the contract for Philadelphia's official printing, he was unafraid to criticize those in authority. In addition, he began to develop advertising support,

▲ The first daily newspaper to appear in the 13 colonies, *Publick Occurrences Both Forreign and Domestick* lasted all of one edition.

Courtesy of John Frost Historical Newspapers

▲ Benjamin Franklin published America's first political cartoon— "Join, or Die," a rallying call for the colonies—in his *Pennsylvania Gazette* in 1754.

©*History Archives/Alamy*

which also helped shield his newspaper from government control by decreasing its dependence on official printing contracts for survival. Ben Franklin demonstrated that financial independence could lead to editorial independence. It was not, however, a guarantee.

In 1734 *New York Weekly Journal* publisher John Peter Zenger was jailed for criticizing that colony's royal governor. The charge was seditious libel, and the verdict was based not on the truth or falsehood of the printed words but on whether they had been printed. The criticisms had been published, so Zenger was clearly guilty. But his attorney, Andrew Hamilton, argued to the jury, "For the words themselves must be libelous, that is, false, scandalous and seditious, or else we are not guilty" (in Pusey, 2013). Zenger's peers agreed, and he was freed. The Zenger trial became a powerful symbol of colonial newspaper independence from the Crown.

NEWSPAPERS AFTER INDEPENDENCE   After the Revolution, the new government of the United States had to determine for itself just how free a press it was willing to tolerate. When the first Congress convened under the new Constitution in 1790, the nation's founders debated, drafted, and adopted the first 10 amendments to the Constitution, called the **Bill of Rights**. The **First Amendment** reads:

> Congress shall make no law respecting an establishment of religion, or prohibiting the free exercise thereof; or abridging the freedom of speech, or of the press; or the right of the people peacefully to assemble, and to petition the Government for a redress of grievances.

But a mere eight years later, fearful of the subversive activities of foreigners sympathetic to France, Congress passed a group of four laws known collectively as the **Alien and Sedition Acts**. The Sedition Acts made illegal writing, publishing, or printing "any false scandalous and malicious writing" about the president, Congress, or the federal government. So unpopular were these laws with a citizenry who had just waged a war of independence against similar limits on their freedom of expression that they were not renewed when Congress reconsidered them two years later in 1800. See the chapter on media freedom, regulation, and ethics for more detail on the ongoing commitment to the First Amendment, freedom of the press, and open expression in the United States.

The Modern Newspaper Emerges

At the turn of the 19th century, New York City provided all the ingredients necessary for a new kind of audience for a new kind of newspaper and a new kind of journalism. The island city was densely populated, a center of culture, commerce, and politics, and especially because of the waves of immigrants that had come to its shores, demographically diverse. Add to this growing literacy among working people, and conditions were ripe for the **penny press**, one-cent newspapers for everyone. Benjamin Day's September 3, 1833, issue of the *New York Sun* was the first of the penny papers. Day's innovation was to price his paper so inexpensively that it would attract a large readership, which could then be "sold" to advertisers. Day succeeded because he anticipated a new kind of reader. He filled the *Sun*'s pages with police and court reports, crime stories, entertainment news, and human interest stories. Because the paper lived up to its motto, "The Sun shines for all," there was little of the elite political and business information that had characterized earlier papers.

Soon there were penny papers in all the major cities. Among the most important was James Gordon Bennett's *New York Morning Herald*. Although more sensationalistic than the *Sun*, the *Herald* pioneered the correspondent system, placing reporters in Washington, DC, and other major U.S. cities as well as abroad. Correspondents filed their stories by means of the telegraph,

▲ Volume 1, Number 1 of Benjamin Day's *New York Sun,* the first of the penny papers.
©*North Wind Picture Archives*

invented in 1844. Horace Greeley's *New York Tribune* was an important penny paper as well. Its nonsensationalistic, issues-oriented, and humanitarian reporting established the mass newspaper as a powerful medium of social action.

THE PEOPLE'S MEDIUM People typically excluded from the social, cultural, and political mainstream quickly saw the value of the mass newspaper. The first African American newspaper was *Freedom's Journal*, published initially in 1827 by John B. Russwurm and the Reverend Samuel Cornish. Others soon followed, but it was Frederick Douglass who made best use of the new mass circulation style in his newspaper *The Ram's Horn*, founded expressly to challenge the editorial policies of Benjamin Day's *Sun*. Although this particular effort failed, Douglass had established himself and the minority press as a viable voice for those otherwise silenced. Douglass's *North Star*, founded in 1847 with the masthead slogan "Right is of no Sex—Truth is of no Color—God is the Father of us all, and we are all Brethren," was the most influential African American newspaper before the Civil War.

The most influential African American newspaper after the Civil War, and the first black paper to be a commercial success (its predecessors typically were subsidized by political and church groups), was the *Chicago Defender*. First published on May 5, 1905, by Robert Sengstacke Abbott, the *Defender* eventually earned a nationwide circulation of more than 230,000. After Abbott declared May 15, 1917, the date of "the Great Northern Drive," the *Defender*'s central editorial goal was to encourage southern black people to move north.

"I beg of you, my brothers, to leave that benighted land. You are free men. . . . Get out of the South," Abbott editorialized (as quoted in Fitzgerald, 1999, p. 18). The paper would regularly contrast horrific accounts of southern lynchings with northern African American success stories. Within two years of the start of the Great Drive, more than 500,000 former slaves and their families moved north. Within two more years, another 500,000 followed.

Native Americans found early voice in papers such as the *Cherokee Phoenix*, founded in 1828 in Georgia, and the *Cherokee Rose Bud*, which began operation 20 years later in Oklahoma. The rich tradition of the Native American newspaper is maintained today around the country in publications such as the Oglala Sioux *Lakota Country Times* and the Shoshone–Bannock *Sho-Ban News*, as well as on the World Wide Web. For example, the *Cherokee Observer*, the *Navajo Times*, and *News from Indian Country* can all be found online.

Throughout this early period of the popularization of the newspaper, numerous foreign-language dailies also began operation, primarily in major cities in which immigrants tended to settle. By 1880 there were more than 800 foreign-language newspapers published across America in German, Polish, Italian, Spanish, and various Scandinavian languages (Sloan, Stovall, and Startt, 1993). As you'll see later in this chapter, the modern foreign language press is enjoying significant success in today's era of flat or falling readership for more mainstream papers.

THE FIRST WIRE SERVICES In 1848, six large New York papers, including the *Sun*, the *Herald*, and the *Tribune*, decided to pool efforts and share expenses collecting news from foreign ships docking at the city's harbor. After determining rules of membership and other organizational issues, in 1856 the papers established the first news-gathering (and distribution) organization, the New York Associated Press. Other domestic **wire services**, originally named for their reliance on the telegraph, followed—the Associated Press in 1900, the United Press in 1907, and the International News Service in 1909.

This innovation, with its assignment of correspondents to both foreign and domestic bureaus, had a number of important implications. First, it greatly expanded the breadth and scope of coverage a newspaper could offer its readers. This was a boon to dailies wanting to attract as many readers as possible. Greater coverage of distant domestic news helped unite an expanding country while encouraging even more expansion. The United States was a nation of immigrants, and news from people's homelands drew more readers. As important, newspapers were able to reduce expenses (and increase profits) because they no longer needed to have their own reporters in all locations.

YELLOW JOURNALISM In 1883 Hungarian immigrant Joseph Pulitzer bought the troubled *New York World*. Adopting a populist approach to the news, he brought a crusading, activist style of coverage to numerous turn-of-the-century social problems—growing slums, labor tensions, and failing farms, to name a few. The audience for his "new journalism" was the "common man," and he succeeded in reaching readers with light, sensationalistic news coverage, extensive use of illustrations, and circulation-building stunts and promotions (for example, an around-the-world balloon flight). Ad revenues and circulation figures exploded.

MAINE EXPLOSION CAUSED BY BOMB OR TORPEDO?

Capt. Sigsbee and Consul-General Lee Are in Doubt---The World Has Sent a Special Tug, With Submarine Divers, to Havana to Find Out---Lee Asks for an Immediate Court of Inquiry---Capt. Sigsbee's Suspicions.

CAPT. SIGSBEE, IN A SUPPRESSED DESPATCH TO THE STATE DEPARTMENT, SAYS THE ACCIDENT WAS MADE POSSIBLE BY AN ENEMY.

Dr. E. C. Pendleton, Just Arrived from Havana, Says He Overheard Talk There of a Plot to Blow Up the Ship---Capt Zalinski, the Dynamite Expert, and Other Experts Report to The World that the Wreck Was Not Accidental---Washington Officials Ready for Vigorous Action if Spanish Responsibility Can Be Shown---Divers to Be Sent Down to Make Careful Examinations.

The New York World a day after

who had been Populists and those who became Progressives — clamored for the United States to rescue the Cuban people from the Spanish malefactors.

President William McKinley and the conservative Republican leaders in Congress reluctantly gave way before this pressure. Senator Henry Cabot Lodge warned McKinley, "If the war in Cuba drags on through the summer with nothing done we [the Republican party] shall go down in the greatest defeat ever known."

Already, in November 1897, Spain, at the urging of President McKinley, had granted

▲ Many yellow papers, especially those of Pulitzer and Hearst, used the sinking of the *Maine* as a call to war with Spain, hoping that war coverage would build circulation.

©Bettmann/Getty Images

Soon there were other new journalists. William Randolph Hearst applied Pulitzer's successful formula to his *San Francisco Examiner*, and then in 1895 he took on Pulitzer himself in New York by purchasing the failing *New York Morning Journal*. The competition between Hearst's *Morning Journal* and Pulitzer's *World* was so intense that it debased newspapers and journalism as a whole, which is somewhat ironic in that Pulitzer later founded the prize for excellence in journalism that still bears his name.

Drawing its name from the Yellow Kid, a popular cartoon character of the time, **yellow journalism** was a study in excess—sensational sex, crime, and disaster news; giant headlines; heavy use of illustrations; and reliance on cartoons and color. It was successful at first, and other papers around the country adopted all or part of its style. Although public reaction to the excesses of yellow journalism soon led to its decline, traces of its popular features remain. Large headlines, big front-page pictures, extensive use of photos and illustrations, and cartoons are characteristic even of today's best newspapers.

The years between the era of yellow journalism and the coming of television were a time of remarkable growth in the development of newspapers. From 1910 to the beginning of World War II, daily newspaper subscriptions doubled and ad revenues tripled. In 1910 there were 2,600 daily papers in the United States, more than at any time before or since. In 1923, the American Society of Newspaper Editors issued the "Canons of Journalism and Statement of Principles" in an effort to restore order and respectability after the yellow era. The opening sentence of the Canons was, "The right of a newspaper to attract and hold readers is restricted by nothing but considerations of public welfare." The wire services internationalized. United Press International started gathering news from Japan in 1909 and was covering South America and Europe by 1921. In response to the competition from radio and magazines for advertising dollars, newspapers began consolidating into **newspaper chains**—papers in different cities across the country owned by a single company. Hearst and Scripps were among the most powerful chains in the 1920s. For all practical purposes, the modern newspaper had now emerged. The next phase of the medium's life, as we'll soon see, begins with the coming of television.

Newspapers and Their Audiences

Forty-nine percent of U.S. adults, 121 million people, will read a printed newspaper in an average week (half of them read *exclusively* in print; Meo, 2016); when digital readership is included, newspapers reach 8 in 10 Americans every month (Benninghoff, 2016).

The industry that serves those readers looks quite different from the one that operated before television became a dominant medium. There are now fewer papers. There are now different types of papers. They deliver the news on different platforms, and more newspapers are part of large chains.

The advent of television at the end of World War II coincided with several important social and cultural changes in the United States. Shorter work hours, more leisure, more expendable cash, movement to the suburbs, and women joining the workforce in greater numbers all served to alter the newspaper–reader relationship. When the war ended, circulation equaled 1.24 papers per American household per day; today that figure is 0.37 per household per day (Gitlin, 2013).

The number of daily newspapers also continues to fall. There were more than 1,600 in 1990; the current total is around 1,300. Big-name dailies like the *Baltimore Examiner*,

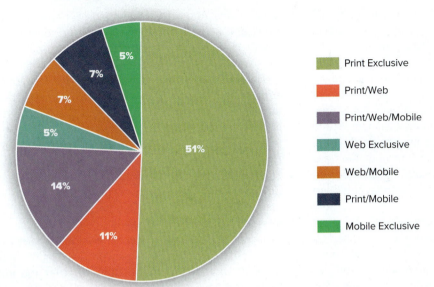

Newspaper readership by platform

- Print Exclusive
- Print/Web
- Print/Web/Mobile
- Web Exclusive
- Web/Mobile
- Print/Mobile
- Mobile Exclusive

51%
11%
14%
5%
7%
7%
5%

◀ **Figure 1** How Readers Access Their Daily Newspaper.
Source: Meo, G., "Newspaper Audience Trends." Nielsen, February 2016 Online: http://www.medialifemagazine.com/wp-content/uploads/2016/03/Nielsen-Newspaper-Audience-Trends-Media-Life-Article-Feb-2016.pptx

Print-only readership still makes up more than half of the newspaper audience.

New York Sun, Honolulu Advertiser, Albuquerque Tribune, Cincinnati Post, Kentucky Post, and *Birmingham Post-Herald* have closed shop. Denver's 150-year-old *Rocky Mountain News* has folded, and the 146-year-old *Seattle Post-Intelligencer* converted to Web-only. The 101-year-old *Christian Science Monitor* shut down its print operation to become an online daily and a weekend newsmagazine. One year alone, 2009, saw 105 newspapers go out of business (Maharidge, 2016). Circulation has suffered years of decline, and ad revenues are falling at a rapid pace. Today's newspapers are buffeted by technological and economic change like no other traditional medium. You can see how readers access the modern newspaper on its different platforms in Figure 1.

Scope and Structure of the Newspaper Industry

Today there are more than 8,000 newspapers operating in the United States. Of these, 14% are dailies, and the rest are weeklies (77%) and semiweeklies (8%). They have a combined print circulation of nearly 130 million. **Pass-along readership**—readers who did not originally purchase the paper—brings 100 million people a day in touch with a daily and 200 million a week in touch with a weekly. But as we've seen, overall print circulation is falling despite a growing population. Therefore, to have success and to ensure their future, newspapers have had to adjust.

USING MEDIA TO MAKE A DIFFERENCE
Nonprofit Newsrooms Fill the Void in Journalism

As newspapers close shop, journalism suffers. "You know who loves this new day of the lack of journalism? Politicians. Businessmen. Nobody's watching them anymore," warns Russ Kendall, a veteran newspaper journalist now self-employed as a pizza maker. "I have a deep fear about what is happening to journalism. No one else is going to do what we do. In that way, we create a community. Television and radio only show up at the big things. They don't show up at school-board meetings, the local drainage board. If your community is going to cut trash collection to every other week, television is not going to come," added another former long-time journalist forced into retirement (Maharidge, 2016, pp. 22–23).

What is it that journalists do that no one else will? They do time-consuming and labor-intensive reporting. They go out and talk to people. They constantly dig for sources and leads; they read documents; they search for facts and information; they ferret out and tell the untold stories. They know the beats they cover; they strive for objectivity, and they have editors who check their facts and guard against unwarranted assumptions and conscious or unconscious bias. Journalists are the people's eyes, ears, and voices. And their numbers are dwindling. In 2007 there were 55,000 full-time journalists working at America's newspapers. Today there are 32,900 (Maharidge, 2016).

But over the last several years, hoping to make a difference, hundreds of nonprofit newsrooms—staffed by veteran and newly minted professional journalists—have sprung up to fill the void. Some are funded by foundations, some receive voluntary payments from their for-profit media partners, and some, for example the *Texas Tribune* (to cover the state legislature) and St. Louis's *Beacon Reader* (to cover race relations in and around St. Louis), practice *crowdfunded journalism*, where journalists pitch stories to readers who contribute small amounts of money for those they want to see completed. Large investigative reporting nonprofits ProPublica and the Center for Public Integrity are backed by major philanthropies like the Ford and Knight Foundations. And while some nonprofit newsrooms are small and serve local communities and local media, many maintain partnerships with major national media. *The New York Times* uses the work of nonprofit newsrooms in Chicago, San Francisco, and other locations to strengthen its reporting in those locales. In addition to the *Times*, major media outlets such as *60 Minutes*, National Public Radio, *Salon*, *USA Today*, NBC-owned television stations, *The Los Angeles Times*, *Bloomberg Businessweek*, and *The Washington Post* make regular use of several nonprofits' investigative reporting on controversial and expensive investigations into issues like natural gas drilling, abuse of federal stimulus dollars, and the failure of many of the nation's coroner and medical examiner offices. Have nonprofit newsrooms made a difference? "We see a lot of legacy publications doing the formulaic press conference stuff—whereas the indie publishers have never felt an obligation to do everything, because they couldn't" answers Matt DeRienzo, executive director of Local Independent Online News Publishers. "What they are doing, in many cases, is more enterprising, more investigative stuff. They step off the hamster wheel and get to what's really at the heart of community. . . . We never want to be the sixth person at a press conference, and we never will be" (in Mullin, 2016b). *Columbia Journalism Review* maintains a list of hundreds of nonprofit newsrooms on their website.

Types of Newspapers

We've cited statistics about dailies and weeklies, but these categories actually include many different types of papers. Let's take a closer look at some of them.

NATIONAL DAILY NEWSPAPERS We traditionally think of the newspaper as a local medium, our town's paper. But two national daily newspapers enjoy large circulations and significant social and political impact. The older and more respected is *The Wall Street Journal*, founded in 1889 by Charles Dow and Edward Jones. It has been ranked the most believable and credible newspaper in every Pew Research newspaper study since 1985. Its focus is on the world of business, although its definition of business is broad. The *Journal* has a circulation of 1.4 million (2.3 million including digital subscribers), and an average household income of its readers of $150,000 makes it a favorite for upscale advertisers. In 2007 it became part of Rupert Murdoch's News Corp. media empire.

The other national daily is *USA Today*. Founded in 1982, it calls itself "The Nation's Newspaper," and despite early derision from industry pros for its lack of depth and apparent dependence on style over substance, it has become a serious national newspaper with significant global influence. Today, the paper's daily circulation of 958,000 (4.1 million including special branded editions and digital subscriptions) suggests that readers welcome its mix of short, lively, upbeat stories; full-color graphics; state-by-state news and sports briefs; and liberal use of easy-to-read illustrated graphs and tables.

LARGE METROPOLITAN DAILIES To be a daily, a paper must be published at least five times a week. The circulation of big-city dailies has dropped over the past 30 years, and they continue to lose circulation at a rate approaching 10% a year. Many old, established papers, including the *Philadelphia Bulletin* and the *Washington Star,* have stilled their presses in recent years. When the *Chicago Daily News* closed its doors, it had the sixth-highest circulation in the country.

As big cities cease to be industrial centers, homes, jobs, and interests have turned away from downtown. Those large metropolitan dailies that are succeeding have used a number of strategies to cut costs and to attract and keep more suburban-oriented readers. Some publish **zoned editions**—suburban or regional versions of the paper—to attract readers and to combat competition for advertising dollars from the suburban papers. But once-customary features like these zoned editions (*Providence Journal*), stand-alone book review sections (*Chicago Tribune*, *The Washington Post*), weekly magazines (*Los Angeles Times*), classified sections (*Cincinnati Enquirer*, *The Boston Globe*), even daily home delivery (*Cleveland Plain Dealer*, Vermont's *Rutland Herald*) are disappearing as papers big and small battle declining ad revenue and rising production and distribution costs.

The *New York Times* is a special large metropolitan daily. It is a paper local to New York, but the high quality of its reporting and commentary, the reach and depth of both its national and international news, and the solid reputations of its features (such as the weekly *Times Magazine* and the *Book Review*) make it the nation's newspaper of record. Its print circulation hovers between 640,000 and 700,000 a day, and its digital subscribers bring that number to more than 3 million daily readers.

▲ High school sports, part of the "holy trinity" of local news buoying community papers' bottom lines. ©Susan Baran

SUBURBAN AND SMALL-TOWN DAILIES   As the United States has become a nation of transient suburb dwellers, so too has the newspaper been suburbanized. Since 1985 the number of suburban dailies has increased by 50%, and one, Long Island's *Newsday*, is the 12th largest paper in the country, with combined print and digital circulation of nearly 700,000.

Small-town dailies operate much like their suburban cousins if there is a nearby large metropolitan paper; for example, the *Eagle-Tribune* publishes in the shadow of Boston's two big dailies. Its focus is the Merrimack River Valley region in Massachusetts, and southern New Hampshire, 25 miles northwest of Boston. If the small-town paper has no big-city competition, it can serve as the heart of its community.

WEEKLIES AND SEMIWEEKLIES   Many weeklies and semiweeklies have prospered because advertisers have followed them to the suburbs. Community reporting makes them valuable to those people who identify more with their immediate environment than they do with the neighboring big city. Suburban advertisers like the narrowly focused readership and more manageable advertising rates. Readers looking for national and international news have countless online sources for that information, but those looking for local and regional news as well as the "holy trinity" of local information—high school sports, obituaries, and the police blotter—do not.

THE ETHNIC PRESS   One hundred and thirty U.S. cities are served by at least one Spanish-language publication. This number has remained constant for some time as publications backed by English-language papers, such as the Tribune Company's *Hoy* (in several cities) and the *Dallas Morning News's Al Día*, join more traditional weekly and semiweekly independent Spanish-language papers, such as the nation's several *La Voz Hispana* papers. This stability is a result of three factors. First, the big dailies have realized, as have all media, that to be successful (and, in this case, to reverse ongoing declines in circulation) they must reach an increasingly fragmented audience. Second, at 18% of the population, self-described Hispanic or Latino people represent not only a sizable fragment of the overall audience but America's fastest-growing minority group. Third, because the newspaper is the most local of the mass media, and nonnative English speakers tend to identify closely with their immediate locales, Spanish-language papers—like most foreign-language

▲ America's foreign language readers are served by a robust ethnic press. ©Susan Baran

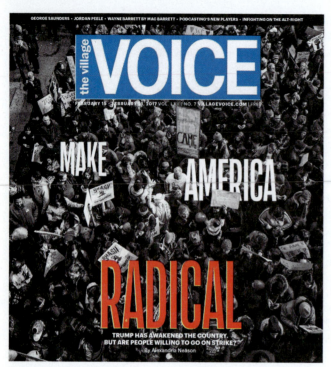

▲ A pioneer of serving a fragmented audience, the *Village Voice*, America's first alternative weekly, became online only in 2017. *Courtesy of* The Village Voice

papers—command a loyal readership, one attractive to advertisers who have relatively few other ways to reach this group. In fact, annual advertising spending on Hispanic and Latino media is growing at a rate of 17%, far exceeding that of overall U.S. ad spending ("Hispanic Ad Spending," 2016).

African American papers, as they have for a century and a half, remain a vibrant part of this country's **ethnic press**. African Americans represent about 12% of the total population. But because English is their native language, African Americans typically read mainstream papers. In fact, after whites they represent the second-largest group of newspaper readers in the country. Still, 200 dailies, weeklies, and semiweeklies aim specifically at African Americans. And papers like the *Amsterdam News* in New York, the *Los Angeles Sentinel*, and the *Minnesota Spokesman-Recorder*, the second-oldest minority publication in America, specialize in urban-based journalism unlike that found in the traditional mainstream dailies.

A robust ethnic press exists beyond Spanish-language and African American papers. For example, New York City is home to foreign-language papers serving nationalities speaking 50 different languages—in the *B*s alone there are Bangladeshi, Bosnian, Brazilian, Bulgarian, and Byelorussian. The *I*s have Indian, Iranian, Irish, Israeli, and Italian. In addition, the United States is home to more than 200 other foreign language papers.

THE ALTERNATIVE PRESS Another type of paper, most commonly a weekly and available at no cost, is the **alternative press**. The offspring of the underground press of the 1960s antiwar, antiracism, pro-drug culture, these papers have redefined themselves. The most successful among them—the *Village Voice*, the *L.A. Weekly*, the *Miami New Times*, and the *Seattle Weekly*—succeed by attracting upwardly mobile young people and young professionals, not the disaffected counterculture readers who were their original audiences. Their strategy of downplaying politics and emphasizing events listings, local arts advertising, and eccentric personal classified ads has permitted the country's 114 alternative weeklies to attract 25 million hard-copy and online readers a week. But this figure masks the fact that the number of hard-copy readers is in decline, as content once considered "alternative" and therefore not suited for traditional newspapers is quite at home on the Web. In response, most alternative papers have a Web presence, and there are now Web-only alternative "papers," leading the industry trade group, the Association of Alternative Newsweeklies, to change its name in 2011 to the Association of Alternative Newsmedia. Beyond declining circulation, the trend that best characterizes the state of contemporary alternative papers is acquisition by the dominant newspaper in their respective cities (Shearer, 2016).

The Newspaper as an Advertising Medium

▲ Newspapers remain a powerful ad medium because they are the most local mass medium and they continue to attract millions of print and online readers.
©*Dave Krieger/Getty Images*

The reason we have the number and variety of newspapers we do is that readers value them. When newspapers prosper financially, it is because advertisers recognize their worth as an ad medium. Nonetheless, the difficult truth for newspapers is that print advertising revenues fell 8% from 2014 to 2015, typical of several years of declining income. A 1% uptick in online advertising hardly compensated for that precipitous drop. Of the industry's nearly $38 billion in income in 2015, two-thirds was from advertising and one-third from subscriptions (Barthel, 2016). Still, over $25 billion in annual ad sales suggests that advertisers find newspapers' readers an attractive audience. One reason is the medium's reach. Eighty percent of all Americans read a print or online paper every month, 4 out of 10 every day, or the equivalent of a daily Super Bowl broadcast. A second reason is newspapers are local. Supermarkets, car dealers, department stores, movie theaters, and other local merchants who want to announce a sale or offer a coupon or circular automatically turn to the local paper. A third reason is newspaper readers, regardless of the platform on which they read, are attractive to advertisers: they are likely to be more educated than are nonreaders and have annual household incomes over $100,000 (Guaglione, 2016).

The News and Feature Services

Much of the 35% of the newspaper that is not advertising space is filled with content provided by outside sources, specifically the news and feature services. News services, as we've already seen, collect news and distribute it to their members. (They are no longer called "wire" services because they no longer use telephone wires. Today material is more likely to come by computer network or satellite.) Unlike the early days of the wire services, today's member is three times more likely to be a broadcast outlet than a newspaper. These radio and television stations receive voice and video, as well as written copy. In all cases, members receive a choice of material, most commonly national and international news, state and regional news, sports, business news, farm and weather reports, and human interest and consumer material.

The feature services, called **feature syndicates**, do not gather and distribute news. Instead, they operate as clearinghouses for the work of columnists, essayists, cartoonists, and other creative individuals. Among the material provided (by satellite, by computer, or physically in packages) are opinion pieces such as commentaries by Ellen Goodman or Garrison Keillor; horoscope, chess, and bridge columns; editorial cartoons, such as the work of Scott Willis and Ben Sergeant; and comics, the most common and popular form of syndicated material. Among the major syndicates, the best known are the *New York Times* News Service, King Features, Newspaper Enterprise Association (NEA), *The Washington Post* News Service, and United Feature Syndicate.

Trends and Convergence in Newspaper Publishing

Loss of competition within the industry, hypercommercialism, convergence, and the evolution of newspaper readership are altering not only the nature of the medium but also its relationship with its audiences.

Loss of Competition

The newspaper industry has seen a dramatic decline in competition. This has taken two forms: loss of competing papers and concentration of ownership. In 1923, 502 American cities had two or more competing (having different ownership) dailies. Today, fewer than 12 have separate competing papers. With print circulation and advertising revenues continuing to fall for urban dailies, very few cities can support more than one paper. Congress attempted to reverse this trend with the 1970 Newspaper Preservation Act, which allowed **joint operating agreements (JOAs)**. A JOA permits a failing paper to merge most aspects of its business with a successful local competitor as long as their editorial and reporting operations remain separate. The philosophy is that it is better to have two more-or-less independent papers in one city than to allow one to close. Six cities, including Detroit, Michigan, and Charleston, West Virginia, currently have JOAs.

The concern that drove the creation of JOAs was editorial diversity. Cities with only one newspaper have only one newspaper editorial voice. This runs counter to two long-held

▲ The *Miami Herald*, a McClatchy paper. Even though newspaper chains have their critics, defenders point to the McClatchy papers as an example of one chain that uses its size to good journalistic ends.
©*Wilfredo Lee/AP Photo*

American beliefs about the relationship between a free press and its readers:

- Truth flows from a multitude of tongues.
- The people are best served by a number of antagonistic voices.

These are the same values that fuel worry over concentration as well. What becomes of political, cultural, and social debate when there are neither multiple nor antagonistic (or at least different) voices? Media critic Robert McChesney offered this answer: "As ownership concentrated nationally in the form of chains, journalism came to reflect the partisan interests of owners and advertisers, rather than the diverse interests of any given community" (2007, p. 13). Today, five chains—Gannett (112 papers), McClatchy (88), Tronc (12), Advance Publications (63), and Media News Group (58)—receive nearly half of all newspaper industry revenue.

Chains are not new. Hearst owned several big-city papers in the 1880s, but at that time most cities enjoyed significant competition between papers. Now that most communities have only one paper, nonlocal chain or conglomerate control of that voice is more problematic. Additional concern is raised about chain ownership when the chain is also a media conglomerate, owning several different types of media outlets, as well as other nonmedia companies. Will the different media holdings speak with one corporate voice? Will they speak objectively, and will they cover at all the doings of their nonmedia corporations?

Chains do have their supporters. Although some critics see big companies as more committed to profit and shareholder dividends, others see chains such as McClatchy, winner of numerous Pulitzer Prizes and other awards, as turning expanded economic and journalistic resources toward better service and journalism. Some critics see outside ownership as uncommitted to local communities and issues, but others see balance and objectivity (especially important in one-paper towns). Ultimately, we must recognize that not all chains operate alike. Some operate their holdings as little more than profit centers; others see profit residing in exemplary service. Some groups require that all their papers toe the corporate line; others grant local autonomy. Gannett, for example, openly boasts of its dedication to local management control.

Conglomeration: Hypercommercialism, Erosion of the Firewall, and Loss of Mission

As in other media, conglomeration has led to increased pressure on newspapers to turn a profit. This manifests itself in three distinct but related ways—hypercommercialism, erasure of the distinction between ads and news, and ultimately, loss of the journalistic mission itself.

Many papers, such as *USA Today*, *The New York Times*, the *Orange County Register,* and Michigan's *Oakland Press* and *Macomb Daily*, sell ad space on their front pages, once the exclusive province of news. Other papers, Rhode Island's *Providence Journal*, for example, take this form of hypercommercialism halfway, affixing removable sticker ads to their front pages. Many papers now permit (and charge for) the placement of pet obituaries alongside those of deceased humans. The *Southeast Missourian* sells letters-to-the-editor placement to those who want to support political candidates.

A second problematic outcome of conglomeration, say critics, is that the quest for profits at all costs is eroding the *firewall*, the once inviolate barrier between newspapers' editorial and advertising missions. Although they find the position of "advertorial editor" at the *Fairbanks Daily News-Miner*—whose salary is split equally between the newsroom and advertising department—strikingly inappropriate, most papers of all sizes face the same problem. "We're all salespeople now," said Mike Wilson, editor of the *Dallas Morning News* (in Parker, 2015).

"There's definitely more interaction as newspapers have come under more financial pressure," said Steve Proctor, deputy managing editor for sports and features at *The Baltimore Sun.* "It used to be if you had a newspaper in town you were able to make a steady profit. Now, like so many other things in the world, newspapers are more at the whim of the opinions of Wall Street analysts. There's a lot more pressure to increase the profit margin of the paper, and so that has led to a lot more interplay between the newsroom and the business side of the paper" (quoted in Vane, 2002, pp. 60–61). One particularly dramatic example of that interplay is **sponsored content**, "content that matches the form and function of editorial but is, in fact, paid for by an advertiser" (Dool, 2017). There are many names for the practice, including branded content, native advertising, brand journalism, and content marketing, but whatever the label, the strategy of permitting advertisers to pay for or even create articles that look like traditional editorial content is common as newspapers try to find new sources of income. Sometimes the material is written by the paper's journalists; other times it is provided by the sponsor or its advertising agency. In either case, the story typically looks in tone and design like content usually found on the paper's site or in its pages and is intended to "take on the form and function of the platform it appears on" (Buscemi, 2016). All papers of size now engage in the practice, and it promises to make up a quarter of the industry's revenues by 2018 (Sass, 2016a). *The Wall Street Journal*, for example, maintains an in-house Custom Studios team staffed with experienced editors, journalists, and designers. The *New York Times* has a 100-person Brand Studio in its ad department. Sponsored content, while now common in all ad-supported media, remains quite controversial, as you'll read in the chapter on magazines. But for now, the question remains, "How can advertising intentionally designed to look like a newspaper's editorial content serve any purpose other than to diminish people faith in its 'real' journalism?"

Newspapers will die, say conglomeration's critics, because they will have abandoned their traditional democratic mission, a failure all the more tragic because despite falling circulation, more newspapers might have remained financially healthy had they invested rather than cut when times were good. In the era of record revenues and record profits, papers were laying off staff, closing state and regional bureaus, hiring younger and less experienced reporters, and shrinking their **newsholes**—the amount of space given to news. Newspaper owners were so focused on profit margins that the editors who worked for them were distracted from finding and running great stories. For example, in 1995, at the time *The Baltimore Sun* closed its 85-year-old, 86,000-circulation afternoon edition, it was achieving 37% profit margins. Nonetheless, it fired nearly 100 editors and reporters. "In the years before the Internet deluge, [these] men and women who might have made *The Sun* a more essential vehicle for news and commentary—something so strong that it might have charged for its product online—were being ushered out the door so that Wall Street could command short-term profits in the extreme," wrote press critic John Nichols (2009, p. C5).

Convergence with the Internet

Why so much talk about money? You and the new digital technologies are why. You are increasingly moving your media consumption online. The Internet has devastated newspapers' advertising income. For example, one social networking site, Facebook, siphoned off $1.3 billion dollars in local ad dollars from newspapers in 2016 alone, with 79% of local advertisers—the lifeblood of the industry's hard-copy business—cutting their print advertising to fund their digital spending (Edmonds, 2016a).

The Internet has proven equally financially damaging in its attack on newspapers' classified advertising business. Before the Internet, classified advertising was the exclusive domain of local newspapers. Today, the Internet overwhelms newspapers' one-time dominance through commercial online classified advertising sites (for example, eBay, Cars.com, and Traderonline.com), advertisers connecting directly with customers on their own sites and bypassing newspapers altogether, and communitarian-minded (that is, free community-based) sites. Craigslist, for example, originating in San Francisco in 1995, is now in more than 700 cities across 70 different countries. Craigslist alone cost local papers more than $5 billion in classified ad revenues from 2000 to 2007, and as a whole, online classified sites have reduced papers' income from classified advertising from $20 billion in 2000 to under $5 billion today (Seamans & Zhu, 2013; Edmonds et al., 2013). Advertising losses are most striking in employment (more than 90%) and auto sales classifieds (more than 80%; Edmonds et al., 2013). To counter career sites like Monster.com, about one-third of the papers across the country created their own national service, CareerBuilder, which rivals Monster's number of listings but not income. Two hundred dailies also have an affiliation with Yahoo!'s HotJobs service. Dozens more work with competitor-turned-partner Monster.com. To counter online auto sales classified sites, as well as real estate and general merchandise sites, virtually every newspaper in the country now maintains its own online classified pages. These efforts, however, have done little to save newspapers' one-time classified dominance.

The problem of the loss of classified ad income is magnified by the exodus of young people, that highly desirable demographic, from print to electronic news sources. Only 5 out of 100 American hard-copy newspaper readers are under 29 years old, as young people favor the Web over print (Mitchell et al., 2016). Not only do the Internet and the World Wide Web provide readers with more information and more depth, and with greater speed, than the traditional newspaper, but they empower readers to control and interact with the news, in essence becoming their own editors in chief. As a result, the traditional newspaper is reinventing itself by converging with these very same technologies. And 2016 seems to have been a watershed year in papers' convergence with the Web as, among other things, the number of people employed in digital publishing exceeded the number working at newspapers for the first time in history (Sass, 2016b); the Newspaper Association of America dropped "newspaper" from its name, becoming the News Media Alliance, and began accepting digital-only news sites as members (Edmonds, 2016b); the American Society of News Editors announced that it would estimate a newspaper's size not by circulation but by monthly web traffic in setting membership dues (Mullin, 2016a); newspaper chain Tribune Publishing reinvented itself as Tronc, a "content curation and monetization company focused on creating and distributing premium, verified content" (Surowiecki, 2016, p. 35); and Facebook began offering free online training for journalists (Albeanu, 2016).

Still, the marriage of newspapers to the Web has not yet proved financially successful for the older medium. The problem is replacing *analog dollars* with *digital dimes.* In other words, despite heavy traffic on newspaper websites—8 in 10 adults who go online will visit a newspaper website—online readers simply are not worth as much as print readers. In fact, newspapers so far have been able to replace every $7 of lost print ad revenue with only $1 of digital ad revenue. Combining subscription fees and advertising, the newspaper industry was earning $1,449 per reader in 2000. Now it takes in under $800 per customer (McChesney, 2013; Chittum, 2014). Still, there are encouraging signs.

The Internet Public Library lists and provides Web links to thousands of online newspapers for every state in the union and most foreign countries. These papers have adopted a variety of strategies to become "relevant on the Internet." *The Washington Post*, for example, has joined with *Newsweek* magazine, cable television channel MSNBC, and television network NBC to share content among all the parties' websites and to encourage users to link to their respective sites. Others (for example, *The Boston Globe*, the *Miami Herald*, and *The Kansas City Star*) have adopted just the opposite approach, focusing on their strength as local media by offering websites specific to their newspapers. Each offers not only what readers might expect to find in these sites' parent newspapers but also significant additional information on how to make the most of the cities they represent. These sites are as much city guides as they are local newspapers.

The local element offers several advantages. Local searchable and archival classified ads offer greater efficiency than do the big national classified ad websites such as Monster.com and Cars.com. No other medium can offer news on crime, housing, neighborhood politics, zoning, school lunch menus, marriage licenses, and bankruptcies—all searchable by street or zip code. Local newspapers can use their websites to develop their own linked secondary sites, thus providing impressive detail on local industry. For example, the *San Jose Mercury News*'s SiliconValley.com focuses on the digital industries. Another localizing strategy is for online papers to build and maintain message boards and chat groups on their sites that deal with important issues. One more bow to the power of the Web—and users' demands for interactivity—is that most papers have begun their own blog sites, inviting readers and journalists to talk to one another.

Despite all this innovation and the readership it generates ("Newspapers don't have a demand problem," said former Google CEO Eric Schmidt, "they have a business-model problem"; in Fallows, 2010, p. 48), papers still face two lingering questions about their online success. The first, as we've seen, is how they will earn income from their Web operations. Internet users expect free content, and for years newspapers were happy to provide their product at no cost, simply to establish their presence online. Unfortunately, they now find that people are unwilling to pay for what the papers themselves have been giving away for free online. So, newspapers have to fix their business models.

Among those "fixes" are papers that rely on advertising for their online revenue. Many continue to provide free access, hoping to attract more readers and, therefore, more advertising revenue. Some papers even offer free online classifieds to draw people to their sites (and their paid advertisers). Other papers, recognizing that the Internet surpassed print papers as readers' source of news in 2009 (Mindlin, 2009), are experimenting with variations of a **paywall**, that is, making all or some of their content available only to those visitors willing to pay. Many papers, large and small, have strict paywalls; readers gain access only by paying for it. *The Wall Street Journal* and *The Newport Daily News* employ this method. *The New York Times* offers a *metered system*—print subscribers get all online content for free, but nonsubscribers are limited to a specified number of free stories before they have to pay. Today, 80% of papers with more than 50,000 circulation maintain a paywall of some form (Lichterman, 2016).

This digital readership raises the second question faced by online newspapers: How will circulation be measured? In fact, if visitors to a newspaper's website are added to its hard-copy readership, newspapers are more popular than ever; that is, they are drawing readers in larger numbers than ever before. Therefore, if many online papers continue to rely on a free-to-the-user, ad-supported model to boost their "circulation," how do they quantify that readership for advertisers, both print and online? Industry insiders have therefore called for a new metric to more accurately describe a paper's true reach, especially as ad rates are determined by how many **impressions**—the number of times an online ad is seen—an individual article can generate. "Circulation," they say, should be replaced by **integrated audience reach**, the total number of readers of the print edition plus those unduplicated Web readers who access the paper only online or via a mobile device. This is not insignificant given the heavy traffic enjoyed by newspaper websites. For example, *The Washington Post* had at its peak a daily circulation of 800,000 but now reaches more than 80 million unique readers a month (Edmonds, 2016b). But there is the danger that new metrics might encourage newspapers to chase **click bait**, stories designed to gain impressions rather than make an impression. You can learn about this potential problem in the box entitled "Attracting Readers with Click Bait."

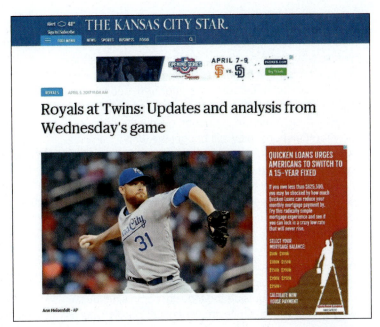

▲ *The Kansas City Star*, one of the more successful online newspapers.
©TJ Photography/PhotoEdit

CULTURAL FORUM
Attracting Readers with Click Bait

Newspaper readers are moving to the Web, but the industry is still struggling to find a way to better monetize that digital migration to make up for the massive loss of print advertising revenue. A question now in the cultural forum, then, is how far should papers go to bring even more readers, especially demographically prized young adults, to their sites? With hard-copy newspapers, the solution to the problem of attracting readers was easy:

In addition to news, offer sports, entertainment news, weather, comics, horoscopes, and lifestyle reporting—something for everyone—and readers who might come for one or more of those features (a) bought the paper

(Continued)

and saw the ads (good for business) and (b) might come across some hard news and opinion of interest as they flipped through the pages in search of their desired content (good for developing an informed public). This model worked well for nearly two centuries. It didn't matter why people bought the paper; even if they bought it only for the sports, they still bought the whole package. And that's how advertising rates were set—how many people bought the whole package.

But the Internet is different. People link directly to the stories that interest them. They can read *only* sports, *only* weather, *only* the crossword puzzle. With the Internet, ad rates are determined by how many impressions a story can generate. Professional reporters researching and writing engaging stories to create more impressions should be good news for journalism, but critics inside and outside the industry complain that isn't what's happening. Quite the opposite is now true as reporters are required to write more sensational stories to attract more readers. Journalist Frédéric Filloux warns, "The audience-building process is shifting its focus from quality to unabated eyeball collection tactics, with pernicious consequences . . . Collecting eyeballs is a diversion of publisher resources. As the ad model loses steam, focusing on page views generates less and less value and leads to commoditized, lowest-common-denominator news content" (2016). Another journalist, Danielle Ryan, is even more critical: "Quantity and speed are vastly superior in importance to quality and factual accuracy. In this self-amplifying social media culture, the number of Twitter followers a reporter has confirms their worthiness. The more retweets we receive, the more we confirm our own bias. The quality journalism that does appear in the midst of it all is fumbling to grab our attention through a mountain of far more appealing trash: listicles, quizzes, stenography masquerading as reporting, opinion masquerading as 'explainer' pieces, propaganda, conspiracy, fake news and cute cat videos" (2017).

Journalists are increasingly judged (and paid) not by the quality of their reporting but by Web metrics—real-time tracking of the number of clicks, impressions, Tweets, and Facebook likes their work can attract. Good, argue some observers; this empowerment of the audience "constitutes a healthy check on the worst habits of journalistic elite" (Christin, 2014).

Enter your voice. Is this good? The newspaper—and the news—have always lived a dual life, simultaneously a commodity *and* a public good. But has the Internet tipped the balance too far in the direction of commodity, simply something to be bought and sold? Could you, as a reporter, resist chasing impressions with click bait? Knowing that the vast majority of this country's professionally reported serious news comes from newspapers (Copps, 2014), does the reliance on Web metrics and the rush toward paying reporters based on their quantity of impressions and page views trouble you? Will it mean more quickly written and less-researched news? More lists of best places to eat, feel-good stories, and articles with more conjecture than facts? Do you agree with *New York Times* media reporter David Carr's warning that "journalism's status as a profession is up for grabs. A viral hit is no longer defined by the credentials of an individual or organization. The media ecosystem is increasingly a pro-am affair, where the wisdom—or prurient interest—of the crowd decides what is important and worthy of sharing" (2014, B1)? Defend your answer.

Smartphones, Tablets, and e-Readers

Half of all adult Americans own at least one e-reader or tablet. In addition, nearly 80% of all online adults have a smartphone (Smith, 2017). Data such as these have added to the newspaper industry's optimism about its digital future, especially because not only do a large majority of U.S. adults, 81%, get their news from websites, apps, and social networking sites, more than half of those folks prefer to get their news on mobile devices (Mitchell et al., 2016). Most smartphone and tablet users access the news via apps, and 82% use more than one news app per day (Ault, 2016). You can see the most popular news apps in Figure 2. "There will always be improvements in technology, but it's hard to beat a lightweight, portable and highly legible, multimedia-driven delivery vehicle," said American Society of News Editors former president Ken Paulson, speaking specifically about tablets, "It's a newspaper amplified" (in Johnson, 2012, p. 20).

The industry shares Mr. Paulson's enthusiasm. Eighty-eight percent of U.S. newspapers make their content available for mobile devices, up from just about half in 2009. In fact, some papers, the *Philadelphia Inquirer* and the *Philadelphia Daily News*, for example, have experimented with programs to subsidize their readers' purchase of tablets. These mobile technologies are of great interest to newspapers because they are especially attractive to

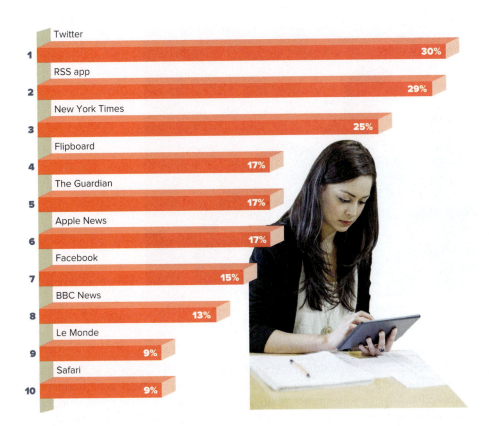

◀ **Figure 2** News App Users' Most-Used News Apps, 2016
Source: Ault, S., "All the News That Fits," Variety, *February 9, 2016, 25.*
©Maskot/Getty Images RF

young readers who otherwise have abandoned print. In fact, when *all* technologies are considered, young adults not only rival their parents in the amount of news they consume, they are more likely to prefer reading the news than watching or listening to it (Mitchell, 2016), and because 64% of 18- to 24-year-olds claim online as their primary news source, that means they are reading digital news (Richter, 2016).

Access to newspapers on tablets and smartphones has been further encouraged by apps and digital services designed specifically to link mobile readers with the news. With Apple News, for example, readers can select topics and publications and have stories instantly delivered without having to move from app to app. Scroll is a monthly subscription service that collates a selection of stories from a wide variety of news outlets and delivers them, without ads, to people's digital devices. Scroll joined existing digital news delivery options like Blendle, an app that lets users buy individual articles, and Facebook's Instant Articles and Google's AMP, both offering streamlined, fast-loading news articles specifically for mobile users.

Changes in Newspaper Readership

Newspaper publishers know well that print newspaper readership in the United States is least prevalent among younger people. A declining number of young people reads a daily paper. Look at Figure 3. Note the dramatic difference in readership between younger and older folks. How do you feel about the fact that so few young people read the paper? The problem facing newspapers, then, is how to lure young people (readers of the future) to their pages. Online and alternative weeklies might be two solutions, but the fundamental question remains: Should newspapers give these readers what they *should* want or what they *do* want?

▲ Young readers have abandoned print, but their consumption of news rivals that of their parents thanks to mobile communication devices.
©Peathegee Inc LLC/Blend Images RF

▶ **Figure 3** Newspaper Audience by Age, 2015.
©Mixa/PunchStock RF

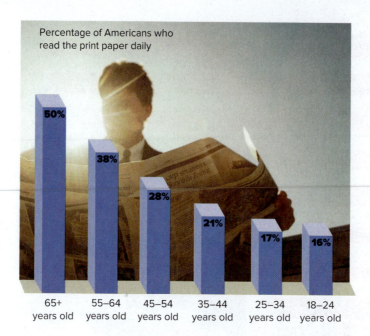

Percentage of Americans who read the print paper daily

65+ years old	55–64 years old	45–54 years old	35–44 years old	25–34 years old	18–24 years old
50%	38%	28%	21%	17%	16%

Some newspapers confront this problem directly. They add inserts or sections directed toward, and sometimes written by, teens and young people. This is good business. But traditionalists disagree with another youth-targeted strategy—altering other, more serious (presumably more important) parts of the paper to cater to the infrequent and non-newspaper reader. As more newspaper professionals adopt a market-centered approach in their pursuit of what media ethicist Jay Black (2001, p. 21) calls (fairly or unfairly?) the "bifurcating, self-indulgent, highly transient, and significantly younger audiences whose pocketbooks are larger than their attention spans"—using readership studies, focus groups, and other tests of customer satisfaction to design their papers—they increasingly find themselves criticized for "cheapening" both the newspaper as a medium and journalism as an institution.

What happens to journalistic integrity, critics ask, to community service, to the traditional role of newspapers in our democracy, when front pages are given over to reports of starlets' affairs, sports heroes' retirements, and full-color photos of plane wrecks because this is what younger readers want? As topics of interest to the 18- to 35-year-old reluctant reader and nonreader are emphasized, what is ignored? What happens to depth, detail, and precision as stories get shorter and snappier? And this is happening, as many major news organizations now require that their reporters keep their stories between 300 and 500 words, allowing only 700 words for the "top two stories" they're covering (Farhi, 2014), and that's when they aren't writing click bait. What kind of culture develops on a diet of **soft news** (sensational stories that do not serve the democratic function of journalism) rather than **hard news** (stories that help citizens make intelligent decisions and keep up with important issues of the day)? Molly Ivins offered a pessimistic answer. The late columnist suggested that newspapers aren't dying; they're committing suicide. "This is the most remarkable business plan," she told *Editor & Publisher*. "Newspaper owners look at one another and say, 'Our rate of return is slipping a bit; let's solve the problem by making our product smaller and less helpful and less interesting'" (in Nichols, 2009, p. 14).

The "softening" of newspapers raises a potential media literacy issue. The media-literate person has an obligation to be aware of the impact newspapers have on individuals and society and to understand how the text of newspapers offers insight into contemporary culture. We might ask ourselves: Are we getting what we asked for? What do we as a people and as individuals want from our newspaper? Do we understand the role newspapers play in our democratic process? Are we fully aware of how newspapers help shape our understanding of ourselves and our world?

In a 1787 letter, Thomas Jefferson wrote to a colleague, "Were it left to me to decide whether we should have a government without newspapers or newspapers without government, I should not hesitate to prefer the latter." Would he write that about today's newspaper, a newspaper increasingly designed to meet the wants, needs, and interests of younger, occasional newspaper readers or those who do not read at all?

There is another view, however—that there is no problem here at all. Ever since the days of the penny press, newspapers have been dominated by soft news. All we are seeing today is an extension of what has always been. Moreover, nonreaders are simply going elsewhere for the hard news and information that were once the sole province of newspapers. They're going online, to television, and to specifically targeted sources, including magazines and newsletters.

DEVELOPING MEDIA LITERACY SKILLS

Interpreting Relative Placement of Stories

Newspapers tell readers what is significant and meaningful through their placement of stories in and on their pages. Within a paper's sections (for example, front, leisure, sports, and business), readers almost invariably read pages in order (that is, page 1, then page 2, and so on). Recognizing this, papers place the stories they think are most important on the earliest pages. Newspaper jargon for this phenomenon has even entered our everyday language. "Front-page news" means the same thing in the living room as in the pressroom.

The placement of stories on a page is also important (Figure 4). English readers read from top to bottom and from left to right. Stories that the newspaper staff deems important tend to be placed above the fold and toward the left of the page. This is an important aspect of the power of newspapers to influence public opinion and of media literacy. Relative story placement is a factor in **agenda setting**—the way newspapers and other media influence not only what we think but also what we think about.

A media-literate newspaper reader should be able to make judgments about other layout decisions. The use of photos suggests the importance the editors assign to a story, as do the size and wording of headlines, the employment of *jumps* (continuations to other pages), and placement of a story in a given section. A report of a person's death on the front page, as opposed to the international section or in the obituaries, carries a different meaning, as does an analysis of an issue placed on the front page as opposed to the editorial page.

Moreover, this "grammar" holds for online newspapers as well, especially when, like the *Philadelphia Inquirer*, they offer a "digital replica" of each edition. Other papers, the *New York Times* for example, provide a digital version of their front page that is not an exact replica but still maintains the traditional values of left-to-right and above-and-below-the-fold. And as you might imagine, many papers, the *Atlanta Journal-Constitution* and *Providence Journal* for example, take advantage of the Web's ease of navigation and present a "front page" that offers a wide array of headlines and images that link to stories throughout the edition, freeing readers to make their own determination of what is newsworthy.

The Daily Mass Communicator

1 Most important story (Especially if accompanied by a photo)

2 Next most important story (Importance can be boosted with a photo)

3 Not quite as important but too significant for the inside pages; can be used for attention-grabbing soft news

4 Least important front page story; can be used for a report that accompanies one of the above-the-fold stories

▲ **Figure 4** Placement of Stories on a Typical Front Page. ©spxChrome/Getty Images RF

MEDIA LITERACY CHALLENGE
Reading the Newspaper: Hard Copy vs. Online vs. Mobile

Two elements of media literacy are *critical thinking skills enabling the development of independent judgments about media content* and *strategies for analyzing and discussing media messages.* Both are involved in this challenge.

Find the Web version of a newspaper with which you are familiar, its app-enabled version for your smartphone or tablet, and its dead-tree version, all from the same day. Compare the three. What content is common to all three? What content exists online or on mobile technology that is unavailable in the printed newspaper?

How would you characterize the Web-specific content? The mobile-specific content? That is, are there specific types of content that seem to appear online and on mobile devices as opposed to appearing in the hard-copy version? Can you speculate why this might be?

How similar or different are the advertisers in the two electronic versions from those in the printed version? Do the Web and mobile versions have different advertisers? Can you speculate why the similarities and differences you found exist? Describe your experience reading the online and mobile newspapers. What did you like about it? What did you dislike? Do the same for the printed version. Despite the demographic trends that might suggest otherwise, do you think you could ever become a regular reader of the hard-copy newspaper? Why or why not?

Resources for Review and Discussion

REVIEW POINTS: TYING CONTENT TO LEARNING OUTCOMES

▶ **Outline the history and development of the newspaper industry and the newspaper itself as a medium.**

- ☐ Newspapers have been a part of public life since Roman times, prospering in Europe, and coming to the colonies in the 1690s.
- ☐ The newspaper was at the heart of the American Revolution, and, as such, protection for the press was enshrined in the First Amendment.
- ☐ The penny press brought the paper to millions of "regular people," and the newspaper quickly became the people's medium.

▶ **Identify how the organizational and economic nature of the contemporary newspaper industry shapes the content of newspapers.**

- ☐ There are several types of newspapers, including national dailies; large metropolitan dailies; suburban and small-town dailies; weeklies and semiweeklies; ethnic and alternative papers; and free commuter papers.
- ☐ Despite falling hard-copy readership, newspapers remain an attractive advertising medium.
- ☐ The number of daily newspapers is in decline, and there are very few cities with competing papers. Chain ownership has become common.

- ☐ Conglomeration is fueling hypercommercialism, erosion of the firewall between the business and editorial sides of the newspaper, and the loss of the newspaper's traditional journalistic mission.

▶ **Describe the relationship between the newspaper and its readers.**

- ☐ Newspaper readership is changing—it is getting older, as young people abandon the paper for the Internet or for no news at all. How newspapers respond will define their future.
- ☐ Localism, that is, providing coverage of material otherwise difficult to find on the Internet, has proven successful for many papers.

▶ **Explain changes in the newspaper industry brought about by converging technologies and how those alterations may affect the medium's traditional role in our democracy.**

- ☐ Newspapers have converged with the Internet. Although most people read news online, still unanswered are questions of how to charge for content and how to measure readership.
- ☐ The industry has found new optimism in the success of their mobile—smartphone, tablet, and e-reader— offerings.

▶ **Apply key newspaper-reading media literacy skills, especially in interpreting the relative placement of stories and use of photos.**

☐ Where content appears—factors such as what page a story is on, where on the page it appears, and the presence of accompanying photos—offers significant insight into the importance a paper places on that content.

☐ This relative placement of stories has influence on what readers come to see as the important news of the day.

KEY TERMS

disruptive transition, 76

Acta Diurna, 76

corantos, 77

diurnals, 77

broadsides (broadsheets), 77

Bill of Rights, 78

First Amendment, 78

Alien and Sedition Acts, 78

penny press, 78

wire services, 79

yellow journalism, 80

newspaper chains, 80

pass-along readership, 81

zoned editions, 83

ethnic press, 84

alternative press, 84

feature syndicates, 85

joint operating agreement (JOA), 85

sponsored content, 87

newshole, 87

paywall, 89

impressions, 89

integrated audience reach, 89

click bait, 89

soft news, 92

hard news, 92

agenda setting, 93

QUESTIONS FOR REVIEW

1. What are Acta Diurna, corantos, diurnals, and broadsheets?

2. What is the significance of *Publick Occurrences Both Foreign and Domestick*, the *Boston News-Letter*, the *New-England Courant*, the *Pennsylvania Gazette*, and the *New York Weekly Journal*?

3. What factors led to the development of the penny press? To yellow journalism?

4. What are the similarities and differences between wire services (or news services) and feature syndicates?

5. When did newspaper chains begin? Can you characterize them as they exist today?

6. What are the different types of newspapers?

7. Why is the newspaper an attractive medium for advertisers?

8. How has convergence affected newspapers' performance?

9. What is the firewall? Why is it important?

10. How do online papers succeed?

To maximize your study time, check out CONNECT to access the SmartBook study module for this chapter and explore other resources.

QUESTIONS FOR CRITICAL THINKING AND DISCUSSION

1. Talk to your parents (or other adults if your parents can't help) about what the paper meant to them before news migrated to the Web. How valuable did they find it and why? Have they abandoned print in favor of the Internet, and if so, why? If they are from a city that no longer has a good newspaper, how have they filled the void?

2. When you go online for news, what kinds of stories most attract you? Do you look for detail and depth, or do you chase click bait? Why? Does it have anything to do with what you have come to expect from online content? Explain your answers.

3. Compare your local paper and an alternative weekly. Choose different sections, such as front page, editorials, and classified ads, if any. How are they similar; how are they different? Which one, if any, speaks to you and why?

REFERENCES

1. Albeanu, C. (2016, October 25). Facebook launches free online training for journalists. *Journalism.com*. Online: https://www.journalism.co.uk/news/facebook-launches -free-online-training-for-journalists/s2/a686060/

2. Ault, S. (2016, February 9). All the news that fits. *Variety*, p. 25.

3. Barthel, M. (2016, June 15). Newspaper: Fact sheet. *Pew Research Center*. Online: http://www.journalism .org/2016/06/15/newspapers-fact-sheet/

4. Benninghoff, E. (2016, July 13). The newspaper media: Not just black and white. *News Media Alliance*.

Online: https://www.newsmediaalliance.org/newspaper-media-not-just-black-white/

5. Black, J. (2001). Hardening of the articles: An ethicist looks at propaganda in today's news. *Ethics in Journalism, 4,* 15–36.

6. Buscemi, J. (2016, March 1). The good and evil of native advertising. *HubSpot.* Online: http://blog.hubspot.com/marketing/good-and-evil-native-advertising#sm.00004173x13qke5npfd1dbkolsyob

7. Carr, D. (2014, March 23). Risks abound as reporters play in traffic. *The New York Times,* p. B1.

8. Chittum, R. (2014, May 28). Reader revenue and the great newspaper bubble. *Columbia Journalism Review.* Online: http://www.cjr.org/the_audit/newspaper_subscription_revenue.php

9. Christin, A. (2014, August 28). When it comes to chasing clicks, journalists say one thing but feel pressure to do another. *Nieman Lab.* Online: http://www.niemanlab.org/2014/08/when-it-comes-to-chasing-clicks-journalists-say-one-thing-but-feel-pressure-to-do-another/

10. Copps, M. J. (2014, March/April). From the desk of a former FCC commissioner. *Columbia Journalism Review,* pp. 35–38.

11. Dool, G. (2017, January 17). How publishers can stay compliant as regulators zero-in on native ads. *Folio.* Online: http://www.foliomag.com/publishers-can-stay-compliant-regulators-zero-native-ads/?hq_e=el&hq_m=3337602&hq_l=8&hq_v=d45892c78f

12. Douglass, Frederick, *The North Star,* December 3, 1847.

13. Dumenco, S. (2008, June 23). Th-th-th-that's all, folks! No more talk of media end-times. *Advertising Age,* p. 48.

14. Edmonds, R. (2016a). A look at Facebook's billion dollar 2016 hit on the news ecosystem. *Poynter Institute.* Online: http://www.poynter.org/2016/a-look-at-facebooks-billion-dollar-2016-hit-on-the-news-ecosystem/440471/

15. Edmonds, R. (2016b, June 10). NAA is getting ready to accept digital-only sites as members. *Poynter Institute.* Online: http://www.poynter.org/2016/naa-is-getting-ready-to-accept-digital-only-sites-as-members/415989/

16. Edmonds, R., Guskin, E., Mitchell, A., & Jurkowitz, M. (2013, May 7). Newspapers: By the numbers. *Pew Research Center.* Online: http://www.stateofthemedia.org/2013/newspapers-stabilizing-but-still-threatened/newspapers-by-the-numbers/

17. Fallows, J. (2010, June). How to save the news. *The Atlantic,* pp. 44–56.

18. Farhi, P. (2014, May 12). New Associated Press guidelines: Keep it brief. *The Washington Post.* Online: http://www.washingtonpost.com/lifestyle/style/new-ap-guidelines-keep-it-brief/2014/05/12/f220f902-d9ff-11e3-bda1-9b46b2066796_story.html

19. Filloux, F. (2016, March 28). Clickbait obsession devours journalism. *Monday Note.* Online: https://mondaynote.com/clickbait-obsession-devours-journalism-1170ba4af65#.hofurslzp

20. Fitzgerald, M. (1999, October 30). Robert Sengstake Abbott. *Editor & Publisher,* p. 18.

21. Gitlin, T. (2013, April 25). The tinsel age of journalism. *Tom Dispatch.com.* Online: http://www.tomdispatch.com/post/175692/

22. Guaglione, S. (2016, December 27). Newspapers record strong readership, print or digital. *MediaPost.* Online: http://www.mediapost.com/publications/article/291865/newspapers-record-strong-readership-print-or-digi.html

23. "Hispanic ad spending: Great expectations." (2016, January 5). *Media Life.* Online: http://www.medialifemagazine.com/hispanic-ad-spending-great-expectations/

24. Johnson, C. (2012, Spring). Second chance. *American Journalism Review,* pp. 18–25.

25. Knolle, S. (2016, June 1). Despite "doom and gloom," community newspapers are growing stronger. *Editor and Publisher.* Online: http://www.editorandpublisher.com/feature/despite-doom-and-gloom-community-newspapers-are-growing-stronger/

26. Lepore, J. (2009, January 26). Back issues. *The New Yorker,* pp. 68–73.

27. Lichterman, J. (2016, July 20). Here are 6 reasons why newspapers have dropped their paywalls. *Nieman Lab.* Online: http://www.niemanlab.org/2016/07/here-are-6-reasons-why-newspapers-have-dropped-their-paywalls/

28. Maharidge, D. (2016, March 21). Written off. *Nation,* pp. 20–25.

29. McChesney, R. W. (1997). *Corporate media and the threat to democracy.* New York: Seven Stories Press.

30. McChesney, R. W. (2013, March 3). Mainstream media meltdown. *Salon.* Online: http://www.salon.com/2013/03/03/mainstream_media_meltdown/

31. Meo, G. (2016, February). Newspaper audience trends. *Nielsen.* Online: http://www.medialifemagazine.com/wp-content/uploads/2016/03/Nielsen-Newspaper-Audience-Trends-Media-Life-Article-Feb-2016.pptx

32. Mindlin, A. (2009, January 5). Web passes papers as news source. *The New York Times,* p. B3.

33. Mitchell, A. (2016, October 6). Younger adults more likely than their elders to prefer reading news. *Pew Research Center.* Online: http://www.pewresearch.org/fact-tank/2016/10/06/younger-adults-more-likely-than-their-elders-to-prefer-reading-news/

34. Mitchell, A., Gottfried, J., Barthel, M., & Shearer, E. (2016, July 7). The modern news consumer. *Pew Research Center.* Online: http://www.journalism.org/2016/07/07/the-modern-news-consumer/

35. Mullin, B. (2016a, October 4). American Society of News Editors undergoes digital revamp. *Poynter Institute.* Online: http://www.poynter.org/2016/american-society-of-news-editors-undergoes-digital-revamp/433269/

36. Mullin, B. (2016b, August 15). As legacy news organizations cut back, local sites are cropping up to fill the void. *Poynter Institute*. Online: http://www.poynter.org/2016/as-legacy -news-organizations-cut-back-local-sites-are-cropping-up-to -fill-the-void/426361/

37. Nichols, J. (2007, January 29). Newspapers . . . and after? *The Nation*, pp. 11–17.

38. Nichols, J. (2009, May 18). Public firms' greed fueled papers' woes. *Providence Journal*, p. C5.

39. Parker, R. (2015, July 23). *Dallas Morning News* editor: "We are all salespeople now." *Columbia Journalism Review*. Online: http://www.cjr.org/united_states_project/dallas _morning_news_mike_wilson.php

40. Pusey, A. (2013, August 1). August 4, 1735: John Peter Zenger acquitted. *ABA Journal*. Online: http://www .abajournal.com/magazine/article/august_4_1735_john_peter _zenger_acquitted

41. Richter, F. (2016, June 20). The generational divide in news consumption. *Statista*. Online: https://www.statista.com/ chart/5067/main-news-source-by-generation/

42. Ryan, D. (2017, January 22). Clickbait culture and groupthink mentality have led to the collapse of journalism—and the rise of Donald Trump. *Salon*. Online: http://www.salon. com/2017/01/22/clickbait-culture-and-groupthink-mentality -have-led-to-the-collapse-of-journalism-and-the-rise-of -donald-trump/

43. Sass, E. (2016a, November 30). One quarter of news revenue will come from native by 2018. *MediaPost*. Online: http:// www.mediapost.com/publications/article/290088/one-quarter -of-news-revenue-will-come-from-native.html

44. Sass, E. (2016b, May 5). Digital publishing headcount passes newspapers. *MediaPost*. Online: http://www.mediapost.com/ publications/article/275191/digital-publishing-headcount -passes-newspapers.html

45. Seamans, R., & Zhu, F. (2013, May 28). Responses to entry in multi-sided markets: The impact of Craigslist on local newspapers. *NET Institute Working Paper no. 10–11*. Online: http://www.gc.cuny.edu/CUNY_GC/media/CUNY-Graduate -Center/PDF/Programs/Economics/Course%20Schedules/ Seminar%20Sp.2013/seamans_zhu_craigslist(1).pdf

46. Shearer, E. (2016, June 15). Alternative weeklies: Fact sheet. *Pew Research Center*. Online: http://www.journalism. org/2016/06/15/alternative-weeklies-fact-sheet/

47. Sloan, W., Stovall, J., & Startt, J. (1993). *Media in America: A history*. Scottsdale, AZ: Publishing Horizons.

48. Smith, A. (2017, January 12). Record shares of Americans now own smartphones, have home broadband. *Pew Research Center*. Online: http://www.pewresearch.org/fact -tank/2017/01/12/evolution-of-technology/

49. Surowiecki, J. (2016, November 14). What's in a name? *The New Yorker*, p. 35.

50. Vane, S. (2002, March). Taking care of business. *American Journalism Review*, pp. 60–65.

51. Zipin, D. (2016, January 7). Why billionaires love to invest in newspapers. *Investopedia*. Online: http://www.investopedia .com/articles/investing/010716/why-billionaires-love-invest -newspapers.asp

Cultural Forum Blue Column icon, Media Literacy Red Torch Icon, Using Media Green Gear icon, Developing Media book in starburst icon: ©McGraw-Hill Education

5 Magazines

◀ Magazines survive, even prosper, by meeting the highly specialized interests of their readers.

©Oleksiy Maksymenko Photography/Alamy

Learning Objectives

Magazines were once a truly national mass medium. But changes in American society and the economics of mass media altered their nature. They are the medium that first made specialization a virtue, and they prosper today by speaking to ever-more-narrowly defined groups of readers. After studying this chapter, you should be able to

▶ Describe the history and development of the magazine industry and the magazine itself as a medium.

▶ Identify how the organizational and economic nature of the contemporary magazine industry shapes the content of magazines.

▶ Describe the relationship between magazines and their readers.

▶ Explain the convergence of magazines with the Internet and mobile technologies.

▶ Apply key media literacy skills to magazine reading.

1729 Ben Franklin's *Pennsylvania Gazette*

1741 ▶ *American Magazine, or a Monthly View of the Political State of the British Colonies* and *General Magazine and Historical Chronicle, for All the British Plantations in America,* the first American magazines

1741–1794 45 new American magazines appear

1821 *Saturday Evening Post*

Source: Library of Congress, Prints and Photographs Division [LC-USZC4-5309]

©John Frost Newsapers/ Mary Evans/The Image Works

1850 ▶ *Harper's*

1857 *Atlantic Monthly*

1879 Postal Act

©Everett Historical/ Shutterstock RF

©Apic/Hulton Archive/ Getty Images.

1910 *Crisis*

1914 Audit Bureau of Circulations founded

1922 *Reader's Digest*

1923 ▶ *Time*

1925 *New Yorker*

1936 *Consumers Union Reports*

1939 NBC unveils TV at World's Fair

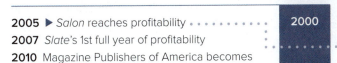

1956 *Collier's* closes

1969 *Saturday Evening Post* closes

1971 ▶ *Look* closes; *Ms.* magazine

1972 *Life* closes

1994 *Salon* goes online

©Creative Crop/Digital Vision/ Getty Images RF

2005 ▶ *Salon* reaches profitability

2007 *Slate's* 1st full year of profitability

2010 Magazine Publishers of America becomes Association of Magazine Media

2012 Audit Bureau of Circulations renamed Alliance for Audited Media; Next Issue

2013 The *Atlantic's* Scientology controversy

2014 Magazine Media 360

2015 Magzter; FTC sponsored guidelines

2016 *Prevention* goes ad-free

©TJ Photography/PhotoEdit

Timeline markers: 1800, 1850, 1900, 1950, 2000

ALTHOUGH YOU'D HEARD THE RUMORS AND THOUGHT YOU WERE READY FOR WHAT MIGHT COME, YOU ARE STILL IN SHOCK AFTER LEAVING THE MEETING WITH YOUR MANAGER. When you started at *More* you thought you'd made it. Twenty years in business and a million subscribers. Stories for smart, professional women, and none of that Photoshop, skinny-model stuff. But now it's gone, closed. She'd like you to move to a new magazine. It's *Eat This, Not That!,* based on an advice column from *Men's Health* magazine that became a book series. It features articles on topics like nutrition-wise recipes and how to make good decisions when eating at fancy restaurants.

But you're thinking this really isn't up your alley; you're a general-interest sort of person. Recipes and nutrition seem, well, narrow. Maybe you'll leave the magazine business altogether. The handwriting seems to be on the wall. In 2015 alone, 35 magazines closed shop. *Jet,* the 63-year-old "bible" of African American readers, closed the year before; so did *Ladies' Home Journal* after 130 years and with more than 3 million subscribers. Over at Interlink Media, the folks who put out *Motor Trend* and *Automobile* killed 12 of their car-related books in one day, including *Popular Hot Rodding* and *Rod & Custom.* But maybe the handwriting isn't so clear; there are quite a few new magazines hitting the stands. In that same dark year there were 237 new print magazines launched, a one-year net gain of 202 magazines (Association of Magazine Media, 2016).

Perhaps you can stay in magazines but move to the digital side. There are a lot of new digital-only publications starting up; *Podster* has been a hit with podcasters, and *SeniorsSkiing* is doing well with aging baby boomers. Maybe the Web *is* the way to go. But even there the evidence is inconclusive. The first Web-only magazines, *Slate* and *Salon,* are profitable, and there has indeed been a lot of exciting activity—*Vice* has a huge online presence, *Allure* and *Vanity Fair* launched digital video channels to enrich their online presence, and traditional books like *The Atlantic* and *Esquire* publish weekly digital mini-mags exclusively for mobile devices. Big magazine companies like Time Inc. and Hearst have even begun dropping the title "publisher" from their organizational charts because, as Time Inc.'s president Mark Ellis explained, *publisher* denotes a "print-centric company" rather than a "digital-first" operation (Sass, 2016b). But although online magazines seem promising, they have yet to replace their lost print ad revenues with money from their digital operations (much like the situation with newspapers). So maybe you'll just stay with what you love. *Eat This, Not That!* it is!

In this chapter we examine the dynamics of the contemporary magazine industry—paper and online—and its audiences. We study the medium's beginnings in the colonies, its pre–Civil War expansion, and its explosive growth between the Civil War and World War I. This was the era of the great mass circulation magazines, and it was also the time of the powerful writers known as muckrakers.

Influenced by television and by the social and cultural changes that followed World War II, the magazine took on a new, more narrowly focused nature, which provided the industry with a growing readership and increased profits. We detail the various categories of magazines, discuss circulation research, and look at the ways the industry protects itself from competition from other media and how advertisers influence editorial decisions. The influence of convergence runs through all these issues. Finally, we investigate some of the editorial decisions that should be of particular interest to media-literate magazine consumers.

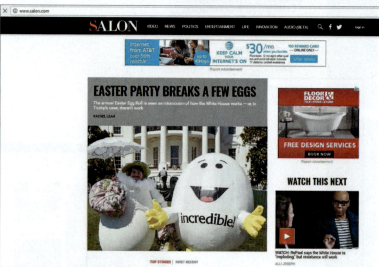

▲ Salon's home page.
©TJ Photography/PhotoEdit

A Short History of Magazines

Magazines were a favorite medium of the British elite by the mid-1700s, and two prominent colonial printers hoped to duplicate that success in the New World. In 1741 in

Philadelphia, Andrew Bradford published *The American Magazine, or a Monthly View of the Political State of the British Colonies,* followed by Benjamin Franklin's *General Magazine and Historical Chronicle, for All the British Plantations in America.* Composed largely of reprinted British material, these publications were expensive and aimed at the small number of literate colonists. Without an organized postal system, distribution was difficult, and neither magazine was successful. *American Magazine* produced three issues; *General Magazine* produced six. Yet between 1741 and 1794, 45 new magazines appeared, although no more than three were publishing at the same time. Entrepreneurial printers hoped to attract educated, cultured, moneyed gentlemen by copying the successful London magazines. Even after the Revolutionary War, U.S. magazines remained clones of their British forerunners.

The Early Magazine Industry

In 1821 *The Saturday Evening Post* appeared. Starting life in 1729 as Ben Franklin's *Pennsylvania Gazette,* it was to continue for the next 148 years. Among other successful early magazines were *Harper's* (1850) and *Atlantic Monthly* (1857). Cheaper printing and growing literacy fueled expansion of the magazine as they had for the book (see the chapter on books for more). But an additional factor in the success of the early magazines was the spread of social movements such as abolitionism and labor reform. These issues provided compelling content, and a boom in magazine publishing began. In 1825 there were 100 magazines in operation; 25 years later there were 600. Because magazine articles increasingly focused on matters of importance to U.S. readers, publications such as the *United States Literary Gazette* and *American Boy* began to look less like London publications and more like a new and unique product. Journalism historians John Tebbel and Mary Ellen Zuckerman called this "the time of significant beginnings" (1991, p. 13); it was during this time that the magazine developed many of the characteristics we associate with it even today. Magazines and the people who staffed them began to clearly differentiate themselves from other publishing endeavors, such as books and newspapers. The concept of specialist writers took hold, and their numbers rose. In addition, numerous and detailed illustrations began to fill the pages of magazines.

Still, these early magazines were aimed at a literate elite interested in short stories, poetry, social commentary, and essays. The magazine did not become a true national mass medium until after the Civil War.

The Mass Circulation Era

The modern era of magazines can be divided into two parts, each characterized by a different relationship between medium and audience.

Mass circulation popular magazines began to prosper in the post–Civil War years. In 1865 there were 700 magazines publishing; by 1870 there were 1,200; by 1885 there were 3,300. Crucial to this expansion was the women's magazine. Suffrage—women's right to vote—was the social movement that occupied its pages, but a good deal of content could also be described as how-to for homemakers. Advertisers, too, were eager to appear in the new women's magazines, hawking their brand-name products. First published at this time are several magazines still familiar today, for example *Good Housekeeping.*

There were several reasons for this phenomenal growth. As with books, widespread literacy was one reason. But the Postal Act of 1879, which permitted mailing magazines at cheaper second-class postage rates, and the spread of the railroad, which carried people and publications westward

▼ This *McClure's* cover captures the spirit of the Roaring Twenties as well as the excitement of the burgeoning magazine industry. ©*Glasshouse Images/Alamy*

▲ Much respected today, *Harper's* gave early voice to the muckrakers and other serious observers of politics and society.
©*Everett Historical/Shutterstock RF*

from the East Coast, were two others. A fourth was the reduction in cost. As long as magazines sold for 35 cents—a lot of money for the time—they were read largely by the upper class. However, a circulation war erupted between giants *McClure's*, *Munsey's Magazine*, and *The Saturday Evening Post*. Soon they, as well as *Ladies' Home Journal*, *McCall's*, *Woman's Home Companion*, *Collier's*, and *Cosmopolitan*, were selling for as little as 10 and 15 cents, which brought them within reach of many working people.

This 1870s price war was made possible by the newfound ability of magazines to attract growing amounts of advertising. Social and demographic changes in the post–Civil War era—urbanization, industrialization, the spread of roads and railroads, and development of consumer brands and brand names—produced an explosion in the number of advertising agencies (see the chapter on advertising). These agencies needed to place their messages somewhere. Magazines were the perfect outlet because they were read by a large, national audience. As a result, circulation—rather than reputation, as had been the case before—became the most important factor in setting advertising rates. Magazines kept cover prices low to ensure the large readerships coveted by advertisers. The fifth reason for the enormous growth in the number of magazines was industrialization, which provided people with leisure time to read and more personal income to spend on that free time.

Magazines were truly America's first *national* mass medium. Like books, they served as an important force in social change, especially in the **muckraking** era of the first decades of the 20th century. Theodore Roosevelt coined this label as an insult, but the muckrakers wore it proudly, using the pages of *The Nation*, *Harper's Weekly*, *The Arena*, and even mass circulation publications such as *McClure's* and *Collier's* to agitate for change. Their targets were the powerful. Their beneficiaries were the poor.

The mass circulation magazine grew with the nation. From the start there were general interest magazines such as *The Saturday Evening Post*, women's magazines such as *Good Housekeeping*, pictorial magazines such as *Life* and *Look*, and digests such as *Reader's Digest*, which was first published in 1922 and offered condensed and tightly edited articles for people on the go in the Roaring Twenties. What these magazines all had in common was the size and breadth of readership. They were mass market, mass circulation publications, both national and affordable. As such, magazines helped unify the nation. They were the television of their time—the dominant advertising medium, the primary source for nationally distributed news, and the preeminent provider of photojournalism.

Between 1900 and 1945, the number of families who subscribed to one or more magazines grew from 200,000 to more than 32 million. New and important magazines continued to appear throughout these decades. For example, African American intellectual W. E. B. DuBois founded and edited *The Crisis* in 1910 as the voice of the National Association for the Advancement of Colored People (NAACP). *Time* was first published in 1923. Its brief review of the week's news was immediately popular (it was originally only 28 pages long). It made a profit within a year. *The New Yorker*, "the world's best magazine," debuted in 1925.

The Era of Specialization

In 1956 *Collier's* declared bankruptcy and became the first of the big mass circulation magazines to cease publication. But its fate, as well as that of other mass circulation magazines, had actually been sealed in the late 1940s and 1950s following the end of World War II. Profound alterations in the nation's culture— and, in particular, the advent of television—changed the relationship between magazines and their audience. No matter how large their circulation, magazines could not match the reach of

▲ The first issue of *Time*.
©*John Frost Newspapers/Mary Evans/The Image Works*

television. Magazines did not have moving pictures or visual and oral storytelling. Nor could magazines match television's timeliness. Magazines were weekly, whereas television was continuous. Nor could they match television's novelty. In the beginning, *everything* on television was of interest to viewers. As a result, magazines began to lose advertisers to television.

The audience changed as well. As we've seen, World War II changed the nature of American life. The new, mobile, product-consuming public was less interested in the traditional Norman Rockwell world of *The Saturday Evening Post* (closed in 1969) and more in tune with the slick, hip world of narrower interest publications such as *GQ* and *Esquire*, which spoke to them about their new and exciting lives. And because World War II had further urbanized and industrialized America, people—including millions of women who had entered the workforce—had more leisure and more money to spend. They could spend both on a wider array of personal interests *and* on magazines that catered to those interests. Where there

A change in people's tastes in magazines reflects some of the ways the world changed after World War II. *Look*'s America was replaced by that of *GQ*.
(left) ©TJ Photography/PhotoEdit; *(right)* ©Apic/Hulton Archive/Getty Images

A wide array of specialized magazines exists for all lifestyles and interests. Here are some of the 7,200 special interest consumer magazines available to U.S. readers.
©Susan Baran

African American Adults
11.90

Lesbian, Gay, Bisexual, and Transgender American Adults
10.50

Hispanic American Adults
9.20

Asian American Adults
8.70

All American Adults
8.60

▲ **Figure 1** Average Number of Print Magazines Read Each Month Per Person, 2016.

Source: Association of Magazine Media, "Magazine Media Factbook 2016." Online: http://www.magazine.org

were once *Look* (closed in 1971) and *The Saturday Evening Post*, there were now *Flyfishing, Surfing, Ski,* and *Easyrider.* The industry had hit on the secret of success: specialization and a lifestyle orientation. All media have moved in this direction in their efforts to attract an increasingly fragmented audience, but it was the magazine industry that began the trend.

Magazines and Their Audiences

Exactly who is the audience for magazines? Industry research indicates that it is a large and demographically attractive audience. Ninety percent of American adults consume magazines either in print or digital form, a proportion that grows to 95% when considering only people younger than 25. They read on average 8.6 *print* magazines a month, and the heaviest readers tend to be younger, under 35. It is a diverse audience, as these data remain near constant across all ethnicities. In fact, African American, Hispanic American, Asian American, and lesbian, gay, bisexual, and transgender adults read more magazines a month than does the overall American population. You can see the level of readership for these different groups in Figure 1. It is also an educated and well-off audience. For example, magazines are the preferred medium among households with incomes over $150,000.

How readers use magazines also makes them an attractive advertising medium. Magazines sell themselves to potential advertisers based not only on the number and demographic desirability of their readers but on readers' engagement with and affinity for magazine advertising. *Engagement* refers to the depth of the relationship between readers and the magazine advertising they see. People choose to read specific magazines for specific reasons. They have an existing interest that brings them to a particular publication. As a result, the magazine and its ads speak to them. In addition, as opposed to many other media, radio and television for example, readers' commitment to the magazine, and by extension its sponsors, is manifested in cash; that is, they pay to access that advertising. The success of publications like *Wine Spectator, Cigar Aficionado, Whisky Advocate,* and *Scrap & Stamp Arts Magazine* rests heavily on readers' passion for their content, both editorial and commercial. *Affinity,* how much readers enjoy magazine advertising, is demonstrated by industry research showing that readers say not only that they trust magazine advertising more than Internet and television advertising but also that they value it as a way to learn about new products. It touches them deeply, gets them to try new things, inspires them to buy things, gives them something to talk about, and brings to mind things they enjoy (all data from Association of Magazine Media, 2016).

Scope and Structure of the Magazine Industry

In 1950 there were 6,950 magazines in operation. The number now exceeds 20,000, some 7,200 of which are general-interest consumer magazines. Of these, 800 produce three-fourths of the industry's gross revenues. Contemporary magazines are typically divided into three broad types:

- *Trade, professional,* and *business magazines* carry stories, features, and ads aimed at people in specific professions and are distributed either by the professional organizations themselves *(American Medical News)* or by media companies such as Whittle Communications and Time Warner *(Progressive Farmer).*

- *Industrial, company,* and *sponsored magazines* are produced by companies specifically for their own employees, customers, and stockholders, or by clubs and associations specifically for their members. *Boy's Life,* for example, is the magazine of the Boy Scouts of America. *VIA* is the travel magazine for AAA auto club members in eight Western states.

- *Consumer magazines* are sold by subscription and at newsstands, bookstores, and other retail outlets, including supermarkets, garden shops, and computer stores. *Sunset* and *Wired* fit here, as do *Road & Track, US, TV Guide,* and *The New Yorker.* See Figure 2 for the top 20 consumer magazines in the United States in 2016.

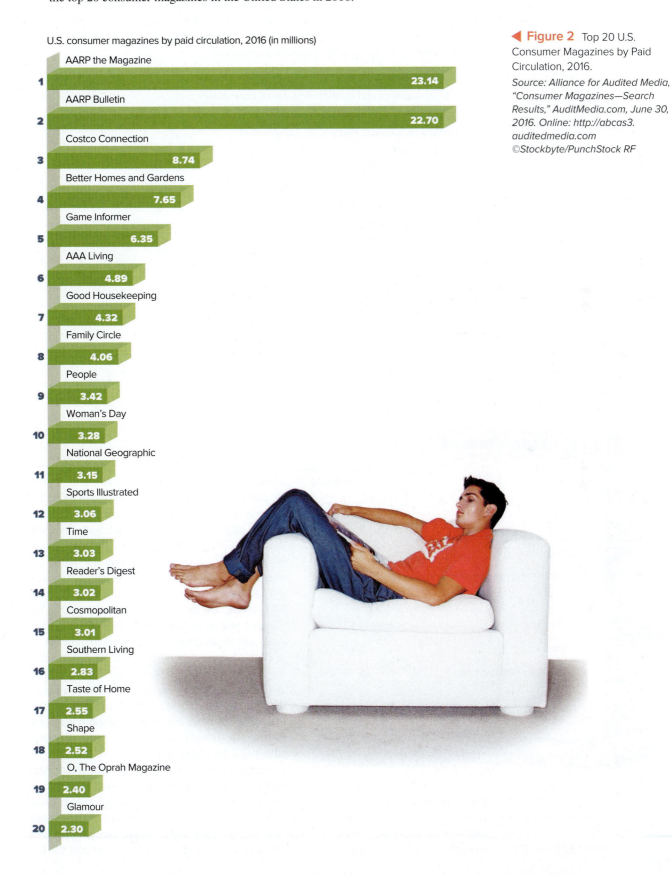

U.S. consumer magazines by paid circulation, 2016 (in millions)

Rank	Magazine	Circulation
1	AARP the Magazine	23.14
2	AARP Bulletin	22.70
3	Costco Connection	8.74
4	Better Homes and Gardens	7.65
5	Game Informer	6.35
6	AAA Living	4.89
7	Good Housekeeping	4.32
8	Family Circle	4.06
9	People	3.42
10	Woman's Day	3.28
11	National Geographic	3.15
12	Sports Illustrated	3.06
13	Time	3.03
14	Reader's Digest	3.02
15	Cosmopolitan	3.01
16	Southern Living	2.83
17	Taste of Home	2.55
18	Shape	2.52
19	O, The Oprah Magazine	2.40
20	Glamour	2.30

◀ **Figure 2** Top 20 U.S. Consumer Magazines by Paid Circulation, 2016.

Source: Alliance for Audited Media, "Consumer Magazines—Search Results," AuditMedia.com, June 30, 2016. Online: http://abcas3. auditedmedia.com ©Stockbyte/PunchStock RF

Categories of Consumer Magazines

The industry typically categorizes consumer magazines in terms of their targeted audiences. Of course, the wants, needs, interests, and wishes of those readers determine the content of each publication. Although these categories are neither exclusive (where does *Chicago Business* fit?) nor exhaustive (what do we do with *Hot Rod* and *National Geographic*?), they are at least indicative of the cascade of options. Here is a short list of common consumer magazine categories, along with examples of each type.

Alternative magazines: *Mother Jones*, the *Utne Reader*

Business/money magazines: *Money*, *Black Enterprise*

Celebrity and entertainment magazines: *People*, *Entertainment Weekly*

Children's magazines: *Highlights*, *Ranger Rick*

Computer magazines: *Wired*, *PC World*

Ethnic magazines: *Hispanic*, *Ebony*

Family magazines: *Fatherhood*, *Parenting*

Fashion magazines: *Bazaar*, *Elle*

General-interest magazines: *Reader's Digest*, *Life*

Geographical magazines: *Texas Monthly*, *Bay Living*

Gray magazines: *AARP The Magazine*

Literary magazines: *The Atlantic*, *Harper's*

Men's magazines: *GQ*, *Men's Fitness*, *Details*

Newsmagazines: *Time*, *U.S. News & World Report*

Political opinion magazines: *The Nation*, *National Review*

Sports magazines: *ESPN the Magazine*, *Sports Illustrated*

Sunday newspaper magazines: *Parade*, *New York Times Magazine*

Women's magazines: *Working Mother*, *Good Housekeeping*, *Ms.*

Youth magazines: *Seventeen*, *Tiger Beat*

Rank	Brand	Amount Spent (in millions)
1	L'Oréal SA	$ 716,709
2	Procter & Gamble Co.	$ 537,125
3	Pfizer Inc.	$ 452,466
4	LVMH Möet Hennessy Louis Vuitton SA	$ 266,747
5	Johnson & Johnson	$ 254,447
6	Unilever	$ 237,830
7	Mars Inc.	$ 200,075
8	Berkshire Hathaway Inc.	$ 197,997
9	Allergan Plc	$ 175,105
10	Estée Lauder Cosmetics Inc.	$ 174,637

▲ **Figure 3** Top 10 Magazine Advertisers, 2015.

Source: Association of Magazine Media, 2016.

©*Creative Crop/Digital Vision/Getty Images RF*

Magazine Advertising

Magazine specialization exists and succeeds because the demographically similar readership of individual publications is attractive to advertisers. Marketers want to target ads for their products and services to those most likely to respond to them. Despite modest revenue declines over the last few years, this remains a lucrative situation for the magazine industry. The average editorial-to-advertising-page ratio is 54% to 46%, and the industry takes in more than $28 billion a year in revenue, about 50% of that amount generated by advertising. Magazines command 7.5% of all the dollars spent on major media advertising in this country (Sass, 2016c; "U.S. Ad Spending," 2016). And of particular importance to marketers, the return on advertising dollars spent is higher for magazines than for any other medium (Guaglione, 2016). The brands that buy the most magazine advertising are shown in Figure 3.

Magazines are often further specialized through **split runs**, special versions of a given issue in which editorial content and ads vary according to some specific demographic or regional grouping. *People,* for example, will sell A-B splits in which every other copy of the national edition will carry a different cover, regional splits by state and by major metropolitan area, and splits targeting the top 10 and top 20 largest metropolitan areas. Magazines work to

THERE ARE NO GUARANTEES IN LIFE.

THE MEREDITH SALES GUARANTEE

Powered by Nielsen, this ground-breaking ROI* tool quantifies the direct impact of your Meredith media investment on product sales. And that's not all. Because we believe so strongly in the power of our magazine brands, we're offering the industry's first and only proof-of-performance guarantee.

To secure your Media Back Guarantee, contact Michael Brownstein, EVP, Chief Revenue Officer, at michael@meredith.com or visit engagingmeredith.com.

*ROI: Incremental sales generated per media dollar spent

meredith SALES GUARANTEE
analytics by nielsen

◀ Like many media companies, Meredith offers accountability guarantees.
Courtesy of the Meredith Corporation

Very few magazines survive today without accepting advertising. Those that are ad-free insist that freedom from commercial support allows them to make a greater difference in the lives of their readers. *Ms.*, for example, cannot advocate development of strong, individual females if its pages carry ads that suggest beauty is crucial for women's success. *Ms.* began in 1972 as a Warner Communications publication and has gone through several incarnations as both a for-profit and a not-for-profit publication. Today it is published four times a year, maintains an online version, carries no advertising, and remains committed to advancing the cause of women and feminism on a global scale. In 2016, *Prevention* decided to go ad-free in order to return "to its historical position as an authoritative, impartial voice in the health and wellness community" (Dool, 2016). But it is *Consumer Reports* that makes the no-advertising case most strongly—it must be absolutely free of outside influence if its articles about consumer products are to maintain their well-earned reputation for fairness and objectivity. As its editors explain on the magazine's website, their mission is to test products and services and inform and protect consumers, all the while remaining independent and impartial. To do this, the magazine accepts no outside advertising, nor does it accept free products for its

USING MEDIA TO MAKE A DIFFERENCE
No Ads? No Problem: *Consumer Reports*

testing. Its only agenda is the interests of consumers. So protective is the magazine of that independence that it refuses to let its ratings be used in any advertising of the products and services it evaluates, even those that it judges superior.

Consumer Reports, first published in 1936 as *Consumer Union Reports* and boasting an initial circulation of 400, charges for access to its Web version. Its 3.2 million online subscribers pay the same rate as its 3.8 million print readers. Nonetheless, its Web readership is among the highest of the world's online magazines, and its print circulation is higher than that of all but a few major magazines, exceeding that of titles like *Good Housekeeping*, *Sports Illustrated*, and *People*.

The Web version does offer a good deal of free information, especially when evaluated products may cause health and safety problems. Also occasionally available for free is special content, such as an ongoing series of media literacy videos examining the persuasive appeals used in consumer drug advertising. But subscribers have access to much more. For example, there are

(Continued)

videos of front and side impact tests on just about every vehicle sold in this country. The Web *Consumer Reports* maintains a searchable archive of all tests and their results as well as up-to-the-minute evaluations of new products.

Because the electronic version has no paper, printing, trucking, or mailing expenses, it actually makes more money than its print sibling. To increase profits on its print version, *Consumer Reports* is produced on less expensive paper rather than the glossy stock used by most magazines, and as a nonprofit group, it pays lower postage rates than other consumer magazines.

Another magazine that, like *Ms.*, *Prevention*, and *Consumer Reports*, eschews advertising because it sees it as inimical to its larger mission of making a difference with its particular category of reader is *Adbusters*. Founded in 1989, *Adbusters* boasts a worldwide print circulation of 120,000 and won the *Utne Reader* Award for General Excellence three times in its first six years of operation. It aims to help stem the erosion of the world's physical and cultural environments by what it views as greed and commercial forces. Its online version allows users to download spoofs of popular ad campaigns and other anticonsumerism spots for use as banner ads on their own sites.

▲ Controlled circulation magazines like United Airlines' *Hemispheres* take advantage of readers' captivity, offering them high-quality travel-oriented fare. They offer advertisers access to a well-educated, affluent readership.
©*Marco Argüello/courtesy of Hemispheres magazine*

make themselves attractive to advertisers in other ways, especially as the industry, like all traditional media, deals with tough economic conditions. One strategy is *single-sponsor magazines*—having only one advertiser throughout an entire issue. Health publication *Walk It Off* uses this technique exclusively, and even venerable titles like *The New Yorker* (Target stores) and *Time* (Kraft foods) publish single-sponsor issues on occasion. Another strategy is to make *accountability guarantees*. *The Week*, for example, promises that independent testing will demonstrate that its readers recall, to an agreed-upon level, a sponsor's ad; if they do not, the advertiser will receive free ad pages until recall reaches that benchmark. Many of the large publishers—Meredith, Hearst, Condé Nast, and Time Inc. for example—also offer similar guarantees. (But for a look at a magazine with no advertising at all, see the essay, "No Ads? No Problem: *Consumer Reports*.")

Types of Circulation

Magazines price advertising space in their pages based on **circulation**, the total number of issues of a magazine that are sold. These sales can be either subscription or single-copy sales. For the industry as a whole, about 90% of all sales are subscription. Some magazines, however—*Woman's Day*, *TV Guide*, and *Penthouse*, for example—rely heavily on single-copy sales. Subscriptions have the advantage of an ensured ongoing readership, but they are sold below the cover price and have the additional burden of postage included in their cost to the publisher. Single-copy sales are less reliable, but to advertisers they are sometimes a better barometer of a publication's value to its readers. Single-copy readers must consciously choose to pick up an issue, and they pay full price for it.

A third form of circulation, **controlled circulation**, refers to providing a magazine at no cost to readers who meet some specific set of advertiser-attractive criteria. Free airline and hotel magazines fit this category. Although they provide no subscription or single-sales revenue, these magazines are an attractive, relatively low-cost advertising vehicle for companies seeking narrowly defined, captive audiences. United Airlines' *Hemispheres*, for example, has 12 million monthly readers with an annual household income of $146,600, the highest of any American print magazine. They're well-educated, too, as half have a college degree (*Hemispheres*, 2016). These "custom publishing" magazines are discussed in more detail later in this chapter.

Measuring Circulation

Regardless of how circulation occurs, it is monitored through research. The Audit Bureau of Circulations (ABC) was established in 1914 to provide reliability to a booming magazine industry playing loose with self-announced circulation figures. In 2012, recognizing that "circulation" should include digital editions and apps, the ABC became platform agnostic and renamed itself the Alliance for Audited Media (AAM). The AAM provides reliable circulation figures as well as important population and demographic data. Circulation data are often augmented by measures of *pass-along readership,* which refers to readers who neither subscribe nor buy single copies but who borrow a magazine or read one in places like a doctor's office or library. The print version of *WebMD Magazine,* for example, has a circulation of 1.4 million, but as it sits in doctors' offices and is passed along, its total monthly readership can reach as high as 10 million (WebMD, 2016).

This traditional model of measurement, however, is under increasing attack. As advertisers demand more precise assessments of accountability and return on their investment, new metrics beyond circulation are being demanded by professionals inside and outside the industry (see the chapter on advertising). Timeliness is one issue. Monthly and weekly magazines can, at best, offer data on how many issues they've shipped, but advertisers must typically wait for days after a particular issue is released for actual readership numbers, and for additional pass-along readership, even longer than that. It can take as long as 10 weeks for a magazine to reach 100% of its total readership (Association of Magazine Media, 2016). Others argue that it is one thing for magazine publishers to boast of engagement and affinity, but how are they measured? As a result, the advertising and magazine industries are investigating new measurement protocols. For example, in 2014 the Association of Magazine Media introduced Magazine Media 360, a metric combining magazines' print and tablet audience, unique visitors to their Web and mobile sites, and unique video views of magazines' video channels (if any). This number is published monthly in addition to a second report that tracks magazines' presence on social media. A spokesperson for the association explained that measures of readership based on printed pages "in a world where 80% of magazine media advertisers invest in other platforms in addition to print reflect only one format and simply aren't comprehensive and therefore not accurate" (Sebastian, 2014, p. 12). Nonetheless, for now, "mere" circulation remains the primary basis for setting magazine ad rates.

Several magazines, most prominently *Time,* offer advertisers the option of choosing between *total audience* and paid circulation when setting advertising rates. Total audience combines print and Web readership. An advertiser may be willing to pay more for those who buy subscriptions, assuming greater commitment to the magazine and its advertisers; another may prefer paying for as many readers as possible, paying a bit less for online readers. In *Time*'s case, for example, the paid circulation number of just over 3 million becomes a total audience of five times that size.

Trends and Convergence in Magazine Publishing

Even though the number of ad pages in print magazines has been declining, total readership of American consumer magazines, both print and digital, continues to grow, reaching 1.19 billion editions read in 2016, up 5.5% from the previous year (Guaglione, 2017). Nonetheless, the forces that are reshaping all the mass media are having an impact on magazines. Alterations in how the magazine industry does business are primarily designed to help magazines compete with television and the Internet in the race for advertising dollars. Convergence, too, has its impact.

Online Magazines

Online magazines have emerged, made possible by convergence of magazines and the Internet. Rare is the magazine that does not produce a digital version, and almost all that do

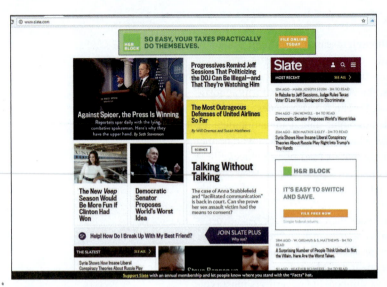

▲ *Slate*'s home page.
©*Barbara Stitzer/PhotoEdit*

offer additional content and a variety of interactive features not available to readers of their hard-copy versions. Different publications opt for different payment models, but most provide online-only content for free and charge nonsubscribers for access to print magazine content that appears online. This strategy encourages readers who might otherwise go completely digital (and drop print) to renew their subscriptions. This is important to publishers and their advertisers because ads in hard-copy magazines are more effective and therefore more valuable: print magazine advertising produces greater increases in brand awareness, brand favorability, and purchase intent than online magazine advertising (Association of Magazine Media, 2016).

Several strictly online magazines have been attempted. In 1996, former *New Republic* editor Michael Kinsley moved from Washington, DC, to Washington State to publish the exclusively online magazine *Slate* for Microsoft. The Washington Post Company bought *Slate* from Microsoft in 2004 to increase its online presence. Two years earlier, several staffers from the *San Francisco Chronicle*, armed with $100,000 in start-up money from Apple Computer, went online with *Salon*. Both *Salon* and *Slate* wanted to do magazine journalism—a mix of breaking news, cultural criticism, political and social commentary, and interviews—at the Internet's speed with the Internet's interactivity and instant feedback.

Although both pioneers regularly draw sizable audiences—*Salon* has 11.4 million unique monthly readers worldwide and *Slate* has 20.4 million—it took them both more than a decade to become profitable. One reason is that, as opposed to sites produced by paper magazines, purely online magazines must generate original content, an expensive undertaking, yet they compete online for readers and advertisers as equals with those subsidized by paper magazines. In addition, these sites must compete with all other websites on the Internet. They are but one of an infinite number of choices for potential readers, and they do not enjoy the security of an audience loyal to a parent publication.

Smartphones, Tablets, and e-Readers

As with books and newspapers, mobile digital media are reshaping the relationship between magazines and readers. In 2012, a group of major magazine publishers came together to create Next Issue, basically a Netflix for magazines. Now called Texture, a relatively low monthly fee gains readers full access to more than 300 magazines. Then in 2015, Magzter, which already offered a "newsstand" of apps that allowed users to buy single issues of more than 5,000 magazines, expanded its service to include the sale of full subscriptions to more than 8,000 titles. Today, there are a number of other digital subscription services operating. Zinio offers access to more than 5,000 magazines. Amazon Prime, through a feature called Prime Reading, gives its members access to a number of high-profile magazines. Although app subscribers make up only 4% of overall magazine circulation (Brustein, 2015), many publications have very sizable mobile readership, for example *ESPN the Magazine*'s 65.5 million monthly unique readers, *Forbes's* 36.2 million, and *WebMD*'s 31.5 million ("Number of Unique," 2016).

▲ Quick response codes have reached near ubiquity in the magazine industry.
©*Onsite/Alamy*

And interestingly, smartphones and tablets now make hard-copy magazines more attractive to readers and advertisers now that **quick response (QR) codes** appear on virtually all consumer magazines. When readers use a scanner app on their smartphones to capture the image of these square barcodes containing smaller squares and rectangles inside, they are instantly directed to a publisher's or marketer's website, increasing engagement. QR code use, while not overwhelming—the average mobile user makes just over four scans a year ("Death of QR," 2016)—nonetheless contributes to the industry's economic stability. Even easier to use are **near-field communication (NFC) chips**, tags embedded in magazines that connect readers to advertisers' digital content when they simply hold their smartphones near an ad; there is no need to have the correct app or to take a picture of a code.

Custom Magazines

Another trend finds its roots in the magazine industry's response to an increasingly crowded media environment. **Custom publishing** is the creation of magazines specifically designed for an individual company seeking to reach a very narrowly defined audience, such as favored customers or likely users or buyers. If you've ever stayed at an Airbnb home-sharing location, for example, you might well have come across *Airbnb Magazine*, distributed for free to member hosts. *WebMD*, the medical information website, distributes for free to 85% of all American doctors' offices a magazine of the same name. Its monthly print circulation of 1.4 million is read by more than 10 million people, a number further expanded by its 78 million digital readers and the more than 53 million unique monthly mobile visitors (WebMD, 2016). Forty-one percent of business-to-customer marketers use custom print magazines, as do 36% of business-to-business marketers (Spaight, 2016). Naturally, such specifically targeted magazines take advantage of readers' engagement with and affinity for magazine advertising.

There are two broad categories of custom publishing. A **brand magazine** is a consumer magazine, complete with a variety of general interest articles and features, published by a retail or other business for readers having demographic characteristics similar to those of consumers with whom it typically does business. These publications carry ad pages not only for the products of their parent business but for others as well. Were you surprised by *Costco Connection*'s inclusion on the list of magazines with the highest print circulations in Figure 2? Its 8.74 million subscribers make it the largest-circulation print monthly in America (the two AARP publications ranked above it are not monthlies). For example, energy drink maker Red Bull publishes *Red Bulletin*; Kraft has been publishing *Food & Family* for more than 20 years; and among others, Dodge, Hallmark, Bloomingdale's, Saks Fifth Avenue, Crunch Fitness, and Sea Ray boats all have successful brand magazines. A small but growing number of brand magazines, for example Enterprise Car Rental's *Pursuits with Enterprise*, are digital-only. Brand magazines recognize two important contemporary realities of today's media environment: (a) The cost of retaining existing customers is significantly lower than that of recruiting new ones, and (b) in an increasingly hypercommercialized and cluttered mass media system, advertisers who want to connect with their customers can rely on the engagement and affinity inherent in a good magazine to overcome growing consumer cynicism and suspicion.

Closely related is the **magalogue**, a designer catalog produced to look like a consumer magazine. Abercrombie & Fitch, J. Crew, Harry Rosen, Saks Fifth Avenue, Net-A-Porter, Asos, Frank & Oak, Bergdorf Goodman, and Diesel all produce catalogs in which models wear for-sale designer clothes. Designers, photographers, writers, and editors from major fashion magazines typically contribute to these publications, and they are occasionally available for sale at newsstands (for example, Net-A-Porter's *Porter*).

▲ The professional organization The Content Council produces its own publication, the high-quality *Content* magazine.
©Content Council

Meeting Competition from Cable Television

As we've seen, the move toward specialization in magazines was forced by the emergence of television as a mass-audience, national advertising medium. But television again—specifically cable television—eventually came to challenge the preeminence of magazines as a specialized advertising medium. Advertiser-supported cable channels survive using precisely the same strategy as magazines—they deliver to advertisers a relatively large number of consumers who have some important demographic trait in common. Similar competition also comes from specialized online content providers, such as ESPN's several sports-oriented sites and the Discovery Channel Online. Magazines are well positioned to fend off these challenges for several reasons.

First is internationalization, which expands a magazine's reach, making it possible for magazines to attract additional ad revenues for content that, essentially, has already been produced. Internationalization can happen in one of several ways. Some magazines, *Time* and *Monthly Review,* for example, produce one or more foreign editions in English. Others enter cooperative agreements with overseas companies to produce native-language versions of essentially U.S. magazines. For example, Hearst and the British company ITP cooperate to publish British and Middle Eastern editions of *Esquire*, two of the 18 international versions of the men's magazine. ITP and Hearst also team up on the Dubai version of the fashion magazine *Harper's Bazaar* and 75 other titles in the Middle East and India. Often, American publishers prepare special content for foreign-language editions. *Elle* has 42 local-language versions of its magazine, including countries like Argentina, Serbia, Poland, Thailand, and Turkey. *Vogue* offers 19 in locales such as China, Greece, and Portugal. *Cosmopolitan* alone has 64 international editions. The internationalization of magazines will no doubt increase as conglomeration and globalization continue to have an impact on the magazine industry as they have on other media businesses.

Second is technology. The Internet and satellites now allow instant distribution of copy from the editor's desk to printing plants around the world. The result—incredibly quick delivery to subscribers and sales outlets—makes production and distribution of even more narrowly targeted split runs more cost-effective.

Third is the sale of subscriber lists and a magazine's own direct marketing of products. Advertisers buy space in specialized magazines to reach a specific type of reader. Most magazines are more than happy to sell those readers' names and addresses to those same advertisers, as well as to others who want to contact readers with direct mail pitches. Many magazines use their own subscriber lists and Web visitors' details for the same purpose, marketing products of interest to their particular readership. Some magazines meet television's challenge by becoming television themselves. Fox Television Studios, for example, produces Web-based programs based on Hearst publications *CosmoGirl* and *Popular Mechanics*. *Allure*, *Maxim*, and *Vanity Fair* maintain video channels; *Teen Vogue* alone has five. *Vice*, which began in 1994 as the 16-page free publication *Voice of Montreal*, has an Emmy Award–winning news show on HBO and more than 50 video series across the Internet. Condé Nast has long had interests in film and video. Its Condé Nast Entertainment division produces films (*No Exit*; *Argo*; *Eat, Pray, Love*) and several scripted and reality TV shows for a number of networks (*The New Yorker Presents* on Amazon Prime and *Whale War* on Animal Planet), and it maintains video channels for 19 of its titles (Steel, 2016).

Advertiser Influence over Magazine Content

Sometimes controversial is the influence that some advertisers attempt to exert over content. This influence is always there, at least implicitly. A magazine editor must satisfy advertisers as well as readers. One common way advertisers' interests shape content is in the placement of ads. Airline ads are moved away from stories about plane crashes. Cigarette ads rarely appear near articles on lung cancer. In fact, it is an accepted industry practice for a magazine to provide advertisers with a heads-up, alerting them that soon-to-be-published content may prove uncomfortable for their businesses. Advertisers can then request a move of their ad, or pull it and wait to run it in the next issue. Magazines, too, often entice advertisers with promises of placement of their ads adjacent to relevant articles.

But **complementary copy**—content that reinforces the advertiser's message, or at least does not negate it—is problematic when creating such copy becomes a major influence in

▲ The look alone of this magazine's cover makes it clear that it is the German version of what we know in the United States as *Psychology Today.*
Courtesy of Psychologie Heute

a publication's editorial decision making. This happens in a number of ways. Editors sometimes engage in self-censorship, making decisions about how stories are written and which stories appear based on the fear that specific advertisers will be offended. Some magazines, *Architectural Digest*, for example, identify companies by name in their picture caption copy only if they are advertisers. But many critics inside and outside the industry see a growing crumbling of the wall between advertising demands and editorial judgment.

This problem is particularly acute today, say critics, because a very competitive media environment puts additional pressure on magazines to bow to advertiser demands. For example, a Sears marketing executive suggested that magazines needed to operate "in much less traditional ways" by allowing advertisers to "become a part of the storyline" in their articles (Atkinson, 2004). Lexus, for example, asks the magazines it advertises in to use its automobiles in photos used to illustrate editorial content. But most troubling are advertisers who institute an **ad-pull policy**, the demand for an advance review of a magazine's content, with the threat of pulled advertising if dissatisfied with that content. The advertising agencies for oil giant BP and financial services company Morgan Stanley shocked the magazine industry by demanding just that—in the case of BP, insisting that it be informed "in advance of any news text or visuals magazines plan to publish that directly mention the company, a competitor, or the oil-and-energy industry" (Sanders & Halliday, 2005). Events like this moved *Advertising Age* to editorialize against what they saw as an attack on magazines' independence and editorial integrity. Ad-pull policies damage trust between readers and magazines, they argued, "the very thing that gives media their value to advertisers to begin with" ("Shame on BP," 2005). This concern is overwrought, say many industry people. When the American Society of Magazine Editors announced in 2008 that it would revise its guidelines to protect magazines' editorial integrity, there was significant pushback. "As long as it's interesting to the reader, who cares?" argued one editor, speaking for the dissenters. "This ivory-tower approach that edit[orial] is so untouchable, and what they're doing is so wonderful and can't be tainted by the stink of advertising just makes me sick" (in Ives, 2008).

The critics' question, however, remains, "How can a magazine function, offering depth, variety, and detail, when BP and Morgan Stanley are joined by scores of other advertisers, each demanding to preview content, not for its direct comment on matters of importance to their businesses, but for controversy and potential offensiveness? What will be the impact on the ideals of a free press and of free inquiry?"

Equally controversial and far more common is sponsored content, articles paid for by advertisers. You can see the depth of the dispute in the essay "Sponsored Content: Deceitful or Necessary . . . or Both?")

◀ Complementing this ad through placement near this story troubles very few people. But when advertisers invoke ad-pull policies, media-literate readers rightfully complain.

(left) ©Image Source/Getty Images RF; (right) Courtesy of The Advertising Archives

CULTURAL FORUM
Sponsored Content: Deceitful or Necessary . . . or Both?

You may have read the story on the future of medicine on *Forbes*'s website, titled "Brand Voice." Maybe you saw the one on the history of hedge funds on the *Wall Street Journal*'s site with the heading "Sponsor Generated Content." Perhaps you caught that piece on the history of Ellis Island, labeled "Paid Post," on the *New York Times* site. As interesting and informative as they might have been, they were actually ads for Showtime, Dell, and Airbnb, respectively. Would you have clicked on these stories had you known they were ads? The Federal Trade Commission (FTC) believes you might not have, judging these labels as intentionally deceptive. As a result, in late 2015 the FTC issued guidelines for the use and labeling of sponsored content—sometimes called branded content, brand journalism, native advertising, or content marketing.

This returned discussion of the practice, expected to annually generate more than one-quarter of news media's ad revenues and $20 billion for all media by 2018, to the cultural forum (Deziel, 2016; Edmonds, 2016). Sponsored content first caused controversy in early 2013, when the online edition of *The Atlantic* ran a long, laudatory article on the Church of Scientology. For several reasons, including the publication of a best-selling book critical of the religion, Scientology was in the news at the time, so the magazine's decision to do the story made good journalistic sense. But it was quickly discovered that the piece was actually a paid placement written not by *The Atlantic*'s journalists but by the Church of Scientology itself.

Since that time, the practice has become not only commonplace across all media but also essential to many magazines' survival. For example, *Slate* relies on sponsored content for 50% of its revenue, *The Atlantic* earns three-quarters of its digital advertising revenue from sponsored content, and *Gawker* makes one-third of its revenue from the practice (Moses, 2016; Herrman, 2016; Deziel, 2016). To be sure, there is significant industry disagreement over its use. Sponsored content "is, at least on some level, inherently contradictory" writes *Folio* magazine senior editor Greg Dool. "Publishers must satisfy their clients' needs by promoting a brand message that blends seamlessly with the articles that surround it, while also being careful to avoid misleading consumers as to the specific nature of the content they're reading" (2017). That's fine, say critics, but an

ad is an ad and should be labeled as such. If "ethical labeling ruins your business model," argued one-time *Atlantic* writer Andrew Sullivan, "it's proof that your business model isn't ethical" (2013). Nonetheless, all seemed well until the FTC issued its guidelines and the debate over sponsored content re-erupted.

The FTC wrote, "Terms likely to be understood include 'Ad,' 'Advertisement,' 'Paid Advertisement,' 'Sponsored Advertising Content,' or some variation thereof. Advertisers should not use terms such as 'Promoted' or 'Promoted Stories,' which in this context are at best ambiguous and potentially could mislead consumers that advertising content is endorsed by a publisher site." But was asking publications to call an ad an ad the equivalent of "asking snipers to wear fluorescent orange," in the words of prominent sponsored-content critic Bob Garfield (2015)? After all, offering these ads in the same visual layout and format as the publication's surrounding editorial content can serve no other purpose than to deceive, especially as the industry's own research demonstrates that 54% of readers do indeed feel deceived (Lazauskas, 2016). But the alternative may not be much better, as research also indicates that seeing "advertisement" in the label "native advertisement" actually damages the reputation of the magazine publishing that content, at least in part because readers see publications working hand-in-hand with advertisers to be somewhat less than honest (McVerry, 2016).

Enter your voice. Is sponsored content intended to deceive? If not, why not identify it using the FTC's preferred labels? Does it alter your opinion knowing that somewhere between 7% and 18% of readers can't identify sponsored stories as paid marketing messages (McVerry, 2016), or that 40% of sponsored stories fail to conform to the FTC's guidelines (Media Radar, 2016)? But the reality for most magazines, and most news media for that matter, is that people work to avoid ads, especially online, and sponsored content may be the only way those outlets can earn sufficient ad revenue to survive. Should they die on the altar of "ethics" or "good journalism"? What's a little deception if the stories are well-written and informative? Do you accept the argument that the magazine industry must loosen its standards, even if only a little and even if only online, in order to compete in a tough media environment? Why or why not? Does the availability of the free app AdDetector, which adds a bright red warning banner to pieces of sponsored content, make a difference in your answer? Would you use it? Why or why not?

DEVELOPING MEDIA LITERACY SKILLS

Recognizing the Power of Graphics

Detecting the use of and determining the informational value of complementary copy and sponsored content is only one reason media literacy is important when reading magazines. Another necessary media-literacy skill is the ability to understand how graphics and other artwork provide the background for interpreting stories. Some notable incidents suggest why.

Kerry Washington, African American actress and star of the television series *Scandal*, appeared on an April 2016 cover of *Adweek*. Her skin had been lightened and her nose photoshopped to appear smaller. *Adweek* denied it had made anything other than "minimal adjustments," but Ms. Washington and her fans felt otherwise. For them, this was especially disconcerting because it had happened to the star just a year earlier when *InStyle* lightened her skin to the point that she appeared to be Caucasian. Then, just a few weeks after the *Adweek* incident, *People*, in declaring tennis champion Serena Williams "one of the world's most beautiful people," published a photo of Ms. Williams that had been altered to slim her waist (Sass, 2016a). A media-literate reader might ask, "Why isn't one of the world's most beautiful people beautiful enough?"

Another example of digital fakery raises a different question, one articulated by an unexpected source. Receiving recognition from *Glamour* magazine at its annual Woman of the Year Awards in 2013, singer Lady Gaga used her time at the winner's podium to challenge the common magazine practice of graphically altering the faces and bodies of the women who appear in their pages and on their covers. Citing her own recent *Glamour* cover, she said, "I felt my skin looked too perfect. I felt my hair looked too soft. . . . I do not look like this when I wake up in the morning. . . . What I want to see is the change on your covers. . . . When the covers change, that's when culture changes" (in Monde, 2013).

The American Medical Association found this common practice of altering images sufficiently harmful that at its 2011 annual meeting it voted to encourage magazine industry efforts to discontinue its use. The AMA board argued not only that altered images of women's bodies create unrealistic expectations in young people, but also that decades of social science research tie these unrealistic media images to eating disorders and other childhood and adolescent health problems. Some in the magazine industry have responded. *Seventeen*, acknowledging a teen-driven online movement to publish more unretouched photos, committed itself to a "Body Peace Treaty" in which it promised to never again change girls' body or face shapes and to begin including in its pages only images of girls and models who appear healthy. *Vogue* instituted its "Health Initiative," stating it would ban from its pages all models under 16 years old and super-skinny models who appear to have an eating disorder.

An additional media literacy issue here has to do with maintaining the confidence of audience members. As digital altering of images becomes more widespread—and its occurrence better known—will viewers and readers come to question the veracity of even unaltered images and the truthfulness of the stories that employ them? "With new technology, faking or doctoring photographs has never been simpler, faster, or more difficult to detect," explains *American Journalism Review*'s Sherry Ricchiardi. "Skilled operators truly are like magicians, except they use tools like Photoshop . . . to create their illusions." John Long, chair of the Ethics and Standards Committee of the National Press Photographers Association, adds, "The public is losing faith in us. Without credibility, we have nothing; we cannot survive" (both in Ricchiardi, 2007, pp. 37–38).

What do you think? Did you see any of these images? Did you know they had been altered? If you did, would that have changed your interpretation of the stories they represented? Does the fact that major media outlets sometimes alter the images they present to you

▲ Although *Adweek* said it had made "minimal adjustments" to its April 2016 cover, actress Kerry Washington and her fans complained that her image had been altered to make her skin lighter and her nose smaller.
©TJ Photography/PhotoEdit

as news lead you to question their overall integrity? Do you believe that media outlets that use altered images have an obligation to inform readers and viewers of their decision to restructure reality? How does it feel to know that almost all of the images that we see in our daily newspapers and news magazines today are altered in some way?

MEDIA LITERACY CHALLENGE
Identifying Digital Alteration

Media-literate magazine readers are *critical thinkers who make independent judgments about content.* They *think critically about media messages,* and they *have heightened expectations of the content they read.* You'll have to have all these skills to complete this challenge.

In print or online, choose your favorite magazine and find all the content, both editorial and advertising, that shows images of people. Identify the images that appear to have been digitally enhanced or changed. Critics and proponents alike acknowledge that just about every image appearing in a consumer magazine has been altered. How many did you find? What were your clues? How do you feel about the practice, and do you think the magazine had the right to make these alterations? What do your answers say about your understanding and respect for the power of media messages, your expectations of magazine content, and your ability to think critically about the messages in magazines? You may want to meet this challenge individually, using your favorite publication, or make it a competition. You can have different people examining the same magazine to see who can find the greatest number of alterations, or you can have teams compete against one another looking at an array of titles.

Resources for Review and Discussion

REVIEW POINTS: TYING CONTENT TO LEARNING OUTCOMES

▶ **Describe the history and development of the magazine industry and the magazine itself as a medium.**
- ☐ Magazines, a favorite of 18th-century British elite, made an easy transition to colonial America.
- ☐ Mass circulation magazines prospered in the post–Civil War years because of increased literacy, improved transportation, reduced postal costs, and lower cover prices.
- ☐ Magazines' large readership and financial health empowered the muckrakers to challenge society's powerful people and institutions.

▶ **Identify how the organizational and economic nature of the contemporary magazine industry shapes the content of magazines.**

- ☐ Television changed magazines from mass circulation to specialized media; as a result, they are attractive to advertisers because of their demographic specificity, reader engagement, and reader affinity for the advertising they carry.
- ☐ The three broad categories of magazines are trade, professional, and business; industrial, company, and sponsored; and consumer magazines.
- ☐ Magazine circulation comes in the form of subscription, single-copy sales, and controlled circulation. Advertiser demands for better measures of readership and accountability may render circulation an outmoded metric.

▶ **Describe the relationship between magazines and their readers.**
  ☐ Custom publishing, in the form of brand magazines and magalogues, is one way that magazines stand out in a cluttered media environment.
  ☐ Magazines further meet competition from other media, especially cable television, through internationalization, technology-driven improvements in distribution, and the sale of subscriber lists and their own direct marketing efforts.

▶ **Explain the convergence of magazines with the Internet and mobile technologies.**
  ☐ Virtually all print magazines have online equivalents, although they employ different financial models.
  ☐ Readers are overwhelmingly positive about electronic magazines.

☐ They are equally enthusiastic about accessing magazines from mobile devices.

▶ **Apply key media literacy skills to magazine reading.**
  ☐ A number of industry revenue-enhancing practices pose different challenges to media-literate readers:
    ▪ Sponsored content is paid-for material that takes on the look and feel of the surrounding editorial content.
    ▪ Complementary copy is editorial content that reinforces an advertiser's message.
    ▪ Ad-pull policies are an advertiser's demands, on threat of removal of its ads, for an advance view of a magazine's content.
    ▪ Heavy reliance on digitally altered graphics is regularly employed in both advertising and editorial content and is highly controversial.

KEY TERMS

muckraking, 102

split runs, 106

circulation, 108

controlled circulation, 108

quick response (QR) codes, 111

near-field communication (NFC) chips, 111

custom publishing, 111

brand magazine, 111

magalogue, 111

complementary copy, 112

ad-pull policy, 113

QUESTIONS FOR REVIEW

1. How would you characterize the content of the first U.S. magazines?

2. What factors fueled the expansion of the magazine industry at the beginning of the 20th century?

3. What factors led to the demise of the mass circulation era and the development of the era of specialization?

4. What are the three broad types of magazines?

5. Why do advertisers favor specialization in magazines?

6. What are engagement and affinity? Why are they important to advertisers?

7. In what different ways do magazines internationalize their publications?

8. Why is the magazine industry optimistic about the effects of new mobile technologies on its relationship with readers?

9. What are the arguments for and against the routine use of sponsored content?

10. What is complementary copy? Why does it trouble critics?

McGraw Hill Education connect

To maximize your study time, check out CONNECT to access the SmartBook study module for this chapter and explore other resources.

QUESTIONS FOR CRITICAL THINKING AND DISCUSSION

1. Can you think of any contemporary crusading magazine or muckraking writers? Compared with those of the era of the muckrakers, they are certainly less visible. Why is this the case?

2. Which magazines do you read? Draw a demographic profile of yourself based only on the magazines you regularly read.

3. Are you troubled by the practice of altering photographs? Can you think of times when it might be more appropriate than others?

REFERENCES

1. Alliance for Audited Media. (2016, June 30). Consumer magazines—search results. *AuditMedia.com.* Online: http://abcas3.auditedmedia.com/ecirc/magtitlesearch.asp

2. Association of Magazine Media. (2016). *Magazine Media Factbook 2016.* Online: http://www.magazine.org/insights-resources/magazine-media-factbook

3. Atkinson, C. (2004, September 27). Press group attacks magazine product placement. *AdAge.com.* Online: http://adage.com/article/media/press-group-attacks-magazine-product-placement/41174/

4. Brustein, J. (2015, January 19). Why almost nobody wants to pay for the "Netflix of magazines." *Bloomberg News.* Online: http://www.bloomberg.com/news/articles/2015-01-19/why-almost-nobody-wants-to-pay-for-the-netflix-of-magazines-

5. "Death of QR codes is greatly exaggerated." (2016). *Structural Graphics.* Online: https://www.structuralgraphics.com/blog/death-of-qr-codes-is-greatly-exaggerated/

6. Deziel, M. (2016, February 10). Why it's time to standardize native ad labels. *Contently.* Online: https://contently.com/strategist/2016/02/10/why-its-time-to-standardize-native-ad-labels/

7. Dool, G. (2017, January 17). How publishers can stay compliant as regulators zero-in on native ads. *Folio.* Online: http://www.foliomag.com/publishers-can-stay-compliant-regulators-zero-native-ads/?hq_e=el&hq_m=3337602&hq_l=8&hq_v=d45892c78f

8. Dool, G. (2016, February 1). Prevention announces plans to go advertising-free with print edition. *Folio.* Online: http://www.foliomag.com/prevention-launches-ad-free-print-edition/

9. Edmonds, R. (2016, October 31). Native ads will provide 25 percent of ad revenues by 2018, says media association. *Poynter Institute.* Online: http://www.poynter.org/2016/native-ads-will-provide-25-percent-of-ad-revenues-by-2018-says-media-association/436556/

10. Garfield, B. (2015, December 28). Unholy and undone. *MediaPost.* Online: http://www.mediapost.com/publications/article/265521/unholy-and-undone.html

11. Guaglione, S. (2017, January 12). MPA: print, digital audience rises 5.5%. *MediaPost.* Online: http://www.mediapost.com/publications/article/292791/mpa-print-digital-audience-rises-55.html

12. Guaglione, S. (2016, June 14). Magazines show highest return on ad spend. *MediaPost.* Online: http://www.mediapost.com/publications/article/278126/magazines-show-highest-return-on-ad-spend.html

13. *Hemispheres.* (2016). *Hemispheres* media kit 2016. *United Airlines.* Online: https://view.publitas.com/ink/hemispheres-media-pack-2016/page/1

14. Herrman, J. (2016, July 24). In media company advertising, sponsored content is becoming king. *The New York Times,* p. B1.

15. Ives, N. (2008, November 17). As ASME fortifies ad/edit divide, some mags flout it. *Advertising Age,* p. 3.

16. Lazauskas, J. (2016, December). Fixing native ads: What consumers want from publishers, brands, Facebook, and the FTC. *Contently.* Online: https://the-content-strategist-13.docs.contently.com/v/fixing-sponsored-content-what-consumers-want-from-brands-publishers-and-the-ftc

17. McVerry, J. (2016, April 18). Native advertising may create negative perceptions of media outlets. *Pennsylvania State University.* Online: http://news.psu.edu/story/407532/2016/04/28/research/native-advertising-may-create-negative-perceptions-media-outlets

18. Media Radar. (2016, November 30). How publishers pivoted to meet FTC's native guidelines. *Folio.* Online: http://www.foliomag.com/how-publishers-pivoted-to-meet-ftcs-native-guidelines/?hq_e=el&hq_m=3312974&hq_l=12&hq_v=d45892c78f

19. Monde, C. (2013, November 12). Lady Gaga slams her own *Glamour* magazine cover for Photoshop: "My skin looked too perfect." *New York Daily News.* Online: http://www.nydailynews.com/entertainment/gossip/lady-gaga-slams-magazine-cover-photoshop-article-1.1514171

20. Moses, L. (2016, July 21). Slate now relies on native ads for nearly 50 percent of its revenues. *Digiday.* Online: http://digiday.com/publishers/slate-now-relies-native-ads-nearly-50-percent-revenue/

21. "Number of unique mobile visitors to websites of select U.S. magazines brands in September 2016 (in millions)." (2016, October). *Statista.* Online: https://www.statista.com/statistics/208813/estimated-mobile-audience-of-popular-magazine-brands/

22. Ricchiardi, S. (2007, August/September). Distorted picture. *American Journalism Review,* pp. 36–43.

23. Sanders, L., & Halliday, J. (2005, May 24). BP institutes "ad-pull" policy for print publications. *AdAge.com.* Online: http://adage.com/article/media/bp-institutes-ad-pull-policy-print-publications/45879/

24. Sass, E. (2016a, April 29). Fans slam "People" for photoshopping Serena. *MediaPost.* Online: http://www.mediapost.com/publications/article/274644/fans-slam-people-for-photoshopping-serena.html

25. Sass, E. (2016b, September 9). Hearst drops "publisher" title at Elle Décor. *MediaPost.* Online: http://www.mediapost.com/publications/article/284374/hearst-drops-publisher-title-at-elle-decor.html

26. Sass, E. (2016c, March 14). Newspaper, magazine revenues fell in 2015. *MediaPost.* Online: http://www.mediapost.com/publications/article/271086/newspaper-magazine-revenues-fell-in-2015.html

27. Sebastian, M. (2014, September 29). MPA: We're about more than pages. *Advertising Age,* p. 12.

28. "Shame on BP and Morgan Stanley ad pull policies." (2005, May 24). *AdAge.com*. Online: http://adage.com/article /viewpoint/shame-bp-morgan-stanley-ad-pull-policies/45888/

29. Spaight, S. (2016, July 29). High-quality branded print magazines among the most effective content marketing tactics. *GS Design*. Online: https://www.gsdesign.com/blog /high-quality-branded-print-magazines-among-most-effective -content-marketing-tactics

30. Steel, E. (2016, April 3). Condé Nast goes into show business. *The New York Times*. Online: http://www.nytimes .com/interactive/2016/04/04/business/media/conde-nast-film -tv-virtual-reality.html?_r=0

31. Sullivan, A. (2013, February 24). Guess which Buzzfeed piece is an ad, ctd. *The Dish*. Online: http://dish .andrewsullivan.com/2013/03/01/guess-which-buzzfeed -piece-is-an-ad-ctd-5/

32. Tebbel, J., & Zuckerman, M. E. (1991). *The magazine in America 1741–1990*. New York: Oxford University Press.

33. "U.S. ad spending by medium and category." (2016, June 27). *Advertising Age*, p. 26.

34. WebMD. (2016). *WebMD magazine media kit 2015*. WebMD.com. Online: http://img.webmd.com/dtmcms/live/ webmd/consumer_assets/site_images/miscellaneous/sales/ webmd_magazine_media_kit_2015.pdf

Cultural Forum Blue Column icon, Media Literacy Red Torch Icon, Using Media Green Gear icon, Developing Media book in starburst icon: ©McGraw-Hill Education

Film

6

◄ 2017 Academy Award Best Picture nominee *Hidden Figures*. Amid the blockbusters, Hollywood can still produce mature, serious movies.

©Entertainment Pictures/Alamy

Learning Objectives

The movies are our dream factories; they are bigger than life. With books, they are the only mass medium not primarily dependent on advertising for their financial support. That means they must satisfy you, because you buy the tickets. As such, the relationship between medium and audience is different from those that exist with other media. After studying this chapter, you should be able to

▶ Outline the history and development of the film industry and film itself as a medium.

▶ Describe the cultural value of film and the implications of the blockbuster mentality for film as an important artistic and cultural medium.

▶ Summarize the three components of the film industry—production, distribution, and exhibition.

▶ Explain how the organizational and economic nature of the contemporary film industry shapes the content of films.

▶ Describe the promise and peril of convergence and the new digital technologies to film as we know it.

▶ Understand how production is becoming more expensive and, simultaneously, less expensive.

▶ Apply film-watching media literacy skills, especially in interpreting merchandise tie-ins and product placements.

1720s Early efforts using chemical salts to capture temporary photographic images

1793 ▶ Niépce begins experimenting with methods to set optical images · · · · · · · · · · · ·

©Pixtal/agefotostock RF

1816 Niépce develops photography

1839 ▶ Daguerreotype introduced; Talbot's calotype (paper film) · · · · · · · ·

1800

©George Eastman House/Getty Images

1877 ▶ Muybridge takes race photos · · · · ·

1887 Goodwin's celluloid roll film

1888 Dickson produces kinetograph

1889 Eastman's easy-to-use camera

1891 Edison's kinetoscope

1895 Lumière brothers debut cinématographe

1896 Edison unveils Edison Vitascope

1850

Source: Library of Congress, Prints and Photographs Division [LC-USZ62-45683]

1902 Méliès's *A Trip to the Moon*

1903 Porter's *The Great Train Robbery* (montage)

1908 Motion Picture Patents Company founded

1915 Lincoln Motion Picture Company; Griffith's *The Birth of a Nation*

1922 Hays office opens

1926 Sound comes to film

1934 Motion Picture Production Code issued

1939 Television unveiled at World's Fair

1947 HUAC convenes

1948 Paramount Decision Cable TV introduced

1900

1950

1969 ▶ Indie film *Easy Rider* · · · · · · · · ·

1976 VCR introduced

1996 ▶ DVD introduced · · · · · · · · · · · ·

Courtesy of Everett Collection

©Howard Kingsnorth/Getty Images RF

2007 *Purple Violets* released directly to iTunes

2009 ▶ *Avatar* · · · · · · · · · · · · · · · ·

2012 For first time, more money spent on online movies than on DVD

2014 Toy manufacturer Hasbro opens Allspark studios; major studios commit to all-digital movie distribution

2015 Netflix and Amazon begin production of feature films; *Tangerine* shot entirely on iPhone

2016 Mobile is top platform for watching Internet video

2017 Apple begins feature film production; *Manchester by the Sea* from Amazon is first movie from a streaming service nominated for an Academy Award

2000

©Moviestore collection Ltd/Alamy

PARIS IS COLD AND DAMP ON THIS DECEMBER NIGHT, THREE DAYS AFTER CHRISTMAS IN 1895. But you bundle up and make your way to the Grand Café in the heart of the city. You've heard that brothers Auguste and Louis Lumière will be displaying their new invention that somehow makes pictures move. Your curiosity is piqued.

Tables and chairs are set up in a basement room of the café, and a white bedsheet is draped above its stage. The Lumières appear to polite applause. They announce the program: *La Sortie des usines Lumière (Quitting Time at the Lumière Factory)*; *Le Repas de bébé*, featuring a Lumière child eating; *L'Arroseur arrosé*, about a practical-joking boy and his victim, the gardener; and finally *L'Arrivée d'un train en gare*, the arrival of a train at a station.

The lights go out. Somewhere behind you, someone starts the machine. There is some brief flickering on the suspended sheet and then . . . you are completely awestruck. There before you—bigger than life-size—photographs are really moving. You see places you know to be miles away. You spy on the secret world of a prankster boy, remembering your own childhood. But the last film is the most impressive. As the giant locomotive chugs toward the audience, you and most of those around you are convinced you are about to be crushed. There is panic. People are ducking under their chairs, screaming. Death is imminent!

The first paying audience in the history of motion pictures has just had a lesson in movie watching.

The Lumière brothers were excellent mechanics, and their father owned a factory that made photographic plates. Their first films were little more than what we would now consider black-and-white home movies. As you can tell from their titles, they were simple stories. There was no editing; the camera was simply turned on, then turned off. There were no fades, wipes, or flashbacks, no computer graphics, no dialogue, and no music; yet much of the audience was terrified by the oncoming cinematic locomotive. And while this story may be the stuff of legends—film historians disagree—it has been around a long time because it reminds us that not only were the first audiences illiterate in the language of film, but also just how far we've come since the medium's earliest days.

We begin our study of the movies with the history of film, from its entrepreneurial beginnings, through the introduction of its narrative and visual language, to its establishment as a large, studio-run industry. We detail Hollywood's relationship with its early audiences and changes in the structure and content of films resulting from the introduction of television. We then look at contemporary movie production, distribution, and exhibition systems and how convergence is altering all three; the influence of the major studios; and the economic pressures on them in an increasingly multimedia environment. We examine the special place movies hold for us and how young audiences and the films that target them may affect our culture. Recognizing the use of product placement in movies is the basis for improving our media literacy skill.

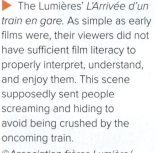

▶ The Lumières' *L'Arrivée d'un train en gare.* As simple as early films were, their viewers did not have sufficient film literacy to properly interpret, understand, and enjoy them. This scene supposedly sent people screaming and hiding to avoid being crushed by the oncoming train.
©Association frères Lumière/ Roger-Viollet/The Image Works

A Short History of the Movies

We are no longer illiterate in the grammar of film, nor are movies as simple as the early Lumière offerings. Consider the sophistication necessary for filmmakers to produce a fantastic feature such as *Rogue One: A Star Wars Story* (2016) and the skill required for audiences to read *Manchester by the Seas*'s (2016) unannounced shifts in time. How we arrived at this contemporary medium–audience relationship is a wonderful story.

Early newspapers were developed by businesspeople and patriots for a small, politically involved elite that could read, but the early movie industry was built largely by entrepreneurs who wanted to make money entertaining everyone. Unlike television, whose birth and growth were predetermined and guided by the already well-established radio industry, there were no precedents, no rules, and no expectations for movies.

Return to the opening vignette. The audience for the first Lumière movies did not "speak film." Think of it as being stranded in a foreign country with no knowledge of the language and cultural conventions. You would have to make your way, with each new experience helping you better understand the next. First you'd learn some simple words and basic customs. Eventually, you'd be able to better understand the language and people. In other words, you'd become increasingly literate in that culture. Beginning with that Paris premiere, people had to become film literate. They had to develop an understanding of cinematic alterations in time and place. They had to learn how images and sound combined to create meaning. But unlike visiting another culture, there was no existing cinematic culture. Movie creators and their audiences had to develop and understand the culture together.

The Early Entrepreneurs

In 1873 former California governor Leland Stanford needed help winning a bet he had made with a friend. Convinced that a horse in full gallop had all four feet off the ground, he had to prove it. He turned to well-known photographer Eadweard Muybridge, who worked on the problem for four years before finding a solution. In 1877 Muybridge arranged a series of still cameras along a stretch of racetrack. As the horse sprinted by, each camera took its picture. The resulting photographs won Stanford his bet, but more important, they sparked an idea in their photographer. Muybridge was intrigued by the appearance of motion created when photos are viewed sequentially. He began taking pictures of numerous kinds of human and

▲ Muybridge's horse pictures. When these plates were placed sequentially and rotated, they produced the appearance of motion.
Source: Library of Congress, Prints and Photographs Division [LC-USZ62-45683]

animal action. To display his work, Muybridge invented the **zoopraxiscope**, a machine for projecting slides onto a distant surface.

When people watched the rapidly projected sequential slides, they saw the pictures as if they were in motion. This perception is the result of a physiological phenomenon known as **persistence of vision**, in which the images our eyes gather are retained in the brain for about 1/24 of a second. Therefore, if photographic frames are moved at 24 frames a second, people perceive them as actually in motion absent any flicker or other interruption.

Muybridge eventually met the prolific inventor Thomas Edison in 1888. Edison quickly saw the scientific and economic potential of the zoopraxiscope and set his top scientist, William Dickson, to the task of developing a better projector. But Dickson correctly saw the need to develop a better system of *filming*. He understood that shooting numerous still photos, then putting them in sequential order, then redrawing the images onto slides was inherently limiting. Dickson combined Hannibal Goodwin's newly invented celluloid roll film with George Eastman's easy-to-use Kodak camera to make a motion picture camera that took 40 photographs a second. He used his **kinetograph** to film all types of theatrical performances, some by unknowns and others by famous entertainers such as Annie Oakley and Buffalo Bill Cody. Of course, none of this would have been possible had it not been for photography itself.

THE DEVELOPMENT OF PHOTOGRAPHY The process of photography was first developed by French inventor Joseph Nicéphore Niépce around 1816. Although there had been much experimentation in the realm of image making at the time, Niépce was the first person to make practical use of a camera and film. He photographed natural objects and produced color prints. Unfortunately, his images would last only a short time.

Niépce's success, however, attracted the attention of countryman Louis Daguerre, who joined with him to perfect the process. Niépce died before the 1839 introduction of the **daguerreotype**, a process of recording images on polished metal plates, usually copper, covered with a thin layer of silver iodide emulsion. When light reflected from an object passed through a lens and struck the emulsion, the emulsion would etch the image on the plate. The plate was then washed with a cleaning solvent, leaving a positive or replica image.

In the same year as Daguerre's first public display of the daguerreotype, British inventor William Henry Fox Talbot introduced a paper film process. This process was more important to the development of photography than the metal film system, but the daguerreotype received widespread attention and acclaim and made the public enthusiastic about photography.

▼ Typical of daguerreotypes, this plate captures a portrait. The method's long exposure time made all but the most stationary subjects impossible to photograph.
©George Eastman House/Getty Images

The **calotype** (Talbot's system) used translucent paper, what we now call the negative, from which several prints could be made. In addition, his film was much more sensitive than Daguerre's metal plate, allowing for exposure times of only a few seconds as opposed to the daguerreotype's 30 minutes. Until calotype, virtually all daguerreotype images were still lives and portraits, a necessity with long exposure times.

The final steps in the development of the photographic process necessary for true motion pictures were taken, as we've just seen, by Goodwin in 1887 and Eastman in 1889 and were adapted to motion pictures by Edison scientist Dickson.

THOMAS EDISON Edison built the first motion picture studio near his laboratory in New Jersey. He called it Black Maria, the common name at that time for a police paddy wagon. It had an open roof and revolved to follow the sun so the performers being filmed would always be illuminated.

The completed films were not projected. Instead, they were run through a **kinetoscope**, a sort of peep show device. Often they were accompanied by music provided by another Edison invention, the phonograph. Patented in 1891 and commercially available three years later, the kinetoscope quickly became a popular feature in penny arcades, vaudeville halls, and big-city Kinetoscope parlors. This marked the beginning of commercial motion picture exhibition.

THE LUMIÈRE BROTHERS The Lumière brothers made the next advance. Their initial screenings demonstrated that people would sit in a darkened room to watch motion pictures projected on a screen. The brothers from Lyon envisioned great wealth in their ability to increase the number of people who could simultaneously watch a movie. In 1895 they patented their **cinématographe**, a device that both photographed and projected action. Within weeks of their Christmastime showing, long lines of enthusiastic moviegoers were waiting for their makeshift theater to open. Edison recognized the advantage of the cinématographe over his kinetoscope, so he acquired the patent for an advanced projector developed by U.S. inventor Thomas Armat. On April 23, 1896, the Edison Vitascope premiered in New York City, and the American movie business was born.

The Coming of Narrative

The Edison and Lumière movies were typically only a few minutes long and showed little more than filmed reproductions of reality—celebrities, weight lifters, jugglers, and babies. They were shot in fixed frame (the camera did not move), and there was no editing. For the earliest audiences, this was enough. But soon the novelty wore thin. People wanted more for their money. French filmmaker Georges Méliès began making narrative motion pictures, that is, movies that told a story. At the end of the 1890s he was shooting and exhibiting one-scene, one-shot movies, but soon he began making stories based on sequential shots in different places. He simply took one shot, stopped the camera, moved it, took another shot, and so on. Méliès is often called the "first artist of the cinema" because he brought narrative to the medium in the form of imaginative tales such as *A Trip to the Moon* (1902).

Méliès had been a magician and caricaturist before he became a filmmaker, and his inventive movies showed his dramatic flair. They were extravagant stage plays in which people disappeared and reappeared and other wonders occurred. *A Trip to the Moon* came to America in 1903, and U.S. moviemakers were quick not only to borrow the idea of using film to tell stories but also to improve on it.

Edwin S. Porter, an Edison Company camera operator, saw that film could be an even better storyteller with more artistic use of camera placement and editing. His 12-minute *The Great Train Robbery* (1903) was the first movie to use editing, intercutting of scenes, and

◄ Scene from A *Trip to the Moon.* Narrative came to the movies through the inventive imagination of Georges Méliès.
©*Star Film/Edison Manufacturing Company/Photofest*

► Scene from *The Great Train Robbery.* Porter's masterpiece introduced audiences to editing, intercutting of scenes, moving cameras, and the Western.
©*Roger-Viollet/The Image Works*

a mobile camera to tell a relatively sophisticated tale. It was also the first Western. This new narrative form using **montage**—tying together two separate but related shots in such a way that they take on a new, unified meaning—was an instant hit with audiences. Almost immediately hundreds of **nickelodeons**, some having as many as 100 seats, were opened in converted stores, banks, and halls across the United States. The price of admission was one nickel, hence the name. By 1905 cities such as New York were opening a new nickelodeon every day. From 1907 to 1908, the first year in which there were more narrative than documentary films, the number of nickelodeons in the United States increased tenfold. With so many exhibition halls in so many towns serving such an extremely enthusiastic public, many movies were needed. To create more films, hundreds of new **factory studios**, or production companies, were started.

Because so many movies needed to be made and rushed to the nickelodeons, people working in the industry had to learn and perform virtually all aspects of production. There was precious little time for, or profitability in, the kind of specialization that marks contemporary filmmaking. Writer, actor, and camera operator D. W. Griffith perfected his craft in this environment. He was quickly recognized as a brilliant director. He introduced innovations such as scheduled rehearsals before final shooting and production based on close adherence to a shooting script. He lavished attention on otherwise ignored aspects of a film's look—costume and lighting—and used close-ups and other dramatic camera angles to transmit emotion.

All his skill came together in 1915 with the release of *The Birth of a Nation.* Whereas Porter had used montage to tell a story, Griffith used it to create passion, move emotions, and heighten suspense. The most influential silent film ever made, this three-hour epic was six weeks in rehearsal and nine weeks in shooting, cost $125,000 to produce (making it the most expensive movie made to that date), was distributed to theaters complete with an orchestral music score, had a cast of thousands of humans and animals, and had an admission price well above the usual 5 cents—$3. It was the most popular and profitable movie made and remained so until 1939, when it was surpassed by *Gone with the Wind.* With other Griffith masterpieces, *Intolerance* (1916) and *Broken Blossoms* (1919), *The Birth of a Nation* set new standards for the American film. They took movies out of the nickelodeons and made them big business. At the same time, however, *The Birth of a Nation* represented the basest aspects of U.S. culture because it included an ugly, racist portrayal of African Americans and a sympathetic treatment of the Ku Klux Klan. The film inspired protests in front of theaters across the

◀ The Ku Klux Klan was the collective hero in D. W. Griffith's *The Birth of a Nation.* This cinematic masterpiece and groundbreaking film employed production techniques never before used; however, its racist theme mars its legacy.
Courtesy of Everett Collection

country and criticism in some newspapers and magazines, and it led African Americans to fight back with their own films (see the essay, "African American Response to D. W. Griffith: The Lincoln and Micheaux Film Companies"). Nevertheless, *The Birth of a Nation* found acceptance by the vast majority of people.

The Big Studios

In 1908 Thomas Edison, foreseeing the huge amounts of money that could be made from movies, founded the Motion Picture Patents Company (MPPC), often simply called the Trust. This group of 10 companies under Edison's control, holding the patents to virtually all existing filmmaking and exhibition equipment, ran the production and distribution of film in the United States with an iron fist. Anyone who wanted to make or exhibit a movie needed Trust permission, which typically was not forthcoming. In addition, the MPPC had rules about the look of the movies it would permit: They must be one reel, approximately 12 minutes long, and must adopt a "stage perspective"; that is, the actors must fill the frame as if they were in a stage play.

Many independent film companies sprang up in defiance of the Trust, including Griffith's in 1913. To avoid MPPC scrutiny and reprisal, these companies moved as far away as they could, to California. This westward migration had other benefits. Better weather meant longer shooting seasons. Free of MPPC interference, people like Griffith who wanted to explore the potential of films longer than 12 minutes and with imaginative use of the camera were free to do so.

The new studio system, with its more elaborate films and big-name stars, was born, and it controlled the movie industry from California. Thomas H. Ince (maker of the William S. Hart Westerns), Griffith, and comedy genius Mack Sennett formed the Triangle Company. Adolph Zukor's Famous Players in Famous Plays—formed when Zukor was denied MPPC permission to distribute one of his films—joined with several other independents and a distribution company to become Paramount. Other independents joined to create the Fox Film Company (soon called 20th Century Fox) and Universal. Although films were still silent, by the mid-1920s there were more than 20,000 movie theaters in the United States—many of them **movie palaces**, elaborately decorated, opulent, architecturally stunning theaters—and more than 350,000 people were making their living in film production. More than 1,240,000 feet of

USING MEDIA TO MAKE A DIFFERENCE
African American Response to D. W. Griffith:
The Lincoln and Micheaux Film Companies

The African American community did not sit passively in the wake of D. W. Griffith's 1915 cinematic but hateful wonder, *The Birth of a Nation.* The NAACP fought the film in court and on the picket line, largely unsuccessfully. But other African Americans decided to use film to combat *Birth.* The first was Emmett J. Scott, a quiet, scholarly man. He sought money from the country's black middle class to produce a short film showing the achievements of African Americans. His intention was to attach his film, *Lincoln's Dream,* as a prologue to screenings of the Griffith film. Together with screenwriter Elaine Sterne, Scott eventually expanded the project into a feature-length movie. He approached Universal Studios with his film but was rejected.

With independent backing from both black and white investors, the film was released in 1918. Produced by an inexperienced cast and crew working on a production beset by bad weather and technical difficulties, the retitled *The Birth of a Race* filled 12 reels of film and ran more than three hours. Its publicity hailed it as "The Greatest and Most Daring of Photoplays. . . The Story of Sin... A Master Picture Conceived in the Spirit of Truth and Dedicated to All the Races of the World" (Bogle, 1989, p. 103). It was an artistic and commercial failure. Scott, however, had inspired others.

Even before *The Birth of a Race* was completed, the Lincoln Motion Picture Company was incorporated, in Nebraska in 1916 and in California in 1917, by brothers Noble and George Johnson. Their tack differed from Scott's. They understood that their "black" films would never be allowed on "white" screens,

so they produced movies designed to tell black-oriented stories to black audiences. They might not be able to convince white America of Griffith's error, but they could reassure African Americans that their views could find expression. Lincoln's first movie was *The Realization of a Negro's Ambition,* and it told the story of black American achievements. The Johnson brothers turned U.S. racism to their advantage. Legal segregation in the South and de facto segregation in the North had led to an explosion of black theaters. These movie houses needed content. Lincoln helped provide it by producing 10 three-reelers between 1916 and 1920.

Another notable film company soon began operation, hoping to challenge, at least in black theaters, Griffith's portrayals. Oscar Micheaux founded the Micheaux Film and Book Company in 1918 in Chicago and soon produced *The Homesteader,* an eight-reel film based on the autobiographical novel he'd written three years earlier. It was the story of a successful black homestead rancher in South Dakota. But Micheaux was not content to boost black self-esteem. He was determined to make "racial photoplays depicting racial life" (as quoted in Sampson, 1977, p. 42). In 1920 he released *Within Our Gates,* a drama about the southern lynching of a black man. Censored and denied a screening in dozens of cities both North and South, Micheaux was undeterred. In 1921 he released the eight-reeler *The Gunsaulus Mystery,* based on a well-known murder case in which a black man was wrongfully accused of murder.

These early film pioneers used their medium to make a difference. They challenged the interpretation of history being circulated by the most popular movie in the world, and they provided encouragement and entertainment to the African American community.

film were shot each year in Hollywood, and annual domestic U.S. box office receipts exceeded $750 million.

The industry prospered not just because of its artistry, drive, and innovation but because it used these to meet the needs of a growing audience. At the beginning of the 20th century, generous immigration rules, combined with political and social unrest abroad, encouraged a flood of European immigrants who congregated in U.S. cities where the jobs were and where people like themselves who spoke their language lived. American farmers, largely illiterate, also swarmed to the cities as years of drought and farm failure left them without home or hope. Jobs in the big mills and factories, although unpleasant, were plentiful. These new city dwellers had money and the need for leisure activities. Movies were a nickel, required no ability to read or to understand English, and offered glamorous stars and wonderful stories from faraway places.

Foreign political unrest proved to be a boon to the infant U.S. movie business in another way as well. In 1914 and 1915, when the California studios were remaking the industry in their own grand image, war raged in Europe. European moviemaking, most significantly the influential French, German, and Russian cinema, came to a halt. European demand for

▲ Millions of fans during the Roaring Twenties enjoyed movies in opulent movie palaces.
©adoc-photos/Getty Images

movies, however, did not. American movies, produced in huge numbers for the hungry home audience, were ideal for overseas distribution. Because so few in the domestic audience could read English, few printed titles were used in the then-silent movies. Therefore, little had to be changed to satisfy foreign moviegoers. Film was indeed a universal language, but more important, the American film industry had firmly established itself as the world leader, all within 20 years of the Lumière brothers' first screening.

Change Comes to Hollywood

As was the case with newspapers and magazines, the advent of television significantly altered the movie–audience relationship. But the nature of that relationship had already been shaped and reshaped in the three decades between the coming of sound to film and the coming of television.

THE TALKIES The first sound film was one of three films produced by Warner Brothers. It may have been *Don Juan* (1926), starring John Barrymore, distributed with synchronized music and sound effects. Or perhaps it was Warner's more famous *The Jazz Singer* (1927), starring Al Jolson, which had several sound and speaking scenes (354 words in all) but was largely silent. Or it may have been the 1928 all-sound *Lights of New York*. Historians disagree because they cannot decide what constitutes a sound film.

There is no confusion, however, about the impact of sound on the movies and their audiences. First, sound made possible new genres—musicals, for example. Second, as actors and actresses now had to really act, performance aesthetics improved. Third, sound made film production a much more complicated and expensive proposition. As a result, many smaller filmmakers closed shop, solidifying the hold of the big studios over the industry. In 1933, 60% of all U.S. films came from Hollywood's eight largest studios. By 1940, they were producing 76% of all U.S. movies and collecting 86% of the total box office. As for the audience, in 1926, the year of *Don Juan*'s release, 50 million people went to the movies each week.

In 1929, at the onset of the Great Depression, the number had risen to 80 million. By 1930, when sound was firmly entrenched, the number of weekly moviegoers had risen to 90 million (Mast & Kawin, 1996).

SCANDAL   The popularity of talkies, and of movies in general, inevitably raised questions about their impact on the culture. In 1896, well before sound, *The Kiss* had generated a great moral outcry. Its stars, John C. Rice and May Irwin, were also the leads in the popular Broadway play *The Widow Jones*, which closed with a climactic kiss. The Edison Company asked Rice and Irwin to re-create the kiss for the big screen. Newspapers and politicians were bombarded with complaints from the offended. Kissing in the theater was one thing; in movies it was quite another! The then-newborn industry responded to this and other calls for censorship with various forms of self-regulation and internal codes. But in the early 1920s more Hollywood scandals forced a more direct response.

In 1920 "America's Sweetheart" Mary Pickford obtained a questionable Nevada divorce from her husband and immediately married the movies' other darling, Douglas Fairbanks, himself newly divorced. In 1920 and 1921 comedian Fatty Arbuckle was involved in legal problems with the police on two coasts. The first was apparently hushed up after a $100,000 gift was made to a Massachusetts district attorney, but the second involved a charge of manslaughter at a San Francisco hotel party thrown by the actor. Although he was acquitted in his third trial (the first two ended in hung juries) and the cause of the woman's death was never fully determined, the stain on Arbuckle and the industry remained. Then, in 1922, actor Wallace Reid died from an addiction to morphine (the studio partly supplied the drug to keep him working through his pain after he was injured in a train wreck), and director William Desmond Taylor was murdered in what the newspapers referred to as "a mysterious fashion" in which drugs and sex were thought to have played a part. The cry for government intervention was raised. State legislatures introduced more than 100 separate pieces of legislation to censor or otherwise control movies and their content.

Hollywood responded in 1922 by creating the Motion Picture Producers and Distributors of America (MPPDA) and appointing Will H. Hays—chair of the Republican Party, a Presbyterian church elder, and a former postmaster general—president. The Hays Office, as it became known, undertook a vast effort to improve the image of the movies. Stressing the importance of movies to national life and as an educational medium, Hays promised better movies and founded a committee on public relations that included many civic and religious leaders. Eventually, in 1934, the Motion Picture Production Code (MPPC) was released. The code forbade the use of profanity, limited bedroom scenes to married couples (although they could not be shown in bed together), required that skimpy outfits be replaced by more complete costumes, delineated the length of screen kisses, ruled out scenes that ridiculed public officials or religious leaders, and outlawed a series of words from "God" to "nuts," all enforced by a $25,000 fine and the demand that scripts be submitted in advance for approval, a form of pre-censorship (Denby, 2016).

NEW GENRES, NEW PROBLEMS   By 1932 weekly movie attendance had dropped to 60 million. The Great Depression was having its effect. Yet the industry was able to weather the crisis for two reasons. The first was its creativity. New genres held people's interest. Feature documentaries such as *The Plow That Broke the Plains* (1936) spoke to audience needs to understand a world in seeming disorder. Musicals such as *42nd Street* (1933) and screwball comedies like *Bringing Up Baby* (1938) provided easy escapism. Gangster movies like *Little Caesar* (1930) reflected the grimy reality of Depression city streets and daily newspaper headlines. Horror films such as *Frankenstein* (1931) articulated audience feelings of alienation and powerlessness in a seemingly uncontrollable time. Socially conscious comedies like *Mr. Deeds Goes to Town* (1936) reminded moviegoers that good could still prevail, and the **double feature** with a **B-movie**—typically a less expensive movie—was a welcome relief to penny-pinching working people.

The second reason the movie business survived the Depression was because of its size and power, both residing in a system of operation called **vertical integration**. Using this system, studios produced their own films, distributed them through their own outlets, and exhibited them in their own theaters. In effect, the big studios controlled a movie from shooting to screening, guaranteeing distribution and an audience regardless of quality.

When the 1930s ended, weekly attendance was again over 80 million, and Hollywood was churning out 500 pictures a year. Moviegoing had become a central family and community activity for most people. Yet the end of that decade also brought bad news for the studios. In 1938 the Justice Department challenged vertical integration, suing the big five studios—Warner Brothers, MGM, Paramount, RKO, and 20th Century Fox—for restraint of trade; that is, they accused the studios of illegal monopolistic practices. The case would take 10 years to decide, but the movie industry, basking in the middle of its golden age, was under attack. Its fate was sealed in 1939 when the Radio Corporation of America (RCA) made the first public broadcast of television from atop the Empire State Building. The impact of these two events was profound, and the medium would have to develop a new relationship with its audience to survive.

▲ Screwball comedies like *Bringing Up Baby* helped Americans escape the misery of the Great Depression.
©20th Century Fox Film Corp./ Courtesy Everett Collection

TELEVISION When World War II began, the government took control of all patents for the newly developing technology of television as well as of the materials necessary for its production. The diffusion of the medium to the public was therefore halted, but its technological improvement was not. In addition, the radio networks and advertising agencies, recognizing that the war would eventually end and that their futures were in television, were preparing for that day. When the war did end, the movie industry found itself competing not with a fledgling medium but with a technologically and economically sophisticated one. The number of homes with television sets grew from 10,000 in 1946 to more than 10 million in 1950 and 54 million in 1960. Meanwhile, by 1955 movie attendance was down to 46 million people a week, fully 25% below even the worst attendance figures for the Depression years.

THE PARAMOUNT DECISION In 1948, 10 years after the case had begun, the Supreme Court issued its Paramount Decision, effectively destroying the studios' hold over moviemaking. Vertical integration was ruled illegal, as was **block booking**, the practice of requiring exhibitors to rent groups of movies, often inferior, to secure a better one. The studios were forced to sell off their exhibition businesses (the theaters). Before the Paramount Decision, the five major studios owned 75% of the first-run movie houses in the United States; after it, they owned none. Not only did they no longer have guaranteed exhibition, but other filmmakers now had access to the theaters, producing even greater competition for the dwindling number of movie patrons.

RED SCARE The U.S. response to its postwar position as world leader was fear. So concerned were some members of Congress that communism would steal the people's rights that Congress decided to steal them first. The Hollywood chapter of the virulent anticommunism movement we now call McCarthyism (after the Republican senator from Wisconsin, Joseph McCarthy, its most rabid and public champion) was led by the House Un-American Activities Committee (HUAC) and its chair, J. Parnell Thomas (later imprisoned for padding his congressional payroll). First convened in 1947, HUAC's goal was to rid Hollywood of communist influence. The fear was that communist, socialist, and leftist propaganda was being secretly inserted into entertainment films by "Reds," "fellow travelers," and "pinkos." Many of the industry's best and brightest talents were called to testify before the committee and were asked, "Are you now or have you ever been a member of the Communist Party?" Those who came to be known as the Hollywood 10, including writers Ring Lardner Jr. and Dalton Trumbo and director Edward Dmytryk, refused to answer the question, accusing the committee, by its mere existence, of being in violation of the Bill of Rights. All were jailed. Rather than defend its First Amendment rights, the film industry abandoned those who were even mildly critical of the "Red Scare," jettisoning much of its best talent at a time when it could least afford to do so. In the fight against television, movies became increasingly tame for fear of being too controversial.

The industry was hurt not only by its cowardice but also by its shortsightedness. Hungry for content, the television industry asked Hollywood to sell it old features for broadcast. The

▶ Warren Beatty eats some lead in the climax of the 1967 hit movie *Bonnie and Clyde.*
©Warner Brothers/Seven Arts/ Photofest

studios responded by imposing on themselves the rule that no films could be sold to television and no working film star could appear on "the box." When it could have helped to shape early television viewer tastes and expectations of the new medium, Hollywood was absent. It lifted its ban in 1958.

FIGHTING BACK The industry worked mightily to recapture audiences from television using both technical and content innovations. Some of these innovations remain today and serve the medium and its audiences well. These include more attention to special effects, greater dependence on and improvements in color, and CinemaScope (projecting on a large screen two and one-half times wider than it is tall). Among the forgettable technological innovations were primitive 3D and smellovision (wafting odors throughout the theater).

Innovation in content included spectaculars with which the small screen could not compete. *The Ten Commandments* (1956), *Ben Hur* (1959), *El Cid* (1960), and *Spartacus* (1960) filled the screen with many thousands of extras and lavish settings. Now that television was catering to the mass audience, movies were free to present challenging fare for more sophisticated audiences. The "message movie" charted social trends, especially alienation of youth (*Blackboard Jungle*, 1955; *Rebel Without a Cause*, 1955) and prejudice (*12 Angry Men*, 1957; *Imitation of Life*, 1959; *To Kill a Mockingbird*, 1962). Changing values toward sex were examined (*Midnight Cowboy*, 1969; *Bob and Carol and Ted and Alice*, 1969), as was the new youth culture's rejection of middle-class values (*The Graduate*, 1967; *Goodbye Columbus*, 1969) and its revulsion/attraction to violence (*Bonnie and Clyde*, 1967). The movies as an industry had changed, which caused the films themselves to become a medium of social commentary and cultural impact.

Movies and Their Audiences

We talk of Hollywood as the "dream factory," the makers of "movie magic." We want our lives and loves to be "just like in the movies." The movies are "larger than life," and movie stars are much more glamorous than television stars. The movies, in other words, hold a very special place in our culture. Movies, like books, are a culturally special medium, an important medium. In this sense the movie–audience relationship has more in common with that of books than with that of commercial television. Just as people buy books, they buy movie tickets. Because the audience, rather than advertisers, is in fact the true consumer, power rests with the audience in film more than it does in television.

Despite changing moviegoer demographics, the major studios continue to create movies as if youngsters and young adults make up the largest portion of the movie audience. There is no question that as age increases, the likelihood of going to the movies decreases ("Changes," 2017), but that fact hides an ongoing and significant fall-off in movie attendance by young people—frequent movie attendance by 12- to 39-year-olds has consistently fallen over the last five years (Lang, 2015; Lang & Rainey, 2016). The reality is that a majority of all movie tickets sold are bought by people 25 and older. So, despite the fact that many in the industry are indeed producing fare for this more mature audience, major studios' attention and the bulk of their resources continue to be directed at the teen audience. As you'll soon read, the reasons are potential income from licensing and product tie-ins (kids love toys, games, and fast food) and overseas ticket sales (audiences don't have to speak English to enjoy superheroes and big explosions). This explains why so many of today's movies and franchises are aimed at youngsters in the form of cartoons (the *Despicable Me* and *Dory* films) and films based on other media such as comic books (the *Avengers* and *Superman* films), popular toys (the *Transformers* franchise), young adult novels (the *Hunger Games* and *Divergent* franchises), television shows (*21 Jump Street* and its sequel *22 Jump Street*), and video games (*Need for Speed* and *Resident Evil*). Look at the top 20 worldwide box office hits of all time in Figure 1, every one of which has earned more than a billion dollars. With the exception of *Titanic* (1997), a special-effects showcase itself, and *Skyfall* (2012), a James Bond action thriller, all are fantastic adventure films that appeal to younger audiences. The question asked by serious observers of the relationship between film and culture is whether the medium is increasingly dominated by the wants, tastes, and needs of what amounts to an audience of children. What becomes of film as an important medium, one with something to say, one that challenges people?

What becomes of film as an important medium, say Hollywood's defenders, is completely dependent on us, the audience; we get the movies we deserve because we tell the studios what we want by how we spend our money. Audiences spent more than $1.5 billion on *Furious 7* in 2015 ($353 million of that in the United States). In 2016 American audiences spent $522 million on *Rogue One: A Star Wars Story* and $408 million on *Captain America: Civil War*. Industry defenders further argue that films aimed at young people aren't necessarily movies with nothing to say. *The Edge of Seventeen* (2016) and *The DUFF* (2015) are "teen films" offering important insight into American society and youth culture, as well as into the topics they explicitly examine, namely, friendship and high-school bullying and digital aggression, respectively. In addition, despite Hollywood's infatuation with younger moviegoers, it still produces scores of movies of merit for a wider audience—*12 Years a Slave* (2013), *American Hustle* (2013), *Selma* (2015), and *The Imitation Game* (2015), for example. All nine Best Picture Academy Award nominees in 2017 were adult, important movies that had much to say about us as a people and as a culture: *Arrival, Fences, Hacksaw Ridge, Hell or High Water, Hidden Figures, La La Land, Manchester by the Sea, Lion,* and *Moonlight*.

If Hollywood is fixated on kid and teen movies, why does it give us such treasures? True, Michael Eisner, as president of Paramount Pictures and then CEO of Disney, famously once wrote in an internal memo, "We have no obligation to make history. We have no obligation to make art. We have no obligation to make a statement. Our only obligation is to make money" (as quoted in Friend, 2000, p. 214). Nevertheless, the movie industry continues to produce films that indeed make history, art, and a statement while they make money. It does so because we buy tickets to those movies.

Scope and Nature of the Film Industry

Hollywood's record year of 1946 saw the sale of more than 4 billion tickets. Today, Americans buy about 1.32 billion movie theater tickets a year. Domestic box office in 2016 was $11.4 billion. Twenty-eight movies in 2016 exceeded $100 million in U.S.–only box office. Fifty-three topped that amount worldwide, and three were billion-dollar movies: *Captain America: Civil War, Finding Dory,* and *Zootopia*. As impressive as these numbers may seem, like other media people, movie industry insiders remain nervous. On a per-capita basis, U.S. moviegoing is at its lowest level in more than a century, and the number of tickets bought by the average moviegoer is the lowest (3.5 tickets a year) that it has been since 1999 (Lang & Rainey, 2016). The question the movie industry is asking about the future, one you can try to answer yourself after reading the essay, is "Will We Continue to Go to the Movies?"

Movie rank and box office revenues (in millions of dollars)

Rank	Movie	Revenue
1	*Avatar* (2009)	$2,784.9
2	*Titanic* (1997)	$2,208.6
3	*Stars Wars Ep. VII: The Force Awakens* (2015)	$2,059.2
4	*Jurassic World* (2015)	$1,670.3
5	*The Avengers* (2012)	$1,519.5
6	*Furious 7* (2015)	$1,514.0
7	*Avengers: Age of Ultron* (2015)	$1,405.8
8	*Harry Potter and the Deathly Hallows: Part II* (2011)	$1,342.2
9	*Frozen* (2013)	$1,274.2
10	*Iron Man 3* (2013)	$1,215.4
11	*Minions* (2015)	$1,164.4
12	*Captain America: Civil War* (2016)	$1,152.3
13	*The Lord of the Rings: The Return of the King* (2003)	$1,141.4
14	*Transformers: Dark of the Moon* (2011)	$1,124.5
15	*Skyfall* (2012)	$1,111.9
16	*Transformers: Age of Extinction* (2014)	$1,104.0
17	*The Dark Knight Rises* (2012)	$1,084.4
18	*Toy Story 3* (2010)	$1,070.2
19	*Pirates of the Caribbean: Dead Man's Chest* (2006)	$1,066.2
20	*Pirates of the Caribbean: On Stranger Tides* (2011)	$1,046.8

▲ **Figure 1** Top 20 All-Time Worldwide Box Office Hits (in millions).

Source: "Top 20 All-Time Worldwide Box Office Hits," Box Office Mojo, 2017. Online: http://www.boxofficemojo.com
©Tony Cordoza/Alamy RF

The data tell a troubling tale. The $11.4 billion box office take of 2016 was a record in dollars but can be attributed "almost entirely to higher ticket prices" (Barnes, 2017, p. C2). In fact, attendance had been flat for years and, in proportion to the growing population, fewer Americans than ever now go to the movies. So an issue often discussed in the cultural forum is "Will people keep going to the movies?" As you might imagine, there is no shortage of answers.

1. *The last several years have seen too many bad movies.* Only big-budget sequels and higher-priced tickets for 3D movies saved box office totals from even greater declines. These made up for flops like *Alice Through the Looking Glass* (2016), *The BFG* (2016), and *CHiPs* (2017). Many critics even saw Hollywood's 2010 announcement that beginning with that year's crop of films, there would be as many as 10 nominees for a "Best Picture" Academy Award instead of the usual five as a cynical attempt to double the number of "acclaimed best pictures," not double the number of actual good movies.

2. Not unrelated, *fewer good movies* mean that not as many people are making it to the theater in the first place, denying them the opportunity to see trailers for and get excited about other films.

3. If there are good films, people go the movies; if not, they go less frequently and they tend to forget about the movies as an option when looking for entertainment. Movie industry people call this *out of sight, out of mind.*

4. This problem is further complicated by people's *skepticism* about just what they will see should they go to the movies. Desperate studios overhyping every new movie as an event or something special or out of the ordinary eventually turns off inevitably disappointed fans.

5. But what faces fans when they do arrive at the movies? A very *expensive* outing. The average ticket price has increased at twice the rate of inflation over the last several years, to $8.50. Add to this the cost of the overpriced Goobers, popcorn, and soda, and an average theater visit costs $28 for two people (Calkins, 2016). Now add the cost of gas to get there plus the price of a trustworthy babysitter (if necessary), and "catching a flick" becomes quite costly at a time when the at-home cost for two hours of on-demand movie viewing has dropped to nearly zero.

6. And what happens when people get to their seats? Chatty neighbors—that is, *an increasingly loud and rude environment*, especially cell phone users, crying babies, and antsy children at age-inappropriate movies.

7. But surely once the house goes dark, all is well. Well, no. People who have just paid handsomely to be at the movies are then faced with *full-length commercials before the trailers.* Almost every theater in America screens these commercials. Advertisers spend over $758 million a year to buy them, with recent annual increases of nearly 6% (Mandese, 2017). Audiences notice this and they're unhappy (Gleiberman, 2017). Why, after just paying a hefty sum for a pair of tickets, would fans want to sit through 20 minutes of commercials? It's the movies, after all, not TV.

8. Speaking of TV, this is, in fact, the industry's greatest fear: *new digital technologies*, especially wired homes (with video on demand; high-definition, big-screen TVs; and pay-per-view movies); increasingly sophisticated DVDs (packed with extra features and now released within weeks of the film's big-screen premiere); dollar-DVD kiosks at retail sites (more than 40,000); and easy-to-use and inexpensive Internet movie downloads. American adults were watching 4 hours and 56 minutes of TV and digital video daily in 2011; today they watch 5 hours and 31 minutes (Lang & Rainey, 2016).

9. People's reliance on sophisticated in-home technologies poses an additional threat to the film industry because it presages a *generational shift away from movies.* It is precisely those young people who will be tomorrow's seat-fillers who are abandoning the theater experience with the least regret. When box office dips, moviegoing among younger fans who have less disposable income drops even more than other groups because they have ready access to and greater facility with attractive and inexpensive options, specifically video games and the Internet.

Enter your voice. Do you go to the movies as much as you once did? If not, why not? If you remain a regular moviegoer, why? What makes the moviegoing experience worth the effort? Many exhibitors are adding amenities such as video arcades, reclining seats, and wine and martini bars. Would moves such as these improve the experience for you?

Three Component Systems

There are three component systems in the movie industry—production, distribution, and exhibition. Each is undergoing significant change in the contemporary digital, converged media environment.

PRODUCTION Production is the making of movies. About 700 feature-length films are produced annually in the United States, a large increase over the early 1980s, when, for example, in 1985, 288 features were produced. As we'll see later in this chapter, significant revenues from home video are one reason for the increase, as is growing conglomerate ownership that demands more product for more markets.

Technology, too, has affected production. Almost all American feature films are shot digitally. The industry had been slow to make the change from film, citing the "coldness" of digital's look and digital's roots in technology rather than art. But the success of digitally shot movies big (all-time box office champ, 2009's *Avatar*) and small (1999's *Blair Witch Project*, made for $35,000, earning $220 million worldwide) has moved filmmakers to greater use of digital capture as a primary shooting format. In fact, even though film is sometimes favored for titles requiring a specific look or feel, the Western *The Hateful Eight* (2015), Forties-style musical *La La Land* (2016), and historical docudrama *Jackie* (2016) for example, film shooting has become sufficiently rare that major providers like Fugifilm and Kodak have ceased production of motion picture stock (Sax, 2016).

Another influence of technology can be seen in most of the top-grossing movies of the last few years. *Guardians of the Galaxy* (2014), *Captain America: The Winter Soldier* (2014), *Transformers: Age of Extinction* (2014), *Jurassic World* (2015), *Avengers: Age of Ultron* (2015), *Star Wars: The Force Awakens* (2015), *Captain America: Civil War* (2016), *Deadpool* (2016), and *Fantastic Beasts and Where to Find Them* (2016) are all marvels of digital effects. Digital filmmaking has made grand special effects not only possible but expected. Stunning special effects, of which *Titanic* (1997) and *Avatar* are fine examples, can make a good movie an excellent one. The downside of computer-generated special effects is that they can greatly increase production costs. *Titanic* cost more than $200 million to make, and *Avatar* more than $300 million. The *average* cost of producing and marketing a Hollywood feature is $140 million, a figure inflated, in large part, by the demands of audience-expected digital spectacles. Many observers see this increase in production costs as a major reason Hollywood studios are less willing to take creative chances in a big-budget film.

But another technology, **cloud computing**, is helping moderate production costs. Cloud computing is the storage of system-operating software, including sophisticated and expensive digital and special-effects programs, on off-site, third-party servers hosted on the Internet that offer on-demand, for-lease access. Access to the cloud frees moviemakers, particularly smaller independent producers, from financial and technical limitations that might otherwise have stymied their productions.

DISTRIBUTION Distribution was once as simple as making prints of films and shipping them to theaters. Now it means supplying these movies to television networks, cable and satellite

▲ Critics assailed *Titanic* for its weak story line and two-dimensional characters—the real stars of the world's first billion-dollar box office hit were the special effects. But grand special effects are no guarantee of success. Special effects-laden *The Lone Ranger* was an all-time box office stinker, costing $375 million to make and promote but earning only $89 million worldwide in 2013, while 2009's *Paranormal Activity*, devoid of technical wizardry and made in seven days for $45,000, earned $170 million in global box office that year.

(left) ©20th Century Fox/Courtesy Everett Collection; (middle) ©Moviestore collection Ltd/Alamy; (right) ©Moviestore collection Ltd/Alamy

networks, makers of DVDs, and Internet streaming companies. In all, a distributor must be able to offer a single movie in as many as 250 different digital formats worldwide to accommodate the specific needs of the many digital retailers it must serve (Ault, 2009). The sheer scope of the distribution business ensures that large companies (most typically the big studios themselves) will dominate. In addition to making copies and guaranteeing their delivery, distributors now finance production and take responsibility for advertising and promotion and for setting and adjusting release dates. The advertising and promotion budget for a Hollywood feature usually equals 50% of the production costs. Sometimes, the ratio of promotion to production costs is even higher. *Avatar* may have cost $300 million to produce, but its studio, Fox, spent another $200 million in marketing and promotion, bringing the total to half a billion dollars, the most expensive movie ever made. Was it worth it? *Avatar* took only 39 days from the day of its release to become the highest-grossing movie of all time ($1.86 billion), accounting for 56 million tickets in the United States alone. Within another month, it had increased that take to $2.36 billion (Cieply, 2010). So spending more to market a film than make it is now standard practice, and the investment is seen as worthwhile, if not necessary (Friend, 2016). In fact, so important has promotion become to the financial success of a movie that studios such as Universal and MGM include their advertising and marketing people in the **green light process**, that is, the decision to make a picture in the first place. These promotion professionals can say yes or no to a film's production, and they must also declare how much money and effort they will put behind the film if they do vote yes.

Another important factor in a film's promotion and eventual financial success is the distributor's decision to release it to a certain number of screens. One strategy, called the **platform rollout**, is to open a movie on a few screens and hope that critical response, film festival success, and good word-of-mouth reviews from those who do see it will propel it to success. Naturally, the advantage of this approach for the distributor is that it can greatly reduce the cost of promotion. Warner Bros. opened *American Sniper* on four screens on Christmas Day, 2014. It went into wide release—3,555 screens—three weeks later on Martin Luther King Day weekend after strong word of mouth and several film festival awards. Its $110 million weekend box office is the all-time best for a January or February weekend (D'Alessandro, 2015). Films likely to suffer at the hands of critics or from poor word of mouth—for example, *Pan* (2015, 11,000 screens) and *Jupiter Ascending* (2015, 2,500 screens)—typically open in thousands of theaters simultaneously. However, it is not uncommon for a potential hit to open on many screens, as *Avatar* did in 2009—on more than 18,300 worldwide—and as did *Rogue One: A Star Wars Story,* opening on 4,100 North American screens in 2016.

EXHIBITION There are currently 43,000 movie screens in the United States spread over 6,000 sites. The four largest American movie chains are Regal Cinemas (7,334 screens), AMC Entertainment (5,206 screens), Cinemark USA (4,457 screens), and Carmike Cinemas (2,917 screens). These four control approximately half of all the country's screens and sell nearly 80% of all tickets (Dawson, 2016b).

It is no surprise to any moviegoer that exhibitors make much of their money on concession sales of items that typically have an 80% profit margin, accounting for 40% of a theater's profits. This is the reason that matinees and budget nights are attractive promotions for theaters. A low-priced ticket pays dividends in overpriced popcorn and Dots. It's also the reason that 60% of moviegoers sneak contraband food into the theater (Friedman, 2014).

▲ Critically acclaimed *American Sniper* opened on four screens; critically panned *Pan* opened on 11,000. Can you guess why?
(Left) ©Moviestore collection Ltd/Alamy (Right) ©Atlaspix/Alamy

Profits from concessions are also why many exhibitors present more than movies to keep seats filled and concessions flowing. Most theaters routinely schedule stand-up comedians, the NFL and NBA in 3D, live opera performances, big-name musical concerts, and classic TV show marathons, sometimes enhanced by wine bars, restaurants and cafés, reserved seating, concierge desks, reclining leather seats, old-fashioned uniformed ushers, and touchpad gourmet-food ordering. Because 5 billion North American theater seats go unsold every year (Barnes, 2016), exhibitors are engaging in a variety of other audience-friendly maneuvers, for example loyalty programs, expanded ticket discounts, and subscription offers. They're also getting into the movie-making business. AMC and Regal joined to create Open Road Films, and the new studio's 2015 film *Spotlight* won that year's Best Picture Academy Award.

The Studios

Studios are at the heart of the movie business, and it's the studios that come to mind when we talk about Hollywood. There are major studios, corporate independents, and independent studios. The majors, who finance their films primarily through the profits of their own business, include Warner Brothers, Columbia, Paramount, 20th Century Fox, Universal, MGM/UA, and Disney. The **corporate independent studios** (so named because they produce movies that have the look and feel of independent films) include Sony Pictures Classics, New Line Cinema (Warner), Fox Searchlight, and Focus Features (Universal). These companies are in fact specialty or niche divisions of the majors, designed to produce more sophisticated—but less costly—fare to (1) gain prestige for their parent studios and (2) earn significant cable, EST, and DVD income after their critically lauded and good word-of-mouth runs in the theaters. Focus Features, for example, is responsible for 2005 Best Picture Oscar-winner *Brokeback Mountain* and 2014 nominee *The Theory of Everything*; Fox Searchlight is home to 2013 Best Picture winner *12 Years a Slave* and 2014's winner *Birdman*; New Line Cinema released the three *Lord of the Rings* films and all the *Rush Hour* movies; Sony Pictures Classics brought to the screen Best Picture nominees *Whiplash* (2014) and *Midnight in Paris* (2011).

Despite the majors' and their specialty houses' big names and notoriety, they produce only about one-fifth of each year's feature films. The remainder come from independent studios, companies that raise money outside the studio system to produce their films. Lionsgate and Weinstein Company are two of the few remaining true independents in Hollywood, producing films like *Silver Linings Playbook*, *The Hateful Eight*, *The Imitation Game*, and the *Halloween* movies (Weinstein), as well as *The Hunger Games* trilogy, the *Twilight Saga*, the *Saw* and Tyler Perry movies, and the *Divergent* series (Lionsgate). Three of the nine Best Picture Academy Award nominations in 2017 were from Lionsgate: *Hacksaw Ridge*, *La La Land*, and *Hell or High Water*. But countless other independents continue to churn out films, often with the hope of winning a distribution deal with one of the Hollywood studios. For example, *Paranormal Activity* was distributed by Paramount, which paid $300,000 for the rights; 2005 Oscar-winner for Best Picture, *Crash*, from Stratus Films, was distributed by

► Corporate indie Fox Searchlight's *12 Years a Slave* earned its parent company an Academy Award Best Picture win and a $190 million global box office take.

©*Pictorial Press Ltd/Alamy*

◀ The smash success of *Easy Rider* (1969) ushered in the indie film boom.
Courtesy of Everett Collection

Lionsgate; and the 2004–2005 $100 million box office hit *Million Dollar Baby*, from independent Lakeshore, was distributed by Warner Brothers.

Independent films tend to have smaller budgets. Often this leads to much more imaginative filmmaking and more risk taking than the big studios are willing to undertake. The 1969 independent film *Easy Rider*, which cost $370,000 to produce and made over $50 million in theater rentals, began the modern independent film boom. *My Big Fat Greek Wedding* (2002) cost $5 million to make and earned over $300 million in global box office receipts. Some independent films with which you might be familiar are *Claire in Motion* (2017), *Magic Mike* (2012), *Before Midnight* (2013), Oscar-winners for Best Screenplay *Pulp Fiction* (1994) and *The Pianist* (2002), 2015 Best Picture nominees *Brooklyn* and *Room*, *Boyhood* (2014), *The Best Exotic Marigold Hotel* (2012), 2017 Best Picture nominee *Moonlight*, and Best Picture Oscar-winner *The Hurt Locker* (2009).

A greater number of independents are now reaching audiences because of several factors, including a dramatic drop in what it costs to shoot and edit a movie on digital equipment (2015's film-festival favorite *Tangerine* was shot entirely on iPhones and edited on Apple's commercially available Final Cut Pro) and a drop in the cost of promoting a movie because of social media and websites like YouTube. A third factor is filmmakers' ability to distribute a movie using the Internet, either independently—as was the case with 2011's *Louis C.K.: Live at the Beacon Theater*—or through established operations like Netflix and iTunes—as did the producers of *Snowpiercer* (2014). This low-cost-of-entry/reasonable-chance-of-success state of affairs has seen entry into the indie movie market from an increasingly wider array of sources. For example, *The Canyons* (2013), starring Lindsay Lohan; Zach Braff's *Wish I Was Here* (2014); Spike Lee's *Da Sweet Blood of Jesus* (2014); and the *Veronica Mars* movie (2013) are all independent films financed through online crowdfunding on Kickstarter, as is 2015's *Kung Fury*. In 2015 Netflix began producing features and Amazon announced plans to produce 12 films a year, screen them in theaters for a month or two, and then make them available to its Amazon Prime subscribers. In 2017 Amazon's *Manchester by the Sea* was the first movie from a streaming service to ever be nominated for an Academy Award. These "new indies" were joined in 2017 by Apple, which began producing feature-length movies for distribution on its Apple Music and Apple TV streaming services.

Trends and Convergence in Moviemaking

Flat box office, increased production costs largely brought about by digital special effects wizardry, and the "corporatization" of the independent film are only a few of the trends reshaping the film industry. There are several others, however, including some that many critics see as contributors to Hollywood's changing future.

Conglomeration and the Blockbuster Mentality

Other than MGM, each of the majors is a part of a large conglomerate. Paramount is owned by Viacom, Warner Brothers is part of the huge Time Warner family of holdings, Disney is part of the giant conglomerate formed in the 1996 Disney/Capital Cities/ABC union, and Universal was bought by NBC's parent company, General Electric, in 2004 and later by cable TV giant Comcast in 2013. Much of this conglomeration takes the form of international ownership. Columbia is owned by Japanese Sony, and Fox by Australia's News Corp. According to many critics, this combination of conglomeration and foreign ownership forces the industry into a **blockbuster mentality**—filmmaking characterized by reduced risk taking and more formulaic movies. Business concerns are said to dominate artistic considerations as accountants and financiers control more decisions once made by creative people. Moviemaking, says former studio CEO Amir Malin, has become "intoxicated with a 'cover my rear' mentality." "All the studio executives who make greenlighting decisions," adds *Variety* magazine, "have bosses higher up the corporate ladder" (both in Lang, 2017, pp. 40–41). There are several common outcomes of this blockbuster mentality.

CONCEPT MOVIES   The marketing and publicity departments of big companies love **concept films**—movies that can be described in one line. *Godzilla* is about a giant, rogue monster. *Jurassic Park* is about giant, rogue dinosaurs. *Transformers* is about good giant alien robots who fight bad giant alien robots.

International ownership and international distribution contribute to this phenomenon. High-concept films that depend little on characterization, plot development, and dialogue are easier to sell to foreign exhibitors than are more sophisticated films. *Fantastic Four* and other Marvel Comics heroes play well everywhere. Big-name stars also have international appeal. That's why they can command huge salaries. The importance of foreign distribution cannot be overstated. Only 2 in 10 U.S. features make a profit on U.S. box office. Much of their eventual profit comes from overseas sales. For example, 2015's *Jupiter Ascending* disappointed at home ($47 million) but earned $125 million overseas. Likewise, 2016's *The Gods of Egypt* earned $31 million in U.S. box office and another $113 million abroad. And it's not just domestic disappointments that do well overseas. *Titanic* doubled its 2009 $601 million U.S. box office, earning $1.2 billion elsewhere. *Avatar* did the same. *Harry Potter and the Deathly Hallows: Part 2* (2011) tripled its domestic take, as did *Furious 7*, globally earning more than a billion dollars in 2015. *Transformers: Age of Extinction* (2014) quadrupled its $245 million domestic box office, taking in nearly $900 million in foreign ticket sales, and *Captain America: Civil War* (2016) nearly doubled its domestic take, earning $1.15 billion worldwide. Overseas box office accounts for 70% of a studio movie's total ticket sales.

AUDIENCE RESEARCH   Before a movie is released, sometimes even before it is made, its script, concept, plot, and characters are subjected to market testing. Often multiple endings are produced and tested with sample audiences by companies such as National Research Group and Marketcast. Despite being "voodoo science, a spin of the roulette wheel," says *Chicago Reader* film critic Jonathan Rosenbaum, audience testing is "believed in like a religion at this point. It's considered part of filmmaking" (quoted in Scribner, 2001, p. D3). This testing produced data indicating that *Fight Club* (1999) would be "the flop of the century"; it made more than $100 million at the box office and has become a cult favorite, earning even more on cable, DVD, VOD, and EST. If the voodoo is so unreliable, ask film purists, what is to become of the filmmaker's genius? What separates these market-tested films from any other commodity? *New York Times* film critic Brooks Barnes explains the dilemma facing blockbuster-driven Hollywood: "Forget zombies," he wrote, "the data crunchers are invading Hollywood. . . . As the stakes of making movies become ever higher, Hollywood leans ever harder on research to minimize guesswork." Research also serves as a "duck-and-cover technique—for when the inevitable argument of 'I am not going to take the blame if this movie doesn't work' comes up" (Barnes, 2013, p. A1). In other words, Hollywood can stand only so much creative freedom when a movie like a $300 million **tentpole** (an expensive blockbuster around which a studio plans its other releases) is in the works and it knows that every year, five films typically produce 25% of all ticket sales (Lang & Rainey, 2016).

SEQUELS, REMAKES, AND FRANCHISES   How many *Batmans* have there been? *Jurassic Parks*? *American Pies* and *Terminators*? *RoboCop* kept the peace in 1987 and again in 2014.

▲ Moviegoers read *The Jungle Book* on the big screen in 1967 and reread it in 2016.
(Left) ©AF archive/Alamy; (Right) ©Atlaspix/Alamy

The surf at *Point Break* was just as gnarly in 2015 as it was in 1991. *Godzilla* flattened cities in 1954 and 1998, as well as in 2014. Hollywood is making increasing use of **franchise films**, movies that are produced with the full intention of producing several more sequels. Classic film franchises like *James Bond* (beginning in 1962) and *Star Wars* (beginning in 1977) continue to churn out sequels over several decades with new casts, and film series based on book series like *Harry Potter* (beginning in 2001) are begun before all of the books are even written. Five of the 10 top-grossing movies in 2016 were continuations of familiar franchises: *Finding Dory, Captain America: Civil War, Batman v Superman: Dawn of Justice, Rogue One: A Star Wars Story,* and *Star Wars: The Force Awakens.* The year before, the top-three grossers were franchise films: *Furious 7, Jurassic World,* and *Avengers: Age of Ultron.* Summer 2017 saw 15 sequels, including reboots of *Guardians of the Galaxy, Transformers, Despicable Me,* and *War of the Planet of the Apes,* giving credence to the old industry saying, "Nobody ever got fired for green-lighting a sequel." But franchises may be losing their luster, as half of all franchises over the last 15 years have seen steady downward box office from the first installment to the last (Dawson, 2016c).

TELEVISION, COMIC BOOK, AND VIDEO-GAME REMAKES Given the fall-off in frequent moviegoing by younger audiences, producer Mike Medavoy worries, "Millennials can play games or watch movies at home on a big screen, so repeating the same kind of content over and over at the movie theater doesn't really make sense. If you don't give people something that's fresh and new, they're not going to show up" (in Lang & Rainey, 2016, p. 43). Nonetheless, teens and preteens still make up a large proportion of the movie audience, and as a result many movies are adaptations of television shows, comic books, and video games. In recent years *CHiPs, Bewitched, Get Smart, Sex and the City, The Simpsons, 21 Jump Street,* and *Star Trek* have moved from small to big screens. *The 6 Million Dollar Man* made it to the movies, too, but with an upgrade to the *Six Billion Dollar Man. The Addams Family, Dennis the Menace, Richie Rich, Spider-Man, Batman,* and *Superman* have traveled from the comics, through television, to the silver screen. *Sin City, Iron Man, Guardians of the Galaxy, Captain America, The Avengers, X-Men, Road to Perdition, 300, Men in Black, Fantastic Four,* and *The Hulk* have moved directly from comic books and graphic novels to movies. *Assassin's Creed, Resident Evil,* and *Mortal Kombat* went from Xbox to box office. But the real reason for the preponderance of TV, comic book, and video-game remakes may well be that these titles are especially attractive to studios because of their built-in merchandise tie-in appeal. The *Resident Evil* franchise, for example, even before the 2017 release of *The Final Chapter,* had already earned its makers $4.9 billion in box office, game sales, and licensing for toys, comic books, novels, and animated films (Verini, 2016).

MERCHANDISE TIE-INS Films are sometimes produced as much for their ability to generate a market for nonfilm products as for their intrinsic value as movies. Kids' 2012 hit *The Lorax* had more than 70 "product partners." The first six *Star Wars* movies have earned more than $20 billion in merchandise sales, and the seventh, *The Force Awakens,* produced $5 billion more on its own (Rainey, 2015). Hollywood makes more than $200 billion a year from merchandise tie-ins to its movie and television shows, a quarter of that amount from character-related merchandise alone (Abrams & Schmidt, 2015). And as almost all of us know, it is nearly impossible to buy a meal at McDonald's, Burger King, or Taco Bell without being offered a movie tie-in product. Studios often believe it is riskier to make a $7 million film with no merchandising potential than a $250 million movie with greater merchandising appeal.

PRODUCT PLACEMENT Many movies are serving double duty as commercials. We'll discuss this $2-billion-a-year phenomenon in detail later in the chapter as a media literacy issue.

Convergence Reshapes the Movie Business

So intertwined are today's movie and television industries that it is often meaningless to discuss them separately. As much as 70% of the production undertaken by the eight largest studios is for smaller screens, and the percentage of their revenues from that source ranges between 35% and 45% (Dawson, 2016a). But the growing relationship between **theatrical films**—those produced originally for theater exhibition—and television is the result of technological changes in the latter. The convergence of film with satellite, cable, VOD, pay-per-view, DVD, and Internet streaming has provided immense distribution and exhibition opportunities for the movies. For example, in 1947 box office receipts accounted for 95% of the studios' film revenues. Now they make up just 20%. Today's distributors make three times as much from domestic home entertainment (DVD, network and cable television, EST, and streaming) as they do from rentals to movie theaters. DVD sales remain a lucrative but declining source of income (Wallenstein, 2016), a trend likely to continue for two reasons. First, in 2012, for the first time, Americans spent more money downloading and streaming movies than they did buying discs, a trend that has since accelerated. Second, because there is nothing to physically manufacture and ship, the profit margin for digital distribution of their movies is much higher than can be realized with DVDs, so studios are increasingly prioritizing digital over disc. Where a solid box office performer—*The Hangover* (2009), for example—could once sell 10 million discs in its first six months of release, today's movies are far more likely to be downloaded for a few dollars on VOD, bought on EST, or streamed from a subscription service rather than purchased as a disc for $15.

The convenience of digital movies has encouraged this digital distribution and exhibition. In 2014 Paramount announced that it would no longer release movies on film in the United States, with the other majors quickly following suit (Scott & Dargis, 2014). As a result, almost all American movie screens have been converted to digital exhibition. Digital exhibition's savings in money and labor to both exhibitor and distributor are dramatic. Rather than making several thousand film prints to be physically transported to individual theaters in metal cans, the electronic distribution of digital movies costs under $100 per screen for the entire process (Stewart & Cohen, 2013).

Although slowed by fears of piracy, the online distribution of feature films to homes is now routine. An American home with Internet and cable access has tens of thousands of full-length movies and television shows to choose from on any given day. Netflix, which originally delivered DVDs to people's homes by mail, has discontinued that service in every country other than the United States. Now focusing on streaming movies, it operates in 45 countries, bringing its subscriber total to nearly 87 million, with 47 million in the United States alone (Smith, 2017). In fact, Netflix-streamed content is the single largest component of American Internet traffic, accounting for more than a third of all the data traveling the Internet at night (Spangler, 2015). And Netflix is not the only source for streamed movies; Internet giants Google Play, Amazon Video and Amazon Prime, and the Comcast cable operation are only four of the scores of sites offering fans everything from classic and niche films to the latest box office hits. And not to be outdone, studios like Disney, Sony, Universal, Warner Brothers, and Lionsgate stream their films via YouTube. You read in the chapter on convergence and the reshaping of mass communication that there are multiple companies offering day-and-date digital home delivery of feature films, and Apple is negotiating with studios to make their movies available in its iTunes stores two weeks after release rather than the standard 90 days (Bednarski, 2016). There are industry analysts, however, who say direct-to-home digital distribution of movies is even more robust than described here because of new technologies that free downloads from the computer screen. For example, Netflix, LG Electronics, Amazon, and TiVo all sell devices that allow downloads directly to TV set-top boxes, avoiding the computer altogether; and with Apple Airplay, you can even send content from your iPhone or iPad to play through an Apple TV on the same WiFi network. See the chapter on the Internet and social media for more about Internet distribution of film and video content.

Digital production has had an additional effect beyond encouraging digital distribution and exhibition. The surprise 1999 hit *The Blair Witch Project* is considered the start of the growing **microcinema** movement through which filmmakers using digital video cameras and desktop digital editing programs are finding audiences, both in theaters and online, for their low-budget (sometimes as little as $10,000) features. The 2009 success of *Paranormal Activity* reinforced interest in microcinema, leading the major studios to create their own in-house microcinema divisions—for example, Paramount's Insurge Pictures. Microcinema has also been boosted by the willingness of A-list talent to get involved with these "small" pictures; for example, Rashida Jones (*Parks and Recreation*), Andy Samberg (*Saturday Night Live*), and Elijah Wood (*The Lord of the Rings*) teamed up on *Celeste and Jesse Forever* (2012).

Smartphones, Tablets, and Social Networking Sites

As they have with all media, smartphones, tablets, and social media are reshaping the relationship between audiences and the movies. Although director David Lynch is skeptical of small-screen viewing, stating, "If you're playing the movie on a telephone, you will never in a trillion years experience the film" (in Kenny, 2016, p. AR16), people are indeed starting to warm to movies on their mobile devices. In late 2016, for the first time, mobile devices accounted for more than 50% of all Internet video views, with half of all that consumption longer than 5 minutes (Ooyala, 2016), and a quarter of all mobile device owners daily watch movies or television shows (eMarketer, 2016).

Exhibitors are also benefiting from mobile technology. There are ticket-buying apps like Fandango (embedded in Facebook and Snapchat feeds and serving 28,000 screens) and those of virtually all the major theater chains. Another app, Atom, offers more than movie times and ticket buying. It provides recommendations based not only on previous theater visits but also on the commentary on linked social network accounts; group discounts for linked purchases, which can be charged to individuals; exclusive merchandise sales to featured movies; concession pre-orders; and **dynamic pricing**, selling seats at varying prices depending on availability and demand.

Major and independent studios are also making use of social networking for the promotion of their films. Fans not only can visit the Miramax, Paramount, Universal Studios, Warner Bros., Lionsgate, and Focus Features official pages on Facebook, they can also use the sites' many features to "like" and share quotations, clips, trailers, and other features of the movies they enjoy with their friends. This use of social networking taps into an audience that is comfortable with the Internet and is more likely to stream movies through their smartphones and tablets with apps like Netflix and Hulu. Of course, with everyone linked by social media, reaction time is instantaneous, so if fans think a movie is a bomb, it will surely be. The industry sees this migration of movies to mobile screens as a mixed blessing. Yes, studios and distributors have many more ways to get content to audiences, but as fans, especially young people already comfortable with relatively small, mobile screens, increasingly watch movies in places other than theaters, what happens to what we have called "the movies" for more than a century?

DEVELOPING MEDIA LITERACY SKILLS
Recognizing Product Placements

Transformers (the toy) may be the stars of several movies by that name, but they share screen time with General Motors cars, apparently the only brand-name vehicles in Los Angeles or whatever other city needs saving. Before it sold a single ticket, 2013's *Man of Steel* had already earned $160 million in promotional support, much of it coming from Superman's co-stars: the National Guard, Gillette, Sears, Chrysler, Hardee's, International House of Pancakes, and Nokia, among others. Its more than 100 "global promotional partners" made it the

▲ Brands covet product placement in hit movies. Here, in 2017's *Kong: Skull Island*, being stalked by a giant gorilla is no reason to ignore the refreshing taste of Coke.

©Warner Bros. Pictures/Courtesy Everett Collection

most commercially branded movie of all time (Morrison, 2013). *Transformers: Age of Extinction* (2014) featured 55 separate brands, including Armani, Budweiser, and Yili milk. Apple, which appeared in 34.4% of all the movies that reached the top of the box office in the decade from 2001 to 2011, was in 23% of 2015's number-one hits; Mercedes-Benz was in 28% (Sauer, 2016). Papa John's is all over New York in 2016's *Ghostbusters* despite that city's reputation for its many quality pizzerias, and Audi had almost as much screen time as star Chris Evans in *Captain America: Civil War* (2016).

The practice of placing brand-name products in movies is not new; Katharine Hepburn throws Gordon's gin into the river in *The African Queen* (1951), and Spencer Tracy is splashed with Coca-Cola in *Father of the Bride* (1950). But in today's movie industry, product placement has expanded into a business in its own right. About 100 product placement agencies are operating in Hollywood, and there's even an industry association, the Entertainment Resources and Marketing Association (ERMA). The attraction of product placements for sponsors is obvious. For one flat fee paid up front, a product that appears in a movie is in actuality a commercial that lives forever—first on the big screen, then on purchased and rented discs and downloads, and then on television and cable. That commercial is also likely to have worldwide distribution.

Many people in and outside the movie industry see product placement as inherently deceptive. "Why not identify the ads for what they are?" From a media literacy standpoint, the issue is the degree to which artistic decisions are being placed second to obligations to sponsors. Scripts are altered and camera angles are chosen to accommodate paid-for placements. For example, laundry detergent Tide replaced Britain's Daz in the script of *The Theory of Everything* (2014) because it was more familiar to American audiences. This may seem like a small adjustment, but what of the many other small and large ones of which the audience is unaware? Media critic Emily Nussbaum sees the problem as even deeper than altered scripts; she sees betrayal:

> There is no art form that doesn't run a three-legged race with the sponsors that support its production, and the weaker an industry gets. . . the more ethical resistance flags. But readers [of novels] would be grossed out to hear that [autobiographical novelist] Karl Ove Knausgaard had accepted a bribe to put the Talking Heads into his childhood memories. They'd be angry if Stephen Sondheim slipped a Dewar's jingle into [his musical] *Company*. That's not priggishness or élitism. It's a belief that art is powerful, that storytelling is real, that when we immerse ourselves in that way it's a vulnerable act of trust. (2015, p. 99)

But, argue defenders of the practice, there is no betrayal; products are part of everything we do in everyday life. All the products around us have brand names. Isn't it a lie to suggest that the things we come into constant contact with don't have logos?

Knowing how media content is funded and how that financial support shapes content is an important aspect of understanding the mass communication process. Therefore, an awareness of the efforts of the movie industry to maximize income from its films is central to good film literacy.

Consider, for example, the following product placements. If you saw these two recent movies, did you recognize the placements?

Batman v Superman: Dawn of Justice (2016)	Airbus, Aston Martin, Bulgari, Chateau Margot, Chrysler, CNN, Converse, Dodge, Dr. Pepper, EMC², Ford, Gucci, Jeep, Jolly Rancher, Marathon Shipping, Microsoft, Moscot, MV Agusta, Nikon, Nortel, Oakley, Oil of Olay, PBS, Ray-Ban, Rolls Royce, Samsung, Tom Davies, Turkish Airlines, Under Armour
Captain America: Civil War (2016)	Apple, Audi, BMW, Cadillac, the CIA, Coca-Cola, FedEx, Ford, Glock, Harley-Davidson, Isuzu, Nestle's Milo, Nike, Massachusetts Institute of Technology, Mercedes-Benz, Mister Softee, MSNBC, Ray-Ban, Salvation Army, *Saveur* (magazine), Tom Ford, Tug Technologies, Under Armour, Vivo, Volkswagen, YouTube

Does it trouble you that content is altered, even if sometimes only minimally, to allow for these brand identifications? To what extent would script alterations have to occur to accommodate paid-for messages before you find them intrusive? Do you think it is fair or honest for a moviemaker who promises you film content in exchange for your money to turn you into what amounts to a television viewer by advertising sponsors' products?

Literate film consumers may answer these questions differently, especially as individuals hold film in varying degrees of esteem—but they should answer them. And what do you make of the recent Hollywood product placement trend, **branding films**, the sponsor-financing of movies to advance a manufacturer's product line. Unilever (Dove soap) co-financed *The Women* (2008), and Chrysler underwrote *Blue Valentine* (2010). Hasbro, the world's second-largest toymaker, was once content to co-finance a picture a year based on its popular board games such as Candy Land and Monopoly. Then, in 2014, it announced it would begin producing movies in its own studio, Allspark Pictures. *My Little Pony* and *Jem and the Holograms* were its first two releases. Former editor in chief of *Variety* Peter Bart laments, "Good movies are hard enough to make without worrying about the branding needs of consumer companies or the script notes of marketing gurus" (2007, p. 58).

MEDIA LITERACY CHALLENGE
Product Placement in Movies

Choose two films. Try for variation, for example, a big-budget blockbuster and a romantic comedy of your choice. List every example of product placement that you can find. In which instances do you believe the film's content was altered, however minimally, to accommodate the placement? Product placement proponents argue that this is a small price to pay for the "reality" that using real brands brings to a film. Do you agree or disagree? Explain your answer in terms of your *expectations of movies' content* and your *ability to recognize when advertising and movie genre conventions are being mixed.* Tackle this one individually, committing your findings to writing, or make it a challenge against one or more classmates.

Resources for Review and Discussion

REVIEW POINTS: TYING CONTENT TO LEARNING OUTCOMES

▶ **Outline the history and development of the film industry and film itself as a medium.**

☐ Film's beginnings reside in the efforts of entrepreneurs such as Eadweard Muybridge and inventors like Thomas Edison and William Dickson.

☐ Photography, an essential precursor to movies, was developed by Hannibal Goodwin, George Eastman, Joseph Nicéphore Niépce, Louis Daguerre, and William Henry Fox Talbot.

☐ Edison and the Lumière brothers began commercial motion picture exhibition, little more than representations of everyday life. George Méliès added narrative, Edwin S. Porter added montage, and D. W. Griffith developed the full-length feature film.

☐ Movies became big business at the turn of the 20th century, one dominated by big studios, but change soon came in the form of talkies, scandal, control, and new genres to fend off the impacts of the Great Depression.

▶ **Describe the cultural value of film and the implications of the blockbuster mentality for film as an important artistic and cultural medium.**

☐ Conglomeration and concentration affect the movie industry, leading to an overreliance on blockbuster films for its success.

☐ Debate exists over whether film can survive as an important medium if it continues to give its youth-dominated audience what it wants.

☐ The annual roster of adult, important movies suggests that film can give all audiences what they want.

▶ **Summarize the three components of the film industry— production, distribution, and exhibition.**

☐ Production is the making of movies, almost universally using digital technology.

☐ Distribution is supplying movies to television and cable networks, DVD makers, Internet streaming and downloading services, and even to individual viewers.

☐ Exhibition is showing movies in a theater, almost universally using digital technologies.

▶ **Explain how the organizational and economic nature of the contemporary film industry shapes the content of its films.**

☐ Studios are at the heart of the movie business and are increasingly in control of the three component systems.

☐ There are major, corporate independent, and independent studios.

▶ **Describe the promise and peril of convergence and the new digital technologies to film as we know it.**

☐ Convergence is reshaping the industry, promising to alter its structure and economics, especially as new distribution models fueled by the Internet and related mobile technologies become even more common than they are now.

▶ **Understand how production is becoming more expensive and, simultaneously, less expensive.**

☐ Distribution is becoming more complex, getting more movies to more people over more platforms.

☐ Exhibition is increasingly out-of-theater and mobile, but is it still "the movies"?

▶ **Apply film-watching media literacy skills, especially in interpreting merchandise tie-ins and product placements.**

☐ The financial benefits of merchandise tie-ins and product licensing are factors in the industry's overreliance on big budget, youth-oriented movies (and the relative scarcity of more mature films).

☐ The inclusion of product placements in films can shape their scripts and production practices, either for better or worse.

KEY TERMS

QUESTIONS FOR REVIEW

1. What are the kinetograph, kinetoscope, cinématographe, daguerreotype, calotype, and nickelodeon?
2. What were Méliès's, Porter's, and Griffith's contributions to film as a narrative medium?
3. What was the Motion Picture Patents Company, and how did it influence the content and development of the movie industry?
4. What societal, technical, and artistic factors shaped the development of movies before World War II?
5. What are the three component systems of the movie industry?
6. What are major and corporate independent studios? What is an independent?
7. What are concept films? Product tie-ins? Product placement?
8. What is platform rollout? When and why is it used?
9. How are digitization and convergence reshaping exhibition? Distribution? Production?
10. What is dynamic pricing? What digital technology makes it possible?

To maximize your study time, check out CONNECT to access the SmartBook study module for this chapter and explore other resources.

QUESTIONS FOR CRITICAL THINKING AND DISCUSSION

1. What do you think of the impact of the blockbuster mentality on movies? Should profit always be the determining factor in producing movie content? Why or why not?
2. Are you a fan of independent movies? When you are watching a movie, how can you tell that it's an independent? If you are an indie fan, do you welcome the microcinema movement? Why or why not?
3. Most industry watchers see the new distribution model promised by digitization of the three component systems as inevitably changing the economics of Hollywood. Some, though, think it will produce better movies. Do you agree or disagree? Why?

REFERENCES

1. Abrams, R., and Schmidt, G. (2015, February 13). Hitching a toy to a star. *The New York Times*, p. B1.
2. Ault, S. (2009, October 16). Studios adjust to digital distribution. *Variety*. Online: http://www.variety.com/article/VR1118010062.html?categoryid=3766&cs=1
3. Barnes, B. (2017, January 2). Film audiences sought fantasy escapes in 2016. *The New York Times*, p. C2.
4. Barnes, B. (2016, December 5). With big help, a movie ticketing start-up hopes to fill empty seats. *The New York Times*, p. B3.
5. Barnes, B. (2013, May 6). Solving equation of a hit film script, with data. *The New York Times*, p. A1.
6. Bart, P. (2007, June 11–17). And now, a scene from our sponsor. *Variety*, pp. 4, 58.
7. Bednarski, P. J. (2016, December 8). Fade out for theaters? Apple angles for quick trip to iTunes. *MediaPost*. Online: http://www.mediapost.com/publications/article/290674/fade-out-for-theaters-apple-angles-for-quick-trip.html
8. Bogle, D. (1989). *Toms, coons, mulattos, mammies, & bucks: An interpretive history of blacks in American films.* New York: Continuum.
9. Calkins, J. (2016, February 16). Exhibitors should open a window to new possibilities. *Variety*, p. 24.
10. "Changes at the multiplex." (2017, March 28). *Variety*, p. 41.
11. Cieply, M. (2010, January 27). He doth surpass himself; *Avatar* outperforms *Titanic*. *New York Times*, p. C1.
12. D'Alessandro, A. (2015, January 20). Eastwood's fistful of dollars: 'Sniper's cume at $110.4M—4-day actuals. *Deadline.com*. Online: http://deadline.com/2015/01/weekend-box-office-american-sniper-kevin-hart-the-wedding-ringer-paddington-blackhat-martin-luther-king-jr-1201349929/
13. Dawson, J. (2016a, October 25). Studios turn up the TV. *Variety*, p. 23.
14. Dawson, J. (2016b, July 26). AMC to slurp up Europe biz. *Variety*, p. 24.
15. Dawson, J. (2016c, June 7). Franchises: A losing bet. *Variety*, p. 20.
16. Denby, D. (2016, May 2). Sex and sexier. *The New Yorker*, pp. 66–72.
17. eMarketer. (2016, April 7). How often are US consumers watching video on their smartphones? Online: https://www.emarketer.com/Article/How-Often-US-Consumers-Watching-Video-on-Their-Smartphones/1013802
18. Friedman, W. (2014, January 10). TV may benefit from decline in moviegoing. *MediaPost*. Online: http://www.mediapost.com/publications/article/217075/tv-may-benefit-from-decline-in-moviegoing.html
19. Friend, T. (2016, January 11). The mogul of the middle. *The New Yorker*, pp. 36–49.
20. Friend, T. (2000, April 24). Mickey Mouse Club. *The New Yorker*, pp. 212–214.

21. Gleiberman, O. (2017, March 28). The singular magic of the big screen. *Variety*, p. 24.

22. Kenny, G. (2016, November 13). Why Netflix is letting movie lovers down. *The New York Times*, p. AR16.

23. Lang, B. (2017, March 28). Anyone in the movie business who tells you they're not scared stiff about the future is probably lying. *Variety*, pp. 40–43.

24. Lang, B. (2015, August 4). Graying auds help seed the specialty biz. *Variety*, p. 14.

25. Lang, B., & Rainey, J. (2016, July 26). Hollywood's summer freeze. *Variety*, pp. 40–45.

26. Mandese, J. (2017, March 30). U.S. cinema ad market expands 5.8%, poised to reach $800 mil. *MediaPost*. Online: http://www.mediapost.com/publications/article/298191/us-cinema-ad-market-expands-58-poised-to-reac.html?edition=101802

27. Mast, G., & Kawin, B. F. (1996). *A short history of the movies*. Boston: Allyn & Bacon.

28. Morrison, M. (2013, June 3). Superman reboot "Man of Steel" snares $160M in promotions. *Advertising Age*. Online: http://adage.com/article/news/superman-reboot-man-steel-snares-160m-promotions/241822/

29. Nussbaum, E. (2015, October 12). The price is right. *The New Yorker*, pp. 95–99.

30. Ooyala. (2016, December). Cord cutters on the march. Online: http://go.ooyala.com/wf-video-index-q3-2016

31. Rainey, J. (2015, December 1). The merchandising force is with Disney. *Variety*, p. 11.

32. Sampson, H. T. (1977). *Blacks in black and white: A source book on black films*. Metuchen, NJ: Scarecrow Press.

33. Sauer, A. (2016, February 24). Announcing the 2016 Brandcameo product placement awards. *Brandchannel*. Online: http://brandchannel.com/2016/02/24/2016-brandcameo-product-placement-awards-022416/

34. Sax, D. (2016, Fall/Winter). The real revenge. *Columbia Journalism Review*, pp. 36–38.

35. Scott, A. O., and Dargis, M. (2014, May 4). Memo to Hollywood. *The New York Times*, pp. 23, 34.

36. Scribner, S. (2001, February 7). Conspiracy to limit the films we see. *Hartford Courant*, pp. D1, D3.

37. Smith, C. (2017, January 2). 105 amazing Netflix statistics and facts. *DMR*. Online: http://expandedramblings.com/index.php/netflix_statistics-facts/

38. Spangler, T. (2015, May 28). Netflix bandwidth usage climbs to nearly 37% of Internet traffic at peak hours. *Variety*. Online: http://variety.com/2015/digital/news/netflix-bandwidth-usage-internet-traffic-1201507187/

39. "Stars diss Hollywood: Clooney, Edgerton & more swipe at commercial movie bombs." *Huffington Post*, Janaury 23, 2012. Online: http://www.huffingtonpost.com

40. Stewart, A., & Cohen, D. S. (2013, April 16). The end. *Variety*, pp. 40–47.

41. Verini, B. (2016, December 14). How Constantin conquered globe. *Variety*, p. 107.

42. Wallenstein, A. (2016, January 6). Why 2015 home entertainment figures should worry studios. *Variety*. Online: http://variety.com/2016/digital/news/home-entertainment-spending-2015-studios-1201673329/

Cultural Forum Blue Column icon, Media Literacy Red Torch Icon, Using Media Green Gear icon, Developing Media book in starburst icon: ©McGraw-Hill Education

Radio, Recording, and Popular Music

7

◀ Homemade YouTube videos brought the then 12-year-old Justin Bieber to music industry attention and then fame.

©Ethan Miller/Billboards2012/Getty Images

Learning Objectives

Radio was the first electronic mass medium, and it was the first national broadcast medium. It produced the networks, program genres, and stars that made television an instant success. But for many years radio and records were young people's media; they gave voice to a generation. As such, they may be our most personally significant mass media. After studying this chapter, you should be able to

▶ Outline the history and development of the radio and sound recording industries and radio and sound recording themselves as media.

▶ Describe the importance of early financing and regulatory decisions regarding radio and how they have shaped the nature of contemporary broadcasting.

▶ Explain how the organizational and economic natures of the contemporary radio and sound recording industries shape the content of both media.

▶ Identify new and converging radio and recording technologies and their potential impact on music, the industries themselves, and listeners.

▶ Apply key music-listening media literacy skills, especially in assessing the benefits and drawbacks of algorithm-based music consumption.

1844 Samuel Morse's telegraph

1860 Scott's phonautograph

1876 Alexander Graham Bell's telephone

1877 ▶ Edison patents "talking machine" • • • • • • • •

1896 Marconi sends wireless signal over 2 miles

1899 Marconi sends wireless signal across the English Channel

©Mooziic/Alamy

~1900 Tesla and Marconi file radio patents — **1900**

1903 ▶ Marconi sends first wireless signal across the Atlantic • • • • • • • • • • •

1905 Columbia Phonograph Company develops two-sided disc

1906 Fessenden makes first public broadcast of voice and music; DeForest invents audion tube

1910 Wireless Ship Act of 1910

1912 Radio Act of 1912

1916 Sarnoff sends Radio Music Box Memo

1919 Radio Corporation of America formed

1920 KDKA goes on air

1922 First radio commercial

©Comstock Images/Alamy RF

1926 NBC, first radio network — **1925**

1927 Radio Act; Federal Radio Commission

1934 Communications Act; Federal Communications Commission

1939 Television introduced at World's Fair; FM goes on air

1946 GIs return from Germany with tape recorder

1947 Columbia Records introduces 33⅓ rpm disc

1949 ▶ Development of the DJ • • • • • • • •

©Michael Ochs Archives/ Getty Images

1951 Car radios exceed home sets — **1950**

Mid-50s Network affiliation halved

1955 ▶ DJ Freed brings R&B to New York • • • • • •

Late-50s National billings drop nearly 80%

©Bettmann/Getty Images

1983 ▶ CD introduced • • • • • • • • • • • — **1975**

1987 MP3 developed

1996 Telecommunications Act

©Digital Vision/Getty Images RF

2001 Satellite radio begins — **2000**

2002 Terrestrial digital radio

2003 ▶ iTunes • • • • • • • • •

2004 Podcasting

2005 *MGM v. Grokster* P2P decision

2008 Sony BMG lifts copy protection from downloads

2009 iTunes becomes DRM free

2011 Digital music sales surpass physical sales

2014 Apple retires the iPod

2015 Catalog sales outpace new releases for first time

©McGraw-Hill Education/Jill Braaten, photographer

"We are listening to the radio."

"I mean something other than this."

"You want music?"

"Yes, please, anything but public radio. Too much talk."

"OK. Here."

"What! That's the classical music station!"

"What's wrong with that?"

"Nothing . . . much."

"What's that supposed to mean, 'Nothing . . . much'?"

"Nothing . . . much. Let me choose."

"OK. You find a station."

"Fine. Here."

"What's that?!"

"It's the New Hot One. All the hits all the time."

"That's not music."

"You sound like my parents."

"I don't mean the stuff they play isn't music; I mean the DJ is just yammering away."

"Hang on. A song is coming up. Anyway, this is funny stuff."

"I don't find jokes about wheelchair races funny."

"It's all in fun."

"Fun for whom?"

"What's *your* problem today?"

"Nothing, I just don't find that kind of stuff funny. Here, I'll find something."

"What's that?"

"The jazz station."

"Give me a break. How about Sports Talk?"

"Nah. How about All News?"

"No way. How about the All Talk station?"

"Why? You need another fix of insulting chatter?"

"How about silence?"

"Yeah, how about it?"

In this chapter we study the technical and social beginnings of both radio and sound recording. We revisit the coming of broadcasting and see how the growth of radio's regulatory, economic, and organizational structures led to the medium's golden age.

The chapter covers how television changed radio and produced the medium with which we are now familiar. We review the scope and nature of contemporary radio, especially its rebirth as a local, fragmented, specialized, personal, and mobile medium. We examine how these characteristics serve advertisers and listeners. The chapter then explores the relationship between radio, the modern recording industry, popular music, and the way new and converging technologies serve and challenge all three. The convenience of algorithm-based music preference—and what that means for the music we hear—inspires our discussion of media literacy.

A Short History of Radio and Sound Recording

The particular stations you and your friend disagree about may be different than those in our opening vignette, but almost all of us have been through a similar conversation. Radio, the seemingly ubiquitous medium, matters to us. Because we often listen to it alone, it is personal.

Radio is also mobile. It travels with us in the car, and we take it everywhere with our smartphones. Radio is specific as well. Stations aim their content at very narrowly defined audiences. But these are characteristics of contemporary radio. Radio once occupied a very different place in our culture. Let's see how it all began.

Early Radio

Because both applied for patents within months of one another in the late 1890s, there remains disagreement over who "invented" radio, Eastern European immigrant Nikola Tesla or Guglielmo Marconi, son of a wealthy Italian businessman and his Irish wife. Marconi, however, is considered the "Father of Radio" because not only was he among the first to send signals through the air, but he was also adroit at gaining maximum publicity for his every success. His improvements over earlier experimental designs allowed him to send and receive telegraph code over distances as great as two miles by 1896. His native Italy was not interested in his invention, so he used his mother's contacts in Great Britain to find support and financing there. England, with a global empire and the world's largest navy and merchant fleets, was naturally interested in long-distance wireless communication. With the financial and technical help of the British, Marconi successfully transmitted wireless signals across the English Channel in 1899 and across the Atlantic in 1901. Wireless was now a reality. Marconi was satisfied with his advance, but other scientists saw the transmission of *voices* by wireless as the next hurdle, a challenge that was soon surmounted.

▲ Guglielmo Marconi (seated).
©AP Photo

In 1903 Reginald Fessenden, a Canadian, invented the **liquid barretter**, the first audio device permitting the reception of wireless voice transmissions. His 1906 Christmas Eve broadcast from Brant Rock, a small New England coastal village, was the first public broadcast of voices and music. His listeners were in ships at sea and a few newspaper offices equipped to receive the transmission.

▼ Lee DeForest.
Source: Library of Congress, Prints and Photographs Division [LC-USZ62-54114]

Later that same year American Lee DeForest invented the **audion tube**, a vacuum tube that improved and amplified wireless signals. Now the reliable transmission of clear voices and music was a reality. But DeForest's second important contribution was that he saw radio as a means of *broadcasting*. The early pioneers, Marconi included, had viewed radio as a device for point-to-point communication—for example, from ship to ship or ship to shore. But in the 1907 prospectus for his radio company DeForest wrote, "It will soon be possible to distribute grand opera music from transmitters placed on the stage of the Metropolitan Opera House by a Radio Telephone station on the roof to almost any dwelling in Greater New York and vicinity. . . . The same applies to large cities. Church music, lectures, etc., can be spread abroad by the Radio Telephone" (as quoted in Adams, 1996, pp. 104–106). Soon, countless "broadcasters" went on the air. Some were giant corporations, looking to dominate the medium for profit; some were hobbyists and hams, playing with the medium for sheer joy. There were so many "stations" that havoc reigned. Yet the promise of radio was such that the medium continued to mature until World War I, when the U.S. government ordered "the immediate closing of all stations for radio communications, both transmitting and receiving."

Early Sound Recording

The late 1800s have long been considered the beginning of sound recording. However, the 2008 discovery in a Paris archive of a

▶ In 1887 Emile Berliner developed the flat disc gramophone and a sophisticated microphone, both important to the widespread public acceptance of sound recordings for the home. Nipper, the trademark dog for his company, RCA Victor, is on the scene even today.
©Mooziic/Alamy

10-second recording by an obscure French tinkerer, Edouard-Leon Scott de Martinville, has some audio historians rethinking recording's roots. Scott recorded a folk song on a device he called a phonautograph in 1860, and he always thought that Thomas Edison had stolen credit that should have been his ("Edison Not," 2008). Nonetheless, in 1877 prolific inventor Edison patented his "talking machine," a device for replicating sound that used a hand-cranked grooved cylinder and a needle. The mechanical movement caused by the needle passing along the groove of the rotating cylinder and hitting bumps was converted into electrical energy that activated a diaphragm in a loudspeaker and produced sound. The drawback was that only one "recording" could be made of any given sound; the cylinder could not be duplicated. In 1887 that problem was solved by German immigrant Emile Berliner, whose gramophone used a flat, rotating, wax-coated disc that could easily be copied or pressed from a metal master. Two equally important Berliner contributions were the development of a sophisticated microphone and later (through his company, RCA Victor Records) the import from Europe of recordings by famous opera stars. Now people had not only a reasonably priced record player but records to play on it. The next advance was introduction of the two-sided disc by the Columbia Phonograph Company in 1905. Soon there were hundreds of phonograph or gramophone companies, and the device, by either name, was a standard feature in U.S. homes by 1920. More than 2 million machines and 107 million recordings were sold in 1919 alone. Public acceptance of the new medium was enhanced even more by the development of electromagnetic recording in 1924 by Joseph P. Maxwell at Bell Laboratory.

The parallel development and diffusion of radio and sound recording is significant. For the first time in history, radio allowed people to hear the words and music of others who were not in their presence. On recordings they could hear words and music that may have been created days, months, or even years before. And the technology changed not only music, but people's relationship with it: individual pieces of music became shorter to fit onto records; on-demand listening, rather than attending scheduled performances, became the norm; listening alone rather than in groups became common; people began defining themselves by their favored genre of music; and despite the fears of the new technology's critics, rather than people giving up making their own music, there was a burst of interest in playing music as listeners were inspired by what they were hearing (Thompson, 2016).

The Coming of Broadcasting

The idea of broadcasting—that is, transmitting voices and music at great distances to a large number of people—predated the development of radio. Alexander Graham Bell's telephone company had a subscription music service in major cities in the late 1800s, delivering music to homes and businesses by telephone wires. A front-page story in an 1877 edition of the *New York Daily Graphic* suggested the possibilities of broadcasting to its readers. The public anticipated and, after DeForest's much publicized successes, was eager for music and voices at home. Russian immigrant David Sarnoff, then an employee of the company American Marconi, recognized this desire and in 1916 sent his superiors what has become famously known as the "Radio Music Box Memo." In this memo Sarnoff wrote of

> a plan of development which would make radio a "household utility" in the same sense as the piano or phonograph. The idea is to bring music into the house by wireless. . . . The receiver can be designed in the form of a simple "Radio Music Box" and arranged for several different wavelengths, which should be changeable with the throwing of a single switch or pressing of a single button. (Sterling & Kitross, 1990, p. 43)

The introduction of broadcasting to a mass audience was delayed in the first two decades of the 20th century by patent fights and lawsuits. Yet when World War I ended, an enthusiastic audience awaited what had become a much-improved medium. In a series of developments that would be duplicated for television at the time of World War II, radio was transformed from an exciting technological idea into an entertainment and commercial giant. To aid the war effort, the government took over the patents relating to radio and continued to improve radio for military use. Thus, refinement and development of the technical aspects of radio continued throughout the war. Then, when the war ended in 1919, the patents were returned to their owners—and the bickering was renewed.

Concerned that the medium would be wasted and fearful that a foreign company (British Marconi) would control this vital resource, the U.S. government forced the combatants to merge. American Marconi, General Electric, American Telephone & Telegraph, and Westinghouse (in 1921)—each in control of a vital piece of technology—joined to create the Radio Corporation of America (RCA). RCA was a government-sanctioned monopoly, but its creation avoided direct government control of the new medium. Twenty-eight-year-old David Sarnoff, author of the Radio Music Box Memo, was made RCA's commercial manager. The way for the medium's popular growth was paved; its success was guaranteed by a public that, because of the phonograph, was already attuned to music in the home and, thanks to the just-concluded war, was awakening to the need for instant, wide-ranging news and information.

On September 30, 1920, a Westinghouse executive, impressed with press accounts of the number of listeners who were picking up broadcasts from the garage radio station of company engineer Frank Conrad, asked him to move his operation to the Westinghouse factory and expand its power. Conrad did so, and on October 27, 1920, experimental station 8XK in Pittsburgh, Pennsylvania, received a license from the Department of Commerce to broadcast. On November 2 this station, renamed KDKA, made the first commercial radio broadcast, announcing the results of the presidential election that sent Warren G. Harding to the White House. By mid-1922, there were nearly 1 million radios in American homes, up from 50,000 just a year before (Tillinghast, 2000, p. 41).

The Coming of Regulation

As the RCA agreements demonstrated, the government had a keen interest in the development, operation, and diffusion of radio. At first government interest focused on point-to-point communication. In 1910 Congress passed the Wireless Ship Act, requiring that all ships using U.S. ports and carrying more than 50 passengers have a working wireless and operator. Of course, the wireless industry did not object, as the legislation boosted sales. But after the *Titanic* struck an iceberg in the North Atlantic in 1912 and it was learned that hundreds of lives were lost needlessly because other ships in the area had left their radios unattended, Congress passed the Radio Act of 1912, which not only strengthened rules regarding

▲ This cover of an 1877 newspaper proved prophetic in its image of speakers' ability to "broadcast" their words.

©Collection of the New-York Historical Society, USA/Bridgeman Images

▲ The wireless-telegraphy room of the *Titanic*. Despite the heroic efforts of wireless operator Jack Philips, hundreds of people died needlessly in the sinking of that great ocean liner because ships in its vicinity did not monitor their receivers.
©Universal History Archive/UIG/ Getty Images

shipboard wireless but also required that wireless operators be licensed by the Secretary of Commerce and Labor.

The Radio Act of 1912 established spheres of authority for both federal and state governments, provided for distributing and revoking licenses, fined violators, and assigned frequencies for station operation. The government was in the business of regulating what was to become broadcasting, a development that angered many operators. They successfully challenged the 1912 act in court, and eventually President Calvin Coolidge ordered the cessation of government regulation of radio despite his belief that chaos would descend on the medium.

He proved prophetic. The industry's years of flouting the 1912 act had led it to the brink of disaster. Radio sales and profits dropped dramatically. Listeners were tired of the chaos. Stations arbitrarily changed frequencies, power, and hours of operation, and there was constant interference between stations, often intentional. Radio industry leaders petitioned Commerce Commissioner Herbert Hoover and, according to historian Erik Barnouw—who titled his 1966 book on radio's early days *A Tower in Babel*—"encouraged firmness" in government efforts to regulate and control the competitors. The government's response was the Radio Act of 1927. Order was restored, and the industry prospered. But the broadcasters had made an important concession to secure this saving intervention. The 1927 act authorized them to *use* the airwaves, which belonged to the public, but not to *own* them. Broadcasters were thus simply the caretakers of the airwaves, a national resource.

The act further stated that when a license was awarded, the standard of evaluation would be the *public interest, convenience, or necessity*. The Federal Radio Commission (FRC) was established to administer the provisions of the act. This **trustee model** of regulation is based on two premises (Bittner, 1994). The first is **spectrum scarcity**. Because broadcast spectrum space is limited and not everyone who wants to broadcast can, those who are granted licenses to serve a local area must accept regulation. The second reason for regulation revolves around the issue of influence. Broadcasting reaches virtually everyone in society. By definition, this ensures its power.

The Communications Act of 1934 replaced the 1927 legislation. The FRC gave way to the Federal Communications Commission (FCC), and its regulatory authority, which continues today, was cemented.

Advertising and the Networks

While the regulatory structure of the medium was evolving, so were its financial bases. The formation of RCA had ensured that radio would be a commercial, profit-based medium. The industry supported itself through the sale of receivers; that is, it operated radio stations in order to sell radios. The problem was that once everybody had a radio, people would stop buying them. The solution was advertising. On August 22, 1922, New York station WEAF accepted the first radio commercial, a 10-minute spot for Long Island brownstone apartments. The cost of the ad was $50.

The sale of advertising led to the establishment of national radio **networks**. Groups of stations, or **affiliates**, all broadcasting identical content from a single distributor, could deliver larger audiences, realizing greater advertising revenues, which would allow them to hire bigger stars and produce better programming, which would attract larger audiences, which could be sold for even greater fees to advertisers. RCA set up a 24-station network, the National Broadcasting Company (NBC), in 1926. A year later it bought AT&T's stations and launched a second network, NBC Blue (the original NBC was renamed NBC Red). The Columbia Broadcasting System (CBS) was also founded in 1927, but it struggled until 26-year-old millionaire cigar maker William S. Paley bought it in 1928, making it a worthy competitor to NBC. The fourth network, Mutual, was established in 1934 largely on the strength of its hit Western *The Lone Ranger*. Four midwestern and eastern stations came together to sell advertising on it and other shows; soon Mutual had 60 affiliates. Mutual differed from the other major national networks in that it did not own and operate its own flagship stations (called **O&Os**, for owned and operated). By 1938 the four national networks had affiliated virtually all the large U.S. stations and the majority of smaller operations as well. These corporations grew so powerful that in 1943 the government forced NBC to divest itself of one of its networks. It sold NBC Blue to Life Saver candy maker Edward Noble, who renamed it the American Broadcasting Company (ABC).

The fundamental basis of broadcasting in the United States was now set:

- Radio broadcasters were private, commercially owned enterprises rather than government operations.
- Governmental regulation was based on the public interest.
- Stations were licensed to serve specific localities, but national networks programmed the most lucrative hours with the largest audiences.
- Entertainment and information (news, weather, and sports) were the basic broadcast content.
- Advertising formed the basis of financial support for broadcasting.

The Golden Age

The networks ushered in radio's golden age. Although the 1929–1939 Great Depression damaged the phonograph industry, with sales dipping to as few as 6 million records in 1932, it helped boost radio. Phonographs and records cost money, but once a family bought a radio, a whole world of entertainment and information was at its disposal, free of charge. The number of homes with radios grew from 12 million in 1930 to 30 million in 1940, and half of them had not one but two receivers. Ad revenues rose from $40 million to $155 million over the same period. Between them, the four national networks broadcast 156 hours of network-originated programming a week. New genres became fixtures during this period: comedy (*The Jack Benny Show*, *Fibber McGee and Molly*), audience participation (*Professor Quiz*, *Truth or Consequences*), children's shows (*Little Orphan Annie*, *The Lone Ranger*), soap operas (*Oxydol's Own Ma Perkins*, *The Guiding Light*), and drama (Orson Welles's *Mercury Theater of the Air*). News, too, became a radio staple.

◀ George Burns and Gracie Allen were CBS comedy stars during radio's golden age. They were among the many radio performers to move easily and successfully to television.
©Bettmann/Getty Images

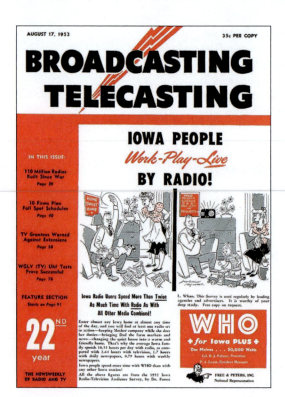

▲ The Iowa radio station that bought space on the cover of industry "bible" *Broadcasting/ Telecasting* wanted readers to believe that all was well in radio-land in 1953. It wasn't.

©*Courtesy of Broadcasting & Cable*

RADIO AND SOUND RECORDING IN WORLD WAR II The golden age of radio shone even more brightly as the United States entered World War II in 1941. Radio was used to sell war bonds, and much content was aimed at boosting the nation's morale. The war increased the desire for news, especially from abroad. The conflict also caused a paper shortage, reducing advertising space in newspapers. No new stations were licensed during the war years, and the 950 existing broadcasters reaped all the broadcast advertising revenues, as well as additional ad revenues that otherwise would have gone to newspapers.

Sound recording benefited from the war as well. Prior to World War II, recording in the United States was done either directly to master metal discs or on wire recorders, literally magnetic recording on metal wire. But GIs brought a new technology back from occupied Germany, a tape recorder that used an easily handled paper tape on a reel. Then, in 1947, Columbia Records introduced a new 33⅓ rpm (rotations-per-minute) long-playing plastic record. A big advance over the previous standard of 78 rpm, it was more durable than the older shellac discs and played for 23 rather than 3⅓ minutes. Columbia offered the technology free to all other record companies. RCA refused the offer, introducing its own 45 rpm disc in 1948. It played for only 3⅓ minutes and had a huge center hole requiring a special adapter. Still, RCA persisted in its marketing, causing a speed war that was settled in 1950 when the two giants compromised on 33⅓ as the standard for classical music and 45 as the standard for pop. And it was the 45, the single (played on cheap plastic record players that cost $12.95; Menard, 2015), that sustained the music business until the mid-1960s, when the Beatles not only ushered in the "British invasion" of rock 'n' roll but also transformed popular music into a 33⅓ album-dominant cultural force, shaping today's popular music and helping reinvent radio.

TELEVISION ARRIVES When the war ended and radio licenses were granted again, the number of stations grew rapidly to 2,000. Annual ad revenues reached $454 million in 1950. Then came television. Network affiliation dropped from 97% in 1945 to 50% by the mid-1950s, as stations "went local" in the face of television's national dominance. National radio advertising income dipped to $35 million in 1960, the year that television found its way into 90% of U.S. homes. If radio were to survive, it would have to find new functions.

Radio and Its Audiences

Radio more than survived; it prospered by changing the nature of its relationship with its audiences. The easiest way to understand this is to see pretelevision radio as television is today—nationally oriented, broadcasting an array of recognizable entertainment program formats, populated by well-known stars and personalities, and consumed primarily in the home, typically with people sitting around the set. Posttelevision radio is local, fragmented, specialized, personal, and mobile. Whereas pretelevision radio was characterized by the big national networks, today's radio is dominated by formats, a particular sound characteristic of a local station.

Who are the people who make up radio's audience? In an average week, approximately 265 million people, 93% of all Americans 12 and over, will listen to the radio. Broadcast radio's audience growth, however, is stagnant. That 93% figure is in fact a decline from the 95.6% who listened in 2009. And while the audience's *size* has remained relatively constant for the last few years, *time spent listening* has fallen, dropping several minutes in that span. But most troubling to radio professionals is that time listening *among young people* is in decline (Washenko, 2016). The industry itself attributes this situation to dissatisfaction with unimaginative programming, hypercommercialization—on average between 12 and 16 minutes of commercials an hour—and the availability of online music sources and mobile technologies like tablets and smartphones. Broadcast veteran Bob Lefsetz explains, "If you don't think new [digital] services will kill [commercial] radio, you must like inane commercials, you must like me-too music, you must think airplay on one of these outlets will sell millions of albums, but that almost never happens anymore" (2013, p. 30). As it is, 68% of Americans now listen to audio on digital devices (Hassan, 2016); and where 96% of U.S. adults owned a radio in 2008, today that number is 79%, 68% if we consider only 18- to 34-year-olds (Owen, 2016). Figure 1 shows the percentage of Americans by age group who listen to the radio each week.

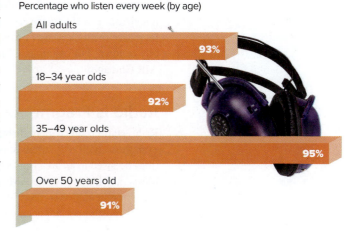

Percentage who listen every week (by age)

All adults — 93%
18–34 year olds — 92%
35–49 year olds — 95%
Over 50 years old — 91%

▲ **Figure 1** Percentage of Americans Who Listen to the Radio Every Week by Age.
Source: Washenko, A., "Nielsen Finds Radio Reach Holds Steady in Q3 2015," Rain News, February 19, 2016. Online: http://rainnews.com/nielsen-finds-radio-reach-holds-steady-in-q3-2015/
©Stockbyte/PunchStock RF

Scope and Nature of the Radio Industry

There are 15,508 broadcast radio stations operating in the United States today: 4,671 commercial AM stations, 6,737 commercial FM stations, and 4,100 noncommercial FM stations. These are joined on the dial by 1,609 **low power FM (LPFM)** stations. There are more than two radios for every person in the United States. The industry as a whole sells more than $17 billion a year of ad time, and radio remains people's primary means of consuming audio content.

FM, AM, and Noncommercial Radio

Although FMs constitute 60% of all commercial stations (to AMs' 40%), as much as 85% of all listening is on FM. In fact, from 2015 to 2016, while the numbers of commercial, noncommercial, and low power FM stations all increased, the number of AM stations actually decreased (Federal Communications Commission, 2016). This has to do with the technology behind each. The FM (frequency modulation) signal is wider, allowing the broadcast not only of stereo (sound perceived from multiple channels, for example bass and drums from the left speaker and guitars and vocals from the right) but also of better fidelity to the original sound than the narrower AM (amplitude modulation) signal. As a result, people attracted to music gravitate toward FM. People favoring news, sports, and information tend to find themselves listening to the AM dial. AM signals travel farther than FM signals, making them perfect for rural parts of the country. But rural areas tend to be less heavily populated, and most AM stations serve fewer listeners.

Many of today's FM stations are noncommercial—that is, they accept no advertising. When the national frequency allocation plan was established during the deliberations leading to the 1934 Communications Act, commercial radio broadcasters persuaded Congress that they alone could be trusted to develop this valuable medium. They promised to make time available for religious, children's, and other educational programming. No frequencies were set aside for noncommercial radio to fulfill these functions. At the insistence of critics who contended that the commercial broadcasters were not fulfilling their promise, in 1945 the FCC set aside all FM frequencies between 88.1 and 91.9 megahertz for noncommercial radio. Today these noncommercial stations not only provide local service, but many also offer national network quality programming through affiliation with National Public Radio (NPR) and Public Radio International (PRI) or through a number of smaller national networks, such as Pacifica Radio.

Radio Is Local

No longer able to compete with television for the national audience in the 1950s, radio began to attract a local audience. Because it costs much more to run a local television station than a local radio station, advertising rates on radio tend to be much lower than on television. Local advertisers can afford radio more easily than they can television, which increases the local flavor of radio. And radio can be localized even more narrowly than by city or town. For example, Chicago's two airports are served by a round-the-clock station, AIR Chicago.

Radio Is Fragmented

Radio stations are widely distributed throughout the United States. Virtually every town—even those with only a few hundred residents—has at least one station. The number of stations licensed in an area is a function of both population and proximity to other towns. Small towns may have only one AM or FM station, and a big city can have as many as 40 stations. This fragmentation—many stations serving many areas—makes possible contemporary radio's most important characteristic, its ability to specialize.

Radio Is Specialized

When radio became a local medium, it could no longer program the expensive, star-filled genres of its golden age. The problem now was how to program a station with interesting content and do so economically. A disc jockey (DJ) playing records was the best solution. Stations soon learned that a highly specialized, specific audience of particular interest to certain advertisers could be attracted with specific types of music. **Format** radio was born. Of course, choosing a specific format means accepting that many potential listeners will not tune in. But in format radio, the size of the audience is secondary to its composition.

American radio is home to about 60 different formats, from the most common, which include Country, Top 40, Album-Oriented Rock, and All Talk, to the somewhat uncommon, for example, World Ethnic. Many stations, especially those in rural areas, offer **secondary services** (formats). For example, a country station may broadcast a religious format for 10 hours on Saturday and Sunday. Figure 2 shows those typical formats. A more precise number and listing is difficult because radio's specialization allows for an infinite variety of formats, for example Houston's B92, whose format changed from News to All-Beyoncé in 2014 (although that experiment lasted only one week).

Format radio offers stations many advantages beyond low-cost operations and specialized audiences that appeal to advertisers. Faced with falling listenership or loss of advertising, a station can simply change DJs and music. Neither television nor the print media have this content flexibility. When confronted with competition from a station with a similar format, a station can further narrow its audience by specializing its formula even more.

▼ In 2014, Houston's B92 changed formats, from News to All-Beyoncé.
©Kevin Mazur/WireImage/Getty Images

Music format radio requires a disc jockey. Someone has to play the music and provide the talk. The modern DJ is the invention of Todd Storz, who bought KOWH in Omaha, Nebraska, in 1949. He turned the radio personality/music formula on its head. Before Storz, radio announcers would talk most of the time and occasionally play music to rest their voices. Storz wanted more music, less talk. He thought radio should sound like a jukebox—the same few songs people wanted to hear played over and over again. His Top 40 format, which demanded strict adherence to a **playlist** (a predetermined sequence of selected records) of popular music for young people, up-tempo pacing, and catchy production gimmicks, became the standard for the posttelevision popular music station. Gordon McClendon of KLIF in Dallas refined the Top 40 format and developed others, such as Beautiful Music, and is therefore often considered, along with Storz, one of the two pioneers of format radio.

Radio Is Personal

With the advent of television, the relationship of radio with its audience changed. Whereas families had previously gathered around the radio to listen together, we

80s Hits
Active Rock
Adult Contemporary (AC)
Adult Hits
Adult Standards/Middle of the Road
Album Adult Alternative
Album-Oriented Rock
All News
All Sports
Alternative
Blues
Children's Radio
Christian AC
Classical
Classic Country
Classic Hits
Classic Rock
Contemporary Christian
Contemporary Inspirational
Country
Easy Listening
Educational
Family Hits
Gospel
Hot Adult Contemporary
Jazz
Latino Urban
Mexican Regional
Modern Adult Contemporary
New Adult Contemporary/Smooth Jazz

New Country
News/Talk/Information
Nostalgia
Oldies
Other
Pop Contemporary Hit Radio
Religious
Rhythmic AC
Rhythmic Contemporary Hit Radio
Rhythmic Oldies
Smooth Adult Contemporary
Soft Adult Contemporary
Southern Gospel
Spanish Adult Hits
Spanish Contemporary
Spanish Contemporary Christian
Spanish Hot Adult Contemporary
Spanish News/Talk
Spanish Oldies
Spanish Religious
Spanish Sports
Spanish Tropical
Spanish Variety
Talk/Personality
Tejano
Urban Adult Contemporary
Urban Contemporary
Urban Oldies
Variety
World Ethnic

▲ **Figure 2**   Radio Formats.
Source: "What Is a Radio Format?" Radio Station World, *2017. Online:* http://radiostationworld.com /directory/Radio_Formats/ © RubberBall Productions RF

now listen to the radio alone. We select personally pleasing formats, and we listen as an adjunct to other personally important activities.

Radio Is Mobile

The mobility of radio accounts in large part for its personal nature. We can listen anywhere, at any time. We listen at work, while exercising, or while sitting in the sun. By 1947 the combined sale of car and alarm clock radios exceeded that of traditional living-room receivers, and in 1951 the annual production of car radios exceeded that of home receivers for the first time. Today, nearly three-quarters of all traditional radio listening occurs away from home; and in the car, where most listening occurs, AM/FM radio rules the road, as you can see in Figure 3.

The Business of Radio

The distinctive characteristics of radio serve its listeners, but they also make radio a profitable business.

Radio as an Advertising Medium

Advertisers enjoy the specialization of radio because it gives them access to homogeneous groups of listeners to whom products can be pitched. Income earned from the sale of airtime

▶ **Figure 3** Percentage of People Who Listen to Audio in Their Primary Car.
Source: Ault, 2016.

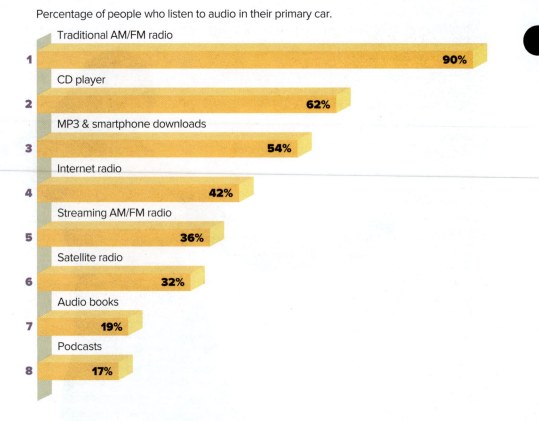

Percentage of people who listen to audio in their primary car.

1	Traditional AM/FM radio — 90%
2	CD player — 62%
3	MP3 & smartphone downloads — 54%
4	Internet radio — 42%
5	Streaming AM/FM radio — 36%
6	Satellite radio — 32%
7	Audio books — 19%
8	Podcasts — 17%

is called **billings**. Local time and national spots (for example, Prestone Antifreeze buys time on several thousand stations in winter areas) account for 97% of all billings; network time makes up the rest (Sass, 2015). The cost of time is based on the **ratings**, the percentage of the total available audience reached.

Radio is an attractive advertising medium for reasons other than its delivery of a homogeneous audience. Radio ads are inexpensive to produce and therefore can be changed, updated, and specialized to meet specific audience demands. Ads can also be specialized to different times of the day. For example, a hamburger restaurant may have one version of its commercial for the morning audience, in which its breakfast menu is touted, and a different version for the evening audience driving home, dreading the thought of cooking dinner. Radio time is inexpensive to buy, especially when compared with television. An audience loyal to a specific format station is presumably loyal to those who advertise on it. Radio is the listeners' friend; it travels with them and talks to them personally.

Deregulation and Ownership

The business of radio is being altered by deregulation and changes in ownership rules. To ensure that there were many different perspectives in the cultural forum, the FCC had long limited the number of radio stations one person or company could own to one AM and one FM locally and seven AMs and seven FMs nationally. These numbers were revised upward in the late 1980s, and controls were almost totally eliminated by the Telecommunications Act of 1996. Now, due to this **deregulation**, there are no national ownership limits, and one person or company can own as many as eight stations in one area, depending on the size of the market. This situation has allowed **duopoly**—one person or company owning and managing multiple radio stations in a single market—to explode. Since the passage of the 1996 act, more than 10,000 radio stations have been sold, and there are now 1,100 fewer station owners, a 30% decline. The vast majority of these sales have been to already-large radio groups such as iHeart Media and Cumulus, with 850 and 459 stations, respectively. As a result, in 25 of the 50 largest radio markets, three companies claim 80% of all listeners. In over 40 cities, one-third of the radio stations are owned by a single company, leading insiders to identify the industry's two biggest problems not as competition from new digital technologies, but first, "control of the industry in the hands of a few giants" and a close second, "decline of local radio with its deep communities ties" (Editors, 2015).

The concern over these issues runs deep. Local public affairs shows now make up less than one-half of 1% of all commercial broadcast time in the United States. "There is a crisis," said FCC Commissioner Michael Copps (2011), "when more than one-third of our commercial broadcasters offer little to no news whatsoever to their communities of license. America's news and information resources keep shrinking and hundreds of stories that could inform our citizens go untold and, indeed, undiscovered." As for the music, a few years ago, when Clear Channel (now iHeart Media) and Cumulus collectively laid off hundreds of DJs in a move toward automated (no live DJ) and nationally syndicated programming, veteran Los Angeles rock DJ Jim Ladd said, "It's really bad news. It was people in my profession that first played Tom Petty, first played the Doors. But the people programming stations now are not music people—they're business people" (in Knopper, 2011, p. 19). LPFM, 10- to 100-watt nonprofit community radio stations with a reach of only a few miles, are one response to "the homogenization of the FM band." As a result of the Local Community Radio Act of 2010, which enjoyed wide bipartisan support in Congress, 1,069 LPFM stations, serving all 50 states, now offer opportunities for additional radio voices to serve their local listenerships. The FCC encourages the growth of LPFM with regular online webinars explaining the application process to potential operators of this local medium designed, in the words of the FCC, "to empower community voices, promote media diversity, and enhance local programming" (in Sokoloct, 2016, p. B1).

▼ Fans debate whether Todd Storz or Gordon McClendon first invented the DJ. But there is no dispute that Alan Freed, first in Cleveland and then in New York, established the DJ as a star. Freed, here in a 1958 photo, is credited with introducing America's white teenagers to rhythm 'n' blues artists like Chuck Berry and Little Richard and ushering in the age of rock 'n' roll. ©*Michael Ochs Archives/Getty Images*

Scope and Nature of the Recording Industry

When the DJs and Top 40 format saved radio in the 1950s, they also changed for all time popular music and, by extension, the recording industry. Disc jockeys were color-deaf in their selection of records. They introduced record buyers to rhythm 'n' blues in the music of African American artists such as Chuck Berry and Little Richard. Until the mid-1950s, the work of these performers had to be **covered**—rerecorded by white artists such as Perry Como—before it was aired. Teens loved the new sound, however, and it became the foundation of their own subculture, as well as the basis for the explosion in recorded music. See the essay "Rock 'n' Roll, Radio, and Race Relations" for more on rock's roots.

Today more than 5,000 U.S. companies annually release around 100,000 new albums on thousands of different labels. American music buyers purchased 1.3 billion pieces of music—digital (70%) and physical (30%)—in 2015 (Friedlander, 2016).

USING MEDIA TO MAKE A DIFFERENCE
Rock 'n' Roll, Radio, and Race Relations

After World War II, African Americans in the United States refused to remain invisible. Having fought in segregated units in Europe and proven their willingness to fight and die for freedom abroad, they openly demanded freedom at home. President Harry Truman, recognizing the absurdity of racial separation in the self-proclaimed "greatest democracy on earth," desegregated the armed forces by executive order in 1948. These early stirrings of equality led to a sense among African Americans that anything was possible, and that feeling seeped into their music. What had been called *cat*, *sepia*, or *race* music took on a new tone. While this new sound borrowed from traditional black music—gospel, blues, and laments over slavery and racial injustice—it was different, much different. Music historian Ed Ward said that this bolder, more aggressive music "spoke to a shared experience, not just to black (usually rural black) life," and it would become the "truly biracial popular music in this country" (Ward, Stokes, & Tucker, 1986, p. 83).

Hundreds of small independent record companies sprang up to produce this newly labeled rhythm 'n' blues (R&B), music focusing on Americans' shared experience with topics like sex and alcohol that were part of life for people of all colors. With its earthy lyrics and thumping dance beat, R&B very quickly found an audience in the 1950s, one composed largely of urban blacks (growing in number as African Americans increasingly migrated north) and white teenagers.

The major record companies took notice, and rather than sign already successful R&B artists, they had their white artists cover the black hits. The Penguins' "Earth Angel" was covered by the reassuringly named Crew Cuts, who also covered the Chords' "Sh-Boom." Chuck Berry's "Maybellene" was covered by both the Johnny Long and Ralph Marterie orchestras. Even Bill Haley and the Comets' youth anthem "Shake, Rattle and Roll" was a cover of a Joe Turner tune.

But these covers actually served to introduce even more white teens to the new music, and these kids demanded the original versions. This did not escape the attention of Sam Phillips, who in 1952 founded Sun Records in an effort to bring black music to white teens. "If I could find a white man who had the Negro sound, I could make a billion dollars," he is reported to have mused (in Menard, 2015, p. 83). In 1954 he found that

man: Elvis Presley, whose breakout hit, *Hound Dog*, was a cover of R&B singer Big Mama Thornton's 1953 song.

The situation also caught the attention of Cleveland DJ Alan Freed, whose nationally distributed radio (and later television) show featured black R&B tunes, never covers. Freed began calling the music he played rock 'n' roll (to signify that it was black and white youth music), and by 1955, when Freed took his show to New York, the cover business was dead. Black performers were recording and releasing their own music to a national audience, and people of all colors were tuning in.

Now that the kids had a music of their own, and now that a growing number of radio stations were willing to program it, a youth culture began to develop, one that was antagonistic toward their parents' culture. The music was central to this antagonism, not only because it was gritty and real but also because it exposed the hypocrisy of adult culture.

For young people of the mid-1950s and 1960s, the music of Little Richard, Fats Domino, Ray Charles, and Chuck Berry made a lie of all that their parents, teachers, and government leaders had said about race, the inferiority of African Americans, and African Americans' satisfaction with the status quo.

Ralph Bass, a producer for independent R&B label Chess Records, described the evolution to historian David Szatmary. When he was touring with Chess's R&B groups in the early 1950s, "they didn't let whites into the clubs. Then they got 'white spectator tickets' for the worst corner of the joint. They had to keep the white kids out, so they'd have white nights sometimes, or they'd put a rope across the middle of the floor. The blacks on one side, the whites on the other, digging how the blacks were dancing and copying them. Then, hell, the rope would come down, and they'd all be dancing together. Salt and pepper all mixed together" (Szatmary, 2000, p. 21).

R&B and rock 'n' roll did not end racism. But the music made a difference, one that would eventually make it possible for Americans who wanted to do so to free themselves of racism's ugly hold. Rock music (and the radio stations that played it) would again nudge the nation toward its better tendencies during the antiwar and civil rights movements of the late 1960s. And it is against this backdrop, a history of popular music making as real a difference as any piece of official legislation, that contemporary critics lament the homogenizing of popular music. Music can and has made a difference. Can and will it ever again? they ask.

The Major Recording Companies

Three major recording companies control 63% of the global recorded music market. Two (Sony and Universal) control nearly half of the world's $15 billion global music sales. Two of the three are foreign-owned:

- Sony, controlling about 21% of the world music market, is a Japanese-owned corporate group. Its labels include Columbia, Epic, RCA, and Arista.
- New York–based Warner Music Group, controlling about 15%, is owned by billionaire Len Blavatnik's Access Industries and several private investors. Its labels include Atlantic, Asylum, and Warner Brothers.
- Universal Music Group, controlling about 27%, is owned by French conglomerate Vivendi Universal and controls labels such as EMI, MCA, Capitol, and Def Jam Records ("Market Share," 2016).

Critics have long voiced concern over conglomeration in the music business, a concern that centers on the traditional cultural value of music, especially for young people. Multibillion-dollar conglomerates typically are not rebellious in their cultural tastes, nor are they usually willing to take risks on new ideas. These duties have fallen primarily to the independent labels, companies such as Real World Records and Epitaph. Still, problems with the music industry–audience relationship remain.

Cultural homogenization is the worrisome outcome of virtually all the world's influential recording being controlled by a few profit-oriented giants. If bands or artists cannot immediately deliver the goods, they aren't signed. So derivative artists and manufactured groups dominate—for example, Miley Cyrus and One Direction. Moreover, popular music is increasingly the product not of individual genius or artistry but of **mathematical songwriting**, songs written specifically to be commercial hits. They are "written to track, which means a producer makes a beat. Then a songwriter listens to it and attempts to generate words that fit that beat, sometimes singing nonsense until the language begins to take shape. It's more about how lyrics sound than what they mean. This has become a bedrock part of the industry" (Lansky, 2015/2016, p. 124).

The *dominance of profit over artistry* worries many music fans. When a major label must spend millions to sign a bankable artist such as Michael Jackson ($250 million to his estate) or Jay Z ($150 million) or Adele ($130 million), it typically pares lesser-known, potentially more innovative artists from its roster. The chase for profit has also produced an increase in the number of product placements in songs (Timberg, 2015a) and the use of computer algorithms to determine which songs are sufficiently similar to existing hits to warrant production (Timberg, 2015b). Critics and industry people alike see these practices as problems for the industry, as well as for the music and its listeners. Record industry sales have dropped consistently over the past two decades, with small gains in 2015 for both the U.S. (0.09%) and global (3.2%) markets finally halting the decline (Friedlander, 2016; Richter, 2016b). The reason for this state of affairs, say many music critics, is not Internet piracy, as is often asserted by the recording industry, but the industry itself. As the industry relies more heavily on superficial, disposable pop stars, it tells people that the music is superficial and disposable. As they increasingly rely on the same big stars, there is little new music for fans to discover and buy. In 1981, for example, 31 songs from 29 different artists hit *Billboard*'s Number 1; in 2016, only 11 songs from 10 different artists reached Number 1 (Justin Bieber appeared twice, and Drake, with others, three times; Timberg, 2016a). What helps keep the industry afloat is continued strength in sales of **catalog albums**, albums more than 18 months old. In fact, catalog albums outsold new releases for the first time in 2015 (Singleton, 2016). But new releases cannot become catalog albums unless the artists and their music are worthy of fans' devotion and money. Look at the names of the best-selling albums and artists in Figure 4. How many current artists and albums do you think will ever join these ranks? Critics of the ascendance of profits over artistry argue that the industry simply lacks the patience to develop new sounds and careers.

Promotion overshadows the music, say the critics. If groups or artists don't come across well on television or are otherwise a challenge to promote (for example, they do not fit an easily recognizable niche), they aren't signed. Again, the solution is to create marketable

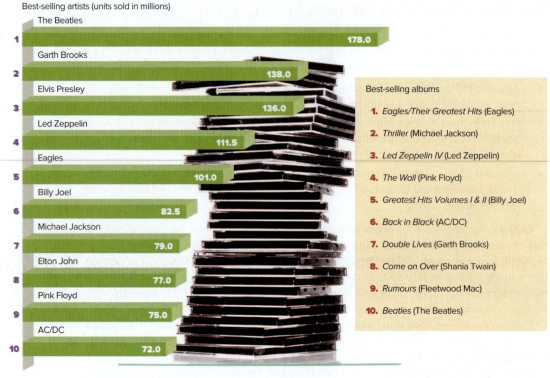

▶ **Figure 4** The Top 10 Best-Selling Albums and Artists of All Time, U.S. Sales Only.

Source: Recording Industry Association of America (www.riaa .com).

©P. Ughetto/ PhotoAlto RF

Best-selling artists (units sold in millions)

Rank	Artist	Units
1	The Beatles	178.0
2	Garth Brooks	138.0
3	Elvis Presley	136.0
4	Led Zeppelin	111.5
5	Eagles	101.0
6	Billy Joel	82.5
7	Michael Jackson	79.0
8	Elton John	77.0
9	Pink Floyd	75.0
10	AC/DC	72.0

Best-selling albums

1. *Eagles/Their Greatest Hits* (Eagles)
2. *Thriller* (Michael Jackson)
3. *Led Zeppelin IV* (Led Zeppelin)
4. *The Wall* (Pink Floyd)
5. *Greatest Hits Volumes I & II* (Billy Joel)
6. *Back in Black* (AC/DC)
7. *Double Lives* (Garth Brooks)
8. *Come on Over* (Shania Twain)
9. *Rumours* (Fleetwood Mac)
10. *Beatles* (The Beatles)

artists from scratch. Promoting tours is also an issue. If bands or artists do not have corporate sponsorship for their tours, there is no tour. If musicians do not tour, they cannot create an enthusiastic fan base. But if they do not have an enthusiastic fan base, they cannot attract the corporate sponsorship necessary to mount a tour. This makes radio even more important for the introduction of new artists and forms of music, but radio, too, is increasingly driven by profit-maximizing format narrowing and is therefore dependent on the major labels' definition of playable artists. As a result, when the Internet began to undermine a complacent industry's long-profitable business model, it was ill prepared to meet the challenges that came its way. Radio veteran Lefsetz comments again, "Music has become a second-class citizen because it's got no self-respect. . . . The enemy is not the techies, but those who make the music and promote it—who have no conviction and can't say no to a payday. We judge everything by money, and however much we've got is never enough" (2015, p. 26).

Trends and Convergence in Radio and Sound Recording

Emerging and changing technologies have affected the production and distribution aspects of both radio and sound recording.

The Impact of Television

We have seen how television fundamentally altered radio's structure and relationship with its audiences. Television, specifically the cable channel MTV, changed the recording industry, too. MTV's introduction in 1981 helped pull the industry out of its disastrous 1979 slump, but at a price. First, the look of concerts has changed. No longer is it sufficient to pack an artist or group into a hall or stadium with a few thousand screaming fans. Now a concert must be an extravagant multimedia event approximating the sophistication of a music video. The set for Lady Gaga's recent "Born This Way Ball" tour, for example, required 15 moving trucks to haul it from venue to venue. This means that fewer acts take to the road, changing the relationship between musicians and fans. Second, the radio–recording industry relationship has changed. Even as MTV began to program fewer and fewer music videos, record companies grew even more reliant on television to introduce new music. For example, labels now time record releases to artists' television appearances, and new and old tunes alike find heavy play on television shows. *American Idol* contestants and the cast of *Glee* sold tens of millions of songs before both shows left the air (Barker, 2014), with newer programs such as *America's Got Talent*, *Star*, *Empire*, and *Nashville* taking their place introducing and selling music to fans. And if television has become the new radio, so has the Internet. YouTube, the world's largest source of streaming music (Richter, 2016a), served as the career launchpad for pop star Justin Bieber, who in 2007 used a series of home-made videos of his 12-year-old self singing in the mirror and around his hometown to catch the eye of the star-hungry record industry, as it did for 16-year-old New Zealander Lorde. Her success as a self-release, free-download Internet music star led Universal to commercially distribute her work, making both the song "Royals" and the artist global smash hits. Universal has since established Awesomeness Music, a label specifically designed to record YouTube talent like Cimorelli, singing sisters from California whose channel has more than 2.7 million subscribers.

▲ TV is the new radio. TV shows like *Empire*, pictured here, *Star*, and *Nashville* introduce and sell new music to their fans.
©Fox Network/Photofest

Satellite and Cable

The convergence of radio and satellite has aided the rebirth of the radio networks. Music and other forms of radio content can be distributed quite inexpensively to thousands of stations. As a result, one "network" can provide very different services to its very different affiliates. Sports broadcaster ESPN, for example, maintains its own radio network, and Westwood One distributes the Rick Dees Weekly Top 40. In addition, Westwood One, through its **syndication** operations, delivers thousands of varied network and program syndication services to almost every commercial station in the country. The low cost of producing radio programming, however, makes the establishment of other, even more specialized networks possible. Satellites, and sometimes now fiber optic Internet, make access to syndicated content and formats affordable for many stations. Syndicators can deliver news, top 10 shows, and other content to stations on a market-by-market basis. They can also provide entire formats, requiring local stations, if they wish, to do little more than insert commercials into what sounds to listeners to be a local broadcast.

Satellite has another application as well. Many listeners now receive "radio" through their cable televisions in the form of satellite-delivered services such as DMX (Digital Music Express) and Music Choice. Direct satellite home, office, and automobile delivery of audio by **digital audio radio service (DARS)** brings Sirius XM Radio to more than 30 million American subscribers by offering hundreds of commercial channels—primarily talk, sports, and traffic—and commercial-free channels—primarily music. Those numbers will likely continue to grow because the company has arrangements with every major carmaker in the country to offer its receivers as a factory-installed option. DARS has proven to be sufficiently inexpensive, reliable, and technologically sophisticated that Norway, in 2017, ceased all terrestrial broadcasting, making DARS its standard radio-delivery technology. Several other European countries are considering the same move.

Terrestrial Digital Radio

Since late 2002, thousands of radio stations have begun broadcasting **terrestrial** (land-based) **digital radio**. Relying on digital compression technology called **in-band-on-channel**

(IBOC), terrestrial digital radio allows broadcasters to transmit not only their usual analog signal but one or more digital signals using their existing spectrum space. And although IBOC also improves sound fidelity, making possible high-definition radio, many stations using the technology see its greatest value in pay services—for example, subscription data delivery. IBOC has yet to completely replace analog radio, as many stations today continue to air both digital and analog services.

Web Radio and Podcasting

Radio's convergence with digital technologies is nowhere more pronounced and potentially profound than in **Web radio**, the delivery of "radio" directly to individual listeners over the Internet, and in **podcasting**, streaming or downloading of audio files recorded and stored on distant servers.

First, we'll discuss Web radio. Tens of thousands of "radio stations" exist on the Web in one of two forms: radio simulcasts and bitcasters. *Radio simulcasts* are traditional, over-the-air stations transmitting their signals online. Some simply re-create their original broadcasts, but more often, the simulcast includes additional information, such as song lyrics or artists' biographical information and concert dates. **Bitcasters**, Web-only radio stations, can be accessed only online. There are narrowly targeted bitcasts, such as Indie 103.1, a Los Angeles alternative rock station, and allworship.com, a Christian station webcasting from Birmingham, Alabama. But the most dramatic evidence of the popularity of bitcasting exists in the success of the scores of **streaming** services that allow the simultaneous downloading and accessing of music.

The most successful streaming service, Pandora, is platform agnostic, available on virtually every new digital device, not only the obvious ones like smartphones, televisions, and car radios, but also the less obvious devices, for example WiFi-enabled refrigerators. Listeners, who collectively log more than 1.9 billion hours a month (Smith, 2016), can pay a small monthly fee to hear the service without commercials, but the vast majority of its 250 million subscribers (78 million active monthly users) tune in for free and hear demographic- and taste-specific commercials. Pandora accomplishes this ad specificity by coupling it with its Music Genome Project. After listeners tell Pandora what artists they like, the Genome Project, according to the company, "will quickly scan its entire world of analyzed music, almost a century of popular recordings—new and old, well known and completely obscure—to find songs with interesting musical similarities to your choice." Listeners can create up to 100 unique "stations," personally refining them even more if they wish, and at any time, they can purchase the tune they are hearing with a simple click.

With 50 million paying subscribers worldwide (100 million overall), Spotify came to the United States in 2011. Using a "freemium model," it offers listeners more than 30 million songs. They can listen for free, hearing commercials and living with limits on how much music they can stream, or they can pay a small monthly fee for premium limitless, commercial-free listening. Including other streaming services such as Slacker, Amazon Music Unlimited, Apple Music, Napster, Deezer, and Tidal, half of U.S. Internet users stream music, and this on-demand radio is the country's fastest-growing way to listen to music, as the number of individual songs streamed increased more than 76% from 2015 to 2016, to 251 billion (Friedman, 2017). You can see the shifts in how people consume recorded music in Figure 5.

Podcasts can also be streamed, but because they are posted online, they do not necessarily require streaming software. They can be downloaded, either on demand or automatically (typically by subscription), to any digital device that has an MP3 player, including PCs, laptops, and smartphones. There are tens of thousands of active podcasters online, and they cover every conceivable topic on which an individual or organization cares to comment, with Christian, Music, Comedy, TV/Film, and News/Politics being the most popular genres (Ault, 2015). And while podcasting was begun in earnest in 2004 by individual techies, audio bloggers, and DJ-wannabes, within a year they were joined by "professional" podcasters such as record companies, commercial and public radio stations, and big media companies like

ESPN, CNN, Bravo, and Disney. Listenership has also exploded as smartphones and Bluetooth-enabled cars have become ubiquitous and as more people have broadband Internet access. Fifty-seven million Americans listen to podcasts every month. They tend to be younger, loyal to their chosen podcast, and comfortable with advertising, ensuring the financial future of the form (Herrman, 2016).

Smartphones, Tablets, and Social Networking Sites

One of radio's distinguishing characteristics, as we've seen, is its portability. Smartphones and tablets reinforce that benefit. For example, more than half of all streaming music listening is mobile, and there are scores of free iPhone and Android music apps. Two-thirds of U.S. smartphone users stream music daily, averaging 45 minutes of listening (Hassan, 2016).

Much smartphone and tablet listening occurs via social networking sites; for example, you can link your Spotify and Pandora accounts to your Facebook account. But social networking sites actually play a much more important role in connecting fans to musical artists and their work. Artists themselves are using the Internet in general for their own production, promotion, and distribution, bypassing radio and the recording companies altogether. Musicians create their own sites and connect with sites designed specifically to feature new artists, such as purevolume.com, both allowing fans to hear (and in some cases, even download) new tunes for free; buy music downloads, CDs, and merchandise; get concert information and tickets; and chat with artists and other fans. They build their own YouTube channels to connect directly with listeners and use crowd-funding sites like Kickstarter to finance production and distribution of their art ($153 million for music projects since 2009; Johnson, 2015). On the world's largest social networking site, Facebook, musicians communicate directly with listeners on fan pages, create and manage their own profiles, offer music apps, and showcase performance events. They use Twitter to reach fans with news and other short notes of interest to keep them involved and encourage retweets to grow the size of their listening community. Instagram and Snapchat serve much the same function, but with the benefit of photos and video. On Periscope artists can create live audio and video content and broadcast it from their mobile devices anywhere, anytime. And like any other social networking site, Periscope connects fans with one another through sharing and live discussions. You may never have heard of the bands Hawthorne Heights, Pomplamoose, or Nicki Bluhm and the Gamblers, but using social networking and the Internet, they have created commercially and artistically meaningful careers. Big-name artists, too, have been gravitating to the Web for years. In 1999, Public Enemy released "There's a Poison Goin' On" exclusively online for the first four weeks of the album's release and was the first band to have music available for download. Thom Yorke also released his album "Tomorrow's Modern Boxes" online, as did U2 with "Songs of Innocence" and Beyoncé with her fifth solo album, "Beyoncé." Artists like Lady Gaga, Kanye West, and Jay Z have exclusive deals with digital stores like Amazon and iTunes. Adele's "Hello" had more than 2 billion YouTube views in its first two months of release.

▲ **Figure 5** Year-over-Year U.S. Music Consumption, by Format, 2015–2016.
Source: Richter, F., "The Rise of Music Streaming Continues," Statista, January 16, 2017.
©L. Mouton/PhotoAlto RF

Percentage of units
76.4% Audio streams
10.0% Vinyl album sales
7.5% Music video streams
−16.3% CD album sales
−20.1% Digital album sales
−25.0% Digital track sales

▶ Even the stars are bypassing the big labels. Kanye West and Jay Z have exclusive distribution deals with Amazon and iTunes. *©Jason Squires/WireImage/Getty Images*

The Internet and the Future of the Recording Industry

In the 1970s the basis of the recording industry changed from analog to **digital recording**. That is, sound went from being preserved as waves, whether physically on a disc or tape, to conversion into 1s and 0s logged in millisecond intervals in a computerized translation process. When replayed at the proper speed, the resulting sound was not only continuous but pristine—no hum, no hiss. The CD, or compact disc, was introduced in 1983 using digital coding on a 4.7-inch disc read by a laser beam. In 1986 "Brothers in Arms" by Dire Straits became the first million-selling CD. In 1988 the sale of CDs surpassed that of vinyl discs for the first time; by 1999 they accounted for 88% of industry revenues; today, CDs account for only 22% of that income (Friedlander, 2016; Perry, 2016).

Convergence with computers and the Internet offers other challenges and opportunities to the recording industry. The way the recording industry operates has been dramatically altered by the Internet. Traditionally, a record company signed an artist, produced the artist's music, and promoted the artist and music through a variety of outlets but primarily through the distribution of music to radio stations. Then listeners, learning about the artist and music through radio, went to a record store and bought the music. But this has changed. Music fans now have access to more music from a greater variety of artists than ever before. And while it is true that the top 1% of all bands and solo artists collects more than three-quarters of all the revenue from recorded music (Hunter-Tilney, 2016), more artists than ever are building profitable musical careers by finding new ways of interacting with their fans and the music industry, as you can read in the essay "The Future of the Music Business?"

The Internet music revolution began with the development of **MP3**, compression software that shrinks audio files to less than a tenth of their original size. Originally developed in 1987 in Germany, it began to take off in the early 1990s as more users began to hook up to the Internet with increasingly faster **modems**. This **open source software**, or freely downloaded software, permits users to download recorded music. Today, given the near-universal presence of computers, smartphones, and tablets, rare is the American—especially young American—who cannot access online music.

The crux of the digital problem for recording companies was that they sold music "in its physical form," whereas MP3 permitted music's distribution in a nonphysical form.

First discussed as "merely" a means of allowing independent bands and musicians to post their music online where it might attract a following, MP3 became a headache for the recording industry when music from the name artists they controlled began appearing on MP3 sites, making **piracy**, the illegal recording and sale of copyrighted material and high-quality recordings, a relatively simple task. Not only could users listen to their downloaded music from their hard drives, but they could make their own CDs from MP3 files and play those discs wherever and whenever they wished.

Rather than embrace MP3, the Recording Industry Association of America (RIAA), representing all of the United States's major labels, responded to the threat by developing their own "secure" Internet technology, but by the time it was available for release it was too late: MP3, driven by its availability and ease of use, had become the technology of choice for music fans already unhappy with the high cost of CDs and the necessity of paying for tracks they didn't want in order to get the ones they did. "The industry thought it was selling music," industry analyst James McQuivey explains. "It was really selling physical objects containing music—CDs—and it wasn't prepared for people buying fewer of them" (in Sommer, 2014, p. BU1). The CD is quickly going the way of the audio tape and 8-track cartridge. It has been replaced by the download. Downloading occurs in two forms: industry-approved and **P2P** (peer-to-peer).

CULTURAL FORUM
The Future of the Music Business?

The recording industry has seen a 25% decline in revenue in the last 10 years (Richter, 2016b); that is a fact. But how it, artists, and fans will shape the future of the music business is less certain. Legendary recording executive David Geffen explained, "The music business, as a whole, has lost its faith in content. Only 10 years ago, companies wanted to make records, presumably good records, and see if they sold. But panic has set in, and now it's no longer about making music, it's all about how to sell music. And there's no clear answer about how to fix that problem." Columbia Records head Rick Rubin added, "Fear is making the record companies less arrogant. They're more open to ideas" (both in Hirschberg, 2007, pp. 28–29). There is, in fact, no shortage of ideas, and they are being debated in the cultural forum.

Talking Heads leader David Byrne wrote, "What is called the music business today is not the business of producing music. At some point it became the business of selling CDs in plastic cases, and that business will soon be over. But that's not bad news for music, and it's certainly not bad news for musicians" (2008, p. 126). He detailed six ideas for reshaping the relationship between the recording industry, musical artists, and fans:

1. *The 360 deal* (sometimes called an equity or multiple rights deal) renders artists brands. Every aspect of their careers—recording, merchandising, marketing, touring—is handled by the label. Because artists and their music are "owned" by the label, that company, freed from the tyranny of the hit CD, will ostensibly take a long-term perspective in its artists' careers. The Pussycat Dolls have a 360 deal with Interscope Records. Madonna left Warner after 25 years with that label to sign a $120 million 360 deal with concert promoter Live Nation.

2. *The standard distribution deal* is how the music business operated for decades. The label pays for the recording, manufacturing, distribution, and promotion of its artists' music. The label owns the copyright to the music, and artists earn their percentage of profits only after all the recording, manufacturing, distribution, and promotion costs have been recouped by the label.

3. *The license deal* is the same as a standard distribution arrangement except that artists retain the copyright to their music and ownership of the master recordings, granting the rights to both to a label for a specified period of time, usually seven years. After that, artists are free to do with their music what they wish. Canadian rockers Arcade Fire have such an arrangement with indie label Merge Records.

4. *The profit-sharing deal* calls for a minimal advance from a label, and as such, it agrees to split all profits with the artist before deducting its costs. Artists maintain ownership of the music, but because the label invests less in them than it might otherwise, they may sell fewer records. Both sides benefit, however.

(Continued)

The label takes a smaller risk; the artist receives a greater share of the income. Byrne's Talking Heads has a profit-sharing arrangement with label Thrill Jockey for its album *Lead Us Not into Temptation.*

5. *A manufacturing and distribution deal* requires artists to undertake every aspect of the process except manufacturing and distribution. They retain ownership and rights to their music but assume all other costs, for example, recording, marketing, and touring. Big labels avoid these deals because there is little profit in it for them. Smaller labels benefit from association with well-known artists, such as Aimee Mann, and artists have the benefit of artistic freedom and greater income (although they take on greater risk).

6. *The self-distribution model* grants artists the greatest freedom. They play, produce, market, promote, and distribute the music themselves. Byrne calls this "freedom without resources—a pretty abstract sort of independence" (2008, p. 129), but many artists big and small, aided by the Internet, have opted for this model. Musicians are using their own sites, social networking sites, and sites designed specifically to feature new artists to connect directly with listeners. Fans can hear and buy music and merchandise, check concert schedules and buy tickets, and chat with artists and other fans. Bouquet is one of the thousands of musical artists using the Internet to self-distribute and connect with fans, and today there are 45% more people self-identifying as "self-employed musician" than there were in 2001 (Johnson, 2015).

Enter your voice. After all, the success of any or all of these different ideas depends on your willingness to buy the music that they produce. Which of these models do you think will dominate music's future, if any? The first, a 360 deal, gives musicians the least artistic freedom but the greatest guarantee of success. The last, self-distribution, grants the greatest freedom but the smallest guarantee of success. Which of the six options would you choose? Why? Might different models work better for different kinds of acts or for artists at different levels of notoriety? In which form would you be most comfortable buying your favorite music? If it were up to you, what would you pay for a download of your favorite artist's latest release? Why? Byrne thinks the upheaval in the music business is "not bad news for music, and it's certainly not bad news for musicians." Do you agree? Will independence from the big labels and their demand for profitable hits free artists to make the music they want? Will there be more or less music of interest to you?

Industry-Approved Downloading

▲ The now-retired iPod, Apple's answer to piracy: cheap, permanent, go-anywhere downloads.
©Realimage/Alamy

Illegal file sharing proved the popularity of downloading music from the Internet. So the four major labels combined to offer "approved" music download sites. None did well. They offered downloads by subscription, that is, a certain number of downloads per month for a set fee. In addition, they placed encrypted messages in the tunes that limited how long the song would be playable and where the download could be used and copied. As a result, illegal file sharing continued. But it was Apple's 2003 introduction of its iPod and iTunes Music Store that suggested a better strategy. Yes, Apple ceased production of the iPod in 2014, largely because of the ubiquity of other mobile music devices, but it taught fans that they could simply buy and own albums and individual songs for as little as 99 cents. Apple controlled only 5% of the PC market, yet it sold over a million tunes in its first week of operation, signaling the inevitability of the cyber revolution. Still, the major labels insisted that their music be downloaded with copy protection built in. But when Sony became the last of the major labels to relent, announcing in 2008 that it would allow the sale of much of its catalog free of copy protection, the distribution and sale of music by Internet became standard, aided by the 2009 announcement from the world's leading music retailer, iTunes, that it would sell downloads from its 10-million-title catalog without antipiracy restrictions. There are now hundreds of legally licensed sites selling tens of millions of different music tracks. Digital music sales surpassed physical sales for the first time in 2011, and the CD's 9% share of sales is a far cry from its dominance of 60% to 70% of all sales just a few years ago. In fact, downloads now account for 34% of the U.S. music industry's recording revenues. And as you read earlier, streaming services like Slacker, Amazon

Music Unlimited, Apple Music, Spotify, and Pandora offer an additional means of access to digital music beyond downloading. These free and subscription sites now account for 34.4% of the industry's revenue (Friedlander, 2016). Not coincidentally, the number of brick-and-mortar record stores in America has been halved since 2003, their function—that which hasn't been displaced by the Internet—taken over by retail giants like Walmart and Target that account for a majority of all physical music retail sales. But even they are stocking fewer CDs, and Starbucks, in 2015, went as far as to stop selling discs altogether.

P2P Downloading

Despite the availability of industry-approved music downloads, illegal downloading still occurs. The 53 million U.S. Internet users who admit to piracy annually download as much as $20 billion worth of digitally pirated recorded music (Resnikoff, 2016). Sites such as Gnutella and Freenet use P2P technologies, that is, peer-to-peer software that permits direct Internet-based communication or collaboration between two or more personal computers while bypassing centralized servers. P2P allows users to visit a constantly and infinitely changing network of machines through which file sharing can occur. The record companies (and movie studios) challenged P2P by suing the makers of its software. In 2005, the Supreme Court, in *MGM v. Grokster*, unanimously supported industry arguments that P2P software, because it "encouraged" copyright infringement, rendered its makers liable for that illegal act. The industry's next challenge, then, is **BitTorrent**, file-sharing software that allows anonymous users to create "swarms" of data as they simultaneously download and upload "bits" of a given piece of content from countless untraceable servers. And while these P2P sharing sites account for the large majority of music theft, their share, once as high as 99%, is being eroded by another form of piracy, **stream ripping**—saving streamed media to a file on a personal device to be accessed locally—from sites like YouTube and music streaming sites. Half of 16- to 24-year-olds admit to regularly stream ripping (Garrahan, 2016).

No matter what model of music production and distribution eventually results from this technological and financial tumult, serious questions about the Internet's impact on **copyright** (protecting content creators' financial interest in their product) will remain. See the chapter on media freedom, regulation, and ethics for more on copyright.

DEVELOPING MEDIA LITERACY SKILLS
You Are What You Listen To

There is scientific evidence that the music you listen to is a reflection of who you are. Psychologist Adrian North's research shows that jazz fans generally have high self-esteem and are creative, outgoing, and at ease; classical music fans have high self-esteem, are creative, introverted, and at ease; rap fans have high self-esteem and are outgoing; rock and heavy metal fans often have low self-esteem, are creative, not hard-working, not outgoing, gentle, and at ease; and pop music fans have high self-esteem, are hardworking, outgoing, and gentle but are not creative and not at ease. As Professor North explains, "People do actually define themselves through music and relate to other people through it" (in Collingwood, 2016). But what if you are choosing your music not because it reflects who you are, but because it's all you know? Keeping in mind that an important element of media literacy is an understanding that media content is a text that provides insight into culture and our lives, you might have a difficult time disputing influential French sociologist Pierre Bourdieu's argument that "nothing more clearly affirms one's 'class,' nothing more infallibly classifies, than tastes in music" (1979, p. 18). And how would you answer novelist Nick Hornby's question, " If you own all the music ever recorded in the entire history of the world [because of streaming], then who are you?" (in Thompson, 2016, p. 35).

So why do you listen to the music you do? At a time when almost every song ever recorded is equally accessible, are you making a personally meaningful decision on your choices of this particular form of media content? Maybe not. This is the age of *music by algorithms*, writes popular culture critic Scott Timberg, "Algorithms—whether driving your streaming playlists, your Amazon recommendations, or suggestions on iTunes—are about driving you closer and closer to what you already know. And instead of taking you toward what you want to listen to, they direct you toward slight variations of what you're already consuming" (2016b). So how will you ever find that new sound, the one that reflects the true or maybe evolving you? It's not easy. Because of downloads and streaming, songs, rather than albums, are the new musical currency. You may have bought Adele's album "25" because you liked *Hello*, but you would also have been introduced to other forms of musical expression, up-beat versus ballad, for example. You might have gone into a music store and serendipitously discovered new music because a knowledgeable clerk turned you on to it, or you heard something interesting over the store's speakers, or you happened upon a CD filed next to the one you were originally looking for. You might have tuned in to an independent radio station (now rare) or read a newspaper's coverage of the local music scene (even rarer). Pandora has its Genome Project; Google Play

matches data points with your location to give you what it thinks you want to hear given where you are and its prediction of what you are doing; and Spotify boasts of employing a trillion data points from 35 million songs and 2.5 million artists to help it tell you what you want to listen to (Hunter-Tilney, 2016). That may be great if that's all you want—more of what the data points say you want—but is that what music is supposed to be? If you are what you listen to, are you content with Spotify's data-driven version of you? Remember the lesson from this chapter's discussion of race and rock 'n' roll—music can be a powerful force of community and social change. But if music is just another well-researched, technology-delivered commodity, how does it become important to and for you?

Media-literate music fans understand that they don't know what they don't know. If you've never heard klezmer, how do you know you don't like it? You might "hate" jazz, but does that mean Kenny G, Arturo Sandoval, Miles Davis, Duke Ellington, or Diana Krall? How can you say you dislike jazz, or country, pop, or classical, if you've never exposed yourself to its many forms? Media literacy means making personally meaningful use of media content. Relying on a distant algorithm's trillions of pieces of data to dictate that use diminishes not only music's social and cultural function but music's entertainment value as well. So, what will you listen to next?

▲ John Cusack and Jack Black in *High Fidelity* (2000) remind us that knowledgeable music store personnel were once the inspiration for finding new music.
©United Archives GmbH/Alamy

MEDIA LITERACY CHALLENGE
Finding New Music

Here are a few musical forms that you might be unfamiliar with: Americana, bluegrass, gospel, neo-classical, alternative country, electronic, ambient, chillwave, techno, Latin rap, indie electronic, Afro beat, bebop, post-punk, and ska. There are literally hundreds more, as a quick Internet search will demonstrate. Challenge yourself to find a genre you've never listened to before and explore it—listen not to just one tune, but five. Now discuss with a friend or your class what you heard. Did you like it? Why or why not? Were you inspired to further investigate this form or another form of music? Why or why not? Now do a little experiment. Find these tunes on Spotify, Pandora, or another streaming site. Listen to five or more in a given genre. Leave that site for a while and then go back. Does the site "recognize" the new musical you? If so, who does it think you are? You're media literate, so you know that music *provides context and insight into who you are*. Having these *heightened expectations of music*, will you continue to experiment with new forms? Why or why not?

Resources for Review and Discussion

REVIEW POINTS: TYING CONTENT TO LEARNING OUTCOMES

▶ **Outline the history and development of the radio and sound recording industries and radio and sound recording themselves as media.**

☐ Guglielmo Marconi's radio allowed long-distance wireless communication; Reginald Fessenden's liquid barretter made possible the transmission of voices; Lee DeForest's audion tube permitted the reliable transmission of voices and music broadcasting.

☐ Thomas Edison possibly developed the first sound-recording device, a fact now in debate; Emile Berliner's gramophone improved on it as it permitted multiple copies to be made from a master recording.

▶ **Describe the importance of early financing and regulatory decisions regarding radio and how they have shaped the nature of contemporary broadcasting.**

☐ The Radio Acts of 1910, 1912, and 1927 and the Communications Act of 1934 eventually resulted in the FCC and the trustee model of broadcast regulation.

☐ Advertising and the network structure of broadcasting came to radio in the 1920s, producing the medium's golden age, one drawn to a close by the coming of television.

▶ **Explain how the organizational and economic natures of the contemporary radio and sound recording industries shape the content of both media.**

☐ Radio stations are classified as commercial and noncommercial, AM and FM.

☐ Radio is local, fragmented, specialized, personal, and mobile.

☐ Deregulation has allowed concentration of ownership of radio into the hands of a relatively small number of companies.

☐ Three major recording companies control 89% of the world's recorded music market.

▶ **Identify new and converging radio and recording technologies and their potential impact on music, the industries themselves, and listeners.**

☐ Convergence has come to radio in the form of satellite and cable delivery of radio, terrestrial digital radio, Web radio, podcasting, and music streaming from a number of different types of sites.

☐ Digital technology, in the form of Internet creation, promotion, and distribution of music, legal and illegal downloading from the Internet, and mobile phone downloading, promises to reshape the nature of the recording industry.

☐ Personal technologies such as smartphones and tablets reinforce radio's mobility and expand its audience.

▶ **Apply key radio-listening media literacy skills, especially in assessing the benefits and drawbacks of algorithm-based music consumption.**

☐ Streaming services offer you what they think you want to hear based on mountains of data about your listening habits and the music you favor. But how do you find new, interesting, or different music? What becomes of music as a personally and culturally important medium when it is data-driven?

KEY TERMS

liquid barretter, 153

audion tube, 153

trustee model, 156

spectrum scarcity, 156

networks, 156

affiliates, 156

O&O, 157

low power FM (LPFM), 159

format, 160

secondary services, 160

playlist, 160

billings, 162

ratings, 162

deregulation, 162

duopoly, 162

cover, 163

mathematical songwriting, 165

catalog albums, 165

syndication, 167

digital audio radio service (DARS), 167

terrestrial digital radio, 167

in-band-on-channel (IBOC), 167

Web radio, 168

podcasting, 168

bitcasters, 168

streaming, 168

digital recording, 170

MP3, 170

modem, 170

open source software, 170

piracy, 171

P2P, 171

BitTorrent, 173

stream ripping, 173

copyright, 173

QUESTIONS FOR REVIEW

1. What were the contributions made to radio by Guglielmo Marconi, Nikola Tesla, Reginald Fessenden, and Lee DeForest?

2. How do the Radio Acts of 1910, 1912, and 1927 relate to the Communications Act of 1934?

3. What were the five defining characteristics of the American broadcasting system just before it entered the golden age of radio?

4. How did World War II and the introduction of television change radio and recorded music?

5. What does it mean to say that radio is local, fragmented, specialized, personal, and mobile?

6. What are catalog albums?

7. How have cable and satellite affected the radio and recording industries? Computers and digitization?

8. Is the size of radio's audience in ascendance or in decline? Why?

9. What is streaming audio?

10. What is P2P technology? Stream ripping?

To maximize your study time, check out CONNECT to access the SmartBook study module for this chapter, watch videos, and explore other resources.

QUESTIONS FOR CRITICAL THINKING AND DISCUSSION

1. Have you ever illegally downloaded music? If you have never done so, what keeps you from engaging in the quite common practice? If you have, do you consider it stealing? If you don't see it as stealing, why not? But if you do consider it theft, how do you justify your action?

2. What do you think of the argument that control of the recording industry by a few multinational conglomerates inevitably leads to cultural homogenization and the ascendance of profit over music?

3. How much regulation do you believe is necessary in U.S. broadcasting? If the airwaves belong to the people, how can we best ensure that license holders perform their public service functions?

REFERENCES

1. Adams, M. (1996). The race for radiotelephone: 1900–1920. *AWA Review, 10*, 78–119.

2. Ault, S. (2016, May 3). Drive toward digital. *Variety*, p. 14.

3. Ault, S. (2015, September 15). Rise of the pod people. *Variety*, p. 31.

4. Barker, A. (2014, March 18). Turning kitsch into classics. *Variety*, p. 40.

5. Barnouw, E. (1966). *A tower in Babel: A history of broadcasting in the United States to 1933*. New York: Oxford University Press.

6. Bittner, J. R. (1994). *Law and regulation of electronic media*. Englewood Cliffs, NJ: Prentice Hall.

7. Bourdieu, P. (1979). *Distinctions: A social critique of the judgment of taste*. Cambridge, MA: Harvard University Press.

8. Byrne, D. (2008, January). The fall and rise of music. *Wired*, pp. 124–129.

9. Collingwood, J. (2016, December 14). Preferred music style is tied to personality. *Psych Central*. Online: http://psychcentral.com/lib/preferred-music-style-is-tied-to-personality/

10. Copps, M. J. (2011, June 9). Statement of Commissioner Michael J. Copps on release of FCC staff report "The Technology and Information Needs of Communities." *Federal Communications Commission*. Online: https://www.fcc.gov/document/commissioner-copps-statement-release-staff-report

11. "Edison not 'the father of sound'?" (2008, March 28). *Providence Journal*, p. A5.

12. Editors of Media Life. (2015, September 17). Radio's big problem: Big radio. *Media Life*. Online: http://www.medialifemagazine.com/radios-big-problem-big-radio/

13. Federal Communications Commission. (2016, October 19). Broadcast station totals as of September 30, 2016. Online: https://apps.fcc.gov/edocs_public/attachmatch/DOC-341807A1.pdf

14. Friedlander, J. P. (2016). News and notes on 2015 RIAA music industry shipment and revenue statistics. *Recording Industry of America*. Online: http://www.riaa.com/wp-content/uploads/2016/03/RIAA-2015-Year-End-shipments-memo.pdf

15. Friedman, W. (2017, January 6). Music streaming doubles in 2016, song sales dive. *MediaPost*. Online: http://www.mediapost.com/publications/article/292374/music-streaming-doubles-in-2016-song-sales-dive.html

16. Garrahan, M. (2016, September 12). Music industry faces "stream ripping" piracy threat. *Financial Times*. Online: https://www.ft.com/content/d31ff954-793a-11e6-a0c6-39e2633162d5

17. Hassan, C. (2016, March 11). 68% of smartphone owners stream music daily, study finds. *Digital Music News*. Online: http://www.digitalmusicnews.com/2016/03/11/parks-associates-68-of-u-s-smartphone-owners-listen-to-streaming-music-daily/

18. Herrman, J. (2016, May 8). The Apple podcast problem. *The New York Times*, pp. BU1, BU7.

19. Hirschberg, L. (2007, September 2). The music man. *The New York Times Magazine*, pp. 28–33, 46–49.

20. Hunter-Tilney, L. (2016, June 10). Music in the age of the algorithm. *Financial Times*. Online: https://www.ft.com/content/fc9db5d6-2cc9-11e6-bf8d-26294ad519fc

21. Johnson, S. (2015, August 23). The creative apocalypse that wasn't. *The New York Times Magazine*, pp. 29–49, 51.

22. Knopper, S. (2011, November 24). Rock radio takes another hit. *Rolling Stone,* p. 19.

23. Lansky, S. (2015/2016, December 28–January 4). Adele is music's past, present, and future. *Time*, pp. 120–126.

24. Lefsetz, B. (2015, January 28). True art must be about the band, not the brand. *Variety*, p. 26.

25. Lefsetz, B. (2013, June 21). Radio digs its own grave as cultural currents shift. *Variety*, p. 30.

26. "Market share of record companies in the United States from 2011 to 2015, by label ownership." (2016) *Statista*. Online: https://www.statista.com/statistics/317632/market-share-record-companies-label-ownership-usa/

27. Menard, L. (2015, November 16). The elvic oracle. *The New Yorker*, pp. 80–88.

28. Owen, L. H. (2016, April 18). Left on the dial: With young people trading AM/FM for streaming, will radio find a home in your next car? *Nieman Lab*. Online: http://www.niemanlab.org/2016/04/left-on-the-dial-with-young-people-trading-amfm-for-streaming-will-radio-find-a-home-in-your-next-car/

29. Perry, M. J. (2016, September 15). Recorded music sales by format from 1973–2015, and what that might tell us about the limitations of GDP accounting. *AE Ideas*. Online: https://www.aei.org/publication/annual-recorded-music-sales-by-format-from-1973-2015-and-what-that-tells-us-about-the-limitations-of-gdp-accounting/

30. Radio Station World. (2017). What is a radio format? Online: http://radiostationworld.com/directory/Radio_Formats/

31. Resnikoff, P. (2016, May 5). How music piracy is completely changing in 2016. *Digital Music News*. Online: http://www.digitalmusicnews.com/2016/05/05/what-music-piracy-really-looks-like/

32. Richter, F. (2017, January 16). The rise of music streaming continues. *Statista*. Online: https://www.statista.com/chart/7604/music-consumption-in-the-united-states/?utm_source=Infographic+Newsletter&utm_campaign=583c9a666d-InfographicTicker_EN_Late_00024&utm_medium=email&utm_term=0_666fe64c5d-583c9a666d-295452301

33. Richter, F. (2016a, September 15). The world's largest music streaming service? *Statista*. Online: https://www.statista.com/chart/5866/online-music-listening-platforms/

34. Richter, F. (2016b, April 22). Rise of digital music stops the industry's decline. *Statista*. Online: https://www.statista.com/chart/4713/global-recorded-music-industry-revenues/

35. Sass, E. (2015, February 20). Radio slipped in 2014, digital growth slowed. *MediaPost*. Online: http://www.mediapost.com/publications/article/244222/radio-slipped-in-2014-digital-growth-slowed.html

36. Singleton, M. (2016, January 22). Old albums outsold new releases for the first time ever. *The Verge*. Online: http://www.theverge.com/2016/1/22/10816404/2015-album-sales-trends-vinyl-catalog-streaming

37. Smith, C. (2016, October 6). By the numbers: 72 interesting Pandora statistics. *DMR Stats*. Online: http://expandedramblings.com/index.php/pandora-statistics/

38. Sokoloct, B. (2016, October 15). Short range, deep reach. *The New York Times*, p. B1.

39. Sommer, J. (2014, May 18). The harmony they want to hear. *The New York Times*, p. BU3.

40. Sterling, C. H., & Kitross, J. M. (1990). *Stay tuned: A concise history of American broadcasting*. Belmont, CA: Wadsworth.

41. Szatmary, D. P. (2000). *Rockin' in time: A social history of rock-and-roll* (4th ed.). Upper Saddle River, NJ: Prentice-Hall.

42. Thompson, C. (2016, January/February). Rocking the house. *Smithsonian*, pp. 35–41.

43. Tillinghast, C. H. (2000). *American broadcast regulation and the First Amendment: Another look*. Ames: Iowa State University Press.

44. Timberg, S. (2016a, June 30). The revenge of the monoculture: The Internet gave us more choices, but the mainstream won anyway. *Salon*. Online: http://www.salon.com/2016/07/30/the_revenge_of_monoculture_the_internet_gave_us_more_choices_but_the_mainstream_won_anyway/

45. Timberg, S. (2016b, June 10). Spotify is making you boring: When algorithms shape music taste, human curiosity loses. *Salon*. Online: http://www.salon.com/2016/06/10/spotify_is_making_you_boring_when_algorithms_shape_music_taste_human_curiosity_loses/

46. Timberg, S. (2015a, May 28). Pop music's biggest sellout: How many brands paid for product placement in your favorite songs. *Salon*. Online: http://www.salon.com/2015/05/28/pop_musics_biggest_sellout_how_many_brands_paid_for_product_placement_in_your_favorite_songs/

47. Timberg, S. (2015b, May 6). Radio is killing the guitar solo—and we'll lose more than our air-guitar skills when it's gone. *Salon*. Online: http://www.salon.com/2015/05/06/radio_is_killing_the_guitar_solo_%E2%80%94%C2%A0and_well_lose_more_than_our_air_guitar_skills_when_its_gone/

48. Ward, E., Stokes, G., & Tucker, K. (1986). *Rock of Ages: The Rolling Stone history of rock & roll*. New York: Rolling Stone Press.

49. Washenko, A. (2016, February 19). Nielsen finds radio reach holds steady in Q3 2015. *RAIN News*. Online: http://rainnews.com/nielsen-finds-radio-reach-holds-steady-in-q3-2015/

Cultural Forum Blue Column icon, Media Literacy Red Torch Icon, Using Media Green Gear icon, Developing Media book in starburst icon: ©McGraw-Hill Education

Television, Cable, and Mobile Video

8

◄ Amazon's *Transparent*. Innovative and challenging streamed and cable programming helps improve the quality of all television.

©Amazon Studios/Photofest

Learning Objectives

No one is neutral about television. We either love it or hate it. Many of us do both. This is because it is our most ubiquitous and socially and culturally powerful mass medium. Several recent and converging technologies promise to make it even more so. After studying this chapter, you should be able to

▶ Outline the history and development of the television and cable television industries and television itself as a medium.

▶ Describe how the organizational and economic nature of the contemporary television and cable industries shapes the content of television.

▶ Explain the relationship between television in all its forms and its viewers.

▶ Identify new and converging video technologies and their potential impact on the television industry and its audience.

▶ Describe the digital and mobile television revolution.

▶ Apply key television-viewing media literacy skills to satirical news.

1884 ▶ Nipkow invents his disc

1900

1923 ▶ Zworykin demonstrates electronic iconoscope tube

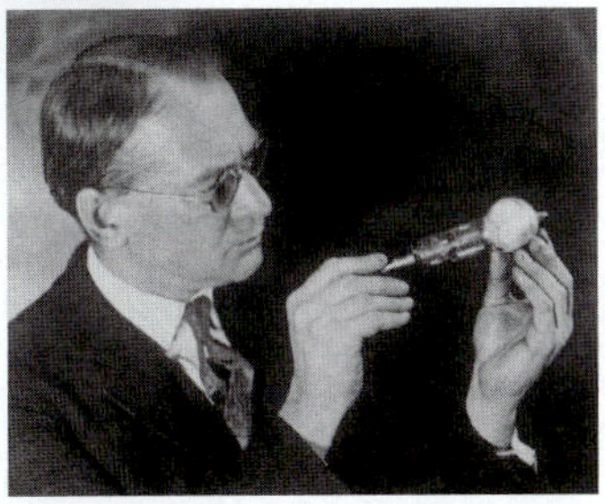

©Bettmann/Getty Images

©Bettmann/Getty Images

1925

1927 Farnsworth demonstrates electronically scanned television images

1928 ▶ Baird transmits mechanical video image across Atlantic

1939 Sarnoff introduces regular television broadcasting at World's Fair

1941 First two commercial stations approved

©Ingram Publishing RF

1950

1950 *Red Channels*; Nielsen ratings

1951 U.S. wired coast-to-coast; ▶ *I Love Lucy*

1954 Army–McCarthy Hearings telecast

1959 Quiz show scandal

1962 All-channel legislation

1963 FCC begins regulation of cable

1975

1975 HBO begins national distribution

1976 VCR introduced

1996 DVD introduced; Telecommunications Act

1998 First digital TV broadcast

1999 ▶ DVR introduced

(TV): ©Interfoto/Alamy;
(image on the screen):
©CBS/Photofest

2000

2002 FCC mandates digital receivers by 2007

2005 Networks begin selling program downloads

2009 All TV stations are digital

2010 *Comcast v. FCC;* Hulu premieres first original show; Mobile digital television

2011 ▶ Netflix, Hulu, and YouTube begin original programming

2012 Online movie transactions exceed discs

2015 HBO, Nickelodeon, and others begin OTT streaming

2016 *Sesame Street* moves to HBO; VCR declared dead; video streaming revenues exceed DVD revenues for first time; House of Representatives protest broadcast by apps

2017 Nielsen's Total Content Ratings

©Handout/KRT/Newscom

©McGraw-Hill Education/
Mark Dierker, photographer

"WHAT'S WITH THE CAMERA AND LIGHTS? YOUR PHONE'S NOT GOOD ENOUGH FOR MAKING VIDEOS ANYMORE?"

"Not for what I'm doing. I'm going to be a TV star."

"A TV star?"

"Well, first a YouTube star, then a TV star, and maybe then the movies, like Roman Atwood."

"Who?"

"Roman Atwood. He has more than 10 million subscribers to his YouTube pranks channel and 11 million subscribers to his vlog YouTube channel."

"Wait, is this the guy who tricked his girlfriend into thinking that one of their kids was killed in an accident? That's some prank."

"For real. It got him a movie deal from Lionsgate. His movie, *Natural Born Pranksters*, was number 2 on the 2016 iTunes movie chart, right behind the *Star Wars* movie. And I bet you never heard of PewDiePie either. He has nearly 40 million subscribers to his YouTube video game channels and makes about $7 million a year. Tyler Oakley? Eight million subscribers; he went from YouTube to *The Amazing Race*. Have you heard of Andrea Russett? She's an actress whose YouTube videos earned her more than 2.5 million subscribers and a role in the movie *Mike and Dave Need Wedding Dates* (all in "10 Standout," 2016). I'm using YouTube's Creator Hub to help me get started and make my mark. YouTube even has YouTube Spaces where people like me can go to produce their shows and maybe even get funding for good ideas. Then they help you get bigger. They have an originals division that connects its stars with big-time movie and TV producers."

"OK. So what are you going to do for your show? I imagine those folks who made it had some talent, right?"

"I haven't figured that out yet. But I have a camera and lights. Action's sure to follow!"

Whether or not our aspiring star will ever benefit from it, there is indeed quite a bit of action surrounding contemporary television and video. In the last few years, Netflix outbid established video giants HBO and AMC for *House of Cards*, originally ordering two seasons for over $100 million. YouTube committed $100 million to commission original programming designed exclusively for some two dozen new channels. Online retailer Amazon commissions program pilots, offers them free to viewers who vote on which should be turned into full series, and then produces the winners for its Amazon Prime subscribers. Its show *Transparent* won a Golden Globe for Best TV series in 2015, and its star, Jeffrey Tambor, won Best Actor, both firsts for streaming television. Hulu Plus streams original shows like *Casual* and *The Handmaid's Tale*. Viewers have enthusiastically taken to this new form of television—half of all U.S. households now subscribe to at least one of these services (Richter, 2016), and the top four television series among 18- to 24-year-olds in 2016 were all from Netflix (Ault, 2016). The "new" television also offers a great deal of creative freedom to those who produce its content. "It's much harder to bring innovation to network television because network television works as a strong corporate entity where change is maybe not as easily applied," explains *House of Cards* cinematographer Igor Martinovic. Streaming companies are "willing to experiment; they're willing to take chances" (in Khatchatourian, 2014, p. 79).

Yes, television is changing, and this chapter details that change, from early experiments with mechanical scanning to the electronic marvel that sits in our homes to the mobile screens we carry in our pockets. We trace the rapid transformation of television into a mature medium after World War II and examine how the medium, the entire television industry in fact, was altered by the emergence and success of cable television. And significant change is once again remaking what we currently know as television . . . and what we once knew as the audience. All of us are now TV executives, choosing *our* programs and *our* schedules, no longer limited by what some distant network television executives think is the schedule that best serves their advertisers' needs.

▼ Netflix's *House of Cards*. Free from network television's commercial restrictions, producers of streamed content can take creative chances.
©Photos 12/Alamy

The remarkable reach of television—in all its forms—accounts for its attractiveness as an advertising medium. We discuss this reach, and we explore the structure, programming, and economics of the television and cable industries. We consider new technologies, their convergence with television, and how they promise to change the interaction between the medium and its audiences. Finally, we discuss media literacy in terms of the role of satirical television news in the cultural forum.

A Short History of Television

Television has changed the way teachers teach, governments govern, and religious leaders preach, and shaped how we organize the furniture in our homes. Television has changed the nature, operation, and relationship to their audiences of books, magazines, movies, and radio. Television even shapes how we think of the Internet. Will the promise of the Web be drowned in a sea of commercials? Can online news services deliver faster, better, and more accurate information than television? Even the computer screens we use look like television screens; we participate in online video conferencing, play new and improved online video games, and of course, stream hours and hours of video. Before we delve deeper into the nature of this powerful medium and its relationship with its audience, let's examine how television developed as it did.

Mechanical and Electronic Scanning

In 1884 Paul Nipkow, a Russian scientist living in Berlin, developed the first workable device for generating electrical signals suitable for the transmission of a scene that people could see. His **Nipkow disc** consisted of a rotating scanning disc spinning in front of a photoelectric cell. It produced 4,000 **pixels** (picture dots) per second, producing a picture composed of 18 parallel lines. Although his mechanical system proved too limiting, Nipkow demonstrated the possibility of using a scanning system to divide a scene into an orderly pattern of transmittable picture elements that could be recomposed as a visual image. British inventor John Logie Baird was able to transmit moving images using a mechanical

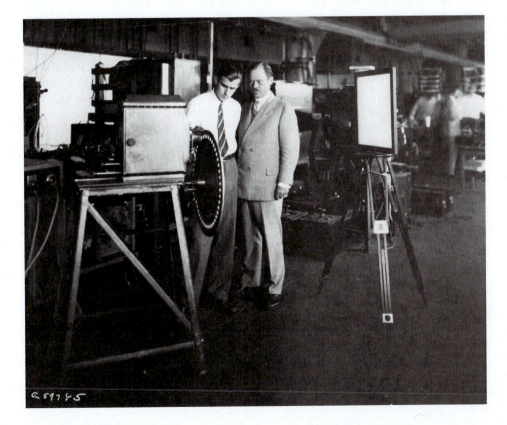

◀ A Nipkow disc.
©*Bettmann/Getty Images*

▶ Philo Farnsworth and Vladimir Zworykin, pioneers in the development of television.
(left, right): ©Bettmann/Getty Images

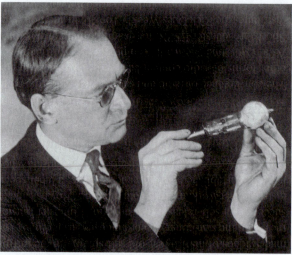

disc as early as 1925, and in 1928 he successfully sent a television picture from London to Hartsdale, New York.

Electronic scanning came either from another Russian or from a U.S. farm boy; historians disagree. Vladimir Zworykin, a Russian immigrant living near Pittsburgh and working for Westinghouse, demonstrated his **iconoscope tube**, the first practical television camera tube, in 1923. In 1929 David Sarnoff lured him to RCA to head its electronics research lab, and it was there that Zworykin developed the **kinescope**, an improved picture tube. At the same time, young Philo Farnsworth had moved from Idaho to San Francisco to perfect an electronic television system, the design for which he had shown his high school science teacher when he was 15 years old. In 1927, at the age of 20, he made his first public demonstration—film clips of a prize fight, movie scenes, and other graphic images. The "Boy Wonder" and Zworykin's RCA spent the next decade fighting fierce patent battles in court. In 1939 RCA capitulated, agreeing to pay Farnsworth royalties for the use of his patents.

In April of that year, at the World's Fair in New York, RCA made the first true public demonstration of television in the form of regularly scheduled two-hour NBC broadcasts. These black-and-white telecasts consisted of cooking demonstrations, singers, jugglers, comedians, puppets—just about anything that could fit in a hot, brightly lit studio and demonstrate motion. People could buy television sets at the RCA Pavilion at prices ranging from $200 for the 5-inch screen to $600 for the deluxe 12-inch-screen model. The FCC granted construction permits to the first two commercial stations in 1941, and then World War II intervened. But as was the case with radio during World War I, technical development and improvement of the new medium continued.

The 1950s

In 1952, 108 stations were broadcasting to 17 million television homes. By the end of the decade, there were 559 stations, and nearly 90% of U.S. households had televisions. In the 1950s more television sets were sold in the United States (70 million) than there were children born (40.5 million) (Kuralt, 1977). The technical standards were fixed, stations proliferated and flourished, the public tuned in, and advertisers were enthusiastic. The content and character of the medium were set in this decade as well:

- Carried over from the radio networks, television genres included variety shows, situation comedies, dramas (including Westerns and cop shows), soap operas, and quiz shows.
- Two new formats appeared: feature films and talk shows. Talk shows were instrumental in introducing radio personalities to the television audience, which could see its favorites for the first time.
- Television news and documentary remade broadcast journalism as a powerful force in its own right, led by CBS's Edward R. Murrow (*See It Now*, 1951) and NBC's David

Brinkley and Chet Huntley. Huntley and Brinkley's 1956 coverage of the major political conventions gave audiences an early glimpse of the power of television to cover news and history in the making.

- AT&T completed its national **coaxial cable** and **microwave relay** network for the distribution of television programming in the summer of 1951. The entire United States was now within the reach of the major television networks, and they came to dominate the medium.

Four other events from the 1950s would permanently shape how television operated: the quiz show scandal, the appearance of *I Love Lucy*, McCarthyism, and the establishment of the ratings system. Another, in 1948, would permanently *reshape* the television industry. That development, as you'll soon see, was cable television.

THE QUIZ SHOW SCANDAL AND CHANGES IN SPONSORSHIP Throughout the 1950s the networks served primarily as time brokers, offering airtime and distribution (their affiliates) and accepting payment for access to both. Except for their own news and sports coverage, the networks relied on outside agencies to provide programs. An advertising agency, for example, would hire a production company to produce a program for its client. That client would then be the show's sponsor—*The Kraft Television Theatre* and *Westinghouse Studio One* are two examples. The agency would then pay a network to air the program over its national collection of stations. This system had enriched the networks during the heyday of radio, and they saw no reason to change.

But in 1959 a quiz show scandal (enveloping independently produced, single-advertiser-sponsored programs) changed the way the networks did business. When it was discovered that popular shows like *The $64,000 Question* had been fixed by advertisers and producers to ensure desired outcomes, the networks, mindful of their reputations, were determined to take control of their schedules. They, themselves, began commissioning or buying the entertainment fare that filled their broadcast days and nights. Now, rather than selling blocks of time to ad agencies and sponsors, the networks paid for the content they aired through **spot commercial sales** (selling individual 60-second spots on a given program to a wide variety of advertisers).

As a result, the content of television was altered. Some critics argue that this change to spot sales put an end to the golden age of television. When sponsors agreed to attach their names to programs, *Alcoa Presents* or the *Texaco Star Theater*, for example, they had an incentive to demand high-quality programming. Spot sales, with network salespeople offering small bits of time to a number of different sponsors, reduced the demand for quality. Because individual sponsors were not identified with a given show, they had no stake in how well it was made—only in how many viewers it attracted. Spot sales also reduced the willingness of the networks to try innovative or different types of content. Familiarity and predictability attracted more viewers and, therefore, more advertisers.

There is a counterargument, however. Once the financial well-being of the networks became dependent on the programming they aired, the networks themselves became more concerned with program quality, lifting television from its dull infancy (remembered now as the golden age only by those small, early audiences committed to serious character-driven televised drama). Different historians and critics offer arguments for both views.

I LOVE LUCY **AND MORE CHANGES** In 1951 CBS asked Lucille Ball to move her hit radio program, *My Favorite Husband*, to television. Lucy was willing but wanted her real-life husband, Desi Arnaz, to play the part of her on-air spouse. The network refused (some historians say the network objected to the prime-time presentation of an interracial marriage—Desi Arnaz was Cuban—but CBS denies this). But Lucy made additional demands. Television programming at the time was broadcast live: Images were typically captured by three large television cameras, with a director in a booth choosing among the three available images. Lucy wanted her program produced in the same manner—in front of a live audience with three simultaneously running cameras—but these cameras would be *film* cameras. Editors could then review the three sets of film and edit them together to give the best combination of action and reaction shots. Lucy also wanted the production to take place in Hollywood, the nation's film capital, instead of New York, the television center at the time.

▶ Running from 1947 until 1958, NBC's *Kraft Television Theatre* aired some of the golden age's most respected live anthology dramas. *Top*, Richard Kiley and Everett Sloane; *left*, Ossie Davis; *right*, Walter Matthau and Nancy Walker.

(top, bottom left and right): Courtesy Everett Collection

CBS was uncertain about this departure from how television was typically produced and refused these requests as well.

Lucy and Desi borrowed the necessary money and produced *I Love Lucy* on their own, selling the broadcast rights to CBS. In doing so, the woman now best remembered as "that zany redhead" transformed the business and look of television:

- Filmed reruns were now possible, something that had been impossible with live television, and this, in turn, created the off-network syndication industry.
- The television industry moved from New York, with its stage drama orientation, to Hollywood, with its entertainment film mind-set. More action and more flash came to the screen.

◀ *I Love Lucy* was significant for far more than its comedy. Thanks to Lucille Ball's shrewd business sense, it became the foundation for the huge off-network syndicated television industry. ©*CBS/Photofest*

- Weekly series could now be produced relatively quickly and inexpensively. A 39-week series could be completed in 20 or 24 weeks, saving money on actors, crew, equipment, and facilities. In addition, the same stock shots—for example, certain exterior views—could be used in different episodes.

MCCARTHYISM: THE GROWING POWER OF TELEVISION   The Red Scare that cowed the movie business also touched television, aided by the publication in 1950 of *Red Channels: The Report of Communist Influence in Radio and Television*, the work of three former FBI agents operating a company called American Business Consultants. Its 200 pages detailed the alleged pro-Communist sympathies of 151 broadcast personalities, including Orson Welles and journalist Howard K. Smith. Advertisers were encouraged to avoid buying time from broadcasters who employed these "Red sympathizers." Like the movie studios, the television industry caved in. The networks employed security checkers to look into people's backgrounds, refused to hire suspect talent, and demanded loyalty oaths from performers. In its infancy, television had taken the safe path. Many gifted artists were denied not only a paycheck but also the opportunity to shape the medium's content.

Ironically, it was this same Red Scare that allowed television to demonstrate its enormous power as a vehicle of democracy and freedom. Joseph McCarthy, the Republican junior sen-

▶ The Army–McCarthy Hearings. Wisconsin's Republican junior senator, Joseph McCarthy, was called in 1954 to give testimony before his fellow senators regarding his claims that the army was rife with Communists, Reds, and "fellow travelers." Network coverage of the senator's erratic behavior helped bring the despot into disrepute.

©Everett Collection Historical/Alamy

ator from Wisconsin whose tactics gave this era its name, was seen by millions of viewers as his investigation of Reds in the U.S. Army was broadcast by all the networks for 36 days in 1954. Daytime ratings increased 50% (Sterling & Kittross, 1990). At the same time, Edward R. Murrow used his *See It Now*, a documentary series broadcast by CBS, to expose the senator's lies and hypocrisy. As a consequence of the two broadcasts, McCarthy was ruined; he was censured by his Senate colleagues and later died a lonely alcoholic's death. Television had given the people eyes and ears—and power—where before they had had little. The Army–McCarthy Hearings and Murrow's challenge to McCarthyism are still regarded as two of television's finest moments.

THE NIELSEN RATINGS The concept of measuring audience was carried over from radio to television, but the ratings as we know them today are far more sophisticated (see the chapter on radio, recording, and popular music for more on ratings). The A. C. Nielsen Company began in 1923 as a product-testing company but soon branched into market research. In 1936 Nielsen started reporting radio ratings and was doing the same for television by 1950.

To produce the ratings today, Nielsen selects 41,000 households, about 100,000 people, thought to be representative of the entire U.S. viewing audience. To record data on what people in those TV households are watching, Nielsen employs the **Global Television Audience Metering (GTAM) meter**, which actively (requiring viewer input) and passively (automatically reading digital codes embedded in video content) measures viewing as people, with increasing mobility, consume video on a growing array of technologies. The data are then sent to Nielsen via the Internet, and the company determines the programs watched, who watched them, and the amount of time each viewer spent with them. But the same convergence that required the development of the GTAM meter is upsetting the business of audience measurement in many ways. In fact, many television and advertising people see the ratings as worthless, "a relic of television's rabbit-ears past" on which more than $70 billion in ad money a year is traded (Steel, 2016).

To present a fuller picture of a show's total audience by accounting for multiplatform and **nonlinear TV** viewing (people watching on their own schedules), many broadcasters are calling for a new rating that measures a program's seven-day performance, called **L+7**, for live plus seven days of viewing. With this ratings system, a single episode of Fox's *Empire*, for example, sees its ratings among coveted 18- to 49-year-old viewers boosted by 2.3%; CBS's *Big Bang Theory* gets a 2.2% bump (Littleton & Kissell, 2016). The four major broadcast networks believe that a truer measure of their viewership will show the much-discussed falloff in its prime-time audience to be something of a fiction. Nielsen has responded with several fixes, including its **C3 rating**, counting audiences across three screens—TV (original airing plus DVR), Internet, and mobile video. The "3" (and for the occasional C7, the "7") represents the viewing of the commercials that appear in a specific program within three days (or seven) of its premiere telecast. Facing pressure from competitor ComScore, who can measure viewing across all screens, stationary and mobile, from more than 10 million homes, even to the extent that it can count viewing of individual Web videos, Nielsen rolled out its Total Content Ratings in 2017. The new measure captures all viewing across all possible devices, including traditional TV, video-on-demand, DVR playback, Internet-connected devices like Roku, Xbox, and Apple TV, smartphones, desktop computers, laptops, and tablets. Nonetheless, there remains great dissatisfaction with Nielsen's ratings, leading many networks to augment them with their own measures, for example levels of Twitter activity and other social network metrics. Some networks have gone as far as to drop Nielsen altogether, most notably cable channel CNBC. Still, as it has been from the earliest days of television, the Nielsens remain the *coin of the realm*, that is, they are, despite their limitations, the agreed-upon currency on which the vast majority of television advertising sales are based.

Another important measure of television's audience is its **share**, which is a direct reflection of a particular show's competitive performance. Share doesn't measure viewers as a percentage of *all* television households (as do the ratings). Instead, the share measures a program audience as a percentage of the *television sets in use* at the time it airs. It tells us what proportion of the *actual* audience a program attracts, indicating how well a particular program is doing on its given night, in its time slot, and against its competition (Figure 1). For example, *The Tonight Show with Jimmy Fallon* normally gets a rating of around .8—terrible by prime-time standards—but because it airs when fewer homes are tuned in, its share of 5 (5% of the homes with sets in use) is quite respectable.

Ratings and shares can be computed using these formulas:

$$\text{Rating} = \frac{\text{Households tuned in to a given program}}{\text{All households with television}}$$

$$\text{Share} = \frac{\text{Households tuned in to a given program}}{\text{All households tuned in to television at that time}}$$

Here's an example. Your talk show is aired in a market that has 1 million television households; 400,000 are tuned in to you. Therefore,

$$\frac{400,000}{1,000,000} = .40, \text{ or a rating of 40.}$$

At the time your show airs, however, there are only 800,000 households using television. Therefore, your share of the available audience is

$$\text{Share} = \frac{400,000}{800,000} = .50, \text{ or a share of 50.}$$

If you can explain why a specific program's share is always higher than its rating, then you understand the difference between the two.

▲ **Figure 1** Computing Ratings and Shares.

The Coming of Cable

In 1948 in Mahanoy City, Pennsylvania, appliance sales representative John Walson was having trouble selling televisions. The Pocono Mountains sat between his town and Philadelphia's three new stations. But Walson was also a powerline worker, so he convinced his bosses to let him run a wire to his store from a tower he erected on New Boston Mountain. As more and more people became aware of his system, he began wiring the homes of customers who bought his sets. In June of that year, Walson had 727 subscribers for his **community antenna television (CATV)** system (Chin, 1978). Although no one calls it CATV anymore, cable television was born.

The cable Walson used was a twin-lead wire, much like the cord that connects a lamp to an outlet. To attract even more subscribers, he had to offer improved picture quality. He accomplished this by using *coaxial cable* and self-manufactured boosters (or amplifiers). Coaxial cable—copper-clad aluminum wire encased in plastic foam insulation, covered by an aluminum outer conductor, and then sheathed in plastic—had more bandwidth than did twin-lead wire. As a result, it allowed more of the original signal to pass and even permitted Walson to carry a greater number of channels.

With expanded bandwidth and new, powerful signal boosters developed by Milton Jerrold Shapp, who would later become Pennsylvania's governor, these systems began experimenting

▲ John Walson.
©*The Barco Library of The Cable Center, Denver, CO*

with the **importation of distant signals**, using wires not only to provide improved reception but also to offer a wider variety of programming. They began delivering independent stations from as far away as New York to fill their then-amazing 7 to 10 channels. By 1962, 800 systems were providing cable television to more than 850,000 homes.

The industry today is composed of 5,208 individual cable systems delivering video to 53 million households, high-speed Internet to 61 million, and digital telephone to 31 million. The industry generates revenues of over $108 billion, with about 10% of that amount earned through advertising (Internet & Television Association, 2017).

Television and Its Audiences

The 1960s saw some refinement in the technical structure of television, which influenced its organization and audience. In 1962 Congress passed **all-channel legislation**, which required that all sets imported into or manufactured in the United States be equipped with both VHF and UHF receivers. This had little immediate impact; U.S. viewers were now hooked on the three national networks and their VHF affiliates. Still, UHF independents and educational stations were able to at least attract some semblance of an audience. The UHF independents would have to wait for the coming of cable to give them clout. Now that the educational stations were attracting more viewers, they began to look less educational in the strictest sense of the word and began programming more entertaining cultural fare (see the essay "The Creation of *Sesame Street*"). The Public Broadcasting Act of 1967 united the educational stations into an important network, the Public Broadcasting Service (PBS), which today has 350 member stations.

The 1960s also witnessed the immense social and political power of the new medium to force profound alterations in the country's consciousness and behavior. Particularly influential were the Nixon–Kennedy campaign debates of 1960, broadcasts of the aftermath of Kennedy's assassination and funeral in 1963, the 1969 transmission of Neil Armstrong's walk on the moon, and the use of television at the end of the decade by civil rights and anti–Vietnam War leaders.

The 1960s also gave rise to a descriptive expression sometimes used today when television is discussed. Speaking to the 1961 convention of the National Association of Broadcasters, John F. Kennedy's new FCC chair, Newton Minow, invited broadcasters to

> sit down in front of your television set when your station goes on the air and stay there without a book, magazine, newspaper, profit and loss sheet, or ratings book to distract you, and keep your eyes glued to that set until the station signs off. I can assure you that you will observe a **vast wasteland**.

Whether or not one agrees with Minow's assessment of television, then or now, there is no doubt that audiences continue to watch:

- There are more than 123 million television households in the United States, 96% of all U.S. homes.
- The average American watches television 32 hours and 1 minute a week.
- Television reaches more adults each day than any other medium, and those people spend more time with television than with any other medium (all from Television Advertising Bureau, 2016).
- Traditional television watching accounts for 78% of all time spent with video (Bednarski, 2016).
- Seventy percent of TV viewers admit to binge viewing, watching five or more episodes of a series in one sitting (Sharma, 2016).

There can be no doubt, either, that television is successful as an advertising medium:

- Total annual billings for television are around $80 billion, with approximately two-thirds generated by broadcast and one-third by cable television. Together they collect 40% of all U.S. ad spending.

- The average 30-second prime-time network television spot costs more than $300,000 (*Sunday Night Football* gets $673,664; spots on *Empire* run $437,100; 30 seconds on *Star* run $300,000).

- Prime ad time on the February 2017 Patriots–Falcons Super Bowl broadcast cost a minimum of $5 million for 30 seconds, or more than $166,666 per second. Advertisers consider the annual Super Bowl broadcast "the single most important communication channel a marketer can exploit" (Schultz, 2017).

- Television has the greatest reach of all ad-supported media, and consumers cite it as the medium most likely to influence their purchasing decisions (Television Advertising Bureau, 2016).

USING MEDIA TO MAKE A DIFFERENCE
The Creation of *Sesame Street*

In 1968 a public affairs program producer for Channel 13 in New York City identified a number of related problems that she believed could be addressed by a well-conceived, well-produced television show.

Joan Ganz Cooney saw that 80% of 3- and 4-year-olds and 25% of 5-year-olds in the United States did not attend any form of preschool. Children from financially disadvantaged homes were far less likely to attend preschool at these ages than their better-off peers. Children in these age groups who did go to preschool received little academic instruction; preschool was the equivalent of organized recess. Large numbers of U.S. children, then, entered first grade with no formal schooling, even though education experts had long argued that preschool years were crucial in children's intellectual and academic development. In addition, the disparity in academic preparedness between poor and other children was a national disgrace.

What did these children do instead of going to preschool? Cooney knew that they watched television. But she also knew that "existing shows for 3- through 5-year-old children . . . did not have education as a primary goal" (Ball & Bogatz, 1970, p. 2). Her idea was to use an interesting, exciting, visually and aurally stimulating television show as an explicitly educational tool "to promote the intellectual and cultural growth of preschoolers, particularly disadvantaged preschoolers," and to "teach children how to think as well as what to think" (Cook et al., 1975, p. 7).

Cooney established a nonprofit organization, the Children's Television Workshop (CTW), and sought funding for her program. Several federal agencies, primarily the Office of Education, a number of private foundations including Carnegie and Ford, and public broadcasters, contributed $13.7 million for CTW's first four years.

After much research into producing a quality children's television show and studying the best instructional methods for teaching preschool audiences, CTW unveiled *Sesame Street* during the 1969 television season. It was an instant hit with children and parents. The *New Republic* said, "Judged by the standards of most other programs for preschoolers, it is imaginative, tasteful, and witty" (cited in Sedulus, 1970). Originally scheduled for one hour a day during the school week, within months of its debut *Sesame Street* was being programmed twice a day on many public television stations, and many ran the entire week's schedule on Saturdays and Sundays. Today, nearly 45 years after its debut, *Sesame Street* airs 35 new episodes a year, and in 2016 it made HBO (including its streaming service) its new home network. Episodes were trimmed to 30 minutes and run on HBO for 9 months before being aired on free public television.

Did Cooney and her show make a difference? Several national studies demonstrated that academic performance in early grades was directly and strongly correlated with regular viewing of *Sesame Street*. The commercial networks began to introduce educational fare into their Saturday morning schedules. ABC's *Grammar Rock, America Rock* (on U.S. history), and *Multiplication Rock* were critical and educational successes at the time, and much of the programming on today's kids channels like Nickelodeon trace their pacing and production techniques to the show. The program has been nominated for more than 250 Emmy Awards, winning nearly 110 times. It recently expanded its preschool curriculum to include subjects such as nature, math, science and engineering concepts, and problem solving. The curriculum for its first season on HBO revolved around kindness.

Scope and Nature of the Broadcast Television Industry

Today, as it has been from the beginning, the business of broadcast television is dominated by a few centralized production, distribution, and decision-making organizations. These networks link affiliates for the purpose of delivering and selling viewers to advertisers. The large majority of the 1,387 commercial stations in the United States are affiliated with a national broadcasting network: ABC, NBC, and CBS each have over 200 affiliates, and Fox has close to that number. Many more stations are affiliated with the CW Network, jointly owned by CBS and Warner Bros. Entertainment. Although cable has introduced us to dozens of popular cable networks—ESPN, MTV, Comedy Central, and A&E, to name a few—for decades most programs that came to mind when we thought of television were either conceived, approved, funded, produced, or distributed by the broadcast networks. Although, as you read at this chapter's outset, that's quickly changing. More on that soon.

Local affiliates carry network programs (they **clear time**). Until quite recently, affiliates received direct payment for carrying a show, called compensation, and the right to keep all income from the sale of local commercials on that program. But loss of network audience and the rise of cable have altered this arrangement. Now networks receive **reverse compensation**, a fee paid by the local station for the right to be that network's affiliate. It is typically based on the amount of money the local cable operation pays to the station to carry its signal, called **retransmission fees**.

The Networks and Program Content

Networks control what appears on the vast majority of local television stations, but they also control what appears on non-network television, that is, when affiliates program their own content. In addition, they influence what appears on independent stations and on cable channels. This non-network material not only tends to be network-*type* programming but most often is programming that originally aired on the networks themselves (called **off-network** programs).

Why do network and network-type content dominate television? *Availability* is one factor. There is 75 years' worth of already successful network content available for airing on local stations. A second factor is that the *production and distribution* mechanisms that have long served the broadcast networks are well established and serve the newer outlets just as well as they did NBC, CBS, and ABC. The final reason is us, the audience. The formats we are most comfortable with—our television tastes and expectations—have been and continue to be developed on the networks.

How a Program Traditionally Gets on the Air

The national broadcast and cable networks look at about 4,000 proposals a year for new television series. Many, if not most, are submitted at the networks' invitation or instigation. Of the 4,000, about 90 will be filmed as **pilots**, or trial programs, at a cost of $3 million for a 30-minute pilot to $7 million for an hour drama. Perhaps 20 to 30 will become one of the 400 scripted series on air at any time. The networks spend over $500 million a season to suffer this process. For this reason, they prefer to see ideas from producers with established track records and financial and organizational stability—for example, Jerry Bruckheimer is the source of *CSI*, *CSI: Miami*, *CSI: NY*, *The Amazing Race*, *Cold Case*, and *Without a Trace* in addition to nearly 20 other prime-time series aired in recent years.

The way a program typically makes it onto the air differs somewhat for those who have been asked to submit an idea and for producers who bring their concepts to the networks. First, a producer has an *idea*, or a network has an idea and asks a proven producer to propose a show based on it (possibly offering a **put**, a deal that guarantees the producer that the network will order at least a pilot or have to pay a hefty penalty). The producer must then *shop* the idea to one of the networks; naturally, an invited producer submits the proposal only to the network that asked for it. In either case, if the network is persuaded, it *buys the option* and asks for a written *outline* in which the original idea is refined. If still interested, the network will order a full *script*.

If the network approves that script, it will order the production of a pilot. Pilots are then subjected to rigorous testing by the networks' own and independent audience research organizations. Based on this research, networks will often demand changes, such as writing out characters who tested poorly or beefing up story lines that test audiences particularly liked.

If the network is still interested, that is, if it believes that the show will be a hit, it orders a set number of episodes and schedules the show. In television's early days, an order might be for 26 or 39 episodes. Today, however, because of escalating production costs, the convention is at first to order six episodes. If these are successful, a second order of nine more is placed. Then, if the show is still doing well, a final nine episodes (referred to as *the back nine*) will be commissioned.

The reason television program producers participate in this expensive enterprise is that they can make large amounts of money in syndication, the sale of their programs to stations on a market-by-market basis. Even though the networks control the process from idea to scheduling and decide how long a show stays in their lineups, producers continue to own the rights to their programs. Once enough episodes are made (generally about 88, which is the product of four years on a network), producers can sell the syndicated package to the highest bidder in each of the 210 U.S. television markets, keeping all the revenues for themselves. This is the legacy of Lucille Ball's business genius (CBS still earns about $15 million a year from *I Love Lucy* syndication). The price of a syndicated program depends on the market size, the level of competition between the stations in the market, and the age and popularity of the program itself. The station buys the right to a specified number of plays, or airings. After that, the rights return to the producer to be sold again and again. A program that has survived at least four years on one of the networks has proven its popularity, has attracted a following, and has accumulated enough individual episodes so that local stations can offer weeks of daily scheduling without too many repeats. In a word, it is a moneymaker. Paramount has already earned more than $2 billion from its syndication of *Frasier*; Warner Brothers collected more than $5.8 million an episode from its original syndication of *Friends* and today gets $4 million an episode for *The Big Bang Theory*, although it is still in its network run.

So attractive is syndication's income potential, especially when coupled with the promise of profits from digital downloads, the sale of DVD collections, and pick up by streaming services like Hulu and Netflix, that the networks themselves have become their own producers (and therefore syndicators). In fact, the major broadcast networks now produce the vast majority of all the prime-time programming on their own and the top 20 cable networks.

▼ Two of syndication's biggest winners, *The Big Bang Theory* and *Friends*.
(left) ©CBS/Photofest; (right) ©NBC/ Courtesy Everett Collection

Top 10 Most-Watched Nonsports Television Broadcasts

Rank

		Rating/Share
	M*A*S*H (final episode), 1983	
1	60.2/77	
	Dallas ("Who Shot JR?"), 1980	
2	53.3/76	
	Roots (Part VIII), 1977	
3	51.1/71	CBS
	Gone with the Wind (Part 1), 1976	
4	47.7/65	ABC
	Gone with the Wind (Part 2), 1976	
5	47.4/64	NBC
	Bob Hope Christmas Show, 1970	
6	46.6/64	
	The Day After (movie), 1983	
7	46.0/62	
	The Fugitive (last episode), 1967	
8	45.9/72	
	Roots (Part VI), 1977	
9	45.9/66	
	Roots (Part V), 1977	
10	45.7/71	

▲ **Figure 2** Top 10 Most-Watched Nonsports Television Broadcasts.

Source: Television Bureau of Advertising (www.tvb.org)

It is important to note that there is another form of syndicated programming. **First-run syndication** is programming produced specifically for sale into syndication on a market-by-market basis. It is attractive to producers because they don't have to run the gauntlet of the network programming process, and they keep 100% of the income. Game and talk shows, long staples of the business, have been joined by programs such as *Judge Judy*, court shows distributed daily to hundreds of stations. They are inexpensive to make, inexpensive to distribute, and easily **stripped** (broadcast at the same time five evenings a week). They allow an inexhaustible number of episodes with no repeats and are easy to promote (for example, "Watch the case of the peeping landlord. Tune in at 5:30.").

And despite the fact that the most-watched programs in history were all aired by the traditional television networks (Figure 2), the process by which programs now come to our screens is changing because the central position of networks in that process has been altered. Because they must compete with the streaming services, the networks are no longer the only game in town for top talent, so they themselves are increasingly offering producers more straight-to-series production deals. NBC's *The Good Place*, Fox's *Son of Zorn*, and ABC's *Designated Survivor* and *Somewhere Between* were beneficiaries of these arrangements. In addition, much quality programming gets to us not because a network elected to air it, but as you saw in this chapter's opening, because a streaming service asked its subscribers which shows they wanted to watch or simply paid quality artists to come work with them. For example, after rejection by the traditional network and cable channels, the producers of *House of Cards* approached Netflix. Kevin Spacey, the star of the show, said Netflix was the only network that told them, "We believe in you. . . . We don't need you to do a pilot. How many [episodes] do you wanna do?" (Auletta, 2014, p. 58). Netflix alone spends more than $5 billion a year on original programming, triple HBO's outlay, and requires no pilots (Nocera, 2016). Of course, all this change is the product of the introduction of new technologies—cable, VCR, DVD, digital video recorders, satellite, the Internet and digitization, and smartphones—that have upset the long-standing relationship between medium and audience. Convergence is also reshaping that relationship.

Cable and Satellite Television

John Walson's brainchild reshaped the face of modern television. During cable's infancy, many over-the-air broadcasters saw it as something of a friend. It extended their reach, boosting both audience size and profits. Then, in November 1972, Sterling Manhattan Cable launched a new channel called Home Box Office. Only a handful of homes caught the debut of what we now call HBO, but broadcasters' mild concern over this development turned to outright antagonism toward cable in 1975, when new HBO owner Time Inc. began distributing the movie channel by satellite. Now **premium cable** was eating into the broadcasters' audience by offering high-quality, nationally produced and distributed content. The public enthusiastically embraced cable, which, coupled with the widespread diffusion of **fiber optic** cable (the transmission of signals by light beam over glass, permitting the delivery of hundreds of channels), brought the medium to maturity.

Programming

Cable's share of the prime-time audience exceeded that of the Big Four broadcast networks for the first time in 2002. Its total audience share has exceeded that of ABC, CBS, NBC, and Fox every year since. What attracts these viewers is programming, a fact highlighted by two pieces of recent industry data: cable shows annually garner the majority of all prime-time Emmy Awards nominations (HBO's *Game of Thrones* earned 38 Emmy Awards in 2016, an industry record for a single show), and cable viewing exceeds network viewing for every single American age demographic.

As we've seen, cable operators attract viewers through a combination of basic and premium channels, as well as with some programming of local origin. There are more than 900 national and regional cable networks. We all know national networks such as CNN, Lifetime, HBO, and the History Channel. Regional network North-West Cable News serves Washington, Oregon, Idaho, Montana, northern California, and parts of Alaska; New England Cable News serves the region that gives it its name; and several regional sports-oriented channels serve different parts of the country. The financial support and targeted audiences for these program providers differ, as does their place on a system's **tiers**, groupings of channels made available to subscribers at varying prices.

BASIC CABLE PROGRAMMING In recognition of the growing dependence of the public on cable delivery of broadcast service as the spread of cable increased, Congress passed the Cable Television Consumer Protection and Competition Act of 1992. This law requires operators to offer a truly basic service composed of the broadcast stations in their area and their public access channels. Cable operators also offer another form of basic service, **expanded basic cable**, composed primarily of local broadcast stations and services with broad appeal such as TBS, TNT, the USA Network, and Comedy Central. These networks offer a wide array of programming not unlike that found on the traditional, over-the-air broadcast networks. Ad-supported cable networks such as these want to be on cable's basic tiers because sponsors covet those large potential audiences. This is the dispute, for example, at the heart of the NFL Network's frequent battles with many of the nation's cable operators. Most operators want to put the network on a premium tier to attract more subscribers. NFL Network wants placement on basic cable where more viewers means more ad dollars.

Because of concentration, operators are increasingly choosing to carry a specific basic channel because their owners (who have a financial stake in that channel) insist that they do. **Multiple system operators (MSOs)** are companies that own several cable franchises. Time Warner owns truTV. Comcast has an interest in numerous prime channels. Viacom owns BET. Naturally, these networks are more likely to be carried by systems controlled by the MSOs that own them and are less likely to be carried by other systems.

The long-standard concept of different pricing for different packages or tiers of channels is frequently under attack by the FCC and some members of Congress. Concerns over viewers' accidental access to unwanted, offensive content and rising cable prices are leading to calls for **à la carte pricing**—that is, paying for cable on a channel-by-channel basis. The industry itself is split on the issue, system operators versus programmers. You can read more about the dispute in the box entitled "Bundle or À la Carte . . . or Skinny Bundle?"

▲ HBO's *Game of Thrones* won 38 Emmy Awards in 2016, a record for a single program.
©HBO/Courtesy Everett Collection

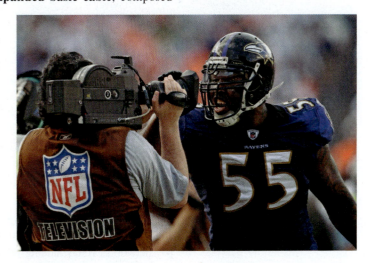

▲ MSOs want the NFL Network on a premium tier; the NFL is happy to stay on basic cable.
©Joe Robbins/Getty Images

CULTURAL FORUM
Bundle or À la Carte . . . or Skinny Bundle?

The debate over how to price a cable subscription has entered the cultural forum because of a perfect storm of concern. Many consumers are upset over rising subscription rates, which are growing at more than four times the rate of inflation (Adamczyk, 2016). Some politicians worry about people accidentally seeing material they find offensive, and more than a few MSOs are chafing under big hikes in what they have to pay for the channels they carry. For them, programming costs have escalated between 6% and 10% a year for the last decade, and for popular channels like ESPN, for example, MSOs must pay $7.86 for each of their cable households ("Net Worth," 2017). One solution to meeting these different concerns is to let the market (meaning viewers) decide with à la carte pricing. That way, consumers wouldn't have to pay for unwatched channels (an average household will watch only 20 of its available 206 channels; Mandese, 2016), there would be reduced risk of exposure to unwanted content, and MSOs wouldn't have to pay programming costs for all their subscribing households, only for those deciding to watch specific channels.

But, argue cable network programmers like Disney and Viacom, our costs have escalated dramatically as well. ESPN, for example, spends more than $5 billion a year on programming, and viewers have decided that this expensive content is what they want. In addition, they argue, à la carte would actually raise consumers' costs because those expensive popular channels make possible the smaller, niche channels. There might be a lot of people willing to pay $12 for ESPN (its projected à la carte price; Kline, 2016), but how many viewers would pay for C-SPAN, or a foreign-language channel, or a religious channel, and how much would they be willing to pay? À la carte means the menu gets much, much smaller. And besides, continues the programmers' position, people are already comfortable with video bundles. Subscription channels like HBO and Cinemax are bundles—we pay for all their programs, not just the ones we watch (and of course, HBO and Cinemax are themselves already available à la carte from MSOs).

Enter your voice, à la carte or bundle? Would you be happier paying for only the channels you watch, or do you find value in having a lot of options, even if you don't take advantage of them all the time? And what about *serendipitous viewing,* running across something you might not have thought to watch, but it catches your eye? Isn't this one of the great gifts of cable?

And what if there were a third option, a *skinny bundle*, a pared-down collection of the most popular channels for a lower price? Using the Internet or an app, you can get Brit Box with scores of English shows from ITV and the BBC; for $40 a month Hulu will deliver Disney, Turner, ESPN, and Fox channels; Google's Unplugged runs between $25 and $50; DirecTV NOW will give you 100 channels for $35; PlayStation Vue will sell you 60 channels for $30 or 110 for $75. Sling TV goes skinnier, 28 networks for $20. Even MSO Verizon offers a skinny bundle, Custom TV, and traditional television network CBS provides all its programming for $6 a month (Spangler, 2016). Is a skinny bundle a better choice for you than paying for hundreds of channels you don't watch or spending much more for individual channels you do?

PREMIUM CABLE As the FCC lifted restrictions on cable's freedom to import distant signals and to show current movies, HBO grew and was joined by a host of other satellite-delivered pay networks. Today, among the most familiar and popular premium cable networks are HBO, Showtime, Sundance Channel, and Cinemax.

In addition to freedom from regulatory constraint, two important programming discoveries ensured the success of the new premium channels. After television's early experiments with over-the-air **subscription TV** failed, many experts believed people simply would not pay for television. So the first crucial discovery was that viewers would indeed pay for packages of contemporary, popular movies. These movie packages could be sold less expensively than could films bought one at a time, and viewers were willing to be billed on a monthly basis for the whole package rather than pay for each viewing.

The second realization boosting the fortunes of the premium networks was the discovery that viewers not only did not mind repeats (as many did with over-the-air television) but welcomed them as a benefit of paying for the provider's slate of films. Premium channel owners were delighted. Replaying content reduced their programming costs and solved the problem of how to fill all those hours of operation.

Premium services come in two forms: movie channels (HBO, Starz!, and Encore, for example) that offer packages of new and old movies along with big sports and other special events—all available for one monthly fee—and pay-per-view channels, through which viewers choose from a menu of offerings (almost always of very new movies and very big sporting events) and pay a fee for the chosen viewing.

People enjoy premium channels in the home for their ability to present unedited and uninterrupted movies and other content not usually found on broadcast channels—for example, adult fare, championship boxing, ultimate fighting, and wrestling. Increasingly, however, that "content not usually found on broadcast channels" often consists not of movies and sports but of high-quality serial programming—content unencumbered by the need to attract the largest possible audience possessing a specific set of demographics. Premium cable series such as *Game of Thrones*, *Westworld*, *Veep*, *Homeland*, *Curb Your Enthusiasm*, and *Power* attract large and loyal followings.

The other dominant multichannel service is direct broadcast satellite (DBS). First available to the public in 1994, it has brought cable's subscriber growth to a standstill because, from the viewer's perspective, what is on a DBS-supplied screen differs little from what is on a cable-supplied screen.

DBS in the United States is dominated by two companies, DirecTV (owned by AT&T) and Dish Network. DirecTV has 25.3 million subscribers; Dish Network has 13.9 million. These two companies, along with Verizon's fiber optic FiOS-TV and its 4.7 million subscribers, have recently been peeling away subscribers from cable. Look at the list of the 10 largest pay-TV services in Figure 3. Note that Dish and DirecTV are among that group. But DBS providers, like other MSOs, face the troubling problem of **cord-cutting**, viewers leaving cable and DBS altogether and relying on Internet-only television viewing. From 2011 to 2016, cable lost 6.7 million subscribers, and more than a quarter of Millennials report never having subscribed to cable, that is, they are **cord-nevers** (Nocera, 2016). Much of this decline is attributed to what the industry calls **over-the-top (OTT)** television, delivery of video without the involvement of an MSO, as in "over (avoiding) the set-top box." Because of OTT, which also makes skinny bundles possible, the number of **zero-TV homes**, those with sets

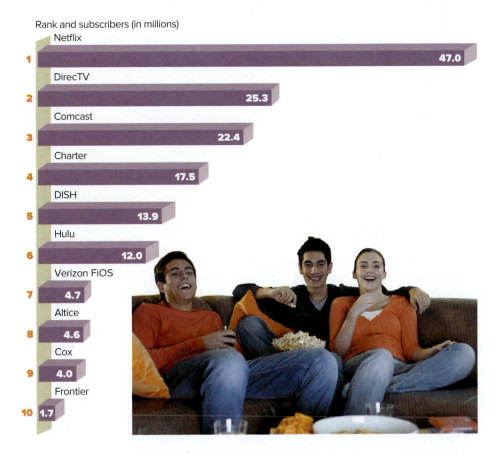

Rank and subscribers (in millions)

Rank	Service	Subscribers
1	Netflix	47.0
2	DirecTV	25.3
3	Comcast	22.4
4	Charter	17.5
5	DISH	13.9
6	Hulu	12.0
7	Verizon FiOS	4.7
8	Altice	4.6
9	Cox	4.0
10	Frontier	1.7

◀ **Figure 3** Top 10 Pay-TV Services, 2017.
Source: Internet & Television Association, 2017.
Photo ©Juice Images Ltd/ Shutterstock RF

▲ Viewers and critics agree that much of television's most sophisticated (and enjoyable) programming is available on premium cable. Unafraid of offending advertisers, cable networks can present challenging, often controversial content. Here are *Westworld*, *Homeland*, *Veep*, and *Power*.

Photos (clockwise from top left): ©HBO/Photofest; ©Showtime Networks/Photofest; ©AF archive/Alamy; ©Pictorial Press Ltd/Alamy

that receive neither over-the-air nor cable/satellite television, now account for 6% of all TV homes, including 13% of homes with 18- to 34-year-olds (Friedman, 2016a).

Look again at Figure 3. You'll notice that there were two non-MSO services, Netflix and Hulu, among the country's top 10 providers of pay television in 2017. One OTT, Netflix, was number one by a very wide margin.

Trends and Convergence in Television and Cable

The long-standing relationship between television and its audiences is being redefined. This profound change, initially wrought by cable and satellite, has been and is being driven by other technologies as well—VCR, DVD, DVR, the Internet, digitization, and even the smartphone.

VCR

Introduced commercially in 1976, videocassette recorders (VCRs) quickly became common in American homes but were declared dead in 2016 as the last manufacturer, Japan's Funai Electronics, ceased production. Still, in its prime, this technology further eroded the audience for traditional over-the-air television, as people, for the first time, could now watch rented and purchased videos on their own schedules. VCR also introduced the public to **time-shifting**, taping a show for later viewing, and **zipping**, fast-forwarding through taped commercials. As a result, people became comfortable with, and in fact came to expect, more control over when, what, and how they watched television.

DVD

In March 1996 the **digital video disc (DVD)** went on sale in U.S. stores. Using a DVD, viewers can stop images with no loss of fidelity; can subtitle a movie in a number of languages; can search for specific scenes from an on-screen menu; and can access bonus features that give background on the movie, its production, and its personnel. Scenes and music not used in the theatrical release of a movie are often included on the disc.

Innovations such as these made DVD at the time of its introduction the fastest-growing consumer electronic product of all time. DVD players now sit in about 50% of U.S. homes, down from 80% just a few years ago. Because of the many viewing options now available, DVD sales and rentals have fallen dramatically for the last several years. In 2012, the number of online movie transactions (sales and rentals) exceeded the number of physical, that is disc, transactions for the first time, 3.4 billion to 2.4 billion (Smith, 2012); and in 2016, video streaming subscription revenues surpassed those from physical disc sales and rentals for the first time (Richter, 2017). Despite its looming obsolescence, DVD served to further alter the relationship between television and its audiences. Viewers became accustomed to having greater control over what they watched, when they watched, and how they watched on a platform much more satisfying than the earlier VCR. In addition, people watching DVDs were viewers that broadcasters could not sell to advertisers, helping to erode television's dominance as an advertising medium.

DVR

In March 1999 Philips Electronics unveiled the **digital video recorder (DVR)**. It contains digital software that puts a significant amount of control over content in viewers' hands. They can "rewind" and play back portions of a program while they are watching and recording it without losing any of that show. By designating their favorite shows, viewers can instruct DVR to automatically record and deliver not only those programs but all similar content over a specified period of time. This application can even be used with the name of a favorite actor. Type in Shemar Moore, and DVR will automatically record all programming in which he appears.

DVR does not deliver programming the way broadcasters, cablecasters, and DBS systems do. Rather, it is employed *in addition to* these content providers. Both DBS providers and almost every MSO now offer low-cost DVR as part of their technology platform, significantly hastening its diffusion into American homes. Today, about half of all TV households have DVR. Naturally, traditional broadcast and ad-supported cable networks found the rapid diffusion of DVR troubling, and while it is true that DVR dramatically changed television viewing as we knew it, it has not had as negative an effect on those traditional programming sources as originally anticipated. While DVR does allow viewers to fast-forward through commercials, we saw earlier in this chapter that traditional broadcasters rely on DVR playback to boost their ratings and therefore profits.

Streaming Video

Television on the Internet was slow to take off because of copyright and piracy concerns, and because few viewers had sufficient **bandwidth**, space on the wires bringing content into their homes. So for several years the most typical video fare on the Internet was a variety of short specialty transmissions such as movie trailers, music videos, and news clips. But the development of increasingly sophisticated video compression software and the parallel rise of homes with **broadband** Internet connections (73% of all U.S. Internet homes have broadband; Smith, 2017) have changed that. Because broadband offers greater information-carrying capacity (that is, it increased bandwidth), watching true television on the Internet is now common. Much of that viewing is of content that originated on network and cable television, but much is also Web-only video (*most* if streaming service video is considered; half of all U.S. TV homes subscribe to a streaming video service; Friedman, 2016b).

And as we saw in this chapter's opening, the distinction between Web-only and broadcast/cable programming is disappearing. Internet video sites Netflix, Hulu, Amazon, and YouTube commission original content. We stream 5 billion videos every day on YouTube, and we also stream 8 billion a day on Facebook (Savage, 2016). And there are many other successful, more narrowly targeted video streaming sites. Crackle, for example, offers new and classic television comedy, and Fandor and Mubi serve die-hard independent movie fans. This wealth of Internet video is altering viewing habits, especially among young people. You can see the steady and precipitous decline in weekly traditional TV viewing among 18- to 24-year-olds in Figure 4.

Ultimately, the convergence of the Internet and television will be even more seamless as there are other technologies further discouraging the distinction between the two. Slingbox and Roku, for example, allow users to "sling" television content to their computers and mobile devices. Viewers can also sling video in the other direction with devices such as Apple TV—digital content from apps like Netflix, Hulu, YouTube, and other streaming services; video from the streaming operations of the NBA, NHL, and MLB; and streamed video from a number of broadcast and cable channels—and send it to home television sets. In addition, using video-game consoles and Internet-enabled HDTVs (commonly called Smart TVs), 74% of all U.S. TV homes have direct Web-to-TV connections (Martin, 2017).

▶ **Figure 4** Weekly Traditional TV Viewing among 18- to 24-year-olds, Q2 of 2011–2016.
Source: Marketing Charts, "Traditional TV Viewing Trends Among 18–24-year-olds," Marketing Charts, 2016.

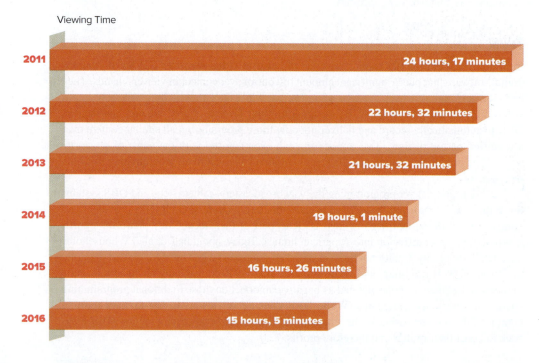

Viewing Time

Year	Viewing Time
2011	24 hours, 17 minutes
2012	22 hours, 32 minutes
2013	21 hours, 32 minutes
2014	19 hours, 1 minute
2015	16 hours, 26 minutes
2016	15 hours, 5 minutes

▶ Who has time for TV when there's so much video to watch?
HI & LOIS ©2011 by King Features Syndicate, Inc. World rights reserved. Reprinted by permission.

Interactive Television

The Internet is not the only technology that permits interactivity. Cable and satellite also allow viewers to "talk back" to content providers. But it is **digital cable television**, the delivery of digital images and other information to subscribers, that offers the truest form of interactive television. There are 61 million digital cable subscribers in the United States (Internet & Television Association, 2017).

Cable's digital channels permit multiplexing, carrying two or more different signals over the same channel. This, in turn, is made possible by *digital compression*, which "squeezes" signals to permit multiple signals to be carried over one channel. Digital compression works by removing redundant information from the transmission of the signal. For example, the set behind two actors in a movie scene might not change for several minutes. So why transmit the information that the set is there? Simply transmit the digital data that indicate what has changed in the scene, not what has not.

This expanded capacity makes possible *interactive cable*, that is, the ability of subscribers to talk back to the system operator (extra space on the channel is used for this back talk). And *this* permits the following services, many of which you already use: one-click shopping (you see it, you click on it, you buy it), local information on demand (news, traffic, and weather), program interactivity (choose a camera angle, learn more about an actor's career, play along with game show contestants), interactive program guides, and video games. But it is **video-on-demand (VOD)**—the ability to access pay-per-view movies and other content that can be watched at any time—that best shows the economic advantage of putting more control into viewers' hands. American television homes annually log 4.4 billion hours of on-demand movies and TV shows via cable (Friedman, 2014).

Phone-over-Cable

Another service offered by many MSOs is phone service over cable wires. Currently there are 31 million cable-delivered residential telephone subscribers (Internet & Television Association, 2017). Phone-over-cable offers a special benefit to MSOs. If telephone service can be delivered by the same cable that brings television into the home, so too can the Internet. And what's more, if the cable line is broadband and capable of handling digitally compressed data, that Internet service can be even faster than the service provided over traditional phone lines. Cable, in other words, can become a one-stop communications provider: television, VOD, audio, high-speed Internet access, long-distance and local phone service, multiple phone lines, and fax. This is **bundling**.

How valuable is a bundle-receiving subscriber to an MSO? Add together the bills you're probably paying right now—basic or premium cable, your Internet service provider, and your phone bill. What does that total? Now speculate how much pay-per-view and VOD you might buy now that you have broadband and a superfast cable modem. And what would you pay for home delivery of real-time sports or financial data? And the MSO would collect each time you accessed an interactive classified or commercial ad. That's how valuable a bundled subscriber will be.

▼ When Republican leaders ordered the cameras turned off, Democratic representatives turned to Periscope and Facebook Live to broadcast their anti-gun-violence demonstration from the House floor to C-SPAN and social networking sites.
Source: Rep. Beto O'Rourke/C-SPAN/Facebook

U.S. HOUSE SIT-IN PROTEST ON GUN LEGISLATION

LIVE Facebook Video from Rep. Beto O'Rourke (D-TX)

Smartphones, Tablets, and Social Networking Sites

Smartphones and tablets (and all contemporary handheld video game consoles) have made television watching an anywhere, anytime activity. We've already seen that watching streamed video on mobile devices is now quite routine, but it is likely to become even more common as social networking sites increase their commitment to video. Twitter live streams NBA basketball games. The league has also developed original programming for the site, which also live streams, among other content, NFL football games, Wimbledon tennis matches, CBS News, the NHL, major league baseball, and the Pac-12 Network. In 2016 Twitter live streamed the Republican and Democratic national conventions. Facebook Live streams professional soccer and the U.S. men's and women's national basketball teams. In addition, all the major professional sports leagues offer free apps that let mobile users access their content while on the go.

There are several apps that encourage not only mobile viewing but mobile broadcasting as well. Periscope and Facebook Live permit their users to connect to their social networking accounts and stream live video directly to their followers. These apps vaulted into public consciousness in 2016 when Democratic members of the U.S. House of Representatives used Periscope and Facebook Live to broadcast their House-floor protest over gun violence after the Republican leadership declared a recess, shutting off C-SPAN's coverage (Kantrowitz, 2016).

DEVELOPING MEDIA LITERACY SKILLS
Watching Satirical News

No matter whom you might have favored in the 2016 presidential election, you were likely among the 60% of Americans dissatisfied with the performance of the traditional press ("Low Marks," 2016). But what about television's satirical news shows? Have you considered their performance? HBO's *Last Week Tonight with John Oliver*, TBS's *Full Frontal with Samantha Bee*, Comedy Central's *The Daily Show with Trevor Noah*, CBS's *The Late Show with Stephen Colbert*, and NBC's *Saturday Night Live* and *Late Night with Seth Meyers* all played significant roles in helping people make sense of what was a confusing and dramatic political season (Robinson, 2016). But should they? Of course, when it's your candidate being lampooned, you might argue "no."

You, however, are a media-literate television viewer, so you understand and respect the power of media messages, you have knowledge of television's genre conventions and recognize when they are being mixed, and above all, you enjoy television content. And this is what makes televised satirical news such an interesting genre for consideration. Satirical television news, by definition, mixes genre conventions, is specifically wielded to have an impact (to reach people's consciences by poking fun at the powerful), and is designed to be enjoyed.

The popularity of these programs raises a number of questions for media-literate TV viewers. First, did they have an impact on the outcome of the election? At a time when so few Americans saw merit in the traditional media's coverage of political campaigns, was the satirists' influence magnified? Another question often raised about TV's satirical news is why it so often seems to have a liberal orientation. "Could it be that American political satire is biased toward liberals in the same way that American political talk radio is biased toward conservatives?" asks cultural critic Oliver Morrison (2015). He points to research "that found liberals and conservatives seemed to have different aesthetic tastes. Conservatives seemed to prefer stories with clear-cut endings. Liberals, on the other hand, had more tolerance for . . . uncertainty and ambiguity," the makings of good comedy in general and satire in specific. Or is it that satire—by definition— challenges the status quo, something traditionally valued by conservatives? Morrison quotes humor researcher Alison Dagnes: "Conservatism supports institutions, and satire aims to knock these institutions down a peg."

How do you answer these questions? There is little doubt that satirical television news is an important voice in the cultural forum. But is it a voice that adds to the conversation, or does it diminish how we talk about our world and how we talk to one another? Does the fact that satirical news comedians like Jon Stewart and Stephen Colbert are consistently ranked among the country's "most trusted" journalists change your answers (Meyers, 2015; Linkins, 2009)?

▲ What is the role and value of satirical television news like that delivered by John Oliver?
©*Jesse Dittmar*/The Washington Post/*Getty Images*

MEDIA LITERACY CHALLENGE
No Video for a Week

There is no better way to *become aware of the impact of the media on you and society* than to do without them. As a media-literate individual, you can test for yourself just how free you are of the power of one specific medium, video. See if you control your viewing or if your viewing controls you. To start, pick a five-day period and simply stop watching. No television. No videos on the Internet or your smartphone. No video games. Simply put, don't watch or even look at any video screen anywhere for five entire days. If you are adventurous, enlist one or more friends, family members, or roommates.

Simply changing your routine viewing behavior will not do very much for you unless you reflect on its meaning. Ask yourself (and any others you may have enlisted) these questions. How easy or difficult was it for you to break away from all video? Why was it easy or difficult? What did you learn about your video consumption habits? How did you use the freed-up time? Were you able to find productive activity, or did you spend your time longing for a screen? Be sure to describe how not watching affected your other life habits (eating, socializing with family and friends, news gathering, and the like). Describe your interactions with other people during this week. Did your conversations change? That is, were there alterations in duration, depth, or subject matter? If you were unable to complete the week of nonviewing, describe why. How easy or difficult was it to come to the decision to give up? Do you consider it a failure to have resumed watching before the five days were up? Why or why not? Once you resume your normal video habits, place yourself on a scale of 1 to 10, with 1 being "I Control Video" and 10 being "Video Controls Me." Explain your self-rating.

Resources for Review and Discussion

REVIEW POINTS: TYING CONTENT TO LEARNING OUTCOMES

▶ **Outline the history and development of the television and cable television industries and television itself as a medium.**

- ☐ In 1884 Paul Nipkow developed the first device for transmitting images. John Logie Baird soon used this mechanical scanning technology to send images long distance. Vladimir Zworykin and Philo Farnsworth developed electronic scanning technology in the 1920s, leading to the public demonstration of television in 1939.

- ☐ In the 1950s, the quiz show scandal, the business acumen of Lucille Ball, McCarthyism, and the ratings system shaped the nature of broadcast television. Cable, introduced in 1948, would soon effect even more change.

- ☐ Cable, designed initially for the importation of distant signals, became a mature medium when it began offering movies and other premium content.

▶ **Describe how the organizational and economic nature of the contemporary television and cable industries shapes the content of television.**

- ☐ Cable, dominated by large MSOs, offers programming in tiers that include basic, expanded basic, and premium cable. Some favor a new pricing scheme, à la carte.

- ☐ Direct broadcast satellite is the primary multichannel competitor to cable, now joined by fiber optic systems like FiOS.

▶ **Explain the relationship between television in all its forms and its viewers.**

- ☐ Once described as a vast wasteland, television is immensely popular, Americans' most used medium.

- ☐ Television has the greatest reach of all ad-supported media, and consumers cite it as the medium most likely to influence their purchasing decisions.

▶ **Identify new and converging video technologies and their potential impact on the television industry and its audience.**
   ☐ A host of technologies influence the television–viewer relationship, including DVD, DVR, video on the Internet, and interactive television.

▶ **Describe the digital and mobile television revolution.**
   ☐ Mobile video on smartphones, tablets, and other portable video devices is now common, aided by the availability of

streaming and live broadcasting apps and the delivery of video via social networking sites.

▶ **Apply key television-viewing media literacy skills to satirical news.**
   ☐ Satirical television news makes a significant contribution to the cultural forum, but is it for the better?

KEY TERMS

Nipkow disc, 181

pixel, 181

iconoscope tube, 182

kinescope, 182

coaxial cable, 183

microwave relay, 183

spot commercial sales, 183

Global Television Audience Metering (GTAM) meter, 186

nonlinear TV, 186

L+7, 186

C3 rating, 187

share, 187

community antenna television (CATV), 187

importation of distant signals, 188

all-channel legislation, 188

vast wasteland, 188

clear time, 190

reverse compensation, 190

retransmission fees, 190

off-network, 190

pilot, 190

put, 190

first-run syndication, 192

stripping, 192

premium cable, 192

fiber optics, 192

tiers, 193

expanded basic cable, 193

multiple system operator (MSO), 193

à la carte pricing, 193

subscription TV, 194

cord-cutting, 195

cord-never, 195

over-the-top (OTT), 195

zero-TV homes, 195

time-shifting, 197

zipping, 197

digital video disc (DVD), 197

digital video recorder (DVR), 197

bandwidth, 197

broadband, 197

digital cable television, 199

video-on-demand (VOD), 199

bundling, 199

QUESTIONS FOR REVIEW

1. What is the importance of each of the following to the history of television: Paul Nipkow, John Logie Baird, Vladimir Zworykin, Philo Farnsworth, and Newton Minow?

2. What was the impact on television of the quiz show scandal, *I Love Lucy*, McCarthyism, and the Nielsen ratings?

3. How are the ratings taken? What are some complaints about the ratings system?

4. How does a program typically make it to the air? How does syndication figure in this process?

5. How have cable, VCR, DVD, DVR, and DBS affected the networks?

6. What are some of the changes in television wrought by cable?

7. Explain the difference between basic cable, expanded basic cable, premium cable, pay-per-view, à la carte pricing, and skinny bundles.

8. What are importation of distant signals, premium cable, and fiber optics? How are they related? What do they have to do with cable's maturity as a medium?

9. What is OTT, and how does it affect what we see on the screen?

10. In what ways can viewers access video on the Internet? Via mobile devices? What kinds of content are available on these platforms?

To maximize your study time, check out CONNECT to access the SmartBook study module for this chapter, watch videos, and explore other resources.

QUESTIONS FOR CRITICAL THINKING AND DISCUSSION

1. As an independent producer, what kind of program would you develop for the networks? How immune do you think you could be from the pressures that exist in this process?

2. Are you a cable subscriber? Why or why not? At what level? Would you prefer à la carte pricing? Why or why not?

3. Could you be a cord-never or live in a zero-TV home? If not, what keeps you committed to your MSO? What would it take to get you to cut the cord?

REFERENCES

1. "10 standout digital stars." (2016, June 21). *Variety*, pp. 52–57.

2. Adamczyk, A. (2016, February 17). Cable prices are rising at four times the rate of inflation. *Time*. Online: http://time.com/money/4227133/cable-price-four-times-inflation/

3. Auletta, K. (2014, February 3). Outside the box. *The New Yorker*, pp. 54–61.

4. Ault, S. (2016, April 26). Young eyes on Netflix. *Variety*, p. 17.

5. Ball, S., & Bogatz, G. A. (1970). *The first year of* Sesame Street: *An evaluation.* Princeton, NJ: Educational Testing Service.

6. Bednarski, P. J. (2016, April 14). Digital viewing going up; TV still has a lock. *MediaPost*. Online: http://www.mediapost.com/publications/article/273526/digital-viewing-going-up-tv-still-has-a-lock.html

7. Chin, F. (1978). *Cable television: A comprehensive bibliography.* New York: IFI/Plenum.

8. Cook, T. D., Appleton, H., Conner, R. F., Shaffer, A., Tamkin, G., & Weber, S. J. (1975). *Sesame Street Revisited.* New York: Russell Sage Foundation.

9. Friedman, W. (2016a, July 13). Broadcast-only TV, no-TV reception homes grow. *MediaPost*. Online: http://www.mediapost.com/publications/article/280205/broadcast-only-tv-no-tv-reception-homes-grow.html

10. Friedman, W. (2016b, March 8). SVOD reaches critical mass, penetrates half of U. S. homes. *MediaPost*. Online: http://www.mediapost.com/publications/article/270739/svod-reaches-critical-mass-penetrates-half-of-us.html

11. Friedman, W. (2014, April 8). Video-on-demand viewing on the rise. MediaPost. Online: http://www.mediapost.com/publications/article/223237/video-on-demand-viewing-on-the-rise.html

12. Internet & Television Association. (2017). Industry data. Online: https://www.ncta.com/industry-data

13. Kantrowitz, A. (2016, June 22). C-SPAN is airing the House's sit-in using Periscope and Facebook Live. *BuzzFeed*. Online: https://www.google.com/?gws_rd=ssl#q=facebook+live

14. Khatchatourian, M. (2014, June 3). It's not just TV, it's OTT! *Variety*, p. 79.

15. Kuralt, C. (1977). *When television was young* (videotape). New York: CBS News.

16. Linkins, J. (2009, August 22). Online poll: Jon Stewart is America's most trusted newsman. *Huffington Post*. Online: http://www.huffingtonpost.com/2009/07/22/time-magazine-poll-jon-st_n_242933.html

17. Littleton, C., and Kissell, R. (2016, May 3). Big data changes numbers game. *Variety*, p. 20.

18. "Low marks for major players in 2016 election—including the winner." (2016, November 21). *Pew Research Center*. Online: http://www.people-press.org/2016/11/21/low-marks-for-major-players-in-2016-election-including-the-winner/

19. Mandese, J. (2016, September 23). Percent of TV channels viewed drops to single digits, Nielsen attributes digital choices. *MediaPost*. Online: http://www.mediapost.com/publications/article/285348/percent-of-tv-channels-viewed-drops-to-single-digi.html

20. Marketing Charts. (2016). Traditional TV viewing trends among 18–24-year-olds. Online: http://www.marketingcharts.com/television/are-young-people-watching-less-tv-24817/attachment/nielsen-traditional-tv-weekly-viewing-trends-among-18-24-q12011-q22016-oct2016/

21. Martin, C. (2017, January 29). Internet-connected TV penetration reaches 74%. *MediaPost*. Online: http://www.mediapost.com/publications/article/293854/internet-connected-tv-penetration-reaches-74.html?utm_source=newsletter&utm_medium=email&utm_content=readmore&utm_campaign=100036

22. Meyers, J. (2015, January 16). The 10 most trusted personalities in TV news. *Newsmax*. Online: http://www.newsmax.com/TheWire/10-most-trusted-personalities-tv/2015/01/16/id/619016/

23. Morrison, O. (2015, February 14). Waiting for the conservative Jon Stewart. *The Atlantic*. Online: http://www.theatlantic.com/entertainment/archive/2015/02/why-theres-no-conservative-jon-stewart/385480/

24. National Association of Broadcasters, John F. Kennedy's new FCC chair, Newton Minow.

25. "Net worth." (2017, March 21). *Variety*, pp. 40–41.

26. Nocera, J. (2016, May 19). Screen grab. *The New York Times Magazine*, pp. 40–47, 55–57.

27. Richter, F. (2017, January 18). Netflix & co. surpass DVD & Blu-ray sales. *Statista*. Online: https://www.statista.com/chart/7654/home-entertainment-spending-in-the-us/?utm_source=Infographic+Newsletter&utm_campaign=22cf6e09df-InfographicTicker_EN_Late_00026&utm_medium=email&utm_term=0_666fe64c5d-22cf6e09df-295452301

28. Richter, F. (2016, February 23). The state of video streaming in the United States. *Statista*. Online: https://www.statista.com/chart/4400/the-state-of-video-streaming-in-the-united-states/

29. Robinson, J. (2016, November 9). Without Jon Stewart, TV's political satire let us down. *Vanity Fair*. Online: http://www.vanityfair.com/hollywood/2016/11/president-donald-trump-jon-stewart-daily-show-weekend-update

30. Savage, J. (2016, April 10). Top 5 Facebook video statistics for 2016. *Social Media Today*. Online: http://www.socialmediatoday.com/marketing/top-5-facebook-video-statistics-2016-infographic

31. Schultz, E. J. (2017, January 10). Mercedes jumps back into the Super Bowl. *Advertising Age*. Online: http://adage.com/article/special-report-super-bowl/mercedes-heading-super-bowl/307446/?utm_source=daily_email&utm_medium=newsletter&utm_campaign=adage&ttl=1484610028?utm_visit=100067

32. Sedulus, "Sesame Street," *New Republic*, June 5, 1970.

33. Sharma, A. (2016, March 23). 70 percent of US consumers binge watch TV, bingers average five episodes per sitting. *Deloitte*. Online: https://www2.deloitte.com/us/en/pages/about-deloitte/articles/press-releases/digital-democracy-survey-tenth-edition.html

34. Smith, A. (2017, January 12). Record shares of Americans now own smartphones, have home broadband. *Pew Research Center*. Online: http://www.pewresearch.org/fact-tank/2017/01/12/evolution-of-technology/

35. Smith, S. (2012, March 23). End of an age: Netflix, Hulu, Amazon will beat physical video viewing in 2012. *MediaPost*. Online: http://www.mediapost.com/publications/article/170863/end-of-an-age-netflix-hulu-amazon-will-beat-phy.html

36. Spangler, T. (2016, November 15). Thin is in. *Variety*, pp. 47–49.

37. Steel, E. (2016, February 3). Nielsen plays catch-up as streaming era wreaks havoc on TV raters. *The New York Times*, p. A1.

38. Sterling, C. H., & Kitross, J. M. (1990). *Stay tuned: A concise history of American broadcasting*. Belmont, CA: Wadsworth.

39. Television Advertising Bureau. (2016). TV basics. Online: https://www.tvb.org/Default.aspx?TabID=1585

Cultural Forum Blue Column icon, Media Literacy Red Torch Icon, Using Media Green Gear icon, Developing Media book in starburst icon: ©McGraw-Hill Education

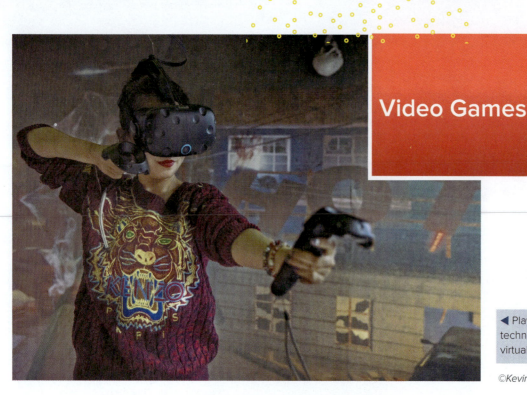

Video Games

9

◀ Players' comfort with technology fuels the boom in virtual reality game play.

©Kevin Frayer/Getty Images

Learning Objectives

Video games are accelerating the five trends reshaping mass communication and the mass media industries. They are the product of a highly concentrated industry, they are luring people away from the more traditional media (audience fragmentation), they are used as and filled with advertising (hypercommercialization), they know no borders (globalization), and they are played on numerous technologies, from game consoles to personal computers to the Internet to smartphones and tablets (convergence). And even though the U.S. game industry grosses nearly twice as much as Hollywood does every year, mass communication experts are only recently taking this medium seriously. After studying this chapter, you should be able to

▶ Outline the history and development of games and the gaming industry.

▶ Describe how the organizational and economic nature of the contemporary gaming industry shapes the content of games.

▶ Explain the relationship between games and their players.

▶ Identify changes in the game industry brought about by new and converging technologies.

▶ Apply key game-playing media literacy skills to understanding and combating the frequent mistreatment of female gamers by some male players.

1931 ▶ *Baffle Ball*, first mass-produced arcade game
1933 *Contact*, first electric pinball game

1940

1947 ▶ Flippers come to pinball
1951 Japanese playing-card company Marufuku changes its name to Nintendo

©Wayne Namerow Collection, photograph Courtesy of Wayne Namerow

1955

1961 Russell creates *Spacewar*
1964 Sega formed
1966 Sega exports *Periscope* to United States and Europe; first amusement game export;
▶ 25 cents per play established as arcade game standard
1968 Baer patents interactive television game

1970

1971 ▶ *Computer Space*, first arcade computer game
1972 *Odyssey* released; Atari formed, develops *Pong*
1975 *Home Pong* debuts; *Gunfight*, first game to use a microprocessor
1976 *Channel F*, first programmable, cartridge-based home game
1977 First handheld video game
1979 First handheld programmable game system
1980 Home *Space Invaders*, first arcade game for home systems; *Pac-Man*
1981 *Donkey Kong*

©Brand X Pictures/ PunchStock RF

©Wayne Namerow Collection, photograph Courtesy of Wayne Namerow

1985

1985 Nintendo's NES introduced
1986 *Legend of Zelda*
1987 PC games introduced
1989 ▶ Game Boy
1990 *Super Mario Bros. 3*
1993 *Doom* released
1994 ESRB ratings established; *Myst* released
1995 PlayStation in United States

©Ken Hively/Los Angeles Times/Getty Images

2000

2000 ▶ Xbox
2001 Game Cube
2003 *Second Life* launched
2004 *Halo 2* released; PlayStation Portable introduced
2006 Nintendo Wii
2011 *Call of Duty: Modern Warfare 3* earns $1 billion in 16 days
2012 Xbox entertainment use surpasses gaming; GamerGate erupts
2013 Wii U, PlayStation 4, Xbox One
2014 *Destiny* earns $500 million in 24 hours
2015 Global mobile gaming revenues overtake console revenues for the first time
2016 Virtual reality gaming

©Digital Vision/PunchStock RF

©Toy Alan King/Alamy

"WHY ARE YOU PLAYING VIDEO GAMES? Don't you have homework or a paper due or something?"

"This is more important. And anyway, what are you, my mother?"

"Nope, I just don't want to have to dig up another roommate when you flunk out, that's all."

"Glad to know you care. And anyway, it may look like I'm playing video games, but I'm really doing research for my global politics class. Check it out. This is a game that the U.S. Navy put out, MMOWGLI. It stands for Massively Multiplayer Online Wargame Leveraging the Internet, and the idea is to combat Somali pirates."

"A game from the government about thwarting Somali pirates?"

"That's this one. There are others, depending on what problem the Office of Naval Research wants help with. They created a game environment where players like us and experts on all kinds of issues can share new ideas and collaborate with other players. We earn points to win the game."

"Why does the Navy care what you think?"

"It doesn't, not really. But it cares about what all of us think. It's Web-based, so MMOWGLI lets the Navy strategize with way more people than it could ever assemble face-to-face. Navy people know Navy stuff. Africa experts know Africa stuff. Other people like us know other stuff. So we all go online and play out different solutions and unimagined possibilities. You know, let a whole network of people, the crowd, get involved in the process. Wanna play?"

"No thanks. If I'm going to play games, I'd like to kill bad guys with a vast array of magnificent weapons and be able to leap over tall buildings in a single bound."

In this chapter we examine games played on a variety of electronic, microprocessor-based platforms. But before we get deeper into our discussion of the sophisticated, entertaining, and sometimes (as you can tell from our opening vignette) not very playful games that abound today, let's look at their roots in the convergence of pinball machines and military simulators. This is fitting because, as with other media, possibly even more so, converging technologies define video games' present and future.

A Short History of Computer and Video Games

Carnival man David Gottlieb invented the first mass-produced arcade game, *Baffle Ball*, in 1931. A small wooden cabinet, it had only one moving part, a plunger. Players would launch a ball into the playing field, a slanted surface with metal "pins" surrounding "scoring holes." The object was to get the ball into one of the holes. Gottlieb was soon manufacturing 400 cabinets a day. Just as quickly, he had many imitators. One, Harry Williams, invented *Contact*, the first electronic pinball game. Williams was an engineer, and his 1933 gaming innovations were electronic scoring (*Baffle Ball* players had to keep their scores in their heads) and scoring holes, or pockets, that threw the ball back into the playing field (in *Baffle Ball,* when a ball dropped into a hole it was gone). The popularity of arcade games exploded, and players' enthusiasm was fueled even more when slot-machine makers entered the field, producing games with cash payouts. With the Depression in full force in the 1930s, however, civic leaders were not much in favor of this development, and several locales, most notably New York City, banned the games. Pinball was considered gambling.

David Gottlieb had the answer. Games of skill were not gambling, nor were games that paid off in additional games. In 1947, he introduced *Humpty Dumpty*, a six-flipper game that rewarded high-scorers with replays. Bans were lifted, pinball returned to the arcades, even more players were attracted to the skills-based electronic games, and the stage was set for what we know today as video games. As Steven Baxter of the *CNN Computer Connection* wrote, "You can't say that video games grew out of pinball, but you can assume that video games wouldn't have happened without it. It's like bicycles and the

Gottlieb's *Baffle Ball* and *Humpty Dumpty*.
(left, right): ©Wayne Namerow Collection, photograph Courtesy of Wayne Namerow

automobile. One industry leads to the other and then they exist side-by-side. But you had to have bicycles to one day have motor cars." Games writer Steven Kent adds, "New technologies do not simply spring out of thin air. They need to be associated with familiar industries or ideas. People may have jokingly referred to the first automobiles as 'horseless carriages,' but the name also helped define them. The name changed them from nebulous, unexplainable machines to an extension of an already accepted mode of transportation" (both quotes from Kent, 2001, pp. 1–2).

Today's Games Emerge

Throughout the late 1950s and 1960s, computers were hulking giants, filling entire rooms (see the chapter on the Internet and social media). Most displayed their output on paper in the form of teletype. But the very best, most advanced computers, those designed for military research and analysis, were a bit sleeker and had monitors for output display. Only three universities—MIT, the University of Utah, and Stanford—and a few dedicated research installations had these machines. At MIT, a group of self-described nerds, the Tech Model Railroad Club (TMRC), began writing programs for fun for a military computer. Club members would leave their work next to the computer so that others could build on what had come before. One member, Steve Russell, decided to write the ultimate program, an interactive game. It took him 200 hours over six months to produce the first interactive computer game, *Spacewar*, completed in 1961. This version featured toggle switches that controlled the speed and direction of two spaceships and the torpedoes they fired at each other. His final version, completed the next year, had an accurate map of the stars in the background and a sun with a mathematically precise gravitational field that influenced play. Russell and his clubmates even built remote control units with switches for every game function, the first game pad. "We thought about trying to make money off it for two or three days but concluded that there wasn't a way that it could be done," said Russell (quoted in Kent, 2001, p. 20).

But another college student, Nolan Bushnell, thought differently (DeMaria & Wilson, 2004). For two years after the completion of Russell's game, the TMRC distributed it to other schools for free. Bushnell, who worked in an arcade to pay for his engineering studies at the University of Utah, played *Spacewar* incessantly. After graduation he dedicated himself to developing a coin-operated version of the game that had consumed so much of his time. He knew that to make money, it would have to attract more than computer enthusiasts, so he designed a futuristic-looking fiberglass cabinet. The result, *Computer Space*, released in 1971, was a dismal failure. It was far too complicated for casual play, doing good business

Nolan Bushnell and a few of his toys.
©Ken Hively/Los Angeles Times/Getty Images

▲ Original *Pong*.
©Mike Derer/AP Photo

near college campuses but bombing in bowling alleys and beer halls. Yet Bushnell was undeterred. With two friends and investments of $250 each, he quit his engineering job and incorporated Atari in 1972.

Long before this, in 1951, Ralph Baer, an engineer for a military contractor charged with developing "the best TV set in the world," decided a good set should do more than receive a few channels (remember, this was before cable's rise). He suggested building games into the receivers. His bosses were unimpressed. Fifteen years later Baer was working for another defense contractor when he drafted the complete schematics for a video-game console that would sell for about $20. He patented it in 1968 and licensed his device to Magnavox, which, in 1972, marketed the first home video-game system as *Odyssey* and sold it for $100.

Odyssey was a simple game offering two square spots to represent two players (or paddles), a ball, and a center line. It had six plug-in cartridges and transparent, colored screen overlays producing 12 games, all very rudimentary. Its high cost and Magnavox's decision to sell it through its television set dealers—leading to the incorrect perception that it could be played only on Magnavox sets—limited its success. Only 100,000 units were sold. But with *Odyssey* and Atari,

> the stage was set for the introduction of a new art form, and a new industry. The technological foundation was built. The earliest pioneers had seen farther than any others and had made their tentative steps along the path. The world was in flux, as new politics, new music, and new social consciousness began to spread throughout the United States and Europe. The 60s were over. A generation of young people dreamed new dreams and broke down the status quo. It was into that world that first Ralph Baer and then Nolan Bushnell made their humble offerings, and changed the world in ways no one could have foreseen. (DeMaria & Wilson, 2004, p. 17)

The spark that set off the game revolution was *Pong*, Atari's arcade ping-pong game, introduced in 1972. Bushnell had seen *Odyssey* at an electronics show and set his people to creating a coin-operated version (Atari later agreed to pay a licensing fee to Magnavox). The two-player game was an overnight hit, selling 100,000 units in its first year—and twice as many knockoffs (Burnham, 2001, p. 61). Players poured quarters into games looking remarkably like *Pong*, including Harry Williams's *Paddle-Ball*, Rally's *For-Play*, and then in an effort to head off what Nolan Bushnell called "the jackals," Atari's own *Pong Doubles*, *Super Pong*, and *Quadrapong* (Sellers, 2001).

Rapid-Fire Developments

What followed, partly as a result of the swift advance of the microchip and computer industries (and a healthy dose of technological genius from a thriving game industry in Japan), was a rapid-fire succession of innovation and development. In 1975 Atari, by marketing *Home Pong* through Sears, made its first steps toward bringing arcade games into the home. Its 1980 release of home *Space Invaders* cemented the trend. Also in 1975, Midway began importing *Gunfight* from Japanese manufacturer Taito. *Gunfight* was significant for two reasons. Although Sega, with *Periscope*, began importing arcade games into the United States in 1966, *Gunfight* was the first imported video game. It was also the first game to use a computer microprocessor. In 1976, Fairchild Camera and Instrument introduced *Channel F*, the first programmable, cartridge-based home game. Mattel Toys brought true electronic games to handheld devices in 1977, with titles like *Missile Attack*, *Auto Race*, and *Football* played on handheld, calculator-sized **LED (light-emitting diode)**, and **LCD (liquid crystal display)**, screens. In 1979 Milton Bradley released Microvision, the first programmable handheld game system. Two Japanese arcade imports, Namco's *Pac-Man* in 1980 and

▲ Nintendo's *Legend of Zelda*, introduced in 1986, pioneered open structure play, now standard in modern games.
Source: Nintendo

Nintendo's *Donkey Kong* in 1981, became instant classics, all-time best sellers, and with the introduction of Nintendo's groundbreaking game console NES in 1985, home-version successes. The Japanese company further advanced gaming with its 1986 release of home console game *Legend of Zelda*, revolutionary because it introduced open structure play—that is, players could go wherever they wanted and there were multiple routes to winning, now standard in modern games.

Arcade games, handheld systems, and home game consoles were joined by personal computer games, beginning with the 1987 release of NEC's hybrid PC/console in Japan. With games being played on microprocessor-based consoles, producing them for microprocessor-based PCs was a simple matter. By the early 1990s, CD-ROM-based computer games were common and successful. *Doom* (1993) and *Myst* (1994) were among the first big personal computer game hits. *Doom* hinted at a development soon to come in games because it could be played over **LANs (local area networks)** of computers, typically in a single building; that is, it was an interactive game played by several people over a computer network. It was also the first **first-person perspective game** as well as the first first-person shooter game; gamers "carried" the weapon, and all action in the game was seen through their eyes.

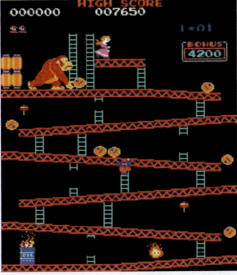

◀ Namco's *Pac-Man* and Nintendo's *Donkey Kong*, introduced as arcade games in the early 1980s, became instant home-version classics when Nintendo introduced its NES game console in 1985.
Sources: (left) Namco; (right) Nintendo

▲ Two of the first interactive games, iD Software's *Doom (left)* and Cyan, Inc.'s *Myst (right)*, introduced gaming to first-person play.
Sources: (left) iD Software; (right) Cyan, Inc.

Games and Their Players

Two-thirds of all American households are home to at least one person who regularly plays video games, that is, for 3 or more hours a week (Entertainment Software Association, 2016). But before we look at these people a bit more closely, we need to define exactly what constitutes a video game.

What Is a Video Game?

As technologies converge, the same game can be played on an increasing number of platforms. *Myst*, for example, was originally a computer game written for Macintosh computers, then IBM PCs, then external CD-ROM drives, and then video-game consoles such as PlayStation. Now it can be played online. Versions of *Donkey Kong* can be played in arcades and on consoles, on the Internet, on Macs and PCs, and on handheld game consoles. *Q*bert* can be played on arcade machines and on collectible Nelsonic game wrist watches. Thousands of games can be played on smartphones and tablets. For our purposes, then, a game is a **video game** when the action of the game takes place interactively onscreen. By this definition, an online text-based game such as a **MUD (multiuser dimension)**, which has no moving images (games like 1977's *Zork* and 2016's *Azereth*), is a video game, but the home version of *Trivial Pursuit*, employing a DVD to offer video hints to those playing the board game, is not.

That takes care of the technologically based half of the word (*video*), but what is a *game*? For our purposes, a video game is a game when a player has direct involvement in the on-screen action to produce some desired outcome. In a MUD, for example, players use text—words—to create personalities, environments, even worlds in which they interact with others toward some specific end. That's a game. But what about *Mario Teaches Typing*, a cartridge-based learning aid? Even though its goal is teaching, because it has gamelike features (in this case, the famous Super Mario and the manipulation of on-screen action to meet a particular end), it's a game. The essay titled "Using Games for Good" looks at games that function as more than entertainment.

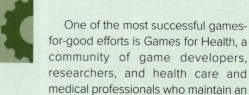

USING MEDIA TO MAKE A DIFFERENCE
Using Games for Good

The video-game industry has reached a level of legitimacy and respectability equal to that of other mass media. Now it is being asked the same questions regarding content as the older media are: What is the impact on kids? What regulations should be imposed? How is the medium used? And just as important, how can we use the medium to make a positive difference?

Game industry professionals, social scientists, educators, and parents regularly examine this last question. Their efforts focus on the use of games for policy change, training, and learning. Their products include initiatives such as Cisco Systems' *Peter Packet Game and Challenge,* designed to confront poverty, and the work of nonprofit Global Kids Inc., which has teamed with organizations such as Lego, Microsoft, and PBS in an effort to encourage kids to create their own educational video games. Persuasive Games is yet another example of a provider building electronic games designed for instruction and activism, as is P.O.V. Interactive, which uses interactive games in coordination with PBS documentaries to explore environmental and other issues. The National Academy of Sciences is funding game development by the Federation of American Scientists, designed to build enthusiasm for science as a discipline and a career.

One of the most successful games-for-good efforts is Games for Health, a community of game developers, researchers, and health care and medical professionals who maintain an ongoing "best practices" conversation—online and in annual conferences—to share information about the impact existing and original games can have on health care and policy. Japanese game maker Konami's *Dance Dance Revolution*, for example, is an existing **exergame** that invites people to exercise while they play. Players follow cascading arrows on a video screen, mimicking their movements on a large footpad attached by a cable to a game console. Sony and Nike teamed up to produce another beneficial exergame, *EyeToy Kinetic*, that encourages users to kickbox, practice yoga, or engage in a number of other physical activities in a variety of simulated environments. Other existing games—just about anything played on a handheld console—are frequently used to reduce children's anxiety before anesthesia, dialysis, or chemotherapy. Research has shown that time on a portable game relaxes preoperative children even more than their parents do.

New games, too, are developed specifically to meet people's health needs. They are particularly effective in matters of health because of their interactivity. "One of the great strengths of video games is that automatically a player goes into a game expecting to have some agency [control]," wrote Amy Green, one of the developers of *That Dragon, Cancer*, a game designed to aid people dealing with a family member's cancer (in Suellentrop, 2016, p. C1). For example, Nintendo's *GlucoBoy* and *Dr. Mario* help children and other patients manage their own diabetic needs. Another games-for-good practitioner, Games for Change, joined forces with the Half the Sky Movement, a global effort to reduce oppression and build opportunity for poor women, to bring *Half the Sky Movement: The Game* to Facebook. Players take on virtual tasks such as collecting books for young girls in Kenya. Their in-game success leads to real-world payoff; for example, collecting enough books unlocks a donation of actual books to a nonprofit that brings improved literacy and gender equality to developing countries.

These efforts are examples of the **gamification** of society, using video-game skills and conventions to solve real-world problems in medicine, health, policy, personal responsibility, and in fact, any issue that humans face. In this sense, gamification is the ultimate use of games for good.

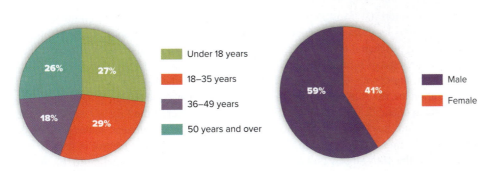

◀ **Figure 1** Game Players' Demographics, 2016.
Source: Entertainment Software Association, 2016

Under 18 years
18–35 years
36–49 years
50 years and over

Male
Female

26% 27% 18% 29%

59% 41%

Who Is Playing?

What do we know about the 190 million regular American video-game players? For one thing, they are not necessarily the stereotypical teenage boys gaming away in their parents' basements, as you can see in Figure 1 and from these data (Entertainment Software Association, 2016):

- The average game player is 35 years old; 44% of American game players are over 36.
- Women 18 or older represent a greater proportion of the gaming population (31%) than boys 18 or younger (17%).
- Forty-eight percent of U.S. households own a dedicated game console.
- Fifty-four percent of gamers play with others, either in-person or online, and a majority play with friends and family (Figure 2).
- Fifty-three percent feel video games help them connect with friends; 42% say games help them spend time with family.

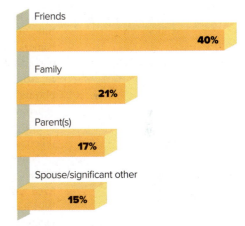

Friends **40%**
Family **21%**
Parent(s) **17%**
Spouse/significant other **15%**

▲ **Figure 2** With Whom Do Players Play?
Source: Entertainment Software Association of America, 2016.

◀ The skinny, sun-deprived teen boy gamer stereotype may persist, but it doesn't reflect the reality.
GET FUZZY ©2007 Darby Conley. Used by permission of ANDREWS MCMEEL SYNDICATION. All rights reserved.

Scope and Nature of the Video-Game Industry

Players in the United States spend more than $16.5 billion a year on game content, another $4.9 billion on hardware, and $2.1 billion more on accessories (Entertainment Software Association, 2016). Globally, gaming is a $100 billion-a-year industry, overshadowing all other forms of entertainment (Gilsdorf, 2016). A championship video-game tournament can easily draw 70,000 live spectators, and more than 70 million people across the globe watch high-level game play on the Internet—as many as 8 million at the same time—an audience sufficiently large to encourage Amazon to buy Twitch, a game streaming site with 9.7 million active daily viewers who watch on average 106 minutes a day (Schultz, 2017). Several college sports conferences, for example, the Big Ten, sanction intercollegiate **e-sports**, streamed online game competition. Half of YouTube's top 100 channels are gaming-focused, as is every one of its top 10 ("Most Popular," 2016). *Grand Theft Auto V* made $1 billion in 3 days in 2013, 14 days faster than the amount of time it took the movie *Avatar* to make $1 billion, and 16 days faster than it took the film *The Avengers* to reach the same goal; it earned $800 million in its first day, selling 16.5 million units, both records.

As is the case with every media industry we've studied so far, concentration and globalization are the rule in gaming. In 2014 alone, major game-design shops bought $15 billion worth of smaller operations; in 2015 Activision, owner of the *Call of Duty* and *World of Warcraft* franchises, paid $5.9 billion for King Digital Entertainment, makers of mobile game hits like *Candy Crush*; and in 2016 Warner Bros. acquired full control of game-based Machinima, the 10th-largest online video company in America (Spangler, 2016). As for game console sales, they are the sole province of three companies—the United States' Microsoft, best known for Xbox and Kinect, and two Japanese companies, Nintendo (Wii) and Sony (PlayStation). Versions of PlayStation and Xbox have long dominated sales and time-of-play. But Wii, introduced in 2006 to appeal specifically to new, nontraditional gamers, has gained significant popularity, primarily because it permits full-body, interactive play using a variety of control wands rather than the typical game's button-laden controller. In 2010 Microsoft met Wii's challenge with Kinect, a motion-sensitive game that reads players' body movements without controllers or wands of any kind. Equipped with facial- and voice-recognition capabilities, Kinect is the fastest-selling consumer electronics device in history, selling 8 million units in its first 60 days of availability (besting former champs iPhone and iPad; Kato, 2012).

Nintendo's cartridge-based Game Boy Advance, multimedia DSi (released in 2009), and glasses-free 3-D, Internet-capable 3DS (2011) have dominated handheld devices. Sony countered with PlayStation Portable (2004), offering Internet access for multiplayer gaming, and Wi-Fi–capable PlayStation Vita (2012), boasting the power and graphics of a console and video streaming. But note that all these consoles and handhelds were released in relatively rapid succession. Why? Because hardware makers are struggling to recapture players' loyalty as gamers increasingly abandon consoles and handhelds for smartphones and tablets. Thus, in addition to the frequent upgrades of their mobile devices, all three manufacturers introduced powerful new consoles in 2013 and 2014 and then very quickly introduced even more powerful devices. Sony's PlayStation 4 and PlayStation 4 Pro, introduced in 2016, let players broadcast their games in real time to the Internet, encouraging friends to join in. Its PlayStation Suite offers an array of games that can be played across consoles, handhelds, tablets, and smartphones. Microsoft's Xbox One S, also released in 2016, while maintaining Kinect's features, is a home entertainment hub, integrating gaming, television, the Internet, and movie and music streaming services. When joined with its SmartGlass application, players' tablets become second game and video screens. Nintendo's Switch, released in 2017, is a fully Internet-capable hybrid console/handheld device that can also play cartridge games.

Their dominance in hardware provides Microsoft, Nintendo, and Sony with more than sales revenue. **Third-party publishers**, companies that create games for existing systems, naturally want their best games on the most popular systems. And just as naturally, better games attract more buyers to the systems that support them. Third-party publishers produce their most popular titles for all systems. For example, Activision's *Call of Duty* is available for all consoles and Macs and PCs; the hugely popular *Madden NFL*, which sells more than 5 million copies a year, and the *MVP Baseball* series come from EA Sports; *Metal Gear* is from Konami; *Tony Hawk* is from Activision; *Elder Scrolls* is from Bethesda Softworks; and *Batman* is from Warner Bros. Interactive. Conversely, Codemaster's *MTV Music Generator* is available only for PlayStation and Xbox, and several third-party publishers produce Wii-only software—for example, Ubisoft and EA's Headgate division. Console makers do produce their own titles. Nintendo has the *Pokémon, Super Mario,* and *Pikmin* series. Sony publishes the *Gran Turismo* line, and Microsoft offers titles such as *XNS Sports* and *Halo.* Concentration exists in the game software business just as it does on the hardware side. Atari owns several game makers, including Infogrames, and EA controls nearly 50% of all video-game sales. In mid-2011 EA further increased its dominance of the content side of the industry with its purchase of casual game developer PopCap, source of some of the most popular free online games such as *Bejeweled* and *Plants vs. Zombies.* In an effort to counter this trend, however, a number of websites for independent game designers has sprung up. Most notable is Humble Indie Bundle. Small developers who cannot afford to distribute and market their games on the scale of the big companies upload their games to its website. Interested players can buy them free of copy- and other theft-protection so that they can be shared with other gamers. The games are designed for all platforms and, once bundled with other games, are for sale at whatever price a buyer wishes to pay, with a portion of the proceeds going to charity. In its first two years of operation it earned more than $11 million for the site operators, game designers, and charities, and *PC Gamer* magazine named the Humble Indie Bundle its 2011 community hero for its support of the indie game development market (Francis, 2011).

A serious problem faced by third-party game creators is that, as in the more traditional media, especially film, production and marketing costs are skyrocketing. Not only has the production technology itself become more sophisticated and therefore expensive, but games, like movie franchises build followings. Given that, the creative forces behind them can demand more recognition and compensation. In 2001, the average game cost $5 million to produce and $2 million to promote. Today, the cost of development *alone* averages between $25 and $50 million, and a blockbuster like *Destiny,* with its musical score by Paul McCartney, cost $500 million to produce (but consider that *Destiny* returned that much in sales in its first 24 hours on the market; Graser, 2014). Again, as with film, industry insiders and fans are expressing concern over the industry's reliance on sequels of franchises and licensed content, including movie- and television-based games. For example, there are over 100 different *Mario* games,

▲ A championship game tournament can easily draw 70,000 spectators.
©Robyn Beck/AFP/Getty Images

▲ Two of video game's most popular titles, EA Sports' *Madden NFL* and Activision's *360 Call of Duty,* are from third-party publishers.
(left) Source: EA Sports; (right) Source: Activision

and money is increasingly diverted to pay for licensed properties like *James Bond 007* and *Spider-Man.* And while industry research indicates that a majority of players want game makers to rely less on licensed content and sequels, those wants are in conflict with three important realities of the contemporary game industry: production, promotion, and distribution costs are soaring; 50% of all games introduced to the market fail; and 39 of the top 40 best-selling video and computer games of 2015 were either a franchise sequel or a licensed title. Buffeted by difficult economic times like other media, the game industry wants to mitigate its risks, and when franchise titles such as *Call of Duty* and *Grand Theft Auto* can top half a billion dollars in sales in their first few days of availability, insiders see sequels as a reasonable strategy.

Trends and Convergence in the Video-Game Industry

Like every media industry we've studied, the game industry is experiencing significant change, most of it driven by convergence and hypercommercialism.

Convergence Everywhere

Cable television giants Comcast and Cox each offer game services for their broadband customers; both direct broadcast satellite (DBS) providers also offer interactive game services. Most Internet service providers offer some form of online interactive games (see the chapter on the Internet and social media). AOL Games, for example, provides scores of games from designers such as EA Sports and Funkitron. Newspapers *USA Today*, the *Los Angeles Times*, and *The New York Times* maintain gaming platforms to foster loyalty, sell advertising, and connect with their readers. Games account for 15% of the sponsored material on gossip/news site BuzzFeed (Willens, 2016). Many game makers, too, offer online interactive gaming. EA's Pogo.com offers board, puzzle, word, casino, sports, and card games (some for free and some for a fee) and can be linked to your Facebook account. Facebook itself provides Instant Games to its 650 million game players through their New Feeds and Messenger (O'Malley, 2016a).

We've already seen that the new generation of handheld game devices is Internet capable. And in an obvious bow to convergence, all new consoles are designed to perform a wide range of game and nongame functions, including playing DVDs, burning music CDs, and providing Internet access with music and video streaming capability, all in widescreen HDTV and digital multichannel sound. For example, iHeart Radio brings more than 800 live concert broadcast and digital-only radio stations to Xbox users who, if they have Kinect, can control their listening through voice and body movements. Xbox users can also access Slacker's personal radio service and its tens of millions of music tracks, and if they subscribe to Microsoft's SmartGlass service, they can stream any and all content from their smartphones and tablets to their televisions through their gaming consoles. Manufacturer Samsung sells television sets that connect viewers directly to its cache of games housed on its distant, dedicated servers (see *cloud computing* in the chapter on film). Cable companies Verizon and Comcast and program providers like HBO, Epix, Netflix, and Hulu stream content via game consoles. In fact, in 2012, for the first time, entertainment usage passed multiplayer game usage on the Xbox; that is, users spent more time with online video and music than playing games (Tsukayama, 2012). You can see how players use their consoles in Figure 3.

Home computer users, able to interact with other gamers for decades via MUDs, have been joined by console players in flocking to **massively multiplayer online roleplaying games (MMOs)** such as *Ultima Online*, *World of Warcraft*, *EverQuest*, and *Second Life*.

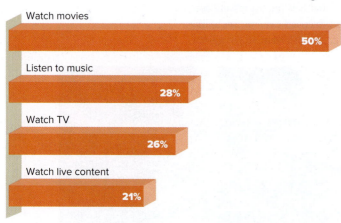

▲ Figure 3 How Gamers Use Their Consoles When Not Playing Games.

Source: Entertainment Software Association of America, 2016.

- Watch movies **50%**
- Listen to music **28%**
- Watch TV **26%**
- Watch live content **21%**

Thirty million people worldwide play these **virtual worlds games**, and one, the hugely popular *World of Warcraft*, has more than 12 million subscribers.

Technology and players' comfort with it are two reasons for this wave of convergence—games can be played on cable television; on game consoles; on handheld devices; and online through social networking sites, game developers' websites, tablets, smartphones, and personal computers.

TECHNOLOGY As smaller, faster, more powerful microprocessors were developed and found their way into game consoles, the distinction between game consoles and personal computers began to disappear. A game console with high-speed microprocessors attached to a television set is, for all intents and purposes, a computer and monitor.

COMFORT WITH TECHNOLOGY As the distinction between the technologies on which games are played has diminished, players' willingness to play games on different platforms has grown. Demographics help account for this trend. Today's typical high school and college-age players have grown up with computer, console, and handheld games as routine parts of their lives; they have a lifetime of familiarity with playing interactive games. In addition, especially since the relatively recent introduction of mobile devices like smartphones and tablets, they are largely platform agnostic in their choice of game platform. In fact, there may be no better evidence of people's comfort playing games across a variety of technologies than that which resides in the smartphone you most probably already use. As it is, 78% of all U.S. smartphone users play games on their devices (PayPal, 2016).

Players' comfort with technology has also been a factor behind the early growth of **virtual reality games**, which through the use of a headset generate realistic images, sounds, and other sensations that replicate an actual or imaginary environment, simulate players' physical presence there, and make it possible for them to interact with the space. Sony offers PlayStation VR, and Microsoft has Scorpio, an enhanced version of its Xbox One. Virtual reality gaming generated more than $5 billion in hardware and software revenues in 2016 ("Virtual Reality," 2016), and industry research indicates that a majority of gamers are not only familiar with VR, but that they intend to play games on this new technology (Entertainment Software Association, 2016).

Smartphones, Tablets, and Social Networking Sites

Smartphones and tablets are revolutionizing the video-game industry. In 2015 worldwide revenues from mobile gaming—$30 billion—overtook those from console gaming—$26 billion—for the first time (Gaudiosi, 2015), and mobile gaming is expected to account for 42% of industry revenue by 2020 (O'Malley, 2016b). Hugely popular mobile location-based *Pokémon Go*, for example, has 500 million downloads, has 20 million active daily users, and generates $2 million a day from in-game purchases for developer Nintendo who, based on the game's massive early success, saw its stock price rise 90%, adding more than $15 billion to the company's value (Dawson, 2016).

Much, if not most, of today's mobile gaming takes the form of **casual games**—classic games such as card games (poker, cribbage, solitaire), table games (checkers, pool), matching games, and word and trivia games. Casual matching game *Candy Crush Saga* has been downloaded more than half a billion times and has more than 400 million regular monthly users (Kelion, 2016). Globally, there are 1.9 billion mobile casual game players. More than half of all Americans ages 13 and older, nearly 70% of the country's smartphone owners, play casual games on their mobile devices, the majority of whom (63%) are female (Tapjoy, 2017).

Games are the single largest category of mobile apps, accounting for 23% of the 1.5 million apps available from the Apple store, 21% of the 1.8 million at Google Play, and 21% of the 400,000 available at Amazon's app store (Dogtiev, 2016). Casual games can be played in spurts and are easily accommodated by the phone's small screen. To be sure, however, casual games are a hit among Internet players as well, with more than 100 million online casual game players regularly visiting sites such as realarcade.com and pogo.com. They are joined by 650 million gamers, again primarily female, playing at social networking sites such as Facebook (O'Malley, 2016a). Ten million Facebookers a day play *Clash of Clans*; 5 million play *8 Ball Pool* and *Farm Heroes Saga*; and games like *Words with Friends* and *Trivia Crack* draw 1 million daily players ("Top Games," 2016).

▲ Social networking games like King's *Candy Crush Saga* and Zynga's *Farmville* attract tens of millions of daily players.
(left) ©IanDagnall Computing/Alamy; *(right)* ©PhotoEdit/Alamy

Hypercommercialism

Hypercommercialism has come to all media. Advertisers' desire to find new outlets for their messages and avoid the advertising clutter in traditional media has combined with gamers' attractive, segmented demographics to make video games particularly appealing vehicles for many types of commercial and other persuasive campaigns. Advertisers have come to think of games as much like magazines.

Different titles attract different demographics—*Mortal Kombat* and *Grand Theft Auto* draw different players than do *Spider-Man* and *Viva Piñata*. Another reason advertisers are attracted to online games is that they are **sticky**. Players tend to stay (stick) with a game site longer than with other websites. Players don't just "visit" sites so much as they seek them out to stay and play a while. Sponsors—and the games they advertise on—hope to monetize this attention. Regardless of the platform, industry research indicates the average console or online gamer spends two to four hours playing a single game in a single sitting. Sponsors use games to reach their targets in four ways—product placement, freemium games, advergaming, and advocacy gaming.

PRODUCT PLACEMENT Advertisers like product placement for several reasons. First, a product used in a game is there forever—every time the game is played, the advertiser's brand appears. Second, the placement is not only permanent, it's DVR-proof; it can't be skipped. Third, a brand's association with a game renders it "cool," but equally important, games' interactivity creates a stronger emotional connection and therefore a more positive association for players with brands—more so, for example, than simply viewing a TV spot. Fourth, players don't seem to mind the ads and even welcome them if it means a game costs less or can be played online for free (Handrahan, 2016). Fifth, they are effective, and that effectiveness can be measured for online games because the response, clicking through to the sponsor, can be precisely measured. And finally, where in-game ads were once static—a billboard atop a building or a logo on the side of a race car—today's online game product placements are dynamic, that is, a sponsor can alter them remotely and on the fly, tailoring them to players' specific real-life locations and times of day.

But why, beyond the cash they earn, do game designers want product placements in their creations, a practice begun in the 1980s when Sega put Marlboro banners in its arcade racing games? First, brand names add a bit of realism to the game's virtual world, presumably enhancing the player's enjoyment. Second, advertisers and game makers frequently engage in cross-promotion. For example, retail store Target offers several mobile games on behalf of the brands it sells, and each new edition of *Madden NFL* brings with it a new set of cross-promotions from companies like GMC trucks' Never Say Never Moment of the Week and Papa John's *Madden NFL* sweepstakes. Players of the massively multiplayer online *EverQuest II* and Pizza Hut have a cross-promotion that lets players order a pizza in real life using an in-game command.

So mutually beneficial has game product placement become that placements, which can cost more than $1 million in a popular game, are frequently bartered for free; that is, the game maker and the brand advertiser exchange no money. The brand image is provided to the designer (for realism) and the sponsor gets placement (for exposure).

FREEMIUM GAMES Even more deeply integrating products into games are **freemium games**, in which consuming advertising or even spending actual cash allows players to progress in their play. Freemiums happen in a number of ways. In some games, in exchange for watching a commercial, players can obtain virtual goods, like weapons or armor, rather than work to earn the credits necessary to buy them (this is the most popular form of freemium reward). In others, choosing to use a brand-name product imbues players with special in-game attributes unavailable to players content with generic products. There is a third form of freemium games in which players can spend actual money in order to advance. A game like *World of Warriors*, for example, has energy meters; when players run out of energy-giving food or elixirs, they must recharge their depleted energy levels to continue their quest to vanquish the Skull Army. There are three primary ways to do this: wait, barter for energy with in-game earned crystals, or buy it with actual cash. Spending real-world money is the least favored form of freemium activity (Handrahan, 2016).

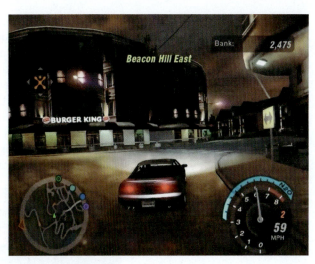

▲ In-game product placement is ubiquitous.
©TJ Photography/Photoedit

ADVERGAMING Product placement in games has proven so successful that, in many instances, brands have become the games themselves in **advergames**. Brand-specific game websites are sometimes downloadable and sometimes played online, and many brands offer mobile app versions of their games. Their goal is to produce an enjoyable experience for players while introducing them to the product and product information. Chipotle Mexican Grill's *The Scarecrow*, a free iPhone game app designed to deliver the message that the chain uses only natural products, is a well-known award-winning effort. Using the Tic Tac game on your smartphone, you can design your own dispenser, and you can play Kia's automotive game to win free test drives in real life (and of course, become a hot lead for the car dealers). *Uber Drive* gives you the thrill of being a virtual Uber driver, but the game's true intent is to recruit you to work for the company, as you can fill out your application from inside the game. Cable television's Hallmark Channel goes in even another direction, establishing its own game site, *Fun & Games*, which offers scores of games, all conveniently designed to promote its basic cable programming.

▲ Chipotle's *The Scarecrow* advergame.
Source: Chipotle

ADVOCACY GAMING Companies or organizations wanting to get their noncommercial messages out turn to **advocacy games**, primarily on the Web and for mobile devices. Many national political candidates are "supported" by advocacy games. You can still play the arcade game *Obama Race for the White House*, or you might prefer to fight "big money, special interests, fat cats, and mudslingers" on Vermont senator Bernie Sanders's *Bernie Arcade*. Dr. Ian Bogost, who created the genre with his 2004 release of the *Howard Dean for Iowa Game*, said, "I didn't get into games because I wanted to reach a demographic. I did it because I think games can communicate political concepts and processes better than other forums" (quoted in Erard, 2004, p. G1).

Supporters of political advocacy games see three significant strengths. First, the games are relatively inexpensive. A good political game can be created in a few weeks for about $20,000, well under the cost of television time. Second, like other advergames, they are sticky, and the message is reinforced with each play (broadcast ads are fleeting). Finally, they are interactive, making them a powerful means of communicating with potential voters, especially younger ones. More traditional forms of advocacy messaging, such as radio and television ads and campaign fliers, passively engage voters with their campaign rhetoric. But games encourage potential voters to interact with the message.

Not all advocacy games are about politics, however. There are games advocating the use of energy alternatives to oil (*Oiligarchy*), religious freedom (*Faith Fighter*), a more flexible application of copyright (*The Free Culture Game*), and improving kids' nutrition (*Fatworld*). Retired Supreme Court Justice Sandra Day O'Connor's nonprofit education group iCivics offers a series of games and accompanying lesson plans designed to introduce middle-school kids to the Constitution and encourage civic involvement. You can read about the gaming industry's efforts to make games a safer and more inviting environment for children in the box "Using the ESRB Ratings."

▶ *Fatworld*, from ITVS Interactive, is an advocacy game exploring the relationships between obesity, nutrition, and socioeconomics in the United States.

Source: ITVS Interactive/ Independent Lens/Persuasive Games

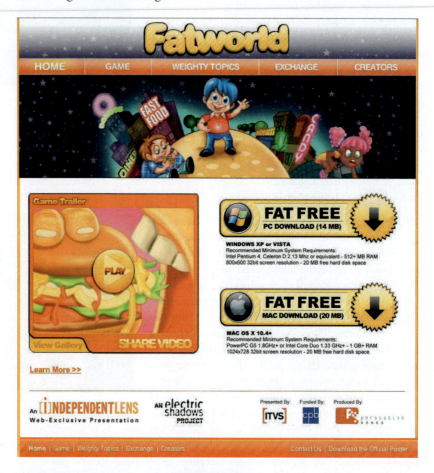

CULTURAL FORUM
Using the ESRB Ratings

The link between video games and antisocial behavior has been at issue ever since there have been video games, finding particular urgency after dramatic events like those in Jonesboro and at Columbine High, where mass shootings of school-aged kids were perpetrated by dedicated gamers. In both these instances, the teen-aged shooters' "addiction" to games was prominently noted. The Columbine shooters had even created a custom *Doom* to represent the killing of their classmates.

And while the argument is not "video games *cause* violence," there is significant scientific evidence (and agreement) that they can be a contributing factor (see, for example, Anderson et al., 2003, and Swing et al., 2010). Given this link, Congress first investigated the effects of video games in 1993, the same year that *Doom* was released for home computers. In an effort to head off government restrictions, in 1994 the industry established the Entertainment Software Ratings Board (ESRB) rating system. It has six ratings (a seventh, RP for Rating Pending, is the equivalent of "this film has not yet been rated"):

EC	Early Childhood	ages 3 and up
E	Everyone	ages 6 and up
E10+	Everyone 10 and Up	ages 10 and up
T	Teen	ages 13 and up
M	Mature	ages 17 and up
AO	Adults Only	ages 18 and up

Like the movie rating system, the ESRB system requires that games offer content descriptors somewhere on the front or back of the game package explaining why a particular rating was assigned. Although the Federal Trade Commission has lauded the ESRB ratings as the most comprehensive of the three rated industries (games, recordings, movies), media-literate gamers (or friends and parents of gamers) should understand the strengths and weaknesses of this system. Depending on your perspective, this self-regulation is either a good thing because it keeps government's intrusive hand out of people's lives and protects game makers' First Amendment rights, or a bad thing because it is self-serving and rarely enforced. The value of the content descriptors, too, is in dispute. All a game maker is required to list is *any one* of the descriptors that has led to a given rating—for example, *strong lyrics*. For some, this is useful information. For others, it masks potential problems. First, according to the ESRB system, if this content is sufficient to give the game an M rating, no other content that might have contributed to that rating, such as *mature sexual themes* or *violence*, need be listed. Second, *strong lyrics* might apply to song lyrics about sex, violence, alcohol, or drug use. Only when the game is played will the player identify the reason for the rating and descriptor.

An additional concern over the rating system is that it is poorly enforced, but this concern may not be well founded. There's no doubt that some underage buying does occur, but the Federal Trade Commission's own undercover investigation of the problem revealed that video-game retailers do an effective job of enforcing age-based ratings; only 13% of underage shoppers are usually able to purchase M-rated video games (Lordan, 2013). This is no doubt due in part to the fact that 91% of parents of gamers are present when their kids buy video games, apparently aware of the medium's benefits as well as risks (Entertainment Software Association, 2016).

DEVELOPING MEDIA LITERACY SKILLS
The Treatment of Female Gamers

GamerGate thrust the issue of the mistreatment of female gamers into the cultural forum in 2012. It has remained there ever since because of the sexist portrayal of females in the games themselves and the continued bullying of female players, especially in live online play (Waterlow, 2016).

In 2012 feminist media critic Anita Sarkeesian began a Kickstarter campaign, wanting to raise $6,000 to produce a series of videos on female representation in games. She clearly hit a nerve among female gamers, because she attracted $158,000 from enthusiastic backers. But she also drew relentless online harassment from many male gamers, including threats of murder and rape. An enraged community of hardcore gamers, using the hashtag #GamerGate and supposedly in the name of fighting censorship and political correctness, unleashed brutal harassment of Sarkeesian and others, such as female game developers Zoë Quinn and Briana Wu and gaming journalist Leigh Alexander, who had written in their defense. News site Reddit and messaging sites 4chan and 8chan became platforms for coordinated harassment campaigns. All these women had their social networking sites hacked and their personal information published online. Facing constant and detailed threats of harm, all were forced to leave their homes. But why? As Sarkeesian explained, "There's a toxicity within gaming culture . . . that drives this misogynist hatred, this reactionary backlash against women who have anything to say, especially those who have critiques or who are feminists. There's this huge drive to silence us, and if they can't silence us, they try to discredit us in an effort to push us out." GamerGate is "trying to hold on to this status quo, this illusion that gaming is for men" (in Collins, 2014).

The status quo does disfavor women. They may make up 41% of the gaming community, but they are underrepresented in the making of games (only 22% of game developers are female; Sinclair, 2016). That may be one reason women are so poorly represented in games. As most players know, there is a very common look in games for female characters: very large breasts, very small waists, very curved hips, and very little clothing.

Enter your voice. Apart from the harassment, which is never even remotely appropriate, is the issue of the treatment of female players much ado about nothing, just more political correctness? Does gaming's status quo favor men over women? Keeping your answers in mind, test your commitment to gender diversity in gaming by using the Video Game Sexism Scale developed by Communication researchers Jesse Fox and Wai Yen Tang (2014). Answer each question on a 1 to 7 scale, with 1 being "completely disagree" and 7 being "completely agree."

Video Game Sexism Scale

1. Most women who play video games just do so with their boyfriends.
2. Most women who play video games are not very good at them.
3. Women who play video games are actually seeking special favors from men.
4. Women who play video games just do it to get attention from men.
5. Women are too easily offended by what goes on in video games.
6. Women get too offended by sexual comments in games.
7. Women are too sensitive about sex jokes and nude pictures of women that circulate in games.
8. Women who call themselves gamer girls think they deserve special treatment.
9. Having a woman play brings down the quality of the game.
10. If a woman plays with a team or guild, she is almost always the weakest link.
11. Women can't handle trash talking in games like men can.
12. Having women around makes the game less fun.
13. Video games are a man's world, and women don't belong.
14. Women are more worried about socializing than anything else in a game.
15. Women prefer spending time dressing up their character rather than playing.
16. Women don't play games to kill or achieve.

Add each number to calculate your score. A score higher than 56 suggests some discomfort with female players—the higher the number the more discomfort—and below 56 suggests otherwise. What does your score tell you about yourself and your reaction to GamerGate? Re-enter your voice in the debate surrounding the treatment of women in gaming, now with a bit more knowledge about where you really stand.

MEDIA LITERACY CHALLENGE
Masculinity and Femininity in Game World

Select five games that feature both male and female characters. For each of those characters, list the first three descriptors that come to mind as you look at them. Are there common traits among the men? Among the women? If so, why do you think they exist? How realistic are the portrayals of the men? Of the women? Can you explain your findings and your reactions to those findings in terms of these media literacy skills: Your *ability and willingness to pay attention to and understand video-game content*, your *respect for the power of games' messages,* and your *ability to distinguish emotional from reasoned reactions when playing video games*?

Media-literate game players have *an understanding of the ethical and moral obligations of those who design the games they play.* Critics of the portrayal of gender in games agree that games are protected speech, but they argue this does not mean that developers are free of responsibility for their contribution to the culture in which we all live. Given what you've learned in this exercise about games' portrayal of men and women, can you address the question of the ethics of gender representation in video games?

Resources for Review and Discussion

REVIEW POINTS: TYING CONTENT TO LEARNING OUTCOMES

▶ **Outline the history and development of games and the gaming industry.**
  - □ While the pinball games developed by David Gottlieb and Harry Williams are the precursors to video games, Steve Russell, Nolan Bushnell, and Ralph Baer are most responsible for what we now call electronic video games.
  - □ A game is a video game when a player has direct involvement in some on-screen action to produce a desired outcome.

▶ **Describe how the organizational and economic nature of the contemporary gaming industry shapes the content of games.**
  - □ Games are most frequently played on game consoles (home and portable), PC and Mac computers, and the Internet, but increasingly smartphones are serving as a popular game platform.
  - □ Game consoles are the sole province of Microsoft, Nintendo, and Sony.
  - □ Third-party publishers design games for the most popular systems.
  - □ Rising costs in the production of games have led to hypercommercialism and a reliance on blockbusters, franchises, and sequels.
  - □ Hypercommercialism in games takes the form of product placement and advergaming.

▶ **Explain the relationship between games and their players.**
  - □ Two-thirds of all American households are home to at least one person who regularly plays video games.

  - □ Game players' demographics are changing; women 18 or older represent a greater proportion of the gaming population than boys 18 or younger, primarily because of the growth of casual games.

▶ **Identify changes in the game industry brought about by new and converging technologies.**
  - □ Convergence, driven by more powerful technology and people's comfort with it, has overtaken gaming, as games can be played on a host of platforms including virtual reality devices.
  - □ Wi-Fi–capable handheld devices, smartphones, and tablets have not only freed games from the console but have also fueled the rise of casual games and swelled the ranks of female and adult players.
  - □ Social networking sites like Facebook further encourage these changes.

▶ **Apply key game-playing media literacy skills to understanding and combating the frequent mistreatment of female gamers by some male players.**
  - □ GamerGate, the controversy surrounding the mistreatment of female game players, revealed widespread misogyny among male gamers.
  - □ Not only are women gamers subject to attack and disrespect, they also make up a distressingly small proportion of the game-designer community.
  - □ The misrepresentation of women in video games may well be the result of this mistreatment and exclusion.

KEY TERMS

LED (light-emitting diode), 210

LCD (liquid crystal display), 210

LAN (local area network), 211

first-person perspective game, 211

video game, 212

MUD (multiuser dimension), 212

exergame, 212

gamification, 213

e-sports, 214

third-party publishers, 214

QUESTIONS FOR REVIEW

1. Who are David Gottlieb and Harry Williams? What were their contributions to the development of pinball?

2. How did *Pong* affect the development of video gaming?

3. What makes a video game a video game?

4. What are the most frequently employed platforms for game playing?

5. What is a third-party publisher?

6. How are movie studios and game developers similar in their efforts to reduce the financial risks involved in creating their products?

7. How does product placement occur in games?

8. What are the different forms of advergaming?

9. What is advocacy gaming?

10. What are the levels of the ESRB rating system?

To maximize your study time, check out CONNECT to access the SmartBook study module for this chapter, watch videos, and explore other resources.

QUESTIONS FOR CRITICAL THINKING AND DISCUSSION

1. What is your favorite game platform? Why? Do you think different types of players gravitate toward different platforms? Why or why not?

2. Does advergaming, especially where children are the players, bother you? Do you find advergaming inherently deceptive for these young players? Why or why not?

3. Have you ever played an advocacy game? If so, what was it? Was it from a group with which you were sympathetic? What would it take to get you to play a game from a site with which you disagree?

REFERENCES

1. Anderson, C. A., Berkowitz, L., Donnerstein, E., Huesmann, L. R., Johnson, J. D., Linz, D., et al. (2003). The influence of media violence on youth. *Psychological Science in the Public Interest, 4,* 81–110.

2. Burnham, V. (2001). *Supercade: A visual history of the videogame age 1971–1984.* Cambridge: MIT Press.

3. Collins, S. T. (2014, October 17). Anita Sarkeesian on GamerGate: "We have a problem and we're going to fix this." *Rolling Stone.* Online: http://www.rollingstone.com/culture /features/anita-sarkeesian-gamergate-interview-20141017

4. Dawson, J. (2016, July 20). How to make Pokémon go on and on. *Variety,* p. 26.

5. DeMaria, R., & Wilson, J. L. (2004). *High score: The illustrated history of electronic games.* New York: McGraw-Hill.

6. Dogtiev, A. (2016, February 29). App store statistics roundup. *Business of Apps.* Online: http://www.businessofapps.com /app-store-statistics-roundup/

7. Entertainment Software Association. (2016). Essential facts. Online: http://essentialfacts.theesa.com/

8. Erard, M. (2004, July 1). In these games, the points are all political. *The New York Times,* p. G1.

9. Fox, J., & Tang, W. Y. (2014). Sexism in online video games: the role of conformity to masculine norms and social dominance orientation. *Computers in Human Behavior, 33,* 314–320.

10. Francis, T. (2011, December 26). The Humble Bundle guys— *PC Gamer*'s community heroes of the year. *PC Gamer.* Online: http://www.pcgamer.com/2011/12/26/the-humble -bundle-guys-pc-gamers-community-heroes-of-the-year/

11. Gaudiosi, J. (2015, January 15). Mobile game revenues set to overtake console games in 2015. *Fortune.* Online: http:// fortune.com/2015/01/15/mobile-console-game- revenues-2015/

12. Gilsdorf, E. (2016, October 2). Players gonna play. *The New York Times Book Review,* p. 16.

13. Graser, M. (2014, December 2). Studios to unwrap digital viewing riches. *Variety,* pp. 14–15.

14. Handrahan, M. (2016, April 7). IAP the least popular form of monetisation among players. *Gamesindustry.biz.* Online: http://www.gamesindustry.biz/articles/2016-04-07-iap-the -least-popular-form-of-monetisation-among-players

15. Kato, M. (2012, January). Arrested development. *Game Informer*, pp. 10–12.

16. Kelion, L. (2016, September 28). Candy Crush Saga: Life beyond level 2,000. *BBC.* Online: http://www.bbc.com/news /technology-37484114

17. Kent, S. L. (2001). *The ultimate history of video games.* New York: Three Rivers Press.

18. Lordan, B. (2013, March 25). FTC undercover shopper survey on entertainment ratings enforcement finds compliance highest among video game sellers and movie theaters. *Federal Trade Commission.* Online: https://www.ftc.gov/news-events/ press-releases/2013/03/ftc-undercover-shopper-survey -entertainment-ratings-enforcement

19. "Most popular YouTube gaming channels as of October 2016, ranked by number of subscribers (in millions)." *Statista.* Online: https://www.statista.com/statistics/453461/leading -youtube-gaming-channels-subscribers/

20. O'Malley, G. (2016a, November 29). Facebook adds instant games to Messenger, News Feeds. *MediaPost.* Online: http://www.mediapost.com/publications/article/289995/ facebook-adds-instant-games-to-messenger-news -fee.html

21. O'Malley, G. (2016b, January 25). Mobile driving gaming growth. *MediaPost.* Online: http://www.mediapost.com /publications/article/267433/mobile-driving-gaming-growth .html

22. PayPal. (2016, November). Digital media consumers. Online: https://www.paypalobjects.com/digitalassets/c/website /marketing/global/shared/global/media-resources/documents /paypal-us-gaming-and-ebooks-study.pdf

23. Schultz, E. J. (2017, April 3). You game? *Advertising Age*, pp. 13–16.

24. Sellers, J. (2001). *Arcade fever.* Philadelphia: Running Press.

25. Sinclair, B. (2016, February 18). Percentage of women devs "not good enough"—ESA CEO. *Gamesindustry.biz.* Online: http://www.gamesindustry.biz/articles/2016-02-18- percentage-of-women-devs-not-good-enough-esa-ceo

26. Spangler, T. (2016, November 17). Warner Bros. acquires full control of Machinima. *Variety.* Online: http://variety.com /2016/digital/news/warner-bros-acquires-machinima -1201920793/

27. Steven Baxter of the CNN Computer Connection

28. Suellentrop, C. (2016, February 5). This game will break your heart. *The New York Times*, p. C1.

29. Swing, E. L., Gentile, D. A., Anderson, C. A., & Walsh, D. A. (2010). Television and video game exposure and the development of attention problems. *Pediatrics, 126*, 214–221.

30. Tapjoy. (2017, January). The changing face of mobile gamers. Online: http://hello.tapjoy.com/Modern-Mobile-Gamer- Research-Report.html

31. "Top games on Facebook 2016." *GameHunters.club.* Online: https://gamehunters.club/top-games/on-facebook

32. Tsukayama, H. (2012, March 28). Xbox adds HBO Go, MLB. TV, Xfinity, as it evolves from game console. *The Washington Post.* Online: https://www.washingtonpost.com/business /technology/xbox-adds-hbo-go-mlbtv-xfinity-as-it-evolves -from-game-console/2012/03/28/gIQASdAWgS_story. html?utm_term=.dfd3489a9e13

33. "Virtual reality video game industry to generate $5.1 billion in 2016." (2016, January 5). *Fortune.* Online: http://fortune .com/2016/01/05/virtual-reality-game-industry-to-generate -billions/

34. Waterlow, L. (2016, February 13). "Rape and death threats are common": Women gamers reveal the vile online abuse they receive EVERY DAY from men who say they should "get back in the kitchen." *Daily Mail.* Online: http://www .dailymail.co.uk/femail/article-3454588/Women-gamers -reveal-vile-online-abuse-receive-DAY-men-say-kitchen.html

35. Willens, M. (2016, December 15). Publishers are playing around with games again. *Digiday.* Online: http://digiday .com/publishers/publishers-playing-around-games/

Cultural Forum Blue Column icon, Media Literacy Red Torch Icon, Using Media Green Gear icon, Developing Media book in starburst icon:
©McGraw-Hill Education

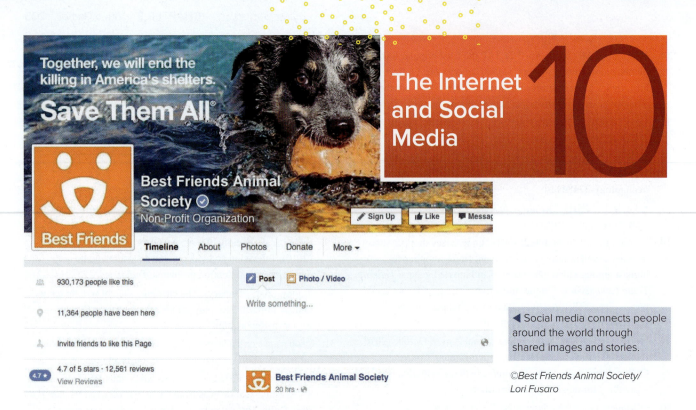

◄ Social media connects people around the world through shared images and stories.

©*Best Friends Animal Society/ Lori Fusaro*

Learning Objectives

It is not an overstatement to say that the Internet and social media have changed the world, not to mention all the other mass media. In addition to being powerful communication media themselves, these technologies sit at the center of virtually all the media convergence we see around us. After studying this chapter, you should be able to

▶ Outline the history and development of the Internet and social media.

▶ Describe how the organizational and economic natures of the contemporary Internet and social media industries shape their content.

▶ Answer a number of questions about how and why individuals use social media.

▶ Analyze social and cultural questions posed by the Internet, social media, and related emerging technologies.

▶ Apply key Internet social media literacy skills, especially in protecting your privacy and reflecting on the Internet's double edge of (potentially) good and troublesome change.

1885 ▶ Babbage designs "computer"

Source: Library of Congress, Prints and Photographs Division [LC-USZ62-66023]

1940 **1940s** British develop Colossus and binary code
1946 ▶ ENIAC
1950 UNIVAC
1951 Census Bureau makes first successful commercial use of computers

©Apic/Hulton Archive/Getty Images

1955 **1957** ▶ *Sputnik* launched
1960 Licklider's *Man–Computer Symbiosis;* IBM mainframe technology
1962 ARPA commissions Baran to develop computer network
1964 McLuhan's *Understanding Media*
1969 ARPAnet goes online

©AP Photo

1970 **1972** E-mail
1974 Internet emerges
1975 ▶ Gates develops PC operating system
1977 Jobs and Wozniak develop Apple II
1979 BITNET
1981 IBM PC introduced

©Doug Wilson/Getty Images

1985 **1990** HTTP developed
1992 Internet society chartered
1994 ▶ Spam appears; first banner ad
1995 Classmates.com

©Y H Lim/Alamy RF

2000 **2000** ▶ U.S. women pass men as users
2004 Facebook launched
2006 Twitter
2007 Laptops outsell desktops; Apple app store opens
2009 Internet surpasses newspapers as news source; social networking surpasses e-mail for person-to-person communication
2010 First popular tablet computer
2012 25th billion app download from Apple app store; Facebook buys Instagram; mobile becomes top e-mail platform
2013 Tablets outsell laptops; smartphones outsell cell phones
2015 Search engines overtake traditional media as most trusted news source; tablets outsell laptops and desktops
2016 Fake news plague
2017 Number of Internet of Things devices surpasses world population

©Onoky Photography/ SuperStock RF

▲ William Gibson.
©Christopher Morris/Corbis/
Getty Images

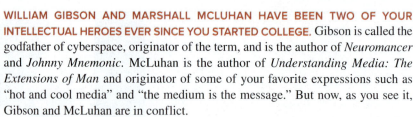

WILLIAM GIBSON AND MARSHALL MCLUHAN HAVE BEEN TWO OF YOUR INTELLECTUAL HEROES EVER SINCE YOU STARTED COLLEGE. Gibson is called the godfather of cyberspace, originator of the term, and is the author of *Neuromancer* and *Johnny Mnemonic*. McLuhan is the author of *Understanding Media: The Extensions of Man* and originator of some of your favorite expressions such as "hot and cool media" and "the medium is the message." But now, as you see it, Gibson and McLuhan are in conflict.

For example, another of McLuhan's famous expressions is "the global village." You understood this to mean that as media "shrink" the world, people will become increasingly involved in one another's lives. As people come to know more about others who were once separated from them by distance, they will form a new, beneficial relationship, a global village.

Then you saw an interview with Gibson on television. His vision of technology's impact on the globe was anything but optimistic. He said, "We're moving toward a world where all the consumers under a certain age will . . . identify more with their consumer status or with the products they consume than they would with an antiquated notion of nationality. We're increasingly interchangeable" (as cited in Trench, 1990).

Maybe you were wrong about McLuhan's ideas. He did his influential writing a long time ago. Where was it you read about the global village? In a magazine interview? You Google it to confirm that you understood him correctly. There it is, just as you thought: "The human tribe can become truly one family and man's consciousness can be freed from the shackles of mechanical culture and enabled to roam the cosmos" (in Norden, 1969, p. 158). McLuhan's global village is an exciting place, a good place for people enjoying increased contact and increased involvement with one another aided by electronic technology. Gibson's nationless world isn't about involving ourselves in one another's lives and experiences. It's about electronic technology turning us into indistinguishable nonindividuals, rallying around products. We are united by buyable things, identifying not with others who share our common culture but with those who share common brands. McLuhan sees the new communication technologies as expanding our experiences. Gibson sees them more negatively. You respect and enjoy the ideas of both thinkers. How can you reconcile the disagreement you have uncovered?

▲ Marshall McLuhan.
©Bettmann/Getty Images

We begin this chapter with an examination of the Internet, the "new technology" that helped bring Gibson to prominence and gave renewed life to Marshall McLuhan's ideas. We study the history of the Internet, beginning with the development of the computer, and then we look at the Internet as it exists today. We examine its formats and its capabilities, especially the World Wide Web and social media.

Many of the issues discussed here will be familiar to you. Given the fundamental role that the Internet plays in encouraging and permitting convergence, concentration, audience fragmentation, globalization, and hypercommercialism, you should not be surprised that we've "met" the Internet, the Web, and social media before now in discussing the more traditional media.

These technologies are significantly reshaping the operation of those media; and as the media with which we interact change, the role they play in our lives and the impact they have on us and our culture will likewise be altered. We will look at the new technologies' double edge (their ability to have both good and bad effects), their ability to foster greater freedom of expression, efforts to control that expression, changes in the meaning of and threats to personal privacy, and the promise and perils of practicing democracy online.

Finally, our discussion of improving our media literacy takes the form of an examination of the Declaration of Internet Freedom. But first, the Internet.

A Short History of the Internet

There are conflicting versions about the origins of the Internet. In the words of media historian Daniel J. Czitrom, they involve "the military and the counterculture, the need for command and control and the impulse against hierarchy and toward decentralization" (2007, p. 484). The more common story—the command-and-control version—is that the Internet is a product of the Cold War. In this version, the air force in 1962, wanting to maintain the military's ability to transfer information around the country even if a given area was destroyed in an enemy attack, commissioned leading computer scientists to develop the means to do so. But many researchers and scientists dispute this "myth that [has] gone unchallenged long enough to become widely accepted as fact," that the Internet was initially "built to protect national security in the face of nuclear attack" (Hafner & Lyon, 1996, p. 10).

In the decentralization version, as early as 1956 psychologist Joseph C. R. Licklider, a devotee of Marshall McLuhan's thinking on the power of communication technology, foresaw linked computers creating a country of citizens "informed about, and interested in, and involved in, the process of government" (as quoted in Hafner & Lyon, 1996, p. 34). He foresaw "home computer consoles" and television sets connected in a nationwide network. "The political process would essentially be a giant teleconference," he wrote, "and a campaign would be a months-long series of communications among candidates, propagandists, commentators, political action groups, and voters. The key," he added, "is the self-motivating exhilaration that accompanies truly effective interaction with information through a good console and a good network to a good computer" (p. 34).

In what many technologists now consider to be the seminal essay on the potential and promise of computer networks, *Man–Computer Symbiosis*, Licklider, who had by now given up psychology and devoted himself completely to computer science, wrote in 1960, "The hope is that in not too many years, human brains and computing machines will be coupled . . . tightly, and the resulting partnership will think as no human brain has ever thought and process data in a way not approached by the information handling machines we know today" (as quoted in Hafner & Lyon, 1996, p. 35). Scores of computer experts, enthused by Licklider's vision (and many more who saw networked computers as a way to gain access to the powerful but otherwise expensive and unavailable computers just beginning to become available), joined the rush toward the development of what we know today as the **Internet**, a global network of interconnected computers that communicate freely and share and exchange information.

▼ Joseph C. R. Licklider envisioned a national system of interconnected home computers as early as 1956.
From the MIT Museum, ©Koby-Antupit Studio, Cambridge/Belmont, MA

Development of the Computer

The title "originator of the computer" resides with Englishman Charles Babbage. Lack of money and unavailability of the necessary technology stymied his plan to build an "analytical engine," a steam-driven computer. But in the mid-1880s, aided by the insights of mathematician Lady Ada Byron Lovelace, Babbage did produce designs for a "computer" that could conduct algebraic computations using stored memory and punch cards for input and output. His work provided inspiration for those who would follow.

Over the next 100 years a number of mechanical and electromechanical computers were attempted, some with success. But Colossus, developed by the British to break the Germans' secret codes during World War II, was the first electronic **digital computer**. It reduced information to a **binary code**—that is, a code made up of the digits 1 and 0. In this form information could be stored and manipulated. The first "full-service" electronic computer, ENIAC (Electronic Numerical Integrator and Calculator), based on the work of Iowa State's John V. Atanasoff, was introduced by scientists John Mauchly and John Presper Eckert of the Moore School of Electrical Engineering at the University of Pennsylvania in 1946. ENIAC hardly resembled the computers we know today: 18 feet tall, 80 feet long, and weighing 60,000 pounds, it was composed of 17,500 vacuum tubes and 500 miles of electrical wire. It could fill an auditorium and ate up 150,000 watts of electricity. Mauchly and Eckert eventually left the university to form their own computer company, later selling it to the Remington Rand Corporation in 1950. At Remington they developed UNIVAC (Universal Automatic Computer), which, when bought for and used by the Census Bureau in 1951, became the first successful commercial computer.

▶ ENIAC.
©Apic/Hulton Archive/Getty Images

▼ The Soviet Union's 23-inches-in-diameter, 184-pound Sputnik was not only the first human-made satellite to orbit Earth; it also sent shudders throughout the American scientific and military communities.

©AP Photo

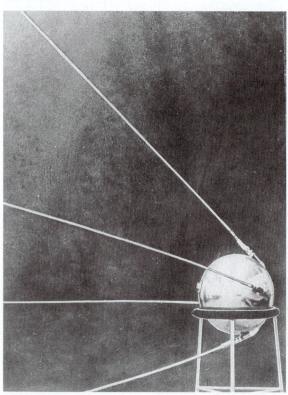

The commercial computer explosion was ignited by IBM. Using its already well-entrenched organizational system of trained sales and service professionals, IBM helped businesses find their way in the early days of the computer revolution. One of its innovations was to sell rather than rent computers to customers, boosting diffusion of the new technology.

Military Applications

In 1957 the Soviet Union launched Sputnik, Earth's first human-constructed satellite. The once-undisputed supremacy of the United States in science and technology had been usurped, and U.S. scientists and military officials were in shock. The Advanced Research Projects Agency (ARPA) was immediately established to sponsor and coordinate sophisticated defense-related research. In 1962, as part of a larger drive to promote the use of computers in national defense (and giving rise to one of the stories of the Internet's origins), ARPA commissioned Paul Baran of the Rand Corporation to produce a plan that would enable the U.S. military to maintain command over its missiles and planes if a nuclear attack knocked out conventional means of communication. The military thought a decentralized communication network was necessary. In that way, no matter where the bombing occurred, other locations would be available to launch a counterattack. Among Baran's plans was one for a "packet switched network." He wrote,

> Packet switching is the breaking down of data into datagrams or packets that are labeled to indicate the origin and the destination of the information and the forwarding of these packets from one computer to another computer until the information arrives at its final destination computer. This (is) crucial to the realization of a computer network. If packets are lost at any given point, the message can be resent by the originator. (As cited in Kristula, 1997, p. 1)

The genius of the system Baran envisioned is twofold: (1) common communication rules (called **protocols**) and common computer

◄ A 1960s-vintage IBM mainframe computer. The personal computer in your home probably carries more computing power than this giant machine.
©Agence France Presse/Getty Images

languages would enable any type of computer, running with any operating system, to communicate with another; and (2) destination or delivery instructions embedded in all information sent on the system would enable instantaneous "detours" or "rerouting" if a given computer on the network became unavailable.

Using Honeywell computers at Stanford University, UCLA, the University of California–Santa Barbara, and the University of Utah, the switching network, called ARPAnet, went online in 1969 and became fully operational and reliable within one year. Other developments soon followed. In 1972 an engineer named Ray Tomlinson created the first e-mail program (and gave us the ubiquitous @ symbol). In 1974 Stanford University's Vinton Cerf and the military's Robert Kahn coined the term "the Internet." In 1979 a graduate student at the University of North Carolina, Steve Bellovin, created Usenet and, independent of Bellovin, IBM created BITNET. These two networking software systems enabled virtually anybody with access to a Unix or IBM computer to connect to others on the growing network. By the time the Internet Society was chartered and the World Wide Web was released in 1992, there were more than 1.1 million **hosts**—computers linking individual personal computer users to the Internet. Today there is an ever-expanding number of hosts, 100 million and growing, serving more than 3.7 billion users across the globe, or 50.1% of the world's population ("Internet Usage," 2017).

The Personal Computer

A crucial part of the story of the Internet is the development and diffusion of personal computers. IBM was fantastically successful at exciting businesses, schools and universities, and other organizations about computers. But IBM's and other companies' **mainframe** and **minicomputers** employed **terminals**, and these stations at which users worked were connected to larger, centralized machines. As a result, the Internet at first was the province of the people who worked in those settings.

When the semiconductor (or integrated circuit, or chip) replaced the vacuum tube as the essential information processor in computers, its tiny size, absence of heat, and low cost made possible the design and production of small, affordable **microcomputers**, or **personal computers (PCs)**. This, of course, opened the Internet to anyone, anytime. Laptop computers, which outsold desktop models for the first time in 2007, extended that reach to anywhere. The tablet computer was first introduced in 2006 by Microsoft. It remained a niche computer

▲ The originators of the personal computing revolution—Bill Gates, Steve Jobs, and Stephen Wozniak.
(left) ©Doug Wilson/Getty Images; (center) ©Paul Sakuma/AP Photo; (right) ©Mickey Pfleger/The LIFE Images Collection/Getty Images

▲ The desktop computer opened the Internet to anyone, anytime. The laptop extended that reach to anywhere. The tablet made anytime, anywhere more convenient.
(left) ©Canadapanda/Shutterstock RF; (top right) ©PSL Images/Alamy; (bottom) ©sdecoret/Shutterstock RF

favored by medical professionals for years. But the 2010 introduction of the iPad (operated not by mouse but by touch screen) not only continued the expansion of computing to anyone, anywhere, but it also made it even more convenient. In 2013 tablets outsold laptops for the first time and outsold both laptops and PCs in 2015 (Anthony, 2014).

The leaders of the personal computer revolution were Bill Gates and the duo of Steve Jobs and Stephen Wozniak. As a first-year college student in 1975, Gates saw a magazine story about a small, low-powered computer, the MITS Altair 8800 (developed by Micro Instrumentation and Telemetry Systems, an American electronics company), that could be built from a kit and used to play a simple game. Sensing that the future of computing was in these personal computers and that the power of computers would reside not in their size but in the software that ran them, Gates dropped out of Harvard University and, with his friend Paul Allen, founded Microsoft Corporation. They licensed their **operating system**—the software that tells the computer how to work—to MITS. With this advance, people no longer had to know sophisticated operating languages to use computers. At nearly the same time, in 1977, Jobs and Wozniak, also college dropouts, perfected Apple II, a low-cost, easy-to-use microcomputer designed specifically for personal rather than business use. It was immediately and hugely successful, especially in its development of **multimedia** capabilities—advanced sound and image applications. IBM, stung by its failure to enter the personal computer business, contracted with Microsoft to use its operating system in its IBM PC, first introduced in 1981. All of the pieces were now in place for the home computer revolution.

The Internet Today

The Internet is most appropriately thought of as a "network of networks" that is growing at an incredibly fast rate. These networks consist of LANs (local area networks), connecting two or more computers, usually within the same building, and **WANs (wide area networks)**, connecting several LANs in different locations. When people access the Internet from a computer in a university library, they are most likely on a LAN. But when several universities (or businesses or other organizations) link their computer systems, their users are part of a WAN.

As the popularity of the Internet has grown, so has the number of **ISPs (Internet service providers)**, companies that offer Internet connections at monthly rates depending on the kind and amount of access needed. There are hundreds of ISPs operating in the United States, including some of the better known such as SuddenLink and CenturyLink. Americans increasingly find that their ISP and video (cable or FiOS) provider are one and the same—for example, Comcast and Verizon. Half of all U.S. Internet users are served by the five largest ISPs. Through providers, users can avail themselves of numerous services, among them e-mail, instant messaging, and VoIP.

With an Internet **e-mail** account, users can communicate with anyone else online, any place in the world. Each person online has a unique e-mail address that works just like a telephone number. There are even online "Yellow Pages" and "White Pages" to help users find other people by e-mail. You may be surprised that 295 billion e-mails are sent each day. But if you are a regular e-mail user, you aren't surprised to learn that 89% of all e-mails, about 260 billion a day, are **spam**, unsolicited commercial e-mails ("Spam Statistics," 2017). **Instant messaging**, or **IM**, is the real-time version of e-mail, allowing two or more people to communicate instantaneously and in immediate response to one another. IM can also be used for downloading text, audio, and video files and for gaming.

Voice over Internet Protocol (VoIP), pronounced "voyp," is telephone whereby calls are transferred in digital packets over the Internet rather than on circuit-switched telephone wires. Think of it as "voice e-mail." Vonage (primarily residential) and Ring Central (primarily business) are two of the better-known VoIP providers. More than 224 million people have residential VoIP, a number boosted by Facebook's introduction of free VoIP in its messaging app in 2014 ("VoIP Market," 2016).

The World Wide Web

Although we often use the terms interchangeably, the Internet and the World Wide Web aren't the same thing. The Internet is a massive network of networks, a networking infrastructure connecting billions of computers across the globe, allowing them to communicate with one another. However, the **World Wide Web** (usually referred to as "the Web") is a means of accessing information on the Internet. Think of the Internet as "composed of the machines, hardware and data, and the World Wide Web is what brings this technology to life," suggests technology writer Jessica Toothman (2017). The Web is not a physical place, or a set of files, or even a network of computers. The heart of the Web lies in the protocols that define its use. The World Wide Web (WWW) uses hypertext transfer protocols (HTTP) to transport files from one place to another. Hypertext transfer was developed in the early 1990s by England's Tim Berners-Lee, who was working at CERN, the international particle physics laboratory near Geneva, Switzerland. Berners-Lee gave HTTP to the world for free. "The Web is more a social creation than a technical one," he wrote. "I designed it for a social effect—to help people work together—and not as a technical toy. The ultimate goal of the Web is to support and improve our web-like existence in the world" (Berners-Lee & Fischetti, 1999, p. 128).

The ease of accessing the Web is a function of a number of components: hosts, URLs, browsers, search engines, and home pages.

HOSTS (COMPUTERS CONNECTED TO THE INTERNET) Most Internet activity consists of users accessing files on remote computers. To reach these files, users must first gain access to the Internet through "wired-to-the-Net" hosts. These hosts are often called servers.

Once users gain access to a host computer on the Internet, they then have to find the exact location of the file they are looking for *on* the host. Each file or directory on the Internet (that is, on the host computer connected to the Internet) is designated by a **URL (uniform resource locator)**. A URL is, in effect, a site's official address. But as any user of the Web knows, sites are more commonly recognized by their **domain names**. The last part of a site's address, the *.com* or *.org*, is its top-level domain name, so we know that .com is a business and .org is a nonprofit. But in 2012 the Internet Corporation for Assigned Names and Numbers, or ICANN, authorized the use of a virtually unlimited number of generic top-level domains to include almost any word or name, for example *.defibrillator* or *.newyorkcity*. It also permits, for the first

▶ Web inventor Tim Berners-Lee.
©Catrina Genovese/WireImage/ Getty Images

time, the use of non-Latin language scripts, such as Arabic, Chinese, and Cyrillic. The number of individual domains, or websites, changes by the minute, but a 2012 analysis by a Google engineer counted 30 trillion unique URLs operating on the Internet ("Google Search," 2017).

BROWSERS Software programs loaded onto the user's computer and used to download and view Web files are known as **browsers**. Browsers take separate files (text files, image files, and sound files) and put them all together for viewing. Google Chrome, Firefox, and Internet Explorer are three of the most popular Web browsers.

SEARCH ENGINES Finding information on the Web is simple thanks to **search engines**, software that allows users to navigate the Internet simply by entering a search word and selecting a page from the results. Among the better known are Ask and Bing, but the best known and most frequently used—65% of all searches worldwide, or 3.5 billion searches a day—is Google, which produces its results with technology that uses the collective intelligence of the Web itself; that is, search results are presented and ranked based primarily on how frequently a given site is linked to others ("Google Search," 2017).

HOME PAGES Once users reach the intended website, they are greeted by a **home page**—the entryway to the site itself. It not only contains the information the site's creators want visitors to know but also provides **hyperlinks** to other material in that site, as well as to material in other sites on other computers linked to the Internet anywhere in the world.

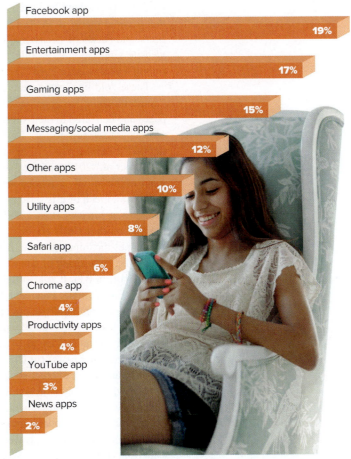

Percentage of Mobile Time

Facebook app 19%
Entertainment apps 17%
Gaming apps 15%
Messaging/social media apps 12%
Other apps 10%
Utility apps 8%
Safari app 6%
Chrome app 4%
Productivity apps 4%
YouTube app 3%
News apps 2%

▲ **Figure 1** Proportion of Mobile Internet Time Spent on Apps.
Source: Chaffey, 2016.
©*Hero/Corbis/Glow Images RF*

Smartphones

Smartphones make connecting to the Internet, already an anytime, anywhere activity thanks to laptops and tablets, even more convenient. There is no need to search for a site or use a browser because an app on your smartphone will take you directly to its designated content; in fact, 90% of all mobile Web access is through apps (Chaffey, 2016). You can see detail of that usage in Figure 1. In 2013, for the first time, users bought more smartphones than cell phones (Walsh, 2013), and smartphones—not PCs, not laptops—are now the most frequently used platform for sending and receiving e-mail (Fluent, 2016). In fact, in 2014 mobile devices accounted for more than half of all U.S. Internet usage, 60%, the first time that has ever happened (Hessinger, 2014).

Social Media

Of course, much mobile use is devoted to social media. Where e-mail was long the Internet's most common and fastest-growing use, it was surpassed in 2009 by **social networking sites**, websites that function as online communities of users. Today they account for 1 out of every 5 minutes Americans spend on mobile Internet and 1 out of every 6 minutes of all Internet time (Bolton, 2016). And it was Facebook's specific desire to make itself even more attractive to mobile users that drove the company in 2012 to buy the two-year-old, purely mobile photo start-up Instagram for $1 billion. Instagram now has more than 89 million U.S. users, 600 million worldwide (C. Smith, 2017a). Classmates.com's 1995 launch began the social networking movement, and it was soon followed by similar sites, most notably Friendster in 2002 and LinkedIn in 2003. MySpace also launched in 2003 and, hipper and more feature-filled than the earlier efforts, became a favorite of young people around the world until it was unseated by Facebook, which was Harvard University–specific at birth in 2004 and became global in 2006. Of all adult Americans on social media, 90.4% are Facebook users, and Facebook occasionally alternates with YouTube as the world's second most-visited website after Google; it collects 67.9% of the world's social networking ad revenues, $33 billion a year in 2016 ("Ad Age Social," 2016).

These "old line" sites were joined in 2006 by Twitter, a social media site designed for "micro-blogging," posts of up to 140 characters (called *tweets*) displayed on senders' profile pages and delivered to their subscribers (*followers*). In 2017, Twitter began testing a doubling of its character limit to 280. Delivery can be restricted to a specific circle of followers, or, by default, it can be public. There are 67 million active monthly users in the United States ("Number of," 2017) and they send 500 million tweets a day ("Twitter Usage," 2017). While much of the activity is innocuous, like following a celebrity (singer Katy Perry has 95 million followers), much of it is serious. It was Twitter activity that alerted the national media to the shooting of Michael Brown and the protests that followed in Ferguson, Missouri, in 2014. MSNBC anchor Chris Hayes said that Twitter "is a heat map and a window, a place where sometimes the things that are 'trending' offer very real insight into the current informational needs of a huge swath of news consumers, some of whom traditional outlets often miss" (in Carr, 2014, p. B1). It is also the medium of choice for many world leaders and other news makers. For example, President Trump regularly uses it to bypass what he calls the "dishonest press" to communicate directly with the public, though the traditional media will often report on his tweets. Trump explained, "I can go *bing bing bing* and I just keep going and they put it on and as soon as I tweet it out—this morning on television, Fox: *Donald Trump, we have breaking news*" (in Uberti & Vernon, 2017).

There are scores of other social networking sites. Some are general interest and growing in popularity, especially with younger users, for example Snapchat (users post images and video that are viewable for only a short time) and Pinterest (users upload or search, save, sort, and manage images and videos into collections called *boards* that serve as personalized media platforms). Others are narrower communities built around specific interests, for example CafeMom (for mothers), BlackPlanet (for the African American community), and Foursquare (for those who want their followers to know where they are and make recommendations of nearby services and activities).

The Debate over Social Media's Value

Just as the benefits and risks—the double edge—of the Internet as a whole continue to be debated, a number of issues specific to social media are generating their own disagreement. We'll take a brief look at some of the most common questions surrounding our use of social media: Why do we engage others on social media, and how realistically do we present ourselves when we do? Do Facebook depression and Facebook envy exist? And are we substituting social media interaction for real-world relationships?

PRESENTATION OF SELF There must be a reason that 70% of all U.S. adults belong to at least one social networking site (A. Smith, 2017), just as there must be a reason that 70% of smartphone users check their phones to read personal e-mails and check social media within an hour of getting out of bed, 61% regularly sleep with their phones turned on under their pillow or next to their bed, and 51% check their devices continuously during their vacations (Durden, 2016).

One answer to the *why* of our engagement with social networking sites resides in the **dual-factor model of social media use**, which claims that this engagement is motivated by two basic social needs. The first is *the need to belong*, our natural desire to associate with other people and gain their acceptance. The second, the *need for self-presentation*, is our ongoing effort to shape what others think of us. The two operate simultaneously because social media activity not only tells us we belong (that's where our friends are), but it increases our sense of acceptance and, therefore, our self-esteem (Nadkarni & Hofmann, 2012). In fact, the simple act of updating and reading our own profiles boosts our self-esteem (Gonzales & Hancock, 2011).

But once we've made the decision to use social media, we must decide *how* we present ourselves. As you'll soon read, many people worry about their privacy when online, but in our everyday use of social media we willingly offer even the minutest details about our lives, taking pains to update those offerings, and even supporting those entries with visual evidence. When we do this we make judgments about the self we choose to reveal. We select our screen names and profile pictures to identify ourselves as we wish to be identified. But do we openly try to deceive? If you think most social media users do, you subscribe to the **idealized virtual identity hypothesis**, which argues that social media users tend to show idealized characteristics that do not reflect who they really are. But this may not happen as much as you might think. For most users, their time on social media constitutes "an extended social context in which to express [their] actual personality characteristics, thus fostering accurate interpersonal perceptions. [Social media] integrate various sources of personal information that mirror those found in personal environments, private thoughts, facial images, and social behavior, all of which are known to contain valid information about personality" (Back et al., 2010, p. 372). As a result, social media use makes it very difficult to hide who we actually are, and as such it's more likely that the **extended real-life hypothesis**, the idea that we use social media to communicate our actual identities, holds true. The openness of social media makes it impossible for us to control information about ourselves and our reputations—others can post information about us—and our friends constantly provide accountability and feedback on our profiles and other material we post. That is, those who know us keep us honest.

FACEBOOK DEPRESSION AND FACEBOOK ENVY Can all this effort to present our best, truthful selves carry too much of a toll? For many young people the answer seems to be "yes." The American Academy of Pediatrics recognizes **Facebook depression**, "depression that develops when preteens and teens spend a great deal of time on social media sites, such as Facebook, and then begin to exhibit classic symptoms of depression. Acceptance by and contact with peers is an important element of adolescent life. The intensity of the online world is thought to be a factor that may trigger depression in some adolescents" (O'Keeffe & Clarke-Pearson, 2011, p. 802).

Indeed, Christina Sagioglou and Tobias Greitmeyer, whose research led them to express surprise "that Facebook enjoys such great popularity," demonstrated that **affective forecasting error**—the discrepancy between the expected and actual emotions generated by Facebook activity—produces a decline in users' mood after using the social networking site (2014, p. 361). Other research has shown that Facebook users, after one week away from the site, had higher levels of life satisfaction, felt happier and less sad and lonely, were more satisfied with their social lives, had less trouble concentrating, and were more likely to feel present in the moment (Tromholt et al., 2015).

There is also evidence of another emotional downside to social networking: **Facebook envy**. As many as one in three Facebook users say they are sometimes resentful of the happiness others show on social media. Commentary on "travel and leisure," "social interactions," and "happiness" are the three most frequent generators of envy (Krasnova et al., 2013, p. 7). And if you use social media, you know that these are the topics your friends usually emphasize in their posts; who wants friends who report where they didn't go, who they didn't spend time with, and how unhappy they are?

SOCIAL ISOLATION Finally, this raises the question: What is a "friend" on social media? What does *friendship* mean when the average Facebook user has 350 friends (649 for 18- to 24-year-olds; "Average Number," 2016)? Are we connected online but disconnected in real life? Why are 18- to 33-year-olds, among the heaviest social media users, more detached from traditional social, political, and religious institutions and far less trusting of others than are their seniors? Only 19% say that "generally speaking, most people can be trusted" ("Millennials in Adulthood," 2014). Psychologist John Cacioppo has indeed demonstrated that "the greater the proportion of face-to-face interactions, the less lonely you are. The greater the proportion of online interactions, the lonelier you are." But, recognizing social media's double edge, he concluded that social media are not at the root of social isolation; they are merely tools, good or bad, depending on how they are used. "If you use Facebook to increase face-to-face contact, it increases social capital," he said. "Facebook can be terrific, if we use it properly. It's like a car. You can drive it to pick up your friends. Or you can drive alone" (in Marche, 2012).

The Internet, Social Media, and Their Users

We typically think of people who access a medium as audience members, but social media and the Internet have *users*, not audience members. At any time—or even at the same time—a person may be both *reading* online content and *creating* content. E-mail, social media, and chat rooms are obvious examples of online users being both audience and creators, but others exist as well. For example, massively multiplayer online roleplaying games (MMOs) enable entire alternative realities to be simultaneously constructed and engaged (see the chapter on video games for more on MMOs), and computer screens that have multiple open windows enable users to read one site while writing on another and uploading audio and video to even another. With ease we can access the Web, link from site to site and page to page, and even build our own sites. The Internet makes us all journalists, broadcasters, commentators, critics, filmmakers, and advice columnists.

It is almost impossible to tell exactly how many users there are on the Internet. People who own computers are not necessarily linked to the Internet, and people need not own computers to use the Internet, as many users access the Internet through devices at school, a library, or work. Current best estimates indicate that there are at least 3.7 billion users worldwide—51% of Earth's population and a 918% increase since 2000. Eighty-seven percent of Americans use the Internet, a 196% increase since 2000, a rapid rate of growth due in large part to the spread of smartphones ("Internet Usage," 2017). The Internet's demographics have undergone a dramatic shift in the last several years as well. In 1996, for example, 62% of U.S. Internet users were men. In 2000, women became the Internet's majority gender for the first time (Hamilton, 2000). Today, women in every age group use the Internet more than men do, and not surprisingly, the younger a person, the greater the likelihood is that he or she has access to the Internet.

Changes in the Mass Communication Process

Concentration of ownership, globalization, audience fragmentation, hypercommercialism, and convergence are all influencing the nature of the mass communication process (see the chapter on convergence and the reshaping of mass communication). Each redefines the relationship between audiences and media industries. For example, elsewhere in this text we have discussed the impacts of concentration on newspaper readership, of globalization on the type and quality of films available to moviegoers, of audience fragmentation on the variety of channel choices for television viewers, of convergence on the music industry's reinvention, and of hypercommercialism on all media.

The Internet is different from these more traditional media. Rather than changing the relationship between audiences and industries, the Internet changes the *definition* of the different components of the process and, as a result, changes their relationship. We are the people formerly known as the audience, and many of us are **digital natives**, people who have never known a world without the Internet. On the Internet a single individual can communicate with as large an audience as can the giant, multinational corporation that produces a network television program. That corporation fits our earlier definition of a mass communication source—a large, hierarchically structured organization—but the Internet user does not. Feedback in mass communication is traditionally described as inferential and delayed, but online feedback can be, and very often is, immediate and direct. It is more similar to feedback in interpersonal communication than to feedback in mass communication.

This Internet-induced redefinition of the elements of the mass communication process is refocusing attention on issues such as freedom of expression, privacy, responsibility, and democracy.

▲ Technologies, even those with as much potential as the Internet and social media, are only as good as the uses we make of them.

DILBERT ©2009 Scott Adams. Used by permission of ANDREWS MCMEEL SYNDICATION. All rights reserved.

The Double Edge of Technology

The solution to the McLuhan–Gibson conflict in the opening vignette is one of perspective. McLuhan was writing and thinking in the relative youth of the electronic media. When *Understanding Media* was published in 1964, television had just become a mass medium, the personal computer was years away, and Paul Baran was still envisioning ARPAnet.

Gibson, writing much later in the age of electronic media, was commenting from a more experienced position and after observing real-world evidence. McLuhan was optimistic because he was speculating on what electronic media *could do.* Gibson was pessimistic because he was commenting on what he had seen electronic media *doing.*

Still, neither visionary is completely right or completely wrong. Technology alone, even the powerful electronic media that fascinated both, cannot create new worlds or new ways of seeing them. *We* use technology to do these things. This is why technology is a double-edged sword. Its power—for good and for bad—resides in us. The same aviation technology that we use to visit relatives halfway around the world can also be used to drop bombs in a war zone. The same communication technologies used to create a truly global village can be used to dehumanize and demean the people who live in it.

Reconceptualizing Life in an Interconnected World

What happens to people as they are increasingly interconnected? What becomes of audiences and users as their roles are electronically intertwined? How free are we to express ourselves? Does greater connectivity with others mean a loss of privacy? These are only a few of the questions confronting us as we attempt to find the right balance between the benefits and drawbacks that come from the new communication technologies.

The Internet and Freedom of Expression

By their very nature the Internet and social media raise a number of important issues of freedom of expression. There is no central location, no on-and-off button for these technologies, making it difficult for those who want to control them. For free expression advocates, this freedom from control is these media's primary strength. The anonymity of their users provides their expression—even the most radical, profane, and vulgar—great protection, giving voice to those who would otherwise be silenced. But this anonymity, say advocates of strengthened Internet control, is a breeding ground for abuse. Opponents of control counter that the Internet and social media's affordability and ease of use make them our most democratic media. Internet freedom-of-expression issues, then, fall into two broad categories. The first is the potential of the Internet and social media to make the First Amendment's freedom-of-the-press guarantee a reality for greater numbers of people. The second is the problem of setting boundaries of control.

Freedom of the Press for Whom?

Veteran *New Yorker* columnist A. J. Liebling, author of that magazine's "Wayward Press" feature and often called the "conscience of journalism," frequently argued that freedom of the press is guaranteed only to those who own one. Theoretically, anyone can own a broadcast outlet or cable television operation. But the number of outlets in any community is limited, and they are unavailable to all but the richest people and corporations. Theoretically, anyone can own a newspaper or magazine, but again the expense involved makes this an impossibility for most people. Newsletters, like soap-box speakers on a street corner, are limited in reach, typically of interest to those who already agree with the message, and relatively unsophisticated when compared with the larger commercial media.

The Internet, however, turns every user into a potential mass communicator. Equally important, on the Internet every "publisher" is equal. The websites of the biggest government agency, the most powerful broadcast network, the newspaper with the highest circulation, the richest ad agencies and public relations firms, the most far-flung religion, and the lone user with an idea or cause figuratively sit side by side. Each is only as powerful as its ideas.

In other words, the Internet can give voice to those typically denied expression. The Internet is fast, far-reaching, easy to use, and perfect for activism at all levels from local to global. This digitally inspired civic engagement is dramatically demonstrated by **flash mobs** (sometimes called **smart mobs**), geographically dispersed groups connected only by communications technology, quickly drawn together to perform collective action. The 8-million-member MoveOn.org is the best-known site for the coordination of flash mobs and, as it has matured, online political action. Using e-mail and social media, MoveOn.org has a history of generating large-scale protests and civic action on issues of social justice and the environment. For example, it successfully mobilized Californians to move their state assembly to pass a bill requiring public disclosure of political donations and Hawaiians to raise the state's minimum wage. And since 2010, GoFundMe has used **crowdfunding**, the practice of using digital technology to solicit donations from a large number of people for a cause or project, to attract financial and other support for those in need because of calamities big and small. Its 2016 funding pages for victims of flooding in Louisiana attracted $11.2 million, and the pages for the victims of the Pulse nightclub shooting in Orlando collected $9 million. When the Islamic Center in Victoria, Texas, was destroyed in a fire under suspicious circumstances in January 2017, a GoFundMe campaign to rebuild it drew more than a million dollars from over 22 thousand donors in its first five days, easily exceeding the $850,000 goal (Link, 2017).

But it doesn't take an activist website to connect people and move them to action. There is much individually inspired online activism, derogatorily called **slacktivism** because it seems to require little real effort. Social movement scholar Jennifer Earl argues that "slacktivists" have no need to apologize for their work, because slacktivism can affect significant social good given that the Web provides slacktivists with two important benefits: It greatly reduces the costs for creating, organizing, and participating in protests, and it erases the need for activists to be physically together in order to act collectively (2016). Slacktivists moved thousands of people to descend on several major U.S. airports in January 2017 to protest what they saw as an unconstitutional and inhumane temporary ban on citizens from seven predominantly Muslim countries, including refugees from war-torn countries, announced only hours before by President Trump (Kuns, 2017). They stopped Bank of America from instituting a $5 debit card fee, motivated the National Federation of State High School Associations to develop materials to educate coaches about sexual assault and how to reduce assaults by those in their charge, and moved *Seventeen* to commit to a "Body Peace Treaty" in which it promised to stop changing models' body and face shapes (as you read in the chapter on magazines).

The Internet also offers expanded expression through Weblogs, or blogs. Before September 11, 2001, blogs were typically personal online diaries. But after that tragic day, possibly because millions of people felt that the traditional press had left them unprepared and clueless about what was really going on in the world, blogs changed. *Blogs* now refers to regularly updated online journals of commentary, often containing links to the material on

▲ When a suspicious fire destroyed the Islamic Center in Victoria, Texas, a GoFundMe campaign to rebuild drew more than a million dollars from over 22 thousand donors in its first five days.
©Barclay Fernandez/The Victoria Advocate/AP Photo

▲ Slacktivists used Twitter, Facebook, and other social media to mobilize thousands of protestors across the country to jam major airports in protest of a Muslim travel ban.
©Handout/ZUMA Press/Newscom

which they are commenting. There are more than 100 million active blogs worldwide. Technology writer and conservative activist Andrew Sullivan saw blogging's potential in those early days: "Blogging is changing the media world and could foment a revolution in how journalism functions in our culture," not only because individual bloggers have earned their readers' respect, but also because their "personal touch is much more in tune with our current sensibilities" than are those of traditional media outlets (Sullivan, 2002, p. 43).

Blogs have become such an important part of the cultural and political conversation that Internet-security company CloudFlare now provides Project Galileo, a full array of protections against cyberattack, to politically or artistically important small, independent blogs as identified by a committee of 15 freedom-of-expression and journalism nonprofits. Blogs can also be more agile than the traditional media. More so than these older, more cumbersome media, they encourage citizen action in a newly *see-through society*. For example, millions of bloggers constantly and in real time fact-check political candidates. Some track the flow of money to politicians, connecting it to how they vote on important public issues. They remind the powerful that "little brother" is watching. Images caught by chance on a smartphone, arcane public data that goes otherwise unexamined, and citizen video taken at official events all make their way to the Internet and social media and to the people. As Web activist Micah Sifry explained, "Even without central direction, the crowd is sourcing the world for interesting news and sharing tidbits constantly" (in Melber, 2008). This is no small matter, as the Internet has surpassed newspapers as Americans' primary news source (Mindlin, 2009) and, in 2015, search engines, primarily Google, overtook the traditional media as Americans' most-trusted way to find news (Sterling, 2015).

Controlling Internet Expression

Of course, the very same technologies that can empower users who wish to challenge those more powerful than themselves can also be used to lie and cheat. The Internet and social media do not distinguish between true and false, biased and objective, trivial and important. Once misinformation has been loosed online, it is almost impossible to catch and correct it.

The *smear forward* has plagued countless people and organizations. Procter & Gamble was victimized by stories that its cleaners killed pets. Starbucks was falsely accused of refusing to provide coffee to marines serving in Iraq. Other Internet-sustained falsehoods can have far more damaging real-world effects, such as the scientifically discredited belief that vaccines cause autism, leading many parents to deny their children potentially life-saving vaccinations. Actress Jenny McCarthy, the most visible face of the anti-vaccine movement, boasts that her education on the issue comes from "the University of Google." She routinely

▶ The Internet's freedom may give lies great reach, but the Internet also has ways of dealing with them. Snopes, one of the first debunking sites, is one of the best. Reprinted by permission of Snopes.com

©Spencer Grant/PhotoEdit

passes on her knowledge to her 1.3 million Twitter followers. Reduced vaccination rates have led to a recurrence of measles outbreaks, once completely eradicated in the United States, and locale-specific outbreaks of mumps, whooping cough, and chicken pox traced to unvaccinated individuals.

Lies and rumors have always been part of human interaction; the Internet only gives them greater reach. But there is little the government can do to control this abuse. Legal remedies already exist in the form of libel laws and prosecution for fraud. Users can help by teaching themselves to be more attentive to unfamiliar Web addresses and by ignoring messages that are sent anonymously or that have suspicious origins. There are e-based solutions as well. Factcheck.org maintains an exhaustive, alphabetically organized list of debunkings of the Internet's biggest lies. Also of value is Snopes.com, the self-proclaimed "definitive Internet reference source for urban legends, folklore, myths, rumors, and misinformation." Individual sites, too, have taken up the cause of precision and fact. Wikipedia's tens of thousands of editors, for example, review new and altered entries in search of erroneous or public-relations-written material. You can read about the controversy swirling around **fake news** —inaccurate Internet news stories designed to deceive and be spread—and what many observers claim was its very real impact on the 2016 presidential election in the essay entitled "Did Fake News Help Elect a President?"

USING MEDIA TO MAKE A DIFFERENCE
Did Fake News Help Elect a President?

Did you hear that presidential candidate Hillary Clinton ran an underground child sex-slave network out of the basement of a pizzeria near the White House? Did you read that President Barack Obama laundered money for Muslim terrorists and that Pope Francis endorsed Donald Trump for president in the 2016 election? These stories, all obviously false, were shared millions of times on the Internet, especially on social networking sites. But did these stories, many designed primarily to help one candidate win the presidency, have their intended effect?

In a political race marked by acrimony and distrust, not only between the candidates but between large portions of the American electorate, it is nearly impossible to single out any one reason Republican Trump defeated Democrat Clinton. But given her nearly 3-million-vote plurality in the popular vote and his narrow wins in the three traditionally Democratic states that gave him the Electoral College victory, many observers saw fake news, largely anti-Clinton, as a deciding factor in what was, until the final days, a very close race (deBuys, 2017).

Fake news had many authors. Some were pranksters who saw their jokes taken seriously. Some were "entrepreneurs" at home and abroad attempting to draw clicks, and therefore ad dollars, with outrageous stories. Some were satirists mocking the gullibility of those in government and the media who were too quick to accept any "news" that fit their preconceptions (Sydell, 2016). Some were "planted" by opposition political operatives (Moylan, 2017), and some were agents of the Russian government determined to assist their favored candidate, as acknowledged by Director of National Intelligence James Clapper (Bruno, 2017; Oremus, 2017). Regardless of their motives for creating fake news, these writers quickly discovered that favorable Trump stories and those damaging to Clinton would be shared far more widely on Facebook and other social networking sites than would stories sympathetic to Clinton (Silverman, 2016). "It's all Trump. People go nuts for it," marveled Canadian satirical fake news writer John Eagan (in Higgins, McIntyre, & Dance, 2016, p. A1).

After the election, the American public learned that Facebook users were two-and-a-half times more likely to read fake news than news from reputable journalism sites (Mandese, 2016) and that 23% of their fellow citizens shared fake political news, about half of whom knew at the time they passed it on that it was false (Mullin, 2016). They saw that during the last three months of the campaign the 20 top fake news stories on Facebook generated more shares, likes, and comments than the top 20 stories from actual news sites ("The Digital," 2016), and that the 23 best-performing fake news stories on Facebook in 2016 combined for 10.6 million engagements—shares, reactions, and comments—or about 460,000 each (Uberti, 2017).

There was fake news; it was read and it was shared. But did it make a difference? It certainly did to the owners and customers of the Comet Ping Pong pizzeria when a man armed with a semi-automatic rifle "self-investigated" the site of Clinton's supposed sex ring, firing three shots while inside (Zapruder, 2016). Facebook, Twitter, and Google believed it made a difference, as all three companies implemented a number of technological and human-based solutions to identify, fact-check, and limit the spread of fake news. CNN and the BBC thought it did, establishing reporting units to chase down and debunk false news stories. The American public believed it did, as 64% said it had "the power to sow confusion" (Loesche, 2017). Ultimately, while it may be impossible to definitely determine if fake news helped elect a president, there is little doubt that fake news did make a difference in an alternative and more insidious way. Philosophy professor Michael Lynch explains, "There are an alarming number of people who tend to be credulous and form beliefs based on the latest thing they've read, but that's not the wider problem. The wider problem is fake news has the effect of getting people not to believe real things." People, he said, think, "There's no way for me to know what is objectively true, so we'll stick to our guns and our own evidence. We'll ignore the facts because nobody knows what's really true anyway" (in Tavernise, 2016, p. A1).

That is how fake news really made a difference; it damaged our democracy by weakening our ability to govern ourselves because we, as citizens, are left with little common, objective reality from which to engage in civic—and civil—discourse.

Pornography on the Internet

Most efforts at controlling the Internet are aimed at indecent or pornographic Web content. You can read more about how indecent and pornographic expression is protected in the chapter on media freedom, regulation, and ethics. The particular concern with the Internet, therefore, is shielding children.

The Child Pornography Prevention Act of 1996 forbade online transmission of any image that "appears to be of a minor engaging in sexually explicit conduct." Proponents argued that the impact of child porn on the children involved, as well as on society, warranted this legislation. Opponents argued that child pornography per se was already illegal, regardless of the medium. Therefore they saw this law as an unnecessary and overly broad intrusion into freedom of expression on the Internet. In April 2002 the Supreme Court sided with the act's opponents. Its effect would be too damaging to freedom of expression. "Few legitimate movie producers or book publishers, or few other speakers in any capacity, would risk distributing images in or near the uncertain reach of this law," wrote Justice Anthony Kennedy. "The Constitution gives significant protection from over-broad laws that chill speech within the First Amendment's vast and privileged sphere" (in "Justices Scrap," 2002, p. A3). Kennedy cited the antidrug film *Traffic,* Academy Award–winning *American Beauty,* and Shakespeare's *Romeo and Juliet,* all works containing scenes of minors engaged in sexual activity, as examples of expression that would disappear from the Internet.

The primary battleground, then, became protecting children from otherwise legal content. The Internet, by virtue of its openness and accessibility, raises particular concerns. Children's viewing of sexually explicit material on cable or streaming television can theoretically be controlled by parents. Moreover, viewers must specifically order this content and typically pay an additional fee for it. The purchase of sexually explicit videos, books, and magazines is controlled by laws regulating vendors. But computers sit in homes, schools, and libraries. Children are encouraged to explore their possibilities. A search for a seemingly innocent term may have multiple meanings and might turn up any number of pornographic sites.

Proponents of stricter control of the Internet liken the availability of smut online to a bookstore or library that allows porn to sit side by side with books that children *should* be reading. In actual, real-world bookstores and libraries, professionals, whether book retailers or librarians, apply their judgment in selecting and locating material, ideally striving for appropriateness and balance. Children are the beneficiaries of this professional judgment. No such selection or evaluation is applied to the Internet. Opponents of control accept the bookstore/library analogy but argue that, as troubling as the online proximity of all types of content may be, it is a true example of the freedom guaranteed by the First Amendment.

The solution seems to be in technology. Filtering software, such as Net Nanny, can be set to block access to websites by title and by the presence of specific words and images. Few free speech advocates are troubled by filters on home computers, but they do see them as problematic when used on more public machines—for example, in schools and libraries. They argue that software that can filter sexual content can also be set to screen out birth control information, religious sites, and discussions of racism. Virtually any content can be blocked. This, they claim, denies other users—adults and mature teenagers, for example—their freedoms.

Congress weighed in on the filtering debate, passing the Children's Internet Protection Act in 2000, requiring schools and libraries to install filtering software. But First Amendment concerns invalidated this act as well. A federal appeals court ruled in June 2002 that requiring these institutions to install filters changes their nature from places that provide information to places that unconstitutionally restrict it. Nonetheless, in June 2003 a sharply divided Supreme Court upheld the Children's Internet Protection Act, declaring that Congress did indeed have the power to require libraries to install filters.

Copyright (Intellectual Property Ownership)

Another freedom-of-expression issue that takes on a special nature on the Internet is copyright. Copyright protection is designed to ensure that those who create content are financially compensated for their work. The assumption is that more "authors" will create more content if assured of monetary compensation from those who use it. When the content is tangible (books, movies, magazines, CDs), authorship and use are relatively easy to identify. But in the cyberworld, things become a bit more complex. John Perry Barlow (1996), a cofounder of the Electronic Frontier Foundation, explained the situation relatively early in the life of the Internet:

> The riddle is this: If our property can be infinitely reproduced and instantaneously distributed all over the planet without cost, without our knowledge, without its even leaving our possession, how can we protect it? How are we going to get paid for the work we do with our minds? And, if we can't get paid, what will assure the continued creation and distribution of such work? (p. 148)

Technically, copyright rules apply to the Internet as they do to other media. Material on the Internet belongs to the author, so its use, other than fair use, requires permission and possibly payment. But because material on the Internet is not tangible, it is easily, freely, and privately copied. This renders it difficult, if not impossible, to police those who do copy.

Another confounding issue is that new and existing material is often combined with other existing material to create even "newer" content. This makes it difficult to assign authorship. If a user borrows some text from one source, combines it with images from a second, surrounds both with a background graphic from a third, and adds music sampled from many others, where does authorship reside?

To deal with these thorny issues, in 1998 the U.S. Congress passed the Digital Millennium Copyright Act. Its primary goal was to bring U.S. copyright law into compliance with that of the World Intellectual Property Organization (WIPO), headquartered in Geneva, Switzerland. The act does the following:

- Makes it a crime to circumvent antipiracy measures built into commercial software
- Outlaws the manufacture, sale, or distribution of code-breaking devices used to illegally copy software
- Permits breaking of copyright protection devices to conduct encryption research and to test computer security systems
- Provides copyright exemptions for nonprofit libraries, archives, and educational institutions under certain circumstances
- Limits the copyright infringement liability of Internet service providers for simply transmitting information over the Internet, but ISPs are required to remove material from users' websites that appears to constitute copyright infringement
- Requires webcasters (those who broadcast music over the Internet) to pay licensing fees to record companies
- States explicitly that **fair use**—instances in which copyrighted material may be used without permission or payment, such as taking brief quotes from a book—applies to the Internet

What the debate over Internet copyright represents—like concern about controlling content that children can access and efforts to limit troublesome or challenging expression—is a clash of fundamental values that has taken on added nuance with the coming of computer networks. Copyright on the Internet is discussed more fully in the chapter on media freedom, regulation, and ethics.

Privacy

The issue of privacy in mass communication has traditionally been concerned with individuals' rights to protect their privacy from invasive, intrusive media. For example, should newspapers publish the names of rape victims and juvenile offenders? When does a person become a public figure and forfeit some degree of privacy? In the global village, however, the issue takes on a new character. Whereas Supreme Court Justice Louis Brandeis could once argue that privacy is "the right to be left alone," today privacy is just as likely to mean "the right to maintain control over our own data." Privacy in the global village has two facets. The first is protecting the privacy of communication we wish to keep private. The second is the use (and misuse) of private, personal information willingly given online. Refer to the chapter on media freedom, regulation, and ethics for more on privacy.

PROTECTING PRIVACY IN COMMUNICATION The 1986 Electronic Communication Privacy Act guarantees the privacy of our e-mail. It is a criminal offense to either "intentionally [access] without authorization a facility through which an electronic communication service is provided; or intentionally [exceed] an authorization to access that facility." In addition, the law "prohibits an electronic communications service provider from knowingly divulging the contents of any stored electronic communication." The goal of this legislation is to protect private citizens from official abuse; it gives e-mail "conversations" the same protection that phone conversations enjoy. If a government agency wants to listen in, it must secure permission, just as it must get a court order for a telephone wiretap.

And while the 1986 act is still the law, whistle-blower Edward Snowden's 2013 revelation that the National Security Agency, in its efforts to thwart terrorism, was collecting virtually every piece of data that traveled the Internet made it clear that privacy of communication on the Internet is, at best, a hoped-for ideal. Debate has raged over whether Snowden is a hero or traitor, but no one disputes the fact that U.S. government agencies constantly and ubiquitously track our online activity. You can argue that this benign surveillance—computers recording what other computers are doing to look for suspicious patterns—is more beneficial than harmful; it's keeping us safe. Or you might argue, as does reporter Chris Hedges, that "the relationship between those who are constantly watched and tracked and those who watch and track them is the relationship between masters and slaves" (2014). In either case, as a media-literate Internet user, you should be aware of what national security reporter Robert Sheer calls "the great contradiction of our time: the unprecedented liberating power of the supercomputer combined with the worldwide Internet . . . also contain[s] the seeds of freedom's destruction because of the awesome power of this new technology to support a surveillance state that exceeds the wildest dream of the most ingenious dictator" (2015). This tension between ensuring our national security and protecting our personal privacy is, in the words of Amazon founder Jeff Bezos, the "issue of our age" (in Tsukayama, 2016).

PROTECTING PRIVACY OF PERSONAL INFORMATION   Every online act leaves a "digital trail," making possible easy **dataveillance**—the massive collection and distillation of consumer data. Ironically, we willingly participate in this intrusion into our privacy. Online marketer Shelly Palmer explains, "Most of us are willing to give up our data—location, viewing, purchasing, or search history—for our online enjoyment. We can call this the 'willing suspension of our privacy' because if you spent a moment to consider what your data was actually being used for, you would refuse to let it happen" (2017, p. 18). She wants us to understand that because of computer storage, networking, and cross-referencing power, the information we willingly give to one entity is easily and cheaply given to countless unknown others.

One form of dataveillance is distributing and sharing personal, private information among organizations other than the one for whom it was originally intended. Information from every credit card transaction (online or at a store), credit application, phone call, supermarket or other purchase made without cash (for example, with a check, debit card, or "club" card), newspaper and magazine subscription, and cable television subscribership is digitally recorded, stored, and most likely sold to others. The increased computerization of medical files, banking information, job applications, and school records produces even more salable data. Eventually, anyone who wants to know something about a person can simply buy the necessary information—without that person's permission or even knowledge. These data can then be used to further invade people's privacy. For example, employers can withhold jobs for reasons unknown to applicants.

Recognizing the scope of data collection and the potential problems that it raises, Congress passed the 1974 Federal Privacy Act, restricting *governments'* ability to collect and distribute information about citizens. The act, however, expressly exempted businesses and other nongovernmental organizations from control. As a result, 45% of Internet users say privacy and security concerns have stopped them from engaging in routine Internet activities such as posting on social networks, expressing opinions, and buying online (Peterson, 2014), and 86% have taken steps online to remove or mask their digital footprints (Raine, 2016).

The Internet industry and the federal government responded in 2012 with a "Consumer Privacy Bill of Rights," voluntary guidelines suggesting sites place a "do not track" button on their Web pages. Critics contend that these guidelines are insufficient protection, as not all sites comply, and even those with the button may still collect and hold users' personal data for their own market research. They object to the idea that websites should provide us that security only if we specifically ask for it, called **opt-out**. "When did privacy become a choice rather than the default?" they ask. Instead, sites should have to get our permission before they collect and disseminate our personal data, that is, we should be able to **opt-in**, as is the case in Europe. While American ISPs and marketers find opt-in "onerous" (Mandese, 2017), European Union privacy law not only requires Internet companies to get explicit user consent before using their data, it also grants all citizens the "right to be forgotten," that is, the right to ask to have all their collected personal data deleted forever. Privacy advocates ask the question, "If we have legislation to bring our copyright laws into compliance with those of other nations, why shouldn't we do the same with our privacy laws?" You can read about other data-privacy discrepancies between the United States and Europe in the box entitled, "Why Not Here?"

Four relatively new technological advances pose additional privacy problems: the **radio frequency identification (RFID) chip**; **augmented reality (AR)**; cloud computing; and the **Internet of Things (IoT)** in which everyday objects have built-in network connectivity, allowing them to send and receive data. The first, RFID, already used by many retailers, is a grain-of-sand-sized microchip and antenna embedded in consumer products that transmits a radio signal. The advantage to retailers is greater inventory control and lower labor costs. The retailer has an absolute, up-to-the-minute accounting of how many boxes of widgets are on the shelf, and consumers simply walk out the door with their boxes while the RFID sends a signal charging the correct amount to the proper credit card; no checkout personnel is needed. Privacy advocates' concern should be clear. That signal keeps on sending. Now marketers, the government, and others will know where you and your box of widgets are at all times, how quickly you go through your box of widgets, and where you are when you run out of widgets. How soon until your e-mail's inbox fills up with offers of widgets on sale? What if a burglar could use an RFID reader from outside your house to preview its contents? What happens when these data are networked with all your other personal information? What if you buy a case of beer rather than a box of widgets? Will your employer know?

The second advance, introduced in 2009 and available in smartphones containing the program Layar, augmented reality (AR) permits users to point their smartphones at a real-world location, person, or scene and be instantly linked to hundreds of websites containing information about those things, superimposed over the screen image. Very cool, say proponents—instant restaurant reviews, nearby flu-shot locations, related Instagram photos, and the names of relatives you might know in the area. Very scary, say privacy advocates: "Fold in facial-recognition [already extant] and you could point your phone at Bob from accounting, whose visage is now 'augmented' with the information that he has a gay son and drinks Hoegaarden" (Walker, 2009, p. 32). In other words, everything that exists on the Internet is linkable. When anyone and everyone can access these data by simply pointing a phone at someone, privacy, already on life support, dies.

A third advance worrying privacy advocates is the growing use of cloud computing and its storage of data, including personal information, on third-party environments. Google, Microsoft, and numerous independent providers offer cloud computing, and advocates tout the increased power and memory of the cloud, arguing that even if your laptop is lost or destroyed, you lose nothing. But privacy advocates counter that data stored online has less privacy protection both in practice and under the law. Cloud services claim data is protected by **encryption**, the electronic coding or masking of information that can be deciphered only by a recipient with the proper decrypting key. Yet there are no guarantees, argue online privacy advocates, given repeated revelations that not only does the federal government tap into the files of Internet search engines and e-mail and cloud service providers, but many of these companies willingly provide people's data to the authorities. For example, it was recently discovered that Yahoo has a secret custom software program that searches all of its customers' incoming e-mails for specific information requested by U.S. intelligence officials (Menn, 2016). Privacy experts say there's simply no way to ever be completely sure your data will remain secure once you've moved it to the cloud.

Finally, almost any everyday device we use today—consumer electronics, cars, utility meters, refrigerators, automatic coffee makers, vending machines, thermostats, lights, clothes and wearable devices, baby monitors—can be connected to the Internet. In 2017 the number of IoT devices surpassed the number of people living on Earth, an expansion encouraged in part by its low cost, about $1 per device. It is only people's concern about their privacy that keeps the growth rate of IoT from being even faster than it is (Martin, 2017). If everything that exists on the Internet is linkable, IoT means that others will have access to an ever greater array of the most personal and intimate aspects of our lives. There is, for example, an IoT bag from corn-chip maker Tostitos that contains a sensor that detects even small traces of alcohol on the breath of nearby snackers. If it does so, it turns red, changes into the image of a steering wheel, and delivers the message, "Don't drink and drive." A simple tap of the bag with a smartphone hails a car from Uber (Nudd, 2017). As convenient as that may be, if it can connect to a ride-sharing service, it can connect to the police, your employer, your insurance company, or anyone interested in how you spend your free time. Privacy advocates' IoT fears seemed to be confirmed with the revelation that Vizio's Internet-connected TV sets were secretly collecting their owners' viewing information and selling it to advertisers (C. Smith, 2017b).

▲ Cool and safety conscious use of IoT or another giveaway of our privacy?

©Spencer Grant/PhotoEdit

Another form of dataveillance is the electronic tracking of the choices we make when we are online, called our **click stream**. Despite the anonymity online users think they enjoy, every click of a key can be, and often is, recorded and stored. This happens whether or not the user actually enters information—for example, a credit card number to make a purchase or a Social Security number to verify identity. This tracking is made possible by **cookies**, an identifying code added to a computer's hard drive by a visited website. Normally, only the site that has sent the cookie can read it—the next time you visit that site it "remembers" you. But some sites bring "third-party" cookies to your computer. Maintained by big Internet advertising networks like DoubleClick and Engage, these cookies can be read by any of the thousands of websites also belonging to that network, whether you've visited them or not, and without your knowledge. As a result, this software is more commonly referred to as **spyware**, identifying code placed on a computer by a website without permission or notification. Spyware not only facilitates tracking by unknown sites and/or people (those "third parties") but opens a computer to unwanted pop-up ads and other commercial messages.

At any given time, a regular Web user will have dozens of cookies on his or her hard drive, but most commercial browsers come equipped with the capacity to block or erase them. The Anti-Spyware Coalition offers information and assistance on how to deal with cookies and spyware. In addition, users can purchase cookie-scrubbing software. Commercial firms such as Anonymizer sell programs that not only block and erase spyware but also allow users to surf the Web anonymously.

CULTURAL FORUM
Why Not Here?

The security and use of our online information, a topic that has roiled the public forum since the Internet was in its infancy, was once again a topic of debate in late 2016 when Google, Amazon, and other American online businesses agreed to a "safe harbor" arrangement with the European Union that would allow the transfer of people's digital data, previously strictly limited, back and forth across the Atlantic only if those companies promised not to make that data available to U.S. intelligence agencies, a protection not available to American Internet users. European Internet users sued to stop the agreement because for many, "an individual's right to privacy [is] almost on par with freedom of expression" and they believed that there was too great a risk that those promises would not be kept (Scott, 2016).

Other online privacy differences exist, even though American companies are bound by Europe's rules when doing business there. For example, not only do Americans not have the right to have their personal data erased and not only must they opt out of data tracking rather than opt in, but Google offers on-screen information to European users giving them details on the cookies a site is using and what information is being collected. In addition, all European Union Internet and social media users have the right to demand that a site provide a detailed account of every bit of information it has collected on them, and that material must be supplied. Europe's "right to be forgotten" rule also gives people the power to have search engines delete listings they consider outdated or irrelevant. Whether you think that is a good idea or not (should a drunk driver who killed an innocent pedestrian have the right to demand the erasure of links to online news sources that reported that event?), these discrepancies raise an important question for Web privacy advocates: Why do American-based Internet and social media companies offer their overseas users greater privacy protection than they do their U.S. customers?

"Europe's data protection rules have become the default privacy settings for the world," said Billy Hawkes, one-time Irish data protection regulator (in Scott, 2014, p. SR5). Hong Kong, for example, now requires opt-in. The Philippines, Indonesia, Malaysia, and even China have adopted data-privacy rules much like those in Europe, some backed by serious financial penalties for violators. But the situation in the United States remains as it has been since the Internet's inception; the government generally prefers to let the industry regulate itself on privacy matters.

Enter your voice. Why should this be the case? As you've read, a large number of Americans do not feel secure in much of their online activity. Why can't we have the privacy controls that American Internet companies grant to others? Is it our basic distrust of government intervention in mass communication issues? If so, why do 64% of Internet users want greater regulatory protection for their online data (Raine, 2016)? Is it

that we trust our social media companies to do the right thing? Then how do you explain the fact that half of American social media users do not trust the sites they use to protect their personal data (Olmstead & Smith, 2017)? Is it our own ambivalence? Are we the authors of our own online fate? How else can you explain the fact that one-third of Americans say they are willing to exchange basic personal information with a website in exchange for "compelling content" (Faw, 2016)?

Virtual Democracy

The Internet and social media are characterized by freedom and self-governance, which are also the hallmarks of true democracy. It is no surprise, then, that these technologies are often trumpeted as the newest and best tools for increased democratic involvement and participation. This enthusiasm for a technological solution to what many see as increased disenchantment with politics and the political process mirrors that which followed the introduction of radio and television. A September 3, 1924, *New Republic* article, for example, argued that the high level of public interest in the radio broadcast of the 1924 political party conventions brought "dismay" to "the most hardened political cynic" (in Davis, 1976, p. 351). In 1940 NBC founder and chairman David Sarnoff predicted that television would enrich democracy because it was "destined to provide greater knowledge to larger numbers of people, truer perception of the meaning of current events, more accurate appraisals of men in public life, and a broader understanding of the needs and aspirations of our fellow human beings" (in Shenk, 1997, p. 60).

Some critics argue that the Internet will be no more of an asset to democracy than have been radio and television because the same economic and commercial forces that have shaped the content and operation of those more traditional media will constrain the Internet just as rigidly. They point to the endless battles to keep the Internet open and free. There are frequent fights over **network neutrality** (often just net neutrality), the requirement that all ISPs, including cable MSOs (multiple system operators), allow free and equal flow of all Web traffic. For example, if all sites were not equal, one that was willing (and able) to pay would have its content transmitted to people's computers more quickly. Another, a political activist site for example, that was unwilling (or unable) to pay would have its content slowed down. Their pessimism also resides in part in concentration and conglomeration of the Internet—Google's acquisition of popular (and democratic) YouTube; Microsoft's purchase of Internet video phone company Skype and social networking sites LinkedIn and Yammer; Facebook's purchase of Instagram and WhatsApp; Yahoo's purchase of blogging service Tumblr and its later acquisition by Verizon; AT&T's merger with DirecTV and its efforts to acquire Time Warner, to list a few.

Others argue that, by its very nature, the Internet is ill suited for the task of serving democracy. Wael Ghonim, one of the "fathers" of the Arab Spring, the short-lived technology-fueled rebellion against Middle East repression, saw the medium's potential and its failure: "The same medium that so effectively transmits a howling message of change also appears to undermine the ability to make it. Social media amplifies the human tendency to bind with one's own kind. It tends to reduce complex social challenges to mobilizing slogans that reverberate in echo chambers of the like-minded rather than engage in persuasion, dialogue, and the reach for consensus. Hate speech and untruths appear alongside good intentions and truths" (in Amanpour, 2016).

THE TECHNOLOGY GAP An important principle of democracy is "one person, one vote." But if democracy is increasingly practiced online, those lacking the necessary technology and skill will be denied their vote. This is the **technology gap**—the widening disparity between the communication technology haves and have-nots. Even with its rapid diffusion, 13% of

Demographics of the 13% of U.S. adults without Internet access

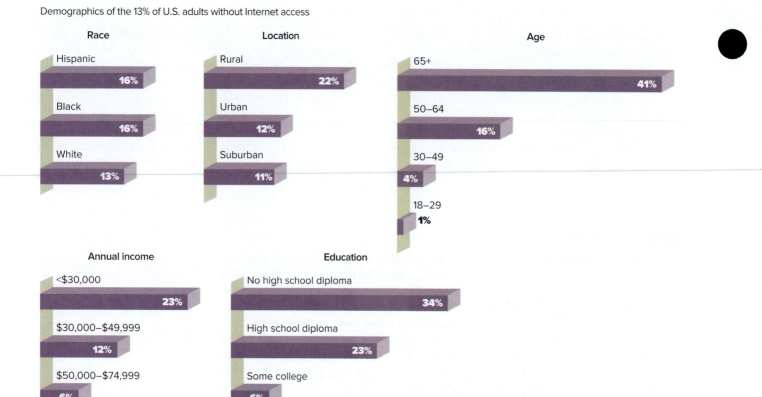

▲ **Figure 2** Who's Not on the Internet.
Source: Anderson, 2016.

people in the United States do not use the Internet. The "democratization" of the Internet still favors those who have the money to buy the equipment needed to access the Internet as well as to pay for that connection. This leaves out many U.S. citizens—those on the wrong side of the **digital divide**, the lack of technological access among specific groups of Americans. Although 87% of all Americans regularly access the Internet, usage rates lag for those less educated, people with disabilities, those with lower incomes, those in rural areas, Hispanic and African American households, and less affluent elderly people with disabilities. You can see the demographics of the divide in Figure 2.

THE INFORMATION GAP Another important principle of democracy is that self-governing people govern best with full access to information. This is the reason our culture is so suspicious of censorship. The technology gap feeds a second impediment to virtual democracy, the **information gap**. Those without the requisite technology will have diminished access to the information it makes available. In other words, they will suffer from a form of technologically imposed censorship.

Critics of the information gap point to troubling examples of other media failures to deliver important information to all citizens. Cable television subscribership is lowest among urban working-class and poor people. Many newspapers, uninterested in these same people because they do not possess the demographic profile coveted by advertisers, do not promote their papers in the neighborhoods in which they live and, in some large cities, do not even deliver there. For the same reason, there are precious few consumer magazines aimed at less well-off people. If the technology gap creates an even wider information gap than already exists between these audiences and other citizens, democracy will surely suffer from what social scientists call the **knowledge gap**, growing differences in knowledge, civic activity, and literacy between better-informed and less-informed Americans.

The best way to bridge the technology, information, and knowledge gaps is to close the digital divide, an effort that has taken up the interest of several private and public entities. For example, the FCC, through its E-Rate program, invests about $1 billion a year to provide, expand, and upgrade broadband Internet access to American schools and libraries with money raised from the universal service fee you see on your phone bill. Cable giant Comcast offers low-cost broadband service, as little as $10 a month, for families living in poverty. Despite significant resistance from local MSOs (the same people who continue to fight net neutrality), 300 cities and towns across America offer their citizens low-cost broadband. In 2015 the Obama administration signaled its intention to forbid state legislatures from outlawing this so-called **municipal broadband**. The attempt was defeated by a 2016 court decision, so these restrictions remain on the books in 23 states. Still, municipal broadband continues to expand; for example, New York City maintains LinkNYC, 10,000 kiosks occupying spots that once housed pay phones, to give its citizens and visitors free Wi-Fi and free domestic phone calling. Other than the fundamental fairness of granting all people equal access to information, these efforts are encouraged by evidence that there is a definite financial benefit to the municipalities and regions that provide expanded broadband access (Koebler, 2016).

DEVELOPING MEDIA LITERACY SKILLS

The Declaration of Internet Freedom

Given its importance to virtually all aspects of human endeavor, many people believe that the Internet should be treated as a basic human right. This philosophy is contained in the Declaration of Internet Freedom, originally developed by a coalition of 1,500 of the world's leading technology and Internet freedom advocates. Among the 2,000 organizational and 75,000 individual signatories in 150 different countries are the Electronic Frontier Foundation, Amnesty International, Reporters without Borders, and the Mozilla Foundation. Translated into 72 languages, the Declaration is posted at www.internetdeclaration.org. It sets out five principles that all governments and corporations should follow to keep the Internet free:

- *There must be no censorship of the Internet.* All expression is free and equal, and users must be free to access it as they wish. Today, scores of national governments continue to censor content because, they say, they wish to impose traditional social values, keep political stability, or maintain national security ("Top 10," 2016).

- *There must be universal access to fast and affordable networks.* The Internet is the most democratizing of all media; to remain so, access—technological and economic—must be available to all, regardless of locale or financial situation. Despite its impressive reach, 3.7 billion of the Earth's people have no access to the Internet ("Internet Usage," 2017).

- *There must be freedom to connect, communicate, create, and innovate over the Internet.* The Internet renders us all creators as well as consumers, generators of innovations as well as their recipients. There should be no barriers to entry or dissemination. You'll recognize this as a call for net neutrality; today 74% of all nations have no such guarantee (Ansip, 2015).

- *There must be protection for new technologies and innovators whose innovations are abused by other users.* The Internet is a benign technology; it is its use that brings value, good or bad. Advances and those who make them must be free from censure if others misuse their work.

- *There must be privacy rights and the ability for users to control how information about them is used.* We are all humans with dignity. The remarkable power of the Internet does not change the inherent value of being free—absent surveillance—to be who and what we want to be. In 84% of the world's countries, laws that prevent mass online surveillance are "weak or nonexistent" (Hui, 2014).

As the Internet, World Wide Web, and social media increasingly become necessities and even life-sustaining utilities, media-literate users have an obligation to do more than know and support this declaration. We must make our own declaration of intent to make the most of our online freedom.

It is important to remember that culture is neither innate nor inviolate. *We* construct culture—both dominant and bounded. Increasingly, we do so through mass communication, and the Internet has given us voice once unimaginable. So before we can enter the forum in which those cultures are constructed and maintained, we must understand where we stand and what we believe. We must be able to defend our positions. The hallmarks of a media-literate individual are analysis and self-reflection. Reread the five principles. After having read this chapter's discussion of privacy, freedom of expression, fake news, the digital divide, net neutrality, and municipal broadband, how well do you think they are being met? Are you aware, for example, that several ISPs, notably Comcast, Frontier Communications, and Time Warner Cable, have either tried or announced they would begin **metering** Internet use? That is, they would charge users "by the byte"—heavier users would pay more and more modest users would pay less. Is this consistent with the promise of full access?

MEDIA LITERACY CHALLENGE
Internet Addiction Self-Diagnosis

The American Psychiatric Association lists "Internet Addiction Disorder" as a recognized mental illness in its *Diagnostic and Statistical Manual of Mental Disorders*. And while you no doubt have tried to unplug for a while, like 67% of U.S. Internet users every year, somehow you just can't seem to do it (Birth, 2016). But you're a media-literate Internet user, so you should be able to explain why it's so hard to ditch your technology. After all, you certainly are *aware of the impact of the Internet on your life*. Possibly you are addicted. No, you say? Then take the Internet Addiction Test, developed by Kimberly S. Young of the Center for Online Addiction (2004). Before answering its eight questions, keep in mind that this is a measure of *Internet* addiction, not *computer* addiction. So consider your Internet usage on all devices—computers, smartphones, tablets, and game consoles—when replying. Be sure to count only recreational usage over the last six months; Internet time for school or work doesn't count.

1. Do you feel preoccupied with the Internet (think about previous online activity or anticipate next online session)?
2. Do you feel the need to use the Internet for increasing amounts of time to achieve satisfaction?
3. Have you repeatedly made unsuccessful efforts to control, cut back, or stop Internet use?
4. Do you feel restless, moody, depressed, or irritable when attempting to cut down or stop Internet use?
5. Do you stay online longer than originally intended?
6. Have you jeopardized or risked the loss of a significant relationship, job, educational or career opportunity because of the Internet?
7. Have you lied to family members, therapists, or others to conceal the extent of your involvement with the Internet?
8. Do you use the Internet as a way of escaping from problems or of relieving feelings of helplessness, guilt, anxiety, or depression?

Interpreting your answers is simple: Addiction is present if you answered "yes" to at least five of the questions. If that was your situation, consider why that is the case. Why are you so dependent on the Internet? What can you do to shed your addiction? Do you even want to? If not, why not? As a media-literate Internet, Web, and social media user you understand that any medium is only as beneficial as you make it; therefore, these are questions, regardless of any level or absence of addiction, that you should ask and re-ask yourself. Doing so will improve your media literacy and increase the benefits you derive from these technologies.

Resources for Review and Discussion

REVIEW POINTS: TYING CONTENT TO LEARNING OUTCOMES

▶ **Outline the history and development of the Internet and social media.**

- ☐ The idea for the Internet came either from technological optimists like Joseph C. R. Licklider or from the military, hoping to maintain communication networks in time of enemy attack—or from both.
- ☐ Paul Baran devised a packet-switching network, the technological basis for the Internet, to be used on powerful computers developed by John V. Atanasoff, John Mauchly, and John Presper Eckert.
- ☐ The personal computer was developed by Bill Gates and the team of Steve Jobs and Stephen Wozniak.
- ☐ Classmates.com started the social media revolution in 1995; Facebook made social media mainstream in 2004.

▶ **Describe how the organizational and economic natures of the contemporary Internet and social media industries shape their content.**

- ☐ The Internet facilitates e-mail, VoIP, social networking, and the World Wide Web, all greatly facilitated by the rapid diffusion of smartphones and tablets.
- ☐ The Web relies on a system of hosts, browsers, and search engines to bring users to websites, characterized by URLs and home pages.
- ☐ Many of us are digital natives; we've never known a world without the Internet and social media.
- ☐ Our messages on the Internet and social media sit side by side with those of the largest and most powerful organizations in the world.
- ☐ Feedback on the Internet and social media is instant and direct, more like that in interpersonal rather than mass communication.

▶ **Answer a number of questions about how and why individuals use social media.**

- ☐ We use social media for self-presentation and because of our need to belong.

- ☐ We tend to present a realistic version of ourselves when on social media.
- ☐ Some users may suffer from Facebook depression or Facebook envy.
- ☐ Social media use can lead to social isolation, or it may not; the outcome is dependent on how we choose to participate in social media.

▶ **Analyze social and cultural questions posed by the Internet, social media, and related emerging technologies.**

- ☐ The Internet and social media make freedom of expression a reality for anyone linked to them. But abuse of that freedom has led to calls for greater control.
- ☐ Restrictions on access to pornography, protection of copyright, and threats to identity are primary battlegrounds for opponents and proponents of control.
- ☐ The Internet and social media's potential contributions to participatory democracy are also in debate, as problems such as the technology and information gaps and the digital divide have yet to be resolved.

▶ **Apply key Internet and social media literacy skills, especially in protecting your privacy and reflecting on the Internet's double edge of (potentially) good and troublesome change.**

- ☐ The Internet and social media, especially with their power to reshape all the mass media, raise multiple issues for media-literate users hoping to effectively make their way in an interconnected world, guidance for which can be found in the Declaration of Internet Freedom:
  - There must be no censorship of the Internet.
  - There must be universal access to fast and affordable networks.
  - There must be freedom to connect, communicate, create, and innovate over the Internet.
  - There must be protection for new technologies and innovators whose innovations are abused by other users.
  - There must be privacy rights and the ability for users to control how information about them is used.

KEY TERMS

QUESTIONS FOR REVIEW

1. What is the importance of each of these people to the development of the computer: Charles Babbage, John Atanasoff, John Mauchly, and John Presper Eckert?

2. What were the contributions of Joseph C. R. Licklider, Paul Baran, Bill Gates, Steve Jobs, and Stephen Wozniak to the development and popularization of the Internet?

3. What are digital computers, microcomputers, and mainframe computers?

4. What is the dual-factor model of social media use? How does it explain our affinity for social media?

5. Differentiate between the idealized virtual identity and the extended real-life hypotheses of social media use.

6. What are Facebook depression and Facebook envy?

7. What are the two primary privacy issues for online communication? What are some of the new technological threats?

8. What is a blog? How might blogs alter journalism?

9. What are some of the arguments supporting the idea that the Internet will be a boost to participatory democracy? What are some of the counterarguments?

10. What are the technology and information gaps? What do they have to do with Internet-based virtual democracy? What is the digital divide?

To maximize your study time, check out CONNECT to access the SmartBook study module for this chapter and explore other resources.

QUESTIONS FOR CRITICAL THINKING AND DISCUSSION

1. Are you an active social media user? If so, how accurate a representation of yourself do you tend to present? Do you show the "real you" because that's what you want to do, or do you feel restricted in your presentation of yourself by the presence of your online friends?

2. Do you ever make personal information available online? If so, how confident are you of its security? Do you take steps to protect your privacy?

3. Do you believe online communication technologies will improve or damage participatory democracy? Why? Can you relate a personal experience of how the Internet or social media increased or limited your involvement in the political process?

REFERENCES

1. "Ad Age social media facts 2016." (2016, September 26). *Advertising Age*, insert.

2. Amanpour, C. (2016, November 22). International Press Freedom Awards speech. *Committee to Protect Journalists*. Online: https://cpj.org/awards/2016/christiane-amanpour.php

3. Anderson, M. (2016, September 7). 13% of Americans don't use the Internet. Who are they? *Pew Research Center*. Online: http://www.pewresearch.org/fact-tank/2016/09/07/some-americans-dont-use-the-internet-who-are-they/

4. Ansip, A. (2015, February 2). Guest blog: Sir Tim Berners-Lee, founding director, World Wide Web Foundation. *European Commission*. Online: http://ec.europa.eu/commission/2014-2019/ansip/blog/guest-blog-sir-tim-berners-lee-founding-director-world-wide-web-foundation_en

5. Anthony, S. (2014, July 8). In 2015 tablet sales will finally surpass PCs, fulfilling Steve Jobs' post-PC prophecy. *Extreme Tech*. Online: http://www.extremetech.com/computing/185937-in-2015-tablet-sales-will-finally-surpass-pcs-fulfilling-steve-jobs-post-pc-prophecy

6. "Average number of Facebook friends of users in the United States as of February 2014, by age group." (2016). *Statista*. Online: https://www.statista.com/statistics/232499/americans-who-use-social-networking-sites-several-times-per-day/

7. Back, M. D., Stopfer, J. M., Vazire, S., Gaddis, S., Schmukle, S. C., Egloff, B., & Gosling, S. D. (2010). Facebook profiles reflect actual personality, not self-idealization. *Psychological Science*, 21, 372–374.

8. Barlow, J. P. (1996). Selling wine without bottles: The economy of mind on the global Net. In L. H. Leeson (Ed.), *Clicking in: Hot links to a digital culture*. Seattle, WA: Bay Press.

9. Berners-Lee, T., & Fischetti, M. (1999). *Weaving the Web: The original design and ultimate destiny of the World Wide Web by its inventor*. New York: HarperCollins.

10. Birth, A. (2016, February 25). Unplugging: Majority of Americans try to disconnect from tech; 45% try weekly. *Harris Poll*. Online: http://www.theharrispoll.com/health-and-life/Unplugging-Americans-Disconnect-Tech.html

11. Bolton, D. (2016, April 6). Here is how people actually use their smartphones. *Applesauce*. Online: https://arc.applause.com/2016/04/06/smartphone-behavior-patterns-2016/

12. Bruno, J. (2017, January 13). Tinker. Tailor. Mogul. Spy? *Washington Monthly*. Online: http://washingtonmonthly.com/2017/01/13/tinker-tailor-mogul-spy/

13. Carr, D. (2014, August 17). Views of #Ferguson thrust Michael Brown shooting to national attention. *The New York Times*, p. B1.

14. Chaffey, D. (2016, April 27). Percent time spent on mobile apps 2016. *Smartinsights.com*. Online: http://www.smartinsights.com/mobile-marketing/mobile-marketing-analytics/mobile-marketing-statistics/attachment/percent-time-spent-on-mobile-apps-2016/

15. *The Child Pornography Prevention Act of 1996*

16. Czitrom, D. J. (2007). Twenty-five years later. *Critical Studies in Media Communication*, 24, 481–485.

17. Davis, R. E. (1976). *Response to innovation: A study of popular argument about new mass media*. New York: Arno Press.

18. deBuys, W. (2017, January 19). New from Trump University: Election Rigging 101. *Alternet*. Online: http://www.alternet.org/election-2016/election-rigging-101?akid=15126.131137.SBIdI1&rd=1&src=newsletter1070817&t=15

19. "The digital virus called fake news." (2016, November 20). *The New York Times*, p. SR10.

20. Durden, T. (2016, May 9). Cell phone addiction: 15 numbers that show the ridiculous obsession Americans have with their phones. *ZeroHedge.com*. Online: http://www.zerohedge.com/news/2016-05-09/cell-phone-addiction-15-numbers-show-ridiculous-obsession-americans-have-their-phone

21. Earl, J. (2016, December 24). Slacktivism for everyone: How keyboard activism is affecting social movements. *Salon*. Online: http://www.salon.com/2016/12/24/slacktivism-how-online-activism-is-affecting-social-movements_partner/

22. Electronic Communications Privacy Act of 1986 (ECPA), 18 U.S.C. § 2510–22.

23. Faw, L. (2016, December 5). Third of consumers say they would exchange personal info for content. *MediaPost*. Online: http://www.mediapost.com/publications/article/290340/a-third-of-consumers-say-they-would-exchange-perso.html

24. Fluent. (2016, November 16). The Inbox Report 2016: Consumer perceptions of email. *Fluentco.com*. Online: http://www.fluentco.com/insight/inbox-report-2016-consumer-perceptions-email/

25. Gonzales, A. L., & Hancock, J. T. (2011). Mirror, mirror on my Facebook wall: Effects of exposure to Facebook on self-esteem. *Cyberpsychology, Behavior, and Social Networking*, 14, 79–83.

26. "Google search statistics." (2017). *Internet Live Stats*. Online: http://www.internetlivestats.com/google-search-statistics/

27. Hafner, K., & Lyon, M. (1996). *Where wizards stay up late: The origins of the Internet*. New York: Simon & Schuster.

28. Hamilton, A. (2000, August 21). Meet the new surfer girls. *Time*, p. 67.

29. Hedges, C. (2014, February 24). Edward Snowden's moral courage. *Truthout.org*. Online: http://www.truthdig.com/report/item/edward_snowdens_moral_courage_20140223

30. Hessinger, S. (2014, July 8). 60 percent of online traffic now comes from mobile. *Smallbiztrends.com*. Online: http://smallbiztrends.com/2014/07/online-traffic-report-mobile.html

31. Higgins, A., McIntire, M., & Dance, G. J. X. (2016, November 26). Websites hit a "gold mine" in fake news. *The New York Times*, p. A1.

32. Hui, S. (2014, December 12). The Web's inventor says affordable Internet should be a 'human right.' *PhysOrg*. Online: http://phys.org/news/2014-12-web-inventor-internet-human.html

33. "Internet usage statistics." (2017). *Internet World Statistics*, June 30. Online: http://www.internetworldstats.com/stats.htm

34. Justice Anthony Kennedy, senior Associate Justice of the Supreme Court of the United States

35. "Justices scrap Internet child porn law." (2002, April 17). *Providence Journal*, p. A3.

36. Koebler, J. (2016, October 27). The city that was saved by the Internet. *Motherboard*. Online: http://motherboard.vice.com/read/chattanooga-gigabit-fiber-network

37. Krasnova, H., Wenninger, H., Widjaja, T., & Buxmann, P. (2013, March). *Envy on Facebook: A hidden threat to users' life satisfaction?* Paper presented to the 11th International Conference on Wirtschaftsinformatik, Leipzig, Germany.

38. Kristula, D. (1997, March). *The history of the Internet*. Online: http://www.davesite.com/webstation/net-history.shtml

39. Kuns, K. (2017, January 28). Live stream: Protests break out over Muslim ban at major airports. *Crooks and Liars*. Online: http://crooksandliars.com/2017/01/live-stream-protests-break-out-over-muslim

40. Link, T. (2017, February 1). Texas mosque destroyed in fire will be rebuilt after $1 million in online donations. *Salon*. Online: http://www.salon.com/2017/02/01/texas-mosque-destroyed-in-fire-will-be-rebuilt-after-1-million-in-online-donations/

41. Loesche, D. (2017, January 12). Americans think fake news has an impact. *Statista*. Online: https://www.statista.com/chart/7541/americans-think-fake-news-has-an-impact/?utm_source=Infographic+Newsletter&utm_campaign=08eb9b509d-InfographicTicker_EN_Early_00004&utm_medium=email&utm_term=0_666fe64c5d-08eb9b509d-295452301

42. Mandese, J. (2017, January 3). Ad groups petition consumer Internet privacy rules, call opt-in requirement "onerous." *MediaPost*. Online: http://www.mediapost.com/publications/article/292165/ad-groups-petition-consumer-internet-privacy-rules.html?utm_source=newsletter&utm_medium=email&utm_content=headline&utm_campaign=99328

43. Mandese, J. (2016, November 25). Facebookers 2.5 times more likely to read fake news, millennials least prone. *MediaPost*. Online: http://www.mediapost.com/publications/article/289778/facebookers-25-times-more-likely-to-read-fake-new.html

44. Marche, S. (2012, May). Is Facebook making us lonely? *The Atlantic*. Online: http://www.theatlantic.com/magazine/archive/2012/05/is-facebook-making-us-lonely/308930/

45. Martin, C. (2017, February 7). IoT devices to surpass world population this year; consumer segment leads. *MediaPost*. Online: https://www.mediapost.com/publications/article/294645/iot-devices-to-surpass-world-population-this-year.html

46. Melber, A. (2008, October 30). Web puts dog-whistle politics on a leash. *The Nation*. Online: https://www.thenation.com/article/web-puts-dog-whistle-politics-leash/

47. Menn, J. (2016, October 4). Exclusive: Yahoo secretly scanned customer emails for U.S. intelligence—sources. *Reuters*. Online: http://www.reuters.com/article/us-yahoo-nsa-exclusive-idUSKCN1241YT

48. "Millennials in adulthood." (2014, March 7). *Pew Research Center*. Online: http://www.pewsocialtrends.org/2014/03/07/millennials-in-adulthood/

49. Mindlin, A. (2009, January 5). Web passes papers as news source. *The New York Times*, p. B3.

50. Moylan, B. (2017, January 19). CNN is hiring a real reporter to investigate fake news. *Vice News*. Online: https://www.vice.com/en_us/article/cnn-is-hiring-a-real-reporter-to-investigate-fake-news-vgtrn?mod=djemCMOToday

51. Mullin, B. (2016, December 15). Nearly a quarter of Americans say they have shared fake political news. *Poynter Institute*. Online: https://www.poynter.org/2016/nearly-a-quarter-of-americans-say-they-have-shared-fake-political-news/442972/

52. Nadkarni, A., & Hofmann, S. G. (2012). Why do people use Facebook? *Personality and Individual Differences*, 52, 243–249.

53. Norden, E. (1969, March). A candid conversation with the high priest of popcult and metaphysician of media. *Playboy*, pp. 53–74, 158.

54. Nudd, T. (2017, January 24). Tostitos' new party bag knows when you've been drinking and will even call you an Uber. *Ad Week*. Online: http://www.adweek.com/creativity/tostitos-new-party-bag-knows-when-youve-been-drinking-and-will-even-call-you-uber-175727/

55. "Number of monthly active Twitter users in the United States from 1st quarter 2010 to 3rd quarter 2016 (in millions)." (2017, January). *Statista*. Online: https://www-statista-com.bryant.idm.oclc.org/statistics/274564/monthly-active-twitter-users-in-the-united-states/

56. O'Keeffe, G. S., & Clarke-Pearson, K. (2011). Clinical report—the impact of social media on children, adolescents, and families. *Pediatrics*, *127*, 800–804.

57. Olmstead, J., & Smith, A. (2017, January 27). Americans and cybersecurity. *Pew Research Center*. Online: http://www.pewinternet.org/2017/01/26/americans-and-cybersecurity/?utm_source=Pew+Research+Center&utm_campaign=8353c6f74e-EMAIL_CAMPAIGN_2017_01_26&utm_medium=email&utm_term=0_3e953b9b70-8353c6f74e-399750965

58. Oremus, W. (2017, January 5). Russia used fake news to influence the election, says U.S. intelligence chief. *Slate*. Online: http://www.slate.com/blogs/future_tense/2017/01/05/russia_used_fake_news_to_influence_the_election_james_clapper_says.html

59. Palmer, S. (2017, January 9). Just how dangerous is Alexa? *Advertising Age*, p. 18.

60. Peterson, T. (2014, January 9). Consumers becoming less trusting of Google, warier of Facebook, Twitter. *Advertising Age*. Online: http://adage.com/article/consumer-electronics-show/consumers-trusting-google-warier-facebook-twitter/290992/

61. Raine, L. (2016, September 21). The state of privacy in post-Snowden America. *Pew Research Center*. Online: http://www.pewresearch.org/fact-tank/2016/09/21/the-state-of-privacy-in-america/

62. Sagioglou, C., & and Greitmeyer, T. (2014). Facebook's emotional consequences: Why Facebook causes a decrease in mood and why people still use it. *Computers in Human Behavior*, *35*, 359–363.

63. Scott, M. (2016, February 2). Deal struck to balance U.S.–Europe data fears. *The New York Times*, p. B1.

64. Scott, M. (2014, December 14). Where tech giants protect privacy. *The New York Times*, p. SR5.

65. Sheer, R. (2015, March 7). The Internet killed privacy: Our liberation, and our capture, are within the same tool. *Salon*. Online: http://www.salon.com/2015/03/07/the_internet_killed_privacy_our_liberation_and_our_capture_are_within_the_same_tool/

66. Shenk, D. (1997). *Data smog: Surviving the information glut*. New York: Harper Edge.

67. Silverman, C. (2016, November 3). How teens in the Balkans are duping Trump supporters with fake news. *BuzzFeed*. Online: https://www.buzzfeed.com/craigsilverman/how-macedonia-became-a-global-hub-for-pro-trump-misinfo?utm_term=.up3dw93Xj#.thVkmM39y

68. Smith, A. (2017, January 12). Record shares of Americans now own smartphones, have home broadband. *Pew Research Center*. Online: http://www.pewresearch.org/fact-tank/2017/01/12/evolution-of-technology/

69. Smith, C. (2017a, January 5). By the numbers. 220+ interesting Instagram statistics (December 2016). *DMR*. Online: http://expandedramblings.com/index.php/important-instagram-stats/

70. Smith, C. (2017b, February 7). Vizio admits to spying on you through your smart TV. *BRG*. Online: http://bgr.com/2017/02/07/vizio-smart-tv-spying-case/

71. "Spam statistics." (2017). *Anti-Spam Engine*. Online: https://antispamengine.com/spam-statistics/

72. Sterling, G. (2015, January 20). Google overtakes traditional media to become most trusted news source. *Searchengineland.com*. Online: http://searchengineland.com/google-over-takes-traditonal-media-become-trusted-source-news-online-213176

73. Sullivan, A. (2002, May). The blogging revolution. *Wired*, pp. 43–44.

74. Sydell, L. (2016, November 23). We tracked down a fake-news creator in the suburbs. Here's what we learned. *NPR*. Online: http://www.npr.org/sections/alltechconsidered/2016/11/23/503146770/npr-finds-the-head-of-a-covert-fake-news-operation-in-the-suburbs

75. Tavernise, S. (2016, December 7). As fake news spreads lies, more readers shrug at truth. *The New York Times*, p. A1.

76. Toothman, J. (2017). What's the difference between the Internet and the World Wide Web? *HowStuffWorks*. Online: http://computer.howstuffworks.com/internet/basics/internet-versus-world-wide-web1.htm

77. "Top 10 censors of the Internet." (2016, June 1). *Le VPN*. Online: https://www.le-vpn.com/top-10-censors-internet-avoid-internet-censorship/

78. Trench, M. (1990). *Cyberpunk*. Mystic Fire Videos. New York: Intercon Production.

79. Tromholt, M., Lundby, M., Andsbjerg, K., & Wiking, M. (2015). The Facebook experiment. *The Happiness Research Institute*. Online: https://media.wix.com/ugd/928487_680fc12644c8428eb728cde7d61b13e7.pdf

80. Tsukayama, H. (2016, May 18). Amazon CEO Jeffrey Bezos: Debate between privacy and security is "issue of our age." *The Washington Post*. Online: https://www.washingtonpost.com/news/the-switch/wp/2016/05/18/amazon-ceo-jeffrey-bezos-debate-between-privacy-and-security-is-issue-of-our-age/?utm_term=.e6da8beafefc

81. "Twitter usage statistics." (2017, January). *Internet Live Stats*. Online: http://www.internetlivestats.com/twitter-statistics/

82. Uberti, D. (2017, January 9). Focus more on fighting bad journalism, less on fake news. *Columbia Journalism Review*. Online: http://www.cjr.org/criticism/bad_journalism_fake_news.php?CJR

83. Uberti, D., & Vernon, P. (2017, January 19). The coming storm for journalism under Trump. *Columbia Journalism Review*. Online: http://www.cjr.org/special_report/trump_media_journalism_washington_press.php

84. "VoIP market stats—a growing industry." (2016, July 11). *IronPaper.com*. Online: http://www.ironpaper.com/webintel/articles/voip-market-stats/

85. Walker, R. (2009, November 13). Reality bytes. *The New York Times Magazine*, p. 32.

86. Walsh, M. (2012, May 1). Mobile to become top email platform. *MediaPost*. Online: http://www.mediapost.com/publications/article/173702/#axzz2Y0dA8xnn

87. Young, K. S. (2004). Internet addiction: A new clinical phenomenon and its consequences. *American Behavioral Scientist*, *48*, 402–415.

88. Zapruder, A. (2016, December 11). No child sex slaves at my pizza parlor. *The New York Times*, p. SR5.

Cultural Forum Blue Column icon, Media Literacy Red Torch Icon, Using Media Green Gear icon, Developing Media book in starburst icon: ©McGraw-Hill Education

One for One

TOMS

◀ Cause marketing at its best. Buy a pair of TOMS and a kid in need gets a pair too.

©Grant Rooney/Alamy

Public Relations

11

Learning Objectives

It is no small irony that public relations (PR) has such poor PR. We criticize the flacks who try to spin the truth because PR is most obvious when used to reclaim the reputation of someone or some organization in need of such help. But public relations is essential for maintaining relationships between organizations and their publics. In fact, much PR is used for good. After studying this chapter, you should be able to

▶ Outline the history and development of the public relations industry.

▶ Describe how the organizational and economic nature of the contemporary public relations industry shapes the messages with which publics interact, especially in an increasingly converged media environment.

▶ Identify different types of public relations and the different publics each is designed to serve.

▶ Explain the relationship between public relations and its various publics.

▶ Apply key media literacy skills when consuming public relations messages, especially fake online reviews.

1773 ▶ Boston Tea Party

Source: The Library of Congress (LC-DIG-ds-03379)

1833 ▶ Andrew Jackson hires Amos Kendall, first presidential press secretary

1800

Source: Library of Congress, Prints and Photographs Division [LC-USZC2-2402]

1896 ▶ William Jennings Bryan and William McKinley launch first national political campaigns

1889 Westinghouse establishes first corporate public relations department

1850

Source: Library of Congress, Prints and Photographs Division [LC-DIG-ppmsca-28850]

1906 The Publicity Bureau, first publicity company

1913 Lee's *Declaration of Principles*

1915 Cadillac's Penalty of Leadership

1917 ▶ President Wilson establishes Committee on Public Information

1929 Torches of Liberty

1938 Foreign Agents Registration Act

1941 Office of War Information

1946 Federal Regulation of Lobbying Act

1947 Public Relations Society of America (PRSA); *The Hucksters*

1900

Source: Library of Congress, Prints and Photographs Division [LC-USZC4-10221]

1954 PRSA Code of Ethics

1962 PRSA accreditation program

1980 ▶ MADD

1950

©Tony Freeman/PhotoEdit

2005 VNR controversy

2006 TOMS begins buy-one-give-one program

2007 Rise of the transparentists

2010 ▶ GM crisis

2013 Lobbyists become government relations professionals

2014 Coalition of PR firms rules out work for climate-change deniers

2000

©Mark Wilson/Getty Images

"YOU'RE BUYING NEW SHOES? DON'T YOU HAVE ENOUGH?"

"You never can have enough nice footwear."

"Agreed, but those are sneakers, and they aren't even high end; they're kinda casual."

"A, the world needs more casual, and B, they're better than high end. They're TOMS."

"Why's that make them better?"

"If I buy a pair, a kid with no shoes somewhere in the world gets a free pair. Buy one, give one."

"Then I'm in, too. I'd like to help."

Your friend, like you, was moved to help kids in more than 60 countries get the shoes they need through TOMS's efforts, mirrored by thousands of other companies, to team up with public service and humanitarian organizations to do good for others while burnishing its corporate image, not unimportant at a time when confidence in the corporate world is a bit shaky. Since 2006, TOMS's buy-one-give-one program has delivered more than 60 million pairs of shoes to kids in need, with footwear based on the terrain and weather where they live. The program has gone even further, creating local jobs by producing the shoes in the countries in which they are used. TOMS eventually launched TOMS Eyewear, again giving one free pair of eyeglasses to someone in need for every pair of sunglasses or optical frames it sells. It does the same with TOMS Roasting Company, joining with Water for People to deliver one week's worth of free water to the areas from which the beans are sourced for every pound of coffee people buy. These efforts have spread beyond TOMS. Diaper maker Pampers, for example, partners with UNICEF for "1 pack = 1 vaccine," a program to donate one tetanus vaccine for every package it sells. It has delivered more than 300 million vaccines to 36 countries and has seen the elimination of maternal and neonatal tetanus in 14 of those nations. Department store Macy's "Buy 1 & We'll Give 1" campaign annually donates about 50,000 coats nationwide to Clothes4Souls, donating one new, never-worn coat for every coat purchased in-store and online during the campaign's fall run.

In this chapter we investigate the public relations industry and its relationship with mass media and their audiences. We first define public relations. Then we study its history and development as the profession matured from its beginnings in hucksterism to a full-fledged, communication-based industry. We see how the needs and interests of the profession's various publics became part of the public relations process, and we also define exactly who those publics are. We then detail the scope and nature of the industry and describe the types of public relations activities and the organization of a typical public relations operation. We study trends such as globalization and specialization, as well as the impact of new, converging communication technologies on the industry. Finally, we discuss trust in public relations. As our media literacy skill, we learn how to recognize fake online reviews.

Defining Public Relations

UNICEF and Water for People, like Mothers Against Drunk Driving, Save Venice, Handgun Control Incorporated, the National Environmental Trust, and countless other nonprofit organizations, are interest groups that use a variety of public relations tools and strategies to serve a variety of publics. They want to use public relations to do good. The companies that sponsor their activities also want to do good—do good for their communities *and* for themselves. Even the most cynical person must applaud their efforts on behalf of helping people in need.

But for many people, efforts such as these serve to demonstrate one of the ironies of public relations, both as an activity and as an industry: Public relations has terrible public relations. We dismiss information as "just PR." Public relations professionals are frequently equated with snake oil salespeople, hucksters, and other willful deceivers. They are referred to both inside and outside the media industries as **flacks**. They are often accused of engaging in **spin**, outright lying or obfuscation. Yet virtually every organization and institution—big and small, public and private, for-profit and volunteer—uses public relations as a regular part of its operation. Many have their own public relations departments. The term "public relations" often carries such a negative connotation that most independent companies and company PR departments now go by the name "public affairs," "corporate affairs," or "public communications."

The problem rests, in part, on confusion over what public relations actually is. There is no universally accepted definition of public relations because it can be and is many things—publicity, research, public affairs, media relations, promotion, merchandising, and more. Much of the observable contact media consumers have with public relations occurs when the industry defends people and companies who have somehow run afoul of the public. China sought help from Ogilvy Public Relations when it was discovered that the toys it was exporting to the United States were coated with dangerous lead paint and the toothpaste it was also sending was tainted with diethylene glycol, a toxin. In the wake of outrage over its 2016 beheading of 27 political dissidents, the Saudi Arabian government enlisted public relations companies Qorvis and Targeted Victory to help it calm criticism of what is supposed to be America's strongest ally in the Middle East (Fang & Jilani, 2016). Washington PR giant Qorvis's positive representation of repressive Middle Eastern regimes Yemen and Bahrain recently led to a much-publicized walk-out by a third of its partners. Journalists recently revealed that the Global Energy Balance Network, a grassroots group of concerned scientists wanting to promote "science-based" solutions to obesity, was in fact quietly funded by $1.5 million from soda maker Coca-Cola. Coke handpicked the group's leaders, edited its mission statement, and suggested material for its website, which in fact was registered to Coke (Malkan, 2016). The Global Energy Balance Network is actually **astroturf** (a fake grassroots organization), its true mission to thwart state and national regulatory efforts to crack down on the sale of sugary drinks. And although a coalition of several of the world's top 25 PR firms mutually agreed in 2014 to no longer work for clients who would use their services to deny climate change (Goldenberg & Karim, 2014), the book and 2014 documentary *Merchants of Doubt* created a public stir with its revelations that PR companies were employing the same techniques that they had used for decades in the debates over the harmful effects of tobacco and asbestos to muddy public opinion on climate change—paying scientists to do supporting research, creating astroturf groups, and training media savvy "experts" to challenge scientists or to provide "balance" to news reports (Beale, 2015).

Yet when seven people died from cyanide poisoning after taking tainted Tylenol capsules in 1982, a skilled and honest public relations campaign by Johnson & Johnson (makers of Tylenol) and its public relations firm, Burson-Marsteller, saved the brand and restored trust in the product. In 2014, when General Motors was rocked by a 1.6-million-car recall and 13 deaths linked to a faulty ignition switch, the company took not only to traditional media—letters to customers, blogs, call centers, and news media—in its efforts to better serve its customers and save its reputation, but it also mounted a massive social-media public relations campaign—connecting with owners, getting them loaner cars, and even paying for public transit. In this way the auto giant "fundamentally redefine[d] themselves as an open, transparent, listening organization," saving the brand and thousands of jobs (Goel, 2014). The public relations campaign by Mothers Against Drunk Driving (MADD) led directly to passage of tougher standards in virtually every state to remove drunk drivers from the road and to provide stiffer sentences for those convicted of driving under the influence. Dramatic reductions

▲ *Merchants of Doubt*, the book and 2014 documentary, focused public attention on PR tactics sometimes used to obfuscate debate on important public health issues.
©*Sony Pictures Classics/Photofest*

▼ General Motors' powerful public relations campaign, conducted by traditional means and on social media, helped save the brand's reputation and thousands of its employees' jobs. Here, CEO Mary Barra testifies before the Energy and Commerce Committee to explain how GM would make things right.
©*Mark Wilson/Getty Images*

in the number of alcohol-related traffic accidents resulted from this effort (see the essay "The MADD Campaign").

"P.R. has a P.R. problem," says Syracuse University public relations professor Brenda Wrigley. "We have to get our own house in order. . . . We are advocates and there's no shame in that as long as it's grounded in ethics and values." Public Relations Society of America president Judy Phair adds, "For public relations to be effective, it has to be built on public trust" (both in O'Brien, 2005, p. 31). Accepting, therefore, that public relations should be honest and ethical, our definition of public relations is drawn from the Public Relations Society of America's "widely accepted" definition:

Public relations is a strategic communication process that builds mutually beneficial relationships between organizations and their publics. (PRSA, 2017)

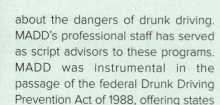

USING MEDIA TO MAKE A DIFFERENCE
The MADD Campaign

After her child was killed in a drunk-driving accident in 1980, Candy Lightner sought out others like herself, mothers who had lost children to the volatile mix of cars and alcohol. She hoped they could provide one another with emotional support and campaign to ensure that other parents would never know their grief. Thus, Mothers Against Drunk Driving (MADD) was born.

Among MADD's publics are teenagers. With its parallel organization, Students Against Destructive Decisions (SADD), MADD targets this high-risk group through various educational campaigns and in the media that attract teen audiences. The organization also conducts public information campaigns aimed at adult drivers and repeat drunk drivers, often in conjunction with state and other authorities. It also assists legislators in their efforts to pass drunk-driving legislation. Two more of MADD's publics are public servants such as police and paramedics who must deal with the effects of drunk driving, and the families and friends who have lost loved ones in alcohol- or drug-related driving accidents.

Has MADD made a difference? Since 1988, numerous prime-time television programs have featured episodes about the dangers of drunk driving. MADD's professional staff has served as script advisors to these programs. MADD was instrumental in the passage of the federal Drunk Driving Prevention Act of 1988, offering states financial incentives to set up programs that would reduce alcohol- and drug-related automobile fatalities. This legislation also made 21 the national minimum legal drinking age. MADD successfully campaigned for the Victim's Crime Act of 1984, making compensation from drunk drivers to victims and their families federal law.

There are two even more dramatic examples of how successful Lightner's group has been. According to the U.S. Department of Transportation, in the 30-plus years since MADD's founding, more than 300,000 lives have been saved, and in 2011, for the first time, the annual number of American drunk-driving fatalities fell below 10,000 ("Drunk Driving," 2012). But MADD's cultural impact shows most strongly in the way people treat drunk drivers. It is no longer cool to talk about how smashed we got at the party, or how we can't believe we made it home. Almost every evening out with a group of friends includes a designated driver. Drunk drivers are considered nearly as despicable as child molesters. Many in public relations, traffic safety, and law enforcement credit MADD's public relations efforts with this change.

A Short History of Public Relations

The history of this complex field can be divided into four stages: early public relations, the propaganda–publicity stage, early two-way communication, and advanced two-way communication. These stages have combined to shape the character of this industry.

Early Public Relations

Archaeologists in Iraq have uncovered a tablet dating from 1800 B.C.E. that today we would call a public information bulletin. It provided farmers with information on sowing, irrigating, and harvesting their crops. Julius Caesar fed the people of the Roman Empire constant reports

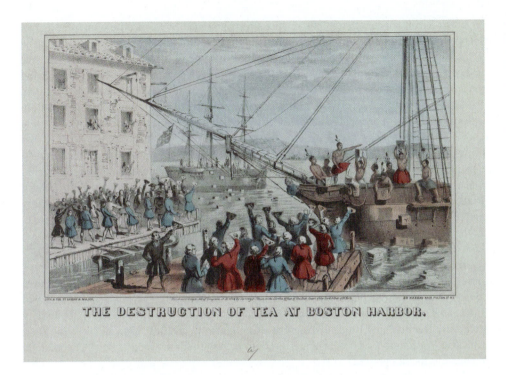

◀ The December 16, 1773, Boston Tea Party was one of the first successful pseudo-events in the new land. Had cameras been around at the time, it would also have been a fine photo op.

Source: The Library of Congress (LC-DIG-ds-03379)

of his achievements to maintain morale and to solidify his reputation and position of power. Genghis Khan would send "advance men" to tell stories of his might, hoping to frighten his enemies into surrendering.

Public relations campaigns abounded in pre-Revolutionary War America and helped create the colonies. Merchants, farmers, and others who saw advantage in a growing colonial population used overstatement, half-truths, and lies to entice settlers to the New World; *A Brief and True Report of the New Found Land of Virginia* by Thomas Hariot and John White was published in 1588 to lure European settlers. The Boston Tea Party was a well-planned media event organized to attract public attention for a vital cause. Today we'd call it a **pseudo-event**, an event staged specifically to attract public attention. Benjamin Franklin organized a sophisticated campaign to thwart the Stamp Act, the Crown's attempt to limit colonial press freedom, using his publications and the oratory skills of criers (see the chapter on books). The *Federalist Papers* of John Jay, James Madison, and Alexander Hamilton were originally a series of 85 letters published between 1787 and 1789, which were designed to sway public opinion in the newly independent United States toward support and passage of the new Constitution, an early effort at issue management. In all these examples, people or organizations were using communication to inform, to build an image, and to influence public opinion.

The Propaganda–Publicity Stage

Mass circulation newspapers and the first successful consumer magazines appeared in the 1830s, expanding the ability of people and organizations to communicate with the public. In 1833, for example, Andrew Jackson hired former newspaper journalist Amos Kendall as his publicist and the country's first presidential press secretary in an effort to combat the aristocrats who saw Jackson as too common to be president.

Abolitionists sought an end to slavery. Industrialists needed to attract workers, entice customers, and enthuse investors. P. T. Barnum, allegedly convinced that there's a sucker born every minute, worked to lure those suckers into his shows. All used the newspaper and the magazine to serve their causes.

Politicians recognized that the expanding press meant that a new way of campaigning was necessary. In 1896 presidential contenders William Jennings Bryan and William McKinley both established campaign headquarters in Chicago from which they issued news releases, position papers, and pamphlets. The modern national political campaign was born.

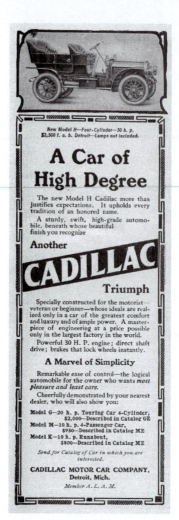

A Car of High Degree

New Model H—Four-Cylinder—30 h. p.
$2,500 f. o. b. Detroit—Lamps not included.

The new Model H Cadillac more than justifies expectations. It upholds every tradition of an honored name.

A sturdy, swift, high-grade automobile, beneath whose beautiful finish you recognize

Another

CADILLAC

Triumph

Specially constructed for the motorist—veteran or beginner—whose ideals are realized only in a car of the greatest comfort and luxury and of ample power. A masterpiece of engineering at a price possible only in the largest factory in the world.

Powerful 30 H. P. engine; direct shaft drive; brakes that lock wheels instantly.

A Marvel of Simplicity

Remarkable ease of control—the logical automobile for the owner who wants *most pleasure and least care.*

Cheerfully demonstrated by your nearest dealer, who will also show you:

Model G—20 h. p. Touring Car 4-Cylinder,
  $2,000—Described in Catalog GE
Model M—10 h. p. 4-Passenger Car,
  $950—Described in Catalog ME
Model K—10 h. p. Runabout,
  $800—Described in Catalog ME

Send for Catalog of Car in which you are interested.

CADILLAC MOTOR CAR COMPANY,
Detroit, Mich.

Member A. L. A. M.

▲ 1906 Car of High Degree Cadillac. This campaign was an early but quite successful example of image advertising—using paid ads to build goodwill for a product.
©*Jay Paull/Archive Photos/Getty Images*

It was during this era that public relations began to acquire its deceitful, huckster image. PR was associated more with propaganda than with useful information. A disregard for the public and the willingness of public relations experts to serve the powerful fueled this view, and public relations began to establish itself as a profession during this time. The burgeoning press was its outlet, but westward expansion and rapid urbanization and industrialization in the United States were its driving forces. As the railroad expanded to unite the new nation, cities exploded with new people and new life. Markets, once small and local, became large and national.

As the political and financial stakes grew, business and government became increasingly corrupt and selfish—"The public be damned" was William Vanderbilt's official comment when asked in 1882 about the effects of changing the schedule of his New York Central Railroad (Gordon, 1989). The muckrakers' revelations badly tarnished the images of industry and politics. Massive and lengthy coal strikes led to violence and more antibusiness feeling. In the heyday of the journalistic exposé and the muckraking era, government and business both required some good public relations.

In 1889 Westinghouse Electric established the first corporate public relations department, hiring a former newspaper writer to engage the press and ensure that company positions were always clear and in the public eye. Advertising agencies, including N. W. Ayer & Sons and Lord and Thomas, began to offer public relations services to their clients. The first publicity company, The Publicity Bureau, opened in Boston in 1906 and later expanded to New York, Chicago, Washington, St. Louis, and Topeka to help the railroad industry challenge federal regulations that it opposed.

The railroads also had other problems, and they turned to *New York World* reporter Ivy Lee for help. Beset by accidents and strikes, the Pennsylvania Railroad usually responded by suppressing information. Lee recognized, however, that this was dangerous and counterproductive in a time when the public was already suspicious of big business, including the railroads. Lee escorted reporters to the scene of trouble, established press centers, distributed press releases, and assisted reporters in obtaining additional information and photographs.

When a Colorado coal mine strike erupted in violence in 1913, the press attacked the mine's principal stockholder, New York's John D. Rockefeller Jr., blaming him for the shooting deaths of several miners and their wives and children. Lee handled press relations and convinced Rockefeller to visit the scene to talk (and be photographed) with the strikers. The strike ended, and Rockefeller was soon being praised for his sensitive intervention. Eventually Lee issued his *Declaration of Principles*, arguing that public relations practitioners should be providers of information, not purveyors of publicity.

Not all public relations at this time was damage control. Henry Ford began using staged events such as auto races to build interest in his cars, started *Ford Times* (an in-house employee publication), and made heavy use of image advertising.

Public relations in this stage was typically one-way, from organization to public. Still, by the outbreak of World War I, most of the elements of today's large-scale, multifunction public relations agency were in place.

Early Two-Way Communication

Because the U.S. public was not particularly enthusiastic about the nation's entry into World War I, President Woodrow Wilson recognized the need for public relations in support of the war effort (Zinn, 1995, pp. 355–357). In 1917 he placed former newspaper journalist George Creel at the head of the newly formed Committee on Public Information (CPI). Creel assembled opinion leaders from around the country to advise the government on its public relations efforts and to help shape public opinion. The committee sold Liberty Bonds and helped increase membership in the Red Cross. It engaged in public relations on a scale never before seen, using movies, public speakers, articles in newspapers and magazines, and posters.

It was about this time that public relations pioneer Edward Bernays began emphasizing the value of assessing the public's feelings toward an organization. He would then use this knowledge as the basis for the development of the public relations effort. Together with

Creel's committee, Bernays's work was the beginning of two-way communication in public relations—that is, public relations practitioners talking to people and, in return, listening to them when they talked back. Public relations professionals began representing their various publics to their clients, just as they represented their clients to those publics.

There were other advances in public relations during this stage. During the 1930s, President Franklin D. Roosevelt, guided by adviser Louis McHenry Howe, embarked on a sophisticated public relations campaign to win support for his then-radical New Deal policies. Central to Roosevelt's effort was the new medium of radio. The Great Depression plaguing the country throughout this decade once again turned public opinion against business and industry. To counter people's distrust, many more corporations established in-house public relations departments; General Motors opened its PR operation in 1931. Public relations professionals turned increasingly to the newly emerging polling industry, founded by George Gallup and Elmo Roper, to better gauge public opinion as they constructed public relations campaigns and to gather feedback on the effectiveness of those campaigns. Gallup and Roper successfully applied newly refined social science research methods—advances in sampling, questionnaire design, and interviewing—to meet the business needs of clients and their publics.

The growth of the industry was significant enough and its reputation sufficiently fragile that the National Association of Accredited Publicity Directors was founded in 1936. The American Council on Public Relations was established three years later. They merged in 1947, creating the Public Relations Society of America (PRSA), the principal professional group for today's public relations professionals.

World War II saw the government undertake another massive campaign to bolster support for the war effort, this time through the Office of War Information (OWI). Employing techniques that had proven successful during World War I, the OWI had the additional advantage of public opinion polling, fully established and powerful radio networks and their stars, and a Hollywood eager to help. Singer Kate Smith's war-bond radio fundraiser brought in millions, and director Frank Capra produced the *Why We Fight* film series for the OWI.

During this era both public relations and Ivy Lee suffered a serious blow to their reputations. Lee was the American public relations spokesman for Germany and its leader, Adolf Hitler. In 1934 Lee was required to testify before Congress to defend himself against charges that he was a Nazi sympathizer. He was successful, but the damage had been done. As a result of Lee's ties with Germany, Congress passed the Foreign Agents Registration Act in 1938, requiring anyone who engages in political activities in the United States on behalf of a foreign power to register as an agent of that power with the Justice Department.

▲ World War I brought government into large-scale public relations. Even today, the CPI's posters—like this one encouraging citizens to support the war effort through war bonds—are recognized.
Source: Library of Congress, Prints and Photographs Division [LC-USZC4-10221]

Advanced Two-Way Communication

Post–World War II U.S. society was confronted by profound social change and expansion of the consumer culture. It became increasingly important for organizations to know what their clients were thinking, what they liked and disliked, and what concerned and satisfied them. As a result, public relations turned even more decidedly toward integrated two-way communication, employing research, advertising, and promotion.

As the public relations industry became more visible, it opened itself to closer scrutiny. Best-selling novels such as *The Hucksters* and *The Man in the Gray Flannel Suit* (and the hit movies made from them) painted a disturbingly negative picture of the industry and those who worked in it. Vance Packard's best-selling book *The Hidden Persuaders*, dealing with both public relations and advertising, further eroded PR esteem. As a result of public distrust

▲ Better known for hits such as *Mr. Smith Goes to Washington* and *It's a Wonderful Life*, director Frank Capra brought his moviemaking talents to the government's efforts to explain U.S. involvement in World War II and to overcome U.S. isolationism. His *Why We Fight* documentary series still stands as a classic of the form.

Courtesy Everett Collection

of the profession, Congress passed the Federal Regulation of Lobbying Act in 1946, requiring, among other things, that those who deal with federal employees on behalf of private clients disclose those relationships. And as the industry's conduct and ethics came under increasing attack, the PRSA responded with a code of ethics in 1954 and an accreditation program in 1962. Both, with modification and improvement, stand today.

Public relations's contemporary era is characterized by other events as well. More people buying more products meant that greater numbers of people were coming into contact with a growing number of businesses. As consumer markets grew in size, the basis of competition changed. Texaco, for example, used advertising to sell its gasoline. But because its gasoline was not all that different from that of other oil companies, it also sold its fuel using its good name and reputation. Increasingly, then, advertising agencies began to add public relations divisions. This change served to blur the distinction between advertising and PR.

Women, who had proved their capabilities in all professional settings during World War II, became prominent in the industry. Anne Williams Wheaton was associate press secretary to President Eisenhower; Leone Baxter was president of the powerful public relations firm Whitaker and Baxter. Companies and their executives and politicians increasingly turned to television to burnish their images and shape public opinion. Nonprofit, charitable, and social activist groups also mastered the art of public relations. The latter used public relations especially effectively to challenge the PR power of targeted businesses. Environmentalist, civil rights, and women's rights groups as well as safety and consumer advocate organizations were successful in moving the public toward their positions and, in many cases, toward action.

Shaping the Character of Public Relations

Throughout these four stages in the development of public relations, several factors combined to shape the identity of public relations, influence the way the industry does its job, and clarify the necessity for PR in the business and political world.

Advances in technology. Advances in industrial technology made possible the mass production, distribution, and marketing of goods. Advances in communication technology (and their proliferation) made it possible to communicate more efficiently and effectively with ever larger and more specific audiences.

Growth of the middle class. A growing middle class, better educated and more aware of the world around it, required more and better information about people and organizations.

Growth of organizations. As business, organized labor, and government grew bigger after World War II, the public saw them as more powerful and more remote. As a result, people were naturally curious and suspicious about these forces that seemed to be influencing all aspects of their lives.

Better research tools. The development of sophisticated research methodologies and statistical techniques allowed the industry to know its audiences better and to better judge the effectiveness of its campaigns.

Professionalization. Numerous national and international public relations organizations helped professionalize the industry and burnish its reputation.

◀ Criticism of public relations found its way into popular culture through a number of popular films and books. This scene is from the movie *The Hucksters.*
Courtesy Everett Collection

Public Relations and Its Audiences

Virtually all of us consume public relations messages on a daily basis. Increasingly, the video clips we see on the local evening news are provided by a public relations firm or the PR department of some company or organization. The content of many of the stories we read online or hear on local radio news comes directly from PR-provided press releases. As one media relations firm explained in a promotional piece sent to prospective clients, "The media are separated into two categories. One is content and the other is advertising. They're both for sale. Advertising can be purchased directly from the publication or through an ad agency, and the content space you purchase from PR firms" (quoted in Jackson & Hart, 2002, p. 24). In addition, the feed-the-hungry campaign we support, the poster encouraging us toward safer sex, and the corporation-sponsored art exhibit we attend are all someone's public relations effort. Public relations professionals interact with seven categories of publics, and a **public** is any group of people with a stake in an organization, issue, or idea. Who are those publics?

Employees. An organization's employees are its lifeblood, its family. Good public relations begins at home with company newsletters, social events, and internal and external recognition of superior performance.

Stockholders. Stockholders own the organization (if it is a public corporation). They are "family" as well, and their goodwill is necessary for the business to operate. Annual reports and stockholder meetings provide a sense of belonging as well as information.

Communities. An organization has neighbors where it operates. Courtesy, as well as good business sense, requires that an organization's neighbors are treated with consideration and support. Information meetings, company-sponsored safety and food drives, and open houses strengthen ties between organizations and their neighbors.

Media. Very little communication with an organization's various publics can occur without the trust and goodwill of professionals in the mass media. Press packets, briefings, and the facilitation of access to an organization's newsmakers build that trust and goodwill.

Government. Government is "the voice of the people" and, as such, deserves the attention of any organization that deals with the public. From a practical perspective, governments have the power to tax, regulate, and zone. Organizations must earn and maintain the goodwill and trust of the government. The providing of information and access through reports, position papers, and meetings with official personnel keeps government informed and builds trust in an organization. The government is also the target of many PR efforts, as organizations and their lobbyists seek favorable legislation and other action.

Investment community. Corporations are under the constant scrutiny of those who invest their own money or the money of others or make recommendations on investment. The value of a business and its ability to grow are functions of the investment community's respect for and trust in it. As a result, all PR efforts that build an organization's good image speak to that community.

Customers. Consumers pay the bills for companies through their purchase of products or services. Their goodwill is invaluable. That makes good PR, in all its forms, invaluable.

Scope and Structure of the Public Relations Industry

Today some 240,700 people in the U.S. identify themselves as working in public relations, and virtually every major American company or organization has a public relations department, some housing as many as 400 employees. There are over 8,300 public relations firms in the United States, the largest employing as many as 2,000 people. Most, however, have fewer employees, some employing as few as four people. Globally, PR firms had $14.2 billion in revenue in 2015 (Bureau of Labor Statistics, 2015; Sudhaman, 2016). Figure 1 shows the 10 largest public relations firms in the world.

There are full-service public relations firms and those that provide only special services. Media specialists for company CEOs, Web commentary monitoring services, and makers of

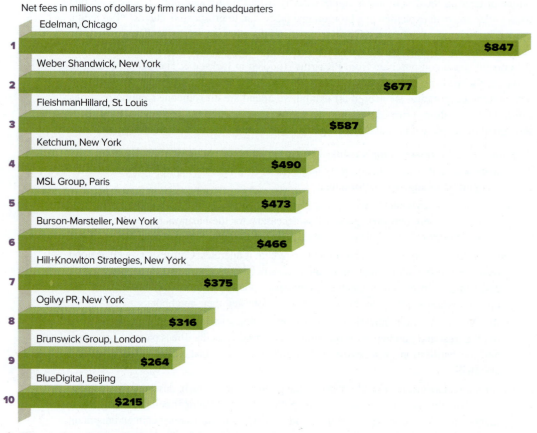

▲ **Figure 1** 10 Largest PR Firms in the World, 2016.
Source: "Public Relations Worldwide," 2016.

video news releases (VNR), preproduced reports about a client or its product that are distributed free of charge to television stations, are special service providers. Public relations firms bill for their services in a number of ways. They may charge an hourly rate for services rendered, or they may be on call, charging clients a monthly fee to act as their public relations counsel. Hill+Knowlton, for example, charges a minimum fee of several thousand dollars a month. Another way to bill is through **fixed-fee arrangements**, wherein the firm performs a specific set of services for a client for a specific and prearranged fee. Finally, many firms bill for **collateral materials**, adding a surcharge as high as 17.65% for handling printing, research, and photographs. For example, if it costs $3,000 to have a poster printed, the firm charges the client $3,529.50 to cover the cost of the poster plus 17.65% of that cost.

Public Relations Activities

Regardless of the way public relations firms bill their clients, they earn their fees by offering all or some of these 14 interrelated services.

1. *Community relations.* This type of public affairs work focuses on the communities in which the organization exists. If a city wants to build a new airport, for example, those whose property will be taken or devalued must be satisfied. If they are not, widespread community opposition to the project may develop.

2. *Counseling.* Public relations professionals routinely offer advice to an organization's management concerning policies, relationships, and communication with its various publics. Management must tell its publics "what we do." Public relations helps in the creation, refinement, and presentation of that message.

3. *Development/fundraising.* All organizations, commercial and nonprofit, survive through the voluntary contributions in time and money of their members, friends, employees, supporters, and others. Public relations helps demonstrate the need for those contributions. This **corporate social responsibility**, the integration of business operations and organizational values, sometimes take the form of **cause marketing**—work in support of social issues and causes—and their importance to clients is evidenced by data indicating that when deciding between two brands of equal quality and price, 90% of U.S. shoppers are likely to choose the cause-branded product (Cause Good, 2016). Figure 2 offers a

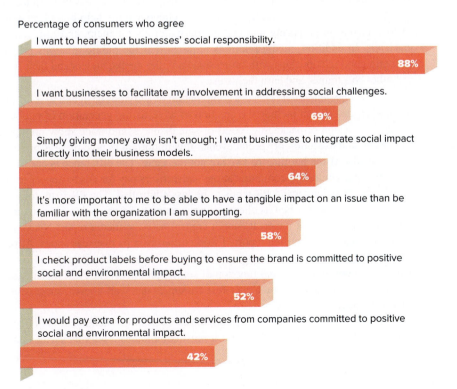

Percentage of consumers who agree

I want to hear about businesses' social responsibility.
88%

I want businesses to facilitate my involvement in addressing social challenges.
69%

Simply giving money away isn't enough; I want businesses to integrate social impact directly into their business models.
64%

It's more important to me to be able to have a tangible impact on an issue than be familiar with the organization I am supporting.
58%

I check product labels before buying to ensure the brand is committed to positive social and environmental impact.
52%

I would pay extra for products and services from companies committed to positive social and environmental impact.
42%

◀ **Figure 2** Consumers' Attitudes toward Corporate Social Responsibility.
Source: Cause Good, 2016.

deeper look at the value of informing the public about clients' efforts at cause marketing and other forms of corporate social responsibility.

4. *Employee/member relations.* This form of public relations responds specifically to the concerns of an organization's employees or members and its retirees and their families. The goal is maintenance of high morale and motivation.

5. *Financial relations.* Practiced primarily by corporate organizations, financial PR is the enhancement of communication between investor-owned companies and their shareholders, the financial community (for example, banks, annuity groups, and investment firms), and the public. Much corporate strategy, such as expansion into new markets and acquisition of other companies, is dependent upon good financial public relations.

6. *Government affairs.* This type of public affairs work focuses on government agencies. **Lobbying**—directly interacting to influence elected officials or government regulators and agents—is often a central activity. The term *lobbyist*, however, has developed a bit of a negative connotation. As such, in 2013 the American League of Lobbyists changed its name to the Association of Government Relations Professionals, and its members, no longer *lobbyists*, became *government relations professionals* (Clines, 2013).

7. *Industry relations.* Companies must interact not only with their own customers and stockholders but also with other companies in their line of business, both competitors and suppliers. In addition, they must also stand as a single voice in dealing with various state and federal regulators. For example, groups as disparate as the Texas Restaurant Association, the American Petroleum Institute, and the National Association of Manufacturers all require public relations in dealing with their various publics. The goal is the maintenance and prosperity of the industry as a whole.

8. *Issues management.* Often an organization is as interested in influencing public opinion about some larger issue that will eventually influence its operation as it is in the improvement of its own image. Issues management typically uses a large-scale public relations campaign designed to move or shape opinion on a specific issue. Usually the issue is an important one that generates deep feelings. Anti-death-penalty activists, for example, employ a full range of communication techniques to sway people to their side. Exxon-Mobil frequently secures paid media placements that address environmentalism and public transportation—important issues in and of themselves, but also important to the future of a leading manufacturer of fossil fuels.

9. *Media relations.* As the number of media outlets grows and as advances in technology increase the complexity of dealing with them, clients require help in understanding the various media, in preparing and organizing materials for them, and in placing those materials. In addition, media relations requires that the public relations practitioner maintain good relationships with professionals in the media, understand their deadlines and other constraints, and earn their trust.

10. *Marketing communication.* This is a combination of activities designed to sell a product, service, or idea. It can include the creation of advertising; generation of publicity and promotion; design of packaging, point-of-sale displays, and trade show presentations; and design and execution of special events. It is important to note that PR professionals often use advertising but that the two are not the same. The difference is one of control. Advertising is controlled communication—advertisers pay for ads to appear in specific media exactly as they want. PR tends to be less controlled. The PR firm, for example, cannot control how or when its client's announcement of a new minority outreach effort is reported by the local paper. It cannot control how the media report Nike's ongoing insistence that it has rectified reported worker abuses in its overseas shops. Advertising becomes a public relations function when its goal is to build an image or to motivate action, as opposed to the usual function of selling products. The Ad Council's seat-belt safety campaign featuring the Crash Test Dummies is a well-known, successful public relations advertising campaign.

Advertising and public relations obviously overlap for manufacturers of consumer products. Chevrolet must sell cars, but it must communicate with its various publics as well. General Motors, too, must sell cars. But in the wake of the ignition switch recall, it needed serious public relations help. One result of the overlap of advertising and public relations is that advertising agencies increasingly own their own public relations departments or firms or associate closely with a PR company. Especially in an age of slacktivism and social media, public relations professionals, says Jackie Cooper, head of global creative strategy at Edelman, are "getting not just a seat at the table, we're getting half the table" (Stein, 2016). You may see his point after reading the essay, "Protecting a Company's Good Name in the Era of Social Media."

Another way that advertising and public relations differ is that advertising people typically do not set policy for an organization. Advertising people *implement* policy after organization leaders set it. In contrast, public relations professionals usually are part of the policy-making process because they are the liaison between the organization and its publics. Effective organizations have come to understand that even in routine decisions the impact on public opinion and subsequent consequences can be of tremendous importance. As a result, public relations has become a management function, and a public relations professional typically sits as a member of a company's highest level of management. You'll soon read more about this.

11. *Minority relations/multicultural affairs.* Public affairs activities are directed toward specific racial and ethnic minorities in this type of work. For example, Chili's Grill & Bar offers free meals on Veterans Day to those who have been in the military. It served more than 200,000 veterans' meals in 2016, but failure to provide one more caused the company significant embarrassment. A manager at a Texas location refused to give a meal to an African American veteran because another customer said that, as a black man, he could not have served in World War II and must be lying about his veteran status, despite the former soldier having showed his military ID and discharge papers. As soon as the story went viral, helped along by a video of the incident that rang up 400,000 views in four days, the company undertook a campaign to speak to those who felt insulted by the event. A secondary goal of its efforts was to send a message to its own employees and the larger public that everybody is welcome at their restaurants (Guarino, 2016).

12. *Public affairs.* The public affairs function includes interacting with officials and leaders of the various power centers with whom a client must deal. Community and government officials and leaders of pressure groups are likely targets of this form of public relations. Public affairs emphasizes social responsibility and building goodwill, such as when a company donates money for a computer lab at the local high school.

▲ You might recognize the Crash Test Dummies, seen here at their introduction into the Smithsonian National Museum of American History, from their long-running seat-belt safety public relations advertising campaign.
©The Washington Post/*Getty Images*

13. *Special events and public participation.* Public relations can be used to stimulate interest in an organization, person, or product through a well-planned, focused "happening," an activity designed to facilitate interaction between an organization and its publics.

14. *Research.* Organizations often must determine the attitudes and behaviors of their various publics in order to plan and implement the activities necessary to influence or change those attitudes and behaviors.

CULTURAL FORUM
Protecting a Company's Good Name in the Era of Social Media

An unfortunate 2013 incident between an airline and a Twitter user thrust the issue of public relations in the social media age into the cultural forum.

When British Airways lost his luggage and was, in his view, unresponsive to his problem, Hasan Syed took to Twitter as thousands, if not millions, of unhappy consumers often do. He posted several tweets, including "@British_Airways is the worst airline ever. Lost my luggage & can't even track it down. Absolutely pathetic #britishairways." Syed then took his social media fight a step further; when there was no response he bought sponsored tweets (anyone can do this directly from Twitter's homepage) and began running them as part of British Airways' Twitter feed to be read by the company's 300,000 followers. "Don't fly @ BritishAirways. Their customer service is horrendous," read his first purchased tweet; "Yes. I'm promoting my tweets to all BA followers since their Customer Service is horrendous. It's not about the money at this point. I'm going to run promoted ads until BA fixes this mess," read another (all in Bennett, 2013). The airline eventually responded, apologized, and explained that its customer service department was open only from 9:00 a.m. to 5:00 p.m. on business days (a terrible admission, as its Twitter followers quickly informed the multibillion-dollar company with customers in every time zone on Earth).

This drama played out against a new reality for public relations professionals working to protect their brands' reputations—instant, immediate, unfiltered consumer commentary. With the advent of social media, "public relations truly became public," in the words of Lorrie Ross of the International Association of Business Communicators (2016). Syed had no advertising budget and no PR team, and even if he had, it's unlikely either would have matched those available to British Airways. But he did have $1,000 and knowledge of social media. He used them to speak directly to British Airways' Twitter followers, garnering 77,000 impressions. His success is good news for consumers, but many PR professionals see this event as good news for their industry as well. A level playing field between clients and their publics puts PR practitioners in the role of *facilitators of conversations*, rather than mere protectors of clients' reputations. Their job becomes less one of spinning a bad situation and more one of encouraging meaningful communication. Given the industry's own definition of public relations that you encountered earlier in this chapter—a strategic communication process that builds mutually beneficial relationships between organizations and their publics—this is how most would rather operate.

Enter your voice. Are we seeing the end of spin, as new, instant consumer media enforce candor? Do you think that companies will more openly engage their consumers in authentic communication about expectations, reputation, and service? If it took a public battering at the hands of a social media–savvy customer to move this airline to better service, will the embarrassment always have to come first, or will the mere existence of social media encourage companies to proactively improve their products and services? Before you answer, keep in mind the bad news for companies—78% of those who complain to a brand via Twitter expect a response within an hour—and the good news—71% of consumers who have had a good social media service experience with a brand are likely to recommend it to others (Hainla, 2016).

Public Relations' Management Function

We saw earlier that public relations people help *establish* communication strategies and advertising people *implement* them. This is public relations' management function, and it is critical to any organization's success. According to the Public Relations Society of America, this function calls on public relations professionals to do the following:

- *Anticipate, analyze, and interpret* public opinions and issues that could have an impact on their organizations.
- *Counsel* their organizations' management on policies, public communication, and courses of action, keeping in mind their larger social responsibilities.
- *Research* and *conduct* public relations efforts and *evaluate* them on an ongoing basis to ensure they meet their organizations' goals.
- *Plan* and *implement* their organizations' efforts to influence or change public policy.
- *Manage* resources necessary to perform these objectives (adapted from PRSA, 2017).

The fictitious Acme Fishhook Research Council in this Robotman & Monty cartoon is a good example of an organization that engages in industry relations activities.

MONTY ©1997 Jim Meddick. Used by permission of ANDREWS MCMEEL SYNDICATION for UFS. All rights reserved.

Organization of a Public Relations Operation

Public relations operations come in all sizes. Regardless of size, however, the typical PR firm or department will have these types of positions (but not necessarily these titles):

Executive. This is the chief executive officer who, sometimes with a staff, sometimes alone, sets policy and serves as the spokesperson for the operation.

Account executives. Each account has its own executive who provides advice to the client, defines problems and situations, assesses the needs and demands of the client's publics, recommends a communication plan or campaign, and gathers the PR firm's resources in support of the client.

Creative specialists. These are the writers, graphic designers, artists, video and audio producers, web designers, and photographers—anybody necessary to meet the communication needs of the client.

Media specialists. Media specialists are aware of the requirements, preferences, limitations, and strengths of the various media used to serve the client. They find the right media for clients' messages.

Larger public relations operations may also have these positions as need demands:

Research. The key to two-way public relations communication rests in research—assessing the needs of a client's various publics and the effectiveness of the efforts aimed at them. Polling, one-on-one interviews, and **focus groups**, in which small groups of a targeted public are interviewed, provide the PR operation and its client with feedback.

Government relations. Depending on the client's needs, lobbying or other direct communication with government officials may be necessary.

Financial services. Very specific and sophisticated knowledge of economics, finance, and business or corporate law is required to provide clients with dependable financial public relations.

Trends and Convergence in Public Relations

As you've read throughout this text, digital technologies—the Internet, the Web, and social media—are altering the relationship between media and their audiences. In those instances, what was once primarily one-way communication—content producer to audience member—is increasingly becoming a conversation. Modern public relations, although already a conversation based on the two-way flow of communication, is equally susceptible to digital technologies' transformative influence.

Globalization, Concentration, and Specialization

As they have in the media industries themselves, globalization and concentration have come to public relations in the form of foreign ownership, reach of PR firms' operations into foreign countries, and the collection of several different companies into giant marketing organizations. Dentsu Aegis Network alone has 23,000 employees serving clients in more than 100 countries. New York–based independent Edelman PR has 5,000 employees in 51 offices around the world. Marketing giant Omnicom Group operates in 100 countries, has over 100,000 employees, and serves more than 5,000 clients. It accomplishes this with three of the world's top-seven-earning PR firms and several specialty PR shops (for example, Brodeur Worldwide, Clark & Weinstock, Gavin Anderson & Company, and Cone). But Omnicom is also parent to several national and international advertising agencies, including three of the top 10 global earners (BBDO Worldwide, DDB Worldwide, and TBWA Worldwide); several media planning and buying companies; event branding and planning companies; outdoor, direct marketing, and online advertising specialty shops; and the global marketing company Diversified Agency Services, which itself is home to more than 160 companies offering services through its 700 offices in 71 countries. Six of the world's 10 largest marketing organizations have ownership outside the United States, as you can see in Figure 3.

Another trend in public relations is specialization. We've seen the 14 activities of public relations professionals, but specialization can expand that list. This specialization takes two forms. The first is defined by issue. Environmental public relations is attracting ever-larger

▼ **Figure 3** World's 10 Largest Marketing Companies, 2015. *Source: "Agency Companies,"* Advertising Age, *May 2, 2016, 14.*

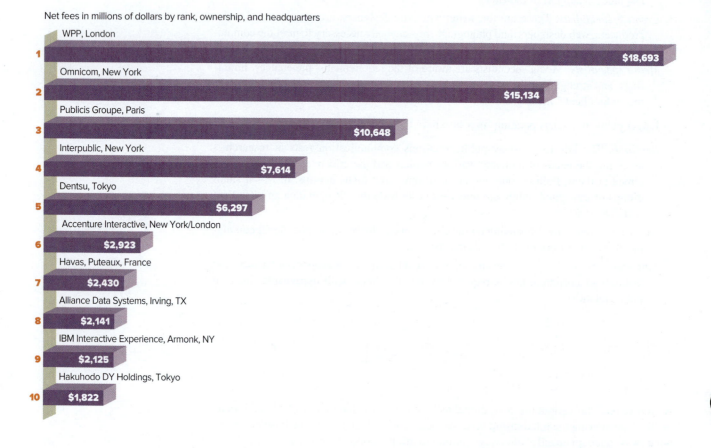

Net fees in millions of dollars by rank, ownership, and headquarters

Rank	Company	Net fees
1	WPP, London	$18,693
2	Omnicom, New York	$15,134
3	Publicis Groupe, Paris	$10,648
4	Interpublic, New York	$7,614
5	Dentsu, Tokyo	$6,297
6	Accenture Interactive, New York/London	$2,923
7	Havas, Puteaux, France	$2,430
8	Alliance Data Systems, Irving, TX	$2,141
9	IBM Interactive Experience, Armonk, NY	$2,125
10	Hakuhodo DY Holdings, Tokyo	$1,822

numbers of people, both environmentalists and industrialists. E. Bruce Harrison Consulting attracts corporate clients in part because of its reputation as a firm with superior **greenwashing** skills. That is, Harrison is particularly adept at countering the public relations efforts aimed at its clients by environmentalists. Health care and pharmaceuticals has also recently emerged as a significant public relations specialty.

Convergence

The second impetus driving specialization has to do with the increasing number of media outlets used in public relations campaigns that rely on new and converging technologies. Online information and advertising and a social media presence are growing parts of the total public relations media mix, as are video news releases. In addition, Web publishing has greatly expanded the number and type of available media outlets. All require professionals with specific skills.

The public relations industry is responding to the convergence of traditional media with the Internet in other ways as well. One is the development of **integrated marketing communications (IMC)**. We saw earlier how advertising and PR often overlap, but in IMC, firms actively combine public relations, marketing, advertising, and promotion functions into a more or less seamless communication campaign that is as at home on the Web as it is on the television screen and magazine page. The goal of this integration is to provide the client and agency with greater control over communication (and its interpretation) in an increasingly fragmented but synergized media environment. For example, a common IMC tactic is to employ **viral marketing**, a strategy that relies on targeting specific Internet users with a given communication and relying on them to spread the word through the communication channels with which they are most comfortable. This is IMC, and it is inexpensive and effective.

The industry has had to respond to the Internet in another way. The Internet has provided various publics with a new, powerful way to counter even the best public relations effort, as we saw in British Airways' social media dust-up. Tony Juniper of the British environmental group Friends of the Earth calls the Internet "the most potent weapon in the toolbox of resistance." As Peter Verhille of PR giant Entente International explains, "One of the major strengths of pressure groups—in fact the leveling factor in their confrontation with powerful companies—is their ability to exploit the instruments of the telecommunication revolution. Their agile use of global tools such as the Internet reduces the advantages that corporate budgets once provided" (both quotes from Klein, 1999, pp. 395–396). For example, the Internet is central to United Students Against Sweatshops' ongoing efforts to monitor the child labor, safety, and working conditions of U.S. apparel and shoe manufacturers' overseas operations. USAS used the Internet to build a nationwide network of students that organized protests and boycotts, resulting in several victories—for example, forcing Nike and Reebok to allow workers at one of its Mexican factories to unionize. Public relations agencies and in-house PR departments have responded in a number of ways. One is IMC. Another is the hiring of in-house Web monitors; a third way is the growth of specialty firms such as eWatch, whose function is to alert clients to negative references on the Web and suggest effective countermeasures.

Smartphones, Tablets, and Social Networking Sites

We've already seen in this chapter how the Internet and social media are changing the PR landscape; industry professionals have also taken note. "Welcome to a new wired world of empowered consumers," says Cone Communications' chief reputation officer Mike Lawrence (in Magee, 2011). Mobile technology and social networking combine to grant publics "free megaphones that carry a customer's complaint around the world," writes *New York Times* technology writer Randall Stross (2011, p. BU3). Yelp, for example, is a website and mobile app for smartphones and tablets that allows the instantaneous posting of complaint or praise to a business's Yelp review page, as well as to the poster's Facebook friends and Twitter followers. In addition, it provides data about local businesses, including health inspection scores, and to foster better relationships between customers and businesses, hosts social events for reviewers, serves as a reservations and food-delivery app, and trains businesses on how to respond to reviewers.

Smartphones and tablets give PR's publics instant, on-the-spot opportunities to pan or praise its clients; that's obvious. But just as important, they give people, especially young people, a greater sense of involvement with a company or organization. "Millennials demand fairness, transparency and clear, consistent rules in every aspect of life," writes Nick Shore, vice president of MTV's research group. He continues, "As consumers they feel comfortable leveraging their power (individually and collectively) to 'level the playing field'" (in Goetzl, 2011).

Trust in Public Relations

We began our discussion of public relations with the industry's self-admission that the profession sometimes bears a negative reputation. Edward Bernays's call for greater sensitivity to the wants and needs of the various publics and Ivy Lee's insistence that public relations be open and honest were the industry's first steps away from its huckster roots. The post–World War II code of ethics and accreditation programs were a second and more important step. Yet Bernays himself was dissatisfied with the profession's progress. The father of public relations died in 1995 at the age of 103. He spent the greater part of his last years demanding that the industry, especially the PRSA, police itself. In 1986 Bernays wrote,

> Under present conditions, an unethical person can sign the code of the PRSA, become a member, practice unethically—untouched by any legal sanctions. In law and medicine, such an individual is subject to disbarment from the profession. . . . There are no standards. . . . This sad situation makes it possible for anyone, regardless of education or ethics, to use the term "public relations" to describe his or her function. (p. 11)

▼ The father of public relations, Edward Bernays, used the last years of his long career and life to campaign for improved industry ethics.

©Bettmann/Getty Images

Many people in the profession share Bernays's concern, especially when the industry's own research shows that 69% of the public does not trust public relations, while only 12% said they do. As a result, Laurence Evans, chief executive of PR firm Reputation Leaders, is adamant about restoring trust in PR, declaring that "distrust is bad for business. High levels of public distrust affect PR businesses, from recruitment to the regulatory environment they inhabit. In addition, PR professionals depend on public credibility to get their clients' message across" (Griggs, 2015).

Today in the United States PR professionals outnumber journalists four to one, and because of the economic stress on the traditional press that you've read about throughout this text, they are better paid (by an average of about $20,000 a year), better financed, and better equipped. Estimates are that 60% of the news we receive comes directly from government press releases and spokespeople, 23% from PR firms, and only 14% from journalists' independent efforts (Pan, 2014). "The widening employment and income disparities have left journalists underpaid, overworked, and increasingly unable to undertake independent, in-depth reporting," write the Center for Public Integrity's Erin Quinn and Chris Young. As a result, many news organizations that once engaged in serious coverage of important topics like science and health, for example, no longer have the resources to do so adequately, "and special interests have filled the void" (2015). This puts a particularly heavy burden on public trust because, as many PR professionals argue, the only bad public relations effort is one that people recognize as PR, so the best PR, therefore, is invisible.

But a growing number of public relations professionals take little comfort in the invisibility of their work or in the public's inability to distinguish between news and PR. In 2007, after Wal-Mart's and Sony's PR operations were discovered paying authors of fake blogs (**flogs**) to promote their brands (and attack competitors'), there were calls from **transparentists** who, according to PR executive Eric Webber, demanded that the industry "adopt a position of full and total disclosure, driven by the innate openness and accessibility to information available on the Internet." If public relations is to hold consumer (and client) trust, Webber argued, its professionals must recognize that "it's too easy now for journalists, pro and amateur alike, to figure out when companies and their PR people lie, so we'd better tell the truth" (2007, p. 8).

Nonetheless, if people *are* lied to by public relations, the cultural implications could not be more profound. What becomes of the negotiation function of culture, wherein we debate and discuss our values and interests in the cultural forum, if public relations gives some voices advantages not available to others? The remedy for this potential problem is that consumers must make themselves aware of the sources of information and the process by which it is produced. As we've seen throughout this book, we would expect nothing less of a media-literate person.

DEVELOPING MEDIA LITERACY SKILLS
Recognizing Fake Online Reviews

In just the past few years the Federal Trade Commission fined a car-shipping service for paying for positive online reviews; travel website Trip Advisor was fined by the Italian government for misrepresenting the authenticity of its online reviews and failing to police false reviews; New York's attorney general fined 19 "reputation management" companies for paying people to write fake reviews on Yelp and other ratings sites; researchers discovered that as many as 16% of Yelp restaurant reviews are fake; and Amazon filed several lawsuits against fake reviewers (Giorgianni, 2015; Thomas, 2016). In other words, there is a lot of questionable information online, and although the Internet and social media have empowered customers and clients, that empowerment is only as good as the information on which it is based.

So how can media-literate consumers know when a review is authentic or not? There are a number of strategies:

1. *Find more than one source.* There are quite a few review sites, including user forums, product evaluation sites, paid membership sites like Angie's List, and Amazon's product reviews. If you find only positive reviews, look again somewhere else, and the more reviews the better.
2. *Look for copycat reviews.* Too much common phrasing and too many nearly identical adjectives and adverbs suggest complaint or praise mills.
3. *Avoid all caps reviews.* IF THEY HAVE TO SCREAM THEIR OPINION IT'S PROBABLY NOT WORTH MUCH.
4. *Look for links.* A reviewer has no need to link you to a product or service. A faker or a plant does.
5. *Look for balanced comments.* Too positive, too good to be true. Too negative, too bad to be true. Reviews that discuss both pros and cons tend to be authentic.
6. *Look for experts.* A review that demonstrates technical knowledge probably comes from someone with some expertise as opposed to a plant.
7. *Look for verifiable information.* Look for facts and details that can be verified.

8. *Read professional reviews.* The Internet abounds with interest-specific sites for everything from consumer electronics to kitchen appliances to photography. And there is always *Consumer Reports* if you're willing to pay for a subscription.

9. *Ask questions.* Many review sites, Amazon.com for example, permit conversations between reviewers and their readers. There are also user forums set up explicitly to foster question asking.

10. *Seek consensus.* Find agreement from professional and nonprofessional reviews alike.

MEDIA LITERACY CHALLENGE
Ferreting Out Fake Online Reviews

An important component of media literacy is *possessing critical thinking skills that enable a person to develop independent judgments about media content.* Naturally, this encompasses *the ability to recognize when genre conventions are mixed,* in this case, public relations promotional material and authentic online reviews. Challenge your media literacy skills, then, by choosing a product, a juicer or vacuum cleaner for example, or service, possibly a restaurant or comedy club, and find as many online reviews as you can. Begin with the target's own website and go from there. What sites did you visit? Were there Yelp reviews? Does your local newspaper, alternative weekly, or area-based magazine offer reviews? Did you visit established review sites like Amazon or product-specific sites like CNET for consumer electronics and appliances, Edmunds for cars, or Steve's Digicams for photography equipment?

Having amassed your collection of review sites, apply the various techniques you learned in this chapter to ferreting out fake reviews. You can take this challenge as either an opportunity for personal reflection, committing your thoughts to paper, or you can duel with classmates to see who can find the greatest number of fake reviews or possibly the most egregious example of deception for the chosen product or service. Honorable mention goes to the classmate with the greatest number and greatest variety of review sites.

Resources for Review and Discussion

REVIEW POINTS: TYING CONTENT TO LEARNING OUTCOMES

▶ **Outline the history and development of the public relations industry.**

☐ The history of public relations can be divided into four stages: early public relations, the propaganda–publicity stage, early two-way communication, and advanced two-way communication.

☐ The evolution of public relations has been shaped by advances in technology, the growth of the middle class, growth of organizations, better research tools, and professionalization.

▶ **Describe how the organizational and economic nature of the contemporary public relations industry shapes the messages with which publics interact, especially in an increasingly converged media environment.**

☐ Public relations tells an organization's "story" to its publics (communication) and helps shape the organization and the way it performs (management).

☐ Advertising executes an organization's communication strategy; public relations provides several important management functions.

☐ Firms typically are organized around an executive, account executives, creative specialists, and media specialists. Larger firms typically include research, government relations, and financial service professionals.

▶ **Identify different types of public relations and the different publics each is designed to serve.**

☐ The publics served by the industry include employees, stockholders, communities, media, government, investment communities, and customers.

☐ Public relations firms provide all or some of these 14 services: community relations, counseling, development and fundraising, employee/member relations, financial relations, government affairs, industry relations, issues management, media relations, marketing communication, minority relations and multicultural affairs, public affairs, special events and public participation, and research.

▶ **Explain the relationship between public relations and its various publics.**

☐ Globalization, specialization, and convergence—in the form of video news releases, integrated marketing communications, and viral marketing—are reshaping contemporary PR's relationships with its clients and its publics.

☐ Trust in public relations is essential if the industry is to perform its role for its clients and publics.

▶ **Apply key media literacy skills when consuming public relations messages, especially fake online reviews.**

☐ Recognizing fake online reviews is difficult, but media-literate viewers look for a variety of clues and seek multiple evaluations from professionals and customers alike.

KEY TERMS

flack, 260

spin, 260

astroturf, 261

pseudo-event, 263,

public, 267

video news release (VNR), 269

fixed-fee arrangement, 269

collateral materials, 269

corporate social responsibility, 269

cause marketing, 269

lobbying, 270

focus groups, 273

greenwashing, 275

integrated marketing communications (IMC), 275

viral marketing, 275

flog, 277

transparentists, 277

QUESTIONS FOR REVIEW

1. What elements are essential to a good definition of public relations?

2. What are the four stages in the development of the public relations industry?

3. Who were Ivy Lee, George Creel, and Edward Bernays?

4. What is the difference between public relations and advertising?

5. Who are public relations' publics? What are their characteristics?

6. What are the 14 services that public relations firms typically offer?

7. What positions typically exist in a public relations operation?

8. How have new communication technologies influenced the public relations industry?

9. What is integrated marketing communications? What is its goal?

10. What is viral marketing? How does it work?

To maximize your study time, check out CONNECT to access the SmartBook study module for this chapter and explore other resources.

QUESTIONS FOR CRITICAL THINKING AND DISCUSSION

1. Are you familiar with TOMS, the shoe company in the opening vignette? What was your opinion of it before you read of its efforts to help people in need? What is your opinion now? Does corporate social responsibility such as this really work, or do most people see it as self-serving? Do you agree or disagree that a company's precrisis reputation can help it weather a crisis should one occur? Why or why not?

2. Have you ever been part of an Internet-fueled movement against the activities of an organization or in support of some good cause? If so, you were engaged in public relations. Measure your experience against the lessons in this chapter. What kinds of public relations activities did you undertake? Who were your publics? Were you successful? Why or why not?

3. Knowing that many of the online reviews you read might be fake or planted, how likely are you to accept without question their veracity or accuracy? If you too readily accept others' evaluations, they are essentially useless. If you too readily reject them, again they hold little value.

Online information is only as good and useful as *you* make it. Why or why not might you subject the online reviews you read to the kinds of scrutiny you most likely apply to your everyday interactions with the "real" world?

REFERENCES

1. "Agency companies." (2016, May 2). *Advertising Age*, p. 14.

2. Beale, L. (2015, March 3). Meet the merchants of doubt: The PR firms giving you cancer, causing acid rain and killing the planet. *Daily Beast*. Online: http://www.thedailybeast.com/articles/2015/03/03/meet-the-merchants-of-doubt-the-pr-firms-giving-you-cancer-causing-acid-rain-and-killing-the-planet.html

3. Bennett, S. (2013, September 4). The $1,000 promoted tweet that complained about @British_Airways on twitter (and won). *Ad Week*. Online: http://www.adweek.com/socialtimes/british-airways-promoted-tweet-complaint/490348

4. Bernays, E. L. (1986). *The later years: Public relations insights, 1956–1988*. Rhinebeck, NY: H&M.

5. Bureau of Labor Statistics. (2015, December 17). *Occupational outlook handbook, 2016–17 edition*. Online: https://www.bls.gov/ooh/media-and-communication/public-relations-specialists.htm

6. Cause Good. (2016). The case for cause marketing—statistics for businesses & nonprofits. Online: https://causegood.com/blog/cause-marketing-statistics/

7. Clines, F. X. (2013, September 22). Lobbyists look for a euphemism. *The New York Times*, p. SR10.

8. "Drunk driving fatalities fall below 10,000." (2012, December 10). *Mothers Against Drunk Driving*. Online: http://www.madd.org/blog/2012/december/drunk-driving-fatalities-fall.html

9. Fang, L., & Jilani, A. (2016, January 5). After executing regime critic, Saudi Arabia fires up American PR machine. *Intercept*. Online: https://theintercept.com/2016/01/04/saudi-pr-machine/

10. Giorgianni, A. (2015, April 8). Don't be fooled by phony online product reviews: How you can tell fake from real. *Alternet*. Online: http://www.alternet.org/economy/dont-be-fooled-phony-online-product-reviews-how-you-can-tell-fake-real

11. Goel, V. (2014, March 23). GM uses social media to manage customers and its reputation. *The New York Times*, p. BU1.

12. Goetzl, D. (2011, December 23). MTV Research: It's (video) game time for marketers. *MediaPost*. Online: http://www.mediapost.com/publications/article/164789/mtv-research-its-video-game-time-for-marketers.html

13. Goldenberg, S., & Karim, N. (2014, August 4). World's top PR companies rule out working with climate deniers. *The Guardian*. Online: http://www.theguardian.com/environment/2014/aug/04/worlds-top-pr-companies-rule-out-working-with-climate-deniers

14. Gordon, J. S. (1989, October). The public be damned. *American Heritage*. Online: http://www.americanheritage.com/content/%E2%80%9C-public-be-damned%E2%80%9D

15. Griggs, I. (2015, March 19). PR in the dock: Nearly 70 percent of the general public does not trust the industry. *PRWeek*. Online: http://www.prweek.com/article/1339167/pr-dock-nearly-70-per-cent-general-public-does-not-trust-industry

16. Guarino, B. (2016, November 15). Day meal to black veteran after man in Trump shirt accuses him of lying. *The Washington Post*. Online: https://www.washingtonpost.com/news/morning-mix/wp/2016/11/15/restaurant-denies-free-veterans-day-meal-to-black-veteran-after-man-in-trump-shirt-accuses-him-of-lying/?utm_term=.6f051a23f2e7

17. Hainla, L. (2016, December 20). 21 social media marketing statistics you need to know in 2016. *DreamGrow*. Online: https://www.dreamgrow.com/21-social-media-marketing-statistics/

18. Jackson, J., & Hart, P. (2002, March/April). Fear and favor 2001. *Extra!*, pp. 20–27.

19. Klein, N. (1999). *No logo: Taking aim at the brand bullies*. New York: Picador.

20. Magee, D. (2011, October 11). Global consumers voice demand for greater corporate responsibility: Study. *International Business Times*. Online: http://www.ibtimes.com/global-consumers-voice-demand-greater-corporate-responsibility-study-321453

21. Malkan, S. (2016, March 20). *Extra!* p. 3.

22. O'Brien, T. L. (2005, February 13). Spinning frenzy: P.R.'s bad press. *The New York Times*, p. B1.

23. Pan, J. (2014, July). Pink collar. *Jacobin Magazine*. Online: https://www.jacobinmag.com/2014/06/pink-collar/

24. PRSA. (2017). About public relations. *Public Relations Society of America*. Online: https://www.prsa.org/aboutprsa/publicrelationsdefined/#.WGAgnk3ruPw

25. "Public relations worldwide." (2016, May 2). *Advertising Age*, p. 21.

26. Quinn, E., & Young, C. (2015, January 15). Who needs lobbyists? See what big business spends to win American minds. *Huffington Post*. Online: http://www.huffingtonpost.com/2015/01/15/big-business-lobbying_n_6476600.html

27. Ross, L. T. (2016, October 6). PR practice in the social media age. *International Association of Business Communicators*. Online: https://www.iabc.com/pr-practice-in-the-social-media-age/

28. Stein, L. (2016, January 11). How public relations is earning its place in 2016. *Advertising Age*. Online: http://adage.com/article/cmo-strategy/public-relations-earning-place/302060/

29. Stross, R. (2011, May 29). Consumer complaints made easy. Maybe too easy. *The New York Times*, p. BU3.

30. Sudhaman, A. (2016, April 25). Global PR industry hits $14bn in 2016 as growth slows to 5%. *Holmes Report*. Online: http://www.holmesreport.com/research/article/global-pr-industry-hits-$14bn-in-2016-as-growth-slows-to-5

31. Thomas, L. (2016, August 18). Don't be fooled by fake online reviews—here's how to catch them. *DealsPlus*. Online: https://www.dealsplus.com/blog/dont-be-fooled-by-fake-online-reviews-heres-how-to-catch-them/

32. Webber, E. (2007, April 30). No need to bare all: PR should strive for translucence. *Advertising Age*, p. 8.

33. Zinn, H. (1995). *A people's history of the United States, 1492–present*. New York: Harper Perennial.

Cultural Forum Blue Column icon, Media Literacy Red Torch Icon, Using Media Green Gear icon, Developing Media book in starburst icon: ©McGraw-Hill Education

◀ Does ambient advertising cut through the clutter or add to it?

©Viviane Moos/Getty Images

Learning Objectives

Advertising is everywhere. As it becomes more ubiquitous, we tend to ignore it. But as we tend to ignore it, advertisers find new ways to make it more ubiquitous. As a result, and as with television, no one is neutral about advertising. We love it or we hate it. Many of us do both. After studying this chapter, you should be able to

▶ Outline the history and development of the advertising industry.

▶ Evaluate contemporary criticisms and defenses of advertising.

▶ Describe how the organizational and economic nature of the contemporary advertising industry shapes the content of advertising, especially in an increasingly converged media environment.

▶ Identify different types of advertising and their goals.

▶ Explain the relationship between advertising content and its consumers.

▶ Apply key media literacy skills when consuming advertising, especially when interpreting intentional imprecision.

1625 ▶ First newsbooks with ads

1735 Ben Franklin sells ad space in *Pennsylvania Gazette*

1841 ▶ Palmer begins first ad agency

1800

©Hulton Archive/Getty Images

1869 Ayer begins first full-service ad agency

1880s ▶ Brands appear

1850

Source: Library of Congress, Prints and Photographs Division

1914 Federal Trade Commission established

1922 First radio commercial

1923 *The Eveready Hour,* first regularly broadcast sponsored series

1936 Consumers Union established

1938 Wheeler-Lea Act

1941 ▶ War Advertising Council (Ad Council) founded

1948 Television to the public

1900

©Photo Researchers, Inc/Alamy

©Fotosearch/Getty Images

1957 Packard's *The Hidden Persuaders*

1959 Quiz show scandal

1971 National Advertising Review Board established; TV cigarette commercial ban

1980 ▶ Foreign ad spending first exceeds U.S. ad outlay

1994 First banner ad; spam appears

1950

©Brand X Pictures/ PunchStock RF

2005 Chaos scenario

2008 Internet ad spending exceeds radio's

2009 Internet ad spending exceeds magazines'

2012 ▶ Internet ad spending exceeds all print advertising; tobacco companies ordered to run corrective ads

2013 Pay-for-performance deals now in majority of agency/client contracts

2016 Internet ad spending exceeds TV's; online purchases exceed in-store purchases; Trustworthy Accountability Group

2017 Coalition for Better Ads formed

2000

(laptop): ©iStockvectors/Getty Images RF; (books): ©Creative Crop/Digital Vision/Getty Images RF

LAUDANI   1951
WIFE
TTINA   1984

▲ Even in death, it's difficult to
avoid advertising.
©Susan Baran

YOUR ROOMMATES, BOTH ADVERTISING MAJORS, CHALLENGE YOU: "We bet you $10 that you can't go all of tomorrow without seeing an ad." You think, "I'll just stay away from radio and television—no problem, considering I listen to music in my car on my smartphone and I have tons of homework to do." That leaves newspapers and magazines, but you can avoid their ads simply by not reading either for 24 hours. Online ads? You'll simply stay unlinked. Facebook and Twitter? You can survive a day friendless and unfollowed. "What about billboards?" you counter.

"We won't count them," your roomies graciously concede, "but everything else is in."

You shake hands and go to bed planning your strategy. This means no cereal in the morning—the Cheerios box has a McDonald's ad on it. There'll be no bus to school. Not only are the insides packed with ads, but a lot of buses are now covered in vinyl wraps that turn them into gigantic rolling commercials. Can't walk either. There are at least two ad kiosks on the way. It'll cost you more than $10 to take a cab, but this is about winning the bet, not about money. Cab it will be! You sleep well, confident victory will be yours.

The next evening, over pizza, you hand over your $10.

"What was it?" asks one of your friends. "Sneak a peek at TV?"

"No," you say, and then you begin the list: The cab had an ad for a radio station on its trunk and a three-sided sign on its roof touting the pizza joint you're sitting in, a chiropractor, and Southwest Airlines. Inside, it had an electronic digital display pushing the lottery. The sidewalk near campus had the stenciled message "From here it looks like you could use some new underwear—Bamboo Lingerie" in water-soluble iridescent red paint. The restrooms on campus have Volkswagen ads pasted on their walls. Your ATM receipt carried an ad for a brokerage firm. You encountered a Domino's Pizza ad on the back of the receipt you got at the grocery store; the kiwi you bought there had a sticker on it reminding you to buy Snapple. The shopping basket had a realtor's pitch pasted to the side; even the little rubber bar you used to separate your kiwi and mineral water from the groceries of the shopper in front of you had an ad on each of its four sides.

"Easiest $10 we ever made," your roommates gloat.

In this chapter we examine the history of advertising, focusing on its maturation with the coming of industrialization and the Civil War. The development of the advertising agency and the rise of professionalism within its ranks are detailed, as is the impact of magazines, radio, World War II, and television.

We discuss the relationship between consumers and contemporary advertising in terms of how advertising agencies are structured, how various types of advertising are aimed at different audiences, and which trends—converging technologies, audience segmentation, globalization—promise to alter those relationships.

We study the controversies that surround the industry. Critics charge that advertising is intrusive, deceptive, inherently unethical when aimed at children, and corrupting of the culture. We look at industry defenses, too.

Finally, in the media literacy skills section, we discuss advertisers' use of intentional imprecision and how to identify and interpret it.

A Short History of Advertising

Your roommates had the advantage. They know that U.S. advertisers and marketers spend hundreds of billions of dollars a year trying to get your attention and influence your decisions. They also know that you typically encounter an estimated 4,000 to 10,000 commercial messages a day (Marshall, 2015). There are a lot of ads and a lot of advertisers. Almost everyone in the ad business complains about commercial **clutter**, yet, in the words of *Advertising Age* writer Matthew Creamer, "Like a fly repeatedly bouncing off a closed window, the ad industry is trying to fix the problem by doing more of the same. That is, by creating more ads" (2007, p. 1). Often those ads are **ambient advertising**, sometimes referred to as **360 marketing**, and by whatever name, they are showing up in some fairly

◀ Advertising everywhere—Sony hired graffiti artists in several major American cities to spray-paint commercials for its PlayStation Portable on walls and buildings.
©Rusty Kennedy/AP Photo

nontraditional settings. This is because advertisers know that "we, the public, are so good at avoiding or ignoring traditional advertising. We are fickle fish, cynical creatures who have already been hooked so many times that the simpler lures no longer work" (Wu, 2016b). So Sony hires graffiti artists in major cities to spray-paint ads for its PlayStation Portable on walls and buildings. Officials in Brooklawn, New Jersey, sell naming rights to school facilities—the gym at the Alice Costello Elementary School is now the ShopRite of Brooklawn Center. The National Park Service sells naming rights to our national parks, and moviemakers pay pastors to mention their films in their sermons (Wu, 2016a). The rPlate looks like a traditional automobile license plate when a vehicle is moving, but it becomes a digital billboard when it is parked, its message targeted to its location (Martin, 2017). Johnnie Walker premium whiskey Blue Label comes in an NFC (near-field communication) chip–equipped smart bottle that links to drinkers' smartphones to send them targeted, personalized advertising messages. Radio, concert promotion, and outdoor ad company Clear Channel Outdoor maintains a separate Branded Cities division in the business of turning locations—parks, city centers, specific streets—into destinations where people can go for all kinds of activities into which brands can be integrated, a practice called **experiential marketing**, the melding of brands and experiences. Other examples include the U.S. Open American Express Fan Experience and car company Lincoln's Tribeca Interactive & Interlude: A Music Film Challenge, where people at film festivals are invited to create music videos for established recording artists. And of course, folks at these "branded experiences," 98% of them, become "content factory workers," capturing the goings-on with their phones and sharing them across social media, making even more clutter (Whitman, 2016b). We see ads on door hangers, on urinal deodorant cakes, in the mail, behind the batter at a baseball game, and on basketball backboards in city parks. We use digital ad-screen hand driers in public restrooms. It wasn't always like this, but advertising itself has been with us for a long time.

Early Advertising

Babylonian merchants were hiring barkers to shout out goods and prices at passersby in 3000 B.C.E. The Romans wrote announcements on city walls. This ad was discovered in the ruins of Pompeii:

> The Troop of Gladiators of the Aedil
> Will fight on the 31st of May

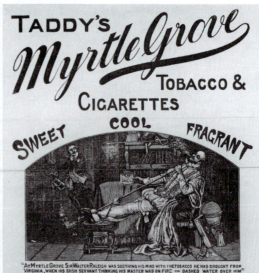

▲ This narrow street in Salzburg, Austria, still exhibits evidence of early European advertising, which often took the form of artistically designed signs announcing the nature of the business below.

©Siepmann/imageBROKER/agefotostock

▲ This early-18th-century tobacco label shows that the British had already mastered the use of celebrities in their advertising.

©Hulton Archive/Getty Images

> There will be fights with wild animals
> And an Awning to keep off the sun. (Berkman & Gilson, 1987, p. 32)

By the 15th century, ads as we know them now were abundant in Europe. **Siquis**—pinup want ads for all sorts of products and services—were common. Tradespeople promoted themselves with **shopbills**—attractive, artful business cards. Taverners and other merchants were hanging eye-catching signs above their businesses. In 1625 the first **newsbook** containing ads, *The Weekly News*, was printed in England. From the beginning, those who had products and services to offer used advertising.

Advertising came to the colonies via England. British advertising was already leaning toward exaggeration and hyperbole, but colonial advertising was more straightforward. Ben Franklin sold advertising space in his *Pennsylvania Gazette*, and this 1735 ad is a typical example for the time:

> A Plantation containing 300 acres of good Land, 30 cleared, 10 or 12 Meadow and in good English Grass, a house and barn & c. [creek] lying in Nantmel Township, upon French-Creek, about 30 miles from Philadelphia. Inquire of Simon Meredith now living on the said place. (Sandage, Fryburger, & Rotzoll, 1989, p. 21)

Advertising, however, was a small business before the Civil War. The United States was primarily an agricultural country at that time, with 90% of the population living in self-sufficiency on farms. Advertising was used by local retailers primarily to encourage area residents to come to their businesses. The local newspaper was the major advertising medium.

Industrialization and the Civil War

The Industrial Revolution and the Civil War altered the social and cultural landscape and brought about the expansion of advertising. By the 1840s the telegraph made communication over long distances possible. Railroads linked cities and states. Huge numbers of immigrants were welcomed to the United States to provide labor for the expanding factories. Manufacturers wanted access to larger markets for their goods. Advertising copywriter Volney B. Palmer recognized in 1841 that merchants needed to reach consumers beyond their local newspaper readership. He contacted several Philadelphia newspapers and agreed to broker the sale of space between them and interested advertisers. Within four years Palmer had expanded his business to Boston, and in 1849, he opened a branch in New York. The advertising agency had been invented.

The Civil War sped industrialization. More factories were needed to produce war material, and roads and railroads were expanded to move that material as well as troops. As farmworkers went to war or to work in the new factories, more farm machinery was needed to compensate for their departure. That meant that more factories were needed to make more machinery, and the cycle repeated.

By the early 1880s the telephone and the electric light had been invented. That decade saw numerous innovations in manufacturing as well as an explosion in the type and availability of products. In the year 1880 alone, there were applications for more than 13,000 U.S. copyrights and patents. Over 70,000 miles of new railroad track were laid in the 1880s, linking cities and towns of all sizes. With more producers chasing the growing purchasing power of more consumers, manufacturers were forced to differentiate their products—to literally and figuratively take the pickle out of the barrel and put it in its own recognizable package. And so brands were born: Quaker Oats, Ivory Soap, Royal Baking Powder, and many more. What advertisers now needed was a medium in which to tell people about these brands.

Magazine Advertising

The expansion of the railroads, the rise in literacy, and advantageous postal rates fueled the explosive growth of the popular magazine just before the end of the 19th century. The marriage of magazines and advertising was natural. Cyrus H. K. Curtis, who founded the *Ladies' Home Journal* in 1883, told a group of manufacturers:

> The editor of the *Ladies' Home Journal* thinks we publish it for the benefit of American women. This is an illusion, but a very proper one for him to have. The real reason, the publisher's [Curtis's] reason, is to give you who manufacture things American women want, a chance to tell them about your product. (in Sandage et al., 1989, p. 32)

By the turn of the century, magazines were financially supported primarily by their advertisers rather than by their readers, and aspects of advertising we find common today—creativity in look and language, mail-order ads, seasonal ads, and placement of ads in proximity to content of related interest—were already in use (see the chapter on magazines for more).

The Advertising Agency and Professionalism

In the years between the Civil War and World War I, advertising had rapidly become more complex, more creative, and more expensive, and it was conducted on a larger scale. Advertising agencies had to expand their operations to keep up with demand. Where Palmer offered merely to broker the sale of newspaper space, F. Wayland Ayer began his "full service" advertising agency in 1869, N. W. Ayer and Sons. He provided clients with ad campaign planning, created and produced ads with his staff of artists and writers, and placed them in the most appropriate media. Several big agencies still operating today started at this time, including J. Walter Thompson, William Esty, and Lord & Thomas.

During this period, three factors combined to motivate the advertising industry to establish professional standards and to regulate itself. First was the reaction of the public and the medical profession to the abuses of patent medicine advertisers. These charlatans used fake claims and medical data in their ads to sell tonics that at best were useless and, at worst, deadly. The second was the critical examination of most of the country's important institutions, led by the muckrakers (see the chapter on magazines). The third factor was the establishment in 1914 of the Federal Trade Commission (FTC), which had among its duties monitoring and regulating advertising. As a result, a number of leading advertising agencies and publishers mounted a crusade against gross exaggeration, false testimonials, and other

▲ Magazines provided the first national medium for advertisers. Here is an imaginative ad for the still popular Pears' soap.
Source: Library of Congress (LC-USZ62-84425)

▲ Reaction to the deception and outright lies of patent medicine advertising—such as this 1880 piece for Pratts Healing Ointment—led to important efforts to professionalize the industry.
©Photo Researchers, Inc/Alamy

▲ A 1930s hard-sell ad from Quaker Oats oatmeal. The hard sell made its debut during the Depression as advertisers worked to attract the little consumer money that was available.
©f8 archive/Alamy

misleading forms of advertising. The Audit Bureau of Circulations was established to verify circulation claims. The Advertising Federation of America (now the American Advertising Federation), the American Association of Advertising Agencies, the Association of National Advertisers, and the Outdoor Advertising Association all began operation at this time.

Advertising and Radio

The first radio ad was broadcast on WEAF in 1922 (the cost was $50 for a 10-minute spot). Radio was important to advertising in three major ways. First, although many people both inside and outside government were opposed to commercial support for the new medium, the general public had no great opposition to radio ads. In fact, in the prosperous Roaring Twenties, many welcomed them; advertising seemed a natural way to keep radio "free." Second, advertising agencies virtually took over broadcasting, producing the shows in which their commercials appeared. The ad business became show business. The 1923 variety show *The Eveready Hour*, sponsored by a battery maker, was the first regularly broadcast sponsored series. Ad agency Blackett-Sample-Hummert even developed a new genre for its client Procter & Gamble—the soap opera. Third, money now poured into the industry. That income was used to expand research and marketing on a national scale, allowing advertisers access to sophisticated nationwide consumer and market information for the first time. The wealth that the advertising industry accrued from radio permitted it to survive during the Depression.

The Depression did have its effect on advertising, however. The stock market crashed in 1929, and by 1933 advertising had lost nearly two-thirds of its revenues. Among the responses were the hard sell—making direct claims about why a consumer *needed* a product—and a tendency away from honesty. At the same time, widespread unemployment and poverty bred a powerful consumer movement. The Consumers Union, which still publishes *Consumer Reports*, was founded in 1936 to protect people from unscrupulous manufacturers and advertisers. And in 1938 Congress passed the Wheeler–Lea Act, granting the FTC extended powers to regulate advertising.

World War II

The Second World War, so important in the development of all the mass media, had its impact on advertising as well. Production of consumer products came to a near halt during the war (1941–1945), and traditional advertising was limited. The advertising industry turned its collective skills toward the war effort, and what product advertising that there was typically adopted a patriotic theme.

In 1941 several national advertising and media associations joined to develop the War Advertising Council. The council used its expertise to promote numerous government programs. Its best-known campaign, however, was on behalf of the sale of war bonds. The largest campaign to date for a single item, the war bond program helped sell 800 million bonds, totaling $45 billion. When the war ended, the group, now called the Advertising Council, directed its efforts toward a host of public service campaigns on behalf of countless nonprofit organizations (see the essay "Effecting Positive Social Change"). Most of us have read or heard, "This message is brought to you by the Ad Council."

The impact of World War II on the size and structure of the advertising industry was significant. A high excess-profits tax was levied on manufacturers' wartime profits that exceeded prewar levels. The goal was to limit war profiteering and ensure that companies did not benefit too greatly from the death and destruction of war. Rather than pay the heavy tariff, manufacturers reduced their profit levels by putting income back into their businesses. Because the lack of raw materials made expansion or recapitalization difficult, many companies invested in corporate image advertising. They may not have had products to sell to the public, but they knew that the war would end someday and that stored-up goodwill would be important. One result, therefore, was an expansion in the number and size of manufacturers' advertising departments and of advertising agencies. A second result was a public primed by that advertising for the return of consumer goods.

Christmas together...Have a Coke

...welcoming a fighting man home from the wars

Time of all times. Home at last ... to wife, to child and to family. With Christmas in the air and the tree lighted brightly. All the dreams of a lifetime rolled into one moment. A home-like, truly American moment where the old familiar phrase *Have a Coke* adds the final refreshing touch.

Coca-Cola belongs to just such a time of friendly, warm family feeling. That's why you find it in homes big and small across the nation ... the drink that adds life and sparkle to living. A happy moment is an occasion for Coke—and the happy American custom, *the pause that refreshes.*

Coca-Cola
·the global
high-sign

Coke = Coca-Cola

◀ Consumer products go to war. Advertisers and manufacturers joined the war effort. This magazine-ad GI is enjoying the comforts of a holiday home—wife, child, and a cold Coke or two. ©*Fotosearch/Getty Images*

USING MEDIA TO MAKE A DIFFERENCE
Effecting Positive Social Change

Advertising can often lead people to do good, and there is no better example of this than the work of the Ad Council, whose mission is to use advertising to bring about beneficial social change. Has it succeeded in making a difference? Who are Smokey Bear, Rosie the Riveter, McGruff the Crime Dog, the Crash Test Dummies, and the Crying Indian (Chief Iron Eyes Cody)? All are creations of the Ad Council. And of course you are aware that friends don't let friends drive drunk and that love has no labels. You certainly understand when to just say no and that a mind is a terrible thing to waste. You know these things because of Ad Council campaigns.

Can the ability of the Ad Council to make a difference be quantified? Consider the following:

· Applications for mentors rose from 90,000 a year to 620,000 in the first nine months after the start of its campaign for Big Brothers/Big Sisters.

- Sixty-eight percent of Americans say that they have personally stopped someone who had been drinking from driving. The old saying, "One More for the Road" has been replaced with "Friends Don't Let Friends Drive Drunk."
- Twenty thousand American kids eight years old and over have been adopted since the 2004 start of the "AdoptUSKids" campaign (all from Ad Council, 2017).

The Ad Council typically has 35 to 40 active public service campaigns running at one time, and it is able to secure about $2 billion a year in donated time and space from 28,000 different media outlets. Its primary focus today is kids' issues, devoting 80% of its resources to its "10-Year Commitment to Children: Helping Parents Help Kids" campaign. But the Ad Council does not shy away from controversial issues. In the 1970s it took on sexually transmitted disease with its "VD Is for Everyone" campaign, an effort attacked by many religious groups, and many broadcasters refused to air its "Help Stop AIDS. Use a Condom" spots in 1987. Its 2015 "Love Has No Labels" campaign challenged racism, homophobia, and intolerance (Tugend, 2015).

The Ad Council is able to make a difference because dozens of ad agencies, big and small, donate their time, energy, and creativity. One ad executive reportedly claimed that he never sees a pitch reel that doesn't contain an Ad Council campaign (Crain, 2016, p. 38).

▲ Among the earliest demonstration ads, Timex took many a licking but kept on ticking.
©Courtesy of The Advertising Archives

Advertising and Television

There was no shortage of consumer products when the war ended. The nation's manufacturing capacity had been greatly expanded to meet the needs of war, but afterwards, that manufacturing capability was turned toward the production of consumer products for people who found themselves with more leisure and more money. People were also having more children and, thanks to the GI Bill, were able to think realistically about owning homes. They wanted products to enhance their leisure, please their children, and fill their houses.

Advertising was well positioned to put products and people together, not only because agencies had expanded during the war but also because of television. Radio's formats, stars, and network structure had moved wholesale to the new medium. Television soon became the primary national advertising medium. Advertisers bought $12 million in television time in 1949; two years later they spent $128 million.

Television commercials, by virtue of the fact that consumers could see and hear the product in action, were different from the advertising of all other media. The ability to demonstrate the product—to do the torture test for Timex watches, to smoothly shave sandpaper with Rapid Shave—led to the **unique selling proposition (USP)**. Once an advertiser discovered a product's USP, it could drive it home in repeated demonstration commercials. Inasmuch as most brands in a given product category are essentially the same—that is, they are **parity products**—advertisers were often forced to create a product's USP. Candy is candy, for example, but M&Ms are unique: They melt in your mouth, not in your hand.

Some observers were troubled by this development. Increasingly, products were being sold not by touting their value or quality but by emphasizing their unique selling propositions. Ads were offering little information about the product, yet people were increasing their spending. This led to growing criticism of advertising and its contribution to the consumer culture (more on this controversy later in the chapter). The immediate impact was the creation of an important vehicle of industry self-regulation. In response to mounting criticism in books such as *The Hidden Persuaders* (Packard, 1957) and concern over increasing scrutiny from the FTC, the industry in 1971 established the National Advertising Review Board (NARB) to monitor potentially deceptive advertising. The NARB, the industry's most important self-regulatory body, investigates consumer complaints as well as complaints made by an advertiser's competitors.

Advertising and Its Audiences

The typical individual living in the United States will spend more than one year of his or her life just watching television commercials. It is a rare moment when we are not in the audience of some ad or commercial. This is one of the many reasons advertisers have begun to place their messages in many venues beyond the traditional commercial media, as we saw earlier, hoping to draw our attention. We confront so many ads every day that we overlook them, and they become invisible. As a result, many people become aware of advertising only when it somehow offends them.

Criticisms and Defenses of Advertising

Advertising does sometimes offend, and it is often the focus of criticism. But industry defenders argue the following:

- Advertising supports our economic system; without it new products could not be introduced and developments in others could not be announced. Competitive advertising of new products and businesses powers the engine of our economy, fostering economic growth and creating jobs in many industries.
- People use advertising to gather information before making buying decisions.
- Ad revenues make possible the "free" mass media we use not only for entertainment but also for the maintenance of our democracy.
- By showing us the bounty of our capitalistic, free enterprise society, advertising increases national productivity (as people work harder to acquire more of these products) and improves the standard of living (as people actually acquire more of these products).

The first defense is a given. Ours is a capitalistic society whose economy depends on the exchange of goods and services. Complaints, then, have less to do with the existence of advertising than with its conduct and content, and they are not new. At the 1941 founding meeting of the Advertising Council, J. Walter Thompson executive James Webb Young argued that such a public service commitment would go far toward improving the public's attitude toward his industry, one "rooted very deep. It is a sort of repugnance for the manifestations of advertising—or its banality, its bad taste, its moronic appeals, and its clamor" (quoted in "Story of the Ad Council," 2001). The second defense assumes that advertising provides information. But much—critics would say most—advertising is devoid of useful information about the product. Rarely does consumer advertising tout the benefits of a product because marketers know well that rather than products, people buy the lifestyles, experiences, and emotions associated with those products. The third defense assumes that the only way media can exist is through commercial support, but many nations around the world have built fine media systems without heavy advertiser support (see the chapter on global media). To critics of advertising, the fourth defense—that people work hard only to acquire more things and that our standard of living is measured by the material things we have—draws an unflattering picture of human nature.

Specific Complaints

Specific complaints about advertising are that it is often intrusive, deceptive, and, in the case of children's advertising, inherently unethical. Advertising is said to demean or corrupt the culture.

ADVERTISING IS INTRUSIVE Many critics fault advertising for its intrusiveness. Advertising is everywhere, and it interferes with and alters our experience. Giant wall advertisements change the look of cities. Ads beamed by laser light onto night skies destroy evening stargazing. School learning aids provided by candy makers asking students to "count the Tootsie Rolls" alter education. Constant commercials diminish the television-viewing experience, leading 83% of DVR users to skip most ads, with 60% of those viewers skipping every ad

Percentage of Internet users who install ad blockers because they

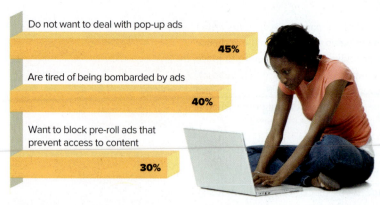

Do not want to deal with pop-up ads

45%

Are tired of being bombarded by ads

40%

Want to block pre-roll ads that prevent access to content

30%

▲ **Figure 1** Why Internet Users Install Ad Blockers.
Source: Faw, 2016.
©Mike Kemp/Rubberball/Getty Images RF

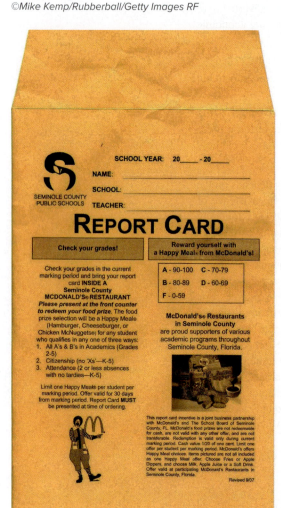

▲ Advertising in schools and on educational material is now common—and quite controversial. It took a parent uprising to end this practice of placing McDonald's ads on report cards in Seminole County, Florida, schools.
Courtesy of Campaign for a Commercial-Free Childhood

(Whitman, 2016a). Many Internet users once believed that "targeted advertising would be a blessing for consumers. Today that vision has soured and even seems like a bad joke given how plagued we are by the rise of stealth advertising, the invasions of privacy, the proliferation of click bait and stalking advertising, and the general degradation of much of the web" (in Wu, 2016b). That's why 70% of those online install ad blockers immediately after hearing about them (Faw, 2016), and why a collection of the Internet's biggest companies and biggest advertisers formed the Coalition for Better Ads in 2017 to promote industry-wide ad blocking "to kill off digital ads" considered the "absolute worst" by users, hoping to protect the Internet as an otherwise valuable advertising medium (Slefo, 2017). There is even a mobile game, *Ad Hunter*, that awards users golden coins if they and their friends hunt down and disable ads in their apps. You can see why people choose to install ad-blocking software in Figure 1.

ADVERTISING IS DECEPTIVE Many critics say that much advertising is inherently deceptive in that it implicitly and sometimes explicitly promises to improve people's lives through the consumption or purchase of a sponsor's products. Communication researchers Kathleen Hall Jamieson and Karlyn Campbell described this as the "If . . . then" strategy: "A beautiful woman uses a certain brand of lipstick in the ad, and men follow her everywhere. Without making the argument explicit, the ad implies that if you use this product you will be beautiful, and if you are beautiful (or use this product), you will be more attractive to men" (1997, p. 242). They called the opposite strategy "If not . . . then not." When Hallmark says, "When you care enough to send the very best," the implication is that when you do not send Hallmark, you simply do not care.

Advertising promises health, long life, sexual success, wealth, companionship, popularity, and acceptance. Industry defenders argue that people understand and accept these as allowable exaggerations, not as deception. Yet 84% of millennials say they do not like advertising, and when asked on a scale of 1 to 5 to rate the level of trust they have in advertising, with 1 being no trust, the average score was a 2.2 (Allen, 2014).

ADVERTISING EXPLOITS CHILDREN The average American child, aged 2 to 11, is exposed to 25,600 television commercials, or 10,700 minutes of ads, a year, and more than 40% of this exposure is in programming not primarily intended for kids (Rideout, 2014). Countries like Norway and Sweden, on the other hand, completely ban television ads aimed at kids, as does the Canadian province of Quebec. Ads and commercialism are increasingly invading schools—90% of American high school students and 70% of American elementary school students attend schools that allow on-campus food advertising, 90% of which is for soda, sports drinks, and other beverages (Morrison, 2014). In 2016 the 35,000-member United Teachers of Los Angeles, representing the nation's second-largest school district, wrote a formal letter to the McDonald's Operators Association of Southern California demanding that it cease its McTeacher's Night, an in-school promotion at which teachers wear McDonald's uniforms and make and serve the fast food to students and their families at full price. The event is billed as a "fund-raiser," but only 15% to 20% of the proceeds are returned to participating schools (Anderson, 2016). Companies spend nearly $20 billion a year targeting children, with a quarter of that amount spent touting "mostly unhealthy products." And not only can a typical first grader recognize 200 logos, but kids ages 3 to 5 show recognition rates as high as 92% for 50 different brands in 16 product categories—McDonald's was most recognizable—demonstrating that children as young as 3 can readily recognize the brands they see advertised (Rettner, 2013; Andronikidis & Lambrianidou, 2010).

Critics contend that children are simply not intellectually capable of interpreting the intent of these ads, nor are they able before the age of 7 or 8 to rationally judge the worth of the advertising claims. This makes children's advertising inherently unethical. Television advertising to kids is especially questionable because children consume it in the home—with implicit parental approval, and most often without parental supervision. The question ad critics ask is, "If parents would never allow living salespeople to enter their homes to sell their children products, why do they allow the most sophisticated salespeople of all to do it for 20 minutes every hour every Saturday morning?" Social critic Henry Giroux argues that advertising directed at children is

> devaluing them by treating them as yet another "market" to be commodified and exploited . . . [It] is conscripting an entire generation into a world of consumerism in which commodities and brand loyalty become the most important markers of identity and primary frameworks for mediating one's relationship to the world . . . Kids may think they are immune to the incessant call to "buy, buy, buy" and to think only about "me, me, me," but what is actually happening is a selective elimination and reordering of the possible modes of political, social, and ethical vocabularies made available to youth. (2011)

The particular issue of fast-food and snack advertising to children is the subject of the essay "Kids' Advertising: Is Self-Regulation Enough?"

CULTURAL FORUM
Kids' Advertising: Is Self-Regulation Enough?

There is no shortage of critics of advertising to children, especially advertising that promotes unhealthy diets. In 1983, companies spent $100 million on child-focused advertising; today they annually spend close to $20 billion, and much of that money is for fast food, cereal, and snacks. Opponents of advertising to kids point to social science evidence demonstrating a strong correlation between exposure to advertising and childhood obesity. One in six children and teens is obese, up threefold from a generation ago, leading the Federal Trade Commission to call childhood obesity the "most serious health crisis facing today's youth." The 65,000-member American Academy of Pediatrics has called for a ban on fast-food commercials on kids' television shows (which the Disney Company agreed in 2012 to do). The U.S. Government Accountability Office has demanded greater FCC oversight of kids' television advertising.

The advertising and fast-food industries have responded with a number of plans that they hope will help protect kids while maintaining their own freedom of expression. Television sponsors have promised to strictly adhere to commercial time limits set by the 1990 Children's Television Act, and the Better Business Bureau's Children's Food and Beverage Advertising Initiative said it would enforce voluntary nutritional standards among its member companies. The National Restaurant Association launched an initiative among its members, including companies such as Burger King and Denny's, to offer and promote healthful kids' meals, a move mirrored by several companies such as Coca-Cola and a number of kid-oriented media outlets like Cartoon Network. The question in the cultural forum, however, is how to find the correct balance between freedom of commercial speech and the protection of children.

Advertisers and the fast-food industry argue that they are entitled to First Amendment protection, so self-regulation is more than enough. Critics say the First Amendment offers no protection to advertising aimed at kids because children do not possess the ability to tell good messages from bad—the bedrock assumption of the First Amendment. Enter your voice. Should children be considered a special class of people in need of extra protection? Or does the First Amendment outweigh all concerns about children's intellectual ability to understand ads?

ADVERTISING DEMEANS AND CORRUPTS CULTURE In our culture we value beauty, kindness, prestige, family, love, and success. As human beings we need food, shelter, and the maintenance of the species, in other words, sex. Advertising succeeds by appealing to these values and needs. The basis for this persuasive strategy is the **AIDA approach**—to persuade consumers, advertising must attract *attention*, create *interest*, stimulate *desire*, and promote *action*. According to industry critics, however, problems arise when important aspects of human existence are reduced to the consumption of brand-name consumer products. Freedom is choosing between a Big Gulp and a canned soda at 7-Eleven. Being a good mother is as simple as buying a bottle of Downy Fabric Softener. Success is drinking Chivas Regal. Love is giving your husband a shirt without ring-around-the-collar or your fiancée a diamond worth two months' salary.

Critics argue that ours has become a **consumer culture**—a culture in which personal worth and identity reside not in ourselves but in the products with which we surround ourselves. The consumer culture is corrupting because it imposes new definitions that serve the advertiser and not the culture on traditionally important aspects of our lives. If love, for example, can be bought rather than being something that has to be nurtured, how important can it be? If success is not something an individual values for the personal sense of accomplishment but rather is something chased for the material things associated with it, how does the culture evaluate success? Name the five most successful people you know. How many teachers did you name? How many social workers? How many wealthy or famous people did you name?

Critics further contend that the consumer culture also demeans the individuals who live in it. A common advertising strategy for stimulating desire and suggesting action is to imply that we are inadequate and should not be satisfied with ourselves as we are. We are too fat or too thin, our hair is in need of improvement, our clothes are all wrong, and our spouses don't respect us. Personal improvement is only a purchase away.

The ad-created consumer culture, according to former Wieden + Kennedy and Martin Agency executive Jelly Helm (his clients included Nike, Coke, and Microsoft), has produced an America that is "sick. . . . We work too hard so that we can buy things we don't need, made by factory workers who are paid too little, and produced in ways that threaten the very survival of the earth." It has produced an America that "will be remembered as the greatest wealth-producer ever. It will be a culture remembered for its promise and might and its tremendous achievements in technology and health. It also will be remembered as a culture of hedonism to rival any culture that has ever existed" (Helm, 2002).

Scope and Nature of the Advertising Industry

The proliferation of the different types of sales pitches described in the opening vignette is the product of an avalanche of advertising. Advertisers are exploring new ways to be seen and heard, to stand out, to be remembered, and to be effective. With so many kinds of commercial messages, the definition of advertising must be very broad. For our purposes, advertising is mediated messages paid for by and identified with a business or institution seeking to increase the likelihood that those who consume those messages will act or think as the advertiser wishes.

The American advertising industry annually spends more than $420 billion to place commercial messages before the public ("U.S. Ad Spending," 2016). This amount does not include the billions of dollars spent in the planning, production, and distribution of those ads. An overwhelming proportion of all this activity is conducted through and by advertising agencies.

The Advertising Agency

There are approximately 6,000 ad agencies operating in the United States, employing roughly 500,000 people, and ad agency employment is at its highest level since 2001 ("Staffing Up,"

2016). Fewer than 500 agencies annually earn more than $1 million, and while the giant agencies garner most of our attention, there is significant growth among **boutique agencies**, smaller, more personalized, and task-specific ad agencies (for example, dealing primarily with social-media marketing) or product-specific agencies (for example, handling only pet supply accounts). Many agencies produce the ads they develop, and virtually all buy time and space in various media for their clients. Production is billed at an agreed-upon price called a **retainer**; placement of advertising in media is compensated through **commissions**, typically 15% of the cost of the time or space. Commissions account for as much as 75% of the income of larger agencies. You can see the ad revenues of the top-earning U.S. agencies in Figure 2.

Ad agencies are usually divided into departments, the number determined by the size and services of the operation. Smaller agencies might contract with outside companies for the services of these typical ad agency departments:

- *Administration* is the agency's management and accounting operations.
- *Account management* is typically handled by an account executive who serves as liaison between agency and client, keeping communication flowing between the two and heading the team of specialists assigned by the agency to the client.
- The *creative department* is where the advertising is developed from idea to ad. It involves copywriting, graphic design, and often the actual production of the piece—for example, radio, television, and Web spots.
- The *media department* makes the decisions about where and when to place ads and then buys the appropriate time or space. (See Figure 3 for a breakdown of ad spending by medium in the United States.) The effectiveness of a given placement is judged by its **cost per thousand (CPM)**, the cost of reaching 1,000 audience members. For example, an ad that costs $20,000 to place in a major magazine and is read by 1 million people has a CPM of $20.

U.S. revenues in millions of dollars by agency rank, parent company, and headquarters

BBDO Worldwide (Omnicom), New York
1    $603

McCann (Interpublic), New York
2    $563

J. Walter Thompson Co.* (WPP), New York
3    $505

Y&R* (WPP), New York
4    $455

TBWA Worldwide (Omnicom), New York
5    $362

Grey* (WPP), New York
6    $336

DDB Worldwide (Omnicom), New York
7    $320

Leo Burnett Worldwide/ARC* (Publicis), Chicago
8    $289

Publicis Worldwide* (Publicis), Paris
9    $288

Saatchi & Saatchi* (Publicis), New York
10    $282

*Denotes non–U.S. ownership

◀ **Figure 2** Largest U.S. Ad Agencies, 2015.
Source: "Ad Agencies: U.S." Advertising Age, *May 2, 2016, 20.*

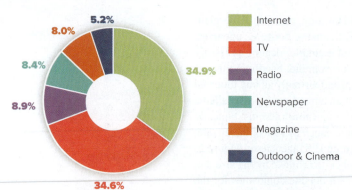

▲ **Figure 3** U.S. Ad Spending, by Medium, 2017.

Source: "Share of U. S. Ad Spending by Medium from Zenith," Advertising Age Marketing Fact Pack, December 19, 2016, 6.

- *Market research* tests product viability in the market, the best venues for commercial messages, the nature and characteristics of potential buyers, and sometimes the effectiveness of the ads.
- Many larger agencies have *public relations departments* as well.

Types of Advertising

The advertising produced and placed by ad agencies can be classified according to the purpose of the advertising and the target market. You may be familiar with the following types of advertising:

Institutional or corporate advertising. Companies do more than just sell products; companies also promote their names and reputations. If a company name inspires confidence, selling its products is easier. Some institutional or corporate advertising promotes only the organization's image, such as "FTD Florists support the U.S. Olympic Team." But some advertising sells the image at the same time it sells the product: "You can be sure if it's Westinghouse."

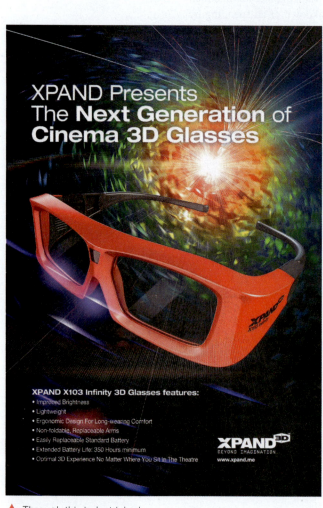

▲ Through this industrial ad appearing in *Variety*, XPAND hopes to attract movie theater owners to its brand of 3D glasses.

©Courtesy of Definition Branding & Marketing

Trade or professional advertising. Typically found in trade and professional publications, messages aimed at retailers do not necessarily push the product or brand but rather promote product issues of importance to the retailer—volume, marketing support, profit potential, distribution plans, and promotional opportunities.

Retail advertising. A large part of the advertising we see every day focuses on products sold by retailers like Sears and Macy's. Ads are typically local, reaching consumers where they live and shop.

Promotional retail advertising. Typically placed by retailers, promotional advertising focuses not on a product but on a promotion, a special event held by a retailer. "Midnight Madness Sale" and "Back to School Sale" are two promotions that often benefit from heavy advertising, particularly in newspapers and local television.

Industrial advertising. Advertising of products and services directed toward a particular industry is usually found in industry trade publications. For example, *Broadcasting & Cable*, the primary trade magazine for the television industry, runs ads from program syndicators hoping to sell their shows to stations. It also runs ads from transmitter and camera manufacturers.

National consumer advertising. National consumer advertising constitutes the majority of what we see in the media we routinely consume. It is usually product advertising, commissioned by the manufacturer—McDonald's, Honda, Cheerios, Sony, Nike—aimed at potential buyers.

Direct market advertising. Product or service advertising aimed at likely buyers rather than at all consumers is called direct market advertising. These targeted consumers are reached through direct mail, catalogs, and telemarketing. This advertising can be personalized—"Yes, BRUCE FRIEDBERG, you can drive a Lexus for less than you think"—and customized. Computer data from credit card and other purchases, zip codes, telephone numbers, and organizational memberships are a few of the ways consumers are identified.

Join **BaZinga** in exploring tomorrow's technology, TODAY!

STANLEY BARAN

Please enjoy a free copy of **BaZinga**, on us.

Dear **Stanley Baran**,

Technology moves at a lightning pace today. It is easy to get left behind in the cosmic dust of our ever evolving digital society. At **BaZinga** we work tirelessly to bring our readers the most up-to-date information even before technology updates hit the market. **BaZinga** was the first magazine to break the news that in 2016 Apple will be coming out with a budget priced line of computers under the Pear label. We were also the first magazine to report the news that the Large Hadron Collider will be hosting next year's *Tour de' France*.

With **BaZinga**, the line *"question everything"* is not just a catch phrase; it is the key to reading our magazine; it is the key to life itself. And **BaZinga** can bring you that key!

Readers of **BaZinga** enjoy many monthly favorites such as *"The Physicist's Conundrum"*, where leading physicists explore whether matter truly matters. *"The IT is IN"* answers questions from readers on why their help desk should be renamed the helpless desk. And who doesn't love *"Can you DIG it?"* where our team of archeologists share all the dirt?

Why are you hesitating? Return the form today with the box marked "YES" and we will rush you your FREE COPY of **BaZinga**, where we explore tomorrow's technology, TODAY!

Sincerely,

Crystal O'Graphy
Editor-in-Chief

> **STANLEY BARAN**
> Send for your FREE issue of **BaZinga** TODAY!

P.S. To receive your free copy of **BaZinga** check the "Yes" box and return your postcard today! You never know when that next issue of BaZinga might report on the next big meteorite headed towards Earth, or worse yet, who might be riding that meteorite!

◀ In this direct marketing piece, the advertiser has not only personalized the pitch—Dear Stanley Baran—but has also targeted this consumer's particular interests in the environment and technology based on its knowledge of his magazine subscriptions.
©Brand X/Superstock RF

◀ Public service advertising allows advertisers to use their skills to serve society. Here is a still from a spot for the National Sexual Violence Resource Center.
©From "Public Service Announcement Posters" by the National Sexual Violence Resource Center, 2012. Available from http://www.nsvrc.org. Copyright 2012 by the National Sexual Violence Resource Center. Reprinted with permission.

Out-of-home advertising. As we saw in the opening vignette, advertising is inescapable. One reason is that we are exposed to advertising even when away from home and otherwise not actually engaged in media consumption. Out-of-home advertising, which globally accounts for more than $49 billion in annual ad spending, can include ads on billboards, street furniture, transit vehicles, and the digital screens we encounter everywhere from the gas pump to the DMV (Friedman, 2017).

Public service advertising. Advertising that does not sell commercial products or services but promotes organizations and themes of importance to the public is public service advertising. Ads for the Heart Fund, the United Negro College Fund, and MADD are typical of this form. They are usually carried free of charge by the medium that houses them.

The Regulation of Advertising

The FTC is the primary federal agency for the regulation of advertising. The FCC regulates the commercial practices of the broadcasting industry, and individual states can police deceptive advertising through their own regulatory and criminal bureaucracies. In the deregulation movement of 1980, oversight by the FTC changed from regulating unfair and deceptive advertising to regulating and enforcing complaints *against* deceptive advertising, typically from a brand's competitor.

The FTC has several options for enforcement when it determines that a false-claim complaint against an advertiser is justified. It can issue a **cease-and-desist order** demanding that the practice be stopped. It can impose fines. It can order the creation and distribution of **corrective advertising**—that is, a new set of ads must be produced by the offender that corrects the original misleading effort. For example, in 2012, U.S. tobacco companies were ordered to run corrective ads containing wording such as "Cigarettes cause cancer, lung disease, heart attacks, and premature death."

One of the greatest difficulties for the FTC is finding the line between false or deceptive advertising and **puffery**—that little lie that makes advertising more entertaining than it might otherwise be. "Whiter than white" and "stronger than dirt" are just two examples of puffery. On the assumption that the public does not read commercials literally—we know that the Jolly Green Giant does not exist—the courts and the FTC allow a certain amount of exaggeration. Puffery may be allowed, but many in the ad industry dislike its slippery slope; puffery, says Keller & Heckman's Richard Leighton, means "never having to say you're sorry for untruths or exaggerated claims" (in Greenberg, 2009).

The FTC and courts, however, do recognize that an advertisement can be false in a number of ways. An advertisement is false if it does any one of the following:

- *Lies outright.* Reebok claimed its EasyTone shoes produced 11% greater strength and tone in hamstring muscles than did regular walking shoes. The FTC said, "Prove it." Reebok couldn't. Ads for POM Wonderful said its pomegranate juice is "backed by $25 million in medical research" and is "proven to fight for cardiovascular, prostate, and erectile health." "Not so," said the FTC.

- *Does not tell the whole truth.* Miller Lite's "new taste protector cap" does indeed better preserve the taste of the beer. But ads touting this feature do not tell the whole truth because Miller Lite's bottle caps are exactly the same as all other bottled beers' and have no taste-protecting characteristics beyond those of ordinary cans and bottles.

- *Lies by implication, using words, design, production device, sound, or a combination of these.* Television commercials for children's toys now end with the product shown in actual size against a neutral background (a shot called an **island**). This is required because production techniques such as low camera angles and close-ups can make these toys seem larger or better than they actually are.

Measuring the Effectiveness of Advertising

It might seem reasonable to judge the effectiveness of an ad campaign by a subsequent increase in sales. But many factors other than advertising influence how well a product fares, including changes in the economy, product quality, breadth of distribution, and competitors' pricing and promotion strategies. Department store magnate John Wanamaker is said to have complained in the late 1880s, "I know that fifty percent of my advertising is wasted. I just don't know which fifty percent." Today's advertisers feel much the same way, and as you might imagine, they find this a less-than-comforting situation. Agencies, therefore, turn to research to provide greater certainty.

A number of techniques may be used before an ad or ad campaign is released. **Copy testing**—measuring the effectiveness of advertising messages by showing them to consumers—is used for all forms of advertising. It is sometimes conducted with focus groups, collections of people brought together to see the advertising and discuss it with agency and client personnel. Sometimes copy testing employs **consumer juries**. These people, considered to be representative of the target market, review a number of approaches or variations of a campaign or ad. **Forced exposure**, used primarily for television advertising, requires advertisers to bring consumers to a theater or other facility (typically with the promise of a gift or other payment), where they see a television program, complete with the new commercials. People are asked their brand preferences before the show and then after. In this way, the effectiveness of the commercials can be gauged.

Once the campaign or ad is before the public, a number of different tests can be employed to evaluate the effectiveness of the ad. In **recognition tests** people who have seen a given publication are asked, in person or by phone, whether they remember seeing specific ads. In **recall testing** consumers are asked, again in person or by phone, to identify which print or broadcast ads they most easily remember. This recall can be unaided, that is, the researcher offers no hints ("Have you seen any interesting commercials or ads lately?"), or aided, that is, the researcher identifies a specific class of products ("Have you seen any interesting pizza commercials lately?"). In recall testing, the advertisers assume that an easily recalled ad is an effective ad. **Awareness tests** make this same assumption, but they are not aimed at specific ads. Their goal is to measure the cumulative effect of a campaign in terms of "consumer consciousness" of a product. A likely question in an awareness test, usually made by telephone, is "What brands of laundry detergent can you name?"

What these research techniques lack is the ability to demonstrate the link that is of most interest to the client—did the ad move the consumer to buy the product? The industry hopes that all-important connection can be better discovered using **neuromarketing research**—biometric measures such as brainwaves, facial expressions, eye tracking, sweating, and heart rate monitoring (Bell, 2015). Because the unconscious accounts for the vast majority of the way peoples' brains process information, these methods tap consumers' unconscious reactions to marketing and advertising. This research is not without its critics, however, who argue that because neuromarketing appeals to the base level of human consciousness, it exploits consumers' nonreasoned, instinctual responses. Still, industry dissatisfaction with more traditional research methods continues to fuel work on neuromarketing research.

Trends and Convergence in Advertising

In the summer of 2005, the world's largest advertiser, Procter & Gamble, announced that it would cut $300 million from its television ad expenditures, a 15% drop from its typical annual spending on that medium. Said Jim Stengel, head of global marketing for the company, "I believe today's marketing model is broken. We're applying antiquated thinking and work systems to a new world of possibilities" (in Auletta, 2005, pp. 35–36). When the country's second-largest advertiser, General Motors, followed suit a year later, slashing its 2006 ad budget by $600 million to shift its marketing resources toward "channels such as direct marketing, websites, online video, event marketing, branded entertainment, and internet advertising," *Advertising Age*'s Jean Halliday called it "a drop so stunning it should convince even the staunchest doubters that the age of mass-media marketing is going the way of the horse and buggy" (2007, p. 1). These public rebukes of the traditional advertising model demonstrated what most industry professionals already knew—their industry was in need of change in, and some even said reinvention of, its *economics*, *creativity*, and *relationship with*

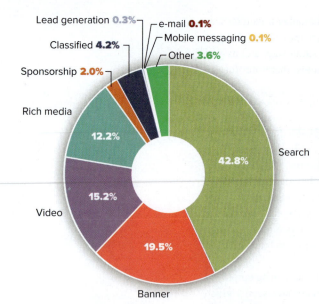

Lead generation **0.3%**
e-mail **0.1%**
Mobile messaging **0.1%**
Classified **4.2%**
Other **3.6%**
Sponsorship **2.0%**
Rich media
12.2%
Search
42.8%
Video
15.2%
19.5%
Banner

▲ **Figure 4** Percentage of U.S. Online Ad Spending, by Format, 2017.

Source: "US Digital Display Ad Spending to Surpass Search Ad Spending in 2016," eMarketer, January 11, 2016. Online: https:// www.emarketer.com/Article /US-Digital-Display-Ad-Spending -Surpass-Search-Ad-Spending -2016/1013442

consumers. The advertising business is facing its "chaos scenario," or as media writer Bob Garfield called it, "a jarring media universe in which traditional forms of mass entertainment swiftly disappear and advertisers are left in the lurch" (in Klosterman, 2005, p. 63). This new, jarring media universe is forged by the interaction of converging technologies and the changes they drive in how, when, and why people consume them (and the ads they contain).

New and Converging Technologies

The production of advertising has inevitably been altered by computers. Computer graphics, morphing (digitally combining and transforming images), and other special effects are now common in national retail television advertising. And the same technology used to change the ads behind the batter in a televised baseball game is now employed to insert product placements into programs where no placement originally existed—a character who was once eating an unbranded cookie can now munch an Oreo.

Computer databases and computerized printing have fueled the rapid growth of direct market advertising, and computerized printing has made possible split runs and other specialized editions of national magazines (see the chapter on magazines). But it is digital advertising, the convergence of all traditional forms of advertising with new digital technologies, that is attracting the most industry interest. In 2007 U.S. online ad spending was $19.5 billion; in 2016 it was $72.1 billion (Figure 4). Internet advertising exceeds that of radio; in 2012 it surpassed that of magazines and newspapers combined (Ives, 2012); and in 2016 it surpassed television (Mandese, 2016b).

Web advertising has matured since the first display advertising, or **banners**, static online billboards placed conspicuously somewhere on a Web page, appeared in May 1994 (D'Angelo, 2009). Other forms are **search marketing**, advertising sold next to or in search results produced by users' keyword searches; **rich media**, sophisticated, interactive Web advertising, usually employing sound and video; **lead generation** directing users who've expressed an interest to a brand's sales website; and online classified advertising.

Smartphones, Tablets, and Social Networking Sites

Boosting all forms of digital advertising is their movement to mobile technologies like smartphones and tablets and the expansion of social networking sites. U.S mobile ad spending was $33 billion in 2016 and is expected to grow to more than $72 billion by 2021, driven primarily by search and social network marketing (O'Malley, 2017).

Industry data indicate that smartphone and tablet advertising encourages **e-commerce**, the buying of products and services online. In 2016, for the first time, people made more of their purchases online than they did in stores, and as online shopping accelerated, so did the use of mobile devices to make purchases. Forty-four percent of mobile device users made at least two purchases over a three-month span (Farber, 2016). That's the good news for advertisers. The bad news is that because the "mobile device experience is a much more intimate experience" and our tablets and smartphones know quite a bit about us, including where we are at the moment, who we communicate with, and what we like, "it's easy to get 'creepy' and alienate customers" (Gray, 2014). Highly targeted mobile marketing, therefore, walks an even finer personalization versus privacy line than do other forms of online commercial interaction.

Social networking sites are clearly a boon to advertisers, as they can direct very specific messages to very specific users based on their freely provided information, a fact that does not make everyone happy. Advertisers also take advantage of sites' interactivity, and virtually every company of any size has at the very least a Facebook and Twitter presence. Social media sites took in more than $10 billion in advertising in 2016 in the United States and $31 billion globally, with Facebook, Twitter, and LinkedIn commanding most of that revenue

("Statistics and Facts," 2016; "Ad Age Social," 2016). Digital advertising in all its forms sits firmly at the center of the change buffeting today's ad industry because of its low cost (relative to traditional media), great reach, and, most important, interactivity, which gives it an accountability unparalleled in the traditional media.

NEW ECONOMICS Consumers are increasingly dissatisfied with hypercommercialism in other media and the lack of relevancy that much advertising has for them. They are becoming resistant to and resentful of much of the marketing they encounter, as you saw earlier in this chapter. As a result, many advertisers are now less interested in CPM, focusing instead on **return on investment (ROI)**. After all, who cares how many thousands you are reaching if they reject your message? Industry professionals who look at Internet and Web advertising and see that it is ideally suited for increased ROI have begun asking why all media can't offer some of that benefit. "As technology increasingly enables fine targeting and interaction between marketer and consumer," Bob Garfield argued, "the old measurement and deployment standards are primitive almost to the point of absurdity" (2005, p. 58).

Rather than simple brand exposure, measured by CPM, advertisers have begun to demand accountability. As such, the Web's **performance-based advertising**, for example, provides the ideal. The website carrying the ad gets paid only when the consumer takes some specific action, making a purchase or linking to the sponsor's site. This Web-inspired demand for accountability led to calls for the development of a new measure of the *effectiveness of all advertising*—**engagement**. Beyond moving advertising dollars to platforms promising greater engagement, demands for accountability can be seen in a number of innovations that threaten the traditional agency–brand relationship described earlier in this chapter: Clients are increasingly demanding from agencies—and receiving—agreements on campaign-specific outcomes and consensus on **accountability metrics**—that is, how the effectiveness of a specific ad or campaign will be judged. Some agencies now offer money-back guarantees if they cannot improve a brand's ROI, and the introduction of **value-compensation programs** in which all or part of the payment of an agency's fees is based on meeting preestablished goals. A majority of all agency/client contracts now contain these pay-for-performance incentives.

One reason there is increased demand for accountability, especially for online advertising, is the growth of **programmatic buying**, automated, data-driven buying of online advertising. Programmatic buying now accounts for over a quarter of all digital ad spending. Because most online advertising is targeted to some degree to specific user demographics (if not specific users), the data used for programmatic buying can be manipulated by the creation of fake impressions or views. These false positives are created primarily by *bots*, in effect "robot" users. Sophisticated bots can take over any computer that's online. They can then simulate human Internet activity, for example commandeering the mouse and moving the cursor over ads to create exposures. They can even fake search histories and cookies to become demographically appealing to programmatic buying algorithms. This **programmatic ad fraud** annually costs advertisers more than $16 billion (O'Reilly, 2017). In response, in 2016 a consortium of advertising industry professional groups created the Trustworthy Accountability Group to identify and eliminate ad fraud, in part through the implementation of an antifraud certification program intended to serve as the industry standard.

NEW CREATIVITY Virtually all advertisers understand that the Internet-fueled fragmentation and democratization of media require a new type of appeal to consumers. If people are increasingly rejecting traditional *mass* media and the commercial messages they carry, the industry must become more creative in its messages and how it gets them to desired consumers. We've already seen many examples—product placement in all media, specially designed and targeted commercials delivered through cable or called up by DVR, online advergames, and the examples of ambient advertising that opened this chapter.

Much of advertising's creative community has learned to distinguish between typical, often unappreciated contextual advertising on the Web and imaginative video advertising delivered by the Web, mobile technologies, and portable game devices. For example, traditional big-time television advertisers like BMW, IKEA, Lincoln-Mercury, Hidden Valley Ranch, and Burger King have moved significant amounts of their advertising dollars to the

▲ *Comedians in Cars Getting Coffee.* One hundred million streams of creative commercials and brand placements for sponsor Acura.

©*Andrew Hetherington 2013/Redux Pictures*

creation and distribution of short online films, sometimes episodic and often featuring well-known actors, to tout their products. Among the best received has been *Comedians in Cars Getting Coffee*, sponsored by Acura. The carmaker gave comedian Jerry Seinfeld free rein on the creation of the show's commercials and brand placements. The 20-minute ad-libbed conversations between Seinfeld and his funny guests as they drive to a coffee shop have drawn more than 100 million streams since the show's 2012 debut (Koblin & Barnes, 2016). Other examples abound. Qualcomm's *Lifeline* is a 30-minute thriller set in Shanghai directed and partly written by an Academy Award–winning writer and featuring actress Oliva Munn. *Ballad of the Dreadnought* is a 40-minute documentary from guitar maker C. F. Martin narrated by actor Jeff Daniels. "You can create content that is compelling, and you don't have to spend money to place it on TV. We think this is the direction advertising is headed," says commercial producer Steve Golin. "There is a lot of resistance to watching bread-and-butter advertising" (in Tugend, 2016, p. B3).

NEW RELATIONSHIP WITH CONSUMERS   The Internet, as we've seen throughout this text, makes mass communication less of a monologue and more of a conversation. Today's consumers are no longer passive media *receivers*, taking whatever the television networks and movie studios insist they should. Instead, they are empowered media *users*, increasingly free to control and shape the content they receive. In the relative youth of Internet advertising, Ogilvy & Mather's vice chair, Steve Hayden, predicted that "as all media becomes addressable, all media becomes refusable." He argued that because the consumer now has the power to accept or reject content, an advertiser has to enter into a transaction with him or her, saying, "'I'll give you this content in exchange for your attention,' which has always been the model of mass advertising. But now, I've got to make that deal on a person-to-person basis" (in Kirsner, 2005). Indeed, 79% of adult American consumers say brands must actively demonstrate "they understand and care about me" before they consider doing business with them (Wunderman, 2017).

This new **permission marketing**, of necessity, has led to a rethinking of the relationship between advertiser and consumer, one in which they act as partners, sharing information for mutual benefit. The new model of advertising is, as Hayden predicted, a conversation between marketers and **prosumers**, proactive consumers who reject most traditional advertising and use multiple sources—traditional media, the Internet, product-rating magazines, recommendations from friends in the know—not only to research a product but also to negotiate price and other benefits. Economists call this *expressing disapproval.* Consumers now have two choices: *exit* (they simply do not buy the product) or *voice* (they explain exactly why they are dissatisfied and what they'd like instead). Active media users, who are at the same time skilled prosumers who have access to interactive technologies, ensure that voice will, indeed, replace exit as the measure of advertisers' success.

Increased Audience Segmentation

Advertisers face other challenges as well. As the number of media outlets for advertising grows, and as audiences for traditional media are increasingly fragmented, advertisers have been forced to refine their ability to reach and speak to ever-narrower audience segments. Digital technology facilitates this practice, but segmentation exists apart from the new technologies. The ethnic composition of the United States is changing, and advertising is keeping pace. African Americans constitute approximately 13% of the total U.S. population, and Hispanics, now the nation's largest minority, make up approximately 18% (more than half of both populations is younger than 30). **Demographic segmentation**—the practice of appealing to audiences defined by varying personal and social characteristics such as race/ethnicity, gender, and economic level—is the ad industry's dominant form of targeting

(Mandese, 2016a). This is no surprise as the number of African Americans with incomes over $60,000 is growing at a faster rate than any other group (Love, 2016); the growth rate in Hispanic "buying power" (disposable income) is double that of all other groups ("Hispanic Influence," 2016), and the buying power of the LGBT community is equal to that of any other minority group (Green, 2016).

Psychographics

In addition to demographic segmentation, advertisers are making increased use of **psychographic segmentation**—that is, appealing to consumer groups with similar lifestyles, attitudes, values, and behavior patterns.

Psychographics entered advertising in the 1970s and has received considerable attention as advertisers work to reach increasingly disparate consumers in increasingly segmented media. **VALS**, a psychographic segmentation strategy that classifies consumers according to values and lifestyles, is indicative of this lifestyle segmentation. Developed by SRI Consulting (2015), a California consulting company, VALS II divides consumers into eight VALS segments. Each segment is characterized by specific values and lifestyles, demographics, and, of greatest importance to advertisers, buying patterns. The segments, including some of their key demographic identifiers, are listed here:

▲ The growing U.S. Hispanic population is increasingly targeted by advertisers in both English and Spanish. Here is an example from Dove from Unilever.
©Spencer Grant/PhotoEdit

Innovators: Successful, sophisticated, high self-esteem; have abundant resources; are change leaders and receptive to new ideas and technologies.

Thinkers: Motivated by ideas; mature, satisfied, comfortable, reflective; value order, knowledge, and responsibility; well educated, actively seek out information.

Achievers: Have goal-oriented lifestyles and deep commitment to career and family; social lives structured around family, place of worship, and work.

Experiencers: Motivated by self-expression; young and impulsive consumers; quickly become enthusiastic about new possibilities but equally quick to cool; seek variety and excitement.

Believers: Motivated by ideals; conservative, conventional, with concrete beliefs based on traditional, established codes: family, religion, community, and nation.

Strivers: Trendy, fun loving; motivated by achievement; concerned about opinions and approval of others; money defines success, but don't have enough to meet their desires; favor stylish products.

Makers: Motivated by self-expression; express themselves through work/projects; practical; have constructive skills; and value self-sufficiency.

Survivors: Live narrowly focused lives; have few resources; comfortable with the familiar; primarily concerned with safety and security; focus on meeting needs rather than fulfilling desires.

Globalization

As media and national economies have globalized, advertising has adapted. U.S. agencies are increasingly merging with, acquiring, or affiliating with agencies from other parts of the world. Revisit Figure 2. You'll see that 6 of the top 10 U.S. agencies are owned by foreign companies. In addition to the globalization of media and economies, a second force driving this trend is the demographic fact that today 80% of the world's population lives in developing countries, and nearly two-thirds of all the people in the world live in Asia alone. The industry

▶ **Figure 5** World's 10 Biggest Global Advertisers, 2016.

Source: "World's 25 Largest Advertisers," Advertising Age, *December 5, 2016, 10.*

©*Brand X Pictures/PunchStock RF*

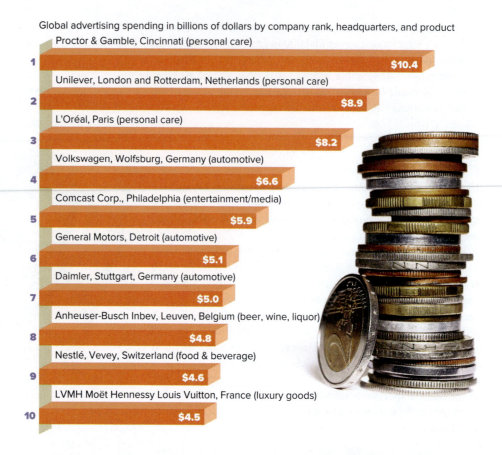

Global advertising spending in billions of dollars by company rank, headquarters, and product

1	Proctor & Gamble, Cincinnati (personal care)	$10.4
2	Unilever, London and Rotterdam, Netherlands (personal care)	$8.9
3	L'Oréal, Paris (personal care)	$8.2
4	Volkswagen, Wolfsburg, Germany (automotive)	$6.6
5	Comcast Corp., Philadelphia (entertainment/media)	$5.9
6	General Motors, Detroit (automotive)	$5.1
7	Daimler, Stuttgart, Germany (automotive)	$5.0
8	Anheuser-Busch Inbev, Leuven, Belgium (beer, wine, liquor)	$4.8
9	Nestlé, Vevey, Switzerland (food & beverage)	$4.6
10	LVMH Moët Hennessy Louis Vuitton, France (luxury goods)	$4.5

is already putting its clients in touch with these consumers. Foreign ad spending first exceeded U.S. totals in 1980, and while major media ad spending in America accounts for a third of the world's total, ad spending in *developing* nations is growing at a faster rate than it is in the developed world. In fact, the Asia-Pacific region surpassed North America as the world's biggest advertising market in 2015, and emerging markets such as the "BRIC" countries (Brazil, Russia, India, and China) routinely post year-to-year rates of growth in advertising that exceed that of the United States. Figure 5 shows the world's 10 biggest global advertisers.

DEVELOPING MEDIA LITERACY SKILLS
Interpreting Intentional Imprecision

Advertisers often use intentional imprecision in words and phrases to say something other than the precise truth, and they do so in all forms of advertising—profit and nonprofit, scrupulously honest and less so. There are three categories of intentional imprecision: unfinished statements, qualifiers, and connotatively loaded words and expressions.

We are all familiar with *unfinished statements*, such as the one for the battery that "lasts twice as long." Others include "You can be sure if it's Westinghouse," "Magnavox gives you more," and "Easy-Off makes oven cleaning easier." A literate advertising consumer should ask, "Twice as long as *what*?" "Of *what* can I be sure?" "Gives me more of *what*?" "Easier than *what*?" Better, more, stronger, whiter, faster—all are comparative adjectives whose true purpose is to create a comparison between two or more things. When the other half of the comparison is not identified, intentional imprecision is being used to create the illusion of comparison.

Qualifiers are words that limit a claim. A product "helps" relieve stress, for instance. It may not relieve stress as well as rest and better planning and organization. But once the qualifier "helps" appears, an advertiser is free to make just about any claim for the product because all the ad really says is that it helps, not that it does anything in and of itself. It's the consumer's fault for misreading. A product may "fight" grime, but there is no promise that it will win. In the statement "Texaco's coal gasification process could mean you won't have to worry about how it affects the environment," "could" relieves the advertiser of all responsibility. "Could" does not mean "will." Moreover, the fact that you *could stop worrying about the environment* does not mean the product does not harm the environment—only that you could stop worrying about it.

Some qualifiers are more apparent. "Taxes not included," "limited time only," "only at participating locations," "prices may vary," "some assembly required," "additional charges may apply," and "batteries not included" are qualifiers presented after the primary claims have been made. Often these words are spoken quickly at the end of radio and television commercials, or they appear in small print on the screen or at the bottom of a newspaper or magazine ad.

Other qualifiers are part of the product's advertising slogan. Boodles gin is "the ultra-refined British gin that only the world's costliest methods could produce. Boodles. The world's costliest British gin." After intimating that the costliest methods are somehow necessary to make the best gin, this advertiser qualifies its product as the costliest "British" gin. There may be costlier, and possibly better, Irish, U.S., Russian, and Canadian gins. Many sugared children's cereals employ the tactic of displaying the cereal on a table with fruit, milk, and toast. The announcer says or the copy reads, "Coco Yummies are *a part of* this complete breakfast"—so is the tablecloth. But the cereal, in and of itself, adds little to the nutritional completeness of the meal. It is "a part of" it.

Advertising is full of words that are *connotatively loaded.* "Best-selling" may say more about a product's advertising and distribution system than its quality. "More of the pain-relieving medicine doctors prescribe most" means aspirin. Cherry-flavored products have no cherries in them. On the ecolabeling front, "no additives" is meaningless; the manufacturer decides what is and is not an additive. "Cruelty free"—again, the company decides. Other connotatively loaded ecolabels are "hypoallergenic" (advertiser-created, scientific-sounding, and meaningless), "fragrance free" (you can't smell the scent because of the chemicals used to hide it), "nontoxic" (won't kill you, but could cause other health problems), and "earth smart," "green," and "nature's friend"—all meaningless. Advertisers want consumers to focus on the connotation, not the actual meaning of these words. And what is "healthy"? Even the U.S. Food and Drug Administration is no longer sure, calling in 2016 for a review of its actual meaning based on "significant scientific agreement" (Forbes, 2016).

Intentional imprecision is puffery. It is not illegal; neither is it sufficiently troubling to the advertising industry to warrant self-regulatory limits. But puffery is neither true nor accurate, and its purpose is to deceive. This means that the responsibility for correctly and accurately reading advertising that is intentionally imprecise rests with the media-literate consumer.

▲ We regularly encounter intentional imprecision in advertising, although maybe not as bad as that practiced by Dogbert.

DILBERT ©2007 Scott Adams. Used by permission of ANDREWS MCMEEL SYNDICATION. All rights reserved.

MEDIA LITERACY CHALLENGE
Finding Those Little White Lies

Finding intentional imprecision—those little white lies—in contemporary advertising can be a challenge, but one that a media-literate consumer should welcome. So, record all the commercials during one hour of either TV watching or radio listening. Then go through them carefully and identify ways in which they might have been intentionally imprecise. Did you find any *unfinished statements* like "It lasts twice as long"? List them and the questions you were left to ponder (Twice as long as what?). How many *qualifiers* like "helps relieve stress" or "this could be the last car you'll ever own" did you find? Were there examples of *connotatively loaded* words like "Coco Yummies are part of a complete breakfast"? How easy were these imprecisions to identify? Do you consider them deceptive or harmless? Why? Can you explain your results and your reaction to those results in terms of media literacy skills such as your *willingness to make an effort to understand ad content and filter out noise* and your *understanding of and respect for the power of commercial messages?*

Resources for Review and Discussion

REVIEW POINTS: TYING CONTENT TO LEARNING OUTCOMES

▶ **Outline the history and development of the advertising industry.**
- Advertising has been a part of commerce for centuries, but it became an industry in its own right with the coming of industrialization and the American Civil War.

▶ **Evaluate contemporary criticisms and defenses of advertising.**
- Advertising suffers from a number of criticisms—it is intrusive, it is deceptive, it exploits children, and it demeans and corrupts culture.
- Advertising is also considered beneficial—it supports our economic system, it provides information to assist buying decisions, it supports our media system, and it improves our standard of living.

▶ **Describe how the organizational and economic nature of the contemporary advertising industry shapes the content of advertising, especially in an increasingly converged media environment.**
- Advertising agencies typically have these departments: administration, account management, creative, media, market research, and public relations.
- There are several ways to measure an ad's effectiveness: copy testing, consumer juries, forced exposure, recognition tests, recall testing, awareness tests, and neuromarketing research.

- The interaction of converging technologies and the changes they drive in how, when, and why people consume them (and the ads they contain) is reshaping the economics and creativity of the advertising industry as well as its relationship with consumers.
- Reshaping of the industry has led to calls for better measures of effectiveness, such as engagement, return on investment (ROI), and performance-based advertising.

▶ **Identify different types of advertising and their goals.**
- There are different types of advertising: institutional or corporate, trade or professional, retail, promotional retail, industrial, national consumer, direct market, out-of-home, and public service.
- Advertisers must deal with consumers increasingly segmented not only by their media choices but also along demographic and psychographic lines.
- As with the media it supports, the advertising industry is increasingly globalized.

▶ **Explain the relationship between advertising content and its consumers.**
- Regulation of advertising content is the responsibility of the Federal Trade Commission, which recognizes that

an ad can be false if it lies outright, does not tell the whole truth, or lies by implication. Puffery, the entertaining "little lie," is permissible.

☐ Largely because of the Internet, people have become proactive consumers who now have two options when dealing with marketers: exit and voice.

▶ **Apply key media literacy skills when consuming advertising, especially when interpreting intentional imprecision.**

☐ Interpreting advertisers' intentional imprecision—unfinished statements, qualifiers, and connotatively loaded words—tests consumers' media literacy skills.

KEY TERMS

clutter, 284

ambient advertising, 284

360 marketing, 284

experiential marketing, 285

siquis, 286

shopbills, 286

newsbook, 286

unique selling proposition (USP), 290

parity products, 290

AIDA approach, 294

consumer culture, 294

boutique agencies, 295

retainer, 295

commissions, 295

cost per thousand (CPM), 295

cease-and-desist order, 298

corrective advertising, 298

puffery, 298

island, 298

copy testing, 299

consumer juries, 299

forced exposure, 299

recognition tests, 299

recall testing, 299

awareness tests, 299

neuromarketing research, 299

banners, 300

search marketing, 300

rich media, 300

lead generation, 300

e-commerce, 300

return on investment (ROI), 301

performance-based advertising, 301

engagement, 301

accountability metrics, 301

value-compensation program, 301

programmatic buying, 301

programmatic ad fraud, 301

permission marketing, 302

prosumer, 302

demographic segmentation, 302

psychographic segmentation, 303

VALS, 303

QUESTIONS FOR REVIEW

1. Why are we seeing so many ads in so many new and different places?

2. Why do some people consider advertising to children unethical and immoral?

3. In what ways can an ad be false?

4. What are the departments in a typical advertising agency? What does each do?

5. What are the different categories of advertising and the goal of each?

6. What is a cease-and-desist order? Corrective advertising? Puffery?

7. What are copy testing, consumer juries, forced exposure, recognition tests, recall testing, and awareness tests? How do they differ?

8. What is a prosumer? How do prosumers change the relationship between advertisers and their audience?

9. In what two ways do consumers express dissatisfaction? How does this affect contemporary advertising?

10. What are demographic and psychographic segmentation?

To maximize your study time, check out CONNECT to access the SmartBook study module for this chapter and explore other resources.

QUESTIONS FOR CRITICAL THINKING AND DISCUSSION

1. If you owned an advertising agency, would you produce advertising aimed at children? Why or why not?

2. If you were an FTC regulator, to what extent would you allow puffery? Where would you draw the line between deception and puffery? Give examples.

3. What do you think of the exit–voice dichotomy of consumer behavior? Can you relate it to your own use of advertising? If so, how?

REFERENCES

1. "Ad Age social media facts 2016." (2016, September 26). *Advertising Age*, insert.

2. "Ad agencies: U.S." (2016, May 2). *Advertising Age*, p. 20.

3. Ad Council. (2017). Our campaigns. Online: http://www .adcouncil.org/Our-Campaigns

4. Allen, K. (2014, June 9). Study: Millennials trust their friends, not advertising. *PR Daily*. Online: https://www.prdaily.com /Main/Articles/Study_Millennials_trust_their_friends_not _advertis_16770.aspx

5. Anderson, O. (2016, November 4). Nation's second-largest school district wants to kick McDonald's out. *Yes Magazine*. Online: http://www.yesmagazine.org/people-power/nations -second-largest-school-district-wants-to-kick-mcdonalds -out-20161104

6. Andronikidis, A. I., & Lambrianidou, M. (2010). Children's understanding of television advertising: A grounded theory approach. *Psychology and Marketing, 27*, 299–332.

7. Auletta, K. (2005, March 28). The new pitch. *The New Yorker*, pp. 34–39.

8. Bell, V. (2015, June 28). The marketing industry has started using neuroscience, but the results are more glitter than gold. *The Guardian*. Online: https://www.theguardian.com /science/2015/jun/28/vaughan-bell-neuroscience-marketing -advertising

9. Berkman, H. W., & Gilson, C. (1987). *Advertising: Concepts and strategies.* New York: Random House.

10. Crain, R. (2016, November 14). *Advertising Age*, p. 38.

11. Creamer, M. (2007, April 2). Caught in the clutter crossfire: Your brand. *Advertising Age*, pp. 1, 35.

12. D'Angelo, F. (2009, October 26). Happy birthday, digital advertising! *Advertising Age*. Online: http://adage.com /digitalnext/article?article_id=139964

13. eMarketer. (2016, January 11). US digital display ad spending to surpass search ad spending in 2016. Online: https://www .emarketer.com/Article/US-Digital-Display-Ad-Spending -Surpass-Search-Ad-Spending-2016/1013442

14. Farber, M. (2016, June 8). Consumers are now doing most of their shopping online. *Fortune*. Online: http://fortune.com /2016/06/08/online-shopping-increases/

15. Faw, L. (2016, July 25). Why consumers use ad blockers and what motivates them not to. *MediaPost*. Online: http://www .mediapost.com/publications/article/281013/why-consumers -use-ad-blockers-and-what-motivates-t.html

16. Forbes, T. (2016, May 11). FDA will review what "healthy" means. *MediaPost*. Online: http://www.mediapost.com /publications/article/275577/fda-will-review-what-healthy -means.html

17. Friedman, W. (2017, January 10). Olympics help push global OOH ad spend up 6.2%. *MediaPost*. Online: http://www .mediapost.com/publications/article/292618/olympics-help -push-global-ooh-ad-spend-up-62.html?utm_source =newsletter&utm_medium=email&utm_content =headline&utm_campaign=99532&hashid=h7Fts3q5i wwjhsRIPgm6Rg2aCgo

18. Garfield, B. (2005, April 4). The chaos scenario. *Advertising Age*, pp. 1, 57–59.

19. Giroux, H. A. (2011, May 5). Youth in a suspect society: Coming of age in an era of disposability. *Truthout*. Online: http://truth-out.org/news/item/923:youth-in-a-suspect-society -coming-of-age-in-an-era-of-disposability

20. Gray, P. (2014, February 19). Don't be creepy—avoid backlash with non-invasive mobile ads. *Tech Republic*. Online: http://www.techrepublic.com/article/dont-be-creepy -avoid-backlash-with-non-invasive-mobile-ads/

21. Green, J. (2016, July 20). LGBT purchasing power near $1 trillion rivals other minorities. *Bloomberg*. Online: https://www.bloomberg.com/news/articles/2016-07-20/lgbt -purchasing-power-near-1-trillion-rivals-other-minorities

22. Greenberg, K. (2009, March 10). ANA discusses line between falsehood, puffery. MediaPost. Online: http://www.mediapost. com/publications/article/101890/

23. Halliday, J. (2007, February 12). GM cuts $600M off ad spend—yes, really. *Advertising Age*, pp. 1, 25.

24. Helm, J. (2002, March/April). When history looks back. *Adbusters* [no page number].

25. "Hispanic influence reaches new heights in the U.S." (2016, August 23). *A. C. Nielsen*. Online: http://www.nielsen.com/us /en/insights/news/2016/hispanic-influence-reaches-new -heights-in-the-us.html

26. Ives, N. (2012, January 19). Online ad spending to pass print for the first time, forecast says. *Advertising Age*. Online: http://adage.com/article/mediaworks/emarketer-online-ad -spending-pass-print-time/232221/

27. Jamieson, K. H., & Campbell, K. K. (1997). *The interplay of influence: News, advertising, politics, and the mass media.* Belmont, CA: Wadsworth.

28. Kirsner, S. (2005, April). Interview: Steve Hayden, Ogilvy & Mather Worldwide. *Magnosticism*. Online: https://magnostic .wordpress.com/best-of-cmo/interview-steve-hayden-ogilvy -mather-worldwide/

29. Klosterman, C. (2005, August). What we have here is a failure to communicate. *Esquire*, pp. 62–64.

30. Koblin, J., & Barnes, B. (2016, Oct. 11). Seinfeld's "Comedians in Cars" is on market. *The New York Times*, p. B5.

31. Love, D. (2016, February 4). 2016 Nielsen Report: Black buying power has reached tipping point, but how will black America leverage it to create wealth? *Atlanta Black Star*. Online: http://atlantablackstar.com/2016/02/04/2016-nielsen -report-black-buying-power-reached-tipping-point-will-black -america-leverage-create-wealth/

32. Mandese, J. (2016a, December 15). Demo targeting still dominant at agencies, behavioral tops with clients. *MediaPost*. Online: http://www.mediapost.com/publications/article

/291159/demo-targeting-still-dominant-at-agencies
-behavio.html

33. Mandese, J. (2016b, September 13). "Digital" poised to overtake TV ad spending earlier than expected. *MediaPost*. Online: http://www.mediapost.com/publications/article /284577/digital-poised-to-overtake-tv-ad-spending-earlie.html

34. Marshall, R. (2015, September 10). How many ads do you see in one day? *Red Crow Marketing*. Online: http://www.red crowmarketing.com/2015/09/10/many-ads-see-one-day/

35. Martin, C. (2017, January 9). Next in connected cars: License plate advertising. *MediaPost*. Online: http://www.mediapost .com/publications/article/292472/next-in-connected-cars -license-plate-advertising.html?utm_source=newsletter&utm _medium=email&utm_content=readmore&utm_campaign =99494

36. Morrison, M. (2014, February 26). Why proposal to limit school marketing does not worry food and beverage companies. *Advertising Age*. Online: http://adage.com/article /news/regulation-groups-applaud-school-marketing-proposal /291888/

37. O'Malley, G. (2017, January 24). Forecast: U.S. mobile ad spend will more than double by 2021. *MediaPost*. Online: http://www.mediapost.com/publications/article/293624 /forecast-us-mobile-ad-spend-will-more-than-doub.html?utm _source=newsletter&utm_medium=email&utm_content=read more&utm_campaign=99906&hashid=Ouetusl3B7Xr8ao LXsXKOov4oIA

38. O'Reilly, L. (2017, March 15). The ad fraud issue could be more than twice as big as first thought—advertisers stand to lose $16.4 billion to it this year. *Business Insider*. Online: http://www.businessinsider.com/thepartnership-msix-and -adloox-ad-fraud-2017-2017-3

39. Packard, V. O. (1957). *The hidden persuaders*. New York: David McKay.

40. Rettner, R. (2013, November 5). Fast food ads: Kids seeing less on TV, more on social media. *Live Science*. Online: http://www.livescience.com/40969-fast-food-advertising -kids.html

41. Rideout, V. (2014). *Advertising to children and teens: Current practices*. New York: Common Sense Media.

42. Sandage, C. H., Fryburger, V., & Rotzoll, K. (1989). *Advertising theory and practice*. New York: Longman.

43. "Share of U.S. ad spending by medium from Zenith." (2016, December 19). *Advertising Age Marketing Fact Pack*, p. 16.

44. Slefo, G. (2017, April 20). The ad industry's great powers consider adopting ad blocking on a wide scale. *Advertising Age*. Online: http://adage.com/article/digital/biggest-players -ad-industry-move-kill-worst-ads/308747/

45. SRI Consulting. (2015). *Understanding U.S. consumers*. Menlo Park, CA: Author.

46. "Staffing up." (2016, May 2). *Advertising Age*, p. 16.

47. "Statistics and facts about social media marketing in the United States." (2016, November 24). *Statista*. Online: https://www.statista.com/topics/1538/social-media -marketing/

48. "The story of the Ad Council." (2001, October 29). *Broadcasting & Cable*, pp. 4–11.

49. Tugend, A. (2016, August 15). An action-packed 30-minute commercial. *The New York Times*, p. B3.

50. Tugend, A. (2015, November 22). Ad Council adapts in an age of activism. *The New York Times*, p. B1.

51. "U.S. ad spending forecast." (2016, June 27). *Advertising Age*, p. 26.

52. Whitman, R. (2016a, September 28). Advertising's no-win: People hate ads but would rather watch ad-supported TV, then skip the ads. *MediaPost*. Online: http://www.mediapost.com /publications/article/285737/advertisings-no-win-people-hate -ads-but-would-ra.html

53. Whitman, R. (2016b, June 6). Marketers' experiential marketing efforts turn consumers into "content factory" workers. *MediaPost*. Online: http://www.mediapost.com /publications/article/277466/marketers-experiential -marketing-efforts-turn-con.html

54. "World's 25 Largest Advertisers." (2016, December 5). *Advertising Age*, p. 10.

55. Wu, T. (2016a, December 4). Mother Nature is brought to you by. *The New York Times*, pp. SR1, SR3.

56. Wu, T. (2016b, November 7). Content confusion. *The New York Times Review of Books*, p. 21.

57. Wunderman. (2017, January). Wantedness. Online: https:// www.wantedness.com/

Cultural Forum Blue Column icon, Media Literacy Red Torch Icon, Using Media Green Gear icon, Developing Media book in starburst icon: ©McGraw-Hill Education

Theories
and Effects
of Mass
Communication

13

◄ The potential of powerful media effects provides a strong argument for increased media literacy.

©Moviestore collection Ltd/Alamy

Learning Objectives

Media have effects. People may disagree about what those effects might be, but media do have effects. Advertisers would not spend billions of dollars a year to place their messages in the media if they did not have effects, nor would our Constitution, in the form of the First Amendment, seek to protect the freedoms of the media if the media did not have important consequences. We attempt to understand and explain these effects through mass communication theory. After studying this chapter, you should be able to

▶ Outline the history and development of mass communication theory.

▶ Explain what is meant by theory, why it is important, and how it is used.

▶ Describe influential traditional and contemporary mass communication theories.

▶ Analyze controversial effects issues, such as violence, media's impact on drug and alcohol consumption, and media's contribution to racial and gender stereotyping.

▶ Apply mass communication theory to your own use of media.

~1900–1938 ▶ Common entertainment seen as corrupting influence that undermines the social order · · · ·

~1930s The Frankfurt School

~1900–1938 Era of mass society theory

©Ronald Grant Archive/Alamy

1938 ▶ Welles's *War of the Worlds* · · · · ·

1941 ▶ Office of War Information · · · · ·

1945 Allport and Postman rumor study

1955 Two-step flow

1960 Klapper's *The Effects of Mass Communication*/reinforcement theory

~1938–1960 Era of limited effects theories

Source: Office of War Information Photograph Collection/Library of Congress

©Ingram Publishing RF

~1960s ▶ Social cognitive theory; symbolic interaction; social construction of reality; British cultural studies · · · · · · ·

~1970s Cultivation analysis

~1970s ▶ Media content seen as having significant cultural influence · · · · · · ·

1972 Agenda setting; Surgeon General's Report on Television and Social Behavior

1975 Uses and gratifications; dependency theory

~1960–1975 Era of cultural theory

©Bill Aron/PhotoEdit

Courtesy of Professor Albert Bandura, Stanford University

2000 National medical and psychological groups' joint report on long-lasting effects of media violence

2002 National Institute of Alcohol Abuse and Alcoholism report on youthful alcohol abuse

2015 ▶ New questions emerge: Why are the poor invisible in our media? Is there a *Will & Grace* effect? · · · · ·

2016 The traditional media badly misinterpret the public mood during the presidential election

1975–today Era of the meaning-making perspective

©NBC/Courtesy Everett Collection

"I KNOW THIS ISN'T LISTED ON THE SYLLABUS. But let's call it a pop quiz." Your instructor has surprised you. "Will this count in our final grade?" you ask. You are seared by the professor's stare.

"Put everything away except a piece of paper and a pen."

You do as instructed.

"Number your paper from 1 to 5. Items 1 through 3 are true or false. One. Most people are just looking out for themselves. Two. You can't be too careful in dealing with people. Three. Most people would take advantage of you if they got the chance. Now, number four. How much television do you watch each week?"

Not too tough, you think, you can handle this.

"Finally, number 5. Draw the outline of a dime as close to actual size as possible."

You think you get the point about watching TV and trusting people, but what's with the dime? What does that have to do with mass communication theory?

In this chapter we examine mass communication theory (and we explain the significance of the dime and the other questions from the quiz). After we define theory and discuss why it is important, we see how the various theories of mass communication that are prevalent today developed. We then study several of the most influential contemporary theories before we discuss the relationship between media literacy and mass communication theory. These theories and their application form the basis of our understanding of how media and culture affect one another.

The Effects Debate

Whether the issue is online hate groups, televised violence, the absence of minority characters in prime-time television programming, or a decline in the quality of political discourse, the topic of the effects of mass communication is—and has always been—hotly debated. Later in this chapter we will take detailed looks at issues surrounding these effects, such as the media's impact on violence, the use of drugs and alcohol, and stereotyping. But before we can examine specific effects issues, we must understand that fundamental disagreement exists about the presence, strength, and operation of these effects. Many people still hold to the position that media have limited or minimal effects. Here are their arguments, accompanied by often-made counterarguments.

1. *Media content has limited impact on audiences because it's only make-believe; people know it isn't real.*

   The counterarguments: (a) News is not make-believe (at least it's not supposed to be), and we are supposed to take it seriously. (b) Most film and television dramas (for example, *CSI: Crime Scene Investigation* and *Modern Family*) are intentionally produced to seem real to viewers, with documentary-like production techniques such as handheld cameras and uneven lighting. (c) Much contemporary television is expressly *real*—reality shows such as *Cops* and *Real Housewives* and talk shows such as *The Jerry Springer Show* purport to present real people. (d) Advertising is supposed to tell the truth. (e) Before they develop the intellectual and critical capacity to know what is not real, children confront the world in all its splendor and vulgarity through television, what television effects researchers call the **early window**. To kids, what they see is real. (f) To enjoy what we consume, we engage the **willing suspension of disbelief**; that is, we willingly accept as real what is put before us.

2. *Media content has limited impact on audiences because it is only play or just entertainment.*

   The counterarguments: (a) News is not play or entertainment (at least it's not supposed to be). (b) Even if media content is only play, play is very important to the way we develop our knowledge of ourselves and our world. When we play organized sports, we learn teamwork, cooperation, the value of hard work, obedience to authority, and respect for the rules. Why should play be any less influential if we do it on the Internet or at the movies?

3. *If media have any effects at all, they are not the media's fault; media simply hold a mirror to society and reflect the status quo, showing us and our world as they already are.*

   The counterargument: Media hold a very selective mirror. The whole world, in all its vastness and complexity, cannot possibly be represented, so media practitioners must make choices. For example, when was the last time you saw a car explode in an accident or police shoot it out with the bad guys on a city street? Most cops will go their entire careers and never fire their guns (Fresh Air, 2016), but our screens are filled with raging gun battles between police and evil-doers, often with heavy weapons and in crowded areas. At best, media hold a fun-house mirror to society and distort what they reflect. Some things are overrepresented, others underrepresented, and still others disappear altogether.

4. *If media have any effect at all, it is only to reinforce preexisting values and beliefs. Family, church, school, and other socializing agents have much more influence.*

   The counterarguments: (a) The traditional socializing agents have lost much of their power to influence in our complicated and fast-paced world. (b) Moreover, *reinforcement* is not the same as having no effects. If media can reinforce the good in our culture, media can just as easily reinforce the bad. Is racism eradicated yet? Sexism? Disrespect for others? If our media are doing no more than reinforcing the values and beliefs that already exist, then they are as empty as many critics contend. Former Federal Communications Commission member Nicholas Johnson has long argued of television in particular that the real crime is not what television is doing *to* us but what it could be doing *for* us, but isn't.

5. *If media have any effects at all, they are only on the unimportant things in our lives, such as fads and fashions.*

   The counterarguments: (a) Fads and fashions are not unimportant to us. The cars we drive, the clothes we wear, and the ways we look help define us; they characterize us to others. In fact, it is media that have helped make fads and fashions so central to our self-definition and happiness. Kids don't kill other kids for their $150 basketball shoes because their mothers told them that Air Jordans were cool. (b) If media influence only the unimportant things in our lives, why are billions of dollars spent on media efforts to sway opinion about social issues such as universal health care, nuclear power, and climate change (see the chapter on public relations)?

▲ The mirror that media hold up to culture is like a fun-house mirror—some things appear bigger than they truly are, some things appear smaller, and some disappear altogether.
©Susan Baran

One reason these arguments about media power and effects continue to rage is that people often come to the issues from completely different perspectives. In their most general form, the debates over media influence have been shaped by three closely related dichotomies: micro- versus macro-level effects, administrative versus critical research, and transmissional versus ritual perspective.

Micro- versus Macro-Level Effects

People are concerned about the effects of media. Does television cause violence? Do beer ads cause increased alcohol consumption? Does pornography cause rape? The difficulty here is with the word *cause*. Although there is much scientific evidence that media cause many behaviors, there is also much evidence that they do not.

As long as we debate the effects of media only on individuals, we risk remaining blind to what many believe is media's more powerful influence (both positive and negative) on the way we live. For example, when the shootings at the Littleton, Colorado, Columbine High School in 1999 once again brought public debate on the issue of media effects, USA Network copresident Steve Brenner was forced to defend his industry. "Every American has seen hundreds of films, hundreds of news stories, hundreds of depictions, thousands of cartoons," he said. "Millions don't go out and shoot people" (as quoted in Albiniak, 1999, p. 8).

Who can argue with this? For most people, media have relatively few *direct* effects at the personal or **micro level**. But we live in a culture in which people *have* shot people or are quick to use violence to settle disputes, at least in part because of the cultural messages embedded in our media fare. The less visible, but much more important, impact of media operates at the cultural or **macro level**. Violence on television contributes to the cultural climate in which real-world violence becomes more acceptable. Sure, perhaps none of us have gone out and shot people. But do you have bars on the windows of your home? Are there parts of town where you would rather not walk alone? Do you vote for the "tough on crime" candidate over the "education" candidate?

The micro-level view is that media violence has little impact because although some people may be directly affected, most people are not. The macro-level view is that media violence has a great impact because it influences the cultural climate. Communication researcher Sut Jhally, speaking specifically about violent video games, highlighted the distinction. Violent games, he said, "don't create violent people; what they do is glorify a violent culture and shut down our capacity as a society to imagine anything different. They short-circuit our ability to think in more productive ways about the real violence in our lives. That is their real tragedy" (2013).

Administrative versus Critical Research

Administrative research asks questions about the immediate, observable influence of mass communication. Does a commercial campaign sell more cereal? Does a heavy dose of celebrity gossip bring more clicks to an online news site? Did video games inspire the killings of the 20 children and six adults at Sandy Hook Elementary School? For decades the only proof of media effects that science (and therefore the media industries, regulators, and audiences) would accept were those with direct, observable, immediate effects. More than 70 years ago, however, Paul Lazarsfeld, the father of social science research and possibly the most important mass communication researcher of all time, warned of the danger of this narrow view. He believed **critical research**—asking larger questions about what kind of nation we are building, what kind of people we are becoming—would serve our culture better. Writing long before the influence of television and information access through the Internet, he stated:

▶ What are the effects of televised violence? The debate swirls as different people mean different things by "effects." This violent scene is from *Supernatural.*
©CW/Courtesy Everett Collection

Today we live in an environment where skyscrapers shoot up and elevateds [commuter trains] disappear overnight; where news comes like shock every few hours; where continually new news programs keep us from ever finding out details of previous news; and where nature is something we drive past in our cars, perceiving a few quickly changing flashes which turn the majesty of a mountain range into the impression of a motion picture. Might it not be that we do not build up experiences the way it was possible decades ago . . .? (1941, p. 12)

Administrative research concerns itself with direct causes and effects; critical research looks at larger, possibly more significant cultural questions. As the cartoon shows, Calvin understands the distinction well.

▲ Calvin understands the difference between administrative and critical research.
CALVIN AND HOBBES ©1995 Watterson. Used by permission of ANDREWS MCMEEL SYNDICATION. All rights reserved.

Transmissional versus Ritual Perspective

Last is the debate that led Professor James W. Carey to articulate his cultural definition of communication. The **transmissional perspective** sees media as senders of information for the purpose of control; that is, media either have effects on our behavior or they do not. The **ritual perspective**, Carey wrote, views media not as a means of transmitting "messages in space" but as central to "the maintenance of society in time." Mass communication is "not the act of imparting information but the representation of shared beliefs" (1975, p. 6). In other words, the ritual perspective is necessary to understand the *cultural* importance of mass communication.

Consider an ad for Skyy vodka. What message is being transmitted? Buy Skyy, of course. So people either do or do not buy Skyy. The message either controls or does not control people's alcohol-buying behavior. That is the transmissional perspective. But what is happening culturally in that ad? What reality about alcohol and socializing is shared? Can young people really have fun in social settings without alcohol? What constitutes a good-looking woman? Is a woman to be admired for more than her looks? The ritual perspective illuminates these messages—the culturally important content of the ad.

Defining Mass Communication Theory

Whether you accept the limited effects arguments or their counterarguments, all the positions you just read are based on one or more **mass communication theories,**

▼ The transmissional message in this liquor ad is obvious—buy Skyy. The ritual message is another thing altogether. What is it?
©Bill Aron/PhotoEdit

explanations and predictions of social phenomena that attempt to relate mass communication to various aspects of our personal and cultural lives or social systems. Your responses to the five quiz questions that opened the chapter, for example, can be explained (possibly even predicted) by different mass communication theories.

The first four items are a reflection of **cultivation analysis**—the idea that people's ideas of themselves, their world, and their place in it are shaped and maintained primarily through television. People's responses to the three true or false items can be fairly accurately predicted by the amount of viewing they do (question 4). The more people watch, the more likely they are to respond "true" to these unflattering comments that others are generally selfish, untrustworthy, and out to get you.

The solution to the dime-drawing task is predicted by **attitude change theory**, which explains how people's attitudes are formed, shaped, and changed and how those attitudes influence behavior. Almost everyone draws the dime too small. Because a dime is an inconsequential coin, we perceive it as smaller than it really is, and our perceptions guide our behavior. Even though every one of us has real-world experience with dimes, our attitudes toward that coin shape our behavior regarding it. Mass communication theorists study media's contribution to the formation of our attitudes on a wide array of issues of far greater importance than the size of a dime.

To understand mass communication theory, you should recognize these important ideas:

1. As we've just seen, *there is no one mass communication theory*. There is a theory, for example, that describes something as grand as how we give meaning to cultural symbols and how these symbols influence our behavior (symbolic interaction), and there is a theory that explains something as individual as how media influence people in times of change or crisis (dependency theory). Mass communication theorists have produced a number of **middle-range theories** that explain or predict specific, limited aspects of the mass communication process (Merton, 1967).

2. *Mass communication theories are often borrowed from other fields of social science*. Attitude change theory (the dime question), for example, comes from psychology. Mass communication theorists adapt these borrowed theories to questions and issues in communication. People's behavior with regard to issues more important than the size of a dime—democracy, ethnicity, government, and gender roles, for example—is influenced by the attitudes and perceptions presented by our mass media.

3. *Mass communication theories are human constructions*. People create them, and therefore their creation is influenced by human biases—the times in which we live, the position we occupy in the mass communication process, and a host of other factors. Broadcast industry researchers, for example, have developed somewhat different theories to explain how violence is learned from television than have university researchers.

4. Because theories are human constructions and the environments in which they are created constantly change, *mass communication theories are dynamic*; they undergo frequent recasting, acceptance, and rejection. For example, theories that were developed before television and computer networks became commonplace have to be reexamined and sometimes discarded in the face of these new technologies.

A Short History of Mass Communication Theory

The dynamic nature of mass communication theory can be seen in its history. All disciplines' bodies of knowledge pass through various stages of development. Hypotheses are put forth, tested, and proven or rejected. Eventually a consensus develops that shapes a discipline's central ideas and, as such, the kinds of questions it asks and the answers it seeks—and expects. However, over time some answers come to challenge those expectations. So new questions have to be asked, new answers are produced, and, eventually, a new consensus emerges. Mass communication theory is particularly open to evolving ideas for three reasons:

- *Advances in technology or the introduction of new media* fundamentally alter the nature of mass communication. The coming of radio and movies, for example, forced rethinking of theories based on a print-oriented mass communication system.

- *Calls for control or regulation* of these new technologies require, especially in a democracy such as ours, an objective, science-based justification.

- As a country committed to protecting *democracy and cultural pluralism*, we ask how each new technology or medium can foster our pursuit of that goal.

The evolution in thinking that resulted from these factors has produced four major eras of mass communication theory: the era of mass society theory, the era of the limited effects perspective, the cultural theory era, and the era of the meaning-making perspective. The first two may be considered early eras; the latter two best represent contemporary thinking.

The Era of Mass Society Theory

As we've seen, several important mass media appeared or flourished during the second half of the 19th century and the first decades of the 20th century. Mass circulation newspapers and magazines, movies, talkies, and radio all came to prominence at this time. This was also a time of profound change in the nature of U.S. society. Industrialization and urbanization spread, African Americans and poor southern whites streamed northward, and immigrants landed on both coasts in search of opportunity and dignity. People in traditional seats of power—the clergy, politicians, and educators—feared a disruption in the status quo. The country's peaceful rural nature was beginning to slip further into history. In its place was a cauldron of new and different people with new and different habits, all crammed into rapidly expanding cities. Crime grew, as did social and political unrest. Many cultural, political, educational, and religious leaders thought the United States was becoming too pluralistic. They charged that the mass media catered to the low tastes and limited reading and language abilities of these newcomers by featuring simple and sensationalistic content. Media, they proclaimed, needed to be controlled to protect traditional values.

The successful use of propaganda by totalitarian governments in Europe, especially Germany's National Socialist Party (the Nazis), provided further evidence of the overwhelming power of media. Social and cultural elites therefore called for greater control of the media to prevent similar abuses at home.

The resulting theory was **mass society theory**—the idea that the media are corrupting influences that undermine the social order and that "average" people are defenseless against their influence. To mass society theorists, "average" people were all those who did not hold their (the theorists') superior tastes and values. Walter Lippmann, a nationally syndicated columnist for *The New York Times* and one of the country's most important social commentators, was indicatively skeptical of average people's ability to make sense of the confusing world around them. Political essayist Eric Alterman explained and summarized Lippmann's thinking as expressed in the legendary social critic's influential 1922 book *Public Opinion*. He said that Lippman saw the average American as akin to a spectator at an event, sitting in the back row: "He lives in a world he cannot see, does not understand and is unable to direct." American journalism, with its devotion to profit and sensationalism, only compounded the problem; therefore, politics and governing were best left to a "specialized class of men," those sitting closer to the action. Alterman summarized Lippmann, "No one expects a steelworker to understand physics, so why should he be expected to understand politics?" (2008, p. 10).

The fundamental assumption of this thinking is sometimes expressed in the **hypodermic needle theory** or the **magic bullet theory**. The symbolism of both is apparent—media are a dangerous drug or a killing force against which "average" people are defenseless.

Mass society theory is an example of a **grand theory**, one designed to describe and explain all aspects of a given phenomenon. But clearly not all average people were mindlessly influenced by the evil mass media. People made consumption choices. They interpreted media content, often in personally important ways. Media did have effects, often good ones. No single theory could encompass the wide variety of media effects claimed by mass society theorists, and the theory eventually collapsed under its own weight.

▶ Agnes Ayers in Rudolph Valentino's arms in the 1921 movie *The Sheik.* Mass society theorists saw such common entertainment fare as debasing the culture through its direct and negative effects on helpless audience members.
©Ronald Grant Archive/Alamy

The Emergence of the Limited Effects Perspective

Shifts in a discipline's dominant thinking usually happen over a period of time, and this is true of the move away from mass society theory. But media researchers often mark the emergence of the limited effects perspective on mass communication as occurring on the eve of Halloween 1938. On that night, actor and director Orson Welles broadcast his dramatized version of the H. G. Wells science fiction classic *The War of the Worlds* on the CBS radio network. Produced in what we would now call docudrama style, the realistic radio play in which Earth came under deadly Martian attack frightened thousands. People fled their homes in panic. Elite media critics argued this was proof of mass society theory, pointing to a radio play with the power to send people into the hills to hide from aliens.

Research by scientists from Princeton University demonstrated that, in fact, 1 million people had been frightened enough by the broadcast to take some action, but the other 5 million people who heard the show had not, mass society theory notwithstanding. More important, however, these scientists determined that different factors led some people to be influenced and others not (Lowery & DeFleur, 1995).

The researchers had the benefit of advances in survey research, polling, and other social scientific methods developed and championed by Austrian immigrant Paul Lazarsfeld. The researchers were, in fact, his students and colleagues. Lazarsfeld (1941) argued that mere speculation about the impact of media was insufficient to explain the complex interactions that mass communication comprised. Instead, well-designed, sophisticated studies of media and audiences would produce more valuable knowledge.

Using Lazarsfeld's work, researchers identified those individual and social characteristics that led audience members to be influenced (or not) by media. What emerged was the view that media influence was limited by *individual differences* (for example, in intelligence and education), *social categories* (such as religious and political affiliation), and *personal relationships* (such as friends and family). The theories that emerged from this era of the first systematic and scientific study of media effects, taken together, are now called **limited effects theories**.

TWO-STEP FLOW THEORY Lazarsfeld's own **two-step flow theory** of mass media and personal influence is a well-known product of this era and an example of a limited effects theory (Katz & Lazarsfeld, 1955). His research on the 1940 presidential election indicated

◀ Orson Welles directs *War of the Worlds.* The 1938 Halloween eve broadcast of this science fiction classic helped usher in the era of the scientific study of mass communication.
©*CBS Radio/Photofest*

that media influence on people's voting behavior was limited by **opinion leaders**—people who initially consumed media content on topics of particular interest to them, interpreted it in light of their own values and beliefs, and then passed it on to **opinion followers**, people like them who had less frequent contact with media (Figure 1).

Two-step flow theory has been rethought since Lazarsfeld's time. For example, television, virtually unavailable in 1940, has given everyone a more or less equal opportunity to consume media content firsthand. There is no doubt that opinion leaders still exist—we often ask friends what they've read or heard about a certain movie, book, or band for example—but because we now have ubiquitous and universal access to information on our own if we wish, their centrality to the mass communication process has diminished.

ATTITUDE CHANGE THEORY   During and after World War II, the limited effects perspective and several theories it supported became more fully entrenched, controlling research and thinking about media until well into the 1960s. As was the case with virtually all the media and support industries we've studied, the war itself was crucial to the development of mass communication theory during this era.

◀ **Figure 1** Model of Two-Step Flow of Media Influence. Media influence passes from the mass media through opinion leaders to opinion followers. Because leaders and followers share common personal and social characteristics, the potential influence of media is limited by their shared assumptions, beliefs, and attitudes.
Source: After Katz & Lazarsfeld, 1955.

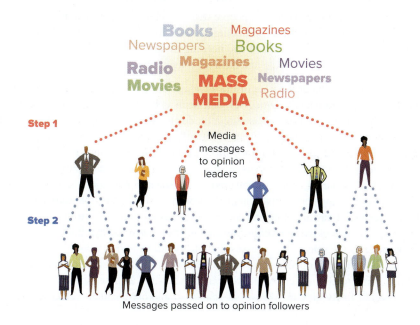

Memories of World War I were still very much alive, and not all Americans were enthused about entering another seemingly remote world conflict. Those who joined or were drafted into the armed forces apparently knew very little about their comrades-in-arms from different regions of the country and from different backgrounds. German propaganda seemed to prove the view of mass society theorists who claimed that mass media wielded remarkable power. The Office of War Information (OWI), therefore, set out to change public opinion about the wisdom of entering the war, to educate the military about their fellow soldiers and sailors, and to counter Nazi propaganda. Speeches and lectures failed. So, too, did informational pamphlets. The OWI then turned to filmmakers such as Frank Capra and radio personalities such as Kate Smith for their audience appeal and looked to social scientists to measure the effectiveness of these new media campaigns.

The army established the Experimental Section inside its Information and Education Division, staffing it with psychologists who were experts on issues of attitude change. Led by Carl Hovland, these researchers tested the effectiveness of the government's mass communication campaigns. Continuing its work at Yale University after the war, this group produced some of our most influential communication research. Their work led to development of *attitude change theory*, which explains how people's attitudes are formed, shaped, and changed through communication and how those attitudes influence behavior (Hovland, Lumsdaine, & Sheffield, 1949).

Among the most important attitude change theories are the related ideas of dissonance and selective processes. **Dissonance theory** argues that when confronted by new or conflicting information, people experience a kind of mental discomfort, a dissonance. As a result, they consciously and subconsciously work to limit or reduce that discomfort through three interrelated **selective processes**. These processes help us "select" what information we consume, remember, and interpret in personally important and idiosyncratic ways:

- **Selective exposure** (or **selective attention**) is the process by which people expose themselves to or attend to only those messages consistent with their preexisting attitudes and beliefs. How often do you read the work of an online pundit who occupies a different place on the political spectrum from you? You're more likely to read those pieces that confirm what you already believe. It's quite common for someone who buys a new car, electronic device, or other expensive item to suddenly start to see more of that product's advertising. You've spent a lot of money; that creates dissonance. The ads confirm the wisdom of your decision, reducing dissonance.

- **Selective retention** assumes that people remember best and longest those messages that are consistent with their preexisting attitudes and beliefs. Television viewers, for example, remember much more detail from the convention broadcasts of the political party to which they are philosophically closer than they do the broadcasts of competing parties.

- **Selective perception** predicts that people will interpret messages in a manner consistent with their preexisting attitudes and beliefs. When your favorite politicians change positions on an issue, they're evolving and heeding the public's will. When those you don't like do so, they're flip-flopping and have no convictions.

The dominant thinking at the time of the development of dissonance theory was limited effects theory; thus, the selective processes were seen as limiting media impact because content is selectively filtered to produce as little attitude change as possible. Contemporary mass communication theorists accept the power of the selective processes to limit the influence of media content when it is primarily informational. But because so much content is symbolic rather than informational, other theorists see the selective processes as relatively unimportant when it comes to explaining media's contribution to some important cultural effects. You will recognize these differing perspectives on media's power in the distinction made earlier in this chapter between the transmissional and ritual views of mass communication.

Here is an example of the distinction between informational and symbolic content and the way they relate to the selective processes. Few television stations would broadcast lecture programs by people who openly espouse the racist opinion that people of color are genetically more prone to commit crime. If we were to see such a show, however, the selective processes would likely kick in. We would change to another channel (selective exposure).

If we did watch, we would interpret the ideas as loony or sick (selective perception); later we would quickly forget the arguments (selective retention).

Fortunately, the media rarely offer such overtly racist messages. The more likely situation in contemporary television is that the production conventions and economic and time demands of television news production lead to the common portrayal of certain people as more likely to be involved in violence and crime. It is easier and cheaper, for example, for stations to cover downtown violent crime—it's handy, it's visual, and it needs no significant research or writing—than to cover nonviolent crime, even though 90% of all felonies in the United States are nonviolent. As a result of these largely symbolic portrayals of crime, our selective processes do not have an opportunity to reshape the "information" in these news reports. There is little information, only a variety of interesting images.

Cultural theorists (we'll meet them later in this chapter) point to official government statistics as proof of the power of the media to shape attitudes toward race. Crime in the United States is committed by all races in near proportion to their presence in the population, yet African American males are disproportionately represented in the prison population and on death row (Quigley, 2016). At traffic stops, African American and Hispanic drivers are more likely to be searched than are whites and Asians, and they are searched on the basis of less evidence even though those more numerous searches are less likely to uncover illegal drugs or weapons than are searches of vehicles with white or Asian drivers (Andrews, 2016). An example of racial bias in the perception of criminals can be found in the 1947 study on rumor that demonstrated the operation of the selective processes. In the famous experiment, psychologists Gordon Allport and John Postman asked people to whisper from one to another the subject of a drawing in which an African American man is clearly being menaced by a razor-wielding white man. Only the first participant saw the image; more often than not, as the story was passed from person to person, the razor shifted from the left hand of the white aggressor to that of the African American. If our criminal laws and our justice system are supposed to be racially neutral, cultural theorists ask, why do these disparities continue to exist?

▲ The race of this driver will determine to a large degree the likelihood that his car will be searched.
©Hill Street Studios/Getty Images RF

REINFORCEMENT THEORY The selective processes, however, formed the core of what is arguably the most influential book ever published on the impact of mass communication. In *The Effects of Mass Communication*, written in 1960 by the eminent scientist and eventual head of social research for CBS Broadcasting Joseph Klapper, the core of the limited effects perspective is articulated firmly and clearly. Klapper's theory is based on social science evidence developed prior to 1960 and is often called **reinforcement theory**. It was very persuasive at a time when the nation's social fabric had yet to feel the full impact of the cultural change brought about by the war in Vietnam. In addition, flush with enthusiasm and optimism for the technology and science that had helped the United States defeat the Axis powers, the public could see little but good coming from the media technologies, and they trusted the work of Klapper and other scientists.

In retrospect, the value of reinforcement theory may have passed with the book's 1960 publication date. With rapid postwar urbanization, industrialization, and the increase of women in the workplace, Klapper's "nexus of mediating factors and influences" (church, family, and school) began to lose its traditional socializing role for many people. During the 1960s, a decade both revered and reviled for the social and cultural changes it fostered, it became increasingly difficult to ignore the impact of media. Most important, however, all the research Klapper had studied in preparation for his book was conducted before 1960, the year in which it is generally accepted that television became a truly mass medium, entering 90%

of American homes. Almost none of the science he examined in developing his reinforcement theory considered television.

THE USES AND GRATIFICATIONS APPROACH Academic disciplines do not change easily. Limited effects researchers were unable to ignore obvious media effects such as the impact of advertising, the media's role in sustaining sentiment against the war in Vietnam and in spreading support for civil rights and the feminist movement, and increases in real-world crime that appeared to parallel increases in televised violence. They turned their focus to media consumers to explain how influence is limited. The new body of thought that resulted, called the **uses and gratifications approach**, claimed that media do not do things *to* people; rather, people do things *with* media. In other words, the influence of media is limited to what people allow it to be.

Because the uses and gratifications approach emphasizes *audience members'* motives for making specific consumption choices and the consequences of that intentional media use, it is sometimes seen as being too apologetic for the media industries. In other words, when negative media effects are seen as the product of audience members' media choices and use, the media industries are absolved of responsibility for the content they produce or carry. Media simply give people what they want. This approach is also criticized because it assumes not only that people know why they make the media content choices they do but also that they can clearly articulate those reasons to uses-and-gratifications researchers. A third criticism is that the approach ignores the fact that much media consumption is unintentional—when we go online for election news, we can't help but see ads. When we go to an action movie, we are presented with various representations of gender and ethnicity that have nothing to do with our reasons for choosing that film. A fourth criticism is that the approach ignores media's cultural role in shaping people's media choices and use.

Despite these criticisms, the uses and gratifications approach served an important function in the development of mass communication theory by stressing the reciprocal nature of the mass communication process. That is, scientists began to take seriously the idea that people are important in the process—they choose content, they make meaning, they act on that meaning.

AGENDA SETTING During the era of limited effects, several important ideas were developed that began to cast some doubt on the assumption that media influence on people and cultures was minimal. These ideas are still respected and examined even today. Among the most influential is **agenda setting**, a theory that argues that media may not tell us what to think, but media certainly tell us what to think *about*. In 1972, based on their study of the media's role in the 1968 presidential election, Maxwell McCombs and Donald Shaw wrote:

> In choosing and displaying news, editors, newsroom staff, and broadcasters play an important part in shaping political reality. Readers learn not only about a given issue, but how much importance to attach to that issue from the amount of information in a news story and its position. . . . The mass media may well determine the important issues—that is, the media may set the "agenda" of the campaign. (1972, p. 176)

The agenda-setting power of the media resides in more than the amount of space or time devoted to a story and its placement in the broadcast or on the page. Also important is the fact that there is great consistency between media sources across all media in the choice and type of coverage they give an issue or event. This consistency and repetition signal to people the importance of the issue or event.

Researchers Shanto Iyengar and Donald Kinder tested the application of agenda-setting theory to the network evening news shows in a series of experiments. Their conclusions supported McCombs and Shaw. "Americans' views of their society and nation," they wrote, "are powerfully shaped by the stories that appear on the evening news" (1987, p. 112). But Iyengar and Kinder took agenda setting a step or two further. They discovered that the position of a story affected the agenda-setting power of television news. As you might expect, the lead story on the nightly newscast had the greatest agenda-setting effect, in part because first stories tend to have viewers' full attention—they come before interruptions and other distractions can occur. The second reason, said the researchers, is that viewers accept the broadcasters' implicit categorization of the lead story as the most important.

DEPENDENCY THEORY In 1975 Melvin DeFleur and Sandra Ball-Rokeach offered a view of potentially powerful mass media, tying that power to audience members' dependence on media content. Their **dependency theory** is composed of several assertions:

- The basis of media's influence resides in the "relationship between the larger social system, the media's role in that system, and audience relationships to the media" (p. 261).

- The degree of our dependence on media and their content is the "key variable in understanding when and why media messages alter audience beliefs, feelings, or behavior" (p. 261).

- In our modern industrial society we are increasingly dependent on media (a) to understand the social world, (b) to act meaningfully and effectively in society, and (c) to find fantasy and escape or diversion.

- Our level of dependency is related to (a) "the number and centrality (importance) of the specific information-delivery functions served by a medium" and (b) the degree of change and conflict present in society (p. 263).

Limited effects theory has clearly been left behind here. Dependency theory argues that, especially in our complex and changing society, people become increasingly dependent on media and media content to understand what is going on around them, to learn how to behave meaningfully, and to escape. Think of a crisis—a natural disaster, for example. We immediately turn to the mass media. We are dependent on the media to understand what is going on around us, to learn what to do (how to behave), and even sometimes to escape from the reality of the situation. Now think of other, more personal crises—reaching puberty, attending high school, beginning dating, or having a child. Dependency theory can explain or predict our media use and its impact in these situations as well, as it can when we rely on media for aid in making a tough decision, such as voting or forming an opinion on a complicated issue like war or health care reform.

SOCIAL COGNITIVE THEORY While mass communication researchers were challenging the limited effects perspective with ideas such as agenda setting and dependency theory, psychologists were expanding **social cognitive theory**—the idea that people learn through observation—and applying it to mass media, especially television (Bandura, 2001).

Social cognitive theory argues that people model (copy) the behaviors they see and that **modeling** happens in two ways. The first is **imitation**, the direct replication of an observed behavior. For example, after seeing cartoon mouse Jerry hit cartoon cat Tom with a stick, a child might then hit his sister with a stick. The second form of modeling is **identification**, a special form of imitation in which observers do not copy exactly what they have seen but make a more generalized but related response. For example, the child might still be aggressive toward his sister but dump a pail of water on her head rather than hit her with a stick.

The idea of identification was of particular value to mass communication theorists who studied television's impact on behavior. Everyone admits that people can imitate what they see on television. But not all do, and when this imitation does occur in dramatic instances— for example, when a Washington-state man strangles his girlfriend and attempts to dissolve her body in a tub of acid as he had seen in an episode of *Breaking Bad* (the police discovered a DVD cued up to that very scene in his home; Terle, 2016)—it is so outrageous that it is considered an aberration. Identification, although obviously harder to see and study, is the more likely way that television influences behavior.

Social cognitive theorists demonstrated that imitation and identification are products of three processes:

Observational learning. Observers can acquire (learn) new behaviors simply by seeing those behaviors performed. Many of us who have never fired a handgun could do so because we've seen it done.

Inhibitory effects. Seeing a model, a movie character, for example, punished for a behavior reduces the likelihood that the observer will perform that behavior. In the media we see Good Samaritans sued for trying to help someone, and it reduces our willingness to help in similar situations. That behavior is inhibited by what we've seen.

Disinhibitory effects. Seeing a model rewarded for prohibited or threatening behavior increases the likelihood that the observer will perform that behavior. This, for example, is the basis for complaints against the glorification of crime and drugs in movies. Behaviors that people might not otherwise make, those that are inhibited, now become more likely to occur. The behaviors are disinhibited.

Cultural Theory—A Return to the Idea of Powerful Effects

The questions asked and the answers produced by the agenda-setting, dependency, and social cognitive theorists were no surprise to their contemporaries, the cultural theorists. These observers were primarily European social theorists and North American humanities scholars such as Marshall McLuhan and James Carey, both of whom we met earlier in this text. As America entered the 1960s, no one could remain unaware of the obvious and observable impact television was having on the culture; the increased sophistication of media industries and media consumers; entrenched social problems such as racial strife and gender inequality; the apparent cheapening of the political process; and the emergence of calls for controls on new technologies such as cable, VCR, satellite, and computer networks. Mass communication theorists were forced to rethink media's influence. Clearly, the limited effects idea was inadequate to explain the media impact they saw around themselves every day. But just as clearly, mass society theory explained very little.

It's important to remember that prominent theories never totally disappear. Joseph McCarthy's efforts to purge Hollywood of communists in the 1950s, for example, were based on mass society notions of evil media and malleable audiences, as was radio preacher Kevin Swanson's assertion that Disney movie *Beauty and the Beast*, like the TV series *Star Trek* before it, encourages "humans to interbreed with other species" (Pennacchia, 2017), and *Fox and Friends* host Steve Doocey's claim that the Disney movie *Frozen* is emasculating men and "empowering women by turning our men into fools and villains" (Walsh, 2015). Social cognitive theory, limited effects, and uses and gratifications are regularly raised in today's

▲ Disney's *Frozen*: Fun for the family or emasculating men?
©Photos 12/Alamy

▲ *Beauty and the Beast*: Popular fairy tale or promoter of inter-species breeding?
©Moviestore/REX/Shutterstock

debates over the regulation of video games and fast-food advertising aimed at kids (see the chapters on video games and advertising).

But the theories that have gained the most support among today's media researchers and theorists are those that accept the potential for powerful media effects, a potential that is *either* enhanced or thwarted by audience members' involvement in the mass communication process. Important to this perspective on audience–media interaction are **cultural theories**. Stanley Baran and Dennis Davis wrote that these theories share "the underlying assumption that our experience of reality is an ongoing, social construction, not something that is only sent, delivered, or otherwise transmitted by some authority or elite" (2015, p. 309). This book's focus on media literacy is based in large part on cultural theories, which say that meaning and, therefore, effects are negotiated by media and audiences as they interact in the culture.

CRITICAL CULTURAL THEORY   A major influence on mass communication theory came from European scholarship on media effects. **Critical cultural theory**—the idea that media operate primarily to justify and support the status quo at the expense of ordinary people—is openly political and is rooted in **neo-Marxist theory**. "Old-fashioned" Marxists believed that people were oppressed by those who owned the factories and the land (the means of production). They called the factories and land the *base*. Modern neo-Marxist theorists believe that people are oppressed by those who control the culture, the *superstructure*—religion, politics, art, literature, and of course the mass media.

Modern critical cultural theory encompasses a number of different conceptions of the relationship between media and culture. But all share these identifying characteristics:

- *They tend to be macroscopic in scope.* They examine broad, culturewide media effects.
- *They are openly and avowedly political.* Based on neo-Marxism, their orientation is from the political left.
- *Their goal is at the least to instigate change in government media policies, and at the most to effect wholesale change in media and cultural systems.* Critical cultural theories logically assume that the superstructure, which favors those in power, must be altered.
- *They investigate and explain how elites use media to maintain their positions of privilege and power.* Issues such as media ownership, government–media relations, and corporate media representations of labor and disenfranchised groups are typical topics of study for critical cultural theory because they center on the exercise of power. You can read a critical cultural theory critique of media coverage of poor and working-class people in the box entitled "Why Were They Invisible?"

CULTURAL FORUM
Why Were They Invisible?

In the aftermath of the 2016 presidential election, there was considerable speculation as to why so many working-class voters abandoned their traditional allegiance to the Democratic Party and voted for Republican Donald Trump. Among the most often cited reasons was the difficult economic situation these folks faced as a result of severe and growing income inequality (Darvis & Konstantinos, 2016). Indeed, the United States has the greatest level of income inequality of any developed democracy in the world, with a wealth gap between the economic top and bottom not seen since the 1920s (Leonhardt, 2016); 43 million Americans, 11 million more than in 2000, live in poverty—more than the combined populations of Texas, Pennsylvania, and Nebraska (Berg, 2017); on any given night in America, nearly 600,000 people will be living on the streets ("The State Of," 2016). Yet in the entire year of 2016, amid a contentious election, not only was there zero coverage of poverty on the three nightly nationally broadcast television news programs (ABC, NBC, and CBS), but the economy in general received less coverage than it had in any of the previous 29 years (Tyndall Report, 2017).

The cultural forum was rightfully roiled by the question of why the traditional media had so badly underestimated the level of frustration felt by Trump voters. "Many in the media, especially me," wrote *New York Times* columnist David Brooks, "did not understand how they would express their alienation. We expected Trump to fizzle because we were not socially intermingled with his supporters and did not listen carefully enough" (2016, p. A27). But *why* did "many in the media" miss this most

(*Continued*)

important story? Was it, as Brooks suggests, that most national journalists are far removed from the real lives of many Americans, with 25% of the country's 40,000 working journalists living in Los Angeles, New York, and Washington? Was it because their relative wealth makes it impossible for them to "fathom the deep, seething, often unspoken economic discontent that afflicts so many Americans" (Gabler, 2016)?

Perhaps it was because working-class people are invisible in our entertainment as well. "These days, there are only a handful of workplace taxonomies in scripted television," writes critic Wesley Morris. "When the economy began to tank in 2007, television was barely equipped to reflect the collapse, in part because the people who make shows were largely immune: They were well-compensated creatures of the entertainment industry, mostly unaffected by a shrinking economy. That disconnection sanitized TV against the complexities of race and class" (2016, pp. 76–79).

Enter your voice. Why had the traditional media— entertainment and news—so badly missed the realities of the lives of working-class people? Why are poverty, homelessness, and the lives of America's least fortunate not news and rarely the material for our dramatic media? Veteran journalist Chris Hedges places much of the blame on concentration and conglomeration: "Journalists long ago gave up trying to describe an objective world or give a voice to ordinary men and women. They became conditioned to cater to corporate demands. News personalities, who often make millions of dollars a year, became courtiers" (2016). Do you agree? How might critical cultural theorists, who have long studied these issues, answer the question?

THE FRANKFURT SCHOOL The critical cultural perspective actually came to the United States in the 1930s when two prominent media scholars from the University of Frankfurt escaped Hitler's Germany. Theodor Adorno and Max Horkheimer were at the heart of what became known as the **Frankfurt School** of media theory (Arato & Gebhardt, 1978). Their approach, centered in neo-Marxism, valued serious art (literature, symphonic music, and theater) and saw consumption of art as a means to elevate all people toward a better life. Typical media fare—popular music, slapstick radio and movie comedies, the soft news dominant in newspapers—pacified ordinary people while assisting in their repression.

Adorno and Horkheimer's influence on U.S. media theory was small during their lifetimes. The limited effects perspective was about to blossom, neo-Marxism was not well received, and their ideas sounded a bit too much like mass society theory claims of a corrupting and debasing popular media. More recently, though, the Frankfurt School has been "rediscovered," and its influence can be seen in two final examples of contemporary critical theory, British cultural theory and news production research.

BRITISH CULTURAL THEORY There was significant class tension in England after World War II. During the 1950s and 1960s, working-class people who had fought for their country were unwilling to return to England's traditional notions of nobility and privilege. Many saw the British media—with broadcasting dominated by graduates of the best upper-crust schools, and newspapers and magazines owned by the wealthy—as supporting long-standing class distinctions and divisions. This environment of class conflict produced theorists such as Stuart Hall (1980), who first developed the idea of media as a public forum in which various forces fight to shape perceptions of everyday reality. Hall and others in British cultural studies trusted that the media *could* serve all people. However, because of ownership patterns, the commercial orientation of the media, and sympathetic government policies toward media, the forum was dominated by the reigning elite. In other words, the loudest voice in the give-and-take of the cultural forum belonged to those already well entrenched in the power structure. **British cultural theory** today provides a home for much feminist research and research on popular culture both in Europe and in the United States.

NEWS PRODUCTION RESEARCH Another interesting strand of critical cultural theory is **news production research**—the study of how economic and other influences on the way news is produced distort and bias news coverage toward those in power. W. Lance Bennett (1988) identified four common news production conventions used by U.S. media that bolster the position of those in power:

1. *Personalized news.* Most news stories revolve around people. If a newspaper wants to do a report on homelessness, for example, it will typically focus on one person or family as

the center of its story. This makes for interesting journalism (and increased ratings or circulation), but it reduces important social and political problems to soap opera levels. The two likely results are that these problems are dismissed by the public as specific to the characters in the story and that the public is not provided with the social and political contexts of the problem that might suggest avenues of public action.

2. *Dramatized news.* News, like other forms of media content, must be attractively packaged. Especially on television, this packaging takes the form of dramatization. Stories must have a hero and a villain, a conflict must be identified, and there has to be a showdown. Again, one problem is that important public issues take on the character of a soap opera or a Western movie. But a larger concern is that political debate is trivialized. Fundamental alterations in tax law or defense spending or any of a number of important issues are reduced to environmental extremists versus greedy corporations or the White House versus Congress. This complaint is often raised about media coverage of campaigns. The issues that should be at the center of the campaign become lost in a sea of stories about the "horse race"—who's ahead; how will a good showing in New Hampshire help Candidate X in her battle to unseat Candidate Y as the front-runner?

3. *Fragmented news.* The daily time and cost demands of U.S. journalism result in newspapers and broadcasts composed of a large number of brief, capsulated stories. There is little room in a given report for perspective and context. Another contributor to fragmented news, according to Bennett (1988), is journalists' obsession with objectivity. Putting any given day's story in context—connecting it to other events of the time or the past—would require the reporter to make decisions about which links are most important. Of course, these choices would be subjective, and so they are avoided. Reporters typically get one comment from somebody on one side of the issue and a second comment from the other side, juxtapose them as if they were equally valid, and then move on to tomorrow's assignment.

4. *Normalized news.* The U.S. newswriting convention typically employed when reporting on natural or human-made disasters is to seek out and report the opinions and perspectives of the authorities. When an airplane crashes, for example, the report invariably concludes with these words: "The FAA was quickly on the scene. The cockpit recorder has been retrieved, and the reason for this tragedy will be determined soon." In other words, what happened here is bad, but the authorities will sort it out. Journalists give little independent attention to investigating any of a number of angles that a plane crash or flood might suggest, angles that might produce information different from that of officials.

The cultural effect of news produced according to these conventions is daily reassurance by the media that the system works if those in power are allowed to do their jobs. Any suggestions about opportunities for meaningful social action are suppressed as reporters serve the powerful as "stenographers with amnesia" (Gitlin, 2004, p. 31).

◀ Normalized news: No media account of a plane crash is complete without assurance that the flight recorder will help officials pinpoint the cause of the crash.
©Mehdi Fedouach/Getty Images

The Meaning-Making Perspective

A more micro-level-centered view of media influence, one paralleling cultural theories in its belief in the power of mass communication, is the **meaning-making perspective**, the idea that active audience members use media content to create meaning, and meaningful experiences, for themselves. Naturally, this use can produce important macro-level, or cultural, effects as well. Cultural and meaning-making theories, taken together, make a most powerful case for becoming media literate. They argue that who we are and the world in which we live are in large part of our own making.

SYMBOLIC INTERACTION Mass communication theorists borrowed **symbolic interaction** from psychology. It is the idea that cultural symbols are learned through interaction and then mediate that interaction. In other words, people give things meaning, and that meaning controls their behavior. The flag is a perfect example. We have decided that an array of red, white, and blue cloth, assembled in a particular way, represents not only our nation but its values and beliefs. The flag has meaning because we have given it meaning, and that meaning now governs certain behavior toward the flag. Very rarely, if ever, will we remain seated when a color guard carries the flag into a room. To do so is considered a mark of disrespect, an insult. This is symbolic interaction.

Communication scholars Don Faules and Dennis Alexander define communication as "symbolic behavior which results in various degrees of shared meaning and values between participants" (1978, p. 23). In their view, symbolic interaction is an excellent way to explain how mass communication shapes people's behaviors. Accepting that these symbolic meanings are negotiated by participants in the culture, mass communication scholars are left with these questions: What do the media contribute to these negotiations, and how powerful are they?

Symbolic interaction theory is frequently used in the study of the influence of advertising because advertisers often succeed by encouraging the audience to perceive their products as symbols that have meaning beyond the products' actual function. This is called **product positioning**. For example, what does a Cadillac mean? Success. A Porsche? Virility. General Foods International Coffees? Togetherness and intimacy.

SOCIAL CONSTRUCTION OF REALITY If we keep in mind James Carey's cultural definition of communication—communication is a symbolic process whereby reality is produced, maintained, repaired, and transformed—we cannot be surprised that mass communication theorists have been drawn to the ideas of sociologists Peter Berger and Thomas Luckmann. In their 1966 book, *The Social Construction of Reality*, they don't directly discuss mass communication, but they offer a compelling theory to explain how cultures use signs and symbols to construct and maintain a uniform reality.

Social construction of reality theory argues that people who share a culture also share "an ongoing correspondence" of meaning. Things generally mean the same to me as they do to you. A stop sign, for example, has just about the same meaning for everyone. Berger and Luckmann call these things that have "objective" meaning **symbols**—we routinely interpret them in the usual way. But there are other things in the environment to which we assign "subjective" meaning. These things they call **signs**. In social construction of reality, then, a car is a symbol of mobility, but a Cadillac or Mercedes Benz is a sign of wealth or success. In either case the meaning is negotiated, but for signs the negotiation is a bit more complex.

Through interaction in and with the culture over time, people bring together what they have learned about these signs and symbols to form **typification schemes**—collections of meanings assigned to some phenomenon or situation. These typification schemes form a natural backdrop for people's interpretation of and behavior in "the major routines of everyday life, not only the typification of others . . . but typifications of all sorts of events and experiences" (Berger & Luckmann, 1966, p. 43). When you enter a classroom, you automatically recall the cultural meaning of its various elements: desks in rows, chalkboard or whiteboard, lectern. You recognize this as a classroom and impose your "classroom typification scheme." You know how to behave: address the person standing at the front of the room with courtesy, raise your hand when you have a question, talk to your neighbors in whispers. These "rules of behavior" were not published on the classroom door. You applied them because they were appropriate to the "reality" of the setting in your culture. In other cultures, behaviors in this setting may be quite different.

Social construction of reality is important to researchers who study the effects of advertising for the same reasons that symbolic interaction has proven valuable. But it is also widely applied when looking at how media, especially news, shape our political realities.

Crime offers one example. What do politicians mean when they say they are "tough on crime"? What is their (and your) reality of crime? It is likely that "crime" signifies (is a sign for) gangs, drugs, and violence. But the statistical (rather than the socially constructed) reality is that there is 10 times more white-collar crime in the United States than there is violent crime. Now think of "welfare." What reality is signified? Is it big corporations seeking subsidies and tax breaks from the government? Or is it unwed, unemployed mothers, unwilling to work, looking for a handout? Social construction theorists argue that the "building blocks" for the construction of these "realities" come primarily from the mass media.

CULTIVATION ANALYSIS Symbolic interaction and social construction of reality provide a strong foundation for *cultivation analysis*, which says that television "cultivates" or constructs a reality of the world that, although possibly inaccurate, becomes meaningful to us simply because we believe it to be true. We then base our judgments about and our actions in the world on this cultivated reality provided by television.

Although cultivation analysis was developed by media researcher George Gerbner and his colleagues out of concern over the effects of television violence, it has been applied to countless other television-cultivated realities such as beauty, sex roles, religion, the judicial process, and marriage. In all cases the assumptions are the same—television cultivates realities, especially for heavy viewers.

Cultivation analysis is based on five assumptions:

1. *Television is essentially and fundamentally different from other mass media.* Unlike books, newspapers, and magazines, television requires no reading ability. Unlike the movies, television requires no mobility or cash; it is in the home, and it is free. Unlike radio, television combines pictures and sound. It can be consumed from people's very earliest to their last years of life.

2. *Television is the "central cultural arm" of U.S. society.* Gerbner and his colleagues wrote that television, as our culture's primary storyteller, is "the chief creator of synthetic cultural patterns (entertainment and information) for the most heterogeneous mass publics in history, including large groups that have never shared in any common public message systems" (1978, p. 178). The product of this sharing of messages is the **mainstreaming** of reality, moving individual and different people toward a shared, television-created understanding of how things are.

3. *The realities cultivated by television are not necessarily specific attitudes and opinions but rather more basic assumptions about the "facts" of life.* Television does not teach facts and figures; it builds general frames of reference. Return to our earlier discussion of the portrayal of crime on television. Television newscasters never say, "Most crime is violent, most violent crime is committed by people of color, and you should be wary of those people." But by the choices news producers make, television news presents a broad picture of "reality" with little regard for how its "reality" matches that of its audience.

4. *The major cultural function of television is to stabilize social patterns.* That is, the existing power relationships of the culture are reinforced and maintained through the meaning-making television images encourage. Gerbner and his colleagues made this argument:

   > The repetitive pattern of television's mass-produced messages and images forms the mainstream of the common symbolic environment that cultivates the most widely shared conceptions of reality. We live in terms of the stories we tell—stories about what things exist, stories about how things work, and stories about what to do—and television tells them all through news, drama, and advertising to almost everybody most of the time. (1978, p. 178)

   Because the media industries have a stake in the political, social, and economic structures as they exist, their stories rarely challenge the system that has enriched them.

5. *The observable, measurable, independent contributions of television to the culture are relatively small.* This is not a restatement of limited effects theory. Instead, Gerbner and his colleagues explained its meaning with an "ice-age analogy":

> Just as an average temperature shift of a few degrees can lead to an ice age . . . so too can a relatively small but pervasive influence make a crucial difference. The "size" of an effect is far less critical than the direction of its steady contribution. (Gerbner et al., 1980, p. 14)

In other words, even though we cannot always see media effects on ourselves and others, they do occur and eventually will change the culture, possibly in profound ways.

▶ **Table 1** Mass Communication Theories

MASS COMMUNICATION THEORY	DESCRIPTION
Mass Society Theory	Idea, propagated by cultural and societal elites, that the media are corrupting influences that undermine the social order; "average" people are defenseless against the influence.
Limited Effects Theory	Media's influence is limited by people's individual differences, social categories, and personal relationships. These factors "limit" media's influence.
Two-Step Flow Theory	Idea that media's influence on people's behavior is limited by opinion leaders, who consume content, interpret it in light of their own values and beliefs, and pass it on to opinion followers. Therefore the source of effects is interpersonal rather than mass communication.
Attitude Change Theory	Collection of theories explaining how people's attitudes are formed, shaped, and changed through communication and how those attitudes influence behavior.
Dissonance Theory	Argument that people, when confronted by new information, experience mental discomfort (dissonance), so they consciously and subconsciously work to limit or reduce that discomfort through the selective processes.
Reinforcement Theory	Joseph Klapper's idea that if media have any impact at all, it is in the direction of reinforcement, especially as important social factors—school, parents, religion—also reinforce cultural norms.
Uses and Gratifications Approach	Idea that media don't do things to people; people do things *with* media. Audience members are powerful agents in either limiting or allowing effects.
Agenda Setting	Theory that media may not tell as what to think, but do tell as what to think about, meaning media can have important effects for individuals and society.
Dependency Theory	Idea that media's power is a function of audience members' dependency on the media and their content.
Social Cognitive Theory	Idea that people learn through observation, either as imitation or identification; actual exhibition of these behaviors is dependent on the reinforcement we associate with them.

Cultural Theory	Idea that meaning and effects are negotiated by media and audiences as they interact in the culture; debate exists over who has the upper hand.
Critical Cultural Theory	Idea that media operate primarily to justify and support the status quo at the expense of ordinary people. Media and other elites have the upper hand in the negotiation of meaning.
The Frankfurt School	Theory that values serious art, viewing its consumption as a means to elevate people toward a better life; but common media content pacifies and represses ordinary people.
British Cultural Theory	Theory of elites' domination over the larger culture, primarily through mass communication, and its influence on bounded cultures, limiting the expression of their values.
News Production Research	Study of how economic and other influences on the way news is produced distort and bias news coverage toward those in power, especially through news practices such as personalized, dramatized, fragmented, and normalized news.
The Meaning-Making Perspective	Idea that active audience members use media content to create meaning and meaningful experiences for themselves. Media-literate consumers can have greater control over the meanings that are made.
Symbolic Interaction	Idea that people give meaning to symbols, which then control people's behavior in their presence.
Social Construction of Reality	Theory that cultures construct and maintain realities by using signs and symbols; people learn to behave in their social world through interaction with it, as those mutually negotiated meanings allow members of a culture to better know one another and predict interactions and behaviors.
Cultivation Analysis	Idea that television "cultivates" or constructs a reality of the world that, although possibly inaccurate, becomes the accepted reality simply because we as a culture believe it to be; we then base our judgments about and our actions in the world on this cultivated reality.

The Effects of Mass Communication— Four Questions

Scientists and scholars use these theories, the earliest and the most recent, to form conclusions about the effects of mass communication. You are of course familiar with the long-standing debate over the effects of television violence. But there are many other fascinating and important media effects questions that occupy researchers' interest beyond that and the others highlighted here.

Does Media Violence Lead to Aggression?

No media effects issue has captured public, legislative, and industry attention as has the relationship between media portrayals of violence and subsequent aggressive behavior. Among the reasons for this focus are the facts that violence is a staple of both television and movies and that the United States experienced an upsurge in real violence in the 1960s, just about the time television entrenched itself as the country's dominant mass medium, and that movies turned to increasingly graphic violence to differentiate themselves from and to compete with television.

The prevailing view during the 1960s was that *some* media violence affected *some* people in *some* ways *some* of the time. Given the dominance of the transmissional perspective of communication and the limited effects theories, researchers believed that for "normal" people—that is, those who were not predisposed to violence—*little* media violence affected *few* people in *few* ways *little* of the time. However, increases in youth violence, the assassinations of Robert F. Kennedy and the Reverend Martin Luther King Jr., and the violent eruption of cities during the civil rights, women's rights, and anti–Vietnam War movements led to creation of the Surgeon General's Scientific Advisory Committee on Television and Social Behavior in 1969. After two years and $1 million worth of research, the committee (whose members had to be approved by the television networks) produced findings that led Surgeon General Jesse L. Steinfield to report to the U.S. Senate:

> While the . . . report is carefully phrased and qualified in language acceptable to social scientists, it is clear to me that the causal relationship between televised violence and antisocial behavior is sufficient to warrant appropriate and immediate remedial action. The data on social phenomena such as television and violence and/or aggressive behavior will never be clear enough for all social scientists to agree on the formulation of a succinct statement of causality. But there comes a time when the data are sufficient to justify action. That time has come. (Ninety-Second Congress, 1972, p. 26)

Despite the apparent certainty of this statement, disagreement persists over the existence and extent of the media's contribution to aggressive behavior. Few would argue that media violence *never* leads to aggressive behavior. The disagreement is about what circumstances are needed for such effects to occur, and to whom.

UNDER WHAT CIRCUMSTANCES? A direct causal relationship between violent content and aggressive behavior—the **stimulation model**—has been scientifically demonstrated in

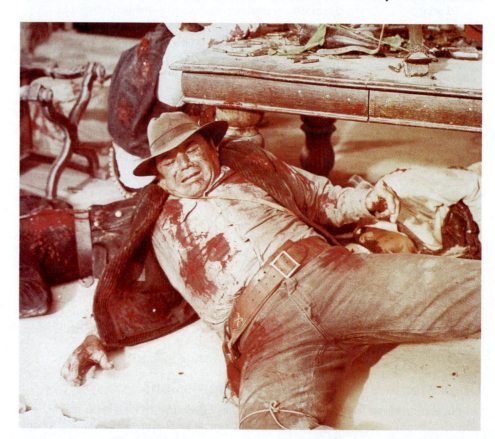

► Ernest Borgnine in Sam Peckinpah's *The Wild Bunch* (1969). In trying to differentiate itself from the television industry, the movie industry turned to graphic violence, fueling the debate over media violence and subsequent real-world aggression.
©Warner Brothers/Photofest

laboratory experiments. So has the **aggressive cues model**—the idea that media portrayals can suggest that certain classes of people, such as women or foreigners, are acceptable targets for real-world aggression, thereby increasing the likelihood that some people will act violently toward people in these groups.

Both the stimulation and aggressive cues models are based on social cognitive theory. Fueled by the research of psychologists such as Albert Bandura, social cognitive theory has made several additional contributions to the violence debate.

Social cognitive theory deflated the notion of **catharsis**, the idea that watching violence in the media reduces people's innate aggressive drive. Social scientists were already skeptical: viewing people eating does not reduce hunger; watching pornography does not decrease sex drive. But social cognitive theory provided a scientific explanation for the research that did show a reduction in aggression after viewing violence. This phenomenon was better explained not by some cathartic power of the media but by inhibitory effects. That is, as we saw in our discussion of social cognitive theory, if media aggression is portrayed as punished or prohibited, it can indeed lead to the reduced likelihood that that behavior will be modeled.

Some people, typically media industry practitioners, to this day defend catharsis theory. But over 40 years ago, respected media researcher and theorist Joseph Klapper, who at the time was the head of social research for CBS television, told the U.S. Senate, "I myself am unaware of any, shall we say, hard evidence that seeing violence on television or any other medium acts in a cathartic . . . manner. There have been some studies to that effect; they are grossly, greatly outweighed by studies as to the opposite effect" (Ninety-Second Congress, 1972, p. 60).

Social cognitive theory introduced the concept of **vicarious reinforcement**—the idea that observed reinforcement operates in the same manner as actual reinforcement. This helped direct researchers' attention to the context in which media violence is presented. Theoretically, inhibitory and disinhibitory effects operate because of the presence of vicarious reinforcement. That is, seeing the bad guy punished is sufficient to inhibit subsequent aggression on the part of the viewer. Unfortunately, what researchers discovered is that in contemporary film and television, when the bad guys are punished, they are punished by good guys who out-aggress them. The implication is that even when media portray punishment for aggressive behavior, they may in fact be reinforcing that very same behavior.

Social cognitive theory also introduced the concept of **environmental incentives**—the notion that real-world incentives can lead observers to ignore the negative vicarious reinforcement they have learned to associate with a given behavior.

In 1965 Bandura conducted a now-classic experiment in which nursery school children saw a video aggressor, a character named Rocky, punished for his behavior. The children subsequently showed lower levels of aggressive play than did those who had seen Rocky rewarded. This is what social cognitive theory would have predicted. Yet Bandura later offered "sticker-pictures" to the children who had seen Rocky punished if they could perform the same actions they had seen him perform. They all could. Vicarious negative reinforcement may reduce the likelihood that the punished behavior will be performed, but that behavior is still observationally learned. It's just that, at the same time it is observed and learned, observers also learn not to repeat it. When the real world offers sufficient reward, the originally learned behavior can be demonstrated.

FOR WHOM? The compelling evidence of cognitive learning researchers aside, it's clear that most people do not exhibit aggression after viewing film or video violence. There is also little doubt that those predisposed to violence are more likely to be influenced by media aggression. Yet viewers need not necessarily be predisposed for this link to occur, because at any time anyone can become predisposed. For example, experimental research indicates that frustrating people before they view media violence can increase the likelihood of subsequent aggressive behavior.

But the question remains, who, exactly, is affected by mediated violence? If a direct causal link is necessary to establish effects, then it can indeed be argued that some media violence affects some people in some ways some of the time. But if the larger, macro-level ritual view is applied, then we all are affected because we live in a world in which there is more violence than there might be without mass media. We live in a world, according to

▲ These scenes from Albert Bandura's media violence research are typical of the laboratory response to portrayals of media violence that social learning researchers were able to elicit from children.

Courtesy of Professor Albert Bandura, Stanford University

cultivation analysis, in which we are less trusting of our neighbors and more accepting of violence in our midst. This need not be the case. As researcher Ellen Wartella said, "Today, we find wide consensus among experts that, of all the factors contributing to violence in our society, violence on television may be the easiest to control" (1997, p. 4). And in a clear sign of that wide consensus, the American Medical Association, the American Academy of Pediatrics, the American Psychological Association, and the American Academy of Child & Adolescent Psychiatry issued a joint report in summer 2000 offering their combined view that the effects of violent media are "measurable and long lasting" and that "prolonged viewing of media violence can lead to emotional **desensitization** toward violence in real life" (as quoted in Wronge, 2000, p. 1E).

Do Portrayals of Drugs and Alcohol Increase Consumption?

Concern about media effects reaches beyond the issue of violence. The claims and counterclaims surrounding media portrayals of drugs and alcohol parallel those of the violence debate.

The wealth of scientific data linking media portrayals of alcohol consumption, especially in ads, to increases in youthful drinking and alcohol abuse led the U.S. Department of Health and Human Services' National Institute of Alcohol Abuse and Alcoholism to report in 1995 that "the preponderance of the evidence indicates that alcohol advertising stimulates higher consumption of alcohol by both adults and adolescents" (Martin & Mail, 1995), a conclusion repeatedly reaffirmed, for example by researchers writing in 2016 in the *Journal of Studies on Alcohol and Drugs*, who demonstrated that "among underage youth, the quantity of brand-specific advertising exposure is positively associated with the total quantity of consumption of those advertised brands" (Naimi et al., 2016). The Center on Alcohol Marketing and Youth (2017) reports the following:

- More youth in the United States drink alcohol than smoke tobacco or marijuana, making it the drug most used by America's young people.
- Every day, 4,750 people under 16 take their first drink of alcohol.

- The average age at which a young person takes his or her first drink is 13 years old.

- Underage drinking is estimated to account for between 11% and 20% of the U.S. alcohol market. Even the lower estimate of 11% represents 3.6 billion drinks each year.

- Youth who start drinking before the age of 15 are five times more likely to develop alcohol dependence or abuse in their lifetimes than are those who begin drinking at age 21 years or later.

- Programming popular with teens is filled with alcohol advertising. Every year since 2001, alcohol ads have appeared on 13 or more of the 15 programs most popular with people ages 12 to 17.

- The neuroscience, psychology, and marketing scientific literature concludes that adolescents, because of how the human brain develops, may be particularly attracted to branded products such as alcohol that are associated with risky behavior and that provide, in their view, immediate gratification, thrills, and/or social status.

- A complete ban on alcohol advertising would result in 7,609 fewer deaths a year from harmful drinking.

BE FABULOUS*

MOËT & CHANDON
CHAMPAGNE

▲ What does this magazine ad say about drinking? About attractiveness? About having fun? About women? Are you satisfied with these representations of important aspects of your life? *Courtesy of The Advertising Archives*

Yet there is a good deal of scientific research—typically from alcohol industry scientists—that discounts the causal link between media portrayals and real-world drinking. Again, researchers who insist on the demonstration of this direct causal relationship will rarely agree on media's influence on behavior. The larger cultural perspective, however, suggests that media portrayals of alcohol, both in ads and in entertainment fare, tell stories of alcohol consumption that predominantly present it as safe, healthy, youthful, sexy, necessary for a good time, effective for dealing with stress, and essential to ceremonies and other rites of passage.

The same scenario exists in the debate over the relationship between media portrayals of nonalcohol drug use and behavior. Relatively little contemporary media content presents the use of illegal drugs in a glorifying manner. In fact, the destructive power of illegal drugs is often the focus of television shows such as *Law and Order: SVU* and *Orange Is the New Black* and is a central theme in movies such as *Sicario* (2015) and *The Wolf of Wall Street* (2013). Scientific concern has centered therefore on the impact of commercials and other media portrayals of legal over-the-counter drugs. Again, impressive amounts of experimental research suggest a causal link between this content and subsequent abuse of both legal and illegal drugs; however, there also exists research that discounts the causal link between media portrayals and the subsequent abuse of drugs. It cannot be denied, however, that media often present legal drugs as a cure-all for dealing with that pesky mother-in-law, those screaming kids, that abusive boss, and other daily annoyances. Prescription drug advertising is enough of a public health issue that the Food and Drug Administration on several occasions has considered banning it. Nonetheless, it is illegal in every country in the world except the United States and New Zealand.

What Is Media's Contribution to Gender and Racial/Ethnic Stereotyping?

Stereotyping is the application of a standardized image or concept to members of certain groups, usually based on limited information. Because media cannot show all realities of all things, the choices media practitioners make when presenting specific people and groups may well facilitate or encourage stereotyping.

Numerous studies conducted over the last 70 years have demonstrated that women, people of color, older people, gays and lesbians—in fact, all of our nation's "out-groups"—are consistently underrepresented or misrepresented in our mass media. For example, Hispanics are significantly underrepresented in American television shows and movies, even more so than 20 years ago (Harding, 2014), African Americans are significantly overrepresented in television crime news (Starr, 2015), and Asian Americans, when they do appear in our media, are usually misrepresented as socially inept, academically aggressive nerds (Zhang, 2010). You read in the chapter on video games about that medium's underrepresentation of women and its sexist portrayal of women and women's bodies (Fox & Tang, 2014). Media effects research over those same 70 years has consistently demonstrated the impact of this underrepresentation and misrepresentation. Jennings Bryant and his colleagues summarized, "Media images of minorities have been shown to have considerable impact. . . . The portrayal of lazy, incompetent, rebellious, or violent persons of color can be an enduring mental image." The result, they conclude, is the creation of harmful stereotypes (Bryant, Thompson, & Finklea, 2013, p. 261).

Any of a number of theories, especially cultivation analysis, symbolic interaction, and social construction of reality, can explain these effects. This underrepresentation and misrepresentation influence people's perceptions, and people's perceptions influence their behaviors. Examine your own perceptions not only of women and people of color but of older people, lawyers, college athletes, and people sophisticated in the use of computers. What images or stereotypes immediately come to mind?

Sure, maybe you were a bit surprised at the data on race and traffic stops and car searches described earlier; still, you're skeptical. You're a smart, modern, college-educated individual. Use the following quiz to test yourself on your stereotypes of crime, marriage, and the poor:

1. Which of these states has the lowest divorce rate: Arkansas, Alabama, or Massachusetts?
2. Which group of Americans—white or African American—has the highest rate of illegal drug use and of selling drugs?
3. Which category of Americans relies most heavily on food stamps—white, Hispanic, or African American?
4. Which is the only American city to rank in the top 10 on the *Economist* magazine's index of the safest cities in the world—Indianapolis, Omaha, or New York City?

Are you surprised to learn that the divorce rate is lowest in liberal, northeast Massachusetts (7 out of every 1,000 people), far lower than heartland states Arkansas and Alabama (both 13 per 1,000; Glass, 2014)? Illegal drug users? According to the National Research Council report on *Growth of Incarceration in the United States: Exploring Causes and Consequences*, "The prevalence of drug use is only slightly higher among blacks than whites for some illicit drugs and slightly lower for others; the difference is not substantial. There is also little evidence, when all drug types are considered, that blacks sell drugs more often than whites" (in Emery, 2016). Food stamps? More than 40% of America's food-stamp recipients are white. African Americans comprise 26% of the program's recipients and Hispanics 10% (Delaney & Scheller, 2015). Safest cities? Using a variety of data, including personal safety, the *Economist*'s Intelligence Unit determined that Tokyo is the world's safest city. New York City, the "Gomorrah of the North," was the only U.S. city to make the top 10 (McGrath, 2015). How did you develop your stereotypes of these people and places? Where did you find the building blocks to construct your realities of their lives?

But can other building blocks, that is, realistic portrayals of out-groups that challenge typical cultural stereotypes, produce beneficial effects? In the case of homosexuality, researchers believe that repeated and frequent exposure to a wide range of realistic media representations can positively influence people's perceptions of gays and issues relating to homosexuality. Some call this the *Will & Grace* effect, where "the single most important indicator of one's support for gay rights is whether one knows someone who is gay, [and a gay person] on TV will do" (Lithwick, 2012, p. 77). Today, having "met" many gay people in real and media life, a majority of Americans (63%) favor same-sex marriage (Cox & Jones, 2017). The question remains, however—as it typically does when discussing media stereotypes—which came first, the culture's perceptions of gay people or gay people's representation in the media? Clearly, television's presentation of gay people has matured over time—from invisible to realistic and sympathetic. But was television's "evolution" in its representation of homosexuality a *mirror* of culture's already changing attitudes, or did the medium *lead* that change?

▲ These images (clockwise from top left) from *Grey's Anatomy*, *Will & Grace*, *Orange Is the New Black*, and *Empire* offer samples of contemporary, nonstereotypical television's portrayals of gay people and homosexuality.
(Clockwise from top left) ©ABC/ Photofest; ©NBC/Courtesy Everett Collection; ©Netflix/Photofest; ©Fox Network/Photofest

Do Media Have Prosocial Effects?

Virtually every argument that can be made for the harmful or negative effects of media can also be applied to the ability of media to do good. A sizable body of science clearly demonstrates that people, especially children, can and will model the good or prosocial behaviors they see in the media, often to a greater extent than they will the negative behaviors. For example, research on the positive impact of media portrayals of cooperation and constructive problem solving (Baran, Chase, & Courtright, 1979) and on prosocial video game play's ability to reduce the propensity for risky driving (Greitemeyer, 2013) indicate that much more than negative behavior can be socially learned from the media (see the essay "Television and the Designated Driver").

Television's ability to serve prosocial ends is obvious in the public service messages we see sprinkled throughout the shows we watch. For example, NBC's *The More You Know* series has been running short, clever PSAs mixed among its regular commercials for more than 20 years. They feature the network's biggest stars, cover issues like quitting smoking, good parenting, remembering to take prescriptions, and good exercise, but you probably remember them from their iconic shooting star and rainbow tail.

USING MEDIA TO MAKE A DIFFERENCE
Television and the Designated Driver

But television writers and producers also more aggressively use their medium to produce prosocial effects by embedding important cultural messages in the entertainment they create. The relationship between the Centers for Disease Control and

Prevention (CDC) and several popular programs is indicative. Aware that most Americans say they learn about health issues from television, experts at the CDC work with the writers of series like *Blackish*, *Grey's Anatomy*, *ER*, *Army Wives*, *Law & Order*, and *Madame Secretary* to include important health information in their scripts. If you watched the episodes of *24* in which Los Angeles suffered a terrorist attack you learned, from this partnership, how infectious agents can be spread by physical contact, how to handle a government-mandated quarantine, and the civil liberty issues involved in such a quarantine. If you watched *Raising Hope*, *The Vampire Diaries*, *Glee*, or *Parenthood*, you've viewed stories written in conjunction with the National Campaign to Prevent Teen and Unplanned Pregnancy designed to promote safe sex.

This "prime-time activism" can be traced to Harvard professor Jay Winsten and his 1988 campaign to get Hollywood to push his novel "designated driver" idea. You know what a designated driver is—he or she is the person among a group of friends who is selected to remain alcohol-free during a get-together and then to drive everyone else home. The concept, much less the term, did not even exist until Professor Winsten, through the intervention of CBS executive Frank Stanton, contacted Stanton's friend Grant Tinker, then chair of NBC, to ask for help. Intrigued by Winsten's plan to develop a new social norm, Tinker put his considerable clout behind the effort, writing letters to the heads of the 13 production companies that did the most business with the networks. Tinker personally escorted Professor Winsten, director of Harvard's Center for Health Communication, to meetings with all 13 producers (Center for Health Communication, 2016).

In the four network television seasons that followed these meetings, designated drivers were part of the story lines of 160 different prime-time shows seen by hundreds of millions of viewers. Professor Winsten was successful in placing his message in entertainment programming, but did his message make a difference? Absolutely. There was a 24% decline in drunk driving fatalities in the four years after the concept was introduced; two years later fatalities reached an all-time low. Estimates are that 50,000 lives have been saved and that 73 million Americans serve as a designated driver or have a designated driver take them home each year ("Designated Driving," 2016).

DEVELOPING MEDIA LITERACY SKILLS

Applying Mass Communication Theory

There are many more theories of mass communication and effects issues than we've covered here. Some apply to the operation of media as part of specific social systems. Some examine mass communication at the most micro level; for example, how do viewers process individual television scenes? This chapter has focused on a relatively small number of theories and effects that might prove useful to people trying to develop their media literacy skills. Among media scholar Art Silverblatt's (2008) elements of media literacy are understanding the process of mass communication and accepting media content as a "text" providing insight into ourselves and our culture. Additionally, one of the most important media literacy skills is to have an understanding of and respect for the power of media messages. See the chapter on mass communication, culture, and media literacy for the full list of Silverblatt's elements of media literacy and the full list of necessary media-literacy skills. Good mass communication theory speaks to these elements and skills. Good mass communication theorists understand media effects. Media-literate people, then, are actually good mass communication theorists. They apply the available conceptions of media use and impact to their own content consumption and the way they live their lives.

MEDIA LITERACY CHALLENGE
Be a News Production Researcher

An awareness of the impact of media on individuals and society is an important component of media literacy, and as you've read, news production research suggests that media do indeed have a powerful effect on people and culture. This work examines economic and other influences on the way news is produced and how these influences distort coverage in favor of society's elites. Like much of critical cultural theory, this is a controversial perspective, but your challenge is to test its validity for yourself. First, choose one of the following media outlets (or if you want to compete against your classmates, divide them between yourselves): a daily newspaper, a local television news broadcast, a national news magazine, and a network television news broadcast. Then, identify as many examples of the four common news production conventions as you can find—personalized, dramatized, fragmented, and normalized news—and discuss their "slant." Once you've completed this exercise, explain why you are more or less likely to accept the arguments of the news production research perspective.

Resources for Review and Discussion

REVIEW POINTS: TYING CONTENT TO LEARNING OUTCOMES

► **Outline the history and development of mass communication theory.**
- ☐ Developments in mass communication theory are driven by advances in technology or the introduction of new media, calls for their control, and questions about their democratic and pluralistic use.

► **Explain what is meant by theory, why it is important, and how it is used.**
- ☐ To understand mass communication theory we must recognize the following:
  - There is no one mass communication theory.
  - Theories are often borrowed from other fields of science.
  - Theories are human constructions and are dynamic.
- ☐ Three dichotomies characterize the different sides in the effects debate:
  - Micro- versus macro-level effects.
  - Administrative versus critical research.
  - Transmissional versus ritual perspective on communication.
- ☐ In the media effects debate, these arguments for limited media influence have logical counters:
  - Media content is make-believe; people know it's not real.
  - Media content is only play or entertainment.
  - Media simply hold a mirror to society.
  - If media have any influence, it is only in reinforcing pre-existing values and beliefs.
  - Media influence only the unimportant things like fads and fashions.

► **Describe influential traditional and contemporary mass communication theories.**
- ☐ The four major eras of mass communication theory are mass society theory, limited effects theory, cultural theory, and the meaning-making perspective. The latter two mark a return to the idea of powerful media effects.

► **Analyze controversial effects issues, such as violence, media's impact on drug and alcohol consumption, and media's contribution to racial and gender stereotyping.**
- ☐ Despite lingering debate, the media violence/viewer aggression link is scientifically well established.
- ☐ The same holds true for the relationship between media portrayals of drug and alcohol use and their real-world consumption.
- ☐ The stories carried in the media can and do contribute to stereotyping of a wide array of people and phenomena.
- ☐ The same scientific evidence demonstrating that media can have negative effects shows that they can produce prosocial effects as well.

► **Apply mass communication theory to your own use of media.**
- ☐ Media-literate individuals are themselves good mass communication theorists because they understand media effects and how and when they occur.

KEY TERMS

QUESTIONS FOR REVIEW

1. What are the four eras of mass communication theory?
2. What are dissonance theory and the selective processes?
3. What is agenda setting?
4. What is the distinction between imitation and identification in social cognitive theory?
5. What assumptions about people and media are shared by symbolic interaction and social construction of reality?
6. What are the five assumptions of cultivation analysis?
7. What four common news production conventions shape the news to suit the interests of the elite?
8. What are the characteristics of critical cultural studies?
9. What are the early window and willing suspension of disbelief?
10. What are the stimulation and aggressive cues models of media violence? What is catharsis?

To maximize your study time, check out CONNECT to access the SmartBook study module for this chapter and explore other resources.

QUESTIONS FOR CRITICAL THINKING AND DISCUSSION

1. Do media set the agenda for you? If not, why not? If they do, can you cite examples from your own experience?
2. Can you find examples of magazine or television advertising that use ideas from symbolic interaction or social construction of reality to sell their products? How do they do so?
3. Do you pay attention to alcohol advertising? Do you think it influences your level of alcohol consumption?

REFERENCES

1. Albiniak, P. (1999, May 3). Media: Littleton's latest suspect. *Broadcasting & Cable*, pp. 6–15.
2. Allport, G. W., & Postman, L. J. (1945). The basic psychology of rumor. *Transactions of the New York Academy of Sciences, 8,* 61–81.
3. Alterman, E. (2008, February 24). The news from Quinn–Broderville. *The Nation*, pp. 11–14.
4. Andrews, E. (2016, June 28). Stanford researchers develop new statistical test that shows racial profiling in police traffic stops. *Stanford News*. Online: http://news.stanford

.edu/2016/06/28/stanford-researchers-develop-new-statistical-test-shows-racial-profiling-police-traffic-stops/

5. Arato, A., & Gebhardt, E. (1978). *The essential Frankfurt School reader.* New York: Urizen Books.

6. Bandura, A. (2001). Social cognitive theory of mass communication. *Media Psychology, 3,* 265–299.

7. Bandura, A. (1965). Influence of models' reinforcement contingencies on the acquisition of imitative responses. *Journal of Personality and Social Psychology, 1,* 589–595.

8. Baran, S. J., Chase, L. J., & Courtright, J. A. (1979). *The Waltons:* Television as a facilitator of prosocial behavior. *Journal of Broadcasting, 23,* 277–284.

9. Baran, S. J., & Davis, D. K. (2015). *Mass communication theory: Foundations, ferment and future* (7th ed.). Boston: Wadsworth Cengage.

10. Bennett, W. L. (1988). *News: The politics of illusion.* New York: Longman.

11. Berg, J. (2017, January 10). U.S. poverty policy is outdated and inefficient. Here's a better approach. *Washington Monthly.* Online: http://washingtonmonthly.com/2017/01/10/u-s-poverty-policy-is-outdated-and-inefficient-heres-a-better-approach/

12. Berger, P. L., & Luckmann, T. (1966). *The social construction of reality: A treatise in the sociology of knowledge.* Garden City, NY: Doubleday.

13. Brooks, D. (2016, March 18). No, not Trump, not ever. *The New York Times,* p. A27.

14. Bryant, J., Thompson, S., & Finklea, B. W. (2013). *Fundamentals of media effects.* Long Grove, IL: Waveland Press.

15. Carey, J. W. (1975). A cultural approach to communication. *Communication, 2,* 1–22.

16. Center for Health Communication. (2016). Harvard alcohol project. *Harvard School of Public Health.* Online: https://www.hsph.harvard.edu/chc/harvard-alcohol-project/

17. Center on Alcohol Marketing and Youth. (2017). Fact sheets: Underage drinking in the United States. Online: http://camy.org

18. Cox, D., & Jones, R. P. (2017, March 10). Majority of Americans oppose transgender bathroom restrictions. *Public Religion Research Institute.* Online: http://www.prri.org/research/lgbt-transgender-bathroom-discrimination-religious-liberty/

19. Darvis, Z., & Konstantinos, E. (2016, November 9). Income inequality boosted Trump vote. *Bruegel.com.* Online: http://bruegel.org/2016/11/income-inequality-boosted-trump-vote/

20. DeFleur, M. L., & Ball-Rokeach, S. (1975). *Theories of mass communication* (3rd ed.). New York: David McKay.

21. Delaney, A., & Scheller, A. (2015, February 28). Who gets food stamps? White people, mostly. *Huffington Post.* Online: http://www.huffingtonpost.com/2015/02/28/food-stamp-demographics_n_6771938.html

22. "Designated driving statistics." (2016). *Designated Driving.net.* Online: http://www.designateddriving.net/designateddrivingstatistics.html

23. Emery, C. E. (2016, July 13). Van Jones claim on drug use, imprisonment rates for blacks, whites is mostly accurate. *Politifact.* Online: http://www.politifact.com/punditfact/statements/2016/jul/13/van-jones/van-jones-claim-drug-use-imprisonment-rates-blacks/

24. Faules, D. F., & Alexander, D. C. (1978). *Communication and social behavior: A symbolic interaction perspective.* Reading, MA: Addison-Wesley.

25. Fox, J., & Tang, W. Y. (2014). Sexism in online video games: The role of conformity to masculine norms and social dominance orientation. *Computers in Human Behavior, 33,* 314–320.

26. Fresh Air. (2016, May 6). After 20 years on the job, NYC police officer tells his intense stories. *NPR.* Online: http://www.npr.org/2016/05/06/476890358/after-20-years-on-the-job-nyc-police-officer-tells-his-intense-stories

27. Gabler, N. (2016, April 24). The mainstream media's big disconnect: Why they don't get Middle America. *Alternet.* Online: http://www.alternet.org/media/mainstream-medias-big-disconnect-why-they-dont-get-middle-america

28. Gerbner, G., Gross, L., Jackson-Beeck, M., Jeffries-Fox, S., & Signorielli, N. (1978). Cultural indicators: Violence profile no. 9. *Journal of Communication, 28,* 176–206.

29. Gerbner, G., Gross, L., Morgan, M., & Signorielli, N. (1980). The "mainstreaming" of America: Violence profile no. 11. *Journal of Communication, 30,* 10–29.

30. Gitlin, T. (2004, July). It was a very bad year. *American Prospect,* pp. 31–34.

31. Glass, J. (2014, January 16). Red states, blue states, and divorce: Understanding the impact of conservative Protestantism on regional variation in divorce rates. *Contemporary Families.org.* Online: https://contemporaryfamilies.org/impact-of-conservative-protestantism-on-regional-divorce-rates/

32. Greitemeyer, T. (2013). Exposure to media with prosocial content reduces the propensity for reckless and risky driving. *Journal of Risk Research, 16,* 583–594.

33. Hall, S. (1980). Cultural studies: Two paradigms. *Media, Culture and Society, 2,* 57–72.

34. Harding, S. (2014, June 19). Columbia University study finds Latinos underrepresented in TV, movie roles; even fewer in top media positions. *Latina Post.* Online: http://www.latinpost.com/articles/15188/20140619/columbia-university-study-finds-latinos-underrepresented-tv-movie-roles-even.htm

35. Hedges, C. (2016, December 26). America is awash in fake news. *Alternet.* Online: http://www.alternet.org/media/america-awash-fake-news

36. Hovland, C. I., Lumsdaine, A. A., & Sheffield, F. D. (1949). *Experiments on mass communication.* Princeton, NJ: Princeton University Press.

37. Iyengar, S., & Kinder, D. R. (1987). *News that matters: Television and American opinion.* Chicago: University of Chicago Press.

38. Jhally, S. (2013). *Joystick warriors.* Online: http://www.mediaed.org/transcripts/Joystick-Warriors-Transcript.pdf

39. Katz, E., & Lazarsfeld, P. F. (1955). *Personal influence: The part played by people in the flow of communications.* New York: Free Press.

40. Klapper, J. T. (1960). *The effects of mass communication.* New York: Free Press.

41. Lazarsfeld, P. F. (1941). Remarks on administrative and critical communications research. *Studies in Philosophy and Social Science, 9,* 2–16.

42. Leonhardt, D. (2016, December 11). The American dream, quantified at last. *The New York Times,* p. SR2.

43. Lithwick, D. (2012, March 12). Extreme makeover. *The New Yorker,* pp. 76–79.

44. Lowery, S. A., & DeFleur, M. L. (1995). *Milestones in mass communication research.* White Plains, NY: Longman.

45. Martin, S. E., & Mail, P. D. (1995). *The effects of the mass media on the use and abuse of alcohol.* Washington, DC: U.S. Department of Health and Human Services.

46. McCombs, M. E., & Shaw, D. L. (1972). The agenda-setting function of mass media. *Public Opinion Quarterly, 36,* 176–187.

47. McGrath, T. (2015, February 4). The 10 safest cities in the world. *Salon.* Online: http://www.salon.com/2015/02/04/the_10_safest_cities_in_the_world_partner/

48. Merton, R. K. (1967). *On theoretical sociology.* New York: Free Press.

49. Morris, W. (2016, May 1). What happened to all the working-class TV characters. *The New York Times Sunday Magazine,* pp. 76–79.

50. Naimi, T. S., Ross, C. S., Siegel, M. B., DeJong, W., & Jernigan, D. H. (2016). Amount of televised alcohol advertising exposure and the quantity of alcohol consumed by youth. *Journal of Studies on Alcohol and Drugs, 77,* 723–729.

51. Ninety-Second Congress. (1972). *Hearings before the Subcommittee on Communications on the Surgeon General's Report by the Scientific Advisory Committee on Television and Social Behavior.* Washington, DC: U.S. Government Printing Office.

52. Pennacchia, R. (2017, April 14). Pastor fears "Beauty and the Beast" is slippery slope to co-ed naked lady bison orgies. *Wonkette.* Online: https://wonkette.com/615578/pastor-fears-beauty-and-the-beast-is-slippery-slope-to-co-ed-naked-lady-bison-orgies

53. Quigley, B. (2016, October 4). 18 examples of racism in the criminal justice system. *Alternet.* Online: http://www.alternet.org/human-rights/racism-criminal-justice-system

54. Silverblatt, A. (2008). *Media literacy* (3rd ed.). Westport, CT: Praeger.

55. Starr, T. J. (2015, March 23). There's a very good reason why black people despise the mainstream media. *Alternet.org.* Online: http://www.alternet.org/media/theres-very-good-reason-why-black-people-despise-mainstream-media

56. "The state of homelessness in America 2016." (2016, April 6). *National Alliance to End Homelessness.* Online: http://www.endhomelessness.org/library/entry/SOH2016

57. Terle, R. (2016, August 23). The 15 most horrific crimes inspired by the media. *The Richest.* Online: http://www.therichest.com/rich-list/most-shocking/the-15-most-horrific-crimes-inspired-by-the-media/

58. Tyndall Report. (2017, January). 2016 year in review. Online: http://tyndallreport.com/yearinreview2016/

59. Walsh, T. (2015, February 5). Fox news segment: Movies like "Frozen" are emasculating America's men. *Talking Points Memo.* Online: http://talkingpointsmemo.com/livewire/fox-news-frozen-movie-emasculating-men

60. Wartella, E. A. (1997). *The context of television violence.* Boston: Allyn & Bacon.

61. Wronge, Y. S. (2000, August 17). New report fuels TV-violence debate. *San Jose Mercury News,* pp. 1 E, 3 E.

62. Zhang, Q. (2010). Asian Americans beyond the model minority stereotype: The nerdy and the left out. *Journal of International and Intercultural Communication, 3,* 20–37.

Cultural Forum Blue Column icon, Media Literacy Red Torch Icon, Using Media Green Gear icon, Developing Media book in starburst icon: ©McGraw-Hill Education

©Nestudio/Shutterstock RF

14 Media Freedom, Regulation, and Ethics

◀ Embedding, the practice of reporters accepting military control over their reporting in exchange for close contact with the troops, is one of many ethical challenges facing media professionals.

Learning Objectives

Free and responsible mass media are essential to our democracy because access to a wide array of information from a wide array of sources is the foundation of our self-governance. But media, because of their power and the conflicting demands of profit and service under which they operate, are (and should be) open to some control. The level and sources of that control, however, are controversial issues for the media, in the government, and in the public forum. After studying this chapter, you should be able to

▶ Outline the history and development of our contemporary understanding of the First Amendment.

▶ Explain the justification for and exercise of media regulation.

▶ Distinguish between a media system that operates under a libertarian philosophy and one that operates under a social responsibility philosophy.

▶ Define and discuss media ethics and how they are applied.

▶ Describe the operation and pros and cons of self-regulation.

▶ Better consider the use of anonymous sources.

1644 Milton's *Areopagitica*
1791 ▶ Bill of Rights ratified

1919 ▶ "Clear and present danger" ruling

1900

Source: National Archives and Records Administration

©Photodisc/PunchStock RF

1931 *Near v. Minnesota* prior restraint ruling

1925

1935 ▶ Hauptmann/Lindbergh trial
1943 NBC "traffic cop" decision
1947 Social responsibility theory of the press

©Bettmann/Getty Images

1964 *New York Times v. Sullivan* public figure ruling

1950

1969 *Red Lion* decision
1971 ▶ Pentagon Papers
1973 *Miller* decision defines obscenity

1979 ▶ *Progressive* hydrogen bomb case

1975

1980 Deregulation of media begins in earnest
1984 *Betamax* decision
1988 Extensive rewriting of copyright law

©Bettmann/Getty Images

2001 Creative Commons founded

2000

2005 *MGM v. Grokster P2P* ruling; Judith Miller jailed
2009 Pirate Bay founders jailed; Supreme Court upholds FCC indecency rules
2011 *Brown v. Entertainment Merchants Assn.*
2012 *FCC v. Fox*
2013 Edward Snowden revelations
2014 SPJ revised Code of Ethics; California anti-paparazzi law
2016 Request for Snowden pardon reopens government surveillance debate; *The New York Times* overhauls confidentiality rules

©Stephanie Dalton Cowan/ Getty Images RF

UP UNTIL NOW, EVERYTHING HAD BEEN RIGHT ABOUT THE JOB. Editor of a major college daily newspaper makes a great résumé entry; you are treated like royalty at school events; and you get to do something good for your campus and, if you do your job well, even for the larger world out there. But as the tension around you grows, you start to wonder if it's all worth it.

First there was the blow-up over your proposed editorial decrying President Obama's refusal to honor Edward Snowden's request for a pardon (Emmons & LaChance, 2016). Snowden was the whistle-blower (most of your staff said traitor) who in May 2013 revealed the existence of a top-secret National Security Agency program that collected the online data of all Americans through access to the servers of the major Internet companies, Web giants like Verizon, Google, Facebook, and Apple. The Prism program, as it was called, was officially aimed at detecting foreign terrorists, but the materials Snowden provided to *The Washington Post*, which won a Pulitzer Prize for its reporting on the surveillance, and to England's *The Guardian* newspaper made it clear that *all* Americans' Internet activity was being collected and stored. Snowden willingly identified himself as the whistle-blower, saying, "I have no intention of hiding who I am because I know I have done nothing wrong." Nonetheless, the government charged Snowden with espionage, bringing with it a possible death sentence. Snowden fled first to Hong Kong and then to Russia as politicians of all political stripes called for his arrest and even his assassination.

You wanted to write that Snowden's revelations were as valuable as those in Daniel Ellsberg's release of the Pentagon Papers. They had generated what you believed to be a much needed public discussion about the balance between liberty and security, as well as important questions about the relationship between journalism and the government.

Then there was the issue of that tweet from Donald Trump, the man who would soon replace Barack Obama in the White House after he won the electoral college but lost the popular vote by almost 3 million votes, a rare occurrence in U.S. elections. The president-elect had just announced on Twitter, "I won the popular vote if you deduct the millions of people who voted illegally." But there was no evidence that illegal voting had occurred, and even Republican voting commissioners around the country confirmed the integrity of the ballot box. So what, you asked your staff, should your paper's headline read? *Politico* used "Trump Claims Millions Voted Illegally." CBS went with "Trump: 'Millions Voted Illegally for Hillary Clinton.'" CNN led with "Trump Falsely Claims 'Millions of People Who Voted Illegally' Cost Him Popular Vote" (all in Calderone, 2016). You wanted something a bit stronger than even CNN's *falsely*. To you, a spurious claim that our elections could be so badly corrupted was a challenge to the people's trust in our democracy. The majority of your staff wanted no adjectives or adverbs at all; they wanted to use only Mr. Trump's words, as did *Politico* and CBS. That, they insisted, ensured objectivity. You argued that *objectivity* and *truthfulness* are not the same. What is our job as journalists? you asked your colleagues. Isn't it to tell the truth?

In these instances you've argued in favor of more, rather than less, public awareness. This is America; who can have a problem with that? You run the Snowden editorial, and your election headline reads, "Trump Lied About Millions of Illegal Votes." You get 181 angry phone calls and e-mails, 17 longtime advertisers pull their regular weekly ads, and your assistant editor and two other staffers quit the paper.

These dilemmas, routinely faced by real college and professional editors, highlight two important lessons offered in this chapter. First, what is legal may not always be what is right. Second, when media practitioners do try to do the right thing, they have to consider the interests, needs, and values of others besides themselves.

In this chapter, we look at how the First Amendment has been defined and applied over time. We study how the logic of a free and unfettered press has come into play in the area of broadcast deregulation. We also detail the shift in the underlying philosophy of media freedom from libertarianism to social responsibility theory. This provides the background for our examination of the ethical environment in which media professionals must work as they strive to fulfill their socially responsible obligations.

A Short History of the First Amendment

The U.S. Constitution mentions only one industry by name as deserving special protection—the press. Therefore, our examination of media regulation, self-regulation, and ethics must begin with a discussion of this "First Freedom."

The first Congress of the United States was committed to freedom of the press. The First Amendment to the new Constitution expressly stated that "Congress shall make no law . . . abridging the freedom of speech, or of the press." As a result, government regulation of the media must be not only unobtrusive but also sufficiently justified to meet the limits of the First Amendment. Media industry self-regulation must be sufficiently effective to render official restraint unnecessary, and media practitioners' conduct should be ethical in order to warrant this special protection.

Early Sentiment for a Free Press

Democracy—government by the people—requires a free press. The framers of the Bill of Rights understood this because of their experience with the European monarchies from which they and their forebears had fled. They based their guarantee of this privileged position to the press on **libertarianism**, the philosophy of the press asserting that good and rational people can tell right from wrong if presented with full and free access to information; therefore, censorship is unnecessary. Libertarianism is based on the **self-righting principle**, originally stated in 1644 by English author and poet John Milton in his book *Areopagitica*. His argument was simple: The free flow or trade of ideas, even bad or uncomfortable ones, will inevitably produce the truth because a rational and good public will correct, or right, any errors. You can see the self-righting principle expressed by Thomas Jefferson in the earliest days of our democracy:

> The people are the only censors of their governors; and even their errors will tend to keep them to the true principles of their institution. To punish these errors too severely would be to suppress the only safeguard of the public liberty. The way to prevent these irregular interpositions of [affronts to] the people is to give them full information of their affairs, through the channel of public papers, and to contrive that those papers should penetrate the whole mass of the people. (in Hartmann, 2017)

But even the First Amendment and libertarian philosophy did not guarantee freedom of the press. The Alien and Sedition Acts were passed a scant eight years after the Constitution was ratified, making it illegal to print criticism of government or its leaders. And Milton himself was to become the chief censor of Catholic writing in Oliver Cromwell's English government.

◀ The 1787 Philadelphia Constitutional Convention. Because they knew democracy could not survive otherwise, the framers of the Constitution wrote the First Amendment to guarantee that the new nation would enjoy freedom of speech and press.
©Archive Photos/Getty Images

Defining and Refining the First Amendment

Clearly, the idea of freedom of the press needed some clarification. One view was (and is) housed in the **absolutist position**, which is expressed succinctly by Supreme Court Justice Hugo Black:

> No law means no law. . . . My view is, without deviation, without exception, without any ifs, buts, or whereases, that freedom of speech means that government shall not do anything to people, either for the views they have or the views they express, or the words they speak or write. (*New York Times v. United States,* 1971)

Yet the absolutist position is more complex than this would suggest. Although absolutists accept that the First Amendment provides a central and fundamental wall of protection for the press and free expression, several questions about its true meaning remained to be answered over time. You can read about a recent controversial Supreme Court First Amendment ruling in the box entitled "First Amendment Protection for Violence but Not for Sex." But for now, let's look at some of history's answers.

CULTURAL FORUM
First Amendment Protection for Violence but Not for Sex

In 2006 California passed a law that would have required the labeling of violent video games and banned their sale to children under 18 years old. The gaming industry sued, and the case, *Brown v. Entertainment Merchants Association* (2011), eventually made its way to the U.S. Supreme Court, where in a 7–2 decision, justices ruled that "a state possesses legitimate power to protect children from harm . . . but that does not include a free-floating power to restrict the ideas to which children may be exposed." In his dissent, Justice Stephen Breyer, citing the scientific evidence linking viewing violent games and aggression, argued that he found "sufficient grounds in these studies and expert opinions for this court to defer to an elected legislature's conclusion that the video games in question are *particularly likely to* harm children."

The issues of free speech and the possible harmful effects of violent video games were of sufficient interest to thrust this decision firmly into the cultural forum, but it was former Justice Antonin Scalia's assertion that drew the most attention: "Because speech about violence is not obscene," it cannot be regulated even when children are involved and even when it involves portraying the sexual assault of a human being, but speech about sex has long been restricted, especially when children are involved, so therefore it is censorable (*Brown v. Entertainment,* 2011). The decision's critics interpreted this as "violence is normal but sex, even nonviolent and consensual, is not." Employing as an example a gruesome game sequence from *Mortal Kombat II* in which a young woman is ripped in two by freakishly large combatants, Jon Stewart explained the decision to his *Daily Show* viewers, "The state has no interest in restricting the sale of [violent video games] to children, but if while being disemboweled, this woman were to [expose her breast], regulate away" (2011). Enter your voice. Is this a "win" for the First Amendment, a loss, or a split decision? Why, in our culture, does media violence merit greater free speech protection than media sex?

WHAT DOES "NO LAW" MEAN? The First Amendment said that the U.S. Congress could "make no law," but could state legislatures? City councils? Mayors? Courts? Who has the power to proscribe the press? This issue was settled in 1925 in a case involving the right of a state to limit the publication of a socialist newsletter. The Supreme Court, in *Gitlow v. New York,* stated that the First Amendment is "among the fundamental personal rights and 'liberties' protected by the due process clause of the Fourteenth Amendment from impairment by the states" (Gillmor & Barron, 1974, p. 1). Given this, "Congress shall make no law" should be interpreted as "government agencies shall make no law." Today, "no law" includes statutes, laws, administrative regulations, executive and court orders, and ordinances from government, regardless of locale.

WHAT IS "THE PRESS"? Just what "press" enjoys First Amendment protection? The Supreme Court, in its 1952 *Joseph Burstyn, Inc. v. Wilson* decision, declared that movies were protected expression. In 1973 Justice William O. Douglas wrote in *CBS v. Democratic National Committee* (1973),

> What kind of First Amendment would best serve our needs as we approach the 21st century may be an open question. But the old fashioned First Amendment that we have is the Court's only guideline; and one hard and fast principle has served us through days of calm and eras of strife, and I would abide by it until a new First Amendment is adopted. That means, as I view it, that TV and radio . . . are all included in the concept of "press" as used in the First Amendment and therefore are entitled to live under the laissez faire regime which the First Amendment sanctions.

Advertising, or commercial speech, enjoys First Amendment protection. This was established by the Supreme Court in 1942. Despite the fact that the decision in *Valentine v. Christensen* went against the advertiser, the Court wrote that just because expression was commercial did not necessarily mean that it was unprotected. Some justices argued for a "two-tiered" level of protection, with commercial expression being somewhat less worthy of protection than noncommercial expression. But others argued that this was illogical because almost all media are, in fact, commercial, even when they perform a primarily journalistic function. Newspapers, for example, print the news to make a profit.

In its 1967 *Time, Inc. v. Hill* decision, the Supreme Court applied similar logic to argue that the First Amendment grants the same protection to entertainment content as it does to nonentertainment content. Is an entertainingly written news report less worthy of protection than one that is dully written? Rather than allow the government to make these kinds of narrow and ultimately subjective judgments, the Supreme Court has consistently preferred expanding its definition of protected expression to limiting it.

WHAT IS "ABRIDGMENT"? **Abridgment** is the curtailing of rights, and even absolutists accept the idea that some curtailment or limits can be placed on the time, place, and manner of expression—as long as the restrictions do not interfere with the substance of the expression. Few, for example, would find it unreasonable to limit the use of a sound truck to broadcast political messages at 4:00 a.m. But the Supreme Court did find unconstitutional an ordinance that forbade all use of sound amplification except with the permission of the chief of police in its 1948 decision in *Saia v. New York*. The permissibility of other restrictions, however, is less clear-cut.

CLEAR AND PRESENT DANGER Can freedom of the press be limited if the likely result is damaging? The Supreme Court answered this question in 1919 in *Schenck v. United States*. In this case involving the distribution of a pamphlet urging illegal resistance to the military draft during World War I, Justice Oliver Wendell Holmes wrote that expression could be limited when "the words used are used in such circumstances and are of such a nature as to create a clear and present danger that they will bring about the substantive evils that Congress has a right to prevent." Justice Holmes added, "Free speech would not protect a man in falsely shouting fire in a theater and causing panic." This decision is especially important because it firmly established the legal philosophy that there is no absolute freedom of expression; the level of protection is one of degree.

BALANCING OF INTERESTS This less-than-absolutist approach is called the **ad hoc balancing of interests**. That is, in individual First Amendment cases several factors should be weighed in determining how much freedom the press is granted. In his dissent to the Court's 1941 decision in *Bridges v. California*, a case involving a *Los Angeles Times* editorial, Justice Felix Frankfurter wrote that free speech and press is "not so absolute or irrational a conception as to imply paralysis of the means for effective protection of all the freedoms secured by the Bill of Rights. . . . In the cases before us, the claims on behalf of freedom of speech and of the press encounter claims on behalf of liberties no less precious."

FREE PRESS VERSUS FAIR TRIAL One example of the clash of competing liberties is the conflict between free press (First Amendment) and fair trial (Sixth Amendment). This debate typically takes two forms: (1) Can pretrial publicity deny citizens judgment by 12 impartial peers, thereby denying them a fair trial? (2) Should cameras be allowed in the courtroom, supporting the public's right to know, or do they so alter the workings of the court that a fair trial is impossible?

Courts have consistently decided in favor of fair trial in conflicts between the First and Sixth Amendments, but it was not until 1961 that a conviction was overturned because of pretrial publicity. In *Irvin v. Dowd* the Court reversed the death sentence conviction of accused killer Leslie Irvin because his right to a fair trial had been hampered by press coverage that labeled him "Mad Dog Irvin" and reported crimes he had committed as a juvenile, his military court-martial, his identification in a police lineup, his failure to pass a lie detector test, his confession to numerous robberies, and his willingness to trade a guilty plea for a life sentence. As a result of this publicity, of 430 potential jurors screened before the trial by attorneys, 370 said they were already convinced Irvin was guilty. Nonetheless, although "tainted" by pretrial publicity, four of the 370 were seated as jurors. The Court determined that Irvin's trial was therefore unfair.

Print reporters have long enjoyed access to trials, but broadcast journalists have been less fortunate. In 1937, after serious intrusion by newspaper photographers during the 1935 trial of Bruno Hauptmann, accused of kidnapping the baby of transatlantic aviation hero Charles Lindbergh, the American Bar Association (ABA) adopted Canon 35 as part of its Code of Judicial Ethics. This rule forbade cameras and radio broadcasting of trials. In 1963 the ABA amended the canon to include a prohibition on television cameras. This, however, did not settle the issue of cameras in the courtroom.

Texas was one of three states that did not subscribe to Canon 35. When Texas financier Billy Sol Estes's conviction for theft, swindling, and embezzlement was overturned by the Supreme Court because of "the insidious influence" (Justice William Douglas's words) of cameras on the conduct of the trial, the wisdom of banning television seemed settled. But Justice Clark counseled, "When advances in [broadcast journalism] permit reporting . . . by television without their present hazards to a fair trial we will have another case" (*Estes v. State of Texas,* 1965). In other words, cameras were back in if they posed no hazard to the principle of fair trial.

In 1972 the ABA replaced Canon 35 with Canon 3A(7), allowing some videotaping of trials for specific purposes but reaffirming its opposition to the broadcast of trial proceedings. But in 1981 the Supreme Court, in *Chandler v. Florida*, determined that television cameras in the courtroom were not inherently damaging to fairness. Today, all 50 states allow cameras in some courts—47 permit them in trial courts—and the U.S. Congress continues to debate opening up federal courts, including the Supreme Court, to cameras. For now, photography and broadcast of federal trials is banned by Federal Rule of Criminal Procedure 53. These limits persist despite the fact that three-quarters of Americans favor cameras in the Supreme Court, whose proceedings are otherwise released in transcripts and audio recordings (Scola, 2014).

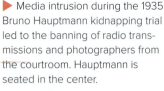

▶ Media intrusion during the 1935 Bruno Hauptmann kidnapping trial led to the banning of radio transmissions and photographers from the courtroom. Hauptmann is seated in the center.

©Bettmann/Getty Images

◀ Is the man here accused of drug dealing guilty or innocent? If he is guilty, he should want to cover his face to hide his identity. But if he is innocent, wouldn't he be just as likely to want to hide his identity? These so-called perp walks raise the issue of unfair pretrial publicity.

©Don Heupel/AP Photo

LIBEL AND SLANDER **Libel**, the false or malicious publication of material that damages a person's reputation, and **slander**, the oral or spoken defamation of a person's character, are not protected by the First Amendment. The distinction between libel and slander, however, is sufficiently narrow that "published defamation, whether it is in a newspaper, on radio or television, in the movies, or whatever, is regarded since the 1990s as libel. And libel rules apply" (Pember, 1999, p. 134). Therefore, if a report (1) defames a person, (2) identifies that person, and (3) is published or broadcast, it loses its First Amendment protection.

A report accused of being libelous or slanderous, however, is protected if it meets any one of three tests. The first test is *truth*. Even if a report damages someone's reputation, if it is true, it is protected. The second test is *privilege*. Coverage of legislative, court, or other public activities may contain information that is not true or that is damaging to someone's reputation. The press cannot be deterred from covering these important news events for fear that a speaker's or witness's comments will open it to claims of libel or slander. The third test is *fair comment*; that is, the press has the right to express opinions or comment on public issues. For example, theater and film reviews, however severe, are protected, as is commentary on other matters in the public eye.

For public figures, however, a different set of rules applies. Because they are in the public eye, public figures are fair game for fair comment. But does that leave them open to reports that are false and damaging to their reputations? The Supreme Court faced this issue in 1964 in *New York Times v. Sullivan*. In 1960 the Committee to Defend Martin Luther King bought a full-page ad in *The New York Times* asking people to contribute to Dr. King's defense fund. The ad detailed abuse of Dr. King and other civil rights workers at the hands of the Montgomery, Alabama, police. L. B. Sullivan, one of three elected commissioners in that city, sued the *Times* for libel. The ad copy was not true in some of its claims, he said, and because he was in charge of the police, he had been "identified."

The Supreme Court ruled in favor of the newspaper. Even though some of the specific facts in the ad were not true, the *Times* had not acted with **actual malice**. The Court defined the standard of actual malice for reporting on public figures as *knowledge of its falsity or reckless disregard* for whether or not it is true.

PRIOR RESTRAINT There is much less confusion about another important aspect of press freedom, **prior restraint**. This is the power of the government to *prevent* the publication or broadcast of expression. U.S. law and tradition make the use of prior restraint relatively rare, but there have been a number of important efforts by government to squelch content before dissemination.

In 1931 the Supreme Court ruled in *Near v. Minnesota* that freedom from prior restraint was a general, not an absolute, principle. Two of the four exceptions it listed were in times of war when national security was involved and when the public order would be endangered by the incitement to violence and overthrow by force of orderly government. These exceptions were to become the basis of two landmark prior restraint decisions. The first, involving *The New York Times*, dealt with national security in times of war; the second, focusing on protecting the public order, involved publishing instructions for building an atomic bomb.

On June 13, 1971, at the height of the Vietnam War, *The New York Times* began publication of what commonly became known as the Pentagon Papers. The papers included detailed discussion and analysis of the conduct of that unpopular war during the administrations of presidents Kennedy and Johnson. President Nixon's National Security Council (NSC) had stamped them top secret. Believing that this was an improper restriction of the public's right to know, NSC staff member Daniel Ellsberg gave copies to the *Times*. After the first three installments had been published, the Justice Department, citing national security, was able to secure a court order stopping further publication. Other newspapers, notably *The Washington Post* and *The Boston Globe*, began running excerpts while the *Times* was silenced until they, too, were enjoined to cease.

On June 30, 1971, the Supreme Court ordered the government to halt its restraint of the *Times*'s and other papers' right to publish the Pentagon Papers. Among the stirring attacks on prior restraint written throughout its decision was Justice Hugo Black's:

> In the First Amendment the Founding Fathers gave the free press the protection it must have to fulfill its essential role in our democracy. The press was to serve the governed, not the governors. The Government's power to censor the press was abolished so that the press would remain forever free to censure the Government. The press was protected so that it could bare the secrets of government and inform the people. Only a free and unrestrained press can effectively expose deception in government. (*New York Times v. United States*, 1971)

Then came the case of the magazine *The Progressive*. In 1979 the magazine announced its intention to publish instructions on how to make a hydrogen bomb. President Jimmy Carter's Justice Department successfully obtained a court order halting publication, even though the article was based on information and material freely obtained from public, nonclassified

▶ Daniel Ellsberg, who gave the Pentagon Papers to *The New York Times*, celebrates that paper's Supreme Court victory.
©Bettmann/Getty Images

sources. Before the case could come to court, several newspapers published the same or similar material. The Justice Department immediately abandoned its restraint, and six months later *The Progressive* published its original article.

OBSCENITY AND PORNOGRAPHY Another form of press expression that is not protected is **obscenity**. Two landmark Supreme Court cases established the definition and illegality of obscenity. The first is the 1957 *Roth v. United States* decision. The Court determined that sex and obscenity were not synonymous, a significant advance for freedom of expression. It did, however, legally affirm for the first time that obscenity was unprotected expression. The definition or test for obscenity that holds even today was expressed in the 1973 *Miller v. State of California* decision. Chief Justice Warren Burger wrote that the basic guidelines must be

> (a) whether the average person, applying contemporary community standards, would find that the work, taken as a whole, appeals to the prurient interest, (b) whether the work depicts or describes, in a patently offensive way, sexual conduct specifically defined by the applicable state law, and (c) whether the work, taken as a whole, lacks serious literary, artistic, political, or scientific value.

The problem for the courts, the media, and the public, of course, is judging content against this standard. For example, what is patently offensive to one person may be quite acceptable to others. What is serious art to one may be serious exploitation to another. And what of an erotic short story written online by an author in New York City but accessed and read by people in Peoria, Illinois? Whose community standards would apply?

An additional definitional problem resides in **pornography**. Pornography is protected expression. The distinction between obscenity and pornography may, however, be a legal one. Sexually explicit content is pornography (and protected) until a court rules it illegal; then it is obscene (and unprotected). The difficulty of making such distinctions can be seen in Justice Potter Stewart's famous declaration in *Jacobellis v. Ohio* (1964), "I may not be able to come up with a definition of pornography, but I certainly know it when I see it," and his dissent two years later in *Ginzburg v. United States* (1966), "If the First Amendment means anything, it means that a man cannot be sent to prison merely for distributing publications which offend a judge's sensibilities, mine or any others." Clearly, the issues of the definition and protection of obscenity and pornography may never be clarified to everyone's satisfaction.

Other Issues of Freedom and Responsibility

The First Amendment has application to a number of specific issues of media responsibility and freedom.

INDECENCY Obscenity and pornography are rarely issues for broadcasters. Their commercial base and wide audience make the airing of such potentially troublesome programming unwise. However, broadcasters frequently do confront the issue of **indecency**. According to the FCC, indecent language or material is that which depicts sexual or excretory activities in a way that is offensive to contemporary community standards.

The FCC recently modified, much to broadcasters' dissatisfaction, its way of handling indecency complaints, making it easier for listeners and viewers to challenge questionable content. Stations must now prove they are innocent; in other words, a complaint has validity by virtue of having been made. To broadcasters, this "guilty until proven innocent" approach is an infringement of their First Amendment rights, as it requires them to keep tapes of all their content in the event they are challenged, even in the absence of evidence that a complaint has merit.

The debate over indecency, however, has been confounded by a number of events. First, a huge surge in complaints (from 111 in 2000 to more than a million in 2004) followed two specific broadcast events: the split-second baring of Janet Jackson's breast at the 2004 Super Bowl football game and rocker Bono's spontaneous award-show utterance of an expletive later that year. And even though the FCC's own data revealed that 99.9% of the complaints, most with identical wording, originated with one group, the conservative Christian Parents Television Council, it still boosted indecency fines by 100% (Rich, 2005; SoundBites, 2005).

Then, faced with penalties of up to $325,000, there was a series of high-profile incidents of broadcaster self-censorship, among them CBS affiliates' refusal to air *9/11 Camera at Ground*

Zero honoring the New York City police, firefighters, and other rescue personnel who lived and died on that tragic day because some on-screen rescuers uttered curses as they fought through the inferno. The award-winning documentary had aired four years earlier without a single complaint. Citing examples such as this, lawsuits by NBC and Fox eventually made their way in 2012 to the Supreme Court which, in its unanimous *FCC v. Fox* decision, overturned the Commission's indecency rulings, not because the FCC had no right to make such judgments but because it did not give broadcasters "fair notice" as to what was and was not permissible; that is, the rules were too vague to be constitutional (Barnes, 2012). Today, the Commission regulates language that is so "grossly offensive" to "members of the public" that it becomes a "nuisance." But language found "grossly offensive" just a few years ago is quite common in our everyday conversations today. As such, the FCC acts in only the most egregious cases.

▶ In 2006, worried about heavy FCC indecency fines, several CBS affiliates chose not to run a documentary honoring the 9/11 rescue effort because several of the police officers and firefighters in it cursed as they fought smoke, debris, and fear. The award-winning movie had aired four years earlier without complaint.

©*Anthony Correia/Getty Images*

DEREGULATION The difficulty of balancing the public interest and broadcasters' freedom is at the heart of the debate over deregulation and the relaxation of ownership and other rules for radio and television. Changes in ownership rules have always been controversial, but relaxation of the regulation of broadcasters' public service obligations and other content controls have provided just as much debate.

The courts have consistently supported the FCC's right to evaluate broadcasters' performance in serving the public interest, convenience, and necessity. Naturally, that evaluation must include some judgment of the content broadcasters air. Broadcasters long argued that such "judgment" amounted to unconstitutional infringement of their First Amendment freedom. Many listeners and viewers saw it as a reasonable and quite small price to pay for the use of their (the public's) airwaves.

The Supreme Court resolved the issue in 1943 in *National Broadcasting Co. v. United States*. NBC argued that the FCC was no more than a traffic cop, limited to controlling the "flow of traffic." In this view, the regulation of broadcasters' frequency, power, times of operation, and other technical matters was all that was constitutionally allowable. Yet the Court turned what is now known as the **traffic cop analogy** against NBC. Yes, the justices agreed, the commission is a traffic cop. But even traffic cops have the right to control not only the flow of traffic but its composition as well. For example, drunk drivers can be removed from the road. Potentially dangerous "content," like cars with faulty brakes, can also be restricted. It was precisely this traffic cop function that required the FCC to judge content. The commission was thus free to promulgate rules such as the **Fairness Doctrine**, which required broadcasters to cover issues of public importance and to be fair in that coverage, and **ascertainment**, which required broadcasters to ascertain or actively and affirmatively determine the nature of their audiences' interest, convenience, and necessity.

But the Fairness Doctrine, ascertainment, and numerous other regulations, such as rules on children's programming and overcommercialization, disappeared with the coming of deregulation during the Reagan and Clinton administrations. License renewal, for example, was once a long and difficult process for stations, which had to generate thousands of pages of documents to demonstrate that they not only knew what their audiences wanted and needed but had met those wants and needs. The burden of proof in their efforts to keep their licenses rested with them. Had they been fair? Had they kept commercial time to acceptable levels? What was their commitment to news and public affairs? Now deregulated, renewal is conducted through a much less onerous process that satisfies broadcasters but angers advocates of greater media responsibility. Broadcasters simply file brief quarterly reports with the commission indicating compliance with technical and other FCC rules. Then, when their licenses are up for renewal (every eight years), they file a short, postcardlike renewal application. This may be convenient for broadcasters, but former FCC commissioner Michael Copps calls this an "automatic, no-questions-asked eight-year extension . . . nothing more than conferring monopoly power with no public oversight" (2014, p. 38).

The deregulation drive began in earnest with President Reagan's FCC chair, Mark Fowler, in the 1980s. Fowler rejected the trustee model of broadcast regulation. He saw many FCC rules as an unconstitutional infringement of broadcasters' rights and believed that "the market" was the audience's best protector. He said that special rules for the control of broadcasting were unnecessary, likening television, for example, to just another home appliance. He called television no more than "a toaster with pictures."

This view of deregulation is not without its critics. Republican and Democratic congressional leaders, liberal and conservative columnists, and numerous public interest groups from across the political spectrum continue to campaign against such fruits of deregulation as concentration, conglomeration, overcommercialization, the abandonment of regulation of children's television, the lowering of decency standards, and the debasement of news. Their argument for rolling back the deregulation of broadcasting rests in the philosophy of noted First Amendment scholar Alexander Meiklejohn (1960), who argued more than half a century ago that what is forbidden is regulation limiting the media's freedom,

> *but not legislation to enlarge and enrich it*. The freedom of mind which benefits members of a self-governing society is not a given and fixed part of human nature. It can be increased and established by learning, by teaching, by the unhindered flow of accurate information, by giving men [*sic*] health and vigor and security, by bringing them together in activities of communication and mutual understanding. And the federal legislature is not forbidden to engage in that positive enterprise of cultivating the general intelligence upon which the success of self-government so obviously depends. On the contrary, in that positive field the Congress of the United States has a heavy and basic responsibility to promote the freedom of speech. (pp. 19–20; italics added)

◄ Broadcast deregulation produced a rush of toy-based children's television shows such as *Pokémon*, which critics contend are inherently unfair to children who cannot recognize them as program-length commercials.
©Warner Bros./Courtesy Everett Collection

COPYRIGHT The First Amendment protects expression. *Copyright*—identifying and granting ownership of a given piece of expression—is designed to protect the creator's financial interest in that expression. Recognizing that the flow of art, science, and other expression would be enhanced by authors' financial interest in their creation, the framers of the Constitution wrote Article I, Section 8 (8), granting authors exclusive rights to their "writings and discoveries." A long and consistent history of Supreme Court decisions has ensured that this protection would be extended to the content of the mass media that have emerged since that time.

The years 1978 and 1998 saw extensive rewritings of U.S. copyright law. Copyright now remains with creators (in all media) for the span of their lives, plus 70 years. During this time, permission for the use of the material must be obtained from the copyright holder, and if financial compensation (a fee or royalty) is requested, it must be paid. Once the copyright expires, the material passes into the **public domain**, meaning it can be used without permission.

The exception to copyright is *fair use*, instances in which material can be used without permission or payment. Fair use includes (1) limited noncommercial use, such as photocopying a passage from a novel for classroom use; (2) use of limited portions of a work, such as excerpting a few lines or a paragraph or two from a book for use in a magazine article; (3) use that does not decrease the commercial value of the original, such as videotaping a daytime football game for private, at-home evening viewing; and (4) use in the public interest, such as *Consumer Reports*'s use of pieces of drug company television commercials to highlight its media literacy efforts.

Two specific applications of copyright law pertain to recorded music and cable television. Imagine the difficulty cable companies would have in obtaining permission from all the copyright holders of all the material they import and deliver to their subscribers. Yet the cable operators do make money from others' works—they collect material from original sources and sell it to subscribers. The solution to the problem of compensating the creators of the material carried by cable systems was the creation of the Copyright Royalty Tribunal, to which cable companies paid a fee based primarily on the size of their operations. These moneys were then distributed to the appropriate producers, syndicators, and broadcasters. Congress abolished the Copyright Royalty Tribunal in 1993, leaving cable copyright issues in the hands of several different arbitration panels under the auspices of the Library of Congress.

Now imagine the difficulty songwriters would have in collecting royalties from all who use their music—not only film producers and radio and television stations, but bowling alleys, supermarkets, and restaurants. Here the solution is the **music licensing company**. The two biggest are the American Society of Composers, Authors and Publishers (ASCAP) and Broadcast Music Inc. (BMI). Both collect fees based on the users' gross receipts and distribute the money to songwriters and artists.

THE INTERNET AND EXPANDING COPYRIGHT The Internet has forced a significant rethinking of copyright, one that disturbs many advocates of free expression. They fear that efforts to protect the intellectual property rights of copyright holders are going too far. The expansion of copyright, argues technology writer Dan Gillmor, gives "the owners of intellectual property vast new authority, simultaneously shredding users' rights" (2000, p. 1C).

For example, in January 2000, a California superior court, citing the Digital Millennium Copyright Act, ruled the posting of DVD decryption software to be illegal (see the chapter on the Internet and social media). The defendants argued that they did not violate copyright. The court ruled against them because they posted "tools" on the Web that might allow others to violate copyright. Tech writer Gillmor scoffed, "Let's ban cars next. Were you aware that bank robbers use them for getaways?" (2000, p. 6C). In August of that same year, a New York court reaffirmed the ban on posting decryption software, adding that even posting links to sites offering the software was a violation of copyright.

Copyright exists, say critics of its expansion, to encourage the flow of art, science, and expression, and it grants a financial stake to creators, not to enrich those creators but to ensure that there is sufficient incentive to keep the content flowing. "It's always important to remember that copyright is a restriction on free speech, and it's a constitutionally granted restriction on free speech," argued copyright expert Siva Vaidhyanathan (in Anderson, 2000, p. 25). In other words, tightening copyright restrictions can have the effect of inhibiting the flow of art, science, and expression.

The **digital rights management (DRM)** debate escalated with the Supreme Court's 2005 *MGM v. Grokster* decision (see the chapter on radio, recording, and popular music). The entertainment industries were heartened by the ruling that a technology was illegal if it "encouraged" copyright infringement; digital rights activists and technologists were appalled. The Court had disallowed Hollywood's 1984 challenge to videotape (*Sony Corp. v. Universal City Studios*, the so-called *Betamax* decision) precisely because VCR, even if some people used it to violate copyright, had "substantial non-infringing uses." But *Grokster*, argued its critics, changed that standard from a technology's primary, noninfringing use to the question of whether innovators "created their wares with the 'intent' of inducing consumers to infringe" (Gibbs, 2005, p. 50).

But as we've seen at several junctures of this text, a reassessment of DRM and copyright is under way, as the involved parties seem to be seeking accommodation. One effort is Creative Commons, a nonprofit corporation founded in 2001 as an easy way for people to share and build on the work of others, consistent with the rules of copyright. Creative Commons provides users with free licenses and other legal tools to mark (copyright) their creative work with the level of freedom they wish it to carry, granting to others specific rights to share, remix, or even use it commercially. As for the traditional media companies, all the major record labels now sell much of their catalogs with limited or no DRM. Low-cost streaming of virtually all movie and television content is ubiquitous. Most of the world's books will soon find themselves living online with quite robust reader access. Most big media companies are embracing websites like YouTube and Facebook, willing to forfeit a bit of DRM control in exchange for exposure of their content. As such, the problem of piracy may be best solved by doing nothing, argues Richard Cooper, who works for an online intelligence company. "A lot of people engaged in video piracy, or at least hacking video piracy, breaking the DRM and so forth, are doing it for the kudos. They see every new anti-piracy measure that comes out as a challenge and something that needs to be cracked. This is their hobby" (in Bednarski, 2016). The future of copyright and DRM, then, is being negotiated in the culture right now. You and other media consumers sit on one side of the table; the media industries are on the other. You will be in a stronger position in these cultural negotiations if you approach these developments as a media-literate person.

Social Responsibility Theory

As we saw at the beginning of this chapter, the First Amendment is based on the libertarian philosophy that assumes a fully free press and a rational, good, and informed public. But we have also seen in this chapter that the media are not necessarily fully free. Government control is sometimes allowed. Corporate control is assumed and accepted. During the 1930s and 1940s, serious doubts were also raised concerning the public's rationality and goodness. As World War II spread across Europe at the end of the 1930s, libertarians were hard-pressed to explain how Nazi propaganda could succeed if people could in fact tell right from wrong. As the United States was drawn closer to the European conflict, calls for greater government control of press and speech at home were justified by less-than-optimistic views of the "average American's" ability to handle difficult information. As a result, libertarianism came under attack for being too idealistic.

Time magazine owner and publisher Henry Luce then provided money to establish an independent commission of scholars, politicians, legal experts, and social activists who would study the role of the press in U.S. society and make recommendations on how it should best operate in support of democracy. The Hutchins Commission on Freedom of the Press, named after its chairperson, University of Chicago chancellor Robert Maynard Hutchins, began its work in 1942 and, in 1947, produced its report "The Social Responsibility Theory of the Press."

Social responsibility theory is a **normative theory**—that is, it explains how media should *ideally* operate in a given system of social values—and it is the standard against which the public should judge the performance of the U.S. media. Other social and political systems adhere to different normative theories, and these will be detailed in the chapter on global media.

Social responsibility theory asserts that media must remain free of government control, but in exchange media must serve the public. The core assumptions of this theory are a cross between libertarian principles of freedom and practical admissions of the need for some form of control on the media (McQuail, 1987):

- Media should accept and fulfill certain obligations to society.
- Media can meet these obligations by setting high standards of professionalism, truth, accuracy, and objectivity.
- Media should be self-regulating within the framework of the law.
- Media should avoid disseminating material that might lead to crime, violence, or civil disorder or that might offend minority groups.
- The media as a whole should be pluralistic, reflect the diversity of the culture in which they operate, and give access to various points of view and rights of reply.
- The public has a right to expect high standards of performance, and official intervention can be justified to ensure the public good.
- Media professionals should be accountable to society as well as to their employers and the market.

In rejecting government control of media, social responsibility theory calls for responsible, ethical industry operation, but it does not free audiences from their responsibility. People must be sufficiently media literate to develop firm yet reasonable expectations and judgments of media performance. But ultimately it is practitioners, through the conduct of their duties, who are charged with operating in a manner that obviates the need for official intrusion.

Media Industry Ethics

A number of formal and informal controls, both external and internal to the industry, are aimed at ensuring that media professionals operate in an ethical manner consistent with social responsibility theory. Among the external formal controls are laws and regulations, codified statements of what can and can't be done and what content is permissible and not permissible, and industry codes of practice. Among the external informal controls are pressure groups, consumers, and advertisers. We have seen how these informal controls operate throughout this text. Our interest here is in examining media's internal controls, or ethics.

Defining Ethics

Ethics are rules of behavior or moral principles that guide our actions in given situations. The word comes from the Greek *ethos*, which means the customs, traditions, or character that guide a particular group or culture. In our discussion, ethics specifically refer to the application of rational thought by media professionals when they are deciding between two or more competing moral choices. "Unlike rules of law," explains media ethicist Patrick Plaisance, "which generally set forth boundaries of our behavior and guide us on what we cannot or should not do, the focus of ethics . . . is more active, or positive: It deals with what we ought to do as moral agents with personal and social obligations" (2014, p. 83).

For example, it is not against the law to publish the name of a rape victim. But is it ethical? It is not illegal to stick a microphone in a crying father's face as he cradles the broken body of his child at an accident scene. But is it ethical?

The application of media ethics almost always involves finding the *most morally defensible* answer to a problem for which there is no single correct or even best answer. Let's return to the grieving father. The reporter's job is to get the story; the public has a right to know. The man's sorrow is part of that story, but the man has a right to privacy. As a human being he deserves to be treated with respect and to be allowed to maintain his dignity. The reporter has to decide whether to get the interview or leave the grief-stricken man in peace. That decision is guided by the reporter's ethics.

Three Levels of Ethics

Because ethics reflect a culture's ideas about right and wrong, they exist at all levels of that culture's operation. **Metaethics** are fundamental cultural values. What is justice? What does it mean to be good? Is fairness possible? We need to examine these questions to know ourselves. But as valuable as they are for self-knowledge, metaethics provide only the broadest foundation for the sorts of ethical decisions people make daily. They define the basic starting points for moral reasoning.

Normative ethics are more or less generalized theories, rules, and principles of ethical or moral behavior. The various media industry codes of ethics or standards of good practice are examples of normative ethics. They serve as real-world frameworks within which people can begin to weigh competing alternatives of behavior. Fairness is a metaethic, but journalists' codes of practice, for example, define what is meant by fairness in the world of reporting, how far a reporter must go to ensure fairness, and how fairness must be applied when being fair to one person means being unfair to another.

Ultimately, media practitioners must apply both the big rules and the general guidelines to very specific situations. This is the use of **applied ethics**, and applying ethics invariably involves balancing conflicting interests.

Balancing Conflicting Interests

In applying ethics, the person making the decisions is called the **moral agent**; she or he, as ethicist Plaisance explained, has specific personal and social obligations that invariably bring together conflicting interests—for example, those of the editor, readers, and advertisers in this chapter's opening vignette.

Media ethicist Louis Day (2006) identified six sets of individual or group interests that often conflict:

- The interests of the moral agent's *individual conscience*; media professionals must live with their decisions.
- The interests of *the object of the act*; a particular person or group is likely to be affected by media practitioners' actions.
- The interests of *financial supporters*; someone pays the bills that allow the station to broadcast or the newspaper or magazine to publish.
- The interests of *the institution*; media professionals have company loyalty, pride in the organization for which they work.
- The interests of *the profession*; media practitioners work to meet the expectations of their colleagues; they have respect for the profession that sustains them.
- The interests of *society*; media professionals, like all of us, have a social responsibility. Because of the influence their work can have, they may even have greater responsibilities than do many other professionals.

In mass communication, these conflicting interests play themselves out in a variety of ways. Some of the most common, yet thorniest, require us to examine such basic issues as truth and honesty, privacy, confidentiality, personal conflict of interest, profit and social responsibility, and protection from offensive content.

TRUTH AND HONESTY Can the media ever be completely honest? As soon as a camera is pointed at one thing, it is ignoring another. As soon as a video editor combines two different images, that editor has imposed his or her definition of the truth. Truth and honesty are overriding concerns for media professionals. But what is truth? Take the case of Chicago television station WBBM. In its coverage of a 2011 night of violence in that city, anchor Steve Bartelstein introduced the story, "Kids on the street as young as four were there to see it all unfold, and had disturbing reactions." The segment included video of an interview with a four-year-old African American boy. When asked by a reporter what he wanted to do when he got older, the boy responded, "I'm going to have me a gun!" On camera back at his news desk Bartelstein exclaimed, "That is very scary indeed." WBBM, however, did not air the remainder of the interview in which the boy explained that he was going to get a gun because he was going to be a police officer. But the boy had indeed said he was going to get a gun, so the station did technically report the truth (Butler, 2011).

PRIVACY Do public figures forfeit their right to privacy? In what circumstances? Are the president's marital problems newsworthy if they do not get in the way of the job? Who is a public figure? When are people's long-ago stints in drug rehab newsworthy? Do you report the names of people who have been raped or the names of juvenile offenders? What about sex offenders? How far do you go to interview grieving parents? When is secret taping permissible?

Our culture values privacy. We have the right to maintain the privacy of our personal information. We use privacy to control the extent and nature of the interactions we have with others. Privacy protects us from unwanted government intrusion. The media, however, by their very nature, are intrusive. Privacy proves to be particularly sensitive because it is almost a metaethic, a fundamental value. Yet the applied ethics of the various media industries allow, in fact sometimes demand, that privacy be denied.

The media have faced a number of very important tests regarding privacy in recent years. Media pursuit of celebrities is one. In 2014, the California legislature passed antipaparazzi legislation designed to make illegal the photography of celebrities' children in a manner that "seriously alarms, annoys, torments, or terrorizes" them. Celebrities are public figures. They therefore lose some right to privacy. But what about their children? How much privacy are they entitled to? People surely want to know about them, and what constitutes *tormenting* and *terrorizing* anyway? Despite complaints that this law infringed on photographers' First Amendment rights, most objective observers would say that the protection of children is more important than selling a few more magazines.

But other privacy issues aren't as clear. For example, what about reporters outing "prominent gay politicians who were in the closet but worked for homophobic causes in the interest . . . of their political careers?" in the words of Michael Rogers, who maintains a blog dedicated to doing just that. Politicians are certainly in the public eye and therefore not entitled to the same degree of privacy as most others, but aren't their private lives their private lives? There is "an important distinction between *outing* and *reporting*," counters Rogers. "Outing is the indiscriminate disclosure of someone's sexual orientation without his or her consent. Reporting is not at all indiscriminate—and it has a higher purpose. What my blog did was reveal the hypocrisy of politicians, to show that people who control the nation's political and legal systems often have different standards for themselves" (2014). As you can imagine, there is more disagreement among media professionals on this issue than there is on photographing celebrities' kids.

▶ There's little disagreement that the children of celebrities should be protected from intrusion into their private lives. Many other privacy issues, however, aren't as clear.

©Paul Bradbury/Getty Images

CONFIDENTIALITY An important tool in contemporary news gathering and reporting is **confidentiality**, the ability of media professionals to keep secret the names of people who provide them with information. Without confidentiality, employees could not report the misdeeds of their employers for fear of being fired; people would not tell what they know of a crime for fear of retribution from the offenders or unwanted police attention. The anonymous informant nicknamed "Deep Throat" would never have felt free to divulge the Nixon White House involvement in the Republican break-in of the Democratic Party's Watergate campaign offices were it not for the promise of confidentiality from *Washington Post* reporters Carl Bernstein and Bob Woodward.

But how far should reporters go to protect a source's confidentiality? Should reporters go to jail rather than divulge a name? Every state in the Union, except Wyoming, and the District of Columbia has either a **shield law**, legislation that expressly protects reporters' rights to maintain sources' confidentiality in courts of law, or court precedent upholding that right. There is no shield law in federal courts, and many journalists want it that way. Their fear is that once Congress makes one "media law" it may want to make another. For example, media professionals do not want the government to legislate the definition of "reporter" or "journalist."

The ethics of confidentiality are regularly tested by reporters' frequent use of quotes and information from "unnamed sources," "sources who wish to remain anonymous," and "inside sources." Often the guarantee of anonymity is necessary to get the information, but is this fair to those who are commented on by these nameless, faceless newsmakers? Don't these people—even if they are highly placed and powerful themselves—have a right to know their accusers?

PERSONAL CONFLICT OF INTEREST As we've seen, ethical decision making requires a balancing of interests. But what of a media professional's own conflicts of interest? Should media personalities accept speaking fees, consulting contracts, or other compensation from groups that may have a vested interest in issues they may someday have to cover? Must media organizations disclose any and all possible conflicts of the commentators who appear in their news shows?

Consider these situations. When the United States in April 2017 launched 59 Tomahawk cruise missiles into Syria in response to that country's chemical gas attack against its own people, pundits were quick to praise the action. Among those cheering on the strike were Fox News military analyst Jack Keane (a member of the board of directors of General Dynamics, maker of the Tomahawk's launch system) and Ed Rogers of *The Washington Post* (a lobbyist for Raytheon, the missile's manufacturer). In neither case did the news outlet acknowledge those potential conflicts of interest (Hananoki, 2017). When Donald Trump's presidential campaign manager Corey Lewandowski was removed from his position in June 2016, he was

▼ *The Washington Post*'s Carl Bernstein and Bob Woodward (left) never would have broken the story of the Nixon White House's involvement in the Watergate break-in if it had not been for an anonymous source. The reporters honored their promise of confidentiality for 35 years, until "Deep Throat," then-FBI Assistant Director Mark Felt (right), revealed himself in 2005.

(left) ©AP Photo; (right) ©Justin Sullivan/Getty Images

quickly hired by CNN as a political commentator. The cable network did not tell its viewers that Lewandowski was bound by a nondisclosure and nondisparagement agreement that was part of the terms of his termination with the Trump campaign and that he remained on the campaign's payroll. Lewandowski not only honored his agreement with his former employer, but he was secretly advising Mr. Trump throughout his time at CNN (Alterman, 2017).

Other conflict-of-interest issues bedevil media professionals. The ongoing wars in the Middle East raise the problem of **embedding**, reporters accepting military control over their reporting in exchange for close contact with the troops. The interests in conflict here are objectivity and access—do reporters pay too high a price for their exciting video or touching personal interest stories? This **access journalism**—reporters acting deferentially toward news sources in order to ensure continued access—is sometimes subtle, as when Chuck Todd, NBC's chief political correspondent and host of *Meet the Press*, explained why he does not ask tough questions of the politicians who sit across from him: "We all sit there, because we all know, the first time we bark is the last time that they do the show. You say something, and sometimes it is last time they will ever come on your show. There is that balance" (2014). Sometimes it is more obvious, as when the Sinclair Broadcast Group promised to televise its interviews with presidential candidate Donald Trump on its 164 stations across the country "without commentary" in exchange for greater access to the candidate himself and the campaign (Dawsey & Gold, 2016). In either case, it offers much more power over journalists than is warranted because, according to *Columbia Journalism Review*'s Ross Barkan, "the best reporting is done on the margins, away from the siren charms of power and prestige." He quotes Pulitzer Prize–winning journalist Robert Caro: "It is more difficult to challenge a man's facts over cocktails than over a conference table" (2016). The box entitled "Journalists as Truth Vigilantes?" offers a look at another ethical issue facing journalists and how well or poorly they deal with the issue.

▶ CNN political commentator Corey Lewandowski. Was his cable news commentary on the 2016 presidential race a conflict of interest because he was on the payroll of one of the candidates? What obligation do media outlets have to reveal those money ties?

©John Lamparski/Getty Images

USING MEDIA TO MAKE A DIFFERENCE
Journalists as Truth Vigilantes?

The New York Times public editor Arthur Brisbane wanted to use his blog to make a difference. With a 2012 post entitled "Should the *Times* be a Truth Vigilante?" he hoped to create a discussion with his readers about the proper role of journalists when the people they cover express obvious falsehoods. So he wrote, "If the newspaper's overarching goal is truth, oughtn't truth be embedded in its principal stories?" What he hoped his readers would consider was how his reporters should respond when politicians lie or dissemble repeatedly; would it be proper for them to identify the misstatement "right at the point where the article quotes it?" (2012).

What had moved him to ask the question was criticism from his own paper's Paul Krugman, who complained that *Times* reporters had repeatedly allowed Republican presidential candidate Mitt Romney to accuse President Obama of the bad habit of apologizing for our country. Not a habit; never happened even once, said Krugman, and Brisbane agreed. The paper's reporters, however, never said so in their coverage of candidate Romney. But here Brisbane was not sure whether they should or should not. Would correcting one politician's view of the facts over another's, he wondered online, violate his paper's standard of objectivity?

The post did indeed make a difference, but not quite the one Brisbane had anticipated. In the words of *Salon*'s Glen Greenwald, it "sparked such intense reaction because it captured and inflamed long-standing anger toward media outlets for mindlessly amplifying statements without examining whether they're true . . . [It's] basically the equivalent of pondering in a medical journal whether doctors should treat diseases, or asking in a law review article whether lawyers should defend the legal interests of their clients, etc.: reporting facts that conflict with public claims (what Brisbane tellingly demeaned as being 'truth vigilantes') is one of the defining functions of journalism" (2012). But journalism has changed, explained media critic Jay Rosen: "Somewhere along the way, truth-telling was surpassed by other priorities the mainstream press felt a stronger duty to. These include such things as 'maintaining objectivity,' 'not imposing a judgment,' 'refusing to take sides' and sticking to what I have called the 'view from nowhere'" (2012).

But did Brisbane really make a difference? Journalist Clay Shirky says yes because, having publicly asked if a journalist should work for her or his readers instead of serving as "a stenographer to politicians, the question cannot now be unasked." Each day that our media continue to "fail at what has clearly surfaced as their readers' preference on the matter," he added, "will be a day in which that gap remains uncomfortably visible" (2012).

PROFIT AND SOCIAL RESPONSIBILITY The media industries are just that—industries. They exist not only to entertain and inform their audiences but also to make a profit for their owners and shareholders. What happens when serving profit conflicts with serving the public?

In 2016, for example, *VeloNews*, a bicycling magazine, planned to publish a story about the specifications of a highly anticipated new bike from manufacturer Shimano. When its editor called Shimano for comment on the then-secret product, the manufacturer demanded that the magazine kill the story or it would cancel all of its advertising for the remainder of the year. *VeloNews* ran the story nonetheless (Herman, 2016). A year earlier, news and entertainment website BuzzFeed was forced to launch an internal review after it was revealed that at least three posts had been deleted because the advertising department complained that they were critical of the site's advertisers (Trotter, 2015). In February 2010, 173 Toyota dealers, primarily in the southeastern United States, shifted their advertising from ABC affiliates to non-ABC stations as "punishment" for the aggressive coverage of Toyota's safety problems by that network and its chief investigative reporter Brian Ross. To its credit, ABC refused to soften its reporting (Rhee & Schone, 2010). In reality, these concessions to advertisers and their interests are rarely acknowledged, nor are they so often so explicitly demanded. As media law expert Charles Tillinghast explained, "One need not be a devotee of conspiracy theories to understand that journalists, like other human beings, can judge where their interests lie, and what risks are and are not prudent, given the desire to continue to eat and feed the family. . . . It takes no great brain to understand one does not bite the hand that feeds—or that one incurs great risk by doing so" (2000, pp. 145–146).

Balancing profit and social responsibility is a concern not just for journalists. Practitioners in entertainment, advertising, and public relations often face this dilemma. Does an ad agency accept as a client the manufacturer of sugared children's cereals even though doctors and dentists consider these products unhealthy? Does a public relations firm accept as a client the trade office of a country that forces prison inmates to manufacture products in violation of international law? Does a syndication company distribute the 1950s television series *The Amos 'n' Andy Show* knowing that it embodies many offensive stereotypes of African Americans?

Moreover, balancing profit and the public interest does not always involve big companies and millions of dollars. Often, a media practitioner will face an ethical dilemma at a very personal level. What would you do in this situation? The editor at the magazine where you work has ordered you to write an article about the 14-year-old daughter of your city's mayor. The girl's addiction to amphetamines is a closely guarded family secret, but it has been leaked to your publication. You believe that this child is not a public figure. Your boss disagrees, and the boss *is* the boss. By the way, you've just put a down payment on a lovely condo, and you need to make only two more installments to pay off your car. Do you write the story?

OFFENSIVE CONTENT Entertainment, news, and advertising professionals must often make decisions about the offensive nature of content. Other than the particular situation of broadcasters discussed earlier in this chapter, this is an ethical rather than a legal issue.

Offensive content is protected. Logically, we do not need the First Amendment to protect sweet and pretty expression. Freedom of speech and freedom of the press exist expressly to allow the dissemination of material that *will* offend. But what is offensive? Clearly, what is offensive to one person may be quite satisfactory to another. Religious leaders on the political right have attacked the cartoon show *SpongeBob Squarepants* for supposedly promoting homosexuality, and critics from the political left have attacked just about every classic Disney cartoon for racial and gender stereotyping. Television stations and networks regularly bleep cusswords that are common on cable television and in the schoolyard but leave untouched images of stabbings, beatings, and shootings. Where do we draw the line? Do we consider the tastes of the audience? Which members of the audience—the most easily offended? These are ethical, not legal, determinations.

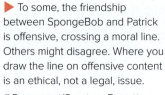

▶ To some, the friendship between SpongeBob and Patrick is offensive, crossing a moral line. Others might disagree. Where you draw the line on offensive content is an ethical, not a legal, issue.

©Paramount/Courtesy Everett Collection

Codes of Ethics and Self-Regulation

To aid practitioners in their moral reasoning, all major groups of media professionals have established formal codes or standards of ethical behavior. Among these are the Society of Professional Journalists' *Code of Ethics*, the American Society of News Editors' *Statement of Principles*, the Radio–Television Digital News Association's *Code of Broadcast News Ethics*, the American Advertising Federation's *Advertising Principles of American Business*, and the Public Relations Society of America's *Code of Professional Standards for the Practice of Public Relations*. These are prescriptive codes that tell media practitioners what they should do. For example, the Society of Professional Journalists in 2014 approved a new *Code of Ethics*. Its preamble reads,

> Members of the Society of Professional Journalists believe that public enlightenment is the forerunner of justice and the foundation of democracy. Ethical journalism strives to ensure the free exchange of information that is accurate, fair, and thorough. An ethical journalist acts with integrity.

To some, these codes are a necessary part of a true profession; to others, they are little more than unenforceable collections of clichés that restrict constitutional rights and invite lawsuits from outsiders. They offer at least two important benefits to ethical media practitioners: They are an additional source of information to be considered when making moral judgments, and they represent a particular media industry's best expression of its shared wisdom. To others, however, they are meaningless and needlessly restrictive. Ethicists Jay Black and Ralph Barney, for example, argue, "The fact should be evident that the First Amendment has a primary purpose of protecting the distribution of ideas . . . from restriction efforts by legions of 'regulators.' Ethics codes should be considered among those 'regulators.'" They continue, "It is indeed not difficult to find examples of codified professional ethics that ultimately become self-serving. That is, they tend to protect the industry, or elements of the industry, at the expense of individuals and other institutions, even of the full society" (1985, pp. 28–29).

In addition to industry professional codes, many media organizations have formulated their own institutional policies for conduct. In the case of the broadcast networks, these are enforced by **Standards and Practices Departments**. Local broadcasters have what are called **policy books**. Newspapers and magazines standardize behavior in two ways: through **operating policies** (which spell out standards for everyday operations) and **editorial policies** (which identify company positions on specific issues). Many media organizations also utilize **ombudsmen**, practitioners internal to the company who serve as "judges" in disputes between the public and the organization. Sometimes they have titles such as public editor or reader advocate. Despite data indicating that having an ombudsman fosters increased credibility among readers and audiences, only 20 American news outlets, half as many as a decade ago, still maintain the position (Rieder, 2013). Some news organizations, for example *The Washington Post*, which eliminated its ombudsman in 2013, use a **readers' representative**, who regularly responds to outside criticism.

These mechanisms of normative ethics are a form of self-regulation, designed in part to forestall more rigorous or intrusive government regulation. In a democracy dependent on mass communication, they serve an important function. We are suspicious of excessive government involvement in media. Self-regulation, however, has certain limitations:

- *Media professionals are reluctant to identify and censure colleagues who transgress.* To do so might appear to be admitting that problems exist; whistle-blowers in the profession are often met with hostility from their peers.

- *The standards for conduct and codes of behavior are abstract and ambiguous.* Many media professionals see this flexibility as a necessary evil; freedom and autonomy are essential. Others believe the lack of rigorous standards renders the codes useless.

- *As opposed to those in other professions, media practitioners are not subject to standards of professional training and licensing.* Again, some practitioners view standards of training and licensing as limiting media freedom and inviting government control. Others argue that licensing has not had these effects on doctors and lawyers.

- *Media practitioners often have limited independent control over their work.* Media professionals are not autonomous, individual professionals. They are part of large, hierarchically structured organizations. Therefore, it is often difficult to punish violations of standards because of the difficulty in assigning responsibility.

Critics of self-regulation argue that these limitations are often accepted willingly by media practitioners because their "true" function is "to cause the least commotion" for those working in the media industries (Black & Whitney, 1983, p. 432). True or not, the decision to perform his or her duties in an ethical manner ultimately rests with the individual media professional. As Black and Barney explain, an ethical media professional "must rationally overcome the status quo tendencies . . . to become the social catalyst who identifies the topics and expedites the negotiations societies need in order to remain dynamic" (p. 36).

DEVELOPING MEDIA LITERACY SKILLS
Judging the Use of Anonymous Sources

As you read in this chapter, the use of anonymous sources for news stories is often essential. Journalists rely on sources to provide information for the stories they publish, and those sources may well be reluctant to share sensitive or critical information in the absence of anonymity because their careers, sometimes even lives, may depend on remaining unnamed. Journalism benefits in another way, as well. The press must always be seen as independent. So if journalists are viewed as extensions of the government because they too easily give up their sources, few people with important but sensitive information will be willing to come forward ever again. But granting anonymity to sources comes with risks. As such, as part of a 2016 overhaul of its policies regarding anonymous sources, the top editors of *The New York Times* sent an e-mail to their journalistic staff that read, in part,

> At best, granting anonymity allows us to reveal the atrocities of terror groups, government abuses or other situations where sources may risk their lives, freedom or careers by talking to us. In sensitive areas like national security reporting, it can be unavoidable. But in other cases, readers question whether anonymity allows unnamed people to skew a story in favor of their own agenda. In rare cases, we have published information from anonymous sources without enough questions or skepticism—and it has turned out to be wrong.

Margaret Sullivan, the paper's public editor, offered her assessment of the practice:

> I'm not in favor of banning anonymous sources, although I've written repeatedly about their overuse. Many important stories—some of the most important, in fact—could never have been written if their sources had not been kept confidential. Reporters risk a lot to protect those sources, and they need to be able to do so. But there's a big difference between, for example, a national security article that simply can't be written with on-the-record sources and the other kinds of anonymity one often sees. That latter category includes allowing unnamed government officials to use the press as a megaphone, to float politically sensitive trial balloons, or to disparage their enemies without accountability. In short, not much rises anywhere near the level of Watergate or an exposé about warrantless government eavesdropping. (Both in Sullivan, 2016)

As such, the *Times* set out its new policy:

1. Special rules apply when the lead of a story—that is, the primary news element—is based entirely on one or more anonymous sources. All such stories must be presented by the department head to one of the paper's top three editors.

2. Every other use of anonymous sourcing anywhere in any story must be personally approved in advance by the department head or deputy.

3. Direct quotes from anonymous sources will be allowed only in rare instances and with the approval of the department head or deputy.

4. As a reminder, it continues to be a hard-and-fast rule that at least one editor must know the specific identity of any anonymous source before publication.

What is your reaction when you read or hear a story based on anonymous sources? Do you tend to be skeptical? Is your skepticism based on the story's content; that is, are you more likely to accept information provided by an unnamed source if it confirms your position on a topic? Do the *Times* rules seem adequate, too much, or too little? Why? If you accept *Times* deputy executive editor Matt Purdy's assertion that anonymously sourced stories are "journalistic I.E.D.s" that could explode unexpectedly and damage the paper and its journalistic credibility, can you make an argument for never using them at all?

If there is any single lesson from this chapter, it is that the legal and regulatory rules that bind mass media organizations are rarely problematic. A law is a law. You may not like it, but you know what it is and what the price for violation may be. But ethics, the values and norms that guide practice where there is no legal bright line, are the dilemmas that challenge media organizations and media-literate consumers the greatest. Yes, reporters' and editors' jobs would be much easier if they did not have to rely on anonymous sources. Our jobs as news consumers would likewise be easier if we always knew a story's sources and their motivations. But that is not the real world of mass communication, nor should it be. A world that is that easy to negotiate would not be interesting enough to engage journalism or us.

MEDIA LITERACY CHALLENGE
Talk to the FCC

The primary telecommunications regulatory agency in the United States is the Federal Communications Commission (FCC). Its website (www.fcc.gov) offers a true bounty of information, including the FCC's efforts to make better use of the Internet to interact with industry and audiences. Inasmuch as *an understanding of the ethical and moral obligations of media practitioners* is an important component of media literacy, your challenge is to access this site and find the links specific to you as an audience member. Then answer these questions: What links did you identify as of particular interest to audience members? Why? Did any of these links offer you an opportunity to "talk" to the Commission's staff? If yes, which ones? Contact the Commission's staff and ask a question (or two or three) that is of interest to you. Detail that question and the FCC's response. Offer a retort. That is, ask another question raised by the Commission's initial response. Detail your question and its answer. Did the Commission offer to provide you with documents or other material to help you with your queries? If so, what were they? Do you think it is important that the FCC stays in touch with audience members? Why or why not? Describe your general reaction to your "conversation" with this federal regulatory agency.

Resources for Review and Discussion

REVIEW POINTS: TYING CONTENT TO LEARNING OUTCOMES

▶ **Outline the history and development of our contemporary understanding of the First Amendment.**

- ☐ The First Amendment is based on libertarianism's self-righting principle.
- ☐ The absolutist position—no law means no law—is not as straightforward as it may seem. Questions have arisen over the definition of the press, what constitutes abridgment, balancing of interests, the definition of libel and slander, the permissibility of prior restraint, and control of obscenity and pornography.

▶ **Explain the justification for and exercise of media regulation.**

- ☐ Media professionals face other legal issues, such as how to define and handle indecent content, the impact of deregulation, and the limits of copyright.

▶ **Distinguish between a media system that operates under a libertarian philosophy and one that operates under a social responsibility philosophy.**

- ☐ Libertarianism assumes a good and rational public with full access to all ideas; social responsibility theory, favoring responsible self-interest over government regulation, is the norm against which the operation of the American media system should be judged.

▶ **Define and discuss media ethics and how they are applied.**

- ☐ Ethics, rules of behavior or moral principles that guide our actions, are not regulations, but they are every bit as important in guiding media professionals' behavior.

- ☐ There are three levels of ethics—metaethics, normative ethics, and applied ethics.
- ☐ Ethics require the balancing of several interests—the moral agent's individual conscience, the object of the act, financial supporters, the institution itself, the profession, and society.
- ☐ Ethics, rather than regulation, influence judgments about matters such as truth and honesty, privacy, confidentiality, personal conflict of interest, the balancing of profit and social responsibility, and the decision to publish or air potentially offensive content.

▶ **Describe the operation and pros and cons of self-regulation.**

- ☐ There is divergent opinion about the value and true purpose of much industry self-regulation.

▶ **Better consider the use of anonymous sources.**

- ☐ Granting anonymity to sources in order to obtain secret or sensitive information is a necessity in contemporary journalism, but it brings with it great risk (for example, powerful sources using it to advance damaging agendas against those less powerful).

KEY TERMS

QUESTIONS FOR REVIEW

1. What are the basic tenets of libertarianism? How do they support the First Amendment?

2. What is the absolutist position on the First Amendment?

3. Name important court cases involving the definition of "no law," "the press," "abridgment," "clear and present danger," "balancing of interests," and "prior restraint."

4. Define obscenity, pornography, and indecency.

5. What is the traffic cop analogy? Why is it important in the regulation of broadcasting?

6. What is copyright? What are the exceptions to copyright? What is DRM?

7. What are the basic assumptions of social responsibility theory?

8. What are ethics? What are the three levels of ethics?

9. What is confidentiality? Why is confidentiality important to media professionals and to democracy?

10. What are some forms of media self-regulation? What are the strengths and limitations of self-regulation?

To maximize your study time, check out CONNECT to access the SmartBook study module for this chapter and explore other resources.

QUESTIONS FOR CRITICAL THINKING AND DISCUSSION

1. How much regulation or, if you prefer, deregulation do you think broadcasters should accept?

2. Of the six individual and group interests that must be balanced by media professionals, which ones do you think would have the most influence over you if you were an investigative reporter for a big-city television station? Explain your answer.

3. In general, and from your own interaction with the mass media, how ethical do you believe media professionals to be—specifically, print journalists? Television journalists? Advertising professionals? Public relations professionals? Television and film writers? Direct mail marketers? Explain your answers.

REFERENCES

1. Alterman, E. (2017, January 30). The serfdom of the press. *Nation*, pp. 10–11.

2. Anderson, M. K. (2000, May/June). When copyright goes wrong. *Extra!*, p. 25.

3. Barkan, R. (2016, November 4). Journalists too easily charmed by power, access, and creamy risotto. *Columbia Journalism Review*. Online: http://www.cjr.org/first_person/podesta_emails_journalists_dinner.php

4. Barnes, R. (2012, June 21). Supreme Court overturns FCC sanctions on networks, sidesteps larger issue. *The Washington Post*. Online: https://www.washingtonpost.com/politics/supreme-court-overturns-fcc-sanctions-on-networks-sidesteps-larger-issue/2012/06/21/gJQAwffxsV_story.html?utm_term=.dae984d52514

5. Bednarski, P. J. (2016, June 16). What to do about piracy? How about nothing? *MediaPost*. Online: http://www.mediapost.com/publications/article/278319/what-to-do-about-piracy-how-about-nothing.html

6. Black, J., & Barney, R. D. (1985). The case against mass media codes of ethics. *Journal of Mass Media Ethics, 1,* 27–36.

7. Black, J., & Whitney, F. C. (1983). *Introduction to mass communications.* Dubuque, IA: William C. Brown.

8. *Bridges v. California,* 314 U.S. 252 (1941).

9. Brisbane, A. S. (2012, January 12). Should the *Times* be a truth vigilante? *The New York Times*. Online: http://publiceditor.blogs.nytimes.com/2012/01/12/should-the-times-be-a-truth-vigilante/?scp=1&sq=Should%20the%20Times%20be%20a%20Truth%20Vigilante&st=cse

10. *Brown v. Entertainment Merchants Association,* U.S. No. 08-1448 (2011).

11. *Burstyn, Inc . v. Wilson,* 343 U.S. 495 (1952).

12. Butler, B. (2011, July 20). Young guns. *Maynard Institute for Journalism Education.* Online: http://mije.org/health/young-guns

13. Calderone, M. (2016, November 27). Media helps boost Donald Trump's false claim that 'millions' voted illegally. *Huffington Post.* Online: http://www.huffingtonpost.com/entry/donald-trump-false-claim-millions-popular-vote_us_583b5ed0e4b09b605600e42a

14. *CBS v. Democratic National Committee,* 412 U.S. 94 (1973).

15. *Chandler v. Florida,* 449 U.S. 560 (1981).

16. Copps, M. J. (2014, March/April). From the desk of a former FCC commissioner. *Columbia Journalism Review,* pp. 35–38.

17. Dawsey, J., & Gold, H. (2016, December 16). Kushner: We struck deal with Sinclair for straighter coverage. *Politico.* Online: http://www.politico.com/story/2016/12/trump-campaign-sinclair-broadcasting-jared-kushner-232764

18. Day, L. A. (2006). *Ethics in media communications: Cases and controversies* (6th ed.). Belmont, CA: Wadsworth.

19. Emmons, A., & LaChance, N. (2016, November 18). Obama refuses to pardon Edward Snowden. Trump's new CIA pick wants him dead. *Intercept.* Online: https://theintercept

.com/2016/11/18/obama-refuses-to-pardon-edward-snowden-trumps-new-cia-pick-wants-him-dead/

20. *Estes v. State of Texas*, 381 U.S. 532 (1965).

21. *Federal Communications Commission v. Fox Television Stations, Inc.*, 556 U.S. 502 (2009).

22. Gibbs, M. (2005, July 18). A new theory with consequences. *Network World*, p. 50.

23. Gillmor, D. (2000, August 18). Digital Copyright Act comes back to haunt consumers. *San Jose Mercury News*, pp. 1C, 6C.

24. Gillmor, D. M., & Barron, J. A. (1974). *Mass communication law: Cases and comments*. St. Paul, MN: West.

25. *Ginzburg v. United States*, 383 U.S. 463 (1966).

26. *Gitlow v. New York*, 268 U.S. 652 (1925).

27. Greenwald, G. (2012, January 13). Arthur Brisbane and selective stenography. *Salon*. Online: http://www.salon.com/2012/01/13/arthur_brisbane_and_selective_stenography/

28. Hananoki, E. (2017, April 11). *Wash. Post* doesn't disclose writer supporting Syria strike is a lobbyist for Tomahawk missile manufacturer. *Media Matters*. Online: https://www.mediamatters.org/blog/2017/04/11/wash-post-doesn-t-disclose-writer-supporting-syria-strike-lobbyist-tomahawk-missile-manufacturer/215976

29. Hartmann, T. (2017, January 16). The Trump story media dare not utter: They sacrificed democracy for ratings. *Alternet*. Online: http://www.alternet.org/election-2016/trump-tv-ratings

30. Herman, M. (2016, April 25). For enthusiast media, ethics can be costly. *Columbia Journalism Review*. Online: http://www.cjr.org/business_of_news/for_enthusiast_media_ethics_can_be_costly.php

31. *Irvin v. Dowd*, 366 U.S. 717 (1961).

32. *Jacobellis v. Ohio*, 378 U.S. 184, 197 (1964).

33. *Joseph Burstyn, Inc. v. Wilson*, 343 U.S. 495 (1952).

34. McQuail, D. (1987). *Mass communication theory: An introduction*. Beverly Hills, CA: Sage.

35. Meiklejohn, A. (1960). *Political freedom*. New York: Harper.

36. *MGM Studios, Inc.v. Grokster, Ltd.*, 545 U.S. 913 (2005).

37. *Miller v. State of California*, 413 U.S. 15 (1973).

38. *National Broadcasting Co. v. United States*, 319 U.S. 190 (1943).

39. *Near v. Minnesota*, 283 U.S. 697 (1931).

40. *New York Times v. Sullivan*, 376 U.S. 254 (1964).

41. *New York Times v. United States*, 403 U.S. 713 (1971).

42. Pember, D. (1999). *Mass media law*. New York: McGraw-Hill.

43. Plaisance, P. L. (2014). *Media ethics*. Los Angeles: Sage.

44. Rhee, J., & Schone, M. (2010, February 8). Toyota dealers pull ABC TV ads; anger over "excessive stories." *ABC News*. Online: http://abcnews.go.com/Blotter/toyota-dealers-pull-abc-tv-ads-anger-excessive-toyota-safety-recall/story?id=9776474

45. Rich, F. (2005, February 6). The year of living indecently. *The New York Times*, p. B.1.

46. Rieder, R. (2013, February 21). Ombudsman role still has a place in newsroom. *USA Today*. Online: http://www.usatoday.com/story/money/columnist/rieder/2013/02/21/rem-rieder-ombudsmen/1934015/

47. Rogers, M. (2014, June 16). Why I outed gay Republicans. *Politico*. Online: http://www.politico.com/magazine/story/2014/06/mike-rogers-outed-gay-republicans-108368

48. Rosen, J. (2012, January 12). So whaddaya think: Should we put truthtelling back up there at number one? *Press Think*. Online: http://pressthink.org/2012/01/so-whaddaya-think-should-we-put-truthtelling-back-up-there-at-number-one/

49. *Roth v. United States*, 354 U.S. 476 (1957).

50. *Saia v. New York*, 334 U.S. 558 (1948).

51. Scola, N. (2014, September 3). Three-quarters of Americans want cameras in the Supreme Court as one federal judge demonstrates why some of his colleagues don't. *The Washington Post*. Online: http://www.washingtonpost.com/blogs/the-switch/wp/2014/09/03/three-quarters-of-americans-want-cameras-in-the-supreme-court-as-one-federal-judge-demonstrates-why-some-of-his-colleagues-dont/

52. Shirky, C. (2012, January 12). *The New York Times* public editor's very public utterance. *The Guardian*. Online: http://www.guardian.co.uk/commentisfree/cifamerica/2012/jan/13/new-york-times-public-editor?CMP=twt_gu

53. Society of Professional Journalists. (2014, September 6). *SPJ code of ethics*. Online: http://www.spj.org/ethicscode.asp

54. *Sony Corp. v. Universal City Studios*, 464 U.S. 417 (1984).

55. SoundBites. (2005, December). A better mousetrap. *Extra! Update*, p. 2.

56. Stewart, J. (2011, June 30). Moral kombat. *The Daily Show*. Online: http://www.cc.com/video-clips/vqgdfb/the-daily-show-with-jon-stewart-moral-kombat

57. Sullivan, M. (2016, March 15). Tightening the screws on anonymous sources. *The New York Times*. Online: http://publiceditor.blogs.nytimes.com/2016/03/15/new-york-times-anonymous-sources-policy-public-editor/

58. Tillinghast, C. H. (2000). *American broadcast regulation and the First Amendment: Another look*. Ames: Iowa State University Press.

59. *Time, Inc. v. Hill*, 385 U.S. 374 (1967).

60. Todd, C. (2014, December 28). Meet the Press transcript—December 28, 2014. *NBC News*. Online: http://www.nbcnews.com/meet-the-press/meet-press-transcript-december-28-2014-n279436

61. Trotter, J. K. (2015, April 18). BuzzFeed deletes posts under pressure from its own business department. *Gawker*. Online: http://tktk.gawker.com/buzzfeed-deleted-posts-under-pressure-from-its-own-busi-1697762873

62. *Valentine v. Christensen*, 316 U.S. 52 (1942).

Cultural Forum Blue Column icon, Media Literacy Red Torch Icon, Using Media Green Gear icon, Developing Media book in starburst icon: ©McGraw-Hill Education

◀ *The BBK Music Phone Supergirl Contest—China's version of American Idol.*

©Wang Jiaowen/ZUMA Press/ Newscom

Learning Objectives

Satellites and the Internet have made mass media truly global. Earth has become a global village. But not all countries use mass media in the same ways. Moreover, many people around the world resent the "Americanization" of their indigenous media systems. After studying this chapter, you should be able to

▶ Outline the development of global media.

▶ Explain the practice of comparative analysis.

▶ Identify different media systems from around the world.

▶ Describe the debate surrounding cultural imperialism and other controversies raised by the globalization of media.

1901 ▶ Marconi sends wireless signal transatlantic	**1900**
mid-1920s European colonial powers use shortwave radio to connect holdings	
1923 Radio comes to China	

©Ingram Publishing RF

1928 ▶ Baird sends television image from London to New York	**1925**
1940 Voice of America goes on air	

©Ingram Publishing RF

1960s ▶ British pirate broadcasters go on air	**1950**
1962 ▶ McLuhan's *The Gutenberg Galaxy*	
1967 McLuhan's *Understanding Media: The Extensions of Man*	

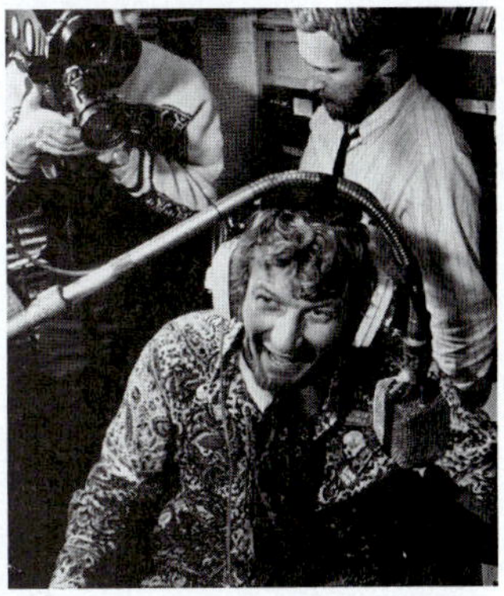

©Hulton-Deutsch Collection/Getty Images

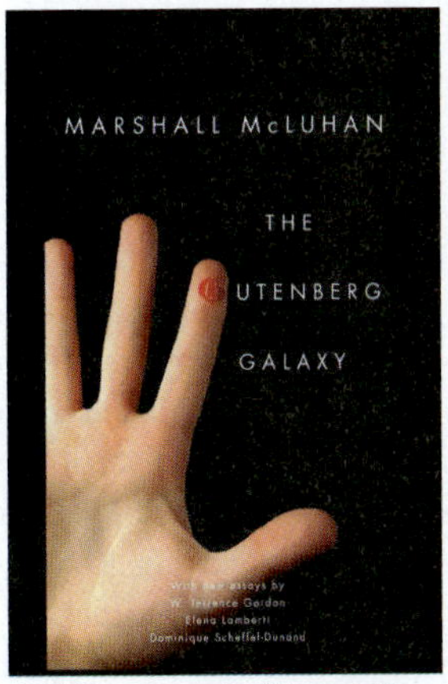

1980 MacBride Report calls for New World Information Order	**1975**
1984 German RTL goes on air	
1985 Radio Martí goes on air	
1989 Fall of European communism	
1990 TV Martí goes on air	
1996 Al Jazeera	
1997 China begins crackdown on the Internet	

MARSHALL McLUHAN THE GUTENBERG GALAXY

©TJ Photography/PhotoEdit

2002 Reporters Without Borders initiates annual press freedom reports	**2000**
2009 UK okays/limits product placement	
2010 Sweden says TV movie commercial breaks may be finable offense; Spain limits TV beauty ads	
2011 ▶ Arab Spring	
2013 Al Jazeera America; Swedish movies must have gender ratings	
2014 French government declares books an "essential good," also puts restrictions on after-work e-mailing	
2015 Call for Universal Charter of Media Freedoms	
2016 Chinese media must serve the Party proclamation; Reporters Without Borders ranks U.S. press as 41st freest in the world	
2017 China becomes world's biggest movie market	

©Nacerdine ZEBAR/Getty Images

HENRI AND YOU HAVE BEEN PEN PALS SINCE SEVENTH GRADE. He's visited you here in the United States, and you've been to his house in the small, walled village of Alet, near Carcassonne in southern France. You treat each other like family. Which means you sometimes fight. But unlike siblings living under the same roof, you have to carry on your dispute by e-mail.

Dear Henri,

What's with you guys and your language police? For everyone else it's e-mail. For you it's *courriel*. People around the world are innovating with Internet start-ups. You have *jeunepousses*. My French isn't as good as yours, but doesn't that mean "little flower" or something? You guys aren't keeping up with the rest of the world. The world's air traffic control systems all use English for their communication.

Three-quarters of all the world's mail is written in English. English is the primary language for the publication of scientific and scholarly reports and for many international organizations such as the European Union and the Association of Southeast Asian Nations. In fact, your own finishing school for future leaders, the National School of Administration, whose alums include your last three presidents, now requires that all its *énarques*, that means "graduates," must be fluent in English "in order to cope with their future roles" (Allen, 2015).

Mon ami,

Close, mais pas de cigare (but no cigar, my linguistically challenged friend). I admit that we may seem a little foolish to the rest of you, but the Académie Française (what you called the language police) is simply trying to protect our language because it represents the deepest expression of our national identity. And we do keep up with the rest of the world! In fact, we are the globe's cultural leaders, the avant-garde. Surely you've recently seen *Le Fabuleux Destin d'Amélie Poulain* and *Un Long Dimanche de Fiançailles* at your local cinema. I think in America they were called *Amélie* and *The Very Long Engagement*. They were worldwide hits. And I'm sure you saw *The Artist*, a little French production that won your Academy Award not too long ago.

Dear Henri,

Say what you will, my friend, but 27 of the world's top 30 money-making movies in 2016 were from America; two of the top three in your own country, in fact: *Zootopia* and *The Revenant* ("Overseas Top," 2017; "The Big," 2016). Want more? The four most popular TV shows in the world are all from *my* culture: *Game of Thrones*, *The Walking Dead*, *Pretty Little Liars*, and *Westworld* (Lubin, 2016).

Not only are American programs like these overseas hits, but American formats are also sold abroad to become local productions. Foreign–language *Hollywood Reporter*, *Dr. Oz*, *Wheel of Fortune*, *Law & Order*, and *Desperate Housewives* clones exist all over the world. *The Apprentice* is another format that has been sold globally. In China it's called *Wise Man Takes All*. China also created a version of *American Idol—The BBK Music Phone Supergirl Contest*. Local versions of foreign shows also travel the other way. *America's Funniest Home Videos* and *Power Rangers* originated in Japan, as did *Shark Tank*. *Shameless*, *House of Cards*, and *The Office* came to the United States via England, and *Homeland* came to America from Israel.

Throughout this text we have seen how globalization is altering the operation of the various mass media industries, as well as the process of mass communication itself. In this chapter, we focus specifically on this globalization and its impact.

In doing so, we will look at the beginnings of international media and their development into a truly global mass media system. To study today's global media we will use comparative analyses to see how different countries establish media systems consistent with their specific people, cultures, and political systems. Naturally, we will discuss the programming available in other countries. And because global media influence the cultures that use them both positively and negatively, we visit the debate over cultural imperialism. Finally, our media literacy discussion deals with contrasting the way other countries handle different media issues with the way we do things here in America.

A Short History of Global Media

It is fair to argue that radio and television were, in effect, international in their earliest days. Guglielmo Marconi was the British son of an Italian diplomat, and among his earliest successes was the 1901 transmission of a wireless signal from England to Newfoundland. American inventors, Philo Farnsworth and Russian immigrant Vladimir Zworykin, improved on the mechanical television design of Scotland's John Logie Baird, among whose greatest achievements was the successful transmission of a television picture from London to New York in 1928. It was not much later in the development of radio and television that these media did indeed become, if not truly global, at least international as they quickly attracted audiences from around the world.

The Beginning of International Mass Media

Almost from the very start, radio signals were broadcast internationally. Beginning in the mid-1920s, the major European colonial powers—the Netherlands, Great Britain, and Germany—were using **shortwave radio** to connect with their various colonies in Africa, Asia, and the Middle East, as well as, in the case of the British, North America (Canada) and the South Pacific (Australia). Shortwave was (and still is) well suited for transmission over very long distances because its low frequencies easily and efficiently reflect—or **skip**—off the ionosphere, producing **sky waves** that can travel vast distances.

CLANDESTINE STATIONS It was not only colonial powers that made use of international radio. Antigovernment or antiregime radio also constituted an important segment of international broadcasting, as illegal or unlicensed broadcast operations were used for political purposes. These **clandestine stations** typically emerged "from the darkest shadows of political conflict. They [were] frequently operated by revolutionary groups or intelligence agencies" (Soley & Nichols, 1987, p. vii). In World War II, for example, Allies operating German-language stations in Britain and other Allied nations pretended to be German and encouraged German soldiers and sailors to sabotage their vehicles and vessels rather than be killed in battle. Allied stations, such as the Atlantic Station and Soldiers' Radio Calais, also intentionally broadcast misleading reports. Posing as two of the many official stations operated by the German army, they frequently transmitted false reports to confuse the enemy or to force official Nazi radio to counter with rebuttals, thus providing the Allies with exactly the information they sought.

But it was in the Cold War that clandestine broadcasting truly flowered. In the years between the end of World War II and the fall of European communism in 1989, thousands of radio, and sometimes television, pirates took up the cause of either revolutionary (procommunist) or counterrevolutionary (anticommunist) movements. In addition, other governments tangentially related to this global struggle—especially the growing anticolonial movements in South and Central America and in Africa—made use of clandestine broadcasting.

During the Cold War, unauthorized, clandestine opposition stations typically operated outside the nations or regions to which they broadcast to avoid discovery, capture, and imprisonment or death. Today the relatively few clandestine operations functioning inside the regions to which they transmit can be classified as **indigenous stations**, and they can make use of technologies other than radio. For example, al-Zawraa (The Gate) was an antigovernment Sunni-operated satellite television station transmitting from constantly changing locations inside Iraq to beam anti-American and anti-Shiite content to Sunni insurgents and other Iraqis involved in that war-torn country's long civil war. Opposition stations transmitting to the regions they hope to influence from outside those areas are **exogenous stations**. Free North Korea Radio, operated primarily by North Korean defectors and refugees, is an example of an exogenous (or international) station. It broadcasts from near Seoul, South Korea, in opposition to the despotic rule of North Korea's Kim Jong Un. But because radios sold in North Korea are pretuned to receive nothing but official government stations and cannot be

▲ Disc jockey Robby Dale broadcasts from pirate station Radio Caroline aboard the MV *Frederika*, anchored off Great Britain's Isle of Man.

©Hulton-Deutsch Collection/ Getty Images

changed, only radios smuggled into the country can deliver FreeNK. FreeNK's response, therefore, is heavier reliance on the Internet, although access to that medium in North Korea is also quite limited. Naturally, many other clandestine operations have migrated to the Internet. Even al-Qaeda maintains a YouTube channel, Red of al Qaeda, which began operation in 1988. But because the difficult terrain in many embattled nations makes telephone lines an impossibility and poverty renders wireless Internet a rarity, radio remains the medium of choice for many out-groups.

PIRATE BROADCASTERS Another type of broadcast operation transmitting from outside its desired audience's geographic location involved something a bit more benign than war and revolution. These were stations that began broadcasting into Great Britain in the 1960s. Called **pirate broadcasters**, they were illegally operated stations broadcasting to British audiences from offshore or foreign facilities. Among the more notable were Radio Caroline, which reached a daily audience of a million listeners with its signal broadcast from the MV *Frederika* anchored 3½ miles off the Isle of Man, and Radio Veronica, broadcasting from a ship off the coast of the Netherlands.

These pirates, unlike their politically motivated clandestine cousins, were powerful and well subsidized by advertisers and record companies. Moreover, much like the commercial radio stations with which we are now familiar, they broadcast 24 hours a day, every day of the year. These pirates offered listeners an alternative to the controlled and low-key programming of the British Broadcasting Corporation's (BBC) stations. Because the BBC was noncommercial, pirate stations represented the only opportunity for advertisers who wanted to reach British consumers. Record companies intent on introducing Britain's youth to their artists and to rock 'n' roll also saw the pirates as the only way to reach their audience, which the staid BBC all but ignored.

Enterprising broadcasters also made use of foreign locales to bring commercial television to audiences otherwise denied. The top-rated network in Germany today, for example, is RTL. Now broadcasting from the German city of Cologne, it began operations in January 1984 in Luxembourg, transmitting an American-style mix of children's programming, sports, talk shows, and action–adventure programming into Germany to compete with that country's two dominant public broadcasters, ARD and ZDF.

THE UNITED STATES AS INTERNATIONAL BROADCASTER World War II brought the United States into the business of international broadcasting. Following the lead of Britain, which had just augmented its colonial broadcast system with an **external service** called the BBC World Service, the United States established in 1940 what would eventually be known as the Voice of America (VOA) to counter enemy propaganda and disseminate information about America. The VOA originally targeted countries in Central and South America friendly to Germany, but as the war became global, it quickly began broadcasting to scores of other nations, attracting, along with Britain's World Service, a large and admiring listenership, first in countries occupied by the Axis powers, and later by those in the Soviet sphere of influence.

It was this Cold War with the Soviets that moved the United States into the forefront of international broadcasting, a position it still holds today. To counter the efforts of the Soviet Union's external service, Radio Moscow, the United States established three additional services. Radio in the American Sector (RIAS), broadcasting in German, served people inside East Berlin and East Germany; Radio Free Europe (RFE) broadcast to all of the other communist-bloc Eastern European countries in their native languages; and Radio Liberty (RL) was aimed at listeners in the Soviet Union itself. When these services were initiated, people both in the United States and abroad were told that they were funded by contributions from American citizens. However, as a result of the furor that arose when it was revealed in 1971 that they were in fact paid for by the Central Intelligence Agency, they were brought openly under government control and funded and administered by the International Broadcasting Bureau, whose members were appointed by the president.

The communist nations targeted by these services attempted to jam their signals by broadcasting on the same frequencies at higher powers, but they were only minimally successful in keeping their people from listening to these Western broadcasts. It was the success of these **surrogate services**—broadcast operations established by one country to substitute for another's own domestic service—that prompted President Ronald Reagan in 1985 to establish a special division of the VOA, Radio Martí, to broadcast into communist Cuba. Radio Martí, still in operation, was joined by TV Martí in 1990.

A final U.S. external service established during World War II and the Cold War, Armed Forces Radio and Television Service (AFRTS), remains active today under its new name, American Forces Radio and Television Service. Maintained by the American military, its stated mission is "to communicate Department of Defense policies, priorities, programs, goals, and initiatives [and to provide] stateside radio and television programming, 'a touch of home' to U.S. service men and women, DoD civilians, and their families serving outside the continental United States" (AFRTS, 2015). It employs shortwave radio, seven Earth-orbiting satellites, and MP3 technology to reach listeners and viewers in 175 countries and aboard U.S. ships with commercial-free fare.

THE VOA TODAY Today, VOA broadcasts in 47 languages draw 236.6 million people a week. Most of that audience is for the VOA itself, but millions of people in 23 developing countries access VOA programming on its surrogate operations, Radio Free Europe and Radio Liberty, serving eastern Europe and central Asia; Radio Martí; the recently added Radio Free Asia; Arabic-language Radio Sawa; Radio Sila, broadcasting in Arabic and French into Darfur from Chad; and Awera24, a 24-hour-a-day satellite channel beamed into Nigeria to counter propaganda from radical groups like schoolgirl kidnappers Boko Haram. Throughout its history, the VOA has frequently vacillated between two roles in response to world events and political pressures at home: (1) disseminating Western propaganda and (2) providing objective information. With the threat of communist world domination now nonexistent, it attempts to meet the far less contradictory goals of spreading American culture and disseminating health and social information.

The VOA's commitment to the spread of American culture is evidenced by the establishment in 1992 of a 24-hour top-40 style service, VOA Europe, and in 1998 of a 24-hour, all-news English-language worldwide radio service characterized by a snappy style reminiscent of domestic commercial stations. The VOA's focus on transmitting health and other practical information can be seen in the increased efforts it devotes to programs aimed at developing nations on AIDS prevention, nutrition, and vaccination. In pursuit of this humanitarian goal, the VOA now frequently strikes agreements with local stations in these countries to broadcast its programs over their AM and FM stations, making them accessible to people who listen outside the shortwave band.

Even in the United States, people may access other countries' surrogate services. Of course, these are more complements than substitutes for domestic media, but their goal is indeed to offer other nations' perspectives on the world. Television's *BBC America* has aired in the United States since 1998, is commercially funded, and is available to a majority of American homes. Iran operates *Press TV*, and like Russia's state-funded and -operated *RT* and China's *Today China*, tends to echo official government talking points. France's *France 24* is more independent.

Global Media Today

The Cartoon Network is satellite- and cablecast in 145 countries in 14 languages. The Discovery Channel has 63 million subscribers in Asia; 35 million in Europe, the Middle East, and Africa; 30 million in India; and 18 million in Latin America. Nickelodeon is the globe's most distributed kids' channel, viewable in more than 320 million households worldwide. In advance of its 2016 television premiere, Fox simultaneously streamed the first episode of

Outcast in 61 countries using dedicated Facebook Live pages. American cable giant Altice USA is actually former cable giant Cablevision under its new French ownership. *The New York Times* sells a hard-copy magazine, *Chinese Monthly*, written in simplified Chinese for readers in Hong Kong and Macau. Britain's Channel 4 pays Fox Television $1 million per episode for *The Simpsons*, and satellite channel BSkyB pays $814,000 an episode for *Glee*. U.S. television network CBS earns more than $1.1 billion a year by selling its programming to overseas broadcasters (Auletta, 2014).

The 2016 biographical movie *Jackie*, about the life of Jacqueline Kennedy in the week after the assassination of her husband President John F. Kennedy, was made for an American studio by Chilean filmmakers and a French production crew. Jackie Kennedy was portrayed by an American actress born in Jerusalem; John F. Kennedy was portrayed by an actor from Denmark; and, as the film was shot in France, Paris stood in for 1960s America. *The New York Times* may be the world's most popular newspaper website, but second and third are England's *Daily Mail* and *The Guardian*. American Spanish-language network Telemundo, owned by NBC, has programming offices in Tokyo; Mexican media conglomerate Televisa has offices in China and coproduction deals with state-run China Central Television, as does Venezuela's Venevision; and Brazilian media company Globo produces content for a number of India's television networks. TV France International, that country's umbrella distribution organization, has partnerships with Fox, Warner Brothers, the Discovery and Sundance channels, and Bravo. Netflix and Amazon Prime produce local-language series for their European subscribers. The Chinese publish *China Daily*, an English-language newspaper, in eight major American cities. *The Washington Post* publishes a daily online newsletter, *Today's WorldView*, specifically for its 25 million international readers. Hundreds of millions of Internet users spread throughout scores of countries can tune in to thousands of Web radio stations originating from every continent except Antarctica. Media know few national borders.

But the global flow of expression and entertainment is not welcomed by everyone. French law requires that 40% of all music broadcast by its radio stations be in French. Iran bans "Western music" altogether from radio and television, going so far as to jail six people in 2014 for making a dance-along video to Pharrell's "Happy"; the accused were forced to issue an apology on state television and were initially sentenced to six months in prison and 91 lashes (Erdbrink & Gladstone, 2014). Jamaica's Broadcasting Commission bans American hip-hop music to, it says, guard against underage sex and juvenile delinquency. America's

▶ *Jackie*, a film about an American First Lady and produced for an American studio, was made by Chilean filmmakers and their French crew.
©Atlaspix/Alamy

You can enjoy *The Simpsons* just about everywhere in the Middle East, but if you do catch it there, you'll never see Homer drink a beer or visit Moe's Bar.
©Fox/Photofest

northern neighbor mandates that all television programming contains at least 15% "Canadian-made content," while the European Union sets its minimum at 20%. While *The Simpsons* is widely distributed across the Middle East by Saudi Arabian DBS provider MBC, all references to Duff Beer have been changed to soda, and Moe's Bar does not appear at all. The Germans and Austrians are wary of *The Simpsons* as well, refusing to air episodes that include the topic of a nuclear accident at the plant where Homer works. To ensure that its people do not access "foreign" or otherwise "counterrevolutionary" Internet content, the Chinese government requires all Internet accounts to be registered with the police. It employs 40,000 "e-police" to enforce its dozens of Internet-related laws (dissidents call it the Great Firewall). Media may know few national borders, but there is growing concern that they at least respect the cultures within them.

One traditional way to understand the workings of the contemporary global media scene is to examine the individual media systems of the different countries around the world. In doing so, we can not only become familiar with how different folks in different places use media but also better evaluate the workings of our own system. Naturally, not every media system resembles that of the United States. As a result, such concepts as audience expectations, economic foundations, and the regulation of mass media differ across nations. The study of different countries' mass media systems is called **comparative analysis** or **comparative studies**.

Comparative Analyses

Different countries' mass media systems reflect the diversity of their levels of development and prosperity, values, and political systems. That a country's political system will be reflected in the nature of its media system is only logical. Authoritarian governments need to control the mass media to maintain power. Therefore, they will institute a media system very different from that of a democratic country with a capitalistic, free economy. The overriding philosophy of how media ideally operate in any given system of social values is called a normative theory (see the chapter on media freedom, regulation, and ethics). You can see where the media systems of different countries rank in their degree of press freedom in the box entitled "We're Number 41! Media Freedom Rankings around the Globe."

CULTURAL FORUM
We're Number 41! Media Freedom Rankings around the Globe

18	Canada
26	Ghana
38	United Kingdom
40	Slovenia
41	USA
42	Burkina Faso
43	Botswana
120	Afghanistan
180	Eritrea

As ongoing violent conflicts around the world endangered reporters as well as combatants and civilians (111 reporters were killed on the job in 2015 alone; Greenslade, 2016), and as governments everywhere sought to control media expression in the name of "the war on terror" (259 journalists were arrested in 2016; Gladstone, 2016), a widely respected report put the issue of global press freedom squarely into the cultural forum.

Reporters Without Borders, or *Reporters Sans Frontières* as it is known outside the United States, is an international nonprofit, nongovernmental organization that promotes press freedom around the world. Since 2002 the Paris-based organization has issued an annual index ranking the level of press freedom in 180 countries. It takes into account factors such as media independence, self-censorship, media transparency, and the quality of the media's physical infrastructure. It looks at official government regulations, official penalties, and the level of independence of public media. It evaluates impediments to the free flow of information on the Internet and violence against journalists.

Its 2016 report was striking because it identified "a deep and disturbing decline in respect for media freedom at both the global and regional levels" (Reporters Without Borders, 2016). But of course that's the rest of the world; the situation in the greatest democracy on Earth must be better than that, right? Maybe not. The United States ranked 41st. Here are a few representative rankings:

1	Finland
2	Netherlands
3	Norway
4	Denmark
16	Germany

How strongly would you disagree, if at all, with the idea that the United States enjoys only the 41st freest media system in the world? In arriving at that score, Reporters Without Borders cited the Obama Justice Department's war on whistle-blowers who leak information about its surveillance activities and record levels of ignoring the Freedom of Information Act's demand of access to government files. It noted the harassment and bullying of reporters online and at the campaign rallies of presidential candidate Donald Trump and the arrest of journalists during Black Lives Matter protests in Baltimore and Minneapolis. It identified the lack of a national shield law to protect journalists and their confidential sources ("The United States," 2016).

Could this evaluation be correct? If so, how and why? If it is, does this low ranking bother you? Why or why not? Why might this sorry situation have come to pass? Media scholar Robert McChesney argues that those nations that have the freest media are invariably those that spend most heavily on public and community media. Top rankings for Scandinavian countries would seem to bear this out. Why doesn't the United States invest more heavily in its journalism to ensure a free press? Would you advocate for this kind of spending? Why or why not? How might the level of press freedom be improved in the United States? Is improvement even possible when 21% of its citizens believe the First Amendment goes too far in the rights it guarantees, and 50% of those without a college degree and 27% with a degree cannot name a single First Amendment freedom (Newseum Institute, 2016)?

William Hachten (1992) offered five concepts that guide the world's many media systems—Western, development, revolutionary, authoritarianism, and communism. We'll examine each and provide a look at places that exemplify them.

THE WESTERN CONCEPT: GREAT BRITAIN The **Western concept** is an amalgamation of the original libertarian and social responsibility models (see the chapter on media freedom, regulation, and ethics). It recognizes two realities: There is no completely free (libertarian) media system on Earth, and even the most commercially driven systems include the expectation not only of public service and responsibility but also of meaningful government oversight of mass communication to ensure that media professionals meet those responsibilities.

Great Britain offers a good example of a media system operating under the Western concept. The BBC was originally built on the premise that broadcasting was a public trust (the social responsibility model). Long before television, BBC radio offered several services—one designed to provide news and information, another designed to support high or elite culture such as symphony music and plays, and a third designed to provide popular music and entertainment. To limit government and advertiser control, the BBC was funded by license fees levied on receivers (currently just under $200 a year), and its governance was given over to a nonprofit corporation. Many observers point to this goal-oriented, noncommercial structure as the reason that the BBC developed, and still maintains, the most respected news operation in the world.

Eventually, Britain, like all of western Europe, was forced by public demand to institute more American-style broadcasting. Fueled by that demand and advances in digital broadcasting, there are now many hundreds of radio stations in the United Kingdom. Most prominent are the 10 domestic BBC networks. The BBC also maintains 40 local stations that program a combination of local news and music, primarily for older listeners. There are also three national commercial radio networks (Virgin Radio, Classic FM, and talkSPORT) and a growing number of local commercial stations. As in the United States, most belong to larger chains.

The BBC also maintains eight television networks, all digital, each having its own character; for example, BBC One carries more popular fare, while BBC Two airs somewhat more serious content. Commercial television exists, too. Independent Television (ITV) programs six digital networks, Channel 4 maintains four, and Channel 5 runs three. These commercial operations accept limits on the amount of advertising they air and agree to specified amounts of public affairs and documentary news programming in exchange for their licenses to broadcast. This is referred to as their **public service remit**.

In terms of other regulation, the media in Great Britain do not enjoy a First Amendment–like guarantee of freedom. Prior restraint does occur, but only when a committee of government officials and representatives of the media industry can agree on the issuance of what is called a **D-notice**. British media are also forbidden to report on court trials in progress, and Parliament can pass other restrictions on the media whenever it wishes—for example, the ban, imposed in 1988 and maintained for several years, on broadcasting the voice of anyone associated with the Irish Republican Army or other paramilitary movements.

THE DEVELOPMENT CONCEPT: HONDURAS The media systems of many Third World or developing African, Asian, Latin and South American, and eastern European nations formerly part of the Soviet bloc best exemplify the **development concept**. Here government and media work in partnership to ensure that media assist in the planned, beneficial development of the country. Content is designed to meet specific cultural and societal needs—for example, teaching new farming techniques, disseminating information on methods of disease control, and improving literacy. This isn't the same as authoritarian control. There is less censorship and other official control of content, but often marginally so.

Honduras offers one example. This small Central American country of 6.4 million people is one of the poorest in the Western Hemisphere; 85% of its population lives in poverty. As a result, the people own only half a million television sets and 2.5 million radio receivers. All of Honduras's 11 television stations are commercial; 290 of its radio stations are commercial, and the government network, Radio Honduras, operates about 20 stations. Radio and printed leaflets have been particularly successful in reducing the number of infant deaths in Honduras caused by diarrheal dehydration and helping people with issues of family planning.

The 1982 Honduras Constitution guarantees freedom of the press, but there is significant control of media content. All the major newspapers are owned by powerful business

▲ Unlike U.S. media, British media do not enjoy First Amendment protections, but as their notorious daily tabloids demonstrate, they nonetheless operate with a great deal of freedom.

©Clynt Garnham Publishing/Alamy

executives or politicians with allegiances to different elites. Because the media in Honduras are constitutionally mandated to "cooperate with the state in the fulfillment of its public functions," journalists must be licensed and adhere to the Organic Law of the College of Journalists of Honduras. As such, they are forbidden to produce reports that "preach or disseminate doctrines that undermine the foundation of the State or of the family." Nor can journalists produce content that "threatens, libels, slanders, insults, or in any other way attacks the character of a public official in the exercise of his or her function." These were the "decrees" invoked by the Honduran military government when it ordered the National Commission of Telecommunications (Conatel), the official body that regulates the country's media, to close down television station Canal 36 and Radio Globo after they broadcast messages from ousted president Manuel Zelaya during a 2009 coup. A recent analysis of media freedom in Honduras by Reporters Without Borders found that its president "often indulges in vicious verbal attacks on the media, thereby setting the tone in what is one of the region's most dangerous countries for media personnel. Journalists working for opposition or community media are the targets of frequent physical violence or death threats. They are also often the targets of abusive judicial proceedings. Defamation is one of the charges routinely brought against them. A law also protects 'official secrets'" (2016). However, you can see how social media have helped people in developing nations in "Social Media and Improving Health Outcomes for Underserved People."

USING MEDIA TO MAKE A DIFFERENCE
Social Media and Improving Health Outcomes for Underserved People

More than 2.5 billion people worldwide use social media, a number likely to rise to just under 3 billion by 2020 ("Number Of," 2017) as several Internet giants are working feverishly to bring the Internet to those most in need. For example, Google uses satellites and even balloons to bring service to remote areas of the globe, and Facebook deploys drones, satellites, and lasers to deliver the Internet to those underserved. Of course, these companies hope to expand their user base, and therefore customer base, but that does not mean that they do not seek significant benefits for those users. Speaking specifically of social media, a World Health Organization study commented,

> Social media, a great information equalizer, is radically transforming the way people communicate around the world. Instant and borderless, it elevates electronic communication to near face-to-face. Until recently the predominant communication model was "one" authority to "many"—i.e. a health institution, the ministry of health, or a journalist communicating to the public. Social media has changed the monologue to a dialogue, where anyone with information and communication technology access can be a content creator and communicator. (McNab, 2009)

Organizations such as Physicians for Peace (PFP) have created groups on social media outlets such as Skype, Facebook, and Google Hangouts to provide online education. "Technology allows us to achieve our goals of strengthening long-distance relationships between our volunteer health care professionals and in-country health care providers," said Lisa Arfaa, PFP's CEO. "Our plan is to continue to bridge the health care chasm through tele-mentoring efforts and other increasingly prevalent technologies" (in Thompson, 2016).

David Risher uses mobile reading apps to make a difference. A former Microsoft and Amazon executive, Risher started nonprofit Worldreader to make digital information available to people in the developing world. Worldreader reaches 2 million people annually with information on a variety of topics from 150 publishers. In the area of health, it digitally delivers crucial information to over 13 million readers in 47 countries through popular children's books such as *Kofi Has Malaria*, young adult titles such as *Growth and Changes*, and easy-to-read health manuals including *Where There Is No Doctor*, a basic training manual for communities lacking health care workers, *Sanitation and Cleanliness for a Healthy Environment*, and *Pesticides Are Poison*.

How else can social media make a difference in people's health outcomes in these remote regions? Eric Williams, a former Democratic congressional staffer involved in global health and human rights issues, says, "Social media provides real-time insight into the lives of people around the world. As a result, when major illnesses occur social media is often the first to know. Clever monitoring of social media can predict disease outbreaks and enable intervention to begin often weeks before the traditional methods would pick up similar results." He cites the use of Twitter to predict flu, Ebola, and cholera outbreaks (2016).

There is no doubt that social media have made and can continue to make a difference in the health outcomes of remote and underserved people. As Williams summarizes, "Social media helps bring access to information to anyone who can see it. In developing countries, this means that people in rural areas, or with little access to services can now obtain educational, mobile health, and financial services in ways that were impossible before mobile technology and the spread of social media."

THE REVOLUTIONARY CONCEPT: POLAND AND THE ARAB SPRING No country "officially" embraces the **revolutionary concept** as a normative theory, but this does not mean that a nation's media will never serve the goals of revolution. International media scholar Robert Stevenson (1994) identified four aims of revolutionary media: ending government monopoly over information, facilitating the organization of opposition to the incumbent powers, destroying the legitimacy of a standing government, and bringing down a standing government. The experience of the Polish democracy movement Solidarity is a well-known example of the use of media as a tool of revolution, as is the Arab Spring, despite its mixed success.

By the first years of the 1980s, the Polish people had grown dissatisfied with the domination of almost all aspects of their lives by a national Communist Party perceived to be a puppet of the Soviet Union. This frustration was fueled by the ability of just about all Poles to receive radio and television signals from neighboring democratic lands (Poland's location in central Europe made it impossible for the authorities to block what the people saw and heard). In addition, Radio Free Europe, the VOA, and the BBC all targeted Poland with their mix of Western news, entertainment, and propaganda. Its people's taste for freedom thus whetted, Solidarity established an extensive network of clandestine revolutionary media. Much of it was composed of technologies traditionally associated with revolution—pamphlets, newsletters, audiotapes, and videocassettes—but much of it was also sophisticated radio and television technology used to disrupt official broadcasts and disseminate information. Despite government efforts to shut the system down, which went as far as suspending official broadcasting and mail services in order to deny Solidarity these communication channels, the revolution was a success, making Poland the first of the Eastern-bloc nations to defy the party apparatus and install a democratically elected government, setting off the ultimate demise of the Soviet bloc.

More recently, the Internet and social media proved to be powerful tools of revolution in what has become known as the Arab Spring. From 2011 to 2014 people in the Middle Eastern countries of Iran, Tunisia, Egypt, Yemen, Libya, Bahrain, Algeria, Morocco, Jordan, Oman, Iraq, Syria, and Saudi Arabia took to Facebook, Twitter, and YouTube to organize protests, monitor abuse, and demand the freedoms enjoyed by most other nations. Many of the movements were met with government brutality, but others produced "voluntary" reform on the part of once-powerful rulers who saw that new media were a growing, uncontrollable check on their authority. It is impossible to isolate the influence of social media from all the other factors—anger at corruption, repression, and torture; joblessness; and lack of opportunity, for example—that led to the Arab Spring. But, wrote *New York Times* reporter Jennifer Preston, there is no doubt that these technologies "offered a way for the discontented to organize and mobilize. . . . Far more decentralized than political parties, the strength and agility of the networks clearly caught [Middle Eastern] authorities . . . by surprise" (2011, p. A10). Unfortunately, those authorities overcame their surprise and learned how to employ those very same revolutionary technologies to destroy the freedom movements they helped spawn. They spread false information to discredit movement leaders, tracked down users, shut down social networking sites, and jailed and tortured site administrators (Hempel, 2016). And according to Freedom House, a nonprofit prodemocracy organization, those governments now understand the revolutionary power of social media even better:

> Public-facing social media platforms like Facebook and Twitter have been subject to growing censorship for several years, but in a new trend, governments increasingly target messaging and voice communication apps such as WhatsApp and Telegram. These services are able to spread information and connect users quickly and securely, making it more difficult for authorities to control the information landscape or conduct surveillance. The increased controls show the importance of social media and online communication for advancing political freedom and social justice. It is no coincidence that the tools at the center of the current crackdown have been widely used to hold governments accountable and facilitate uncensored conversations. Authorities in several countries have even resorted to shutting down all Internet access at politically contentious times, solely to prevent users from disseminating information through social media and communication apps, with untold social, commercial, and humanitarian consequences. (2016)

In fact, governments shut down their nations' Internet more than 50 times in 2016 (Rowlands, 2017).

THE AUTHORITARIANISM AND COMMUNISM CONCEPTS: CHINA Because only five communist nations remain and because the actual operation of the media in these and other **authoritarian systems** is quite similar, we can discuss authoritarianism and communism as a single concept. Both call for the subjugation of media for the purpose of serving the government. China is not only a good example of a country that operates its media according to the authoritarian/communist concepts, but it also demonstrates how difficult it is becoming for authoritarian governments to maintain strict control over media and audiences.

The Chinese media system is based on that of its old ideological partner, the now-dissolved Soviet Union. For a variety of reasons, however, it has developed its own peculiar nature. China has approximately 1.4 billion people living in more than a million hamlets, villages, and cities. As a result, in the early 2000s, the government undertook an extensive program called *Cuncun Tong*, designed to bring at least radio, but preferably radio and television, to every one of those million locales. At the same time, it closed down hundreds of local newspapers and broadcast stations to solidify its control over content through its central and provincial government operations, primarily China Central Television. In fact, all of the country's more than 2,400 radio and 1,200 television stations are owned by or affiliated with the Communist Party of China or a government agency. There is no privately owned television or radio, and state-run Chinese Central TV and the provincial and municipal stations

▶ Arab Spring protesters face off against Algerian police. Social media helped ignite the democracy movements that swept the Middle East.
©Nacerdine ZEBAR/Getty Images

offer more than 2,000 channels. The country's Central Propaganda Department lists subjects that are forbidden to appear on those channels, and the government maintains the authority to approve all programming.

Only relatively recently has the newspaper become an important medium. Widespread rural illiteracy and the lack of good pulpwood restricted the newspaper to the larger cities. Cities and towns were dotted with hundreds of thousands of reading walls where people could catch up on the official news. But when China embarked on its Open Door Policy in the late 1970s, it committed itself to developing the newspaper as a national medium. As a result, most reading walls are now gone, the few remaining used primarily by older people. Today, China is the world's largest newspaper market and, with India, accounts for 62% of global daily print circulation (Henriksson, 2016).

The media exist in China to serve the government. Chairman Mao Zedong, founder of the Chinese Communist Party, clarified the role of the media very soon after coming to power in 1949: The media exist to propagandize the policies of the Party and to educate, organize, and mobilize the masses. In 2016, to counter what he saw as a drift away from that mission, Chinese president Xi Jinping announced, "All news media run by the party must work to speak for the party's will and its propositions, and protect the party's authority and unity." The Chinese news media understood this to mean they exist to serve as a propaganda arm of the Communist Party, and must pledge fealty to Xi (Wong, 2016, p. A1).

Radio came to China via American reporter E. C. Osborn, who established an experimental radio station in China in 1923. Official Chinese broadcasting began three years later. Television went on the air in 1958, and from the outset it was owned and controlled by the Party in the form of Central China Television (CCTV), which in turn answers to the Ministry of Radio and Television. Radio, now regulated by China People's Broadcasting Station (CPBS), and television stations and networks develop their own content, but it must conform to the requirements of the Propaganda Bureau of the Chinese Communist Party Central Committee.

Financially, Chinese broadcasting operates under direct government subsidy. But in 1979 the government approved commercial advertising for broadcasting, and it has evolved into an important means of financial support. Coupled with the Chinese government's desire to become a more active participant in the international economy, this commercialization has led to increased diversity in broadcast content.

For several decades, only the state's China TV Programming Agency could buy foreign content, and it was limited to purchasing no more than 500 hours a year. Rules also restricted stations to programming no more than 25% of their time with imported fare. *The Teletubbies* (*Antenna Babies* in China) is a longtime favorite. Restrictions on *foreign* content still exist, but there is now an emphasis on *domestic* coproduction with foreign programmers. In 2005, the central government began to allow foreign investment in and coproduction of media content for Chinese audiences, with the condition that all content be at least 51% government-owned. This is why producers from across the globe have set up shop in China and why local versions of Western fare like *The Apprentice* now flourish there.

Basic government control over major media and the Internet remains, however. For example, only 34 foreign movies are permitted exhibition in China each year. These films must pass a prerelease censorship screening. And although a foreign studio can take home no more than 25% of a film's box-office income, those studios are still anxious for a crack at what is, as of 2017, the largest movie market in the world (Lang & Rainey, 2016). In December 1997, anticipating the explosive growth of the Internet (China today, with more than 700 million users, has the world's largest and fastest-growing online population), the Party began enforcing criminal sanctions against those who would use the Internet to "split the country," "injure the reputation of state organs," "defame government agencies," "promote feudal superstitions," or otherwise pose a threat to "social stability." The state has established a 24-hour Internet task force to find and arrest senders of "counterrevolutionary" commentary. Popular bulletin boards are shut down when their chat becomes a bit too free. Websites such as Human Rights Watch, *The New York Times*, and publications about China that are independent of government control, such as *China News Digest*, are officially blocked by the government's Cyberspace Administration, but not very successfully, as skilled Internet users can easily traverse the Web by routing themselves through VPNs (virtual private networks) and

► A Chinese reading wall. This 1980-vintage photo shows a rapidly disappearing vestige of an earlier media era.
©Vince Streano/Getty Images

▲ Only 34 foreign movies a year can be exhibited in China. *Resident Evil: The Final Chapter* made the cut in 2017.
©Screen Gems/courtesy Everett Collection

distant servers such as DynaWeb and FreeGate. "It's as if we're shutting down half our brains," said one critic of the government's limits on the Internet, an artist who promotes her work online. "I think that the day that information from the outside world becomes completely inaccessible in China, a lot of people will choose to leave" (in Jacobs, 2015, p. A1).

Programming

Regardless of the particular concept guiding media systems in other countries, those systems produce and distribute content, in other words, programming. In most respects, radio and television programming throughout the world looks and sounds much like that found in the United States. There are two main reasons for this situation: (1) The United States is a world leader in international distribution of broadcast fare, and (2) very early in the life of television, American producers flooded the world with their programming at very low prices. Foreign operators of emerging television systems were delighted to have access to this low-cost content, because they typically could not afford to produce their own high-quality domestic material. For American producers, however, this strategy served the dual purpose of building markets for their programming and ensuring that foreign audiences would develop tastes and expectations similar to those in the United States, further encouraging future sales of programs originally produced for American audiences (Barnouw, 1990).

Naturally, programming varies somewhat from one country to another. The commercial television systems of most South American and European countries are far less sensitive about sex and nudity than are their counterparts in the United States. In Brazil, for example, despite a constitutional requirement that broadcasters respect society's social and ethical values, television networks such as SBT, TV Record, and TV Globo compete in what critics call the *guerra da baixaria*, the war of the lowest common denominator. Guests on variety shows

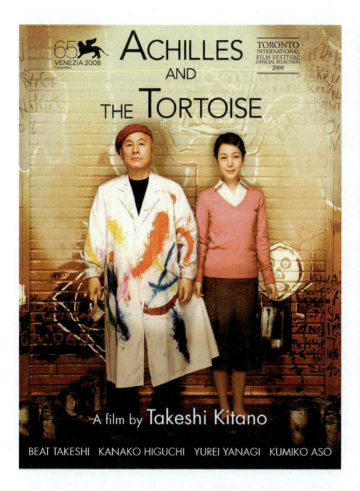

▲ Many countries hope their fare will find a worldwide audience, especially an American one. Here are two posters from Japanese films hoping to make their way to American screens.

(left) ©Tokyo Theatres K.K./ Courtesy Everett Collection; (right) ©Fever Dreams/Courtesy Everett Collection

wrestle with buxom models dressed only in bikinis and eat sushi off women's naked bodies. On game shows, male contestants who give wrong answers can be punished by having patches of leg hair ripped out, while those who answer correctly are rewarded by having a nearly naked model sit on their laps. European commercial operations regularly air shows featuring both male and female nudity, sometimes because it is integral to the plot, sometimes simply for titillation.

Another difference between American programming and that of its global neighbors is how that content is utilized in different places. Naturally, broadcasting systems relying on the sale of commercial time find most value in programming that attracts the greatest number of viewers or a large number of viewers with the desired demographics. Commercial channels are just that, commercial. But many broadcast systems, those relying on license fees or other public support, frequently offer programming specifically designed to have educational, social, or political value. Many nations, even those with commercially supported systems, use a particular genre, the soap opera, for educational and social purposes.

The Global Village and the Debate over Cultural Imperialism

The most famous and oft-considered of communication theorist Marshall McLuhan's many groundbreaking ideas is the concept of the **global village**, introduced in his books *The Gutenberg Galaxy* (1962) and discussed again in *Understanding Media: The Extensions of Man* (1964). As you read earlier, McLuhan predicted that new communication technologies would permit people to become increasingly involved in one another's lives. And as you might

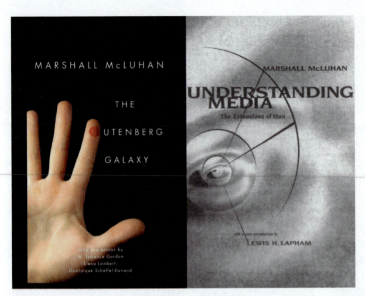

▲ The books that introduced the world to the concept of the global village.

(left): ©TJ Photography/PhotoEdit; (right): Courtesy of MIT Press

imagine, with the subsequent development of the Internet and social media, debates over the global village's double edge have become quite intense. Although McLuhan's critics accuse him of having an unrealistic, utopian infatuation with technology, the theorist himself never said all would be tranquil in the global village. Yes, he did believe electronic media would permit "the human tribe" to become "one family," but he also realized that families fight:

> There is more diversity, less conformity under a single roof in any family than there is with the thousands of families in the same city. The more you create village conditions, the more discontinuity and division and diversity. The global village absolutely insures maximal disagreement on all points. (McLuhan & Stearn, 1967, p. 279)

Involvement does not mean harmony, but it does mean an exchange of ideas. As McLuhan said, the global village is "a world in which people encounter each other in depth all the time" (McLuhan & Stearn, 1967, p. 280). And how does that in-depth-all-the-time interaction play out now that there are few physical borders between countries in a globally mediated world? Governments that could once physically prohibit the introduction and distribution of unwanted newspapers, magazines, and books had to work harder at jamming unwanted radio and television broadcasts. But they could do it, until satellite came along. Governments cannot disrupt satellite signals. Only lack of the necessary receiving technology can limit their reach. Now, with the Internet, a new receiving technology is cheap, easy to use, and available to more and more millions of people in every corner of the world—and because of the universal availability of free translation software like Google Translate, its content is readable, often in spite of government efforts at control, by those millions of people wherever they live. As a result, difficult questions of national sovereignty and cultural diversity are being raised anew.

The MacBride Report and the NWIO

The debate over the global village reached its height with the 1980 release of the MacBride Report by the United Nations Educational, Scientific, and Cultural Organization (UNESCO). The report was named after the chair of the commission set up to study the question of how to maintain national and cultural sovereignty in the face of rapid globalization of mass media. At the time, many developing and communist countries were concerned that international news coverage was dominated by the West, especially the United States, and that Western-produced content was overwhelming the media of developing countries, which lacked sufficient resources to create their own quality fare. The fear was that Western cultural values, especially those of the United States, would overshadow and displace those of other countries. These countries saw this as a form of colonialization, a **cultural imperialism**—the invasion of an indigenous people's culture by powerful foreign countries' cultures.

Fears of cultural imperialism are based in **electronic colonialism theory**, the belief "that cultural products produced, created, or manufactured in another country have the ability to influence, or possibly displace, indigenous cultural productions, artifacts, and media to the detriment of the receiving nations" (McPhail, 2014, p. 291). The MacBride Report, endorsed by UNESCO, was designed to calm these concerns. But it called for the establishment of a New World Information Order (NWIO) that contained several elements problematic to Western democracies. In arguing that individual nations should be free to control the news and entertainment that entered their lands, it called for monitoring of all such content, monitoring and licensing of foreign journalists, and requiring that prior government permission be obtained for direct radio, television, and satellite transmissions into foreign countries. Western nations rejected these rules as a direct infringement on the freedom of the press.

Western allies of the United States may have agreed that the restrictions of the NWIO were a threat to the free flow of information, yet virtually every one had in place rules (in the form of quotas) that limited U.S. media content in their own countries. Canada, our closest cultural neighbor, required that specific proportions of all content—print and broadcast—either be produced in Canada or reflect Canadian cultural identity. Canadian law forbids foreign (read: American) ownership in its commercial broadcasting channels. The French made illegal the printing of certain U.S. words, including "hamburger" and "cartoon" (France maintains an official office to prosecute those who would "debase" its

▲ *The Simpsons Movie* premiered simultaneously in 100 countries and in 50 languages. Its opening weekend box office in the United States was $72 million. Elsewhere, it topped $100 million.
©20th Century Fox. All rights reserved/Courtesy Everett Collection

language, the Académie Française in our opening vignette). The European Union's Television Without Frontiers Directive requires member countries' broadcasters to dedicate a majority of their airtime to European-produced programming and to commission at least 10% of all their shows from local, independent producers. South Korean law mandates that movie houses show native films at least 146 days out of each year. In October 2005, UNESCO approved the *Convention on the Protection and Promotion of the Diversity of Cultural Expressions* by a vote of 148 to 2. The only two dissenters were the United States and Israel (UNESCO, 2005). The convention permits countries to treat "cultural products" such as movies, books, music, and television shows differently than they do other, more durable commodities. That is, countries can legally establish quotas and subsidies to protect their local media industries. And while the convention's text argued that the defense of every country's cultural heritage is "an ethical imperative, inseparable from respect for human dignity," it was clear from the debate preceding its passage that its true goal was protecting other countries' "cultural heritage" specifically from American media ("How They See Us," 2005).

The resistance to U.S. media would not exist among our international friends if they did not worry about the integrity of their own cultures. It is folly, then, to argue that non-native media content will have no effect on local culture—as do some U.S. media content producers. The question today is, how much influence will countries accept in exchange for fuller membership in the global community? In light of instant, inexpensive, and open computer network communication, a parallel question is, have notions such as national sovereignty and cultural integrity lost their meaning? For example, ESPN is carried on 26 networks in 21 languages to 155 million television households in 61 different countries. *The Simpsons* is drawn in South Korea. *The Simpsons Movie* premiered simultaneously in 100 countries and in 50 languages. BBC Radio broadcasts daily to a worldwide audience in 40 languages, as does Radio Beijing from China. CNN uses its satellites to transmit to a billion viewers in almost 200 countries. Two of the three largest U.S. record companies have international ownership. Movie theater chain AMC is owned by a Chinese conglomerate, Dalian Wanda Group. Hollywood's Columbia Pictures is owned by Japanese Sony, and 20th Century Fox is owned by Rupert Murdoch's Australian corporation. Bertelsmann, a German company that controls a large proportion of the U.S. book publishing market, earns more money from the United States than from any other nation, including its homeland.

▲ Proponents of the global flow of communication find value in the local adoption of varied cultures. In Indonesia, *Sesame Street* becomes *Jalan Sesama* and counts among its residents the book-reading orangutan Tantan.
©Bay Ismoyo/AFP/Getty Images

The Case for the Global Village

There are differing opinions about the benefits of this trend away from nation-specific cultures. Global village proponents see the world community coming closer together as a common culture is negotiated and, not incidentally, as we become more economically interconnected. There should be little fear that individual cultures and national identities will disappear, because the world's great diversity will ensure that culture-specific, special-interest fare remains in demand. Modern media technology makes the delivery of this varied content not only possible but profitable. Not only do native-language versions of U.S. television shows like *Jeopardy* exist in virtually every western European country, but other "translations" are taking place. For example, with the worldwide success of the *Spider-Man* movies, Marvel Comics and an Indian company announced the birth of *Spider-Man India*, in which a young Bombay lad, Pavitr Prabhakar, inherits powers from a sacred yogi and accessorizes his Spidey suit with a traditional dhoti. And there exist 120 "translations" of *Sesame Street* across the globe. As a result of these cultural exchanges, argue proponents of globalization, "a global culture is created, piece by piece, but it grows more variegated and complex along the way. And even as geographically based identities blur and fade, new subcultures, based on shared tastes in music or literature or obscure hobbies, grow up" (Bennett, 2004, p. 62).

The Case against the Global Village

The global village is here, say those with a less optimistic view, and the problem is what it looks like. *Time* media writer James Poniewozik calls it "the new cold war—between the Hollywood/Mickey D's axis and every other world culture" (2001, p. 69). When, for example, Mickey D's (McDonald's) recently opened a burger shop in a building owned by the Vatican, there was a good deal of local anger. The Committee for the Protection of Borgo called the restaurant, situated in the Pio Borgo district just outside Vatican City within view of St. Peter's Square, a "decisive blow on an already wounded animal," referring to the commercialization overtaking one of Italy's most hallowed sites (Victor, 2017, p. A9). What locals derisively called "McVatican" was on the ground floor of a building that was home to several senior cardinals, leading one, Cardinal Elio Sgreccia, to call the decision to rent to the fast-food chain "aberrant" and "a perversion." "I repeat, selling mega-sandwiches in Borgo Pio is a disgrace," he said. He argued that the rent money would be better used to help "the area's needy and suffering, as the Holy Father teaches" (Johnson, 2017). Sgreccia's specific complaints centered on two traditional Italian cultural concerns: art and food. The restaurant, he said, was "not at all respectful of the architectural and urban traditions of one of the most characteristic squares overlooking the colonnade of St. Peter," and the lease was

▶ When McDonald's opened a shop in a Vatican-owned building within sight of St. Peter's Basillica, locals called it a "perversion." ©*WENN US/Alamy*

These Malaysian students are encouraged to "Makan" (eat) at their local Kuala Lumpur McDonald's. Although critics of cultural imperialism see this as an intrusion of Western culture into the lives of these people, defenders of globalization of culture see the expansion of opportunity for both the "sending" and the "receiving" cultures. ©Vincent Thian/AP Photo

"a business decision that ignores the culinary tradition of Roman cuisine" (Victor, 2017, p. A9).

There is no simple answer to the debate over protecting the integrity of local cultures. As we've just seen, there is even disagreement over the wisdom of doing so. Media-literate people should at least be aware of the debate and its issues, and they may also want to consider the paradox of what Josef Joffe, editor of Germany's weekly *Die Zeit*, calls the "soft power" of America's exported culture. It "does not bend hearts" as cultural imperialism's critics contend. Rather, "it twists minds in resentment and rage." He points to data collected by the Pew Global Attitudes Project. When asked if they "like American music, movies, and television," large percentages of citizens in England (62%), France (65%), Germany (67%), and Italy (69%) said "yes." But when asked if "it's good that American ideas and customs are spreading," other large percentages of people in England (33%), France (27%), Germany (24%), and Italy (43%) said "no" (2006, p. 15). This may be because, as British journalist Justin Webb explains, the "cultural seduction" of American movies, music, and literature makes Europeans "feel weak," producing a self-loathing that leads them to hate "the seducer" as well as themselves (2015). Like most debates over mass communication, the simple answers aren't always the correct answers.

DEVELOPING MEDIA LITERACY SKILLS

Making the Invisible Visible: Comparative Analysis

While comparative analysis offers us a glimpse of other countries' media systems, it also helps us understand our own. This is because we tend to think that the characteristics of our own media system are "natural," the way it is. Those aspects of media become so familiar that we don't see or perceive them at all. But comparative analysis, comparing the way our media operate to the workings of another country's media, can help us identify aspects of our own system that might require a little more thought. Comparative analysis has the "capacity to render the invisible visible," to draw attention to aspects of any media system, including our own, "that may be taken for granted and difficult to detect when the focus is on only one national case" (Blumler & Gurevitch, 1975, p. 76).

We've seen elsewhere in this text that, with New Zealand, the United States is the only country in the world that permits advertising of prescription drugs; that America is alone among industrialized nations in permitting largely unregulated advertising in children's television programming; and that as opposed to here at home, European nations require that Internet users opt in before their personal data can be shared. Here are a number of other aspects of foreign media systems that differ from our own:

- The Spanish government bans airing television commercials for beauty products and services before 10:00 p.m. "Broadcasters cannot carry advertisements for things that encourage the cult of the body and have a negative impact on self-image—such as slimming products, surgical procedures, and beauty treatments—which are based on ideas of social rejection as a result of one's physical image or that success is dependent on factors such as weight or looks" (Hall, 2010, p. 6).

- The German government is considering setting "binding standards" for how social media companies deal with hate speech on their sites. There would be fines of up to $53 million for failure to swiftly remove offending content (Eddy & Scott, 2017, p. B2).

- Sweden's Supreme Court ruled that inserting commercial breaks into televised movies at particularly dramatic moments "violates the integrity and value of the film" and is punishable by fine (Rehlin, 2010). Movies in Sweden must also carry a gender rating. To earn an A, a film must have at least two women in it who talk to one another about something other than a man (McDonough, 2013).

- The French government has declared books an "essential good," outlawing deep discounts (no more than 5%) and subjecting books to low taxes, just like food. As a result, big chain bookstores like Amazon struggle, Paris averages two bookstores per block, and the average French person reads 25% more books than his or her American counterpart (Mendelsohn & Hamid, 2014).

- The French government prohibits modeling agencies from hiring "dangerously thin" models and requires that altered photographs of models be clearly labeled. Similarly, Britain's Advertising Standards Authority can ban ads featuring models who are "unhealthily thin" (Forbes, 2016).

- The lower parliamentary body in France passed a bill that makes it illegal for companies with more than 50 employees to send after-hours work e-mails (Turner, 2016); in Germany, some government bureaus are forbidden from contacting their employees outside work hours (Sayare, 2014).

- With more than 12 million residents, São Paulo, Brazil, is the seventh most populous city in the world. Its Clean City Law places a total ban on outdoor business signage of any kind: no billboards, no logos, no posters on bus stops. None. More than 70% of its citizens say the law is "beneficial" (Jefferson, 2011).

- Mexico, Bolivia, and France make free newspapers available to young readers, and in an effort to boost circulation, Morocco made it illegal to read a paper you haven't bought yourself (Sass, 2016).

- Annual government funding for public media in the United States amounts to $3.75 per person. In Canada it is $30.42; in Germany, $131.27; in Denmark, $131.27; and in Norway, $133.57 (Benson & Powers, 2011).

Can you explain why these differences might exist? Would any of these rules or practices seem "natural" in our American media system? Why or why not? Are there any that you would like to see adopted by our homegrown system? Why or why not? The hallmarks of a media-literate individual are critical thinking, analysis, and reflection. As such, you should have ready answers to these questions. Do you?

MEDIA LITERACY CHALLENGE
Do Your Own Comparative Analysis

As a media-literate individual, you know that *media content is a text providing insight into contemporary culture*; and as you've just read, comparative analysis is one way to "make visible" aspects of your own culture's media by looking at the media of other places. Here are several facts about other countries' media activities. What do they say to you about those specific countries and their media systems? How do these facts compare to the same situation in the United States? What do any differences say about our media? About us as a culture? Take this challenge either by offering your responses in a brief essay or in debate with one or more classmates.

1. People in Serbia watch more television per day than people in any other country.
2. In Madagascar, barely one in six households has a television.
3. More Peruvian homes have televisions than have electricity—people use batteries to run their sets (1–3 in "Global Media Habits," 2011).
4. Western daily newspapers have the largest circulation declines in the world; circulation is rising fastest in Asia ("Global Newspaper," 2016).
5. Commissioners from the European Union advise people to close their Facebook accounts if they do not want their information collected by America's National Security Agency (Moody, 2015).
6. China leads the world in time spent on PCs, Nigeria leads in time spent on smartphones, and the Philippines tops the world in tablet time (Thompson, 2014).

Resources for Review and Discussion

REVIEW POINTS: TYING CONTENT TO LEARNING OUTCOMES

▶ **Outline the development of global media.**
  □ For decades, international mass media took the form of shortwave radio broadcasts, especially in the form of clandestine stations, both exogenous and indigenous.
  □ Other exogenous operations are pirate broadcasters and many countries' external services such as the BBC and VOA.

▶ **Explain the practice of comparative analysis.**
  □ Different countries rely on different media systems to meet their national needs. The study of these varying models is called comparative analysis.
  □ Naturally, different systems make varying use of different programming as their nations' needs demand.

▶ **Identify different media systems from around the world.**
  □ There are five main models or concepts: Western, development, revolutionary, authoritarianism, and communism.

▶ **Describe the debate surrounding cultural imperialism and other controversies raised by the globalization of media.**
  □ There is serious debate about the free and not-so-free flow of mass communication across borders. The conflict is between those who want the free flow of information and those who worry about the erosion of local culture, a conflict resulting from a technology-created global village.
  □ Much of this controversy, however, has more to do with protecting countries' media systems from American influence than it does with protecting all countries' cultural integrity.

KEY TERMS

shortwave radio, 375

skip, 375

sky waves, 375

clandestine stations, 375

indigenous stations, 375

exogenous stations, 375

pirate broadcasters, 376

external service, 376

surrogate service, 377

comparative analysis
  (studies), 379

Western concept, 380

public service remit, 381

D-notice, 381

development concept, 381

revolutionary concept, 383

authoritarian system, 384

global village, 387

cultural imperialism, 388

electronic colonialism
  theory, 388

QUESTIONS FOR REVIEW

1. What are clandestine broadcast stations? Differentiate between indigenous and exogenous stations.

2. What are pirate broadcasters? What differentiates them from traditional clandestine operators?

3. How did World War II and the Cold War shape the efforts of the United States in terms of its external and surrogate services?

4. What is comparative analysis?

5. What are the main characteristics of media systems operating under Hachten's Western concept?

6. What are the main characteristics of media systems operating under Hachten's development concept?

7. What are the main characteristics of media systems operating under Hachten's revolutionary concept?

8. What are the main characteristics of media systems operating under Hachten's authoritarianism and communism concepts?

9. What is cultural imperialism? What two telecommunications technologies fuel current concern over its operation?

10. What was the MacBride Report? Why did most Western nations reject it? How does it relate to McLuhan's concept of the global village?

To maximize your study time, check out CONNECT to access the SmartBook study module for this chapter and explore other resources.

QUESTIONS FOR CRITICAL THINKING AND DISCUSSION

1. Britain's external service, the BBC, is available on shortwave radio, the Internet, and American public broadcasting and cable and satellite television. Listen to or watch the BBC. How does its content compare to the homegrown radio and television with which you are familiar? Think especially of news. How does its reporting differ from that of cable networks such as CNN and from broadcast networks such as ABC, CBS, and NBC? Why do you think differences exist? Similarities?

2. Do you have experience with another country's media? If so, which one? Can you place that system's operation within one of the concepts listed in this chapter? Describe how that system's content is similar to and different from that with which you are familiar in the United States. Do you favor one system's fare over another's? Why or why not?

3. Do you think countries, especially developing nations, should worry about cultural imperialism? Would you argue that they should use low-cost Western fare to help their developing system get "off the ground," or do you agree with critics that this approach unduly influences their system's ultimate content?

REFERENCES

1. AFRTS. (2015). Purpose/mission. *American Forces Radio and Television Service*. Online: http://afrts.dodmedia.osd.mil/

2. Allen, P. (2015, February 15). France demands that its future leaders must speak English. *Telegraph*. Online: http://www.telegraph.co.uk/news/worldnews/europe/france/11414245/France-demands-that-its-future-leaders-must-speak-English.html

3. Auletta, K. (2014, February 3). Outside the box. *The New Yorker*, pp. 54–61.

4. Barnouw, E. (1990). *Tube of plenty: The evolution of American television*. New York: Oxford University Press.

5. Bennett, D. (2004, February). Our mongrel planet. *American Prospect*, pp. 62–63.

6. Benson, R., & Powers, M. (2011, February). Public media and political independence: Lessons for the future of journalism

from around the world. *Free Press*. Online: http://www
.freepress.net/sites/default/files/stn-legacy/public
-media-and-political-independence.pdf

7. "The big picture." (2016, December 14). *Variety*,
pp. 69–73.

8. Blumler, J. G., & Gurevitch, M. (1975). Towards a
comparative framework for political communication research.
In S. H. Chaffee (Ed.), *Political communication: Issues and
strategies for research*. Beverly Hills, CA: Sage.

9. Eddy, M., & Scott, M. (2017, March 15). Germany threatens
to fine Facebook and Twitter over hate speech. *The New York
Times*, p. B2.

10. Erdbrink, T., & Gladstone, R. (2014, September 18). "Happy
in Tehran" Dancers Are Given Suspended Sentences. *The
New York Times*. Online: http://www.nytimes
.com/2014/09/19/world/middleeast/happy-in-tehran
-dancers-are-given-suspended-sentences.html?_r=0

11. Forbes, T. (2016, April 7). Brits ban Gucci ad; contemplate
"activity icons" on packages. *MediaPost*. Online: http://www
.mediapost.com/publications/article/272980/brits-ban
-gucci-ad-contemplate-activity-icons-o.html?edition=

12. Freedom House. (2016, November). *Silencing the messenger:
Communication apps under pressure*. Online: https://freedom
house.org/report/freedom-net/freedom-net-2016

13. Gladstone, R. (2016, December 13). Record number of
journalists jailed in 2016, press advocacy group says.
The New York Times, p. A6.

14. "Global media habits: A TV in every house." (2011, October
3). *Advertising Age*, p. 8.

15. "Global newspaper circulation and advertising trends in
2015." (2016, June 21). *Marketing Charts*. Online: http://
www.marketingcharts.com/traditional/global-newspaper
-circulation-and-advertising-trends-in-2015-68480/

16. Greenslade, R. (2016, March 11). Journalists must be
protected in order to combat propaganda. *The Guardian*.
Online: https://www.theguardian.com/media/greenslade/2016
/mar/11/journalists-must-be-protected-in-order-to-combat
-propaganda

17. Hachten, W. A. (1992). *The world news prism* (3rd ed.).
Ames: Iowa State University Press.

18. Hall, E. (2010, January 25). Beauty riskier than booze on
Spanish TV. *Advertising Age*, p. 6.

19. Hempel, J. (2016, January 26). Social media made the Arab
Spring, but couldn't save it. *Wired*. Online: https://www
.wired.com/2016/01/social-media-made-the-arab-spring
-but-couldnt-save-it/

20. Henriksson, T. (2016, June 11). Full highlights of world
press trends 2016 survey. *World Association of Newspapers
and News Publishers*. Online: http://www.wan-ifra.org/
articles/2016/06/12/full-highlights-of-world-press-trends
-2016-survey

21. "How they see us." (2005, November 4). *The Week*, p. 19.

22. Jacobs, A. (2015, January 29). China further tightens grip on
the Internet. *The New York Times*, p. A1.

23. Jefferson, C. (2011, December 22). Happy, flourishing city
with no advertising. *Good Cities*. Online: http://www.good.is
/post/a-happy-flourishing-city-with-no-advertising/

24. Joffe, J. (2006, May 14). The perils of soft power. *The New
York Times Magazine*, pp. 15–17.

25. Johnson, A. (2017, January 2). Controversial McDonald's
opens in Vatican building (Wi-Fi is available). *NBC News*.
Online: http://www.nbcnews.com/news/world/controversial
-mcdonald-s-opens-vatican-building-wi-fi-available
-n702166

26. Lang, B., & Rainey, J. (2016, July 26). Hollywood's summer
freeze. *Variety*, pp. 40–45.

27. Lubin, G. (2016, December 30). Data reveals the 20 most
popular TV shows of 2016. *Business Insider*. Online: http://
www.businessinsider.com/most-popular-tv-shows-2016-12

28. McDonough, K. (2013, November 7). Sweden launches
gender ratings for movies. *Salon*. Online: http://www.salon
.com/2013/11/07/sweden_introduces_a_gender_rating
_system_for_films/

29. McLuhan, M. (1962). *The Gutenberg galaxy: The making of
typographic man*. London: Routledge.

30. McLuhan, M. (1964). *Understanding media: The extensions
of man*. New York: McGraw-Hill.

31. McLuhan, M., & Stern, G. E. (1967). A dialogue: Q & A. In
M. McLuhan & G. E. Stearn (Eds.), *McLuhan: Hot and cool:
A primer for the understanding of McLuhan and a critical
symposium with a rebuttal by McLuhan*. New York: Dial
Press.

32. McNab, C. (2009). What social media offers to health
professionals and citizens. *Bulletin of the World Health
Organization, 87*, 566.

33. McPhail, T. L. (2014). *Global communication*. Malden, MA:
Wiley.

34. Mendelsohn, D., & Hamid, M. (2014, November 11). Should
the United States declare books an "essential good"? *The New
York Times*, p. BR31.

35. Moody, G. (2015, March 25). EU: Don't use Facebook if you
want to keep NSA away from your data. *Arstechnica.com*.
Online: http://arstechnica.com/tech-policy/2015/03/eu-dont
-use-facebook-if-you-want-to-keep-the-nsa-away-from
-your-data/

36. Newseum Institute. (2016). *The 2016 state of the First
Amendment*. Online: http://www.newseuminstitute.org
/wp-content/uploads/2016/06/FAC_SOFA16_report.pdf

37. "Number of social network users worldwide from 2010 to
2020 (in billions)." (2017, January). *Statista*. Online: https://
www.statista.com/statistics/278414/number-of-worldwide
-social-network-users/

38. "Overseas top 100 of 2016." (2017). *Variety*, p. 21.

39. Poniewozik, J. (2001, September 15). Get up, stand up. *Time*,
pp. 68–70.

40. Preston, J. (2011, February 6). Movement began with outrage
and a Facebook page that gave it an outlet. *The New York
Times*, p. A10.

41. Rehlin, G. (2010, March 1–7). Swedish court takes uncommercial break. *Variety*, p. 4.

42. Reporters Without Borders. (2016, April 20). *2016 world press freedom index*. Online: https://rsf.org/en/ranking

43. Rowlands, L. (2017, January 5). Governments shut down the Internet more than 50 times in 2016. *Truthout*. Online: http://www.truth-out.org/news/item/38988-more-than-50-internet-shutdowns-in-2016

44. Sass, E. (2016, June 13). Morocco bans sharing newspapers. *MediaPost*. Online: http://www.mediapost.com/publications/article/277992/morocco-bans-sharing-newspapers.html

45. Sayare, S. (2014, April 12). In France, a move to limit off-the-clock work emails. *The New York Times*, p. A4.

46. Soley, L. C., & Nichols, J. S. (1987). *Clandestine radio broadcasting: A study of revolutionary and counterrevolutionary electronic communication*. New York: Praeger.

47. Stevenson, R. L. (1994). *Global communication in the twenty-first century*. New York: Longman.

48. Thompson, D. (2014, May 28). How the world consumes media—in charts and maps. *The Atlantic*. Online: http://www.theatlantic.com/business/archive/2014/05/global-mobile-media-smartphones-tv-maps/371760/

49. Thompson, S. (2016, March 15). How social media is transforming medical care in the developing world. *Fast Company*. Online: https://www.fastcompany.com/3057869/how-social-media-is-transforming-medical-care-in-the-developing-world

50. Turner, K. (2016, May 12). France might pass a law that makes it illegal to send after-hour work emails. *The Washington Post*. Online: https://www.washingtonpost.com/news/the-switch/wp/2016/05/12/france-might-pass-a-law-that-makes-it-illegal-to-send-after-hours-work-emails/?utm_term=.2359f42bb776

51. UNESCO. (2005, October 20). General Conference adopts Convention on the Protection and Promotion of the Diversity of Cultural Expressions. Online: http://portal.unesco.org/en/ev.php-URL_ID=30298&URL_DO=DO_TOPIC&URL_SECTION=201.html

52. "The United States ranks 41st in Reporters without Borders 2016 World Press Freedom Index." (2016, April 20). *Reporters without Borders*. Online: https://rsf.org/en/news/united-states-ranks-41st-reporters-without-borders-2016-world-press-freedom-index

53. Victor, D. (2017, January 3). Despite pleas, new neighbor for Vatican. *The New York Times*, p. A9.

54. Webb, J. (2015, October 30). Those who hate the US actually hate themselves. *The Times of London*. Online: http://www.thetimes.co.uk/tto/opinion/columnists/article4599959.ece

55. Williams, E. (2016, July 25). Can social media help developing countries? Absolutely! *Forum One*. Online: https://forumone.com/ideas/can-social-media-help-developing-countries-absolutely

56. Wong, E. (2016, February 23). Chinese leader's news flash: Journalists media must serve Party. *The New York Times*, p. A1.

Cultural Forum Blue Column icon, Media Literacy Red Torch Icon, Using Media Green Gear icon, Developing Media book in starburst icon: ©McGraw-Hill Education

Glossary

abridgment the curtailing of rights

absolutist position regarding the First Amendment, the idea that no law against free speech means no law

access journalism reporters acting deferentially toward news sources in order to ensure continued access

accountability metrics agreement between ad agency and client on how the effectiveness of a specific ad or campaign will be judged

Acta Diurna written on a tablet, an account of the deliberations of the Roman senate; an early "newspaper"

actual malice the standard for libel in coverage of public figures consisting of "knowledge of its falsity" or "reckless disregard" for whether or not it is true

addressable technology technology permitting the transmission of very specific content to equally specific audience members

ad hoc balancing of interests in individual First Amendment cases, several factors should be weighed in determining how much freedom the press is granted

administrative research studies of the immediate, observable influence of mass communication

ad-pull policy demand by an advertiser for an advance review of a magazine's content, with the threat of pulled advertising if dissatisfied with that content

advergames video games produced expressly to serve as brand commercials

advocacy games primarily online games supporting an idea rather than a product

affective forecasting error discrepancy between the expected and actual emotions generated by Facebook activity

affiliate a broadcasting station that aligns itself with a network

agenda setting the theory that media may not tell us what to think but do tell us what to think about

aggressive cues model of media violence; media portrayals can indicate that certain classes of people are acceptable targets for real-world aggression

AIDA approach the idea that to persuade consumers, advertising must attract *attention*, create *interest*, stimulate *desire*, and promote *action*

à la carte pricing charging cable subscribers by the channel, not for tiers

Alien and Sedition Acts series of four laws passed by the 1798 U.S. Congress making illegal the writing, publishing, or printing of "any false scandalous and malicious writing" about the president, Congress, or the U.S. government

aliteracy possessing the ability to read but being unwilling to do so

all-channel legislation 1962 law requiring all television sets imported into or manufactured in the United States to be equipped with both VHF and UHF receivers

alternative press typically weekly, free papers emphasizing events listings, local arts advertising, and "eccentric" personal classified ads

ambient advertising advertising content appearing in nontraditional venues

applied ethics the application of metaethics and normative ethics to very specific situations

appointment consumption audiences consume content at a time predetermined by the producer and distributor

ascertainment requires broadcasters to ascertain or actively and affirmatively determine the nature of their audiences' interest, convenience, and necessity; no longer enforced

astroturf fake grassroots organization

attitude change theory theory that explains how people's attitudes are formed, shaped, and changed and how those attitudes influence behavior

audience fragmentation audiences for specific media content becoming smaller and increasingly homogeneous

audion tube vacuum tube developed by DeForest that became the basic invention for all radio and television

augmented reality (AR) permits users to point phones at things in the real world and be instantly linked to websites containing information about those things superimposed over the screen image

authoritarian/communism system a national media system characterized by authoritarian control

awareness tests ad research technique that measures the cumulative effect of a campaign in terms of a product's "consumer consciousness"

bandwidth a communication channel's information-carrying capacity

banners online advertising messages akin to billboards

billings total sale of broadcast airtime

Bill of Rights the first 10 amendments to the U.S. Constitution

binary code information transformed into a series of digits 1 and 0 for storage and manipulation in computers

binge viewing watching five or more episodes of a TV series in one sitting

bitcasters "radio stations" that can be accessed only over the World Wide Web

BitTorrent file-sharing software that allows users to create "swarms" of data as they simultaneously download and upload "bits" of a given piece of content

block booking the practice of requiring exhibitors to rent groups of movies (often inferior) to secure a better one

blockbuster mentality filmmaking characterized by reduced risk taking and more formulaic movies; business concerns are said to dominate artistic considerations

blogs regularly updated online journals

B-movie the second, typically less expensive, movie in a double feature

bounded cultures (co-cultures) groups with specific but not dominant cultures

boutique agencies smaller, more personalized, and task-specific ad agencies

brand entertainment when commercials are part of and essential to a piece of media content

branding films sponsor financing of movies to advance a manufacturer's product

brand magazine a consumer magazine published by a retail business for readers having demographic characteristics similar to those consumers with whom it typically does business

British cultural theory theory of elites' domination over culture and its influence on bounded cultures

broadband a channel with broad information-carrying capacity

broadsides (sometimes **broadsheets**) early colonial newspapers imported from England, single-sheet announcements or accounts of events

browsers software programs loaded on personal computers and used to download and view Web files

bundling delivering television, VOD, audio, high-speed Internet access, long-distance and local phone service, multiple phone lines, and fax via cable

C3 rating measure of viewing of commercials that appear in a specific program within 3 days of its premiere telecast

calotype early system of photography using translucent paper from which multiple prints could be made

casual games classic games most often played in spurts and accommodated by small-screen devices

catalog albums in record retailing, albums more than 18 months old

catharsis the theory that watching mediated violence reduces people's inclination to behave aggressively

cause marketing PR in support of social issues and causes

cease-and-desist order demand made by a regulatory agency that a given illegal practice be stopped

censorship when someone in authority limits publication or access to it

cinématographe Lumière brothers' device that both photographed and projected action

circulation the number of issues of a magazine or newspaper that are sold

clandestine stations illegal or unlicensed broadcast operations frequently operated by revolutionary groups or intelligence agencies for political purposes

clear time when local affiliates carry a network's program

click bait Web content designed to attract ad impressions

click stream the series of choices made by a user on the Web

cloud computing storage of all computer data, including personal information and system-operating software, on remote servers hosted on the Internet

clutter overabundance of commercial messages

coaxial cable copper-clad aluminum wire encased in plastic foam insulation, covered by an aluminum outer conductor and then sheathed in plastic

collateral materials printing, research, and photographs that PR firms handle for clients, charging as much as 17.65% for this service

commissions in advertising, method of compensation for the placement of advertising in media, typically 15% of the cost of the time or space

communication the process of creating shared meaning

community antenna television (CATV) outmoded name for early cable television

comparative analysis the study of different countries' mass media systems

comparative studies see **comparative analysis**

complementary copy newspaper and magazine content that reinforces the advertiser's message, or at least does not negate it

concentration of ownership ownership of different and numerous media companies concentrated in fewer and fewer hands

concept films movies that can be described in one line

confidentiality the ability of media professionals to keep secret the names of people who provide them with information

conglomeration the increase in the ownership of media outlets by nonmedia companies

consumer culture a culture in which personal worth and identity reside not in the people themselves but in the products with which they surround themselves

consumer juries ad research technique in which people considered representative of a target market review a number of approaches or variations of a campaign or ad

consumption-on-demand the ability to access any content, anytime, anywhere

controlled circulation a magazine provided at no cost to readers who meet some specific set of advertiser-attractive criteria

conventions in media content, certain distinctive, standardized style elements of individual genres

convergence the erosion of traditional distinctions among media

cookie an identifying code added to a computer's hard drive by a visited website

copyright identifying and granting ownership of a given piece of expression to protect the creators' financial interest in it

copy testing measuring the effectiveness of advertising messages by showing them to consumers; used for all forms of advertising

corantos one-page news sheets on specific events, printed in English but published in Holland and imported into England by British booksellers; an early "newspaper"

cord-cutting viewers leaving cable and DBS altogether and relying on Internet-only television

cord-never viewer who never had cable TV

corporate independent studio specialty or niche division of a major studio designed to produce more sophisticated—but less costly—movies

corporate social responsibility the integration of business operations and organizational values

corrective advertising a new set of ads required by a regulatory body and produced by the offender that correct the original misleading effort

cost of entry amount of money necessary to begin media content production

cost per thousand (CPM) in advertising, the cost of reaching 1,000 audience members, computed by the cost of an ad's placement divided by the number of thousands of consumers it reaches

cottage industry an industry characterized by small operations closely identified with their personnel

cover rerecording of one artist's music by another

critical cultural theory idea that media operate primarily to justify and support the status quo at the expense of ordinary people

critical research studies of media's contribution to the larger issues of what kind of nation we are building, what kind of people we are becoming

crowdfunding the practice of using digital technology to solicit donations from a large number of people for a cause or project

cultivation analysis idea that television "cultivates" or constructs a reality of the world that, although possibly inaccurate, becomes the accepted reality simply because we as a culture believe it to be reality

cultural definition of communication communication is a symbolic process whereby reality is produced, maintained, repaired, and transformed; from James Carey

cultural imperialism the invasion of an indigenous people's culture by the cultures of outside, powerful countries

cultural theory the idea that meaning and therefore effects are negotiated by media and audiences as they interact in the culture

culture the world made meaningful; socially constructed and maintained through communication, it limits as well as liberates us, differentiates as well as unites us, defines our realities and thereby shapes the ways we think, feel, and act

custom publishing publications specifically designed for an individual company seeking to reach a narrowly defined audience

daguerreotype process of recording images on polished metal plates, usually copper, covered with a thin layer of silver iodide emulsion

dataveillance the massive electronic collection and distillation of consumer data

decoding interpreting sign/symbol systems

democracy government by the people

demographic segmentation advertisers' appeal to audiences composed of varying personal and social characteristics such as race, gender, and economic level

dependency theory the idea that media's power is a function of audience members' dependency on the media and their content

deregulation relaxation of ownership and other rules for radio and television

desensitization the idea that viewers become more accepting of real-world violence because of its constant presence in television fare

development concept of media systems; government and media work in partnership to ensure that media assist in the planned, beneficial development of the country

digital audio radio service (DARS) direct home or automobile delivery of audio by satellite

digital cable television delivery of digital video images and other information to subscribers' homes

digital computer a computer that processes data reduced to a binary code

digital divide the lack of technological access among people of color, people who are poor or disabled, and those in rural communities

digital natives people who have never known a world without the Internet

digital recording recording based on conversion of sound into 1s and 0s logged in millisecond intervals in a computerized translation process

digital rights management (DRM) protection of digitally distributed intellectual property

digital video disc (DVD) digital recording and playback player and disc, fastest-growing consumer electronic product in history

digital video recorder (DVR) video recording device attached to a television, which gives viewers significant control over content

dime novels inexpensive late 19th- and early 20th-century books that concentrated on frontier and adventure stories; sometimes called **pulp novels**

disinhibitory effects in social cognitive theory, seeing a model rewarded for prohibited or threatening behavior increases the likelihood that the observer will perform that behavior

disintermediation eliminating gatekeepers between artists and audiences

disruptive transition radical change in an industry brought about by the introduction of some new technology or product

dissonance theory argues that people, when confronted by new information, experience a kind of mental discomfort, a dissonance; as a result, they consciously and subconsciously work to limit or reduce that discomfort through the selective processes

diurnals daily accounts of local news printed in 1620s England; forerunners of our daily newspaper

D-notice in Great Britain, an officially issued notice of prior restraint

domain name on the World Wide Web, an identifying name, rather than a site's formal URL, that gives some indication of the nature of a site's content or owner

dominant culture (mainstream culture) the culture that seems to hold sway with the large majority of people; that which is normative

double feature two films on the same bill

dual-factor model of social media use social media use is motivated by the need for acceptance and the need to belong

duopoly single ownership and management of multiple radio stations in one market

dynamic pricing selling movie seats at varying prices depending on demand and availability

early window the idea that media give children a window on the world before they have the critical and intellectual ability to judge what they see

e-book a book that is downloaded in electronic form from the Internet to a computer or handheld device

e-commerce the buying of products and services online

economies of scale concept that relative cost declines as the size of the endeavor grows

editorial policy newspapers' and magazines' positions on certain specific issues

electronic colonialism theory belief that cultural products from one country will overwhelm those of another

electronic sell-through (EST) buying of digital download movies

e-mail (electronic mail) function of Internet allowing communication via computer with anyone else online, anyplace in the world, with no long-distance fees

embedding war correspondents exchanging control of their output for access to the front

encoding transforming ideas into an understandable sign/symbol system

encryption electronic coding or masking of information on the Web that can be deciphered only by a recipient with the decrypting key

engagement psychological and behavioral measure of ad effectiveness designed to replace CPM

environmental incentives in social cognitive theory, the notion that real-world incentives can lead observers to ignore negative vicarious reinforcement

e-publishing the publication and distribution of books initially or exclusively in a digital format

e-reader digital book having the appearance of a traditional book but with content that is digitally stored and accessed

e-sports streamed online game competition

ethics rules of behavior or moral principles that guide actions in given situations

ethnic press papers, often in a foreign language, aimed at minority, immigrant, and non-English readers

exergame video game designed to encourage beneficial physical activity

exogenous stations clandestine broadcast operations functioning from outside the regions to which they transmit

expanded basic cable in cable television, a second, somewhat more expensive level of subscription

experiential marketing melding of brands and experiences

extended real-life hypothesis predicts that we use social media to communicate our actual identities

external service in international broadcasting, a service designed by one country to counter enemy propaganda and disseminate information about itself

Facebook depression depression resulting from intensity of social media activity

Facebook envy resentfulness of others' social media expressions of happiness

factory studios the first film production companies

Fairness Doctrine requires broadcasters to cover issues of public importance and to be fair in that coverage; abolished in 1987

fair use in copyright law, instances in which material may be used without permission or payment

fake news inaccurate Internet news stories designed to be spread and deceive

feature syndicates clearinghouses for the work of columnists, cartoonists, and other creative individuals, providing their work to newspapers and other media outlets

feedback the response to a given communication

fiber optics signals carried by light beams over glass fibers

First Amendment "Congress shall make no law respecting an establishment of religion, or prohibiting the free exercise thereof; or abridging the freedom of speech, or of the press; or the right of the people peaceably to assemble, and to petition the Government for a redress of grievances."

first-person perspective game video game in which all action is through the eyes of the player

first-run syndication original programming produced specifically for the syndicated television market

fixed-fee arrangement the arrangement whereby a PR firm performs a specific set of services for a client for a specific and prearranged fee

flack a derogatory name sometimes applied to public relations professionals

flash mobs (sometimes **smart mobs**) geographically dispersed groups connected only by communications technology, quickly drawn together to perform collective action

flog fake blog; typically sponsored by a company to anonymously boost itself or attack a competitor

focus groups small groups of people who are interviewed, typically to provide advertising or public relations professionals with detailed information

forced exposure ad research technique used primarily for television commercials, requiring advertisers to bring consumers to a theater or other facility where they see a television program, complete with the new ads

format a radio station's particular sound or programming content

franchise films movies produced with full intention of producing several sequels

Frankfurt School media theory, centered in neo-Marxism, that valued serious art, viewing its consumption as a means to elevate all people toward a better life; typical media fare was seen as pacifying ordinary people while repressing them

freemium games video games in which consuming advertising or even spending actual cash allows players to progress in their play

gamification use of video game skills and conventions to solve real-world problems

genre a form of media content with a standardized, distinctive style and conventions

globalization ownership of media companies by multinational corporations

Global Television Audience Metering (GTAM) meter video ratings technology that will actively and passively measure viewing across all platforms

global village Marshall McLuhan's theory that new communication technologies permit people to become increasingly involved in one another's lives

grand theory a theory designed to describe and explain all aspects of a given phenomenon

green light process the process of deciding to make a movie

greenwashing public relations practice of countering the public relations efforts aimed at clients by environmentalists

hard news news stories that help readers make intelligent decisions and keep up with important issues

home page entryway into a website, containing information and hyperlinks to other material

hostile media effect the idea that people see media coverage of important topics of interest as less sympathetic to their position, more sympathetic to the opposing position, and generally hostile to their point of view regardless of the quality of the coverage

hosts computers linking individual personal computer users to the Internet

hypercommercialism increasing the amount of advertising and mixing commercial and noncommercial media content

hyperlink connection, embedded in a website's content allowing instant access to other material in that site as well as to material in other sites

hypodermic needle theory idea that media are a dangerous drug that can directly enter a person's system

iconoscope tube first practical television camera tube, developed in 1923

idealized virtual identity hypothesis social media users tend to show idealized characteristics not reflective of who they really are

identification in social cognitive theory, a special form of imitation by which observers do not exactly copy what they have seen but make a more generalized but related response

imitation in social cognitive theory, the direct replication of an observed behavior

importation of distant signals delivery of distant television signals by cable television for the purpose of improving reception

impressions the number of times an online ad is seen

imprint book publishing company

in-band-on-channel (IBOC) digital radio technology that uses digital compression to "shrink" digital and analog signals, allowing both to occupy the same frequency

indecency in broadcasting, language or material that depicts sexual or excretory activities in a way offensive to contemporary community standards

indigenous stations clandestine broadcast operations functioning from inside the regions to which they transmit

inferential feedback in the mass communication process, feedback is typically indirect rather than direct; that is, it is inferential

information gap the widening disparity in amounts and types of information available to information haves and have-nots

inhibitory effects in social cognitive theory, seeing a model punished for a behavior reduces the likelihood that the observer will perform that behavior

instant books books published very soon after some well-publicized public event

instant messaging (IM) real-time e-mail, allowing two or more people to communicate instantaneously and in immediate response to one another

integrated audience reach total numbers of the print edition of a newspaper plus unduplicated Web readers

integrated marketing communications (IMC) combining public relations, marketing, advertising, and promotion into a seamless communication campaign

Internet a global network of interconnected computers that communicate freely and share and exchange information

Internet of Things (IoT) everyday objects having built-in network connectivity, allowing them to send and receive data

interpersonal communication communication between two or a few people

island in children's television commercials, the product is shown simply, in actual size against a neutral background

ISP (Internet service provider) company that offers Internet connections at monthly rates depending on the kind and amount of access needed

joint operating agreement (JOA) permits a failing paper to merge most aspects of its business with a successful local competitor, as long as editorial and reporting operations remain separate

kinescope improved picture tube developed by Zworykin for RCA

kinetograph William Dickson's early motion picture camera

kinetoscope peep show devices for the exhibition of kinetographs

knowledge gap growing differences in knowledge, civic activity, and literacy between better-informed and less-informed Americans

L+7 TV rating of live plus seven days of viewing

LAN (local area network) network connecting two or more computers, usually within the same building

LCD (liquid crystal display) display surface in which electric currents of varying voltage are passed through liquid crystal, altering the passage of light through that crystal

lead generation directing users who've expressed an interest into a brand's sales pipeline

LED (light-emitting diode) light-emitting semiconductor manipulated under a display screen

libel the false and malicious publication of material that damages a person's reputation (typically applied to print media)

libertarianism philosophy of the press asserting that good and rational people can tell right from wrong if presented with full and free access to information; therefore, censorship is unnecessary

limited effects theory media's influence is limited by people's individual differences, social categories, and personal relationships

linotype technology that allowed the mechanical rather than manual setting of print type

liquid barretter first audio device permitting the reception of wireless voices; developed by Fessenden

literacy the ability to effectively and efficiently comprehend and use written symbols

lobbying in public relations, directly interacting with elected officials or government regulators and agents

location-based mobile advertising technology allowing marketers to send targeted ads to people where they are in the moment

low power FM (LPFM) 10- to 100-watt nonprofit community radio stations with a reach of only a few miles

macro-level effects media's widescale social and cultural impact

magalogue a designer catalogue produced to look like a consumer magazine

magic bullet theory the idea from mass society theory that media are a powerful "killing force" that directly penetrates a person's system

mainframe computer a large central computer to which users are connected by terminals

mainstreaming in cultivation analysis, television's ability to move people toward a common understanding of how things are

mass communication the process of creating shared meaning between the mass media and their audiences

mass communication theories explanations and predictions of social phenomena relating mass communication to various aspects of our personal and cultural lives or social systems

massively multiplayer online roleplaying game (MMO) interactive online game where characters and actions are controlled by other players, not the computer; also called **virtual worlds games**

mass medium (pl. **mass media**) a medium that carries messages to a large number of people

mass society theory the idea that media are corrupting influences; they undermine the social order, and "average" people are defenseless against their influence

mathematical songwriting songs written specifically to be commercial hits

meaning-making perspective idea that active audience members use media content to create meaning, and meaningful experiences, for themselves

media literacy the ability to effectively and efficiently comprehend and utilize mass communication

media multitasking simultaneously consuming many different kinds of media

medium (pl. **media**) vehicle by which messages are conveyed

meme an online idea or image that is repeatedly copied, manipulated, and shared

metaethics a culture's fundamental values

metering Internet use charged "by the byte"; heavier users pay more, more modest users pay less

microcinema filmmaking using digital video cameras and desktop digital editing programs

microcomputer a very small computer that uses a microprocessor to handle information (also called a **personal computer** or **PC**)

micro-level effects effects of media on individuals

microwave relay audio and video transmitting system in which super-high-frequency signals are sent from land-based point to land-based point

middle-range theories ideas that explain or predict only limited aspects of the mass communication process

minicomputer a relatively large central computer to which users are connected by terminals; not as large as a mainframe computer

modeling in social cognitive theory, learning through imitation and identification

modem a device that translates digital computer information into an analog form so it can be transmitted through telephone lines

montage tying together two separate but related shots in such a way that they take on a new, unified meaning

moral agent in an ethical dilemma, the person making the decision

movie palaces elaborately decorated, opulent, architecturally stunning theaters

MP3 file compression software that permits streaming of digital audio and video data

muckraking a form of crusading journalism that primarily used magazines to agitate for change

MUD (multiuser dimension) online text-based interactive game

multimedia advanced sound and image capabilities for microcomputers

multiple points of access ability of a media-literate consumer to access or approach media content from a variety of personally satisfying directions

multiple system operator (MSO) a company owning several different cable television operations

municipal broadband publically provided low-cost, high-speed Internet access

music licensing company an organization that collects fees based on recorded music users' gross receipts and distributes the money to songwriters and artists

narrowcasting aiming broadcast programming at smaller, more demographically homogeneous audiences

near-field communication (NFC) chip tag embedded in a magazine page that connects readers to advertisers' digital content

neo-Marxist theory the theory that people are oppressed by those who control the culture, the superstructure, as opposed to the base

network neutrality granting equal carriage over phone and cable lines to all websites

networks centralized production, distribution, decision-making organizations that links affiliates for the purpose of delivering their audiences to advertisers

neuromarketing research biometric measures (brain waves, facial expressions, eye tracking, sweating, and heart rate monitoring) used in advertising research

newsbook early weekly British publication that carried ads

news deserts communities starved for news vital to their existences due to a lack of journalistic resources

newshole the amount of space in a newspaper given to news

newspaper chains businesses that own two or more newspapers

news production research the study of how economic and other influences on the way news is produced distort and bias news coverage toward those in power

niche marketing aiming media content or consumer products at smaller, more demographically homogeneous audiences

nickelodeons the first movie houses; admission was one nickel

Nipkow disc first workable device for generating electrical signals suitable for the transmission of a scene

noise anything that interferes with successful communication

nonlinear TV watching television on our own schedules, not the programmer's

normative ethics generalized theories, rules, and principles of ethical or moral behavior

normative theory an idea that explains how media should ideally operate in a given system of social values

obscenity unprotected expression determined by (1) whether the average person, applying contemporary community standards, would find that the work, taken as a whole, appeals to the prurient interest, (2) whether the work depicts or describes, in a patently offensive way, sexual conduct specifically defined by the applicable state law, and (3) whether the work, taken as a whole, lacks serious literary, artistic, political, or scientific value

observational learning in social cognitive theory, observers can acquire (learn) new behaviors simply by seeing those behaviors performed

off-network broadcast industry term for syndicated content that originally aired on a network

offset lithography late 19th-century advance making possible printing from photographic plates rather than from metal casts

oligopoly a media system whose operation is dominated by a few large companies

ombudsman internal arbiter of performance for media organizations

O&O a broadcasting station that is owned and operated by a network

open source software freely downloaded software

operating policy standards for everyday operations for newspapers and magazines

operating system the software that tells the computer how to work

opinion followers people who receive opinion leaders' interpretations of media content; from **two-step flow theory**

opinion leaders people who initially consume media content, interpret it in light of their own values and beliefs, and then pass it on to opinion followers; from **two-step flow theory**

opt-in consumers giving permission to companies to sell personal data

opt-out consumers requesting that companies do not sell personal data

over-the-top (OTT) television delivery without the involvement of an MSO

parity products products generally perceived as alike by consumers no matter who makes them

pass-along readership measurement of publication readers who neither subscribe nor buy single copies but who borrow a copy or read one in a doctor's office or library

payola payment made by recording companies to DJs to air their records

paywall making online content available only to those visitors willing to pay

penny press newspapers in the 1830s selling for one penny

performance-based advertising Web advertising where the site is paid only when the consumer takes some specific action

permission marketing advertising that the consumer actively accepts

persistence of vision images our eyes gather are retained by our brains for about 1/24 of a second, producing the appearance of constant motion

personal computer (PC) see **microcomputer**

pilot a sample episode of a proposed television program

piracy the illegal recording and sale of copyrighted material

pirate broadcasters unlicensed or otherwise illegally operated broadcast stations

pixel the smallest picture element in an electronic imaging system such as a television or computer screen

platform agnostic having no preference where media content is accessed

platform agnostic publishing digital and hardcopy books available for any and all reading devices

platform rollout opening a movie on only a few screens in the hope that favorable reviews and word-of-mouth publicity will boost interest

playlist predetermined sequence of selected records to be played by a disc jockey

podcasting streaming or downloading of audio files recorded and stored on distant servers

policy book delineates standards of operation for local broadcasters

pornography expression calculated solely to supply sexual excitement

premium cable cable television channels offered to viewers for a fee above the cost of their basic subscription

print on demand (POD) publishing method whereby publishers store books digitally for instant printing, binding, and delivery once ordered

prior restraint power of the government to *prevent* publication or broadcast of expression

production values media content's internal language and grammar; its style and quality

product placement the integration, for a fee, of specific branded products into media content

product positioning the practice in advertising of assigning meaning to a product based on who buys the product rather than on the product itself

programmatic ad fraud technological simulation of online activity designed to create billable ad impressions

programmatic buying automated, data-driven buying of online advertising

prosumer a proactive consumer

protocols common communication rules and languages for computers linked to the Internet

pseudo-event event that has no real informational or issue meaning; it exists merely to attract media attention

psychographic segmentation advertisers' appeal to consumer groups of varying lifestyles, attitudes, values, and behavior patterns

P2P peer-to-peer software that permits direct Internet-based communication or collaboration between two or more personal computers while bypassing centralized servers

public in PR, any group of people with a stake in an organization, issue, or idea

public domain in copyright law, the use of material without permission once the copyright expires

public service remit limits on advertising and other public service requirements imposed on Britain's commercial broadcasters in exchange for the right to broadcast

puffery the little lie or exaggeration that makes advertising more entertaining than it might otherwise be

pulp novels see **dime novels**

put agreement between a television producer and network that guarantees that the network will order at least a pilot or pay a penalty

quick response (QR) code small barcode with squares that appear on many media surfaces that direct mobile device users to a specific website

radio frequency identification (RFID) chip grain-of-sand–sized microchip and antenna embedded in consumer products that transmit a radio signal

rating percentage of a market's total population that is reached by a piece of broadcast programming

readers' representative media outlet employee who regularly responds to outside criticism

recall testing ad research technique in which consumers are asked to identify which ads are most easily remembered

recognition tests ad research technique in which people who have seen a given publication are asked whether they remember seeing a given ad

reinforcement theory Joseph Klapper's idea that if media have any impact at all, it is in the direction of reinforcement

remainders unsold copies of books returned to the publisher by bookstores to be sold at great discount

retainer in advertising, an agreed-upon amount of money a client pays an ad agency for a specific series of services

retransmission fee money a local cable operation pays to a broadcast station to carry its signal

return on investment (ROI) an accountability-based measure of advertising success

reverse compensation fee paid by a local broadcast station for the right to be a network's affiliate

revolutionary concept normative theory describing a system where media are used in the service of revolution

rich media sophisticated, interactive Web advertising, usually employing sound and video

ritual perspective the view of media as central to the representation of shared beliefs and culture

RSS (really simple syndication) aggregators allowing Web users to create their own content assembled from the Internet's limitless supply of material

search engines Web- or Net-search software providing on-screen menus

search marketing advertising sold next to or in search results produced by users' keyword searches

secondary service a radio station's second, or nonprimary, format

selective attention see **selective exposure**

selective exposure the idea that people expose themselves to or attend to those messages that are consistent with their preexisting attitudes and beliefs

selective perception the idea that people interpret messages in a manner consistent with their preexisting attitudes and beliefs

selective processes people expose themselves to, remember best and longest, and reinterpret messages that are consistent with their preexisting attitudes and beliefs

selective retention assumes that people remember best and longest those messages that are consistent with their existing attitudes and beliefs

self-righting principle the free flow or trade of ideas, even bad or uncomfortable ones, will inevitably produce the truth because a rational and good public will correct, or right, any errors

share the percentage of people listening to radio or of homes using television tuned in to a given piece of programming

shield laws legislation that expressly protects reporters' rights to maintain sources' confidentiality in courts of law

shopbills attractive, artful business cards used by early British tradespeople to promote themselves

shortwave radio radio signals transmitted at low frequencies that can travel great distances by skipping off the ionosphere

signs in social construction of reality, things that have subjective meaning

siquis pinup want ads common in Europe before and in early days of newspapers

skip ability of radio waves to reflect off the ionosphere

sky waves radio waves that are skipped off the ionosphere

slacktivism derogatory name of online activism

slander oral or spoken defamation of a person's character (typically applied to broadcasting)

smart mobs see **flash mobs**

social cognitive theory idea that people learn through observation

social construction of reality theory explains how cultures construct and maintain their realities using signs and symbols; argues that people learn to behave in their social world through interaction with it

social networking sites websites that function as online communities of users

social responsibility theory normative theory asserting that media must remain free of government control but, in exchange, must serve the public

soft news sensational stories that do not serve the democratic function of journalism

spam unsolicited commercial e-mail

spectrum scarcity broadcast spectrum space is limited, so not everyone who wants to broadcast can; those who are granted licenses must accept regulation

spin in PR, outright lying to hide what really happened

split runs special versions of a given issue of a magazine in which editorial content and ads vary according to some specific demographic or regional grouping

sponsored content content that matches the form and function of an editorial but is, in fact, paid for by an advertiser

spot commercial sales in broadcasting, selling individual advertising spots on a given program to a wide variety of advertisers

spyware identifying code placed on a computer by a website without permission or notification

Standards and Practices Department the internal content review operation of a television network

stereotyping application of a standardized image or conception applied to members of certain groups, usually based on limited information

sticky an attribute of a website; indicates its ability to hold the attention of a user

stimulation model of media violence; viewing mediated violence can increase the likelihood of subsequent aggressive behavior

streaming the simultaneous downloading and accessing (playing) of digital audio or video data

stream ripping saving streaming media to a file on a personal device to be accessed locally

stripping broadcasting a syndicated television show at the same time five nights a week

subscription TV early experiments with over-the-air pay television

subsidiary rights the sale of a book, its contents, even its characters to outside interests, such as filmmakers

surrogate service in international broadcasting, an operation established by one country to substitute for another's own domestic service

symbolic interaction the idea that people give meaning to symbols, and then those symbols control people's behavior in their presence

symbols in social construction of reality, things that have objective meaning

syndication sale of radio or television content to stations on a market-by-market basis

synergy the use by media conglomerates of as many channels of delivery as possible for similar content

targeting aiming media content or consumer products at smaller, more specific audiences

taste publics groups of people or audiences bound by little more than their interest in a given form of media content

technological determinism the idea that machines and their development drive economic and cultural change

technology gap the widening disparity between communication technology haves and have-nots

tentpole an expensive blockbuster around which a studio plans its other releases

terminals user workstations that are connected to larger centralized computers

terrestrial digital radio land-based digital radio relying on digital compression technology to simultaneously transmit analog and one or more digital signals using existing spectrum space

theatrical films movies produced primarily for initial exhibition on theater screens

third-party publishers companies that create video games for existing systems

third-person effect the common attitude that others are influenced by media messages, but we are not

360 marketing see **ambient advertising**

tie-in novels books based on popular television shows and movies

tiers groupings of channels made available by a cable or satellite provider to subscribers at varying prices

time-shifting taping a show on a VCR for later viewing

trade book hard- or softcover book including fiction and most nonfiction and cookbooks, biographies, art books, coffee-table books, and how-to books

traffic cop analogy in broadcast regulation, the idea that the FCC, as a traffic cop, has the right to control not only the flow of broadcast traffic but its composition as well

transmissional perspective the view of media as senders of information for the purpose of control

transparentists PR professionals calling for full disclosure of their practices—transparency

trustee model in broadcast regulation, the idea that broadcasters serve as the public's trustees or fiduciaries

two-step flow theory the idea that media's influence on people's behavior is limited by those who initially consume media content, interpret it in light of their own values and beliefs, and then pass it on to others who have less frequent contact with media

typification schemes in social construction of reality, collections of meanings people have assigned to some phenomenon or situation

unique selling proposition (USP) the aspect of an advertised product that sets it apart from other brands in the same product category

URL (uniform resource locator) the designation of each file or directory on the host computer connected to the Internet

uses and gratifications approach the idea that media don't do things *to* people; people do things *with* media

VALS advertisers' psychographic segmentation strategy that classifies consumers according to values and lifestyles

value-compensation program ad agency/brand agreement that payment of the agency's fees is predicated on meeting preestablished goals

vast wasteland expression coined by FCC chair Newton Minow in 1961 to describe television content

vertical integration a system in which studios produced their own films, distributed them through their own outlets, and exhibited them in their own theaters

vicarious reinforcement in social cognitive theory, the observation of reinforcement operates in the same manner as actual reinforcement

video game a game involving action taking place interactively on-screen

video news release (VNR) preproduced report about a client or its product that is distributed free of charge to television stations

video-on-demand (VOD) service allowing television viewers to access pay-per-view movies and other content that can be watched whenever they want

viral marketing PR strategy that relies on targeting specific Internet users with a given communication and relying on them to spread the word

virtual reality games through the use of a headset, games that generate an imaginary environment, simulating players' physical presence there

virtual worlds games see **massively multiplayer online roleplaying game**

Voice over Internet Protocol (VoIP) phone calls transferred in digital packets over the Internet rather than on circuit-switched telephone wires

WAN (wide area network) network that connects several LANs in different locations

webisode Web-only television show

Web radio the delivery of "radio" over the Internet directly to individual listeners

Western concept of media systems; normative theory that combines libertarianism's freedom with social responsibility's demand for public service and, where necessary, regulation

Wi-Fi wireless Internet

willing suspension of disbelief audience practice of willingly accepting the content before them as real

wire services news-gathering organizations that provide content to members

World Wide Web a tool that serves as a means of accessing files on computers connected via the Internet

yellow journalism early 20th-century journalism emphasizing sensational sex, crime, and disaster news

zero-TV homes homes that have sets but receive neither over-the-air nor cable/satellite television

zipping fast-forwarding through taped commercials on a VCR

zonecasting technology allowing radio stations to deliver different commercials to specific neighborhoods

zoned editions suburban or regional versions of metropolitan newspapers

zoopraxiscope early machine for projecting slides onto a distant surface

Index

Boldfaced locators signify definitions in the text of glossary terms. *Italic* locators signify illustrations